Outside 25

Outside 25

CLASSIC TALES AND
NEW VOICES FROM THE
FRONTIERS OF ADVENTURE

25th Anniversary Edition

Edited and with an Introduction by Hal Espen

W. W. Norton & Company • New York • London

The text of this book is composed in Sabon
with the display set in Tarzana Narrow
Composition by Matrix Publishing
Manufacturing by the The Courier Companies, Inc.
Book design by Chris Welch

Library of Congress Cataloging-in-Publication Data

Outside 25 : classic tales and new voices from the frontiers of
adventure / the editors of Outside magazine.— 25th anniversary ed.
p. cm.
"Outside books."
ISBN 0-393-05186-2 (hard)
1. Outdoor recreation. 2. Outdoor recreation—United States.
I. Outside (Chicago, Ill.)
GV191.6+
790—dc21

2002004815

ISBN-0-393-32503-2 (pbk.)

W. W. Norton & Company, Inc., 500 Fifth Avenue, New York, N.Y. 10110
www.wwnorton.com

W. W. Norton & Company Ltd., Castle House, 75/76 Wells Street, London W1T 3QT

3 4 5 6 7 8 9 0

Contents

At Play

The Fall Line

Around the Bend

Introduction

Fall 2002 marks the 25th anniversary of *Outside*'s plunge into the treacherous rapids of American journalism, and the book in your hands is a proud measure of how the magazine has endured and grown over the past quarter-century. But this anthology is as much about where we're going as where we've been. Unlike two previous collections that drew on work published as far back as 1977—*Out of the Noösphere* (1992) and *The Best of Outside: The First 20 Years* (1997)—almost all of the articles in this volume date from the last five years. Our latest choices celebrate emerging voices and perennial favorites; they reflect the enthusiasm and resourcefulness of a magazine that has flourished by expanding the boundaries of adventure storytelling in new directions.

One secret of *Outside*'s success is that our beat has kept us happily stuck in a state of excitable optimism. We always start with the universal motto of childhood—"Let's go out and play"—and follow the restless arc of its adult expression wherever it leads. This freedom translates into a range of subjects as gloriously open-ended as the word *outside* itself; thankfully, our readers have proven to be up for anything, as long as the story speaks in some way to the infinite variety of exuberant exploration. Even the magazine's darkest stories of tragedy and death honor this impulse, by honestly portraying the cost that such exploration sometimes exacts.

That said, it's no simple thing to define what makes a great *Outside* story. Readers of Jon Krakauer's *Into the Wild* and *Into Thin Air* and Sebastian Junger's *The Perfect Storm*—each of these best-selling books began as an article in *Outside*—might reasonably surmise that catastrophe is the defining element. But we believe that something more vital is at work: a commitment to precisely detailed reporting that brings to life the authentic horror and pathos of those tragedies. Only a few pieces in this collection—including Krakauer's first report on the true tale that became *Into the Wild*—can be typed as part of "the literature of disaster," a genre that has lately spawned more exploiters than masters. But all the writers represented here share a passionate, irreverent, commonsense devotion to the complicated, messy, fact-studded, awful, and frequently funny truth.

It's possible to find truth anywhere, even indoors, but *Outside*'s peculiar literary DNA thrives best in the open air. Perhaps because humans evolved over countless millennia by continuously experiencing a prearchitectural immersion in nature, we still find much of what seems most real when we stand outdoors. Inside is the realm of abstraction, safety, hierarchy, and calculation; inside is where we spend more and more time gazing through the translucent doors of electronic screens at quicksilver data palaces where no sun shines and nothing wild lives. Outside is the analog kingdom, the authentic ground, the necessary antidote to the notional and the virtual.

All *Outside* stories start in the same place: Something real is happening out there somewhere, beyond four walls. Something about an adventure, a physical challenge, a new idea, or a journey reaches our ears, and awakens our curiosity. After that, the rules get more provisional. On principle, we like ruggedness and roughing it, blunt honesty, laughing at the general folly. We don't mind pissing people off when verisimilitude is at stake. We don't preach to the choir. In our editorial lexicon, "earnest" is a quality to be avoided. In the world we cover, celebrity is a nearly worthless commodity. *Outside* stories are about characters, the more provocative the better.

Physical, questing, adventurous characters tend to be athletes of some kind, and *Outside* is a sports magazine—of a sort. (When pressed, we often say, knowing it's not completely true, that we only cover sports that don't involve boundary lines.) All sports began as free play in nature, and *Outside* gravitates toward athletic endeavors that remain close to those origins—sports that involve risk, like climbing, skiing, surfing, endurance racing, sailing, and travel in untamed, uncertain places.

This has less to do with an interest in things "extreme" and more to do with actively seeking wildness. Most of us recall Thoreau's distilled pronouncement: "In Wildness is the preservation of the World." When you read "Walking," the essay in which he wrote those words, you realize the sentence is not a slogan endorsing unpeopled serenity—it's a barbaric yawp affirming the strenuous, assertive, participatory role that human beings play in the wild. Elsewhere in "Walking," the author advises, "We should go forth on the shortest walk, perchance, in the spirit of undying adventure, never to return,—prepared to send back our embalmed hearts only as relics to our desolate kingdoms."

The human soul depends on such moments of total commitment, as the preservation of the world depends on wildness.

In early 1996 I quit a perfectly good job as an editor at *The New Yorker* and went to live for eight months in a borrowed wilderness cabin near the Rogue River in southern Oregon. During that time I never saw the light of another dwelling or camp. I did a little caretaker work, but mostly I hiked and mountain-biked and spent long hours casting for steelhead. And I read books—dozens of books. For a magazine editor, losing the time and the appetite to read serious books for pleasure is a vocational hazard, and I was happy to regain both. A lot of what I read turned out to be good preparation for my next job, especially works by Edward Abbey, Aldo Leopold, Wallace Stegner, Edward Hoagland, Annie Dillard, and David Rains Wallace. But it was lighting out for the woods in the first place that probably landed me at *Outside*. I'm pretty sure my open-ended unemployment impressed the editors at the home offices in Santa Fe—that and the fact that I had no phone. The urge to do what I had been doing is *Outside*'s stock-in-trade; people who followed similar paths (or wanted to) have kept the magazine in business. We were made for each other.

The magazine I signed on with in late 1996 was an operation hitting its stride, big-time. *Outside* had started with a brief run in San Francisco and then spent 15 years in Chicago before Lawrence J. Burke, the magazine's owner and undisputed *jefe grande,* moved the business to northern New Mexico. The move was, I think, congenial to *Outside*'s prospects in ways that are hard to quantify, but the new home underscored the magazine's independence and put the staff in closer proximity to a landscape that encouraged everything the magazine stands for. A bold redesign followed. Then, in the spring of 1996, just as it was winning the first of three consecutive National Magazine Awards for General Excellence—an achievement no other magazine has ever pulled off—*Outside* sent longtime contributor Jon Krakauer to climb Mount Everest. The editors found themselves with the adventure scoop of the decade when a storm killed eight climbers, including two leading guides. Advance copies of the issue featuring Krakauer's 17,000-word cover story had just reached *Outside*'s offices when I arrived to meet editor Mark Bryant and his staff.

A year later, *Into Thin Air* and *The Perfect Storm* were competing for precedence at the top of the best-seller lists, and the publishing industry went slightly mad over any story in which malevolent nature brought doom to plucky adventurers. Soon enough *Vanity Fair* was flirting with disaster and *The New York Times Magazine* was stoking a reflexive backlash with theories about the death of adventure and the rise of "explornography."

Almost all the stories in this anthology were published after this high-water mark in the commercial valuation of true-life adventure tales, but in rereading our selections, I'm pleased to have found no trace of a desire to milk this or any other trend. Nor do these writers seem preoccupied with the idea that adventure itself has become a weary matter of stunt expeditions and third-rate accomplishments in a world where everything's already been done. In fact, you can still go to Timbuktu, where, as Tim Cahill points out in the first story reprinted here, there's "a reasonably comfortable hotel, cold beer for sale, a post office, and a jetport . . . forty-eight hours from any major airport on earth." But getting there the old-fashioned way—overland, passing through the legendary salt mines of Mali, past bandits and camel carcasses and the encampment of a silent warrior named Colonel Yat—can still result in a tale worth repeating. And it always will.

This book opens with a section called "Tracks"—stories of travel to places that deliver a radically different version of reality than everyday America: the Inuit homeland in the Arctic, the famine-and-war crisis zones of sub-Saharan Africa, the Kamchatka Peninsula of Russia's Far East, India's Arunachal Pradesh, the South Pacific, and the front lines of a Maoist insurgency in Nepal. The next section, "Wild Things," offers tales of natural history, threatened places, and hopes of restoration. "At Play," the third section, chronicles athletes and their lives, from intimations of invulnerability to final races. "The Fall Line" features stories that consider risk, danger, crime, and ethics at the sharp end of circumstance. The final section, "Around the Bend," reviews some of the oddities, absurdities, pleasures, and rewards of the outdoor life.

First and last, *Outside* has always been a magazine of audacious storytellers and brave iconoclasts, and it isn't easy following in the footsteps of giants. Writers such as Edward Abbey, Peter Matthiessen, Annie Proulx, Thomas McGuane, Jim Harrison, Barry Lopez, and James Salter showed the way in the magazine's formative years. Stalwarts such as Cahill, Krakauer, David Quammen, Bob Shacochis, Randy Wayne White, Daniel Coyle, Ian Frazier, Bill Vaughn, and Paul Theroux, all of whom are represented in this collection, have made equally important contributions to the magazine's literary treasure-house. Alongside works by these veterans are stories by more recent frequent contributors such as Hampton Sides, Bruce Barcott, Florence Williams, Mark Jenkins, Daniel Duane, William T. Vollmann, Sara Corbett, Bill McKibben, Peter Maass, Patrick Symmes, and David Rakoff—the vanguard of literary journalists advancing the art of magazine writing and "the spirit of undying adventure."

These stories are also the product of the vision and craftsmanship of many remarkable *Outside* editors, past and present, working behind the scenes to make sure that the writers' voices ring clear. Thanks to Mark Bryant, Greg Cliburn, Michael Paterniti, John Tayman, Brad

Wetzler, Andrew Tilin, Adam Horowitz, Susan Casey, and the incomparable Laura Hohnhold. In recent years a new wave of editors has brought good cheer, fierce ambition, and valor to the cause. Among these splendid colleagues, I'm particularly grateful for the talent and spirit of Mary Turner, Elizabeth Hightower, Brad Wieners, Jay Heinrichs, Eric Hagerman, Katie Arnold, and Jay Stowe. I'd also like to thank Kevin Fedarko, James Glave, Leslie Weeden, Stephanie Pearson, Nick Heil, Chris Keyes, Dianna Delling, Eric Hansen, Jason Daley, Christian Nardi, and the rest of the *Outside* crew for their inspiration and energy. And even if their visual work is absent from this book, I'd also like to acknowledge the crucial contributions of the brilliant photographers, illustrators, photo editors, and art directors who give the words their proper accompaniment in the magazine. Special thanks to my partners Hannah McCaughey, Susan Boylan, and Rob Haggart for helping us to see, and to Eileen Rhine for getting the ink on the paper.

I'm grateful to John Barstow of W. W. Norton for his encouragement, guidance, and patience, and to my *Outside* colleague Anne Mollo-Christensen for her wisdom and humor.

Finally, Alex Heard was an ideal reader and shaping force during the planning and editing of this book.

—*Hal Espen, editor*

Tracks

Forbidden

TIM CAHILL

"Teem, wake up. There are some bandits."

An Italian—I don't recall which one—was standing over my sleeping bag and nudging my foot with his. It was about ten o'clock on a cool, clear February night in the Sahara, and I had been asleep for half an hour.

"What?"

"Some bandits have followed us up from Kidal. We have to go back to Aguelhok."

"Tuaregs?" I asked.

"Muhammad said they came from Kidal."

Muhammad, our recently hired security consultant, was a Tuareg himself. Kidal was a Tuareg town. But then again, so was Aguelhok.

I struggled out of my sleeping bag and stumbled around for a few groggy minutes in the dark. We were about three miles west of Aguelhok in the West African country of Mali and a couple of hundred miles north of the Niger River, camped near the central trans-Saharan road leading north to Algeria. This was to be the last stop before a high-speed run to the historic and formerly forbidden salt mines at Taoudenni, which—we didn't know—might not even exist anymore.

Our motorized caravan was parked amid a huge jumble of rocks that had probably formed the narrows of a swift-flowing, ancient river. The rocks were black, river-rounded, the size of large trucks, and many were festooned with drawings of creatures that must have existed here in a forgotten time when the sun-blasted sandscape was a vast and fertile grassland. There were drawings of an elephant, an eland, an ostrich. Giraffes seemed to have been considered the most consequential of the animals depicted. There were two of them etched in ocher onto flat, black rock, set just above the sand as if in a gallery. The figures were five feet high and expertly rendered. Riding beside one of the giraffes was a man on horseback, reining his mount and preparing to throw a spear. There were already four spears in the giraffe.

I had planned to study the rock art in the morning, along with my favorite among the Italians, Luigi Boschian. Gigi, as everyone called him, was the oldest in our group, 67, but nonetheless a strong walker who wanted no help clambering over the rocks and who seemed always to know where he was when we strolled through the desert together. Our bond was this: Gigi and I were interested in the same things—history, astronomy, archaeology, geology, anthropology—the difference between us being that he had taken the trouble to do an immense amount of reading in these areas.

Our common language was Spanish, though neither of us spoke with precision, which was sometimes frustrating. I wondered, for instance, if the men on horseback depicted on the rocks could be the ancestors of the Tuareg people who now populated the deserts of northern Mali, Niger, and southern Algeria. When I asked Gigi about it, he started at the beginning, as he tended to do. Present-day Tuaregs were the descendants of North African Berbers, who invaded the central Sahara about 3,500 years ago. They were originally horsemen, but as the climate changed and the desert claimed the land, the horse gave way to the camel. And wasn't it interesting that while the Berbers had used chariots, the use of the wheel was eventually abandoned? Camels were the better technology.

In the course of his explanations, Gigi often got sidetracked, wandering off on some tangent or other and dithering there for half an hour at a crack. He wore desert khakis, neatly pressed, but a shirttail was always out or a pant leg stuck into a sock. His abundant white hair was properly combed in the morning, but by noon it had degenerated into a finger-in-the-light-socket situation I'd describe as a full Einstein. He was the quintessential absentminded professor, Italian style. In explanation mode, he held his hands in front of his chest, palms up and open, as if weighing a pair of melons. When our mutual incompetence in Spanish defeated us, he'd turn his palms over and drop them to his waist, as if patting two small children on the head. I thought of this as Gigi's I-can-speak-no-more futility gesture.

Now, with bandits presumably chasing us, we had to abandon the rock art.

I gathered my gear, lurched down the sand slope, and began helping with the loads. Our caravan consisted of three four-wheel-drive, one-ton vehicles modified in this manner or that for hard overland desert driving. Lanterns were glowing, and our party of just over a dozen—three West Africans from the land below the Niger River, two local Tuaregs, a cacophony of Italians, myself, and photographer Chris Rainier—was moving very fast, stashing the gear any old way because it was thought the bandits were now very close.

We'd been half expecting the bastards.

No Guarantees

Aguelhok was a small, wind-scoured town of narrow, sandy streets and adobe buildings, none of which would look out of place in Taos, New Mexico. We pulled our vehicles into a large walled courtyard that seemed to be a municipal gathering place, locked ourselves behind the metal gates, and milled around in the dark, unwilling to sleep.

One of the Italians, Dario, said, "Bandits? Ha. They want us to stay here so we have to pay." Dario, I'd guess, was in his early forties, a trim, athletic man I could see snapping out orders in a corporate boardroom.

Muhammad, the Tuareg security consultant we'd hired and the man who'd told us about the bandits, was talking to our Italian guide, Alberto Nicheli.

"I can no longer guarantee you safe passage to the salt mines," he said.

"You could this afternoon," Alberto said.

"That was before the car followed you up from Kidal."

"We can't pay you if you don't come," Alberto explained.

"This is no matter," Muhammad said.

I caught Dario's eye. We'd offered Muhammad $400 for two weeks' work; $400 is the average annual income in Mali.

"Maybe," Dario said, "this is more serious than I thought."

Gigi motioned to me. He had a map draped over the hood of the Land Rover and was displaying what can only be described, given the circumstances, as a singular lack of urgency while he traced the course of the Niger River with a finger. Could I see how it flowed east, starting in the highlands to the west, and then humped north into the Sahara like a hissing cat before turning back south and east to empty into the Atlantic at the Bight of Benin? And here, perched on top of the northern hump of the river, was Timbuktu. Geography made it the great trading city of antiquity. North African Arabs from the Mediterranean coast brought trade goods south, through the desert, while the black African kingdoms sent gold north from the forests and mountains. They met in Timbuktu.

The caravans started about the time of Christ. Around A.D. 1100, Arabs began bringing salt down from the desert to trade in Timbuktu. Salt, used to preserve and flavor food, was then a rare spice, as much in demand in certain circles as cocaine is today, and equally expensive. It was traded weight for weight with gold in the Middle Ages, and for centuries the camel train bringing salt south to Timbuktu was called the Caravan of White Gold.

And while all this was happening, Gigi explained as he weighed a pair of melons in his hands, the climate was changing, changing, changed. The giraffe-littered grassland became a desert, and the Tuareg nomads became great warriors who preyed on the caravans. They developed the mehari camel—the ultimate medieval desert-war machine—a tall, elegant beast with an elongated back that allowed riders to sit in front of the hump, down low, in sword's reach of horsemen and those fleeing on foot.

The Tuaregs, not unreasonably, sought tolls and tributes from the caravans passing through their desert. The Arab caravans—1,000-camel operations and more—were loose confederations of traders, and they did not band together for mutual defense in the manner of American wagon trains facing hostile Indians in John Wayne movies. Tuareg raiders simply rode along with caravans, located the weakest groups, cut them out of the train, and took what they wanted. These affairs were most often bloody.

Today Tuaregs are considered the finest camel breeders and riders on earth. They live the romance of their past, still herding goats, pursuing a nomadic lifestyle, and dressing as they have throughout the whole of recorded history. The men most often wear blue robes—they are sometimes called the Blue Men of the Desert—and blue or black *chèches*, ten-foot-long strips of cloth that are wrapped around the head and neck and can be pulled up over the nose to protect the face from blowing sand. The *chèche* can also be used as a mask, which is no small advantage for those engaged in the business of banditry.

An Ambush

We had started in Gao, on the Niger River, where there was a paved street or two, a market, and crowds of people clamoring for a *cadeau*, a gift. Moving slowly through the streets was a plethora of white Toyota Land Cruisers, all of them belonging to various aid agencies. My traveling companion, Chris, talked with a woman from the UN High Commissioner for Refugees, who said things in northern Mali were settling down nicely. The six-year Tuareg rebellion against the central government in Bamako was essentially over. The rebels had signed a peace treaty in Timbuktu in March 1996, during a ceremony in which 3,000 weapons were burned in a great bonfire.

The droughts of the eighties and early nineties had helped fuel the rebellion, and the government had taken a unique step designed to feed hungry people: Former Tuareg rebels were allowed to enlist in the Malian army. The pay these soldiers earned fed large extended families. In effect, the Malian government had bought off the insurrection.

Which wasn't to say that everything was hunky-dory. The Tuareg rebels were actually a loosely aligned group of several different desert factions—the Popular Movement of this town, the People's Army of that area—and not all of them were in agreement with the peace treaty. Some, it was said, were still fighting. Plus, the army hadn't been able to take every former rebel who wanted a job, so there were still some bands of hard men in the desert, former rebels who were in fact out-and-out bandits.

The woman from the UN told Chris that about a month ago, bandits had ambushed several UNHCR workers, stolen their car, stripped them naked, and driven off. It was winter, and the workers were more likely to freeze to death at night than bake to death in the day. Besides, they weren't far from town, and everyone got back all right, so there wasn't any harm done.

"What town was that?" Chris asked.

"Kidal."

The Sleeping Colonel

The trans-Saharan highway from Gao to Kidal was a thin red line on the map, and the line was a lie. There was no road, only a number of braided tracks in the sand, all of them running vaguely northeast and littered with the rusted and half-buried hulks of vehicles that had surrendered to the desert. In Kidal, a sprawling town of adobe houses only slightly darker than the surrounding sand, we tried to speak with the governor, the army commander, anyone who could give us information on the security situation. We wanted to go to the salt mines. Was it safe? Few answers were forthcoming.

One morning, Alberto, Chris, and I walked the red-dust streets to the largest house in town. It was said to be owned by Colonel Yat, the man thought to be the instigator of the Tuareg rebellion, a fellow, we imagined, who might have some cogent thoughts about security.

The house had a high-walled courtyard punctuated by a pair of large metal doors wide enough to admit a good-size truck. We knocked for a long time until a gentleman inside opened one of the doors a crack. He wore threadbare black pants, a tattered red tunic, a black *chèche,* and rubber flip-flops. His right foot was terribly twisted. We were admitted into a large flagstone courtyard, where dozens of small trees had recently been planted. A satellite TV emblazoned with the RadioShack logo stood to one side of the house near several dozen 55-gallon drums of gasoline. A white Land Cruiser—the modern equivalent of the mehari camel—was parked in front of the door. There was a bullet hole just below the backseat on the driver's side.

One tended to speculate about such vehicles. In June 1990, after soldiers massacred several Tuaregs at a famine-refugee camp just over the border in Niger, rebels ambushed a team of aid workers, stole their Land Cruiser, and used it to attack the town of Ménaka, killing 14 Malian policemen. They escaped with guns and ammunition, and the rebellion was on. Soon there was fighting on the streets of Gao and on the blazing plain of Tanezrouft. Those are the facts. The legend is this: Colonel Yat, the man we had come to see, planned and executed the initial attacks.

The Toyota in the courtyard was white, like most aid agency cars, with a thin red stripe, and it did not carry a Malian license plate. I thought it might be a car with some history to it.

The house itself was unlike anything else in Kidal. It was a large, poured-cement building with flowing Moorish lines, painted brown and white. The man with the twisted foot knocked on an ornately carved wooden door. We stood there for some time until we were admitted by an almost preternaturally handsome Tuareg man who looked to be in his midthirties. He was about six feet tall, slender, wearing black slacks and gold-rimmed aviator sunglasses. His black *chèche* covered his mouth but not his neatly trimmed black mustache, and what we could see of his skin was that curious Tuareg color of charcoal and milk. He looked like a human sword. No names were given. No handshakes.

We said we'd like to speak with Colonel Yat, if it was possible. Wordlessly, the man turned, motioned for us to follow, and led us across highly polished wood floors to a large, dark room completely bare of furniture except for five mattresses pushed against the two far walls. Colonel Yat, we were given to understand, was the man-shaped lump under a sheet on one of the mattresses. It was late in the Muslim fasting month of Ramadan—no food or drink between sunrise and sunset—and the colonel was resting.

In whispers, we said that we could come back later, after sunset, when the colonel had refreshed himself. The man in sunglasses stared at us without expression. Colonel Yat stirred on his mattress and propped himself up on an elbow. He called out. His voice sounded sleep-clogged.

The slender Tuareg walked over, squatted by the bed, and exchanged a few words with the colonel. He walked back across the room, moving with a kind of lethal grace.

"What do you want to talk about?" he asked in heavily accented French.

"We want to talk about the current state of security in the area," Alberto said.

The man glided to the bed, whispered some words, and came back. "Why?"

"We're journalists," I said.

When that bit of information was relayed to the colonel, he pulled the sheet up over his head and turned to the wall.

"He doesn't want to talk to any journalists," the Tuareg said.

"We're not really journalists," Alberto said.

"He won't talk to you," the man replied, and even through his bad French, it sounded like a threat.

Out of Bounds

And so we drove to Aguelhok, where we hired Muhammad, who claimed to have been an intermediary between the government and the rebels during the late war and who now said he could no longer provide security.

Alberto called us all together in the courtyard, and we stood around in the dark, shifting from foot to foot because there were decisions to be made. Alberto's clients, the Italians, were all prosperous men who'd spent dozens of vacations together traveling in the Sahara. Now they wanted to go somewhere no one else had been, someplace unique, and Alberto, a guide with a reputation for getting things done in West Africa, had suggested the salt mines. This is the nature of adventure travel at the turn of the century. Truly exotic journeys, singular and privileged, like the one the Italians had contracted for, are easily arranged. A person standing in any airport on earth is no more than 48 hours from Timbuktu (given the proper connections and no desire to sleep). There, in that dusty desert town, travelers congregate at the post office. Send a card to your Aunt May, postmarked Timbuktu.

These days tourists are enthusiastically welcomed to the fabled city, which was once forbidden to the world outside Africa. Those with the perverse desire to visit currently forbidden sites, people like my Italian friends, must endure various uncertainties regarding their own personal safety.

The salt mines were just such a place. "For one thousand years," Alberto had told his Italian clients, "no one from the outside could go to the salt mines. They were forbidden. You don't tell people where your gold mine is located."

In the seventies, Alberto, like many adventurous young Europeans, had made a living of sorts shipping cars from Europe across the Mediterranean to Africa and then driving them 2,000 miles south through the Sahara and selling them in Mali or Nigeria or Togo or Burkina Faso. At the time, the salt mines were still operating up at Taoudenni, or so he had heard. No one he knew had ever been there. After independence from the French in 1960, the Malian government had used the mines as a political prison. Dissidents, generally from Bamako, were sent to the desert, where they were ill prepared to survive. To be condemned to work in the salt mines was tantamount to a death sentence.

Alberto became obsessed with the Taoudenni salt mine prison during his car-running days. As a political prison it was, of course, off-limits to foreigners. Forbidden. The only outsider Alberto ever talked to who had even gotten close to the prison was an International Red Cross worker who'd driven up from Timbuktu to check on the welfare of the prisoners. A guard stopped the man at gunpoint. The relief worker, staring into the business end of the rifle, explained the concept of international law and reminded the soldier of the strict neutrality of the Red Cross, called the Red Crescent in Muslim Africa. It was his duty to see that political prisoners were treated humanely, in accordance with international law.

"Imbecile," the guard said, "there is no law here."

Alberto hatched an ill-conceived plan to dress as an Arab and try to see the mines. Good sense finally got the better of him.

In 1991, the prison was shut down. Mali, once aligned with the Soviet Union, was now moving toward a multiparty democracy. The elimination of human-rights abuses, such as forced labor in the salt mines, was a first step in securing international aid money. In 1996, a spokesman for the U.S. State Department declared Mali's human-rights record for that year "a bright spot on the African continent."

But, Alberto had heard, there were still people working in the mines, on their own, for money, and since there was a thin red line on the map but no real roads from the mines at Taoudenni to Timbuktu, Alberto figured there still had to be camel caravans, carrying salt across the flowing dunes.

Seeing this medieval anachronism—the Caravan of White Gold— well, Alberto thought and the Italians agreed, it could be the experience of a lifetime. You just didn't want it to be the last experience of a lifetime. And so Alberto gave us a choice: We could go back down south of the Niger River and see, oh, the Dogon cliff dwellings, a nice, culturally captivating trip with no security problems at all—a trip, in fact, that Alberto guided frequently for the company Mountain Travel-Sobek. Mali south of the Niger was very safe.

Gigi and Dario wanted to wait a bit. See what happened. The two other Italians were both named Roberto. The Roberto everybody called Pepino had the heavy, ponderous dignity of a Roman emperor, and he was leaning toward retreat, as was the other Roberto, a man who reminded me of Clint Eastwood.

We decided not to decide.

Security Bandits

The next day was Eid-al-Fitr, a feast day marking the end of Ramadan. The streets of Aguelhok were thronged with people wearing resplendent new robes, all of them moving toward the mosque, where prayers were said outdoors. There were, I noticed, no cars other than our own in town.

After prayers, several families invited me into their homes, where I was invariably served tea, brewed on a charcoal brazier outside the front door. Tuareg tea is heated with an enormous amount of sugar until it boils up out of the pot and then served in a shot glass, which is always refilled twice. The first glass is said to be "strong like a man," the second "mild like a woman," and the third "sweet like love." The convention seemed to be that one shouted "hi-eee" several times during the ingestion of the tea.

So there were people shouting "hi-eee" and drinking tea, while four teenage girls, using a pair of washtubs for drums, sang a series of hauntingly melancholy songs. Two polite boys, about eight years old, had befriended me and were teaching me to say something in Arabic that they obviously considered to be just a bit naughty. Something, I imagined, in the nature of "Hello, my name is Mr. Poopy Pants."

I figured it out by the time they got to the proper name. "Lahidahi ilalahi Muhammad . . ."

I was laughing along with the boys and saying the naughty words—"There is no God but Allah, and Muhammad is his prophet"—when a shadow passed over. I looked up. A man in an iridescent green robe stood above me. He wore a black *chèche* and gold-rimmed aviator sunglasses. It was Colonel Yat's man, the human sword. He turned and walked swiftly away.

I followed at a cautious distance but lost him in the crowd. Two blocks away, parked by a curb, I found the bullet-scarred white Toyota we'd seen at Yat's house. It was the only other car in town, and now we knew who the bandits were. And why Muhammad, the security consultant, had turned down a year's wages for two weeks of work.

Alberto, who'd independently discovered the identity of the bandits, formulated a simple plan, modeled in part on the Malian solution to the Tuareg rebellion. We'd hire the bandits themselves to provide security.

Intarka, a Tuareg desert guide we'd hired on our first trip through Aguelhok, arranged a meeting, and we squatted in the courtyard with Colonel Yat's man and his two shadowy companions. The bandits wore their *chèche*s in mask mode. The human sword was named Mossa ag Ala (Mossa, son of Ala). His two buddies were both named Baye. ("This is my brother Larry and this is my other brother Larry," I thought.) And yes, for the right amount of money, they could get us to the salt mines and then safely down to Timbuktu.

Negotiations began in earnest. The would-be security bandits bargained fiercely but finally agreed upon a price. We walked to an administrative center and typed out what I thought was a fairly impressive-looking contract. Mossa scrawled his name, pulled his *chèche* down over his mouth, and actually smiled.

And then, our security problems presumably solved, we were off to the salt mines, about 500 miles to the north and west. Intarka navigated while Mossa, Baye, and Baye led the caravan in the white Toyota, which was essentially a rolling bomb. The bandits chain-smoked, all three of them in the front seat, while two leaky 55-gallon drums full of gasoline banged around in the back of the car.

The Tuaregs decided to run overland, off the tracks in the sand that were the trans-Saharan highway. They wanted to avoid traffic, because traffic meant cars and cars meant bandits. Once, when we crossed some fresh tracks, the bandit car sped ahead and pulled to a stop just below a rise. Mossa lay on his belly in the sand, glassing the plain ahead. There was a car in the distance, but no—focus, focus—it was simply a rock, glittering in the sun.

I wore a blue *chèche* to filter sand out of the air I was breathing. There are many ways to wrap a *chèche,* but I preferred the romantic Tuareg-bandit look, which left a three-foot-long tail of fabric hanging from the left shoulder. Stand in the desert wind, and the thing blew out behind you, Lawrence of Arabia style.

At one point, a herd of Dorcas gazelles bolted past our car. They were sand-colored animals about the size of elongated Brittany spaniels, sporting rabbity ears and a pair of inward curving horns about two feet long. The gazelles ran at speeds of over 40 miles an hour, making comical straddle-legged leaps every few seconds.

Here's a fashion hint concerning *chèche*s and wildlife photography: Suppose you pull to a stop when a herd of gazelles goes leaping by, jump out of the car with your camera, and slam the door behind you. If you are wearing your *chèche* in the fashionable Tuareg-bandit mode, the tail will catch in the door and abruptly pull you to your rear as you attempt to move forward.

A *chèche* pratfall is a source of great amusement to Tuaregs and Italians, to people from Togo like Daniel, the cook, and Amen, the mechanic (the one indispensable man in our party). An event of this nature will even draw an outright laugh from someone like Omar, the sulky Malian driver, who generally never smiled. Slapstick is universal. Brotherhood through comedy.

We sped over a flat desert plain where pebbly rocks were imbedded in hard sand, and our tires left tracks only half an inch deep. The Sahara provides two environments: *reg,* which is coarse flat sand, like the pea gravel we were driving through, and *erg,* shifting dune sand, which we expected to hit near the mines.

Just before dusk, Intarka had us pull into a large basin behind a low, rocky butte that would hide our campfires. The bandit car had veered off into the distance and was running inexplicable patterns across the sand—wide, curving turns, abrupt stops, sharp 90-degree corners. The bandits rolled into camp after dark with a gazelle they'd run to exhaustion, a method of hunting that didn't entirely appeal to my ideas about sportsmanship. Still, they ate the whole animal, which they grilled over a brush fire, and they gave the rabbity, horned head to Daniel, who felt he could use it in some fetish ceremony.

I asked Intarka, who had worked for the army during the rebellion, if he thought Mossa and his pals had really been planning to rob us. He shrugged. Would they have killed us, or merely taken the cars? Intarka said it didn't matter. "They're with us now," he said, "and their word is good."

Over by the Tuareg fire, Mossa threw down a shot glass of tea and shouted, "Hi-eee!"

The Salt Mines

Two more days of driving, while *reg* turned to *erg.* The dunes sloped gently upward where they faced the wind, then dropped off sharply on the other side. Omar couldn't seem to get the hang of driving the dunes. He'd race up the shallow slope, hit the crest of the dune, see what amounted to a cliff face dropping away below, and slam on the brakes, burying the front end of the truck two feet deep. Then it was sand-ladder time.

We dug out the wheels with shovels and hands and placed two three-foot-long tire-width metal rails in the sand underneath. Everyone pushed. Sometimes the car got going again and we ran after it, carrying the sand ladders, hoping there was some solid sand in the near distance. Often we had to dig out a second time, and a third, and a fourth. We were motoring through the Sahara three feet at a crack.

As we worked, a strong wind out of the northeast drove scouring sand before it. The seasonal harmattan winds carry sand from the Sahara all the way across the Atlantic and dump it on various Caribbean islands. A good blow seems to start low: It comes toward you pushing snakes of sand along the belly of the dune. Look around, and the world under your feet is alive with twisting, streaming sand snakes.

And then, half obscured by the ankle-deep sand snakes, I spied a series of tracks that looked like they had been made by three motorcycles running abreast. A closer look proved that these were camel tracks.

We saw them coming toward us: 60 camels walking single file, in three pack-strings of 20 apiece. Each of the camels carried four blocks of pure white salt. The blocks were rectangular, about two inches thick, two feet high, and three feet wide. They weighed about 80 pounds apiece. Four young Tuaregs walked along with the caravan.

In exchange for *cadeaux* of tea and sugar, the Tuaregs explained the economics of the Caravan of White Gold. Salt cost about $4 a block at the mine. If you were lucky, that same block might sell for $30 in Timbuktu. This 60-camel caravan carried about ten tons of salt and might fetch a price of $6,200.

From Timbuktu, the salt would be ferried up the Niger to the town of Mopti, where there was a paved road system that could get it out to the whole of West Africa. Taoudenni salt was more expensive than the more plentiful sea salt, but West Africans—truly spectacular cooks who combine French technique with African ingredients and creativity—believe it is the best tasting and are willing to pay premium prices.

Alberto and I talked about the realities of the salt trade. Camel caravans still existed, as they had in the Middle Ages, because they were the only economically feasible means of transporting salt from the mines to the Niger. "You could rent a Land Cruiser," Alberto explained. "Say your brother-in-law owns the rental company. You get it for $50 a day, instead of the $100 I pay. Three days at least to drive to the mines from Timbuktu. One day to buy and load. Three days back. Seven days at a rental cost of $350, plus $150 for gas. That's $500, not counting what you pay for a driver, food, oil, and maintenance. A Land Cruiser carries a ton. At your best price, you'd make $650, which wouldn't even cover expenses."

"What about a ten-ton truck?" I wondered.

"Wouldn't make it through the sand."

We were now, we calculated, only miles from the mines. The next morning we rose up over a sandy hillside, crested a dune, and found ourselves staring down into a great yellow-orange basin, an enormous flatland that melted almost imperceptibly into the curve of the earth. Scattered about the sand plain at odd intervals were a number of loony, artificial-looking landmarks: a pink sand-scoured cone, a kind of lopsided pyramid, and toward the center of the plain, a butte that looked like a many-footed sphinx. There were humans and hundreds of camels—tiny toy figures—moving about under the gaze of the sphinx. A vast area of sand and clay was cratered with small excavations, as if the place had suffered some terrible saturation-bombing raid.

A three-mile drive took us a thousand years back into history, to the periphery of the fabled Taoudenni salt mines. Men—there were no women—cautiously approached the cars. There was no electricity, no town, no road, only the desert all about and these men laboring in the sand and clay. A dozen or more of the men accompanied me as I strolled through the mines. They asked for and accepted *cadeaux* of aspirin and antibiotics, all the while pointing out the sights, such as they were.

The excavations were all of a size: rectangular holes about 10 by 20 feet and perhaps 15 feet deep. They'd been dug by hand, and the dirt was piled high around the craters.

The basin surrounding the many-footed sphinx, I imagined, had once been completely underwater: a vast inland lake, something like the Great Salt Lake in Utah. As the climate changed and the water evaporated away, minerals were deposited in the old lake bed. Centuries of blowing sand buried the salt about ten feet deep.

The good, glittering white salt was concentrated in a layer about three feet thick. It was covered over in a layer of dirty brown salt that some workers had chopped out in blocks to make small shelters. The men who dug in the pits were mostly blacks, and they used handmade axes and picks to dig out the salt, to file away the inferior brown mineral, and to smooth the edges of the blocks so they could be loaded on the camels, which knelt obediently in the sand and were loaded right at the pits. The camel drivers were Tuaregs or Arabs. Ringing the mines were 16 different caravans of 60 to 70 camels apiece, at least a thousand animals. In the distance, I counted five more pack strings, three of which were loaded and on their way out.

At sunset, Mossa, in his capacity as security bandit, made a point of gathering everyone up and getting us all out of the mines before dark. We would camp a good distance away from the work crews, far to the northeast, on the edge of an abandoned part of the mine where old excavations were gradually filling with sand. In the morning, we'd walk through the mines one more time and leave early in the afternoon for Timbuktu, so the Italians could catch their flight. Families would be expecting them, Dario told me, and family came first.

By the next morning, the harmattan had kicked into high gear. The goofy landmarks—the cone and pyramid—began to shimmer and fade in the distance. Wind-driven sand snakes raced across the desert floor.

I pulled the neck portion of my *chèche* up over my face. Visibility was down to 200 yards, and I wandered off into the desert to relieve myself in the privacy-veil provided by blowing sand. I walked several hundred yards, then looked back. I couldn't see the camp and assumed they couldn't see me. The wind was on my left shoulder. I did my business and went back, navigating by the simple expedient of putting the wind on my right shoulder.

At camp, Amen had some bad news. Gigi was missing. Clint Eastwood–looking Roberto was sitting on the ground, beside the Land Rover, and he was literally wringing his hands in an agony of guilt. He'd been walking with Gigi. Gigi had dithered. Roberto had left him somewhere in the mines. Now he was gone.

We put together a search party and, with Dario in the lead, retraced the steps Gigi had taken. Alberto, meanwhile, had hired men on camels to ride in a widening spiral around the mines, looking for a man on foot.

Dario, athletic and decisive, ran ahead, scaling the highest of the excavations, where he'd be more likely to see Gigi, especially if he was lying injured in one of the old pits. Clint Eastwood–looking Roberto trudged through the sand in a hopeless fashion. He was known in Italy as a great hunter, but all his skills were useless to him here. The sandstorm had swept the desert floor clear of tracks. To me, the mines seemed a hopeless labyrinth. Including the abandoned sections, I estimated about five square miles of closely spaced pits, more than a thousand of them.

We straggled back into camp well after dark.

There'd been no sign of Gigi.

Strangers in the Night

After dark, Intarka stood on the roof of the Land Rover with a handheld spotlight and spun the beam through a slow 360-degree circuit. He did this tirelessly and for hours. Perhaps Gigi would see the light and follow it to the source.

Alberto drove around the mines to a small collection of salt-block houses directly opposite our camp. It was the only thing that resembled a settlement that we'd seen. Someone, we all felt, must have kidnapped Gigi. Alberto's plan was to offer money, diplomatically, for the return of our friend.

There were no police in the settlement, no soldiers, no secular authorities at all. The men of the mines, however, had submitted themselves to the moral authority of the Maraboot, a minor Muslim cleric who knew the Koran and who settled various disputes. Alberto met him in a salt-block courtyard illuminated by lanterns.

The Maraboot looked the part: an ascetic man of about 50 with an untrimmed beard going to white. He wore a brown robe and a black chèche, and he carried his authority with a degree of nobility. He told Alberto that he knew the kind of men who lived in the mines and that none of them was a killer or a robber or a kidnapper. He felt Gigi was somewhere safe, perhaps staying with people until the morning. The Maraboot offered a prayer for Gigi and said, "I think you will find your friend in one day and that he will not be injured."

Alberto arrived back in our camp and said that he'd been impressed with the Maraboot. Still, he'd organized and paid in advance for a 50-man search party to leave at dawn. In the distance, toward the mines, we could see lights moving in our direction. They were flash-lights, held by people who wanted us to know they were coming to talk and were not sneaking up on us for an ambush. There were dozens of men. We interviewed them one by one.

An Arab with a broken foot said he'd seen one of the white men walk out into the desert about noon, just when the sandstorm was at its worst.

"What did he look like," Alberto asked.

"Blue *chèche*. He was the big one."

"Alberto," I said, "this guy's a moron. I'm standing right in front of him wearing a blue *chèche*. I'm the big one."

"Did you walk out into the desert?"

"To take a crap."

And so it went, for hours.

Clint Eastwood–looking Roberto sat in one of the cars, chain-smoking cigarettes. He blamed himself, and his eyes were red-rimmed from crying. Pepino-Roberto sat with him, assuring the grief-stricken man that Gigi's disappearance wasn't his fault. Things would work out.

At about 2 A.M. a tall Arab mounted elegantly on a sleek camel rode into camp along with four or five men on foot who seemed to be his retinue. The man wore a fine green robe and had the air of a digni-tary. "Your friend," he said, "is staying with some people." He, the Arab, knew these people. He could buy Gigi back for us. It would cost 500,000 African francs, about $1,000.

Dario said, "You see, the Arab people do their business at night." It was less an expression of prejudice than one of hope. Dario had agreed with me earlier in the evening; he, too, thought Gigi was dead. Now, for $1,000, that sorrow could be instantly lifted from his soul.

Alberto bargained with the Arab. He would give only 50,000 francs up front, the rest to be paid when we saw Gigi alive and well. The Arab dismounted, spat on the ground, and stood too close to Alberto. "500,000 now," he said. "Then maybe you will see your friend."

Alberto turned and nodded to the white Land Cruiser behind him, where Mossa, Baye, and Baye were smoking cigarettes and monitor-ing the conversation. Mossa snapped on his headlights, and the tall

Arab stood there blinking in the sudden glare. All three Tuaregs stepped out of the car, their black *chèches* worn up, in mask mode. The tall Arab, half blinded and confused, now looked as if all his internal organs had suddenly collapsed. I have seldom seen such outright fear on a man's face.

Mossa shouted three harsh words, and the tall Arab, along with his entourage, disappeared rapidly into the night.

No one slept. People kept wandering into camp with another tidbit of information. About four in the morning, a young Arab appeared and said that earlier in the evening he'd seen a white man walking toward the well at Taoudenni. This didn't seem right. The well was ten miles away and almost 180 degrees in the wrong direction. Gigi knew how to get around outdoors. Plus, Alberto had already been to the well, and none of the men there had seen Gigi.

Still, the young Arab seemed guileless. He was about 18 and knew nothing about our offer of a reward to anyone who found Gigi alive. The Arab said he had seen an older man walking alone and a spotlight beaming in the distance.

Now a white man walking in the desert at night was an extremely odd circumstance. So was the light. The young Arab had put the two together instantly: The light was for the white man. He had tried to tell him that, but the man just kept walking, staring at the ground and smiling vaguely. He had touched the man's arm and tried to turn him so he could see the light. But the man would not turn. He only made this strange gesture: The Arab dropped his hands to his sides.

"Wait a minute," I said, nearly shouting. "Do that again. Do it the way he did it."

The Arab turned his hands and moved them lightly up and down, as if patting two small children on the head. It was Gigi's futility gesture.

Goddamn! Gigi, still alive, somewhere near the Taoudenni well.

Gigi in the Tormentosa de Sable

Alberto, Pepino-Roberto, Chris, Mossa, and I sped overland in the eerie silver light of false dawn. We skidded to a stop at the well. There was a ruined French fort, an abandoned prison, and a defunct armored personnel carrier parked nearby. The sun was just rising, an enormous sphere balanced on the horizon, and its light, in the lingering haze of the sand-storm, was the lurid red of flowing blood. When I looked back toward the prison, there was a man walking our way. He cast a shadow 30 feet long, and it rose high and red on the whitewashed walls of the prison.

"Gigi!" I screamed.

Mossa had already seen him and was running over the sand, with me sprinting behind and steadily losing ground. Mossa hit Gigi like a linebacker and nearly knocked him over with an embrace. The car sped by me. Alberto was hugging Gigi when I got there, so Mossa hugged me. His eyes were tearing over. He wasn't crying—I couldn't imagine Mossa ever crying—but he was overcome with emotion. Pepino, walking in his heavy, dignified way, was sobbing openly, drying his eyes with a clean white handkerchief.

We offered Gigi some water, and he took a small sip, as if to be polite. He'd been lost in the Sahara, without a canteen, for 22 hours. He drank two more sips, then patted some children on the head to indicate that, no, no, he didn't want any more.

Back at our camp, Alberto paid the Arab the promised reward. Dario and Clint Eastwood–looking Roberto were taking turns embracing Gigi. Their gestures were elegantly expressive, fully Italian. Roberto, weeping, hugged Gigi, patted him on the back, and then pushed him out to arm's length and cocked a fist as if to punch him in the mouth.

Gigi was smiling his vague smile, staring at the ground, and every time Roberto gave him a little room, he began weighing a couple of melons in explanation.

After this orgy of emotion, while everyone else was packing up for what now had to be a doubly high-speed run over the dunes to Timbuktu, Gigi and I spoke for a couple of hours. I wanted to know what happened. We spoke in Spanish, our only common language.

Gigi told me:

He'd been walking, taking pictures, dithering around as usual, when the sandstorm hit. He'd marked his position by the various oddly shaped formations on the horizon—the many-footed sphinx, the pyramid, and the cone—and felt he would be able to tell where he was at any time by using the process of triangulation. Did I understand about triangulation? Gigi began weighing some melons in his hands. "*Por* example," he said, "if I move from here to the west, the cone would change its position on the horizon . . ."

"*Si, si, entiendo*," I said, a bit impatiently. I understood about triangulation.

Well, in a sandstorm, Gigi explained reasonably, a "*tormentosa de sable*," a man cannot see the mountains on the horizon and therefore cannot use the process of triangulation in order to fix his position. He'd been concentrating on his photos, because in the sand there were bits of clay that he was interested in and . . .

"So," I said, hurrying the story along, "when you looked up from your photo . . ."

The sand, Gigi said, was blowing and he couldn't see, so he just began walking but he must have gotten turned around taking the photos, and he walked the wrong way. He was walking almost directly into the wind, to the northeast, the direction of the harmattan, and he should have known that was wrong, but he was thinking about other things.

I almost asked what he was thinking about but quelled the impulse. At this point we'd been working on the story for an hour.

It was actually painful, walking into the blowing sand, so Gigi sat down for an hour or two, with his back to the wind. By late that afternoon, the storm had blown itself out, but the distant mountains, his triangulation points, were still obscured in the harmattan haze. Gigi walked in a large circle, hoping to see the rubble and excavation of the salt mines. But it was just a level plain of sand. He sat down to think again, admired the sunset, and then got up, picked a direction at random, and began walking.

It was dark when a young man came up to him and began speaking in a language Gigi took to be Arabic. Gigi tried to project the image of an Italian gentleman out on an evening stroll, preoccupied with his own thoughts and unwilling to be bothered. The young man grabbed his arm as if he wanted him to turn and go the other way. Gigi had some preconceived notions about Arabs in the dark and so he refused to turn and see the light. In the day, Gigi said, it might have been different. He continued walking, smiling at the ground and making his it-is-useless gesture of patting children on the head. The Arab shrugged and left him. Gigi felt he'd handled the encounter well.

He walked for several more hours until he saw the lights of some campfires reflecting off a whitewashed building in the distance. As he got closer, he could see figures moving around the fires, then he could hear the shouts and laughter of people conversing in Arabic. They seemed to be camped around a well.

In the building nearest him, and farthest from the fires and the people, there were several very small rooms with bars on the windows. It was, Gigi assumed, the old prison. He chose a cell and lay down. The brick building held the heat of the day and it was all quite pleasant. The sky had now cleared, and Gigi could see the stars.

He lay on his back and formulated a plan. His friends had to get to Timbuktu to catch a flight to Bamako and then to Italy, where their families would be waiting. He expected that we would be searching for him, but he hoped we'd leave by noon, so as not to miss the flight. He didn't want to have a lot of families worried on his account.

And if we did leave, Gigi would simply walk over to the Arabs by the well, introduce himself, and ask if he could tag along on the 500-mile trip back to Timbuktu. He'd be home in a couple of months.

Satisfied with his plan, Gigi fell into a sleep so profound that he didn't hear the Land Rover pull into the prison compound at 11 that night. He didn't hear Alberto and Chris and Pepino conversing with the Arabs. He'd hid himself well, and none of the men had seen him.

He woke refreshed just before dawn. As soon as the sun came up, he walked out of the prison, on his way down to the well, to make friends with the Arabs. That's when he saw me and Mossa and Pepino. All these people sprinting over the desert in his direction, crying and shouting. It was strange.

The Maraboot's *Cadeau*

We'd lost a day looking for Gigi, but there was a chance the Italians could still make their flight out of Timbuktu. However, there were thank-yous to be offered, and that would delay us. Alberto stopped at the Maraboot's salt-block house and called off the morning's search. The men he'd hired could keep the money that had been given them. Most of them had searched for Gigi yesterday afternoon anyway, without compensation. We were very grateful.

Alberto thanked the Maraboot for his prayers and asked if there was anything he could do: Would the Maraboot accept a *cadeau*? He would not. The cleric was just happy that everything had turned out well and that our friend was safe. The Maraboot's refusal made him all the more impressive in our eyes. We'd been bombarded by cries for *cadeaux* for weeks.

But no, after a moment's reflection, the Maraboot said there was something we could do. There were two Arab men who had been stranded at the mines and were unaffiliated with any caravan. Could we take them back to their homes about 200 miles north of Timbuktu?

Yes, of course.

Both the Arabs were thin, desiccated-looking men, with strong, coppery planes in their faces and high arched noses. They looked like Moorish versions of Don Quixote, as drawn by El Greco. The man who rode with me in the Land Rover was named Nazim, and he carried a 20-pound bag of dates. If his good luck evaporated and he had to walk, the dates would sustain him for the 300-mile trek.

Nazim had never ridden in a car before. He had to be shown how to work the door latch and the handle that rolled down the window. In 30 seconds, he had pretty much mastered the technological intricacies involved in being an automobile passenger.

The Arabs navigated. They rapidly figured out what sort of terrain was best for the vehicles and chose areas where the wind had packed sand tight to the ribs of the dunes. We flew over a roller coaster of smooth sand at 40 miles an hour. Every few hours we converged on the main camel track leading toward the mines. I counted 12 caravans heading in to the mines and 11 going out, about 1,600 camels in all.

It was near noon, and Nazim was getting nervous, looking around and fidgeting.

"Prayers," I shouted over the rattle of the diesel engine.

Alberto stopped the car, and Nazim, an old hand with door latches by now, jumped out and knelt in the sand, facing east. While the Tuaregs and Arabs prayed together, I scanned the line of dunes ahead, which rose and crested like so many ocean waves about to break. Bright, flashing lights seemed to be moving over the summit of the highest of the dunes, a dozen or more miles away. Although I couldn't

see the camels, I guessed it had to be another caravan, fully loaded,
the salt blocks glinting in the sun like a long line of signal mirrors.

We drove until well after dark and then set up camp at the base of
a high dune that had the rolling sensuality of a line-drawn nude. The
sand was cool and seemed luxurious. The constellations spun above,
almost impossibly bright, and for a moment the Sahara seemed the
most romantic spot on earth.

Many women, I knew, especially French women, travel to the desert
hoping to kindle a romance with a proud desert chieftain, with someone, I imagined, exactly like Mossa. Ah, the handsome features, the
noble warrior's heart, the strong, slender hands stroking under cotton
robes with the hard stars burning overhead . . .

"I heard two American women talking about their affairs with
Tuaregs," Alberto told me. "I was driving a tour. They didn't know I
spoke English."

"What did they say?"

It was pretty much as I had thought. The women agreed the Tuareg
men were physically beautiful, and they took these women, there in
the sand, as if by right. They took them brashly and with a breath of
contempt, which made it that much more exciting.

Just one thing about all that ravishing, Alberto added.

"What?"

"They said it was quick."

Alberto pronounced the word "queek."

"Queek," I repeated, secretly pleased.

"Yes, both of them agreed. Queek, queek, it is all over."

We exchanged a glance, Alberto and I. The glance said, "Maybe we
are not the most desirable specimens of masculinity in this desert, but—
in contrast to every offensively handsome Tuareg male alive—we
would, given the opportunity, conduct this ravishment-under-the-stars
business with a good deal less efficiency."

Such delusions are the salve of wounded pride.

Revenge of the Gazelles

Gradually, grudgingly, the sand began to give way to a sparsely vege-
tated plain that, after miles of *erg*, seemed incredibly lush. There were

a few camels feeding on acacia trees, and then, as we slowed to negotiate a path through a large herd of goats, Nazim pointed to a pair of
blue-and-beige open-fronted tents. He said, "Ah, ah, ah."

We stopped. A woman huddled in the nearest tent, protectively pushing a pair of youngsters behind her. Cars never came this way. Her
expression seemed to say, "Nothing good can come of this." Nazim
stepped out of the Land Rover and carefully closed the door behind
him, as if to demonstrate new skills. The woman stared at Nazim in
a kind of awed astonishment. She rose slowly to her feet, stupefied,
then ran to him and hugged him tightly while the two small children
pulled at the folds of his tunic.

So we delivered the Maraboot's *cadeau*, and thank you, Nazim, but
no time for tea. It was still ten hours to Timbuktu, and 16 hours until
the Italians' flight.

We ran hard. Omar, the surly Malian driver, blew a shock absorber,
there was a flat tire or two on the other vehicles, and our security bandits' gasoline drums were running low, which didn't actually stop them
from chasing gazelles.

We were slaloming up and down a series of sloping dunes in the
dark, about 50 miles north of Timbuktu, when the bandits finally and
irrevocably ran out of gas. Mossa, Baye, and Baye got out and surrounded their vehicle. They stood with their arms crossed over their
chests, staring hard at the Toyota as if it owed them some sort of an
explanation.

It was a tableau I'd entitle "The Revenge of the Gazelles."

Alberto took a GPS reading while Mossa, Baye, and Baye discussed
their options. It was decided that Baye and Baye would stay with the
car while Mossa would come with us, continuing to provide high-class
security all the way to Timbuktu, as agreed. There he'd arrange for
another car and would be back to pick up Baye and Baye by and by.

The two men gave everyone a hug in the abrupt bone-crushing manner of the desert. And then we were off again.

"Bye-bye, Baye Baye," everyone shouted from the windows. I imagine we sounded like a pack of dogs all suffering from the same strange
speech impediment.

"Bye-bye, Baye and Baye."

"Hi-eee, Hi-eee," shouted Baye and Baye.

The vehicles slipped and slid across the shifting sand. They got bogged down. They got pushed out on sand ladders. They slowed near the top of most every dune, engines roaring, slowing, slowing, stopping. We had to back down every third slope and try again. And then, at the summit of a dune that had taken us four tries to climb, I saw our destination only ten miles away. It was spread out below us in all its glittering magnificence, such as it was (I counted 27 lights): the historic and formerly forbidden city of Timbuktu, where there was a reasonably comfortable hotel, cold beer for sale, a post office, and a jetport that was 48 hours from any major airport on earth. Some of which, I thought, were not entirely secure.

October 1997

The Very Short History of Nunavut

WILLIAM T. VOLLMANN

On the first of April 1999, I had the privilege of watching as a new territory came into being, for most of the right reasons. The birth happened at midnight, in Canada's far north, with fireworks instead of bloodshed. I had just returned from Kosovo, and while I was watching the bright detonations over Iqaluit, the new capital of the new Nunavut, NATO bombers were busy over Yugoslavia. I could not help thinking of the faraway blossoms of those incendiary shells as I stood at the edge of the sea-ice that night when Nunavut became real, with Inuit children calling and roaring with happiness at each explosion. The fireworks hung like palm fronds around the full moon, offering green comets instead of leaves, and the silhouettes of gloved and parkaed people standing in the snow took on noonday life for a moment, until the light faded. Snow scuttered like gravel underfoot. There came more and more bursts, celebrated by fur-ruffed kids sitting on a high hillock of snow that had gone glassy with ice. With the windchill it was 40 below; my face was numb; my pen froze. I'll never forget the dark figures on the pale snow, the rapturous cries, the fireworks' remarkable purity and clarity in that cold air. Every fiery star seemed as solid as a shard of glass in a kaleidoscope, and we could see its slowly dimming fall to the ice. Witnessing all around me the joy of the Nunavummiut, who had regained some control over their nation at last—after all, Nunavut means "our land"—I was moved almost to tears.

If you look at a map and take in the vastness of that balsamic paradise called Canada, you will quickly see why Nunavut, huge as it is, remains outside the ken of so many Canadians, let alone the rest of the world.

"Nunavut? What's that?" said a taxi driver in Montreal when I passed through on my way north to Iqaluit. "Le Grand Nord," I tried to explain. "Île de Baffin, Île d'Ellesmere, Île de . . ."

He shrugged. He didn't really care. Because Nunavut lies so far away from almost everything! We're speaking of one-fifth of Canada's landmass, it's true—730,000 square miles with one paved road, only 25,000 people, and 27 times that many caribou. But Canada, like Russia, can scarcely see and count herself in her entirety. Two square miles or two million, it's all the same to Canada. And so until now the conception, the *idea*, of Nunavut has lain neglected, misunderstood. But the actual ground of Nunavut itself? Well, for centuries explorers, whalers, merchants, politicians, and soldiers have been coming here to the frozen edge of the world—first only to where the ice began as they crept and surveyed, clinging to the safety of water, the safety of summer's final channels, dark blue and corduroyed with sunlight, with the white cloud-puzzles overhead, past overhung ice-puzzles—and then the white people calculated, gambled, stepped onto the ice.

Pretty soon some were doing well, like a Quebecer taxi driver I know in Iqaluit who stops by the Navigator Inn late at night when Inuit carvers sell their greenstone animal figures cheap because they crave drunkenness; my acquaintance pays $60 per piece and sends them to his sister down south, who sells them for $400, keeps a 10 percent commission, and returns him the rest, so he clears a tax-free ten grand a year from that racket alone. Decades of cigarette smoking have awarded him the voice of an Inuit throat-singer, and in those ragged tones he always promises to lead me to the best carvers or, if I don't go for that, he can score me drugs, or anoint me a member of a top-secret club whose purpose is to help me get *really close* to Inuit girls.

I rarely stay in Arctic towns on my visits north. I come with my shelter on my back; I get off the plane and I start walking. Two or three miles outside of town I pitch my tent. I come in a few times and try to make friends. I go to church on Sundays and listen to the Inuit pray for the Queen of England in Inuktitut. But mostly I leave them alone. I am here to listen to wind and water.

What does Nunavut look like? This is difficult for me to say, not only because deep down I don't want you to go to the Arctic, and I feel guilty about going myself—Nunavut should be left to the Nunavummiut—but also because so many happy images and memories swirl behind my eyes whenever I think about this land. I wrote a novel set in the Canadian Arctic landscape, and I could write many more: pods of whales, polar bears, caribou running on ridge tops, summer moss, summer berries, mosquito crowds dense enough to blacken your face, cold that hurts, a sun that goes round and round in the sky like a clock without ever setting, long days and nights of winter moonlight bright enough to read a newspaper by (if you could stop shivering), the low elongations of the land, the blues and purples of the frozen sea, the sulphur-smelling crags of Baffin Island, waist- and shoulder-high rivers to ford, herds of musk oxen gathered (their spiked horns pointing out) in circles like immense wagon wheels, fossilized ferns and pine needles in valleys of icy shale, light, closeness to the sky, and above all, solitude.

I love that land, but it is not mine. It can never belong to me. When I was younger I once thought about settling here, in which case I would have become a member of the 15 percent of the Nunavummiut who aren't of Inuit extraction. Few of those people stay for long. So the land is truly not even mine to describe. To do so is to describe the Inuit themselves, because the Inuit are the land and the land belongs to them.

An Inuit woman named Elisapi has been my translator on several visits to the far northern settlement of Resolute; she is gentle, quiet, and plain, a serious, fortyish woman to whom I have always felt I could say anything. What word can describe her better than *pure*? But then I am always saying this about Inuit. To borrow from some idiot's remark about pornography, I can't define purity, but I know it when I see it. In Elisapi's case I think of kindness and patience and an unassuming spirituality. I hate even to write this much; I don't want to invade her soul with my conjectures and blundering definitions. Once, when I asked her what she thought was the most beautiful place in the Arctic, Elisapi looked at me in surprise and said, "Why, the land, of course. *All* the land."

What Elisapi loves above all else is to be "out on the land"—a phrase of almost mystic significance to Nunavummiut. *Out on the land!* On one of my trips to Iqaluit I met the wife of a carver, a slender woman who engraves brooches of walrus ivory. "I love to hunt anything," she said—the same words I'd already heard uttered by so many. "I've killed caribou, seal, walrus. I never killed a whale or a polar bear, but my niece killed both already." She spoke with immense pride.

Elisapi, her husband, Joe, and their children have spent many a summer in a hunting camp on the ice. Even non-Inuit get infected. I've heard a Quebecer schoolteacher here use the same words: She was going to take her children out on the land for Easter, if the wind didn't prove too cold for the little ones. A young Anglo man I met in Apex, a little offshoot of Iqaluit, was always saying, "Man, I wish I were out on the land. Man, I wish I had a machine."

I remember the day Elisapi told me about the way she feels about the land. There was a strange light upon the hills and hollows, the armpits and throats of the white country, with the snow-covered sea pale blue like open water, and when Elisapi spoke, a feeling between love and sadness came over me, the same feeling I have year after year in the Arctic when I'm alone with mountains or musk oxen, far away beneath the sky.

Do I have your permission to compress the history of the Canadian Arctic into nine paragraphs? In 1576 Martin Frobisher sailed from England to seek the Northwest Passage. He anchored off Baffin Island, which now forms the eastern boundary of Nunavut, and loaded up his ship with tons of fool's gold while kidnapping other cargo: a man and an Inuit woman holding a small child by the hand. Frobisher's men carried them away from an elder, perhaps the child's grandmother, who "howled horribly." Perhaps it is no wonder that the capital, the only town of any size (population 4,500), which stands upon the site of the mariner's landing and which for years and years was called Frobisher Bay, changed its name to Iqaluit—"the place of many big fish." The locals would rather not remember him.

In Frobisher's time, Inuit families were self-sufficient, or else they starved. But then whalers from England and Scotland and elsewhere began to trade knives, needles, tea, rifles, and bullets for furs, meat, and ivory. Beginning in the late eighteenth century, subsistence hunting lost ground to the fur trade—although even now, as much as half of what some Nunavummiut eat remains "country food": caribou, seal, whale, ptarmigan, and the like, killed by relatives or friends. It was only in the second half of this century, when Canadian and American World War II air bases and then English-language schools mushroomed in the high Arctic, that the Inuit began to live in towns, 28 little government-created settlements scattered over the snow and ice.

The growing dependence on trading with outsiders proved sometimes beneficial, sometimes pernicious. What happens if, instead of killing caribou to feed my family, I hunt Arctic foxes to sell their skins for bullets? Then we earn a lot of bullets, provided that the price of fox skins stays high in the south and my caribou hunting is easy. But if the price falls, we just might starve, which dozens did in the 1934–35 central Arctic famine. We might also starve, or simply become idle and despondent, if hunting seals or whales were no longer acceptable, as happened in the 1970s and '80s when Greenpeace and other environmental and animal-rights groups crippled the international sealskin trade. These do-gooders are accordingly hated throughout the Arctic; with varying degrees of justification, unemployment and suicides have been blamed on them. Many's the time in Nunavut and Greenland that I've been asked, "Are you a spy from Greenpeace?"

It was in part to protect the Inuit from a drastic boom-and-bust cycle that, in the 1960s, Canada's federal politicians began to encourage the construction of hamlets where people could enjoy medical care, education, warm beds, and an uninterrupted food supply. An old lady who'd been born in an igloo once told me, "In old days we had a very hard time. Government came, and it got easier." We sat on the sofa in her house in Iqaluit's tumble of old military hangars and prefab housing and unnamed gravel roads. I asked her, "If people wanted to live on the land again, would you go with them or would you stay in your house?" Sitting with her hands clasped in her lap, her head trembling, perhaps from Parkinson's disease, she peered at me through her huge and rimless spectacles, and then replied in high-pitched, glottal Inuktitut, "I can't stay in a remote outpost now. From the hospital they're giving me medicine, so I must stay in town."

And so, on southern Nunavut's green-mossed rock, painted oil drums, painted wood-and-metal houses, and garbage dumps rose up in the summer rain. In northern Nunavut, the colored houses appeared upon tan gravel banks. Of course, this new way of life further accelerated the very dependence that had already caused so much harm. I wonder if by then the future was already as evident as a yellow lightbulb in Iqaluit glaring down on rock-hard snow. That future was mass welfare. Animal populations declined near the towns, making hunting less practical and more occasional. Dog teams sickened in the close quarters. More than one hunter came home in those days only to find that the Mounties had shot all his dogs in the interest of public health—for the white people, it seemed, always knew best. Could this have anything to do with the fact that Nunavut has six times the national suicide rate?

The most famous of these resettlement efforts took place between 1953 and 1955, when the government forcibly relocated some 17 extended Inuit families from Inukjuak to new settlements at Resolute and Grise Fiord. Inukjuak lies way down in northern Quebec, nearly 400 miles south of Nunavut as the Arctic raven flies. To me it is almost paradise. It is green, not white. In summer the tundra hangs thick with crowberries and caribou run everywhere. In winter the sun never disappears entirely. Elisapi's mother, Old Annie, who sewed my *kamiks*, the sealskin boots I wear on my feet, was born in a camp there. She never wanted to leave. But they shipped her north.

Some Inuit believe that the Canadian government wanted to assert sovereignty over the high Arctic islands in the face of the American air bases strategically placed there in World War II, and therefore settled them with the indigenous people most likely to survive. But it should also be said that Inukjuak was not so edenic in the late 1940s: The caribou herds were dwindling, the price of fur had fallen, the people were falling deeper into welfare addiction. The government figured, paternalistically, why not just move some Inuit to the northern ice and let them become the self-sufficient hunters of old. For good measure, they also relocated some families from Ellesmere Island's Pond Inlet—northerners to help the southerners settle in. But the relocations were accomplished against people's wills, with misinformation, and with appalling results. The people from Inukjuak were unfamiliar with the hunting strategies they needed to succeed on the Arctic pack ice; they didn't even get along with the Pond Inlet Inuit, who didn't even speak the same dialect. Look at a map of Canada to see how far away from home these people were taken. See Inukjuak on the northeastern shore of Hudson Bay? Now let your eyes sail north as the Canadian Navy sealift-supply ship *C.D. Howe* did, carrying those Inuit families: first 300 miles into what is now Nunavut (we're out of Hudson Bay at last) and then perhaps 1,000 miles farther north and 200 miles west, almost to the magnetic North Pole.

The first time I went to Resolute, it was mid-August, around the same time the settlers had arrived, and it was snowing. By the time I left six weeks later, I had to chop up my drinking water with an ax. "When we arrived it was dark and cold," an old woman told me. "My child was really skinny from starving." The Inukjuak Inuit, who had never built igloos, constructed houses out of old packing crates and foraged for food in the garbage dumps of the whites, a sparse scattering of whom were stationed there with the Mounties, who oversaw a trading post in Resolute. For high prices, payable in furs, an Inuit hunter could obtain a scant few supplies, but sometimes there was an additional price—the sexual services of his wife. The results of the relocations: hunger, tuberculosis, lifelong bitterness.

The communities in Resolute and Grise Fiord survived, because Inuit are pretty damned tough. And in the more than 20-year-long tale of the land-claims negotiations that created Nunavut, one reads a similar tenacity. What Nunavut gained—besides more than a billion Canadian dollars over the next 14 years and valuable mineral rights—was a measure of self-governance. Nunavut is now a territory, exactly like the Yukon, exactly like the Northwest Territories it had been part of. What the Inuit gave up was the land. One of the only native North American groups who had never entered into a land treaty, many Inuit were anxious about extinguishing aboriginal title, and when the matter first came up for election in 1982, only 56 percent voted in favor of division. But what ultimately passed in 1993—the Nunavut Land Claims Agreement Act—was the biggest land deal between a government and an aboriginal people in North American history. Suffice it to say that in the face of federal skepticism and infighting and bureaucratic foot-dragging and worse, a partition line was at long last drawn through the Northwest Territories. What lay east became Nunavut.

To me it was a kind of miracle that this good thing was about to happen. And Iqaluit, which like so many Arctic towns is saturated with militaryspeak from the air-base days, seemed filled instead with joy-speak. Late in the evening on that last night of Northwest Territoriality, the bunkerlike elementary school filled with crowds come to hear the Anglican service in honor of Nunavut's birth. The stage was bedecked with figures in red and white robes, and the minister said, "We must remember that what we call Nunavut, our land, is in fact God's gift to us." In front of me was a little girl, half asleep in her mother's *amauti*, a parka with a hooded pouch in back for carrying babies. "We pray for our new commissioner," the minister went on, "for our new premier, for their families, for our new justices, who will be sworn in in a few moments, and most of all we pray for ourselves." In that cavernous, windowless gymnasium, built on concrete like a shop floor, they rose and prayed in English, French, and Inuktitut. "Now may the blessing of God Almighty be with us, both now and indeed forevermore. Amen." Then the minister smiled, checked his watch, and said, "Twenty-two minutes," and everyone laughed. In Inuktitut they sang "Now Thank We All Our God" in sweet and steady voices. A woman in a crimson vest embroidered with a white polar bear leaned her head upon her husband's shoulder as she sang.

A Nunavut for Nunavummiut—only some of the white cab drivers were sullen about it. Their taxi lights shone slow on the glassy night snow between the still, cold lights of the settlement.

The new territory purports to represent the interests of all residents, but the ultimate goal is to create a de facto self-governing Inuit homeland—not now, of course, but in 20 or 50 years. Today the non-Inuit 15 percent of the population holds a disproportionate number of the government, medical, and teaching jobs. Few Inuit are trained. Only a third of Nunavut's teachers are Inuit; there are no Inuit doctors; there is only one Inuit lawyer in all of Nunavut, 34-year-old Paul Okalik, and he has been elected its first premier. A high-school dropout from Pangnirtung, a little village on the eastern shore of Baffin Island, Okalik wrestled with alcohol problems, jail, and his brother's suicide before going back to school on student loans. Despite his involvement in the Nunavut negotiations, he is as freshly minted a politician as Nunavut is a territory: He passed the bar and became premier within six weeks. The new territory's elder statesman—the father of Nunavut—is John Amagoalik, the journalist-politician who negotiated the land-claims settlement that created it and ran the Nunavut Implementation Commission that shaped its government. Sixteen of Nunavut's 19 legislators are Inuit, too—a few former mayors, some businessmen, a snowplow operator. Starting on Nunavut Day, when a white person in the territorial government wrote a memo to his superiors, the reply might well come back in Inuktitut.

"They cannot just want to throw white people away," a Quebecer teacher named Thérèse, who works at the elementary school in Iqaluit, told me. "Not all of the Inuit are qualified." But then she added quietly, "I know some white people are afraid of losing their jobs, but gradually they should be replaced."

Plenty of Caucasians do fine in Nunavut: Elisapi's husband, Joe, for one, is white and as northern an individual as I have ever met. But many find living in Nunavut difficult. The language daunts them; the mores are so different. Thérèse had spent four years in Iqaluit, but she planned to return south. She had a few Inuit friends, acquaintances really, from work. But Nunavut was not hers.

Meanwhile, in northern Quebec, the Inuit region known as Nunavik (from which the relocations to Resolute and Grise Fiord were carried out) harbors similar, half-concealed aspirations to autonomy. And down in Ottawa, even as Nunavut set off its fireworks, Cree Indians were drumming and singing on Parliament Hill in protest of the new territory, on the grounds that 31,000 square miles of their land have been stolen to create it. And of course, many Quebecers long to secede from Canada and form their own Francophone nation. The white taxi drivers I talked with in Iqaluit are among this number: They told me that this whole Nunavut business was all *shit*. The Inuit weren't ready, one of them opined. Quebec should secede, but not Nunavut. Quebec pays too much in taxes, and Canada just called Quebecers *fucking frogs*. The prime minister was an *asshole*. This last cabbie was an angry, stupid man, but, like the Inuit themselves, all he really wanted was some kind of recognition.

Finally, from what now remains of the Northwest Territories comes talk of further partitions and ethnic homelands. There was a move to rename this region Denedeh because so much of it was Dene Indian land, but the whites (who'd become the majority after the partition of Nunavut) voted down the measure, after which a bitter joke went around the Northwest Territories that the only real way to satisfy them would be to call the territory by the Anglo name of Bob.

Given the desire of so many places to un-Canada themselves to varying degrees, I was all the more impressed when the prime minster of Canada, Jean Chrétien, who had flown up to Iqaluit for the Nunavut Day festivities, rated justice over expediency in his speech that night. "We have come to recognize the right of the people of the north to take control of their own destiny," he proclaimed. And everyone stood up and cheered, and I cheered.

It would be as pleasing as it would be false to end our tale with the close of that inaugural ceremony in one of the concrete military hangar bays, as tiny old Helen Mamyaok Maksagak, first commissioner of Nunavut, hugged to her heart the flag of her territory, presented to her by Inuit boys from Canada's Boy Scouts, the Junior Rangers. Or to conclude on Nunavut Night, the evening after the fireworks, where a heavy-metal band from Kuujuaq was entertaining one crowd with noise and dry-ice vapor while two hangars down the little kids were jigging to banjo and fiddle, and the old ladies in parkas were nodding, smiling, clapping, and everyone was applauding, and Premier Okalik was wandering around in his sealskin vest, floating in a shyly happy dream.

The air grew hot with the fragrance of bubble gum, wet fur, human sweat. Dancers came out, circling and snaking to the repetitive melody;

an old man in a red cap and a collar of wolverine skins with the claws still on jogged happily up and down, watching. So many people with Nunavut hats and T-shirts, so many with the new Nunavut sweatshirts! But finally it was time to go back out among the gray snowdrifts and glaring streetlights of April, back to the steep-roofed houses to sleep. And the next morning and forever the tale of Nunavut must continue, this time without miraculous ceremonies.

"I've already given you enough beer," the white waiter in Iqaluit's Komatik Restaurant told the Inuit grandmother and her toothless boyfriend. "So I'll just put your next beer in the fridge and give it to you next time."

At this, the boyfriend started crying out in Inuktitut, and the grandmother joined in, wailing, "How *come* you? How come?"

"You cannot drink them tonight because you don't need the beer," the waiter insisted. "You've had too much. That's the end of the conversation."

"Where's my beer?" the grandmother demanded. "Where's my goddamned beer?" She wore a T-shirt printed in memory of a friend who'd died. Her eyes were lights glaring on ice; her words were breath-steam in the night. She was 44 years old.

"If you keep this up," the waiter said, "there'll be trouble."

It was two nights after Nunavut Day. I'd seen her earlier that afternoon before she was drunk, a big, squat woman with cropped hair, upslanted eyes, and a down-pouted mouth. She was pale and old; her arms were covered with cooking burns. One of her sisters had died of cancer, another of alcoholism, a brother in a car accident (the car ran over his head). The last brother had hanged himself "because he was crazy," she said.

Now, as the waiter refused to serve her and her boyfriend, I invited them back to my hotel, which stood almost within sight of the restaurant. The grandmother's boyfriend didn't want to come. He stayed on at the Komatik, wiggling his fingers, feebly bewildered.

So the grandmother and I walked and she whined and wept, because she was very cold. Her ancient parka didn't zip anymore, and the alcohol had only pretended to warm her, in much the same fashion that the low sun can gild a house's siding so that it glows and shines against the blue snow with spurious preciousness. I offered to let her wear my parka but she wouldn't. She kept crying: "Too cold! *Ikkii!*" She touched my hand and said: "You cold. Cold! You too cold! *Ikkii!* Better you eat like Inuk. Eat meat. Eat caribou, walrus, seal . . ."

Anytime I wanted her to smile, I only had to ask her what animals she liked to hunt. She'd reply: "Any kind!" and would commence counting off the different animals on her fingers, uttering the Inuktitut names. Earlier that evening, with the beer not yet raging in her, she remained a wise old huntress. Just as caribou are sometimes silhouetted against snow, especially on ridges and when they crouch down to graze, snowy-white-on-white, so her memories stood out or hid, browsing and drowsing within her, living their own life. She could scarcely read or write, but (or perhaps therefore) she could remember. And for her, animals were the most vividly numinous entities.

I said that I wanted to go hunting sometime with her or her family, at which she began to check me out very seriously and soberly, saying, "OK, Bill, you got the mitts, you got the coat; you can come hunting. Your pants gonna be cold, though." Not having planned on hunting again this trip, I'd left my windpants back in America.

We were outside then. It was 20 below zero. Later that night, I wandered wearily through one of Iqaluit's arcade malls, my hood thrown back, my parka unzipped, wearing my *kamiks* since I had no other shoes, my mitts dangling conveniently from strings at my sleeves. A slender young Inuit girl, high or crazed, began mocking me and eventually came running down the hall and punched me and kicked me, shrieking: "Where are you *from,* Daddy-o? What are you doing with all that fuckin' stupid gear?"

She herself was dressed like a southern California girl, and I wondered whether she had been among those serenely happy crowds on Nunavut Day, those people clapping grimy work gloves and sealskin mitts, while the fur ruffs of their parkas swirled in the wind. So angry and sad, did she care about Nunavut?

For her, the beauties of utility had given way to the beauties of fashion. Moreover, in so many young people's eyes, utility and fashion married one another in synthetic apparel. On a walk in Apex, I found myself promenading beside a young Anglo guy with dyed hair along the community's frozen shore, past rocks and trash cans protruding from the snow. He wore camouflage pants and a brand-name American parka. As we approached the frozen drifts on the frozen sea, with the wide, low domes of snow-islands ahead, he was telling me about one of his adventures over the winter. "We were fuckin' set up, man. We had fuckin' beer and the whole fuckin' nine yards. Then we got slammed with a 120-kilometer wind and, well, we lay down between our snowmobiles and we made it." He had no use for caribou-skin clothing, and neither did I.

In that mall, to be sure, I was ludicrously overdressed. My old huntress did not find me so. She was charitable and practical; she was gentle, open, giving. But later that night she was drunk; now she was crazy, too. A hundred years ago, she might have been better off—unless, of course, she'd starved to death. Now she could drink herself to death.

For her, perhaps, Nunavut had arrived too late; it would differ too painfully from her code of life. This new thing, Nunavut, is as beautiful as a woman's parka trimmed with strips of fur and strips of patterned cloth, as ugly as scraps of plastic dancing in an Arctic wind.

But who can foresee Nunavut's future even five years ahead? It's an experiment, full of vigor and nobility, the government resolutely, democratically local, with its ten departments housed in ten widely spread Arctic towns. And Premier Okalik is an *Inuit* leader, as bright and optimistic as the territory. No doubt he and the other young politicians will grow old; perhaps they'll fall into nepotism and inertia until the political landscape freezes like the laundry on a clothesline covered with Easter snow. But for now he seems committed.

On Nunavut Day, the elders gathered in the hangar bays cheered Okalik—he was *their* young man, homegrown. But precisely because he was theirs, they didn't have to stand on ceremony, and so their kids ran loudly in and out. Perhaps Okalik won the election because he exemplified the pragmatic modesty and moderation that have always served Inuit so well, the genial humility that had his colleagues in the territorial negotiations introducing one another's speeches with aw-shucks humor, insisting that at the beginning they didn't even know what a land claim was. Now, when Okalik came to the podium, he declared, "We have achieved our goal through negotiations without civil disobedience. . . . We hope we can contribute to the prosperity and diversity of Canada."

Here was no separatist poison, no threat to the sovereignty of the country at large. Nunavut remained Canadian—with a difference, of course. At the conclusion of the inaugural ceremony, they sang the national anthem, but this rendition of "O Canada" must have startled Prime Minister Chrétien and the other federal politicians, for the Inuit decorated its melody at beginning and end with an ancient *ayah* song, performed by three women.

Nunavut remains her own place, an extended family even after all the decades of damage, the community a superorganism that tries to warm all in its bosom. But can the fresh new super-superorganism truly give itself to all Inuit? Almost 60 percent of the Nunavummiut are under 25 years of age. And the alteration of almost every aspect of material culture has occurred so rapidly that the elders and the kids riding their bikes in the April snow almost constitute two separate societies. Sometimes I think that the old huntress and the girl who kicked me had more in common with me than with one another.

At her house in Resolute, Elisapi's mother, Annie, takes a hunk of frozen raw caribou or seal from the freezer, sets it down on cardboard on the kitchen floor, and chops off splinters of meat with a hatchet. Annie says her favorite boarders are those who eat her "country food," and she always smiles at me because I fall to with relish.

At community feasts, the Inuit drag in whole animal carcasses, and tear out raw intestines with their teeth; so the fact that I'll eat almost anything helped endear me to Annie, one linchpin of her culture being the sharing of home-killed meat. When by happy chance I found Annie and Elisapi living in Iqaluit not long after Nunavut Day, my hair was long and Annie liked that too, because it made me look like a native. She told me this with Elisapi's help, because she cannot speak English.

For the people of Annie's generation, Nunavut is above all a vindication, a gift, a balm to wounded pride. Annie is entering her second childhood. Elisapi and the other sisters will take care of her. She's too frail to sew *kamiks* anymore. She'll never use a computer. She's already home. She'll die safe from the unimaginable changes now looming over Nunavut.

For Annie, and for so many Inuit, men and women alike, to be oneself is to hunt. Everybody hunts for survival: People raised on that basis know how to share, how to kill, and how to handle firearms responsibly. I once went out on a walrus hunt and watched a seven-year-old boy instructing his five-year-old brother in gun safety, with no adults in attendance except me. On that same hunt, I saw a seal killed with three shots and a walrus with one.

Many tourists from down south simply don't possess such attributes, but if the new territory of Nunavut gets what it wants, there will be more white hunters, more white visitors out on the land. The outfitters in Nunavut will soon be swimming in business, I imagine. They will take bird-watchers and whale-lovers out to stalk their prey with binoculars, telephoto lenses, and watercolor brushes. They'll learn to pamper the ones who forgot their warm clothes. They'll learn that legal liability hangs over them at all times. They'll be treated to cries of amazed disgust when somebody from a city sees a hunter butchering a bloody seal on an icy gravel beach. It's all for the good, I suppose, as long as local people make money. Over time, Nunavut will be receiving a diminishing income from the federal government, so why shouldn't tourism make up the shortfall?

Today only about 8,000 tourists a year come to Nunavut, most of them dogsledders, hunters, and wildlife watchers bound for the remote interior or for Baffin Island, and its belugas and killer whales. The adventurous few climb Mount Thor or Mount Asgard, or sea kayak the fjords of Baffin Island. But if it weren't for the shiny glints of increased tourism and development, why were corporate Canada's congratulations on the birth of Nunavut so loud?

Elisapi and Joe were hoping to rent out their house to the rich tourists who undertake expeditions to the North Pole. Elisapi had come to Iqaluit, in fact, to enroll as a communications student. She wanted to go into public relations or journalism. Since public relations is generally employed by businesses and governments rather than by aboriginal hunters, her new career seemed fairly certain, however indirectly, to further "develop" the land.

In that sense Elisapi reminded me of the carver's wife I met in Apex; the woman liked Nunavut, she said, because there would soon be more jobs. According to recent national census and provincial labor figures, 40 percent of the Inuit residents of Nunavut, and 9 percent of the other residents, do not "participate in the labor force (wage economy)." Moreover, the remote Nunavummiut must pay between two and three times more for basic goods and services than southern Canadians do. So the carver's wife was worried about being left out in the economic cold. But she also hungered for solitude, preferring Apex to Iqaluit because it was quieter. Like Annie, she'd been born in a hunting camp.

There was a term for these new Nunavummiut: weekend hunters. Their philosophy was to let the new life come and to benefit from it while living the old life as long as they could. But as new careers and tourism push the caribou back, where will their land be? It made me worry about the next 20 years. I said as much to Elisapi's sister Laila, but she cut me off. "Don't worry about us," she said with an angry smile. "We'll survive."

And why shouldn't Elisapi learn to shape the world's understanding of Inuit? Other people have. One sardonic old Inuit joke used to run that the average Inuit family comprises 6.5 individuals: a husband, a wife, 3.5 children, and a nosy anthropologist from down south.

"Objectivity" may be lost, but much else will be gained, when Elisapi replaces the anthropologist. And if her public relations contribute to the development of Nunavut, who am I to say that's a bad thing? And as Nunavut increasingly caters to tourists, wouldn't it be excellent, given that many of those caterers will doubtless be capital-rich entrepreneurs from Toronto or Sydney or Los Angeles, if Elisapi could make her percentage? As Inuit culture becomes a commodity, can't Elisapi sell it better than I can?

But what is Inuit culture? Endless hunting for the sake of prowess, the sharing of killed food, a knowledge of Inuktitut, sexual easiness and earthiness, old stories, a reserved smile, tenderness with children and confidence in them, respect for family, cheerfulness in the face of physical discomfort, *ayah* songs and throat-songs, animal-skin clothes? I can buy the garments; can I buy the rest?

If in the future they open resorts in Nunavut, remember solitude, and let someone else patronize them. If you must go, expect discomfort, inconvenience, and high prices. If you possess less experience than you will need to survive on your own, by all means find a local outfitter who can help you, and be guided by his advice. Above all, if you visit Nunavut, take care that your actions don't transform the region into a mirror image of the place you left.

For the next three months, Elisapi, with her two sons and Annie, was going to be staying at her daughter Eunice's place, an immaculate house (too much so for Elisapi's taste) with snow-white wall-to-wall carpet. In a corner niche I saw a group photograph, taken by a social worker back in 1955, of Annie and her family waiting to be relocated to Resolute, sitting forlornly on the rocks of Inukjuak.

I'd met Eunice once or twice in Resolute, the first time when she was about 13. She drew for me a picture of a polar bear stalking a baby seal on an Arctic midnight. When I got home I mailed her some colored pencils. She moved down to Iqaluit a few years later, and now, at 24, she has two daughters and is a famous throat-singer whose albums are sold to strangers across the Atlantic. She had performed in traditional dress at the Nunavut gala. She'd already been to Hawaii three times.

Fifteen minutes after I arrived, Eunice said she'd see me around. Her husband had just bought a new snowmobile; they were going for a ride out on the land. This was not rudeness on her part, but the habitual casualness of the Nunavummiut, who come and go as they wish. Eunice told me what I already knew, that I was welcome to stay for as long as I pleased, and indeed I visited with her relatives for another two hours before I went on my way.

Getting ready for their ride, Eunice had slipped her younger daughter into the *amauti*, because it was one of those cold days when breath-steam rose high above everybody's hoods. I had asked Eunice what kind of fur she used for her hood's unfamiliar ruff, and she made a face: "I don't know," she had replied. "Some ugly kind. I should get it replaced." But Elisapi and Annie both knew what kind of animal it came from, and they immediately told her—or told me, I should say, because Eunice wasn't interested. The ruff was coyote, from way down south, like her carpet and her snowmobile.

I never got the chance to ask Eunice if she still hunted, and in a way it doesn't matter. Her strain of Inuitness, like her mother's, will survive even after that hypothetical day when all the shores of Baffin Island have reared up their apartment forests in mocking imitation of the trees that could never have lived here. Fluent in both English and Inuktitut, and deriving both recognition and cold cash from her culture, Eunice seems likely to thrive. Maybe someday she'll be the Voice of Nunavut, emerging from radios and loudspeakers like the muezzins of Pakistan calling people to prayer.

What Nunavut will Eunice live in then? Perhaps the land will be changed, developed. Perhaps she and Elisapi and their family will live in a city of skyscrapers. Perhaps every seal will be tagged by then, transmitting its location and vital signs to wildlife officials, and Eunice's throat-songs will comprise their own signals in a realm of signal, human and animal equal. Why not? Which is to say, who knows? This spring, Nunavut was a promise. Now Nunavut will become a mystery as socioeconomic forces weave their half-blind ravelings.

On the last night of my trip, I stood on a snow-ridge between Iqaluit and Apex, gazing up at the aurora borealis sprinkling itself across the sky like confectioner's sugar, mingling with the city's steam-trails and smoke-trails. After a while it began to ooze slowly downward like white fists and frozen white winds swirling between stars. Far away, the lonely headlight of a snowmobile rushed across the land.

July 1999

Another Day in the Drop Zone

PETER MAASS

Baidoa, Somalia

"*S*alat! Salat!*"

The call to prayer came at 4:30 A.M.

"Pray! Pray! It's better to pray than to sleep!"

I was staying in a house across the street from one of Baidoa's mosques, so there was no chance of dozing. As the echoes from the loudspeaker faded into the darkness, I could hear the neighborhood stirring as people rose to wash their hands and feet and kneel in prayer toward Mecca.

There was a knock at the bedroom door. "You awake?" John Miskell called out.

Miskell and I were leaving Baidoa before dawn on a journey to a town named Tieglo, deep in the Somali hinterland a few miles south of nowhere. Miskell, who oversees CARE International's relief programs in southern Somalia, was planning to rendezvous there with a convoy of 12 trucks bringing 254 tons of food from Mogadishu. Between Baidoa and Tieglo lay 13 hours of Somali bush, dirt-and-boulder roads offering little more than lungfuls of dust and lobe-deadening headaches and the bleak scenery of a country pounded by civil war and famine. It was Miskell's job to make sure the food got to Tieglo safely.

It's been nearly a decade since jeering mobs dragged the body of U.S. Army Ranger Bill Cleveland through the streets of Mogadishu, and in that time little has improved. When the United Nations armed forces departed in 1995, the implicit message was simple: You people want to kill? Go ahead, kill yourselves. Call us when you get tired of it. Since then, northern Somalia has stabilized somewhat, but southern Somalia, with Mogadishu at its heart, remains a nightmarish, Hobbesian realm that once again hovers on the cusp of famine.

Our Toyota Land Cruiser was parked in the house's courtyard behind a steel gate topped with barbed wire and guarded by a couple of teenagers toting AK-47s. Loaded in the rear were 80 liters of gas in plastic containers. We would be traveling in a four-wheel drive, all-terrain bomb. Miskell would have liked to put the gas on the rooftop luggage rack, but that space was reserved for two other militiamen bearing AK-47s, who were to keep an eye out for trouble—of which, unlike food or water or peace or schools or law and order, there is plenty in Somalia.

"Where's the driver?" I asked when we got to the courtyard.

Miskell nodded at a prostrate form on the ground.

"Apparently our driver is praying," he said.

The prayers seemed unusually devout. When he finished, we drove into the center of town and met up with several more Somalis who worked for CARE. They would travel with us in two other Land Cruisers—one in front of our vehicle, the other behind— equipped with the requisite duos of rooftop gunslingers. As dawn broke, our convoy headed into the bush, only to stop after a few miles. We were surrounded by stunted trees covered in dust. Camels plodded past, herders in tow. Finally Cobra, one of the Somalis—everybody has a nickname in Somalia, and his was Cobra—walked back from the lead vehicle to tell us what was happening.

"There is an ambush ahead," he said.

Mangar Angui, Sudan

"It's coming," Sienna Loftus whispered.

The roar grew louder, more insistent. We were standing outside Mangar Angui, a Dinka village in southern Sudan whose name means "den of hyenas." We had not heard mechanical sounds for days. There was no electricity in the village or anywhere nearby, nothing larger than the mud-and-grass huts, nothing with more moving parts than a one-speed bicycle. Even the fighting is primitive here. A civil war between the Muslim government in Khartoum and the largely Christian Sudan People's Liberation Army has been torturing Sudan almost nonstop for decades. In the area around Mangar Angui, which the SPLA controls, a much-feared pro-government militia ransacks villages on horseback. And when the government decides to bomb the rebels, it sends aloft a clunky Soviet-era Antonov transport plane and a soldier rolls artillery shells out of the cargo bay.

The bombing today would be different.

"I don't want those guys under the trees!" Loftus shouted in English, waving at a group of men. "All those guys should move out! There are people under the tree! Move!" A local relief worker hustled the men away.

By now you could look at the sky and see why she was causing a commotion: A C-130 Hercules transport plane lumbered perhaps 700 feet above ground, heading straight for us.

"This is the most nerve-racking part of our job," said Loftus, a field-worker for the UN World Food Program. "Look at those women as they walk behind the drop zone and don't think it's a problem. Someone could die right now." She shouted for them to move away and then pushed the talk button on her radio.

"Fox-one-four, you're clear to drop, you're clear to drop."

"One minute to drop zone," the pilot replied.

"Right now is the crucial time," Loftus said. "When he says, 'One minute to drop,' and you give the OK, you cross your fingers and just hope nothing happens. A little kid can start running into the zone. You're always looking. We're not supposed to kill people while bringing food in."

The WFP plane was overhead now, scaring birds from their nests and prompting villagers to look up openmouthed. Suddenly, hundreds of white 50-kilo bags—325 in all, 16 tons of corn and grain—began tumbling from the Herc's cargo bay. At first they seemed to float like the world's largest bits of confetti, but after a few seconds they began hitting the ground, one after the other, sounding and feeling like a salvo of artillery shells—*boom boom boom boom*—and you realized these things could indeed kill.

But not today. Loftus smiled. "To be in a place where food arrives from the sky," she said, "it's almost magical. It's always exciting, always."

Exciting but not easy. After less than a year as an aid worker, Loftus, 32, who grew up in Montana, has had typhoid once, malaria twice, and a slew of mysterious boils. She's waded through swamps befouled with human waste and disease and endured the sort of bureaucratic nullity in which the UN specializes—like the time a bush plane dropped her off without the trunk of food that was supposed to keep her alive. (It arrived nine days later.) For his part, John Miskell, 53, a native of upstate New York, is a petri dish of tropical ills—he's had dengue fever several times, bacterial and amebic dysentery, giardia, blood poisoning, and most recently cholera, which almost killed him. He's been shot at and cursed. And yet neither he nor Loftus (whom he has never met) would do anything else.

Thanks to the end of the Cold War, aid work has undergone a geometric leap in visibility, controversy, and danger. Aid workers are the first to arrive and the last to leave the world's most chaotic and violent war zones—"complex emergencies," in relief jargon—places routinely filled with hunger and disease and, instead of government soldiers who follow (more or less) the Geneva Conventions on war, gunmen (and gunboys) who don't think twice about kidnapping or killing a Western aid worker. In 1998, for the first time, more UN aid workers were killed than UN peacekeepers, although tinder boxes like Sierra Leone can blow up in peacekeepers' faces at any time. When I was in Sudan with Loftus, ten aid workers were killed. First, two CARE employees were killed outside Khartoum; the government blamed the rebels. A week later, eight aid workers affiliated with African churches were gunned down near the Ugandan border by Ugandan guerrillas from the Lord's Resistance Army. The gunmen simply opened fire on their vehicle. But the victims were Africans, and the tragedy of their execution was compounded by a sad irony: While local aid workers compose the bulk of the aid world's ranks and, at least in Africa, are often at greater risk than white expatriates, the violent deaths of almost a dozen of them didn't (and don't) make the evening news in Europe or America.

Still, First World or Third World, black or white, aid workers often laugh when you ask why they do what they do. It's an ambiguous chuckle, knowing and nervous, that means the answer is either obvious or a mystery, even to them. They'll repeat the line about their profession being composed of missionaries, mercenaries, or maniacs, but that doesn't get you very far, nor them: Missionaries would be crestfallen by the corruption, mercenaries could find easier ways to get their hands on a few pieces of silver, and maniacs could not cope with the discipline the job demands.

So why do they do it? For aid workers from the Third World, the jobs pay quite well, and if they are working in their native countries, they are helping their own people. For First Worlders, there is the thrill of exotic altruism. None of them rejoices in the mines or the kidnappings or the cholera or the misery of starving villagers, but these things catapult them out of the drudgery of nine-to-five life in their tamperproof homelands. They have a front-row seat to history in motion, which is big and terrifying and amazing, like the thrashings of a wounded elephant. Aid workers are bearers of good will and targets for warlords. They are vultures and angels.

Outside Baidoa, Somalia

In Somalia, there is usually an explanation for violence that appears mindless, and in fact an explanation existed for the ambush that awaited us a few hundred yards up the road. CARE, like other humanitarian groups, does not own any of the vehicles it uses in southern Somalia. It is unwise to own a car there unless you also own a private militia that can prevent another private militia from stealing it. CARE rents its vehicles from people connected to various militias, and its written contract requires owners to provide, with each car, "two security guards with necessary hardware." Meaning assault rifles. Pistols will not do.

The gentlemen manning a roadblock a half-mile up the road were representing, in the Somali fashion, the interests of someone in Baidoa who did not win the contract to supply vehicles to CARE. The gunmen didn't want to shoot us; they just wanted us to use different vehicles (theirs) at the going rate of $60 per vehicle per day, a small fortune in Somalia. If we refused their offer, they might, reluctantly, find it necessary to open fire. Cobra, who is in his thirties and used to work for the U.S. embassy in Mogadishu back when there was a U.S. embassy in Mogadishu, calmly explained this to Miskell.

"You've got to be kidding," Miskell said.

"No," Cobra replied. "I'll go back to town and bring the district commissioner here to straighten this out."

Cobra returned with the commissioner, and after 15 minutes of arguing with the guys at the roadblock we all drove back to Baidoa's police station. You could tell it was the police station by the traditional Somali crime-fighting vehicles outside: bullet-pocked pickups with heavy machine guns mounted in back, and a truck with a large antiaircraft gun on its flatbed. These *Mad Max*–style vehicles are known as "technicals." Next to them sat a battered pickup bearing a corpse wrapped in a blanket with a woman wailing beside it.

There's really no difference between the police and the fighters in southern Somalia; policemen just happen to be charged by their warlords with keeping civil order instead of battling other clans. They have no training and no uniforms because there are no government officials to provide them. Public schools no longer exist in southern Somalia, just scattered Islamic schools that teach Arabic and the Koran; nor is there a public health system or anything else that would suggest the presence of a controlling legal authority. In the U.S. State Department's official briefing paper on Somalia, under the heading "Government," there is simply the word "None." The country's legislative system is "Not Functioning." The judiciary is also "Not Functioning." The entry for national holidays reads, "None presently celebrated."

There was certainly no celebrating going on at the Baidoa police station. After another half-hour, the commissioner got fed up and tossed several of the gunmen into jail and sent us on our way.

As we drove off, a few of the men who'd gathered to observe the proceedings began jeering—as far as they were concerned, the wrong guys were being locked up. One pointed a finger at Miskell, who'd come to Baidoa to give away food, and said, "Fuck you."

We were journeying into one of Somalia's larger fiefdoms, an area controlled by the Rahenweyn Resistance Army, which is led by a thin, reportedly diabetic warlord known as Red Shirt. He was wearing a white shirt when Miskell visited him a day before, seeking his blessing to distribute food without being attacked. RRA territory is relatively safe, but that only means no aid workers have been killed there recently. Of course, aid convoys had been attacked, including, a few months earlier, one of Miskell's; he escaped injury because the bandits were shooting at a different vehicle. On another occasion one of Miskell's Somali staffers had not been so lucky. Militiamen ambushed him as he drove through an area north of Mogadishu that had been considered relatively safe—until he was murdered.

The problem is that anyplace in Somalia can turn into a killing ground. On the outskirts of Wajit, halfway on our journey to Tieglo, a child several years away from his first shave presided over yet another roadblock. As our Land Cruisers approached a twisted metal pole cast across the road, the kid told our guards to surrender their guns because, he said, visitors were not allowed to carry weapons into town. When our guards protested, the kid pointed his AK-47 at us. One of our guards—a veteran of such standoffs, though only in his late teens— hopped off the roof and marched toward the boy, pointing his rifle at the youngster.

"What's he doing?" Miskell said under his breath. "Let's not start a war."

The kid retreated into a nearby hut. As we drove past, he came back out, looking as though he were about to cry. He was just a boy, but boys like him have shot adults like us many times. "Don't worry," Miskell had told me, "your chance of being shot to death is greater than being robbed." Then he'd smiled. "And your chance of being shot accidentally is greater than being shot intentionally."

Mangar Angui, Sudan

The men were whipping the women with branches torn from nearby trees. You could hear the lashes cutting through the air. Hundreds of women had lined up on the airstrip to receive the food dropped by the Herc the day before, and here and there pushing and shoving had broken out, as well as tugs-of-war over sacks of grain. That's why the men had whips—to restore order.

There was a festival air, despite the whipping, because food was being given away. The community was gathering en masse, an unusual event for people who spend their days tending meager crops of sorghum and thin herds of cattle or goats. At the moment, there is no wholesale starvation in Mangar Angui, though there was in 1998. The villagers' storehouses, which Loftus had inspected in the past few days, were almost bare; the WFP is not solving the hunger problem, just keeping it at bay. After the distribution, women and children would sift through the dust, looking for stray kernels of corn.

Loftus moved with the quickness of a hummingbird, as did John Kamemia, a Kenyan and veteran aid worker who was partnered with her in Mangar Angui (WFP field-workers travel in pairs for safety). Hundreds of sacks of maize and lentils, as well as tins of vegetable oil, were being handed out at several points spread over an area as large as a few football fields. Loftus and Kamemia wanted, above all, to make sure the food was divided fairly. WFP food is supposed to go to the vulnerable—refugees, nursing mothers, children, and the disabled. Lists had been drawn up with the names of villages, village chiefs, and the number of people to receive food in each village. Local relief workers from the Sudanese Relief and Rehabilitation Association, the humanitarian arm of the SPLA, were attempting to sort it out as Loftus flitted here and there, calling out instructions. "*Dhuok cen! Dhuok cen!*" she shouted, in Dinka, to several men lounging around a stack of food bags. "Everyone around these bags needs to go. *Dhuok cen! Dhuok cen!*" Like most foreign aid workers in southern Sudan, Loftus knows only a few words of Dinka, and the ones she uses most frequently mean "Step back."

She was dressed in her usual bush outfit: a pair of shorts and a white WFP T-shirt. On her feet she wore Ralph Lauren Polo flip-flops; on her head, a Patagonia hat with sun visors in front and back; and on her back, a 3.5-liter CamelBak. In a country where 100 degrees is regarded as cool weather, a water-filled backpack is the sort of thing that makes eminent sense. But when you are a healthy American moving among Africans who are a meal or two away from starvation, you look more like a visitor from another planet.

After a while Loftus took a break under a tree. She looked exhausted; her dark hair was pasted down by sweat and she was covered in dirt. Women with 50-kilo bags on their heads were walking away into the bush, which was problematic. Unless you see food actually given to the people it's intended for, you have no idea whether the village chief will keep much of it for himself and his multiple wives, or whether soldiers may grab it instead.

"We want them to stay here and share the food," Loftus remarked. "We don't want them to go off and share the food under a chief. We want to monitor it."

Merca, Somalia

Aid work is an addiction. Something happens, and your life—which was going to be normal, with a family and a good job that you perform with decreasing enthusiasm over the years—becomes exceptional, forever. And you can't imagine it otherwise.

In 1969 John Miskell, having just graduated from Syracuse University's College of Environmental Science and Forestry, joined the Peace Corps, figuring on a year or two of adventure before settling down. He was sent to Kenya, where his sojourn coincided with a famine. Incompetence and corruption hindered efforts to feed the hungry, so they died, sometimes right in front of Miskell, who was teaching high school in Wajir, a village in the north (and trapping poisonous snakes and selling them to a zoo in his spare time).

"I thought when I joined the Peace Corps that I would do my two years and go home and look for a job as a forester or entomologist," he told me. "My first year in Wajir changed that." He met Zahra Hussein Awale, an enchanting Somali secretary traveling through Kenya, and they got married. When his hitch in the Peace Corps ended, he took a job in the entomology department at the National Museum in Nairobi, where he spent most of his time in a cavernous room with 250,000 beetle specimens. When funds for that job ran out, he decamped with his wife and two young children (two more would come later) to Mogadishu, well before the city devolved into a synonym for anarchy, to conduct a bird survey for the UN.

Eventually funding for that project ran dry, too, so he took a job with CARE. There are thousands of nongovernmental organizations, or NGOs, across the globe, but CARE ranks among the elite, in terms of reliability and efficiency, along with Médecins Sans Frontières, Save the Children, World Vision, the International Rescue Committee, and several others. Founded in 1945 as a vehicle to send aid packages to survivors of World War II, CARE then stood for Cooperative for American Remittances to Europe. The group, headquartered in Atlanta, Georgia, has since changed its name to Cooperative for Assistance and Relief Everywhere; it operates in more than 60 countries with more than 10,000 employees, the vast majority of them Third World citizens working in the Third World.

Most NGOs tend to see the UN, their ubiquitous counterpart in relief operations, as a 900-pound gorilla. And while UN personnel usually get along quite well with NGO workers in the field, their bureaucratic cultures are polar opposites. In Nairobi, an NGO like CARE is based in a rented house filled with a few dozen staffers. The UN agencies occupy a sprawling campus with landscaped grounds and more than a thousand well-paid employees. NGO staffers will tell you that the UN wastes almost as much money as it spends; UN officials sniff that the NGOs are nickel-and-dime amateurs.

Miskell is a pro. He spent four years in Somalia with CARE before shifting to eastern Sudan in 1985 for three years; then, in 1988, to Uganda; then to a remote corner of Bangladesh in 1993, because, as he says, "No one wanted to go there." He stayed for a year and a half, at which point he was asked to take charge of a CARE project in a remote part of Sudan, another place no one wanted to go. Later he was sent to Tanzania for a spell, then back to Sudan in 1998; finally, last year, his pinball trajectory deposited him back in Somalia. His family could not quite keep up: In 1991 they moved to Geneseo, New York, so that his children could attend high school and college in America. One of his sons is now in the U.S. Army, just back from Bosnia; another recently moved to Washington, D.C.; and a third is finishing high school in Geneseo. His ten-year-old daughter, born in Mogadishu, is starting sixth grade this fall. Miskell sees them twice a year, during vacations. Two months with his family, ten in Africa.

Miskell is based on the outskirts of Merca, 60 miles south of Mogadishu; it is too dangerous for him to live in the capital. In many respects, CARE's Merca villa is splendid. If you stand on the balcony, you have a view of the turquoise Indian Ocean a few hundred yards in front of you; if you look to the left, Merca's colonial precincts unfold, a whitewashed mix of African and Arabic and Italian architecture, like an apparition from a Paul Bowles novel. A strong, warm wind blows off the ocean. One hears the regular calls to prayer, occasional ruptures of gunfire, and, when kids in the street catch a glimpse of you, excited shouts of *"Gal! Gal!"*—Somali for "infidel."

It's comfortable, as prisons go. The villa's steel gate is locked at all times. Miskell does not leave without at least three armed bodyguards, and he rarely walks anywhere. There is a handful of foreign aid workers in Merca, mostly Italians rebuilding local schools, and they follow the same rules. One Italian aid worker was assassinated a few years back—the killer slipped into her villa, shot her in the head, and ran out. Last year more than a dozen aid workers were kidnapped in southern Somalia: Ten staffers for the International Committee of the Red Cross were seized in April, threatened with death, and then released after two weeks. (The ICRC says no ransom was paid, but a news report claimed that $150,000 changed hands.) That same month another Italian was abducted and held for three weeks, and a top WFP official traveling in Mogadishu was kidnapped for a few days at the end of 1999. It was his second abduction.

Mangar Angui, Sudan

Just as Sudan has the unfortunate distinction of possessing Africa's longest-running civil war, the food drops Loftus helps oversee are part of Africa's longest-running, and most controversial, aid project. The war itself began in 1956, when Sudan gained independence from British rule; went into remission in 1972; and returned worse than ever in 1983, after the Muslim government in Khartoum imposed Islamic law on the country, including the largely Christian and animist southern half. (The U.S. government supports the rebel Sudan People's Liberation Army.) In the last 17 years the war has cost some two million lives—many from war-induced famines—and turned several million more people into refugees.

Loftus's work is part of Operation Lifeline Sudan, an 11-year-old joint project of the United Nations and some 40 NGOs, including CARE. The operation has run up an estimated $2 billion tab so far through its food and medicine drops, and critics have charged that such projects allow bloody conflicts to continue indefinitely since aid groups strike devil's bargains with warring factions, which inevitably get a cut of the food in exchange for safe passage of their convoys. Refugees get fed, but so do murderers.

Out in the field, Loftus has more important things to worry about than lofty policy debates—things like not dying. Born the year John Miskell joined the Peace Corps, she is relatively new to the game. She came to Sudan via Great Falls, Montana, a place, she says in a mock serious voice, "where a handshake is still the law." Always athletic, she became an expert rock climber in her teens, and after high school moved to Boston and worked as a nanny, an emergency medical technician, a vegetarian chef, and an orderly in a mental institution before getting an anthropology degree from the University of Massachusetts. After college she drifted to Kenya and worked as a guide for luxury safaris, but there was an emptiness to the work—baby-sitting rich white people in Africa is not terribly meaningful. So two years ago she applied for a job with the World Food Program in Sudan and, thanks to some persistence, got it.

Every six weeks Loftus boards a bush plane at the UN base in Lokichokio, Kenya, and is dropped off several hours later in rebel-held territory in southern Sudan. This is assuming the UN plane does not nose-dive into the landing strip and flip over (as one did while I was in Sudan) or that its passengers are not taken hostage by gunmen (as happened to another UN plane shortly after I left). If all goes well Loftus and a partner stay at each drop-off point for a few days to a week. Then another plane takes them to another site. Loftus sleeps in a Kelty tent, cooks over a kerosene burner, and does her best to avoid snakes, scorpions, hyenas, soldiers, and wild dogs. The WFP requires its field-workers to keep a survival bag handy with food, water, first-aid supplies, flashlight, and compass in case they have to flee. In Mangar Angui, I asked Loftus's field partner, John Kamemia, where he keeps his "fast-run kit." He laughed and pointed to his ample belly. "This is my fast-run kit," he said.

If Loftus needs to investigate food conditions in a village ten miles from her camp, she must walk. Paved roads do not, for the most part, exist in southern Sudan, nor do vehicles to drive on them— just the occasional NGO Land Rover or military truck being pounded to death by the baked earth in the dry season or swallowed up by that same earth in the rainy season. Some monitors are sent out with bicycles (one-speed bikes made in China have proven more durable here than American-made mountain bikes), but the terrain tends to be too rutted or too swampy for travel on anything but your own two feet, which will be cracked or infected, depending on the season.

Mosquitoes can be so dense that you inhale them. Sudan also boasts 80 percent of the world's cases of infestation by guinea worm, whose larva enters the human body via unclean drinking water and grows in the bloodstream into a three-foot-long white worm before chewing its way through the skin, usually at the foot, and emerging in its entirety in an agonizing and horribly disgusting process that takes weeks at a minimum, and usually months.

"Sudan," said one WFP field worker, a woman who'd endured cerebral malaria and a mysterious grapefruit-size growth on her neck, "tries to destroy people."

Tieglo, Somalia

Despite white hair and a white beard, John Miskell looks absurdly vigorous for a man who has spent his adult life in the punishing bush. The mystery of his youthful appearance deepened as we drove to Tieglo. In places the road wasn't even dirt, just rocks, and the Land Cruiser jolted up and down as though perched atop a giant jackhammer. Red dust invaded the cabin in clumps; the 100-degree air tasted of gasoline. I placed a bandanna over my mouth; our driver jammed the end of his scarf into his mouth and gnawed on it. Occasionally we passed small towns nearly wiped out in the last decade

of war, a Dresden-like vista of ruin. Small groups of underfed people sat in what shade they could find beside mud huts. They stared
as we passed, our Land Cruisers strange apparitions from the land
of plenty.

Miskell sat up front, seemingly unfazed. Nothing covered his nose
or mouth. He patiently scanned the bush for birds; when he saw one,
he would jot its name in his notebook. I tried to stump him, asking
the names of birds that flew past in a millisecond, but he was miles
ahead of me. "Red-billed hornbill," he said as one zoomed by, and
then he delivered an ornithological trump card: "Female." On occasion he would tell the driver to stop, and he would leave the car,
binoculars in hand, and shuffle toward a creature perched in a tree.
The rooftop guards seemed baffled by this white guy chasing after
birds.

Long-term exposure to other people's suffering can harm aid workers in a process known euphemistically as "vicarious traumatization."
The mind and body have ways of coping: alcohol abuse, withdrawal.
This has not happened to Miskell. His defense mechanism is unique—
he retreats into an alternative universe of wildlife. For him, the bush
isn't full of misery, but of mysteries unsolved. He has coauthored a
book on Somali birds and is updating it for a second edition. He has
discovered three new species of beetles, and two admiring colleagues
named beetles they discovered after him. "Every time a botanist comes
to this country, they find a new species of plant," he enthused. "It's
just amazing."

Miskell has become a man of Africa rather than a visitor to Africa.
He drinks camel milk by the gallon, and almost everywhere he goes,
he carries a six-by-eight-inch picture of his family, a posed studio shot
where he stands proudly with his Somali wife and his half-Somali, half-
American children. It is, in a way, a passport that tells everyone Miskell
is African, that he is not just another white guy with the power to provide free food, that he is more at home in the chaos of Somalia than
in the comfort of America.

Well after sunset, and nearly 14 hours after leaving Baidoa, we pulled
into Tieglo reeking of gasoline and sweat and dust. The food trucks,
which had set out from Mogadishu, were scheduled to arrive the next

day. But as we were to find out, things had not gone according to plan. Miskell was about to get another dose of chaos.

Mangar Angui, Sudan

At six in the evening, Loftus fired up her WFP solar-powered radio and shouted out, "Lima Two, Mike Golf India!" No response. She shouted again, and this time summoned a voice from the ether.

"Sienna?"

"Yes!" she yelled back. "John? How are you doing?"

John Burns, another WFP field-worker, is Loftus's boyfriend. Like lovers meeting on the same bench in a park, they talk on the radio at the same time every evening.

"Great," Burns replied.

"Are you still smoking?" Loftus asked.

"No, but I really crave it."

"That's a good copy. When will you get to the field?" Burns, who was at the UN base in northern Kenya, was waiting to be sent into southern Sudan.

"I don't know. There's nothing for me to do there yet."

"OK," Loftus yelled. "Well, keep on not smoking."

"Right, talk to you tomorrow."

Loftus turned to me. "Now everyone in the SPLA, SRAA, and WFP knows John is trying to quit smoking," she said, laughing. "You'd like to say, 'I love you, I love you, I miss you, I miss you,' but you can't."

Two-way radios are the Internet of the aid world. Virtually every aid worker in southern Sudan—there are hundreds in the field at any time—uses a shortwave radio to stay in touch with headquarters and, if the need arises, as it frequently does, to arrange emergency evacuations for medical or security reasons. At night the airwaves become a vast chat room in which people swap gossip like teenagers burning the phone lines after lights-out. If you flip between channels—and aside from talking with your colleagues, the best form of entertainment is eavesdropping on them—you will hear WFP staffers talking about sports, bitching about the weather, trying to sell each other used cars.

The foreigners work alongside Sudanese whose grasp of English seems to derive, in part, from radio chatter. In Mangar Angui, one of

Loftus's colleagues was a 26-year-old local named John Garang (not to be confused with the head of the SPLA, who has the same name). If Garang wanted to know whether Loftus understood something, he would ask, with a hint of BBC in his accent, "Do you copy?" If he wanted to indicate that things were fine, he might say "Oscar Kilo," radio-ese for "OK."

One day, after a grueling six-hour walkabout to check food conditions, Garang hung around our tents, which we had set up inside mud huts, and leafed through a copy of *Yachting* that Loftus had brought into the field along with a recent copy of *Newsweek* and one of *Shape,* its cover advertising "8 New Moves for a Knockout Tush." Putting his finger on a color picture of a 45-foot sloop, Garang—a man who had likely never seen open water in his life, nor a vessel larger than a canoe—announced enthusiastically, "I want this boat."

Loftus and I were slumped in the shade of a tree, swallowing oral-rehydration salts.

"Aren't you tired?" I asked.

"Negative," Garang said. "Small walk."

The Dinka are known for being exceptionally tall and long-legged. The most famous Dinka in the world is seven-foot, seven-inch retired NBA center Manute Bol.

"How long can you walk?"

"Twenty-four hours," Garang said.

"Twenty-four hours?"

"Affirmative."

Tieglo, Somalia

The town has several hundred mud huts, but no hotels, so Miskell and I stayed in a local merchant's home that had a roof made of tin rather than plastic sheeting, making it deluxe accommodations. In the morning, the CARE team gathered for a breakfast of sweet tea, camel milk, goat meat, and *anjera,* the local bread. Miskell didn't bother saying good morning.

"You haven't heard yet," he told me. "The convoy was attacked."

The news had come over the two-way radio. No one was sure where the convoy was or whether anyone had been injured. After breakfast

Miskell visited the local radio operator, in a lean-to crammed with Somalis waiting in line to talk with friends in other towns, and got through to someone in CARE's office in Merca.

"When do you expect him to reach this location?" Miskell shouted.

"I don't know," came the reply. "There was fighting. Over." The connection broke off abruptly.

"Can you use channel 8044?" Miskell shouted. "Channel 8044! Over." They briefly reestablished contact. Miskell left the hut in disgust. Four guards had been killed, three wounded, and a technical destroyed in the ambush, at a checkpoint about 100 miles from Tieglo. "Why are they doing it?" Miskell fumed. "It's insane."

The rest of the day consisted of quick updates with CARE employees in Merca and Mogadishu. On one occasion, Ahmed Abdulle, the CARE convoy leader, was patched through. Because anyone could listen to the shortwave conversation, including the gunmen who attacked the convoy, little was said about where the convoy was holed up or how it was going to get here intact.

"Are you safe where you are?"

"Yes," Ahmed replied. "I am safe. The convoy is intact and safe."

"Will you be able to leave?"

Static.

Before dinner we listened to the BBC World Service, which reported that the office of a British aid group, ACCORD, had been attacked in a town near Merca. Two people were dead. A militia tracked the gunmen down and killed their leader, but two bystanders were wounded in that shootout. There was silence in the compound.

The next morning, when I wandered into the courtyard for breakfast, Miskell again skipped the pleasantries. "You haven't heard?" he asked.

"What now?" I said.

"A civilian truck that was on the road the convoy was on hit a land mine. We don't know how many were killed." The mine, he explained, was meant for our food convoy.

The ambush appeared to be a business dispute. The trucking firm that CARE hired to transport the food was being attacked by a rival company that wanted CARE's business, we learned. Allies of the vic-

timized firm had already struck back by kidnapping one of the owners of the firm that launched the ambush.

There was more. We soon heard that the CARE convoy had been
attacked a second time the previous evening, as many as ten more
guards killed and another technical destroyed by rocket-propelled
grenades. On top of that, militias linked to the warring trucking firms
had begun fighting in Beledweyn, a town near the ambush sites; shops
in the town had been looted.

"Food is dangerous," Miskell remarked. "If we're not careful, this
convoy is going to start a war, a big war."

There was nothing he could do except return to Merca the next day
and instruct Ahmed to give the food to local charities and go back to
Mogadishu. When he returned from the radio shack, Miskell sat in the
courtyard, ignoring dozens of children who stared at him through the
wooden fence, and began reading a novel by Tony Hillerman. I drew
his attention to a beetle climbing a wall behind him.

"Longhorned wood bore," he said.

Mangar Angui, Sudan

Before the sun had risen much above the horizon, Loftus and I put on
running shoes and headed for the dirt airstrip. We jogged back and
forth for a half-hour, past women lugging jugs of water on their heads,
past thin hunters with spears, past naked, giggling children.

"They think it's the most bizarre thing," Loftus said. And it is. But
in Sudan, where serious illness is a scratch or a sneeze or a dirty fork
away, staying fit (or at least unsick) is important. Loftus travels with
an arsenal of health- and sanity-preserving weapons. She eschews the
beans-and-rice strategy of bush survival, opting instead for jars of garlic and olives, packets of cumin and coriander, powdered coconut milk,
cans of tikka masala, and bags of bulgar and lentils. She carries $60
tubes of Lancôme skin cleanser, toenail polish, and a solar-powered
cassette player. "I have one week off for every six weeks in the field,"
she explains. "If I didn't feel at home, I couldn't work here."

Sadly, these self-protective strategies can widen the gulf between aid
workers and the people they help. It's not a white-versus-black issue;
Kamemia was almost as much of an alien in Mangar Angui as Loftus,

although his knowledge of Arabic, which some educated southern Sudanese speak, brought him closer to a few. Aid workers learn to be insular: The hands extended toward you—and everyone wants to shake your hand—can transmit any number of gastrointestinal diseases. Loftus has already perfected a method of waving in such a friendly way that people don't realize she hasn't shaken their hands.

As we packed up to leave Mangar Angui for another village, we were watched closely by two women who had been employed, during our visit, to wash our dishes and bring water from a well a half-mile away, carrying the 20-liter containers on their heads. They had been paid with a sack of maize, which would fulfill perhaps a quarter of a family's needs for a month, after the women pounded it into powder and cooked it into a sludgy porridge. But they wanted more, and they held out their hands to Loftus as she stowed her food in her trunk. The women wore torn, soiled bits of clothing and, like all but the luckiest of local villagers, had no shoes.

"Don't beg," Loftus said sharply to one, in English. "It doesn't make you look good."

It sounded harsh, and it was. But her words reflected the sort of hardheartedness aid workers must adopt to keep from being driven into utter depression by the insurmountable misery around them. It also reflected an effort to stay sane by following the rules even when doing so seems callous or futile. You can't save everyone, nor can you protect them from vultures in their midst. Sometimes you have little choice but to walk away. During the food distribution, as women left with entire 50-kilo bags, Loftus spoke with local officials who told her the food would be kept nearby and redistributed the next day. By that time, as they well knew, she would be gone. And the chiefs would divide the food however they wished.

Tieglo, Somalia

The elders of Tieglo gathered in the village's television hut, where you pay the equivalent of five cents for an evening of satellite TV, and listened to Miskell explain that the convoy had been attacked twice and dozens killed. Their people—a scattered 10,000 in all—would not be getting any food, not now. The quartet of elders, carrying finely carved wooden staffs and wearing elegant sarongs, sat in plastic lawn chairs and stroked their beards.

"Hunger is increasing," one of them said, as a Somali translated for me. "We didn't get any food in December or January. People are selling their livestock for food." This is true. The WFP was about to appeal for a massive infusion of food aid for countries in the Horn of Africa: According to the UN, roughly eight million people are at risk of starvation in Ethiopia alone, as well as in parts of Kenya and Sudan. Pockets of malnutrition were already developing around Tieglo—indicators of big trouble ahead.

"We have to go," Miskell replied. "We'll come back as soon as we can."

The elder shrugged in the resigned manner of men who have come to expect the worst in a country that has experienced the worst. "It is Allah's will," he said.

It was hard to keep track of all the thievery and corruption. There was the provincial official seeking free food for his orphanage, an empty house filled with kids only when aid workers visited. There was the Baidoa warehouse set on fire to cover up the pilfering of UN supplies by its managers. There was the 370-ton food convoy stolen by a provincial governor's gunmen and used, the rumor goes, to acquire new Land Cruisers. And the WFP official who was so corrupt that, according to a joke making the rounds, WFP stood for "Warlord Food Program."

When the meeting ended, everyone filed away quietly, as though leaving a funeral. Miskell returned to our tin-roofed room, which was stiflingly hot. Outside, a stiff breeze stirred up clouds of dust.

"Most people in this country would like to see the warlords evaporate," he told me. "If you cut the food out, who is going to starve? Not the gunmen. They have guns and they will find ways to get food. The other people will starve. If we pulled out there might be some sort of conclusion reached faster than otherwise, but the number of people who would die would be pretty incredible."

This dilemma is at the heart of the debate over food aid. Perhaps pulling out would be, in the long run, the right thing to do, but doing so would take the ruthlessness of a Machiavellian and the heartlessness of a Malthusian. "Sometimes you feel like packing it in," Miskell admitted. "Some people would tell you I'm crazy, and maybe they're right." But he stays.

"My family keeps telling me to come back to America, that I can find a job, I don't need to do this," he said. "But every time I go to the States I go for about four weeks, and after about a month I know it's time to leave again. Maybe it's because everything is too perfect. I find it boring."

Miskell is no adrenaline junkie. He may be an unpredictability junkie, however—a guy who wants to be surprised by what unfolds in front of him or what flies over his head. And he wants to feel that he is really doing something. As I discovered, he is pathetically out of touch with the rest of the media-saturated First World, out of touch with IPO fever and the latest box-office sensation. He still cares about starvation, the poor bastard, even after 30 years in the field.

We returned to Baidoa the next day and then flew to Merca. After a 30-minute stopover to load some fuel, the plane headed to Nairobi, with me on it. I watched as Miskell climbed into his Land Cruiser and started home with his quartet of bodyguards. His first order of business was to find a trucking company that could get a convoy of food to Tieglo. He will likely be doing that sort of thing for the rest of his working life. He does not plan to return to live in America, ever. When he retires, he wants to build a house on a plot of land that he owns with his wife. The land is in Mogadishu.

Lokichokio, Kenya

It happened quickly, the switch from blighted war zone to bush-camp luxury. Loftus, Kamemia, and I waited at Mangar Angui's airstrip with our gear for the single-engine plane that would take us to the next village. The nine-seater landed with a bump, and the pilot stepped out and told us we wouldn't be going to the other village after all, because the dirt airstrip there, which the villagers had just scratched out of the bush, and over which he had just flown, was too short. We radioed Lokichokio for instructions and were told to return to Kenya.

Loki is a cross between a military camp and a summer camp. The roar of cargo planes is constant, and an army of four-wheel-drive vehicles shuttles between the airstrip and the aid workers' residential compounds a few miles away. The jeeps pass through town, a parched collection of dilapidated storefronts and dome-shaped huts of branches and plastic sheeting inhabited mostly by members of the Turkana tribe.

The main compound has some incongruous Club Med touches: Attractive thatch roofs cover outdoor picnic tables; a disco ball hangs in an open-air bar offering everything from Russian vodka to American cigarettes. There is a volleyball court a few paces away. At night, aid workers unwind over beers kept ice-cold in a refrigerator hooked up to a generator. Later still they might head off in pairs to each others' tents and huts.

Early one evening, Loftus and I sat down for a quiet beer. The bar was crowded with Afrikaner UN pilots bossing around the Kenyan bartender. Friends of Loftus's said hello. A few yards away a swimming pool was surrounded by bougainvilleas in bloom. Outside the perimeter, delineated by a barbed-wire fence patrolled by men with rifles, sat the baked red desolation of northern Kenya.

I asked Loftus to tell me what she was learning, living this life.

"When you see war," she told me, "when you see a culture that has changed into a war culture, you become grateful. People in the States do not know what it's like to not be free. They have no clue. All the issues that I would scream and march and yell about in college—I didn't know shit. You don't know what loss of freedom is until you see people who have no freedom, until you see people whose children are stolen into slavery."

On my last day at Loki, the security guards went on strike and held a protest outside the main gate. The local police were called in, and they fired at the crowd, and after the crowd dove for cover, shots were fired at the police and into the compound. Loftus and her colleagues hardly flinched. They finally retreated into a courtyard after several volleys were fired and after the head of security began yelling, "I suggest you get somewhere safe! Anything can happen!" As sporadic gunfire continued for an hour or two, the aid workers slouched on the ground, so casual they could have fallen asleep.

Earlier, when we talked at the bar, Loftus said, "You know you can be shot, you know it, but you really feel like you're not gonna. Some-

how, because you're here trying to help, somehow you've got this protective armor. Which is bullshit. You almost have to feel that way to
go into it, because if you're constantly thinking, 'Oh, God, I could get
shot,' then it doesn't work." She laughed. "I think it's not going to
happen to me, which is crap."

Loftus has already been evacuated from the field twice—once for
malaria, once because her village was about to be attacked by militiamen. One night in Mangar Angui, when the BBC World Service
reported the deaths of the eight aid workers near the Ugandan border
only about two hundred miles from us, I went to Loftus's hut and told
her; she was less interested than I expected. She didn't know them. I
told Kamemia. "Oh, yeah?" he said, and returned to his book.

Loftus did know Richard Powell, a WFP worker from Australia who
died last year in a plane crash. Powell's ashes were buried in January
at a Sudanese village where he had worked, and Loftus cried at his
funeral. The African ceremony involved the slaughter of a half-dozen
cows, the burial of a live sheep, and at the end of it all, the playing,
on a portable stereo, of Pink Floyd's "The Wall."

It is a form of cognitive dissonance: *I could be killed; I can't be
killed.* John Miskell has this capacity, too. He doesn't scare easily, and
he doesn't have a death wish, but he has paid for extra insurance that
will provide his family, in the event of his death in the field, with a
year of his salary in addition to the three years' salary CARE would
chip in. Like Loftus, he knows the risks, and he carries on. There is a
difference between risking your life and thinking you will lose it. All
aid workers do the former; few do the latter.

Loftus's insurance is a four-leaf clover worn on a pendant around
her neck. She doesn't know how much longer she will last in Sudan.
A year, maybe two. After that, she's not sure. She wants to sail around
the world with her boyfriend and return to aid work, somewhere,
somehow. Perhaps not in a war zone, but in a country with development work, the sunnier side of the humanitarian world. I asked whether
she might return to America and live a life that would fit within the
parameters of "normalcy." If she wanted to help people, she could
work in a soup kitchen; for thrills, she could go climbing, the sort of
thing she used to do before heading to Africa. But Loftus told me that

when she visits home and sees her old climbing buddies, her attention
fades as they talk about mountains they have summited; theirs fades
as she talks about Sudan.

My question lingered in the air. Finally, Loftus shook her head from
side to side.

"You can't go back," she said.

July 2000

Here the Bear
and the Mafia
Roam

BOB SHACOCHIS

I n the central Siberian city of Tomsk, children play a game called Dead Telephone, whispering a sentence around a circle until someone fails to repeat the original wording accurately, and for the child who gets the sentence wrong, the penalty is "You must go live in Kamchatka." Meaning that the loser has been imaginatively banished from the relative comforts of Siberia to the very end of the earth. Kamchatka, perhaps Russia's most famous nowhere, the wild east of the Russian and Soviet empires, nine time zones and 10,000 kilometers distant from Moscow.

Tundra. Shimmering twilight. A slow, high-banked river the color of tea, as if it flowed from the spigot of a samovar.

Where I should have been was on a vodka-clear, rock-bottomed river, fast and wild, somewhere to the north and farther inland with a phantom cadre of biologists, fly-fishing for salmon specimens on the Kamchatka Peninsula. Where I'd ended up was about three klicks inland from the Sea of Okhotsk, on an estuarine section of another river that I'd been advised, by the self-proclaimed criminals who deposited me here, to forget about, or else.

We had come from the end of the road, three hours across tundra and beach, atop my host's—let's call him Misha—GTT, a large, blunt-snouted all-terrain vehicle that came into his possession when the Soviet military began to disintegrate in 1991. Despite Misha's earlier assurances, not only were we not going to the river I'd traveled thousands of miles to fish, in hopes of seeing what I'd never seen before—the phenomenon of a massive salmon run—but we'd be leaving in the morning, a day earlier than I thought had been agreed upon. Misha, who looked like a blond-haired, cornhusking quarterback, had Brandoesque mannerisms; waiting for my tantrum to subside, he tilted his head back and cocked it coolly, peering down the nascent beefiness of his ruddy face, and then chided me in the hushed cadence of the ever-reasonable gangster.

"Robert," he said, "I'm Mafiya, Mafiya, Mafiya—not a tour agent."

Then he wrapped his hands around his throat, as if to strangle himself, and said he would, if I wanted, take care of my inept outfitter back in Petropavlovsk-Kamchatski (P-K), and for a moment I thought, Nice guy!

At the Mafiya's oceanside fish camp, when I explained that, to salvage something out of the trip, I wanted to be ferried across the lagoon to spend the night upriver, Misha considered this desire stupid and pointless, but mostly he considered it dangerous. Bears were as thick as gooseberries over there, he said, and I didn't have a gun, but when I persisted he ordered his boatman to take me across. Rinat, my half-Tatar, half-Russian interpreter/driver, was coming with me. Sergei, our wilderness guide, said he'd rather not.

Now, standing on a tiny tide-swept island in waist-high grass at the end of this remarkably strange day, I cast futilely for silver salmon with my spinning rod, the strong wind sailing the lure within inches of a sandy patch of beach jutting out below the opposite shore. On the steep bank ten feet above me, Rinat had his nose in the food bag, tossing spoiled provisions out onto the ground.

"Rinat! Are you mad? Throw that food in the river."

Kamchatka is said to have more and larger grizzly bears per square mile than any place on earth, but Rinat was churlishly indifferent to their presence. A city boy, born and raised in P-K, the peninsula's largest metropolis, he was employed by a local tourist company trying to bluff its way into the wilderness biz. His employer—my outfitter—let him come out into the ever-perilous, grizzly-roamed outback without a proper food container, without even a tent (I'd brought my own). Earlier in the summer, we'd done soberingly foolish things together, taken risks that Rinat never seemed to recognize—traversed glaciers where one slip would send you plummeting into oblivion; edged ourselves out onto melting ice bridges; stood on the fragile crater floor of the belching Mutnovsky volcano, our lungs seared by sulfurous gases. How, I often wondered, was this puckish, hardworking fellow ever going to survive his occupation, here in one of the last great wild places left on earth?

"Sushi." Rinat giggled irreverently, pitching stale bread and moldy cheese into the river, making a reference to Michiko Honido, the renowned bear photographer, who was eaten by his Kamchatkan subjects last year.

A minute later I hooked up with a good-size silver salmon, which cheered me deeply, here in the land called the Serengeti of Salmon, where I had been consistently thwarted in my (apparently not) simple quest to savor a fine day of fishing. The fish made its freedom run, keeping me well occupied, and when I looked up again, Rinat, the imp, had set the tundra on fire.

I landed the fish, put my rod down, hopped back to the mainland, and began hauling pots of water while Rinat slapped at the rapidly spreading flames with a fiber sack. Though I'd just reeled in the first salmon of my life, the experience had been akin to losing one's virginity while your little brother's in the room, playing with a loaded pistol.

Later, as I planked one of the filets for smoking, Rinat cut the other into steaks for the cookpot. We lolled around the campfire, uncommonly taciturn, because Rinat had found it politic to give away our last bottle of vodka to the boyos.

"Here we are with the criminals," he said, shaking his head morosely. "Here we are with the bears."

Imagine an Alaska sealed tight for 50 years, suspended in isolation, inaccessible to all outsiders until 1990, when the sanctum's doors ease slowly open to the capitalists on the threshold, the carpetbaggers, the tycoon sportsmen, and, of course, the gangsters. Unworldly Kamchatka, with a not-quite-propitious swing of history's horrible pendulum, is called upon to reinvent itself, and not for the first time.

As gold had once inspired the conquest of the New World, the lust for fur—beaver in North America, sable in Russia—accelerated the exploration of two continents and the spread of two empires. Russia's eastward expansion very much mirrored America's westward expansion—the genocidal subjugation of native peoples in the pursuit of natural riches and trade routes. White guys on the move.

Annexed for the czars by a Cossack expedition in 1697, Kamchatka provided Peter the Great with a global monopoly on the fabulously valuable sable. Within 40 years, the ruthless, plundering Cossacks had decimated the coastal-oriented Itelmen and reindeer-herding Koryaks— the likely descendants of indigenous people who had crossed the Bering Strait to North America. A native rebellion in 1731 resulted in a mass suicide, and before long 150,000 tribal people had been reduced to 10,000, their number today, barely 2.5 percent of Kamchatka's population. Racially and culturally, Kamchatka is as Eurocentric as a bottle of Perrier.

In 1725, Peter the Great sent Captain Vitus Bering on an unsuccessful mission to determine the relation of eastern Siberia to the American continent. Bering was recommissioned by Peter's successor, and his Great Northern Expedition, which took years to plan and execute and eventually involved 3,000 people, is rightfully remembered as one of the greatest voyages of discovery. Bering sailed his two packets, the *St. Peter* and the *St. Paul,* into Avachinsky Bay in 1740 and founded the town of Petropavlovsk, named after his ships. The following spring he set sail for the coast of North America, sighting land in July—Kayak Island off the Alaskan coast—and throughout the summer and fall he mapped the Aleutians, charted the Alaskan shoreline, and then turned back toward Kamchatka, discovering the Commander Islands. His efforts had irrevocably opened the Russian Far East and Russian America for development and trade—in particular, the fur trade, which continued to dominate the peninsula's economy until 1912, the year St. Petersburg banned the trapping of sable for three years to restore the species' population.

Surprisingly, no one showed much interest in the more available resource—salmon—until 1896, when the first fish-processing plant, sponsored by the Japanese, was established at the mouth of the Kamchatka River, once the site of the peninsula's most prolific run. By the time the last Japanese left the peninsula 31 years later, Kamchatka had been thoroughly incorporated into the Soviet system, and both the salmon fishery and the sable trade were transformed into state monopolies. Kamchatkans were free to harvest as much salmon as they wanted until 1930, when the state's imposition of limits radically affected subsistence fishing, and by 1960 the official allowance, 60 kilos a year, was barely sufficient to keep a sled dog from starving. Meanwhile the commercial fishery was booming, and by 1990 Kamchatka's total annual salmon catch had increased from 30,000 tons to 1.5 million tons. As in Alaska, the fishery began to develop dry holes—a river here, a bay there, under severe pressure.

As Kamchatka receded behind the curtain of official xenophobia after World War II, Moscow rapidly developed the area's defenses—a submarine base in Avachinsky Bay; ICBM launch sites, satellite-tracking stations, military outposts up and down its coastlines—and expected in return "gross output." Not just salmon and sable; now everything was up for grabs. By the late eighties, central Kamchatka's primary forests, 60 percent old-growth larch, were decimated; the Soviets had managed to annihilate Kamchatka's herring-spawning grounds as well. Today, in a debauchery of joint ventures with foreign companies, Moscow has taken aim at the crab and pollock fisheries, at risk to suffer the same fate as the larch, the sable, the herring. Nor has the end of Communism spelled anything but crisis for Kamchatka's legendary brown bears. By 1997, the peninsula's Cold War population of grizzlies, an estimated 20,000 bears, had been halved by poachers and trophy hunters. At the rate things are going, says Boris Kopylov, the vice-director of Kamchatka's State Environmental Protection Committee, the most powerful federal agency mandated to preserve the peninsula's natural resources, "In the next five years all the endangered species will be at a critical level, the sea otters and bears especially." This year, the agency's staff was halved: Conservation law enforcement in remote areas vanished as helicopter patrols were reduced from

300 flying hours to zero, and the system, as Kopylov lamented, didn't work anymore. "If you want to save Kamchatka," said Robert Moiseev, one of the peninsula's leading environmental scientists, "you're welcome to pay for it."

Shortly after dawn, the criminals returned to collect us, a humorless sense of urgency in their manner. The chiefs were mightily vexed, they told us, having last night discovered that thieves had spirited away 1,200 kilos—one ton—of caviar the gang had cached on the beach.

"Check Rinat's knapsack," I said. The criminals smiled uneasily—heh-heh—and we loaded our gear into the skiff. I'd come to Kamchatka, twice, to fish, and so far I'd been allowed to do damn little of it. In July, a rafting trip on the Kamchatka River quickly devolved into some awful hybrid of absurdity—Samuel Beckett meets Jack London. The rafts were dry-rotted, the river had been dead for ten years, the mosquitoes were nightmarish, our fishing "guide" was actually a hawk-eyed *tayozhnik,* a taiga woodsman, who had given his stern heart to hunting and horses but had probably never seen a sportfisherman in his life.

On my second expedition to Kamchatka, the day I arrived in P-K from Anchorage an M1-2 helicopter crashed, killing everyone aboard, and I no longer had a ride to the mythical river up north. My local outfitter hadn't considered a Plan B. The only alternative, untested, that the outfitter could offer was for Rinat and me to head out to the coast and try to beg a lift across the tundra with anybody we could find in possession of a GTT—the acronym translated as "Tracks Vehicle: Heavy."

First we drove in Rinat's truck to a village south of P-K to collect Sergei, the wilderness guide, a Russian version of Bubba, attired in camouflage fatigues, who was an erstwhile law-enforcement officer for RIVOD, the peninsula's Fish Regulatory Board. He was now employed as a field-worker by TINRO—the Pacific Scientific Research Institute of Fisheries and Oceanography, a state agency operating in association with the Russian Academy of Science but in cahoots with commercial interests. From 1990 to 1996, hard currency gushed in as TINRO became a clearinghouse for the avaricious flow of foreign investment into Kamchatka's fisheries. "Everybody in the institute got very rich. There was so much money they didn't know what to do with it," a TINRO scientist had told me. "The bosses built big dachas, bought expensive cars." The institute's sudden wealth finally attracted the attention of Moscow, which began sucking up 90 percent of the institute's revenues and controlling quotas.

Sergei, as a quasi-scientific government employee, was our insurance, along for the ride not only to steer us clear of official trouble, but to legitimize whatever it was we might end up doing that was a bit too *diki*—wild, independent—for the apparatchiks.

At the last town before the windswept barrenness of the coast, we turned down a dirt road toward a pre-Soviet Dogpatch, a cluster of clapboard and tar-papered houses, stopping in front of the first one we saw with a GTT in its yard. There on the wooden stoop was Misha, barefoot, wearing camouflage bib overalls, one of his forearms intricately tattooed. He could have been any midwestern hayseed waiting for the glory of team sport. Sergei hopped out, explained our mission, and offered to hire Misha and his machine.

"*Nyet*," insisted Misha. Money, he explained, was nothing to him; therefore, yes, he would take us up the coast, but as his guests. I had no way of measuring the offer and began to ask predictable questions, anticipating predictable answers. The house wasn't his, he said; he came here on the weekends from P-K with his friends to relax.

"What do you do in the city?"

"We are criminals," he replied. "Even the FBI knows about us."

"What'd you do," I joked naively, "sell missiles to Iran?"

Misha narrowed his eyes and demanded to know why I asked such a question. I swore I was only kidding around, and he studied me hard for a good long minute before his demeanor changed and, clapping me on the back, he decided, I suppose, that I was good entertainment out here in the hinterlands—an American writer dropped into his lap.

"Robert, you will write your story about me, you will put me on the cover of your magazine, you will tell the truth," he declared matter-of-factly, an extravagant display of hubris.

The truth, as I understood it, went something like this: Years ago Misha had committed a crime, the nature of which he refused to explain except obscurely. The old system—the commies, I suppose—threw him in jail in Siberia for "not fitting in," where he fell in with like-minded troublemakers sharing grandiose, if not exactly morally based, ambitions for a better life. Most significantly, he connected with his fierce partner—let's call him Viktor, and then let's forget that we ever called him anything.

Gorbachev, perestroika, freedom, the implosion of the USSR, crony economics, the democracy scam—Misha and his Siberian Mafiya crew moved to Kamchatka and became underworld oligarchs. These were the days, the early nineties, of the *diki* Mafiya: no rules, every man for himself, and bodies in the streets. As best I could determine, Misha and friends privatized—seized—a huge tract of state property on the coast, an expansive fiefdom containing four or five rivers plus a processing plant, and went into the caviar business. Eventually the Mafiya and the government realized they had to coexist, so now, after massive greasing, the Mafiya had all the requisite documents and licenses they needed in order to legally do what they were doing—harvesting and processing an astonishing 30 tons of caviar a season to ship to their associates in Moscow.

"The Mafiya," explained Misha, "is a state within a state," and perhaps it was destined to morph into the state itself, because if the government ever tries to recover the properties and companies and concerns the Mafiya had sunk its claws into, "there will be a coup d'état," said Misha emphatically, "and there will be a civil war." Which was exactly the sort of dire prediction I'd been hearing from every upright citizen in Kamchatka throughout the week.

We went inside the austere little house, where Misha sat me down at the kitchen table and smothered me in hospitality, happily watching me shovel down the grub he set out—pasta with minced pork and silver salmon dumplings. Someone appeared with a large bowl of fresh curds and whey. Bonbons? asked Misha, sticking a box of chocolates in my face. Out came a bottle of Armenian brandy. The cross-cultural we-are-all-brothers stuff proceeded splendidly until I made the mistake of cussing.

"*Blyat*," I said—shit. I can't even remember about what.

"Robert," Misha objected, "don't hurt my ears with bad words.

Real men," he admonished in his lullaby voice, "don't need to talk to each other this way."

In the morning, Misha double-checked the tide chart he carried folded in his wallet. "Robert, let's have one for the road," he said. What he meant was, Let's have one *bottle* for the *beginning* of the road. Aspirin and vodka, the breakfast of criminals. Afterward we mounted the GTT and crawled headfirst through the hatch covers into the cavernous interior. We bucked and roared out of town, across the east-west highway and onto the much-scarred tundra, stopping long enough for Misha, Rinat, and myself to climb up on the roof, where we each wrapped a hand around safety ropes and held on as the driver slammed the beast into gear and we slopped our way forward through the bogs.

An hour later we arrived at the coast, littered with the shabby sprawl of a government fish operation. We churned onward through the pebbly sand, the blue Sea of Okhotsk to our left, huge slabs of tundra peat eroding from coastal bluffs on our right. Misha, surveying his kingdom, took delight in pointing out the sights—white-tailed eagles swooping down out of the moody heavens, flocks of berry-fat ptarmigans tumbling clumsily out of the scrub, a pod of all-white beluga whales, scores of sea otters bobbing in the waves off a river mouth. We crossed another without a hitch and Misha happily announced that we were entering private property—his.

We saluted the first brigade of his workers, a motley crew of caviar cowboys. They looked like—and perhaps might someday soon be—partisan rebels in their black rubber waders, filthy overcoats, stubbled faces. We cracked open another bottle of vodka, ate lunch, and Misha wanted pictures, group pictures, buddy pictures, and I took out my camera. We went on, conferring with another survivalist cell of workers farther up the coast, always a guy with a rifle or shotgun standing nearby.

Misha had become a bit nervous, his bonhomie turned brittle. Somewhere up ahead was his jack-booted partner Viktor, who had outlawed alcohol in the camps. If you signed onto a brigade, if you were lucky enough to be asked, you came to work, worked yourself to numbing exhaustion, but after a 12-day cycle of setting nets, pulling nets, tear-

ing the roe out of thousands of now-worthless salmon and processing
the eggs into caviar, you went home with a small fortune—$1,500 a
man. Then, and only then, you could drink your Russian self blind,
for all Viktor cared.

Twenty minutes later, we came to a pair of Ural trucks ahead on
the beach. "No pictures!" Misha warned as I followed him to the dune
line, toward a storm-built village of wooden-hulled shipwrecks. At this
moment I had to be honest with myself about Misha's character flaws
relevant specifically to my presence there on the beach: His pride—he
wanted to boast. His gregariousness—he wanted to be liked and appre-
ciated. His generosity—he wanted everyone to understand he was a
big man who looked after his own. Viktor, Misha's partner but apparently the first among equals, had no such flaws.

"Here is Viktor," said Misha. It wasn't an introduction. I glanced
toward Viktor, who looked at me steadily, his round face icy with menace, and I immediately turned and walked away, careful not to
acknowledge him, as he was so clearly offended by my existence. Misha
had erred in bringing me here with my retinue, playing games when
there was serious work to be done, caviar to salt, traitors to whack,
and now he vied for Viktor's forbearance of this cardinal sin. When
we rendezvoused with Misha back at the GTT, he was singing the same
tune of camaraderie, but in a different key.

"Robert," he said, gazing meaningfully into my eyes, "don't write
about us . . . or I will lose all respect for you," which I suppose is how
a real man says I will have your ass.

Which brings everything back to this lagoon behind the Mafiya's
northernmost outpost, where I stood that morning after my night out
on the tundra with Rinat, not caring so much about how the treach-
ery of the stolen caviar might somehow come crashing down on us
when we reunited with Misha and Viktor at low tide, but instead far
more concerned with my new belief that I was destined never to have
a solid day of good fishing here in the angler's paradise of Kamchatka.

When Misha had dropped us here the previous afternoon, we'd spent
a moment discussing the nature of things, fishwise. His men had
gawked at me, the sportfisherman. Not a one had ever brought in a
fish unless he had gaffed, gigged, netted, snagged, or somehow scooped

it out of the water like a bear. When Misha finally understood the style of fishing I was intent on doing, he frowned.

"*Nyet, nyet, nyet,*" he said. "Don't bring that here. We don't want catch-and-release here." We argued: If he kept harvesting the roe at such a pace, where would the fish be for his children, his grandchildren? "Robert"—Misha smiled—"you and I alone are not going to solve this problem."

And then, too quick, always too quick, it was time to go. Back in Misha's orbit, the criminals actually were in high spirits. It had been a good season so far, the silvers were starting to arrive, and the interior of the GTT was packed solid with wooden casks of precious caviar.

"I don't like to catch fish," Misha said breezily. "I like to catch money."

Kamchatka's exploitation was both an old and a new story, but so was the campaign to preserve its wealth of resources. In 1996 Russia bequeathed more than one-fourth of Kamchatkan territory to the UN Development Programme. A stunning gift to mankind—a World Heritage site that includes the Kronotsky Biosphere Nature Preserve, 2.5 million acres of some of the most spectacular landscape on earth. The Kronotsky Preserve contains a geyser field that is second only to Yellowstone's, and the Uzon Caldera, filled with steam vents, smoking lakes, mud cauldrons, and dozens of hot springs. It also is home to three times as many grizzlies as in the entire Yellowstone ecosystem, plus the greatest known populations of Pacific and white-tailed eagles. The park has 22 volcanoes, including the Fuji-like Klyuchevskaya, 15,584 feet of elegant cone, the tallest active volcano in Asia or Europe.

Many Kamchatkans fear that, as the economy plummets and the country opens itself to the unchecked appetites of the free market, the peninsula's natural resources will be raided and areas like Kronotsky overrun by tourists. When I spoke with Boris Sinchenko, vice-governor of the Kamchatka region administration and one of the men at the helm of Kamchatka's future, he told me, "In five to ten years, we expect to host five to ten million tourists annually and to have built the infrastructure to accommodate them. The territory is so large, we can easily lose ten million people in its vastness."

Many Kamchatkans also harbor a corollary fear. The peninsula's total population is less than 500,000, three-quarters of which lives in or around P-K. An environmental scientist told me with a shrug, "When there's no electricity, the people say, 'We don't care about nature, give us heat!'" One day, Rinat had slapped an orange sticker on the front of my notebook, given to him by his ex-wife, who worked for a Canadian gold-mining conglomerate: "Hungry, Homeless, Need a Job? Call the Sierra Club, Ask About Their No Growth Policy." Only the most arrogant conservationist would demand that Kamchatkans remain impoverished in order to preserve their wonderland for a future less hopeless and bleak than the present. Talking with Sinchenko, however, I sensed there was something a bit cynical about signing over a quarter of the peninsula to the enviros at the UN, as if now that it had proved its enlightenment, the state had earned carte blanche to do what it pleased with the rest of its resources.

There were precedents for such cynicism. Twice, in the sixties and the eighties, the Soviets began to erect power plants on swift-flowing rivers inside or near the reserve, destroying spawning grounds and wasting millions of rubles. Nevertheless, a large hydroelectric project is under construction on the Tolmachevo River, and the gorgeous, fish-rich Bystraya River flowing through the village of Esso was stuck with a dam and power station. Sitting below the areas around Esso are some of the richest unmined gold deposits in the world. When I spoke with Boris Kopylov of the State Environmental Protection Committee, he mentioned that his agency had been successful in stopping exploratory drilling on west coast oil deposits and halting placer mining for gold near the mouth of the Kamchatka River, but it was clear that sooner or later the oil was going to be drilled and the Esso gold deposits were going to be extracted, ultimately endangering spawning grounds in central Kamchatka. "In previous years all the [environmental] agencies were completely against all exploration for gas, oil, and gold," said Kopylov. "Now our position is to change a little."

In the salmon fishery, the magnitude of greed, multiplied in many instances by a struggle for survival, was mind-boggling. "Illegal fishing out of Kamchatka yields $2 billion a year," David La Roche, a consultant for the UN's environmental mission to Kamchatka, told me over beers in a P-K café as we talked about the local flowchart for corruption. "The legal fisheries are yielding not as much."

The economic pressures that confront the ordinary Kamchatkan were made viscerally clear to me in July when I met Vladimir Anisimov, the headman of Apacha, a sprawling collective farm about 150 kilometers due west of P-K. A prosperous dairy farm until Gorbachev presided over the nation's demise, Apacha's ability to survive had seriously corroded, its herds whittled away by the state from 4,000 to 400 head, its buildings in sad disrepair. In desperation, the Apacha villagers had signed an experimental one-year contract with the Japanese to collect mushrooms, herbs, and fiddlehead ferns from the surrounding forest. And then, like almost every other collective in Kamchatka, Apacha had gone into the fishing business.

Everyone was waiting, waiting, for the fish to start their run, but when I returned to Apacha in September, I learned that, as in much of Alaska this summer, it never happened—the July run of salmon never really came in from the sea. Nobody in the village had been paid a wage in recent memory. Vladimir was at a loss; the collective hadn't netted half its quota of 1,200 tons when, if truth be told, it had counted on netting its legal quota and then doubling it with another thousand tons off the books, as is the common practice. Apacha was rotting on the hoof, the central government gnawing away at the resources that the people had struggled 50 years to create. Since the middle of August, the ruble had lost two-thirds of its value, and the last day I saw Vladimir, shops were empty of basic foodstuffs, and Apacha was without electricity because there wasn't any fuel to run its generator. Even in such dire straits, the kindness and generosity that all Kamchatkans had shown me did not abandon Vladimir, and he embarrassed me by siphoning gas out of his own vehicle so that I could go fishing.

Sergei, heretofore simply along for the ride, suddenly awoke to the idea that it was time to take control of our half-baked expedition, now that we had parted with the Mafiya and exhausted every option in our one and only plan to head north to that never-fished river. Pointing for Rinat to take a turnoff up ahead on the east-west road, Sergei allowed that if all I truly wanted to do was fish, then he had an idea that might finally relieve me of my obsession.

Sergei disappeared down a path. I sat in Rinat's diesel truck, praying that something good might come of this. Rinat wouldn't look at me, and I could hardly blame him. His country was falling apart around him, and he was stuck chauffeuring a sport-crazed American, one of the nominal victors in an ugly game we had all been forced to play. All he could do was resign himself to an even uglier truth—foreigners equal money equals hope: Drive on.

Sergei reemerged from the trees, beaming. He had a pal, the local *tayozhnik*, who owned a skiff and was caretaker of a hunting cabin about a half-hour's cruise downriver at the base of the mountains, at the mouth of a tributary as thick with char and *mikisha* (rainbows) as the main river itself was obscenely packed with the season's final run of pink salmon. The *tayozhnik* would be willing to take us there.

"But there's a problem," said Sergei, wincing. "No gasoline for the outboard motor."

OK, that was a problem—there was only one gas station within a hundred kilometers, and it was closed. We drove to a shack atop the bluff above an invisible river and picked up the *tayozhnik*, an unshaven backwoods gnome we might have roused from an Appalachian hollow, and together we traveled a half-hour to Apacha, where Vladimir, the destitute headman of his destitute people, came to our rescue with the siphoned gas. Two hours later, back on the bluff, while I repacked my gear for the boat, Sergei and the woodsman suddenly took off to run unspecified errands.

Rinat and I broke out the medicine and resigned ourselves to further delay. Then began the cirque surreal. First to wander across the clearing was a lugubrious old man who stood gaping at me with wet eyes, as if I were the Statue of Liberty. I passed him the bottle of vodka so that he might cheer up. Then a group of hooligans from Apacha screamed up in their battered sedan, disco blasting, apparently convinced we had come to the river to party. Obligingly, I passed around another bottle. Another hour ticked off the clock.

Sergei and the *tayozhnik* returned, followed in short order by a carload of RIVOD inspectors, blue lights flashing, replaced only a few minutes later by the militia, who sprang from their car patting their sidearms. Again, we passed the bottle.

Night was quickly falling. Just as I bent to hoist my duffel bag, a van rolled into the clearing and out flew a not unattractive woman in a track suit and designer eyeglasses. "I heard there was an American here!" she shouted breathlessly and, zeroing in, almost tackled me in her excitement. She dragged me back to the van and shoved me inside, where her three companions rolled their eyes with chagrin, handed me a plastic cup, and apologetically filled it with vodka. My abductor—Marguerite—knelt in front of me, her hands on my knees, babbling flirtatiously.

"What gives?" I said, utterly bewildered. She slipped a business card into my shirt pocket and pleaded that I allow her to represent me, refusing to hear my explanation that there was nothing to "represent." OK, she said, let's do joint venture.

"Robert?" I heard Sergei calling me. They were ready to go, no more endless dicking around.

I tried to get up, but Marguerite pushed me back in my seat. I grabbed her hands, looked her in the eyes, and firmly declared, "I have to go fishing."

"*Nyet,*" she cried, "*nyet, nyet, nyet,*" and she kissed me. Her friends looked straight ahead, as if it were none of their business.

I lurched for the door, but she had me wrapped up. This couldn't be more bizarre, I told myself—until Marguerite began stuffing six-ounce cans of caviar into the pockets of my slicker. OK, I said, if you want to come, fine, but I'm going fishing now. Marguerite relaxed just long enough for me to bolt out of the van, but there she was again, welded to my arm, attached to me in some frightening, unknowable way.

There was a quick, sharp exchange between her and the gnome, and the next I knew I was threading my way, alone and free, down the bluff through the darkening slope of stone birches. The air was warm, but when you inhaled it was the river you breathed, its mountain coldness, and I felt transcendentally refreshed. Then we were all in the boat, sans Marguerite, shoving off into the main current of this perfect river, the Plotnikova, clean and fast and wild enough for any harried soul.

We were carried forward on a swift flow of silver light, stars brightening in the deep blue overhead. Then the light died on the river too, just as the *tayozhnik* beached the bow on the top end of a long gravel bar, bellying out into the stream. It was too late, too dark, to forge on to the hunter's camp, and I said fine. Sergei begged off again, said he'd be back to pick us up tomorrow, and I said fine to that too. Rinat and I threw our gear ashore, and I pushed the skiff back into the current and then stood there, the black cold water swirling around my waders, singing praise on high for the incredible fact of my deliverance. This river made noise; this river sang.

We dug out our flashlights and dragged our packs about a hundred yards up from the water's edge to the trunk of a huge tree ripped from the riverbank and washed onto the bar. Rinat collected wood for a campfire, and soon we squatted in a private dome of firelight, watching a pot of water boil for tea. I hadn't eaten all day, and my stomach growled.

"Rinat, where's the food?"

He cleared his throat and confessed he'd given everything to the Mafiya, mumbling some ridiculous explanation about the code of the wilderness.

"Where's my candy?"

"I gave it to the criminals."

"You gave the Mafiya my candy! They had their own candy."

"It was the least we could do," said Rinat, "since, you know, they didn't kill us when you hurt their ears with bad words."

We rocked into each other with laughter, howling at the absurdities we had endured together. Our assorted adventures, supernaturally screwed up and filled with hazard, were over but for one true and honest day of fishing, out on the sheer edge of a magnificent world, in a nation going to hell. I patted my pocket for cigarettes and discovered a tin of Marguerite's caviar, Rinat produced a hunk of brown bread, and we ate. He rolled out his sleeping mat and bag and tucked himself into the tree trunk. "Let me apologize in advance," I said, "if the bears come to eat you."

And in the morning, the fish—like the trees and the gravel bar, like the screaming birds and humming bottleflies, like the sun and its petticoat of mists and everything else to be found in its rightful place—the fish were there. I had never seen anything remotely like it, the last days of an immense salmon run. What first struck me, as it hadn't last night, was the profound stench. The gravel island was carpeted with the carcasses of pink salmon—humpbacks—from the height of the run, one of the most concentrated runs in recent years, as if so many fish within its banks had made the river overflow. Now the slightest low spot on the island was pooled with rotting eggs where fish had spawned. Maggots were everywhere, a sprinkle of filthy snow across the rocks and mud and weeds, and dead fish everywhere, rimed with a crust of maggots. I slipped into my waders, walked down to the river through shoals of decomposing fish, and entered the water. Humpback salmon nosed my boots as they struggled wearily upstream; like the prows of sinking ships, the gasping jaws of debilitated male humpies poked out of the water as the fish drifted by, their milt spent, their energy spent, the last glimmer of life fading into the sweep of current. In the shallows, gulls sat atop spawned but still-living fish, tearing holes into the rosy flesh. Fish still fresh with purpose threw themselves into the air, I don't know why, but what I did know was that the salmon were bringing the infinite energy of the sea upriver, an intravenous delivery of nutrients funneling into the land, the animals, the insects and birdlife and the very trees.

Here, in a salmon, nature compressed the full breath of its expression, the terrible magnificence of its assault, and I stood in the current, mesmerized. On the far bank at the mouth of a tributary there were poachers. At first glance it seemed that they had built low bonfires on the opposite shore, the red flames licking and twisting, but where was the smoke? I wondered, and as I looked more deliberately I saw my mistake: The writhing flames were actually fish. One poacher worked at the base of the tall bank, poised like a heron above the stream, using a long staff to gaff salmon—females, hens—as they swam past and then flipping the fish overhead to a pile on the top of the bank, where his partner crouched, gutting out the roe.

When the spell broke, I sat down on a log and finally accomplished the one thing I had passionately desired to do for days, months, all my life: I rigged my fly rod for salmon fishing.

I decided to head down the bar to where the currents rejoined at the rapids below its downstream point, an eddy splitting off to create slack water. The island was probed by wayward, dead-end channels, trickling into basins where the sand had flooded out, and as I waded through the biggest pool scores of humpback salmon, coalesced into orgies of spawning, scurried before me in the foot-deep shallows like finned rats. In the deeper holes the season's last reds cruised lethargically in their scarlet and olive-green "wedding dresses," as the Kamchatkans call a fish's spawning colors. I sloshed onward to dry land, the fish gasping, the birds screaming, and everywhere the reek of creation.

On the tail of the bar I planted my feet in the muck and cast into a deep turquoise body of water that resembled nothing so much as an aquarium, waiting for the connection, that singular, ineffable tug that hooks a fisherman's hungry heart into whatever you want to call it— the spirit of the fish, the bigness of life or even the smallness, the euphoric, crazed brutality of existence, or simply a fight: the drama of the battle between man and his world. Not every cast, but most, ended with a fish on my hook, a glorious humpback, three to five pounds each, the hens painted in swaths of mulberry, green, and rose, the males beautifully grotesque with keel-like dorsal humps and hooked jaws like the beak of a raptor.

A day of humpies landed on flies here on this grand river was enough to quench my deepest craving for the sport, but then my rod bent from the pressure, the reel sang its lovely shrill song as the line escaped, and here came the silvers, big and angry, like bolts of electricity, filled with the power of the sea. Rinat finally joined me in this dance, and by the late afternoon, when Sergei and the *tayozhnik* returned, we had two fish apiece, the limit, silvers as long and fat as our thighs.

We gathered more wood, Rinat started the fire, and Sergei brought his cookpot from the boat. "I'm going to show you how to make a poachers' *ukhá*," said Sergei, cutting off the salmon heads and tails and sliding them into the boiling pot with diced potatoes and onion and dill. I had caught dozens of pinks but kept only one, a female, and Sergei slit her belly to make instant caviar, unsacking the eggs into a bowl of heavily salted water.

We sat in the gravel with our backs propped against the fallen tree and gazed lazily out at the fast blue dazzle of the river, slurping our fish soup. A raft floated down from around the bend, paddled by two RIVOD officers. The poachers on the opposite shore vanished into the forest, the wardens paddled furiously into the tributary, and we listened as the crack of gunshots resonated over the river, here in the Wild East.

Sergei, waxing philosophical, quoted a poet: "It's impossible to understand Russia, only to believe in it." Then he lifted a spoon of caviar to my lips, and I recalled the last fish I had caught that day, a hen, which had no business hitting my fly, ripe as she was. When I brought her from the water she sprayed a stream of roe, an arc in the air like a chain of ruby moons, splashing over my feet onto this most eternal, unsettled world of the river.

December 1998

Everest to the Left of Me, Unrest to the Right

EDWARD HOAGLAND

Back to the future, I thought, heading for India again, that kaleidoscopic subcontinent now closing on a billion people, the squeeze of human beings fissured by religious righteousness and rapacious capitalism, with incongruous juxtapositions of seething hustle and mystic symbolism, ten and a half hours' worth of time zones away from New York City. You have to like the idea of people—the chattering crush and possible divinity of myriads of them—to enjoy India. All those separate envelopes of rushing, self-important, self-involved dignity: The cut of the headcloth or glint of the sari denoting caste or class or whatever. People in galaxy numbers have a whole-is-greater-than-the-parts reverberation, at least for me. I'm usually elated by crowds, whether in New York or Cairo, London or Calcutta—the glee, élan vital, and energy. Even amid vistas of poverty, I tend to think I see meaning. Generosity in squalor.

I was headed, however, for the state of Arunachal Pradesh ("Land of the Dawn-Lit Mountains"), a salient of Indian territory in the foothills of the Himalayas extending eastward between Myanmar and Tibet. China, in fact, contests Indian sovereignty in this border region, home to some two dozen animist hill tribes, and invaded in blitzkrieg style in 1962, when Arunachal Pradesh was constitutionally part of the neighboring Indian state of Assam. Eighteen years earlier the Japanese, under General Renya Mutaguchi, had also invaded Assam, to try to sweep the British out of India. You need an internal visa to enter Arunachal Pradesh (it was opened to foreign tourists only in 1995), and tribal insurrections continue to harass the army and plague the police in Assam, where traditionalists want autonomy. At Guwahati, Assam's capital, shortly before our arrival, Bodo rebels blew a hole in the bridge across the Brahmaputra River and, separately, derailed an express train loaded with Guwahati passengers for New Delhi, with great loss of life—all in the name of secession for "Bodoland."

The approach by jet to Bombay from the Arabian Sea still affords views of a lovely diadem of yellow lights—not boastful or bombastic in its wattage like a Western city, but tentative, evocative, and homemade, sort of a glowing crescent. The passengers clapped as we landed safely, as they often do on Third World flights. Then we waited for an hour in a rattletrap bus before transferring five miles to the domestic airport, and five hours there. I was pleased, though, because my friend Trudy and I began meeting the surge of souls you do while on the road in India. A young engineer who was returning to Bangalore after attending a conference in Cincinnati. A cruise ship steward just back for six weeks of home leave in Cochin after six months of sailing in Alaska and the Caribbean. A couple of American Hare Krishna pilgrims en route to an ashram, and a shaky fortysomething Canadian who had come in search of, as he said, "Nada." Also a middle-aged Goan woman who had been living comfortably in London but was now returning to India for the first time in eight years because she had begun to suspect that the half-million-pound estate her family had donated to charity was being converted into a moneymaking scam.

Our next stop was Calcutta, that proverbially dying city and yet India's intellectual and artistic capital. As in a parable, squalor and joy cohabit, while almost everyone over the age of ten swims hard against the tides and density to obtain their daily pound of rice. If you think people are a chip off the old block, embodying a spark of divinity—God's holy chosen tribe straddling like Gulliver the Lilliputian natural world—how many can be too many? India's situation, seen broadly, looks more optimistic than this particular frenetic megalopolis of refugees and street-dwellers collapsing from accrued procrastination and dystopian dilemmas, nearing 300,000 souls per metro square mile, and any spare dirt patch ditched for a rice paddy or dug out to grow carp. By the millennium India's population may triple from what it was at independence in 1947; Calcutta's also, though Calcutta's infrastructure is desperately asthmatic now. Yet the lift my spirits got in Calcutta is memorable because it seemed sanguine.

The next morning we had time to see the city's wholesale flower market, down under Howrah Bridge—cantilevered, ramshackle, and ungainly, and said to be the busiest in all the world. Two million people a day somehow manage to cross it, afoot or squeezed into an assortment of vehicles—omnibuses, gypsy cabs, auto-rickshas, rickshas, mopeds, pedicabs. In the muddy warren of alleys below and south of the bridge, lorry-loads of flowers had been distributed overnight and were being sewed into red religious garlands for temple offerings, feasts, fests, marriages, and burials in a hundred tiny establishments, then tossed into bicycle carts and handcarts for delivery. The brown shoals of the Hooghly River were stained red and yellow from the masses of petals washed in by the rains, plus yesterday's discarded flowers. Where stone steps went down, a lot of people were bathing in it also, though there was floating flotsam and offal. The mix and flux of flowers, people, and offal is of course India's curse and blessing: what distinguishes it from "us."

Another flight took us 325 miles northeast across Bangladesh to Guwahati, the administrative and trading center of Assam. It's a sprawled-out, comparatively prosperous little riverbank city, cupped under choppy green hills. The government hotel overlooked the Brahmaputra River, as wide as the Mississippi even at this driest time of year, with a small temple to Siva on an islet in the middle, and a black-and-white stork stalking the shore. There were dugouts on the Brahmaputra, too, and cormorants diving, harrier hawks and pariah kites scouting about, and vultures sailing high and martins scooting low. In the morning in the garden I saw an owl, and mynahs, common as robins, and drongos, magpies, gray-necked crows, and turtle-doves. Cool, majestic trees decorated the promenade above the waterfront, and peddlers shook nuts into your hand for a rupee or two. Below, a dozen people were washing their clothes, soaking the garments and pounding them on a drift log. Several sampans were floating leaflike out on the vast river, each with a loaf-shaped little shelter in the middle and propelled by a man with a pole standing at each end.

The Brahmaputra flows 1,800 miles from inner Tibet, beyond the Himalayas, in a great loop around to the mouth of the Ganges via the plains of Assam, having drained in the meantime about 626,000 square miles by way of 24 major tributaries. Assam's fertility is much enhanced as a result. Two-thirds of its farmland is planted with rice, and the other best cash crop is harvested from the plantations of tea, though it also produces a sixth of India's petroleum. So the three minor insurrections that were in fitful progress in the state at the moment—and noticeable to us as graffiti in Assamese or bold headlines in the local papers (or else because any vehicle deemed drivable by the military had been seized for transporting soldiers)—were apparently not about hunger, but ethnic pride. The frontier with China, a much larger flashpoint, is north of Assam through the layered mountains of our Arunachal Pradesh and guarded by roadless outposts that the army's helicopters supply. The Brahmaputra is famous for torrential canyons and pugnacious tribes where it crosses wildly through the main chain of the Himalayas from Chinese territory—dropping, for example, 6,000 feet in a curving canyon in just two miles, right at the border, but already more than 700 miles from its source. Yet here on the plains, it looked huge and sedate.

We set out for our adventure, six Americans and Gautam Malakar, our Delhi-based guide, in a stubby blue bus toward the city of Tezpur, a district center six hours upriver on the north bank, which had been the limit of the Chinese advance in the 1962 war. (The Chinese troops withdrew later that year under international pressure, and the border dispute remains unresolved.) Mostly rolling rice country, diked, ditched, and closely cultivated in checkerboard plots, with family fishponds occupying slight depressions amid the paddies, it was more of a breadbasket than claustrophobic. There were banana and betel-nut plantations as well, and we passed a sizable paper mill that was being fed with truckloads of bamboo poles and sal trees. Also the village of Nelli, where Gautam said 3,000 Muslim immigrants from Bangladesh had been slaughtered by Hindu locals 15 years ago.

As we got into higher terrain, the tea plantations began. These were extensive, but some of the hilltops were still wooded naturally, and the paddy fields presented a wide, pretty quiltwork of grays and greens. Scattered humpbacked brown cattle or black buffalo browsed the stubble in the fallow stretches, with dark tick birds and white egrets accompanying them, or straggling, peppy files of goats. A troop train rattled alongside the road for a while, the commanding officer leaning out the door in his military tunic and white pajama pants.

More and more tea plantations replaced the gridwork rice paddies as we climbed away from the Brahmaputra. On our ribbon of road there were two-man handcarts, one-man handcarts, and occasional battered, wheezing trucks painted like carnival wagons, blue with gaudy yellow designs and tinselly tassels hanging over the windshields. Periodically a broken-springed bus barreled by, careening to a stop if somebody walking raised a hand. Wicker fish traps were set in the streams.

After the town of Gohpur there were no main arenas of cultivation, just forested ridges rising into Arunachal Pradesh. At the clamorous border our skinny, lorry-pitted road passed through the small hustlers' towns of Banderdewa and Naharlagun. A billboard greeted us at the roadblock where police checked our papers: ARUNACHAL PRADESH AWAITS TO YOUR ARRIVAL WITH ITS ENTHRALLING VALLEYS. Either our papers were not in order or some "efficiency money" (as bribes are called in India) had to be paid, because we went to a sort of truck stop for barbecued goat meat and Godfather Super Strong High Power Beer while negotiations progressed. Eventually the police chief's brother got hired as our temporary guide.

Arunachal Pradesh (population one million), formerly known as the North East Frontier Agency, became India's 23rd state in 1987. The regional capital, Itanagar, is an ugly, energetic community landlocked among roadless mountains and largely cut off from the rest of the state it's supposed to govern. We shared the dining room of the best hotel with the Minister for Tax and Tourism, who was bellowing drunk, but after supper we drove across town to the comely new yellow-roofed Buddhist monastery atop one of the city's hills. It had recently been dedicated by the Dalai Lama, and the day before we visited, 20 young boys had arrived for their novitiate. They were visibly excited to be assuming the duties of apprenticeship—patrolling the lovely, freshly painted temple counterclockwise in shifts, with prayer flags flying overhead, launching a prayer to heaven with every tremble and flip. Later, they would be sent out individually with begging bowls to subsist for a year on the charity of strangers. Every religion, it seemed to me, should fly prayer flags at its temples and send priests out for long walkabouts to fathom something of the way other people live.

It's not how Americans travel, however. Our group included a likable Fifth Avenue dentist and his school-board-chairman wife. Another man was a business executive; he had been a prep-school roommate of Jack Kennedy's and said he hadn't slept in a sleeping bag since he was 12. We had a staff of ten to care for us: Gautam, a Bengali from New Delhi; four Sherpas from Nepal; three Assamese from Guwahati; and Michi Reni, an Apa Tani from the hill town of Ziro.

Because of the lack of roads, we needed to loop back into the lowlands of Assam for an hour or two in order to reenter Arunachal Pradesh and go farther, climbing along a series of river gorges brocaded in shimmering green. The previous night our little bus had been suddenly requisitioned for moving troops around (we weren't told why or where), and as replacements we'd gotten three shaky, breathless cars, which soon began suffering breakdowns, giving us time to spare in villages such as Licky. The bamboo-slat houses had overhanging thatch roofs, and the villagers had Tibetan faces, not oriented yet to smiling at tourists. Over the next ten days, in fact, we saw only one other party of tourists, a group of Austrians. Being well east of Nepal, and even of Sikkim and Bhutan, Arunachal Pradesh is not a launching pad for mountain-climbing attempts, and politics of the old style had kept it unfrequented—not nuclear bluster, so much in the news recently, but skirmishing rebel bands, tribal fights, and the Chinese infantry along the border. It's also not a druggy hangout, and there are no places to shop, no airports for a quick entry or exit. In every town where we slept over, policemen checked our faces against our passport photos, forgetting that satellites do the spying now.

I'd been in many mountains before, but not the Himalayas. Vertiginous cuts and gorgeous gorges succeeded each other, as we wound round and round, up the watersheds, with serrated ridgetops always rising above us no matter how high the road climbed. And these were the mere foothills. All we'd ever see were foothills, exhilarating and awesome but, at 6,000 feet, only a fourth as high as the farthest ranges. The dirt road was slippery where recent washouts had occurred; the only source of wage employment seemed to be in repairing it. Otherwise, people fed themselves by stump farming (slash-and-burning) or subsistence hunting—the men with old Enfield rifles, the boys with slingshots, their quarry including musk deer, wild boar, songbirds, monkeys, turtles, and miscellany such as caterpillars. The bulky wilderness cattle known as mithuns—which are domesticated gaurs, the wild oxen of India, like short-haired buffalo thriving in the steepest rainforest yet tame when led back to the village to serve as a bride price or funeral sacrifice—were to be seen occasionally, like big black-skinned innocents grazing amid the riot of ferns, vines, rushes, grasses, and sedges, on sidehills pitched at 60 degrees. There had also been some sporadic logging of old-growth trees in the region, but this had just been halted by an environmentalist lawsuit in New Delhi. We saw an army helicopter laboring north to supply a frontier post a hundred miles beyond the nearest road.

We were aiming for Ziro. The Apa Tanis, 20,000 strong, are regarded as perhaps Arunachal Pradesh's most prosperous tribal group. Even before their first contact with Europeans—H. M. Crowe, a British tea planter of redoubtable temperament, ventured into their territory in 1889—the Apa Tanis had shifted from hunting and gathering to an agricultural economy. They occupy an anomalously level plateau of about 20 square miles 5,000 feet up in these otherwise tumultuous mountains, and intensively cultivate it. In the past, though demonstrating less prowess as individual warriors than such neighbors as the Nishis and the Hill Miris, they outnumbered them locally and had more cohesion, raising big families in crowded bamboo villages, and so were able to defend as well as grow an abundance of rice, while their adversaries lived sparsely off wild meats and plants like the sago palm.

In muddy Ziro, we camped next to an experimental orchid farm run by the World Wildlife Fund. (There are hundreds of native species.) But in traditional hamlets like Hang, we saw older Apa Tani women wearing wooden plugs in their nostrils and latticed blue facial tattoos, originally a custom that discouraged raiders from kidnapping them. The Apa Tanis trade rice for livestock and cotton with neighboring tribes and are good weavers. By legend, they originated their patterns by imitating a spider's web, or the shimmering ripples on the Kali River, or a butterfly's beauty, or a snake's paisley skin, or the symmetry of a fish's scales. The loom is a simple one, and the woman sits cross-legged facing it, leaning back against a strap that holds it straight.

Next morning, on the road to the Tagin tribal stronghold of Daporijo, we saw forktails, rollers, and tits; saw fields of millet, maize, sugarcane, pumpkins, ginger, and gourds. The watercourses were not apologetic. They crashed, bashed, and plummeted by the logic of physics. No dams or levees, and the treacherous road tiptoed in tenuous switchbacks high above the torrents.

We first passed through the homeland of the Nishis. "Nishi" means "hill men," and this tribe lives in a scattered fashion. Being aggressive, individualistic hunter-foragers, its members usually forgo the governance of headmen. The men sported talismanic hats that appeared somehow to contain a whole indigenous world. The basic frame was of wickerwork and musk-deer skin, but sewn to the front of that was a sizable tuft of black-bear fur in place of the customary *podum,* or knot, of their own hair that many tribes wear, with a brass skewer through it. Above the bear fur was a huge red-dyed hornbill's bill, projecting forward. Attached to the top of the cap but instead extending back were an eagle's muscular fingers and riveting talons. And a cluster of classy peacock feathers hung down in back. These Nishis wore short, sheathed swords.

After we stopped at one point and scrambled up a mucky rise, we provoked the hilarity of several startled ladies in saris, at work on a steep hilltop with pestle and mortar, or a backstrap loom, by asking through Michi, our narrow-faced Apa Tani translator, if we could tour one of their houses. Big bamboo porches led into the dimly airy interior, ventilated and lit by the spaces between the polework on the sides, and all tied with vines. Though tree posts and logs supported the crosshatched stiltwork below, and though the floor itself was closely laid with halved bamboo poles to furnish a flat surface, the structure moved, nestlike, according to the wind or the influence of our shifting weight. The four or five separate hearths in roomy compartments were partitioned by cane curtains and fireproofed by a mud foundation laid on top of the bamboo floor. Over each little fire there was a blackened canework sling that held the stored food—newly harvested rice that was drying and meat being smoked. The rafters functioned as a closet or as dresser drawers; clothing was hung at a convenient height on them. And on the side wall were a few nails where you'd see a winnowing basket or a cultivating implement or a quiver of slender bird arrows in a bamboo stem or an animal skull.

With Michi's help we chatted, having climbed so sharply through the mud to meet them. Pigs ran around, and a dead goat hung on a fence. The boys wore slingshots round their foreheads, and some men were cutting house posts with bush knives trimmed with monkey fur. Nearby a woman was mixing sand and cement to bolster a small dam at the outlet of a forest spring. Sometimes, she told us as she worked, the villagers took drums and pounded through the forest, driving a congeries of wildlife—frogs, hares, rodents, wild hogs, and deer—into a trap amid the palms, creepers, wild banana, nahor, tita, and silk-cotton trees.

The bottle-green Kamla River demarcated the end of the Nishis' territory from the beginning of the Hill Miris', though after we had crossed the bridge there wasn't an immediate difference to be seen. Unlike the Apa Tanis, who had placed their crowded villages on oddments of the least cultivable land so as to maximize the rice crop, the less numerous, more warlike Hill Miris and Nishis had been primarily concerned with security when they set their settlements on hilltops, a long haul from water but a hard knoll for a band of raiders to get at.

Now that headhunting and skirmishing have ceased and the tribalists have been pacified (as recently as four or five decades ago, encyclopedias described Arunachal Pradesh as scarcely explored), with a couple of languid soldiers posted in every town that the road goes through, these defendable hamlets remain simply glorious vantage spots. Far-off vistas of cloud forest and plummeting slopes spread everywhere, both higher and lower than you, with the slash-and-burn quilting of farm work just occasional: rice, millet, yams, corn, wheat, potatoes, tobacco, peppers, in subsistence parcels. Otherwise, many varieties of bamboo and sal, poma and toon trees, walnuts, chestnuts, pines, spruces, oaks, rhododendrons, and vigorous undergrowth enrich the scenery.

Traditionally, the Hill Miris are said to believe that they found their home by following flights of birds south from Tibet and that, apart from the Sun-Moon Creator God, the most powerful spirit is Yapom, the deity of the forests, who may assume quirky but ominous human form. Hill Miris are flamboyant—the women with beaded necklaces and metal bracelets and earrings, the men bearing on their chests a leopard's or a tiger's jaws with a mirror in the middle and wearing a decorated cane helmet, sometimes with an entire tiger's tail dangling down. We saw one man flaunting an eagle's wing across his chest, and other men with cobra skins draped around their necks and boars' tusks on their heads. Unfortunately, large cats such as tigers are vanishing from Arunachal Pradesh, and it was only the old men who had been able to kill one of them as a rite of passage. The young men either wore the smaller leopards' jaws or else were reduced to using the jaws of mere wildcats the size of an American bobcat. Gautam told us that the Hill Miris are still an aggressive tribe, and they did object to being photographed, with several older men stalking severely out of camera range. Women standing in their dooryards dodged away.

Two gorges were set catty-corner underneath us in this clamor of mountains striped with streaming clouds. Burial in such a setting, as the Hill Miris do it, is performed by members of the opposite sex. Then several stuffed monkeys are placed on a platform above the grave of the person who died, outfitted for the trip to the netherworld with little pack-baskets of food and tubes of rice beer and miniature tobacco pipes stuck in their mouths, as servants for the soul.

We camped on the bluff of the Tagin tribal town of Daporijo for two nights, at the confluence of two splendid rivers, the aquamarine tributary Sippi and the earthier Subansiri. It was more than scenery—it was positively paradisiacal, though the town is the site of an army base: the Ninth Assam Rifles. We saw crag martins stunting below us over the water, and ravens, forktails, white-breasted kingfishers, black drongos (like blue jays), yellow bul-buls, mergansers, a blue whistling thrush, pied wagtails, and a falcon darting, cruising, high above. The Subansiri appears to be lonely and majestic, a sublime, graceful river assembling thousands of square miles of Himalayan watercourses after their tumult is mostly done. All that drenching rainfall, the vertigo of the massifs of the mountain range, collected into just this one of many tributaries of the grander Brahmaputra, curving in quiet python coils toward the Bay of Bengal.

Daporijo had a concrete market street with assorted stalls and flickering electricity. We set off in the morning to visit some Tagins, up a gorge of the Sippi, in the next-to-last village, Nintemuri, that can be reached on four wheels. In two places the mud road had washed out next to horrific precipices where we skidded dangerously. The Tagins, like the Hill Miris and Nishis, were hunter-foragers who are thought to have crossed the Himalayas from Tibet and, also like them, until recently were little known to the outside world. And vice versa—in 1953 a group of Tagins ambushed a government exploration party, killing 47 of its 165 members. They wear round cane hats and build square bamboo houses; hunt barking deer, mountain goats, crocodiles, snakes, wildcats, and hares; lead mithuns about by a woven-vine rope; wear a black-root woven cape that looks like bearskin and sheds rain; and hang straw effigies on a bamboo frame in front of a shrine to ward off malignant *wiyus,* or spirits, which are subsidiary to the benignly indifferent Sun-Moon god, called Daini-Pol.

Verrier Elwin himself, the British explorer-author who, inspired by Gandhi, was the principal champion or protector of these hill tribes after India's independence, wrote that the Tagin area was "the most formidable, the most desolate, in a way the least rewarding country I have visited. . . . The climate is abominable; the people are under-nourished and tormented by diseases of the skin; the tracks are impossible." And the mountains were indeed molar and uninviting, the weather lawless. The V-cut of the valley cleaved the views in each direction very short and left little space for cultivating terraces. At Ninte-muri, some Tagin men were amused to say that their grandfathers had shot arrows at the first survey helicopters that went over in the for-ties. Michi, in chatting, added that his own Apa Tani grandfather had helped fight the first military expedition that showed up near Ziro in the 1950s, having penetrated their territory from Assam, after India won its independence, with a mission to establish a national hegemony. Too young to be in the forefront, he'd stood behind the warriors, preparing and handing forward arrows—though many of them were killed by machine guns or taken away as prisoners.

The bridge over the Subansiri River was a funnelly rattletrap of metal and boards that had recently fallen out under a bus with 82 peo-ple on it and drowned them all. It did us no harm, but another bridge we crossed that day, going toward the town of Along, tore up the undercarriage of one of our cars and halted us for a bit. The steel-and-wood structure was falling apart. Loops of loose wiring and jumbles of nails stuck out from the rusting girders and busted planks.

We were crossing from the territory of the Tagins to that of the Gal-longs and from the drainage of the Subansiri River to that of the Siang, the Arunachali name for the upper Brahmaputra itself. The tributaries of each river had carved giddy, green, orchestral valleys that deserved the august name "Himalayas," and we wound like bugs along the vast margins of these, from pass to pass, and then down again. And begin again.

When the Gallongs—like the Nishis, Hill Miris, and Tagins—were still regarded as fearful cannibals and bestial murderers by the people of the farming floodplains between Guwahati and other populous towns beside the big lowland Brahmaputra after it has straightened out, they were not known by their present names, but as Abhors or Daflas, "savage" appellations bestowed on them by agricultural Assamese, who had long cultivated the protection and good opinion of the English and previous conquerors. And for years, into the middle of the twentieth century, they intimidated intruders, killed the occasional unwary explorer, and maintained a local pattern of hunting, raiding, and sometimes slavery, unsubdued.

The British first came partway up the Siang in force when the Japanese tried to invade Assam. Then, after Independence, the nationalistic expeditions became more punitive and punctilious. Down in Tirap, for instance, 300 villagers were massacred by the Assam Rifles in 1954. And several roads were quickly built after the Chinese invaded India in 1962. The Gallongs, however, seem rather milder, more assimilated, a less bristly people nowadays than the Tagins, Hill Miris, and Nishis.

From Daporijo to Along—home of the Gallongs—was a long, rainy haul. Clouds sopped the mountainsides, up, up around hairpin turns, fishhooks, switchbacks, with valleys set at a tangent like gargantuan elbows, and a peak peeking out at almost moon-height, way beyond. Or we'd skid through a streambed, a pony-size galloping cataract, if the road had washed out, and almost over a drop-off, where the forest, perhaps through sheer, seething density, bound by its cat's-cradle creepers, had still managed to cling. Only birds had much fun negotiating these. The horn on one vehicle failed—as dangerous on mountain curves as losing your headlights at night (which we also once did).

We were just skirting all this immensity, threading the edge. When one of our cars broke down again, we walked uphill awhile to a well-watered settlement of lush fields and banana trees terraced on a slope. I saw a leopard's prints on the track, and a bear's prints, and heard so much birdsong, noticed so many butterflies, smelled the fragrance of so many flowers that it was clear these people had obviously struck a good balance between slash-and-burning for crops and maintaining the overall web of life.

The Gallongs grow grapefruit and oranges, do backstrap looming and mortar-and-pestle milling, but boast an occasional TV aerial on houses close to their capital, or an ornate porch railing and some hanging plants to dress up the primitive bamboo architecture. In the village of Pangin, spread in leisurely fashion along a bench above the Siang River, we saw smoked squirrels and monkeys hanging next to the hearths, and millet and maize fields galore. Yet also jalopies and pick-ups, and several young men who had been to the city.

But the principal boast of Pangin is its two 100-yard-long cane sus-pension bridges, in the splendid pre-Contact engineering tradition. The Siang cuts a good working trench through this part of the valley, so it can rise 30 feet without flooding the mossy ground where the big trees grow. The bridges, constructed of coils of cane, are slung all the way across like a swaying, looping-down, open-topped, V-shaped tube going from one huge tree to another. Bamboo poles are laid end to end on the bottom to provide a bouncing sort of footing, and cane ropes, horizontal but also webbed vertically, furnish handholds at about chest-height, plus a gingerly sense of partial enclosure. You climb up along a huge split log to the jump-off point and look down the narrow incline, which jounces slightly in the wind and slants scarily up again to the stubby platform on the tree over on the other side. Two people can barely slide past each other, if that becomes necessary, holding the vine rails and treading the pole floor.

Forty or fifty feet underneath us were four slim bamboo fishing rafts, each poled by a single man, who combined with the others to set a net and drive fish into it by banging the water. The river was at its most placid stage, despite the daily rains we had had, so a little later Trudy and I stretched out on a drift log on the wide gravel beach for a spell of privacy, letting the tour group move on and watching the tiptoe traffic of women carrying pack baskets of grain or loads of bamboo across the elastic bridge over us. Some little kids came down the bank, questioned us about America, and waded with spears after fish or threw stones at them and scanned the bushes for a bird they could hit with their slingshots. The young men who had been fishing approached us with curiosity as well but asked whether we were afraid. We said no.

"The people here are innocent," one told us. "In Calcutta they would rob you." He moved off without doing so, but when we saw him beat-ing a screaming dog not long afterward, and after Trudy had shouted at him to stop to no avail, I decided we'd better get back nearer the road. This was country where people like us might have been shot full of arrows as recently as when I was in my teens.

I went and sat for a while later on at the mud hearth fires of two lean patriarchs in their longhouses. One was a priest, also the son of a priest, as he told me through Michi. He had decided to become a priest 25 years ago, when he felt his own calling, and had been trained by another shaman. When I asked if he healed sick people with herbs, he told me no, just prayers and animals that he sacrificed. The twisting fingers of firelight, the silence except for our murmuring voices and the wind brushing against the bamboo house-frame, the smell of smoke and forest meats (the canework hammock hanging over the fire, where meat and rice were stored, looked practically fireproof, it had so hardened with soot), made me relax my wristwatch-and-monotheistic rigidity.

I live in the woods without electricity anyway for part of the year, but that is like wading in a swimming pool, next to the ocean of lifelong habituation of people who live by the sun, stars, and fire-flicker from birth to a quiet grave. The spirits of tigers and hollow old trees and the muscling-in weather and mountain massifs are no more implausible than Jehovah of the Pentateuch—though in knee-jerk fashion we repel the thought that nature might be more than geophysics, that it might also be spirit and whimsy. Our own spirit can have no counterpart short of heaven, we think. It sprang full-blown into existence only with us.

The priest was probably fiftyish, though his wiry figure and face looked older by Western standards. His wife and daughter sat cross-legged across the stewpot-size fire in the breezy room, with the sky in its night costume outside. He said, through Michi's translation, that the tiger was the biggest spirit in the forest, among the animals, though if you killed a bear or a leopard you would have to do *puja*, too, lest its spirit haunt you. The trees large enough to have a spirit were malign as well. They were being cut, so when the forests were logged off commercially and the wildlife killed, it would simplify things in the sense that constant propitiation might be at an end. But the undergirdings of the culture, of course, would be gone also. His negotiations were all with the world as it was before agriculture and industry.

The other patriarch, in another bamboo house with a busy, tidy fire as its centerpiece—the ends of two burning logs touching each other, controlled by how far he pulled them back or pushed them together—had worked for the British as a hod-carrier in the 1940s, when they had established a tentative military post at Pasighat, a week's walk downriver on the Siang, about where it changes to the Brahmaputra. (In far Tibet it is called the Yalutsangpo or Tsangpo.) And whereas in the cities there is a tendency to remember Calcutta's Netaji Subash Chandra Bose as a hero who raised an Indian liberation army to fight against the British alongside the Japanese in World War II—exalting him even above Gandhi, who was too pacifist for contemporary tastes—remote tribal peoples such as the Gallongs remember the British more as protectors than oppressors, as they try to resist being swamped and nullified in contemporary India. He spoke in this sort of vein, as I enjoyed again the whickering silence, just the fire's ticking, and the night birds outside. He and his wife muttered to each other in normal voices that were much softer than my ears could easily take in.

The labyrinth of giddy valleys and soaring high country of Arunachal Pradesh harbors 26 major tribes, of which we had encountered only five on the scant road system. We continued east toward Pasighat—maybe the finest drive of all, with the road running a thousand feet up along the Siang's jungly gorge. One's retinas could hardly register the green and white water boiling way down below and the stupendous opposite flank going up to regions that the clouds obscured or sailed alongside. The river twisted like a striped reptile, swelling and roiling—constructing cliffs, flooding meadows. After hours of wild, wonderful grandeur we saw, with reluctance, the gap where the Siang forks onto the plains.

October 1998

The Essential Nature of Islands

PAUL THEROUX

I liked the look of Palawan on a map—the sausagey shape of it, the way it linked Indonesia to the Philippines, its great distance away, its apparent insignificance, its only one town-dot of any size, its fringe of a thousand scattered islands, some in the Sulu Sea, the rest in the South China Sea, the whole place nearer to Borneo than to its own mainland. All this stirred me: It had just the right profile to be a great place for kayaking.

My ideal in travel is you show up and head for the bush, because most cities are snake pits. In the bush there is always somewhere to pitch your tent.

But I knew nothing about Palawan and even the guidebooks were pretty unhelpful. All my ignorance made me want to travel there and hop those islands. Then, whenever I talked about it, people said, "Don't go," because the very mention of the Philippines brings to the narrow mind images of dog-eaters and cockfights, urban blight and rural poverty, and Mrs. Marcos's ridiculous collection of shoes—a place where the visitor industry consists mainly of sex tours and money launderers and decaying old white men looking for doe-eyed Filipinas to marry or else willing catamites in Manila, and of course the furtive visits of European branches of Pedophiles Sans Frontières.

The Philippine general election loomed. Campaigning—so I was told—involved high-caliber cross fire, the supporters of one candidate raking the opposition in a bloody enfilade of horrific gunplay. It was a country of ferry disasters and kiddie porn and government thievery on a grand scale. In other respects it was what Ireland had been in the nineteenth century, a producer of menial workers for the world. Name almost any country and there were Filipinos in it, minding its children and mopping its floors. The Philippines was a place that people fled; so why would anyone want to go there?

Some of this was incontestable, and yet I remained curious. Palawan looked like what it had obviously once been, a land bridge, and I could just imagine the fauna and flora that had tumbled across it. With three weeks free I had it in my head to disappear and go paddling my folding kayak somewhere I had never been.

It did not concern me much that in Hawaii toothy comedians made whole careers out of mimicking the Filipino accent and the funny names and the dog-stew business. Oddly enough, almost the first person I met in Manila was a man named Booby. "An Australian said to me that my name means 'poolish,' but my farents give me this name!"

Booby had a dog recipe. Everyone had one. Just for the record, Dog Stew: "Don't get a dalmatian! Too expensive! Find an *aso kalye*—street dog—chop him up and morrinate in 7-Up. If you can't find 7-Up use Sprite. It takes the smell off. Then drain. Morrinate again in soy sauce and calamansi lemon for one hour. Drain again. Fry the drained *aso* in garlic, onion, and potato. Add tomato sauce and pineapple chunks. Stew for one hour or more. Oh, and before removing it add cheese and wait until it is melted. Serve with rum or strong alcohol, and a pockage of crockers."

But the stereotypes seemed to slip away after Manila and—to skip ahead a bit—I had a wonderful time. I camped on empty islands and went up rivers and saw snakes in trees and had my tent butted by monitor lizards, and in seaside villages everyone complimented me on my tattoos, and I had several proposals of marriage. I teamed up with a man named Acong—Acong was his *palayaw*, or nickname, as Booby was Eduardo's. Filipino friendliness is often expressed in this way; a nickname makes you approachable.

Acong told me, "I am a native. I am a Tagbanua. When I was a small child there were only natives here." He said, "There were so many fish in the lagoons that we killed them by standing and shooting arrows." And: "The rivers were deep when I was a boy, but they started to cut trees and the mud came. And now it is shallow." And: "Most of these people you see in Palawan are not natives. They come from Visaya and Luzon."

He ate dogs, he ate monkeys and monitor lizards, he ate snakes. He loved wild pigs because they tasted so much better than village pigs. He was 40 and looked 60. He knew why. "My face is old because my life is hard." Also his wife had run off three years before and left him to look after his four-year-old. He did not call her a perfidious bitch. He just shrugged and said, "I don't know where she is." He lived in a coastal village. He lamented the changes on Palawan: the loggers, the illegal fishers, the loss of trees and fish. "When I was a small boy . . ." he would begin. It was only 30-odd years ago but Palawan was an Eden then, so he said.

I was camped on a little island in the middle of Pagdanan Bay on Palawan's west coast, six or seven miles out of Port Barton, and Acong and I met almost every day for a week. We paddled along the coast and up the hot, airless rivers, he in his *bangká* with the double outrigger and I in my kayak. We looked for beehives and monitor lizards and monkeys and snakes—of which there were many, coiled in tree branches. Every now and then Acong would call out, "So, what do you think of my place?"

He meant this coast of Palawan, the whole of it.

I said truthfully that it was one of the best places I had ever been.

But all of that was ahead of me when I landed in Manila, the pleasure of island hopping and camping and congratulating myself that I had come.

The shape of Palawan had fascinated the Spanish, too: so long and slender they called it Paragua, because it was shaped like a rolled umbrella. The etymologies of the word *Palawan,* also the name of one of the indigenous peoples, are various. It means "heroic warrior" in Malay, suggesting a lost mythology. A mountain spine runs down the middle. "Few paved roads," my guidebook said. That was promising. "Thinly populated." Even better. "Thousands of uninhabited offshore islands." That was what did it for me. I set off with some hot-weather clothes, camping equipment, snorkeling gear, and my Klepper single.

I happened to be in Hawaii, an 11-hour flight to Manila. I stopped for the night in the Philippine capital—snake pit—and flew the next day to Puerto Princesa, the capital of Palawan. Strung along one long street of pawnshops and grocery stores and offices, the town was dusty and full of election posters. But no matter: The gunplay (29 voters dead so far) was primarily on Mindanao, across the Sulu Sea. On Palawan, as far as I could see, an election meant flapping posters and free T-shirts with slogans.

The prettily named Puerto Princesa was surprisingly tidy. Instead of cars there were motorized tricycles, part motorbike, part ricksha, 20 U.S. cents a ride. The market was vast and dark and full of dried cuttlefish and wild honey and the cashews that with rice and bananas are one of the island's cash crops. I had arrived on a Friday—men were praying at the mosque and a mixed crowd at the cathedral sat listening to a priest holding a bilingual service, reading from John, the miracle of the loaves and fishes. The large, youthful congregation looked hungrily hopeful. Walking on I saw a small neglected marker: "A grim reminder of the realities of war." It went on to say that in December 1944, just in front of the cathedral, soldiers of the Japanese Imperial Army forced 154 American prisoners of war into a tunnel, poured gasoline on them, and set them alight; 143 died, 11 escaped. The survivors' names and hometowns were listed on the plaque.

That massacre and much else in Palawan—its dusty simplicity, its empty mountains, its inaccessible villages, and its indigenous creation myths about the Weaver of the World—made it seem a ghostly place. I had not been there long before I began thinking that there was nowhere else I would rather be and that its air of being haunted only added to my pleasure.

The hauntedness was not merely an aspect of its ambiguous past, its being on the old Spanish and Chinese trade route, the refuge of pirates and scene of wartime cruelty. Off the map and rich in resources, Palawan was the site of a great deal of ecological plunder as well. It was famous for its splendid hardwood forests of mahogany, ipil, narra, and amagong, prized for furniture. The waters were full of fish, and many pods of dugongs—sea cows.

In the 1930s, British loggers began clear-cutting the west coast and giving English names to bays and harbors and islands. Facing west from Port Barton, almost every island and headland you see has an English name, the loggers' nicknames incorporated onto the American charts. After the Spanish-American War, American administrators and missionaries settled on Palawan. One of their enduring legacies is the large rural prison at Iwahig, about 15 miles west of Puerto Princesa. Several buildings, put up in the 1920s, still stand, including an elegant recreation hall. I rode up on a motorcycle and spent a day there marveling at what enlightened prison management can achieve. Prisoners mix with visitors, and I was shown around by Luis, who was serving seven years on a drug-smuggling charge. "A whole jeepney full!" He introduced me to his fellow inmates, all heavily tattooed.

"'To Trust a Woman Is Death,'" I read aloud from one man's arm. "You think that's true, Amado?"

"In my life, yes, Joe."

The word *Sputnik* was tattooed on Amado's belly. Sputnik was a prison protection mob Amado himself had started 29 years ago, when he was imprisoned for murder.

Iwahig, with its 1,500 incarcerated "colonists," is completely self-sufficient in food. Some revenue is earned by inmates making souvenirs—carvings, walking sticks, furniture—that are sold in Puerto Princesa. Many prisoners are lifers or long-termers—multiple murderers, armed robbers, drug dealers—and some of these, 30 at least, live with their families, their children playing on the parade ground while their inmate fathers work in the fields. The inmates have not lost their sense of humor. When I passed one work gang on my motorcycle, they called out, "Daddy! Daddy!"—joking that I was their American GI father—and laughed.

After the war swept through Palawan, and the Japanese, and the chaos, more loggers came, most of them illegal, denuding the mountains and driving the indigenous people deeper into the forest. Drought and misery and overfishing in the rest of the Philippines meant an influx of migrants. I saw these people along the coast and at the edges of many islands. "Officially these villages do not exist," a Dutch geographer told me. "They are not on any census." They were people from the populous and desperate parts of the Philippines, where marine stocks had been depleted, Luzon, Negros, Mindanao. Fishing people, they created instant villages where the waters teemed with fish.

"They say, 'When the fish are gone we will leave and go where the fish are,'" said Yasmin Arquiza, editor of the environmental magazine *Bandillo ng Palawan*. "They always assume there will be another place to go." When times are tough, some hard-pressed village families pass the hat and stump up an airfare, and one of the young, strong, unmarried girls is chosen to go abroad—to Hong Kong, Japan, Singapore, wherever there is work—and send much of her salary back home. But mostly when times get tough, the migrants follow the fish.

It seemed in fact that everyone with status or power or money on Palawan came from somewhere else. Yasmin was from Mindanao. And Puerto Princesa's mayor, Ed Hagedorn, who was just about to be reelected for his third three-year term, was born on Luzon. The two had little else in common. For her investigative journalism, Yasmin had been the object of the mayor's scorn, which he had bestowed on her in an open letter to the local newspaper. A self-confessed crook known to have boasted of his shady past, Hagedorn was out campaigning when I arrived. I sought him out immediately.

"Do you know Fernando Poe?" he asked.

"In West Africa?" I said, thinking he meant the island Fernando Po. "Never been there."

"Fernando Poe the actor," the mayor said. "He starred in my life story."

Hagedorn, the movie, dramatized the colorful life of this reformed gun-toting gambling lord. The Bruce Willis of Filipino cinema, Poe bore very little resemblance to Hagedorn, a small, solid man with a chattering laugh, whose head seemed much too large for his body. He talked fast in the growly voice of a chain-smoker.

"I was a bad boy." He laughed. "I was a mother's worst fear. I grew up with guns. I hadn't even reformed when I got married!"

He admitted to gunplay and gambling and confrontations with the military. ("Because they crossed my path. Some died. I never ran away from trouble—but I changed!") He said he had never been involved in illegal logging, or illegal fishing, or the slaughter of sea cows, but he knew a great deal about these activities. Anyway, he had had a conversion (the high point of the biopic), and the story was that he used his criminally acquired fortune as the controller of an island-wide lotto game called Juedeng to finance his mayoral campaign. The classic example of a poacher turned gamekeeper, Hadegorn was as voluble describing his love of guns as he was about his new career as a green.

"When I took over as mayor there was no law or order," he told me. "Palawan was a microcosm of the Philippines—economic grief and environmental grief. Illegal logging, gambling, fishing, squatting." Sea cows were being killed for their oil and their meat, forests were being chainsawed into oblivion, fish were vanishing from the coastal waters, and migrant villages were mushrooming.

In his telling, it was Mayor Hagedorn who single-handedly turned this situation around. With his violent past, he said, "I was not afraid to tackle it. Take the illegal fishermen. We had 2,000 apprehensions in the first year alone." Others tell a different story and say that Hagedorn is reaping the credit for many people's efforts, including the charismatic Governor Socrates (who would also be reelected); but the fact is that a place that was going to eco-hell had begun to improve.

For a chance to paddle my boat and go camping while I was in Puerto Princesa, I took a ricksha piled high with my equipment about ten miles north to the Honda Bay boat dock at Santa Lourdes Pier. There I found a boatman, who took me to Pandan Island, where there is a tiny village. I stayed for a few days in my tent, set up my boat, and snorkeled and kayaked my way around the bay islands. Every reef I saw showed signs of serious wreckage—massive collapsed coral walls, the litter of broken antlers and blasted-open brain coral. A broken reef has the look of a boneyard, some chunks leveled by dynamite, others killed with poison.

You hear the words *illegal fishing* and you think of nets with small interstices, the snatching of protected species, the encroachment on pre-

serves. You don't think of cyanide or dynamite or shiploads of abused
boys living in semislavery, hundreds of them, spending every waking hour
in the water smashing the reefs with scrap metal attached to rubber tubes
and heavy poles to drive fish into nets. But that's what occurs here.

Then there is the poison. Diners-out in Hong Kong enjoy choosing
their main course by pointing out a fat fish gliding through a restaurant aquarium. Until the 1993 five-year ban on the export of live fish,
many of these creatures came from Palawan. Fishermen squirt a cyanide
mixture on the coral reef, and when the dazed fish float to the surface
they are scooped up and shipped out gasping in barrels. The reef dies.
If no cyanide is handy, there's also the fish-stunning cocktail of air-
freshener and so-called urinal candy. But we won't go into that.

Mayor Hagedorn had set up a "Baywatch" program for monitoring
illegal fishing—one of the sentry posts was nearby on Honda Bay's Snake
Island—but with so many miles of unpoliced coast, it was impossible
to eliminate the use of dynamite or scrap metal or poison entirely.

And then there's the threat from tourism. "Palawan is underdevel-
oped," Yasmin Arquiza told me. "Ironically, that's why it's so nice." She
feared that Palawan would, as she put it, "become a playground for the
rich." Part of it already has: Pamalican Island, one of the northern out-
liers, already boasts the Amanpulo Resort—one of these trophy hotels
that is half obscenity, half joke. The $475 a night is more than most Fil-
ipinos earn in three months. Another oversize and unpromising resort
is going up on the island of Arrecife in Honda Bay, and I went there
in an outrigger pump-boat, bluffed my way through security as "Dr.
Theroux," and made notes on the ridiculous overdevelopment.

So tourism may not be the answer to Palawan's problems, but it
does have an upside: It was partly to attract tourism that Palawan's
politicians went green. It is almost unimaginable that a country with
old-growth forests and a small manufacturing base and limited
resources would agree to stop logging for the sake of the environment;
and it is something that far more prosperous—and forested—countries
(the United States, Canada, Brazil, the Congo) would never consider.
But that is what the Philippines did when it passed a Palawan logging
ban in 1992—a ban that earned the country several well-deserved
awards from the UN, which the mayor fondly listed for me.

Three major timber concessions were given less than a year to wrap up their business. The largest was not far from Acong's village, at the town of San Vicente, north of Port Barton. While the silted-up estuaries remain, the area's essential habitat has been preserved, and it is possible to see monkeys and pigs and bearcats and the Palawan peacock-pheasant and many other birds—the red-headed tree babbler, the white-throated bulbul, the shama, the flycatchers—among the tall trees.

That was where I was headed, up to Port Barton and Pagdanan Bay for ten days of kayaking. My route from Puerto Princesa had taken me through mountain passes across the island's spine to the little harbor of Sabang, where boats take off for Port Barton and almost anywhere on the western coast, the boatmen trading Palawan's execrable roads for smooth runs between harbors. I preferred the west coast over the reputedly pirate-ridden southern province, but the exquisite cluster of islands outside the northern port of El Nido are equally empty and perfect for paddling.

From Sabang, it was a short trip by outrigger up the coast to Port Barton, where I stocked up on provisions in the small settlement's several grocery stores and hopped in my boat. Pagdanan Bay is large enough to contain 20 islands and islets, among them the huge Boayan in the northwest, with a number of empty beaches to camp on. Many of the islands are deserted, some privately owned ("No Trespassing"), others settled by migrants.

One of the advantages of camping in the hot season on Palawan—it was late April and had not rained since December—was that out on the bay mosquitoes were almost nonexistent. But the heat was terrific—in the high nineties most days, in the high eighties at night. I estimated that I would need four or more liters of water on paddling days, and as no fresh water was available on the empty islands, I went ashore or back to Port Barton every few days to fill up.

Setting out in the yellow-pink of the tropical dawn I paddled through still air thick with gnats, the mirror of the sea a flawless reflection of deep green mainland and high outer islands and rocky islets that had no names. There was hardly any wind until midmorning, and I crossed a sea so smooth in air so silent that the only sound was the chuckle of the bow wave and the rattle of passing kingfishers. The winds were predictable in my first week, freshening through the morning and blowing hard in the afternoon. By midafternoon I was supine in the shade of a palm grove, reading Lytton Strachey's *Eminent Victorians* and studying the chart for tomorrow's destination. There was always another island.

The shock of my second week of paddling was the sight of ink-black clouds, the first of the monsoon, looming in the afternoon. The air and water were deranged: The day went dark, there were cannonades of thunder, and often a spatter of windblown rain and a very stiff wind from an odd and vacillating direction. One day the wind veered from west to east. Another I was caught unprepared and had to surf my kayak through three- and four-foot waves to the nearest island. When I didn't see any fishermen, I took it as a sign to stay ashore.

Most days, though, the sun was the strongest I have ever known over a sea, invariably burning down from a clear sky, dazzling on the water and shriveling the leaves on land. The sun was like a weight on my head and shoulders, and I calculated my island crossings in liters per mile. The reward for thrashing through the water on these hot clear days was the sight of a green sea turtle craning its neck or the flight of a dozen flying fish strafing my bow. Now and then I noticed the swift shadow of a ray flashing just below the surface of the water, startling the fish.

Paddling one day about ten miles southwest to a headland, I caught sight of an island that had been hidden from my campsite—a new hump of rock where I saw a sandy beach and some huts. A Germanic-looking man in a green bathing suit stood on the beach to welcome me. "Hi," he said and grabbed my bowline and helped pull my boat to shore.

"Nice kayak," he said. It was salt-smeared and wet from the long haul from the headland. "Isn't that the kind of boat Paul Theroux paddled in his travels around the Pacific?"

Being cautious, I said, "You read that book?"

"Oh, yeah. Great book."

This happens now and then—more often in a remote place like Palawan than in places closer to home.

"I wrote it."

"Cut the shit."

Pretty soon we were sitting under a palm tree, swapping travelers' tales. He was Charlie Kregle and had left a good job in Chicago three years before to ramble around the world. Such was the state of the stock market that even when he was traveling third-class on an Indonesian ferry or an overcrowded jeepney on Mindanao, he had been earning steadily.

Like the stories of many independent travelers I had met, his were vastly more colorful and complex than most I had read: He had traveled in Brazil and Southeast Asia. He had crossed Africa, walking much of the way. His life had been on the line many times, and he had experienced the worst of travel, which is not danger but weeks of excruciatingly inconvenient delay. I liked his judgments on places, epitomized by his summary of Equatorial Guinea: "Great place. Anarchic, though. Not ready for prime time." He traveled on a shoestring, and from time to time, when he was in a place that sold newspapers, he checked the stock quotes and saw that he was worth much more than the last time he had looked.

He laughed when I told him I knew nothing about the stock market and had no investments.

"What about your 401(k)?"

"Nothing."

"Why?" he said. "Are you planning to die soon?"

Coming from a young man in a bathing suit living in a hut on a small island off Palawan, a man whose entire earthly goods fit into a modest-size rucksack, this investment sarcasm seemed odd. A little while later, still interrogating him, I asked him to tell me the most amazing thing that had happened to him in the Philippines and he looked at me and my boat and said, "This!"

It was the next day that I met Acong. I paddled back from Kregle's Island around midafternoon the day before, but an offshore wind had sprung up and it took me almost four hours to get back to my tent. In the morning I was surprised to see a woman holding a yellow umbrella seated in a canoe paddled by three men. The canoe glided onto what I thought of as my beach, and the woman got out, her umbrella upright and stately as she proceeded down the beach. That was how I discovered that I shared this island with a small hidden village.

Looking for a new island, I ran across Acong. He was fishing on the reef, and with his shirt wrapped and folded neatly around his head against the heat, he looked like an Egyptian sitting cross-legged in his canoe. He had learned English at school but had dropped out "in elementary." He used his boat for fishing and for transporting the rattan and coconuts he collected to use as currency. It was too small for taking people out to the islands.

"Those people are from the Visayas," he said of the village on my island. He said it with a trace of bitterness, because it was nonregulated immigration. Many Palaweños told me that squatting was the cause of many land disputes. Yasmin Arquiza had said, "Tribal people here had no homestead patents." Instead of awarding land titles to protect them, the government merely gave them priority when it handed out concessions for rattan and almaciga, or copal, a resin used in varnish. The indigenous people had rights to the concession and could earn from it.

I told Acong that I was looking for a new campsite on an empty island, and he pointed me to the perfect spot—a hidden cove, a sandy beach, a coral reef that had not been dynamited or poisoned. In the coming days, I followed Acong's narrow outrigger through shallow water and up silted-up rivers and around the jutting coral heads of the remote parts of the great bay.

We traveled up the Togdunan, a narrow tributary of the Darapiton, the largest river emptying into the bay. The rivers were muddy, narrow, humid, buggy, and the deeper we went the more shadowy they became, overhung with a tunnel of boughs. In itself the inconvenience of such branches is minor, but coiled on many of these branches were snakes, thick yellow-and-black five-footers Acong called *binturan*. Strung across other branches were spiderwebs with hairy, deep-green, claw-shaped spiders clinging at the level of my face.

"The snakes will not trouble you if you do not trouble them," Acong said.

After a few miles on the tributary we came to an obstruction—a tree lying across the river. Acong was surprised and cautioned: It was not the custom for the people here to block the rivers. It was well known that the Tagbanua and Pala'wan and Batak peoples had no traditional concept of land ownership. Like many indigenous people they did not buy or sell land, because they could not separate themselves from the land: It would be perverse to sell it, something like an amputation. This barrier was a grotesque novelty, obviously brought about by all the encroachment and the new settlers.

"We could slide our boats over the log," I said. But I was just needling him, to see what he would say.

"No. We stop here."

Even though these people were of his own language group, he felt it was a bad idea to go farther. We might be misunderstood.

On the way back Acong told me about the loggers, and how ships from Japan had been moored for years just offshore to pick up the big apitung logs, and how the logging coincided with the mud and the rivers and river-mouths were not deep anymore.

He told me about the word *banua*, which interested me with its similarities to the Fiji word *vanua*, "land" (as in Vanua Levu, the name of Fiji's second-largest island). *Banua* meant "land," Acong said; *Tagbanua*, "people of the land." I had made it a habit to compile word lists whenever I was in a remote Pacific place, to assess the linguistic relationships among islanders who dispersed the Austronesian language over thousands of nautical miles and thousands of years. I asked Acong the words for various numbers and for big, small, dog, fish, canoe, house, moon, water, and so forth; and I discovered that many Tagbanua words were cognate with ones from Sulawesi, and others straight from Malay—*ikan,* for "fish," *lima* for "five," and *mata* for "eye" (as in Mata Hari, "Eye of the Day").

Some days, when it was much too hot to go paddling, there was little else to do except sit under a palm tree and interrogate Acong and his extended family. These people were settled, but some Tagbanua in the north were nomadic.

The other indigenous people of Palawan lived in the interior—the Batak on the slopes of the central mountain chain, the Palawan people farther south. One guidebook reports, "The Tau't Batu in the south of Palawan were only discovered in 1978." This story of the Stone People (and *batu* for "stone" is another Malay cognate) is not quite true. It is fact that these people keep to themselves and live in caves and in a bowl-shaped valley on the slopes of Palawan's highest peak, 6,839-foot Mount Mantalingajan. But this recent first contact was one of several hoaxes attributed to a minister in the Marcos regime, one "Manda" Elizalde, who, the story goes, tried to gain international prominence by pretending to discover hidden ("Stone Age") peoples in the Philippine hinterland. The Tasaday People near Lake Sebu in south Mindanao were another of his "discoveries." This can be put down to a Filipino variation of Munchausen syndrome, attention-seeking by the retailing of tall stories.

But it is indisputable that many indigenous people on Palawan still subsist by traditional means—hunting wild pigs with spears and blowguns, feasting on flying squirrels, and snaring fish in lovely woven traps. And they lament the day that Palawan's resources began to be stripped away by non-Palaweños, its fish to Japanese factory ships and canneries and Hong Kong restaurant aquariums, its trees to chairs and chopsticks.

Palawan had been on the brink of devastation. Its fall had been arrested. Much of the island was still wild, and I prayed that it would remain so. In the course of ten days' paddling I made a circuit of a dozen Pagdanan islands and camped on three of them, island-hopping northwest to the largest one, Boayan. It was on my return, one very hot night, on the uninhabited Double Island that I found myself lying in my mosquito-net tent, the moon bathing the island and the treetops I could see in a lunar fluorescence. There was no wind. I had achieved the ultimate in fresh-air fiendishness. I was flat on my back. I thought, I am a monkey, and—lying there fulfilled, content, stark naked, alone— I was happy.

But I also thought, It is in the remote and vulnerable places like Palawan that you understand the effect of the wealthier world's cynical hunt for lumber and fish. It is reassuring to know that Palawan has begun to understand how rich it is.

September 1998

The Last Days of
the Mountain
Kingdom

PATRICK SYMMES

t is in the nature of communist revolutions, many scholars have noted, to screw up a good cappuccino.

Lying on the hotel bed my second morning in Kathmandu, I find that the medicinal properties of caffeine have assumed heroic proportions in my jet-lagged brain. There was airport Nescafé in New York and London, anemic hotel java in New Delhi, and watery airborne muck everywhere in between. Now, all I really want from life is some strong coffee.

While I wait for room service to deliver the cure, I try the phone number one more time. I've dialed it for a day with no results. The telephone system in Kathmandu is inexplicable. I can't tell if I'm getting no connection, or no one is answering, or I'm dialing the wrong number.

If someone ever does answer, that person is supposed to know where the guerrillas are. The insurgents, elusive revolutionaries from the hills, call themselves Maoists. Nobody paid attention when this hard-line faction of communists declared a "people's war" back in 1996. The guerrillas were almost without weapons, and did little more than organize propaganda rallies for poor farmers in Rolpa district and other remote western zones of Nepal. But they've earned a reputation for severity—banning alcohol, cutting off the hands of hashish dealers, and forcing village gamblers to eat their decks of cards. And last September the revolution entered a new, militant phase. A thousand guerrillas appeared from nowhere to blast their way into Dunai, the remote western town that served as the gateway for Peter Matthiessen's trek into Inner Dolpo in *The Snow Leopard*. The pace of attacks has picked up since then: This April the Maoists stormed two police outposts—known here as POPs—in the western towns of Rukumkot and Dailekh. The posts were overrun at night by hundreds of guerrillas hurling homemade hand grenades in human-wave attacks. Seventy police officers were killed, some of them executed after they had surrendered. On July 7, another 39 were killed in three simultaneous attacks in Lamjung, Gulmi, and Nuwakot districts, west of Kathmandu. Smaller skirmishes are now a weekly event, as the Maoists drive the government out of whole swaths of the countryside, stripping the dead and the prisoners of rifles, ammunition, and shoes. With up to 5,000 full-time fighters, and as many supporters in part-time militias, the biggest problem the Maoists face is having more recruits than equipment.

Most Western tourists and trekkers, including the 40,000 Americans who visit Nepal each year, have dodged the sharp edge of this unsheathed war. But that grows harder every day. In February, a Chinese development worker, the first foreigner, was injured when Maoists raided a dam project to steal dynamite. Still, in Kathmandu, there is denial.

I punch the digits on my phone, and this time someone answers. "Sorry, sir," the voice replies in trembling, terrible English. "No Maoists." He doesn't know what I'm talking about, he's never heard of the Maoists, there's nobody here by the name I'm asking for. I leave a message and hang up. A couple of minutes later, there's a knock on the door. It's room service with the cappuccino, which smells of everything good. I take one sip, and the phone rings.

It was then, with the heavy cup still in my hand, that words began to drift toward other meanings, that reality began to melt into new and unstable forms. Like Alice, I'd swallowed a potion that would take me into a Wonderland, a kingdom of retrocommunism unlocked by secret handshakes and punctuated by thousands of clenched fists. Time would now flow backward, the 21st century giving way to Year Zero,

Boeings yielding to bows and arrows, video night in Kathmandu becoming firelight in mud huts. The forecast for the glorious future would look a lot like 1950.

It is the same voice on the phone, but different. His English and his attitude have suddenly improved. "You want to meet the Maoists?" he asks. Voices argue in the background, and then he announces that it is time for a journey. He can't say what kind of a journey it is, whether it will be to the east or the west, into the Himalayas or down to the subtropical plains. He can't say how long we will be gone. He won't even tell me who he is.

I write down an address. "You must be there in 15 minutes," he says.

This is impossible, but we try. I run downstairs, rip photographer Seamus Murphy from the lunch table, throw money at the front desk, and we walk out with only the clothes we are wearing, spare socks, and the contents of our knapsacks.

The taxi creeps through the crushing traffic of Kathmandu, swerving around bicycle rickshas and sacred cows sleeping in the stream of Toyotas. We go past the Royal Palace, a Himalayan Elsinore surrounded by spear-point fencing that serves not to keep danger out, but to trap it inside. (The massacre of the royal family is less than two weeks away.) Our driver turns down Durbarmarg; we cross a bridge, enter a neighborhood that foreigners never visit, and are dropped on a busy sidewalk, 20 minutes late. I watch the passing stream of humanity, sari-clad shoppers and topee-topped deliverymen, students in jeans and dusty construction workers in sandals. They are remnants of a Nepal that is already fading away.

A young man in a tan shalwar kameez—a Pakistani-style long shirt over pants—steps out of the traffic. His eyes are burning in his brown face, and his smile is a trick. "Hello, sir," he says. "Come with me." Without waiting, he folds back into the flow of people, walking fast. The rabbit hole opens up, and we, soon to be followed by the entire nation, fall in.

They definitely need some new astrologers at the royal court in Kathmandu. It was the seers of the spheres, casting their ancient divina-

tions and decoding the celestial motions, who laid the trap. They ca
culated that the heavens were not in alignment for a royal wedding.
The crown prince had picked the wrong bride. The auspicious date
and the harmonious mate were still years in the future. The queen listened to them too closely—or, some say, they listened to her too
closely—and rejected her son's plan to marry his girlfriend.

Intrigue is the Nepalese national pastime, factionalism the country's
historic curse. Crown Prince Dipendra's bride-to-be, Devyani, and
Queen Aiswarya were both members of the most powerful political
clan in Nepal, the Ranas, who ruled the country from 1846 to 1951
in an inherited dictatorship that allowed the royal Shah Dev family to
retain the crown. But the Ranas long ago split into rival branches, and
Aiswarya could not stomach her son's choosing from the wrong side
of the family tree.

On June 1, 29-year-old Dipendra—popular heir to the throne of the
world's only Hindu kingdom, inheritor of the Lost Horizon—did something that was, the astrologers admitted later, not foreseen in his charts.
He reportedly drank some scotch, smoked some hashish, and then committed regicide, patricide, matricide, fratricide, sororicide, and finally
suicide. Shortly after being ejected from a family dinner for drunkenness, Dipendra returned with a submachine gun, an assault rifle, a shotgun, and a pistol, and killed everyone he could, beginning with his
father, continuing through most of the royal household, and ending
with himself. When it was over, ten people were dead.

Like Hamlet, the crown prince seems to have been driven to violence by the inbred madness of a rotten kingdom. Like Ophelia, the
star-crossed young royal killed himself at a pond in the palace garden.
But you don't have to look to Shakespeare for analogies: Nepal's own
history is littered with examples of blood on the crown, including a
spectacular 1846 massacre, instigated by the queen, that cut down
more than 30 members of the elite.

Still, the murdered king had seemed the very model of a modern
minor monarch. Birendra Bir Bikram Shah Dev, a descendent of the
original Gurkha prince who conquered and united Nepal in the 1760s,
had been educated at Eton and Harvard, and became absolute monarch
at age 26 upon the death of his father, King Mahendra, in 1972. Unlike

his father, who had dissolved Nepal's first constitutional government in 1960, imprisoned most of the dominant Nepali Congress Party leadership, and banned all political activity, Birendra was a relatively liberal ruler, the glue that held together this country of 23 million people—a patchwork of 60 languages and a score of ethnic groups—as it opened to the outside world.

The political system, however, remained tightly restricted until 1990, when street demonstrations forced Birendra's royal hand. He cemented his popularity by assenting to democracy—albeit a system where weak prime ministers are squeezed between an unaccountable monarchy and a parliament of cynical, corrupt coalitions. Democracy has now given birth to 92 registered parties, among them 15 "legitimate" communist parties that have often overlapped in coalitions, and even names. The Kathmandu phone book currently lists the Nepal Communist Party (United Marxist-Leninist)—the main opposition in parliament—as well as the Communist Party of Nepal (Marxist-Leninist), the Nepal Communist Party (Democratic), the Nepal Communist Party (Masal), and its rival-by-one-letter the Nepal Communist Party (Mashal). All of them despise the Communist Party of Nepal (Maoist) for abandoning the electoral process in 1995 to go underground.

Despite the patina of modernity in Kathmandu, the country still suffers the aftereffects of isolation. High-caste Hindu Brahmans and Chetris of Indian descent, called Aryans, control the government, the economy, and much of the best farmland, while low-caste farmers and untouchables are marginalized. Almost half the country's people, including the Sherpas, are "tribals," mountaineers of Tibeto-Burmese descent, usually Buddhist or animist in their beliefs. There are long memories here, and hill people resent that Hindus arrived centuries ago as refugees, only to impose their culture, alphabet, rulers, and religion.

"It is a country made of groups that have long histories of suspicion toward each other," says Joe Elder, director of the Center for South Asia at the University of Wisconsin, Madison. "The farther you go out from the Kathmandu Valley, the more people insist that they are Gurung, or Tamang, or Magar, not Nepalese."

Modern geopolitics plays out along parallel lines. Never conquered by the British, Nepal swelters in the economic and political shadow of India, the regional superpower. Since the enemy of my enemy is my friend, Nepal has reluctantly turned to China. The realpolitik issue for China is Tibet. As long as Nepal clamps down on its tens of thousands of restive Tibetan exiles, Beijing supports Kathmandu, not the Maoists.

Squeezed between giants and pricked by overpopulation, deforestation, and corruption, many resentful Nepalis are vulnerable to conspiracy theories. ("In my experience, there's at least one conspiracy theory for every person in Nepal," Elder notes.) Ideologues who promise a war on "class enemies" and the satisfaction of ancient grievances find willing listeners. The Maoists' elusive leader, Comrade Prachanda (Nepali for "fierce"), constantly denounces the country's Hindu Brahman leaders, despite being a Hindu Brahman leader himself, and has whipped up nationalist paranoia with predictions of an imminent Indian invasion. Most of the time, however, Prachanda leaves the talking to the guerrillas' media-savvy second-in-command, Baburam Bhattarai, an Indian-educated architect fond of gassy vows to "hoist the hammer-and-sickle red flag atop Mount Everest."

The explosion of all these tensions came not with the royal massacre, which left the nation in stunned silence, but three days later, when—as in *Hamlet*—the dead king's brother, 55-year-old Gyanendra, assumed the throne in a ceremony whose very haste prompted suspicion. Many Nepalis did not believe—*would* not believe—the official verdict that the massacre was the act of a single, drug-addled prince. It was a double cross by factions of the Rana family; it was a coup plot by India and the CIA; it was Gyanendra, who, conveniently absent, used his despised son Paras to orchestrate the killings. Comrade Prachanda, rumored to be hiding in India or London, issued a statement calling the carnage and its aftermath "a serious political conspiracy." On June 4, thousands of demonstrators, fronted by communist students, took to the streets. Fourteen curfew violators were shot and wounded by police. Two editors and the publisher of *Kantipur*, a Kathmandu daily, were arrested after publishing an anti-royal article by Baburam Bhattarai. The Maoists launched a string of symbolic bomb attacks, dynamiting the house of the unpopular prime minister, Girija Prasad Koirala, and the chief justice of the supreme court, who led the dubious investigation into the massacre.

When King Birendra, his skin painted pink with tikka paste, was cremated on a funeral pyre, the old Nepal went up in flames with him.

The Maoists are perhaps the only beneficiaries of this national nervous breakdown, with thousands of men and women scattered in the hills, lodged in remote base camps in Rolpa and Jumla districts, settled in small villages down on Nepal's flat southern *terai,* or living over the next ridge somewhere near the Tibetan border. At a time when the entire nation is disarmed by events, the Maoists are bristling with weapons; as the government founders in discord, the guerrillas are laying out five-year plans; while Nepal's archaic social order crumbles under corruption, the insurgents spread hyperrational fantasies of a cultural revolution that will wipe the slate of history clean. The rebels already operate in a third of the country; they will only expand, thanks to the bloody discrediting of the ancien régime.

Despite the evasiveness of our Kathmandu contacts, we gather that there is going to be a big rally somewhere in the foothills. Although the guerrillas don't carry around copies of Mao's Little Red Book, they have adopted the Great Helmsman's essential strategy: using the countryside to encircle the cities. They have chased away the national police and established broad *aadhar ilaka,* or base areas. They have set up "people's courts" and village councils in a few places, but now they are going to declare a new shadow government at the multidistrict level, their biggest step so far. Our role, apparently, is to attend the rally and spread their propaganda.

We're not surprised, therefore, to find ourselves driving westward on the Prithvi Highway that first day. If the Maoists have a homeland, it is a cluster of five districts—Rukum, Rolpa, Salyan, Jajarkot, and Kalikot—in the midwest, a jagged, densely cultivated hill country dominated by the Magar ethnic group, far beyond the tourist orbits of Annapurna and Pokhara. We head out in a taxi—a Korean microbus—crowded with Seamus, our Maoist guide, our driver, and me, plus three Nepali men who turn out to be stringers for Kathmandu dailies. Still unsure of our destination, companions, and prospects, we keep our eyes focused on the countryside, the dry-season rice paddies decorated with tumbledown huts.

We turn south before reaching Gorkha, a region immensely popular with trekkers—and, increasingly, with Maoists. Although the guerrillas have ignored tourists so far, the U.S. Embassy cautions Americans against visiting Gorkha and 16 other districts, from Kalikot in the far west, to Sindhuli, east of Kathmandu; it restricts its own staff from traveling in Jajarkot, Kalikot, Rolpa, Rukum, and Salyan. With Maoists operating in 60 of the country's 75 districts, trekking companies like Geographic Expeditions and Snow Lion Expeditions have canceled or rerouted some excursions.

Not far from Buddha's birthplace of Lumbini, we pass a troop of rhesus monkeys waiting impatiently for the wheels of our taxi to split open the unripe fruit they have deposited on the asphalt. We overtake two long files of teenage soldiers, a 600-man battalion of the Royal Nepalese Army marching westward, clutching automatic rifles. So far the army has stayed in barracks while the demoralized, poorly trained national police have done all the fighting. King Birendra had been reluctant to escalate the conflict, convinced that negotiations were preferable. Within a few weeks of Birendra's death, however, Gyanendra would verify his conservative reputation by proclaiming a draconian National Security Act, permitting the arrest of anyone, anywhere, without any explanation. For now, the soldiers we pass, and the guerrillas we are heading toward, are all blissfully ignorant of the approaching storm.

By dawn the next day we leave behind asphalt and turn up from the flat *terai*. The first thing we see is a cardboard effigy of despised prime minister Koirala dangling from a lamppost: We are in contested country now. We swing up and over the Mahabharata mountains and pick up the Bheri River valley. Our leader, another Kathmandu supporter of the guerrillas, is sweating inside a down vest; he never removes his hat, dark glasses, or the earphones of his cassette player. With rigid discipline he gives no explanations, offers no answers, names no destinations.

The taxi driver, on the other hand, is a verbose fraud. The deeper we get into hostile territory, the more he quivers with fear. He invents a series of imaginary breakdowns, pulling over at any pretext to announce that it is "impossible, sir" to continue. Each time, after crawling under the van for inspections, I shame him into pushing on, but when he begins surreptitiously pumping the gas and brake pedals, ascribing the van's lurching to "clutch broken, sir," I drag him from behind the wheel and start driving myself.

The correspondents are equipped for the mountains in slacks and loafers. They speak Inspector Clouseau English, and pander to us all day with a stream of preposterously false declarations about the terrain, the travel time, and the villages we pass. If you like dust, bumps, bad food, sweaty seatmates, misinformation, near misses with trucks, and Bollywood music, the road trip has its moments.

We rattle down washboard roads and ascend toward the middle hills of the Dhaulagiri Himal. We pass a few POPs, outposts where frightened cops hide behind sandbags, and in the late afternoon we reach a nameless, straggling village where policemen stand on the roofs, scanning the valley. We check into a smoke-filled bunkhouse, and at five the next morning, under an icy half-moon, set off again. After dawn we try to sneak past the capital of Rolpa district, a heavily garrisoned town called Libang. We disembark, somehow manage to convince the authorities that we are just a badly confused trekking expedition, and continue on foot, leaving the road—and electricity, the government, and the taxi driver—behind.

After a couple of hours, we step along a swaying footbridge high over a green, boulder-strewn stream and find a tattered red flag with a hammer and sickle snapping in the breeze. "We are now entering area of topmost Maoist influence," one of the correspondents explains—the *aadhar ilaka,* the home of the revolution.

One more nameless river valley and we trip lightly across a second cable bridge to find an unarmed woman in camouflage sitting at a picnic table, watching the bridge. She pays no attention to us, and we march quietly on, turning left beneath a "Martyrs Arch"—a cement gate dedicated to the 2,000 guerrillas and civilians the Maoists say have been killed in the war so far. Within the hour we are waiting in a farmhouse while messengers are sent. A handful of curious men appear, loitering outside the hut, reluctant to come in. A couple carry astonishing muskets obsolete since the American Civil War. One has a pistol, but most are unarmed. They are wearing flip-flops.

Incredibly, these losers are the guerrillas.

There are three rules of travel in the Maoist heartland. Sitting in the safe house, we are briefed by the leader of the ragtag squadron, a 42-year-old former school principal who speaks fine English. He is an ethnic Gurkha and goes by the nom de guerre of Sanktimon, after the hero of a cartoon on Indian television. Sanktimon means "strong man," but it's not for his muscles. "It is because I am strong in ideology," Sanktimon offers with a wide grin. He explains the route we will follow and then the rules: (1) No taking pictures without permission. (2) No going to the bathroom without a guard. (3) You must give a speech.

Within hours, Seamus will disregard the first rule completely; the second one proves deeply problematic; the third rule is one I immediately reject.

We gloss over these disagreements and seal the deal with an exchange of *lal salaams,* a revolutionary slogan that means "red salute" and is always accompanied by a clenched fist. We quickly march off in single file, crossing more paddies and then heading up through a beech forest onto a switchbacking trail that becomes, eventually, the steepest surface I have ever climbed. Hours later we reach a razor-thin, foggy ridgeline at 5,000 feet. The slopes are stacked with terraces even here, the paddies no wider than a single ox. Nepal's population has tripled since the 1940s, and the relentless search for arable land has increased deforestation and erosion massively while still not producing enough to eat. Exclusively agricultural, western Nepal is nonetheless a net importer of food. Hungry, impoverished peasants are easy recruits to the Maoist cause, with its promise of a government by, for, and of the small farmers.

Sometime after dark, the sky explodes with rain, and we tumble into a puny hamlet where dozens of guerrillas wait in huts. These are real Red Army troops, main force soldiers in neat camouflage uniforms. They carry Lee-Enfield .303 rifles, relics from World War II but state of the art compared to the flintlocks carried by our patrol.

In a dark, smoky room we eat with the soldiers, wolfing down rice and lentils with our fingers. Comrade Strong Man won't answer questions about the movement, its ideology, or his own position within the group—"I am just someone," he says, dismissing my questions. The only foreign correspondent they've seen before, he says, was a dyed-in-the-wool communist from *The Revolutionary Worker,* the weekly newspaper from Chicago, and Strong Man assumes we're here to cheer the revolution on. He is thrilled to host fellow travelers and promises to find two spoons for "the gentlemen comrades" by the next meal. Out here, spoons are still in the future, and metal of any kind is so rare that even plowshares are made of wood. In the soft light of the cooking fire, surrounded by men clutching ancient weapons, we seem to be regressing toward the Bronze Age.

We sleep packed elbow-to-ass amid a dozen snoring guerrillas. At 2 A.M., I am jolted awake by a shower of blows. The guerrilla on my left is twitching in the grip of a nightmare. I lie on the stone floor, staring at the ceiling until 5 A.M., and then we are hiking again.

In meeting the Maoists, we've achieved exactly what most visitors to Nepal have been hoping to avoid. Although few foreigners have heard much about the guerrillas—thanks to a suppressed local news media and a see-no-evil tourism industry—the two groups are already beginning to meet on the remote mountain paths that they share. Some trekking groups have bumped into Red Army patrols, who have pressed them to "donate" binoculars and sleeping bags to the revolution, but in most incidents the guerrillas and hikers have passed without speaking.

The real squeeze is happening back in Kathmandu. In March of last year, many foreign-owned businesses were approached by guerrilla representatives demanding money. Speaking on background, to protect his business, the head of one major American trekking company explained it as "a choice between operating here or holding to your ethical standards." Like several other foreign outfitters, he paid $1,400 to ensure that the Maoists left his clients alone.

Funding the very revolution that threatens you may seem self-defeating, but taking a stand against corruption in Nepal is like pissing up a rope. Extortion was once the privilege of the royal family, but since democracy arrived, in 1990, there are many more hands in the pot. Foreign aid funds evaporate; trekking fees earmarked for irrigation projects and reforestation are siphoned off. Until the practice was exposed in 1995, Queen Aiswarya received three million rupees annually from the oil monopoly and a rake-off from all foreign aid that passed through her powerful Queen's Coordinating Council. The weak do what the powerful teach them: Traffic policemen shake down motorists, and beat cops hit up restaurants for protection money.

By this standard, the Maoists are quite reasonable. They send neatly written, personalized letters to hotels, businessmen, teachers, NGOs, and even government offices requesting the payments. In typical Nepali fashion, they will negotiate the price. The business of extortion has now become so lucrative that the country suffers from a plague of fake Maoists. A group of tourists rafting in the Chitwan nature reserve was robbed last year by "guerrillas," but an American diplomat told me that, of the four to five such encounters reported by tourists so far, only two involved genuine Maoists. In an effort to fight this corruption of their corruption, the Maoists began issuing receipts on official revolutionary letterhead, but they had to abandon this effort when—also in typical Nepali fashion—fake receipts were rushed into circulation.

Pervasive government corruption has become the single greatest source of support for the guerrillas. "Look at Kathmandu," says Barbara Adams, a textile expert living here since the early 1960s. "Most of the palaces were built with corruption money, taken from development funds and foreign aid. It's an aid mafia, literally." Originally from New York, Adams knows the inner workings of the Kathmandu elite better than almost any foreigner, having been the *kanchi swasni*—"unofficial wife"—of a prince in the 1960s. She still has the Sunbeam Alpine sports car given to her by King Mahendra's brother.

Like a surprising number of people in Kathmandu, including intellectuals, members of parliament, and even army officers, Adams is eerily sympathetic to the Maoists in the hills. She believes they are patriots, fighting against a corrupt order. They actually care what happens to the majority of Nepalis, who can't read and have no electricity. She quotes a Nepali friend: "We're all Maoists now; there is no alternative."

But the lack of alternatives is the very problem. King Birendra was quietly sending signals to the Maoists, who praised him and sent condolences on his death. The new government is a cipher, but will likely take a harder line to protect its wealth and position. Even a Sunbeam-driving sympathizer can see that every day that passes without a solution makes things worse. Like the Shining Path, the Khmer Rouge, and Chairman Mao himself, the more the guerrillas fester in mountainous isolation, the more paranoid and intolerant they become. "The longer this goes on," Adams notes, "the harder the Maoists will get. And the next thing you know, we'll have a Taliban."

We summit one of Rolpa's infinite peaks, and suddenly we're looking down on the site of the rally. It is a broad, rounded spur the size of several soccer fields, reaching out over a deep valley. We hike down, pass beneath another Martyrs Arch, and find a half-dozen huts and a long schoolhouse—the hamlet of Babhang. A battery-powered public address system is lashed to poles, and a packed-earth platform with chairs awaits the speakers. After only a few minutes, there is the sound of chanting in the distance.

They come in village by village, spilling down into the rally with unfeigned hoopla. Sixty from one hamlet, 30 from another, 40 from a third, a stream of desperately poor, excited people waving their fists in the air. The men wear bland homespun skirts or worn-out tracksuits; the women dress in saris of royal blue, emerald green, earthen reds, and otherworldly purples. Within minutes, a second column begins to stream over a high peak in the distance. As they spot the rally site, men discharge their blunderbusses in thundering blasts that echo back and forth in the hills. A third column appears, snaking steadily up from the valley floor, hundreds more carrying banners and blasting off their own guns in reply.

The largest guerrilla rally I've read about featured 700 people; within an hour there are a thousand here, and then twice that, delegations from 52 villages across Rolpa. They march in crude military lockstep, barefoot or in blown-out sandals, and arrive chanting call-and-response slogans ("Communist Party of Nepal, LONG LIFE!" and "Marxism-Leninism-Maoism, LONG LIFE!"). Perhaps 200 Red Army soldiers wait, stonefaced. They've got Enfields—like the canvas sneakers on their feet, captured from the national police—and wear counterfeit Lowe Alpine backpacks. Comrade Strong Man appears from time to time to shout, "Here are the masses! The masses are coming!"

Village bands arrive, tooting on horns and banging drums. A group of black-clad boys dances into the rally, bells jangling on their ankles, and girls from the remotest peaks, who walked three days to get here, giggle and cover their faces at the sight. Every few minutes another black-powder gun detonates, launching a huge doughnut of smoke into the sky.

By noon there are 4,000 people, and still they pour in. A village militia arrives from some other century, clutching bows and carrying quivers of neatly fletched arrows, chanting, "No to feudalism!" Next is an entire girls' soccer team armed with blue tracksuits and muskets. Student groups traipse in with neat flags, and associations of untouchables, and women's groups chanting, "Murder and rape must stop!" The Maoists can sound progressive: They vow not only to fight police corruption, but to punish spousal abuse and hunt down rapists, while recruiting women guerrillas and political cadres. Likewise, they challenge the ancient caste system, which is nothing but racism, and the untouchables are among their most eager recruits.

Five thousand, six thousand, eight thousand people. The crowd fills the entire ground, each group parading under the Martyrs Arch with chants, and then marching to an assigned spot where they collapse into densely packed clusters. They open their umbrellas to make shade and light up chillum pipes, little chimneys of tobacco and marijuana casting puffs of smoke over the scene. There's a flurry of excitement when a government helicopter circles (high) overhead, scanning the rally, but they might as well read it in the papers: The Nepali journalists are busy taking notes, and their dispatches will hit the Kathmandu front pages in about four days. ("MAOISTS DECLARE ADMN, VOW TO FIGHT ARMY.")

Strong Man spots me taking my own notes. "You are preparing your speech," he announces. No, I remind him, I won't be giving any remarks. He seems disappointed but counters with the good news that two spoons have been found. A young guerrilla spoon-bearer is assigned to serve us lunch.

In midafternoon, with 10,000 peasants packed onto the spur, the propaganda starts. The main event is the declaration of the shadow government in Rolpa and several adjacent districts, and the new leaders of the revolution's first official government are invited to step forward. There are 19 of them, a cross section of the movement itself—a few tough Magar peasants from Rolpa, much like the attendees at the rally, but also an ambitious student leader from Kathmandu, and several older professional communist politicians. Comrade Strong Man turns out to be Rolpa's new representative of "the intellectuals." Invoking the name of the almighty Prachanda, he delivers a 30-minute speech about the teachings of the leader they follow but never see; after him the new vice-chairman gives a speech, and after him the district's new top man, Chairman Santosh Buddha, gives an amazingly dull, hour-long talk. A typical politician, Buddha is lofty and affected, and seems to have practiced looking thoughtful in a mirror. Despite the sunshine, he preens about in a gray Gore-Tex coat, the only one at the rally. Seamus and I call him Chairman Gore-Tex behind his back.

My speech is a huge hit, although I have no idea what I said. With dusk approaching, Strong Man drags us onto the platform for a ceremonial welcome. Chairman Gore-Tex pins us with red ribbons and smears a thumbful of pink dye between our eyebrows, the traditional tikka blessing. As he lays a garland of lali guras flowers around my neck, he explains that these red blooms grow only at high altitude— "like the revolution." I try to run for it, but it is too late: They push me at the microphone.

The second I open my mouth ("Greetings to the people of Rolpa district") the crowd starts giggling. In a region where even radios are an unknown luxury, most of them have never heard a foreign language, and my brief clichés about peace and justice are buried beneath a rolling wave of laughter. After a *lal salaam* and a pathetic clenched fist, I slink offstage to a ragged cheer. I'll never survive my Senate confirmation hearings now.

I'm replaced by another speaker, and then another, on through dusk, politicians, newly appointed cadres, the women's representative, and then, in the dark night, a string of guerrilla officers, hard men in camouflage speaking hard words about "taking on" the army in a coming war.

By 10 P.M. all 10,000 Maoists—armed men and women, kids and babies—simply lie down where they are, some sleeping, others smoking, everyone wrapped tightly in shawls against the mountain chill. I head for the alfresco bathroom, trailed by the usual guerrilla guard. This time I'm ready. Hidden in my backpack, I've found a handful of chemical light sticks, and I break a green one and give it to him. He's never seen one before and rushes off in delight to show it around, leaving me in peace. The beam of my flashlight illuminates the bushes around me: wild cannabis, the source for Nepal's hashish industry and one explanation for the laughter during my speech.

Back at the hut, my guard sits in a circle of Red Army men, their faces glowing green from the soft chemical light. One of the guerrillas throws an arm around me and says, "Good speech." The valley still echoes with the words of the Red Army's top officer, Comrade Lifwang. "War is a challenge," he says. "Without war, nothing can be changed." So many military terms here are borrowed from English that I can follow along as he describes a battle just days ago, in eastern Nepal. He tells of the first platoon attacking the police. He pantomimes a police helicopter circling overhead, trying to relieve the besieged POP, the machine finally chased away by rifles cracking in the night. The second platoon comes forward, and finally the POP is overrun.

Victory for the revolution. I pass out.

By first light there is not a single person left on the field. I wander over the barren saddle of the mountains, wondering if the 10,000 chanting peasants were a dream, but the proof is on the ground, the dust still imprinted with the shapes of their missing bodies.

The guerrillas' philosophy too is ghostly. So far we've had a propaganda massage without getting to ask any questions ourselves. Finally, at 10 A.M., with cold clouds blowing in, I am summoned to the schoolhouse, where the entire gang is assembled for a press conference. Gore-Tex, Strong Man, some Maoist schoolteachers, and several vice-flunkies are lined up on benches.

I sit on my bench, scuff my feet in the dirt, and finally ask the question I should have asked the crowd yesterday: How many people must die? The guerrillas like to cite the Shining Path as their fellow travelers in the Maoist cause. I point out that 30,000 people have died in Peru, without a Red victory. If that many people die in Nepal, will the revolution still be justified?

Yes, they all nod immediately. The true face of the revolution at last. "To protect a whole thing," a schoolteacher says, "a part can be damaged. It is the rule of nature."

Comrade Strong Man elaborates: "A big part of the people here believe it is not necessary to solve Nepal's problems with violence." He brushes aside this natural reluctance. "We clear their mind of this idea," he says. "The people's war is necessary."

They dismiss offers of peace talks from the government, tricks designed to fool the people, weaken the country, and deliver it to the control of India. Ominously, Gore-Tex vows a "protracted war in rural areas," and "armed . . . urban rebellion," the first hint of a guerrilla war in Kathmandu.

They descend quickly into jargon. They are for dialectical materialism and against reactionary power. Chairman Mao's Cultural Revolution, in which mobs beat "class enemies" through the streets, was good, and will be imitated as soon as they come to power. Colonialism, feudalism, imperialism, capitalism, and revisionism are all bad. Peasants are good and politicians are bad. On this animal farm, four legs are good and two legs are bad.

Their policy about foreign tourists is clear: The more, the better.

"Not any foreign person is to be disturbed," Gore-Tex announces, as Strong Man nods. They actually invite trekkers to visit their areas—with permission—because they believe Westerners will be seduced by Maoism and spread the revolution to Europe and America. It's a Red Tourism offensive. "We will inspire them to flourish the same movement in their country!" Strong Man boasts.

Strong Man presents me with several pages ripped from his notebook. This document begins with an error-riddled manifesto—"the C.P.N. (Moist) is guided the ideology of Marxism-Leninnism-Maosim against the reactionary power of Nepal which is preserved by Indian expansionis and world imperialist"—and continues with an executive

summary of the press conference, which bears no relation to any of
the questions I asked.

Q. *How do you face Royal Army.*
A. *We will face it with the power of the people.*
Q. *How do you forward the production.*
A. *We forward it with the help of people.*
Q. *How do you bring about indigenous society.*
A. *We bring it according to Lenin's ideology.*
Q. *How do you forward Negotiation with the government.*
A. *We are fighting total war.*

As we talk, an early tendril of the monsoon season blows in, a thick,
blasting rain of tropical density and high-altitude chill. We exchange
endless good-byes in the dripping hut, while guards are found to escort
us out of the base area.

During the wait, Strong Man teaches me the secret Red Army handshake (forefingers, pinkies, and thumbs meet in a triangle; then rotate
on the thumbs into a soul shake). A dozen guerrillas crowd around to
give me the shake. Overwhelmed by emotion, I hand out the remaining light sticks.

In a sopping-wet ceremony, Gore-Tex drops more flowers around
our necks and rubs more tikka on our foreheads. He gives all of us,
including the Nepali journalists, sealed airmail envelopes. I naively
assume that these contain a letter, or a certificate, or some propaganda,
and stuff mine into my pocket, ready to get moving. As I walk out the
door, I notice that the Chairman's Gore-Tex coat has soaked through
completely. It's as fake as he is.

The descent is a hallucination. We set off into howling rain, speed-
hiking hour after hour in a downpour. We're still wearing our lunch
clothes from a week before; our raingear consists of garbage bags. We
trudge through mud, ford streams, and cross cliffs on slate paths two
feet wide. At times the guerrilla walking point disappears into fog and
mist. Landscapes open abruptly, and worlds disappear between glances.
There are few people on the trails. A herder driving goats and cows
stands still and looks askance; in one barefoot hamlet, we draw the

entire population in a shy, silent crowd. A patrol of Red Army soldiers hustles past, without even a *lal salaam*. Bells tinkle in the distance, and strange howls float down from the slopes. One long day, and we are out of topmost Maoist country. Climbing now with night coming on, we hit the road and hitch a ride into Libang.

At some point in here I drag the crumbling, soggy envelope from my pants pocket, slide a finger down the seal, and discover that it contains money. Not a letter, not a certificate, not a propaganda flyer, but a bribe. About $5 worth of rupees. Now I'm as dirty as everyone else in Nepal.

Alice wakes up from her dream, and time begins to move forward again, bringing with it small signs of the depressing realities that grip present-day Nepal. In Libang, I meet Chairman Gore-Tex's nemesis, Harikrishna. He's the government's chief district officer for Rolpa, a conceited, high-caste politician who shows up an hour late, awash in flunkies. Although he can't even visit most of his guerrilla-controlled territory, he insists that the Red Army rules by fear alone. "They have no support," he tells me, cleaning his nails with the tip of a key.

We meet a 75-year-old refugee, Ratibhan Oli, one of hundreds of people the Maoists have chased out of their base areas. These are the "revisionists," people who won't, for one reason or another, toe the party line. And at a mud-floored boarding school the same day, 300 students assemble on the parade ground to hear me, at the insistence of their teachers, give another speech. Staring at their upturned faces, beneath guard towers, I am at a loss. Should I tell them to pay no mind to communist dingbats and court astrologers? Should I point out that the Maoist revolution will inevitably turn inward and eat its children, like every revolution everywhere?

I can't think of a damn thing to say.

Another day of brutal road travel and a prop plane back to Kathmandu. In the terminal, I spot a plastic box for donations to the Red Cross and shove the remaining rupees, the Maoist bribe money that we didn't spend on Fantas, through the acrylic slot.

Soon the king will die. Kathmandu, like the countryside, is already seething, as if by premonition. There's another general strike on, one in a series that has paralyzed transport and turned the city into a ghost town. For days we wander avenues so quiet that the holy cows are con-fused by the lack of traffic and moo in despair. Without the pollution of tailpipes, the fresh mountain breeze is a reminder of an old Nepal. But the empty sidewalks and shuttered cybercafés of Thamel also look like another Nepal, some future place where the Maoists have come to power and dispersed the modern world with a harmless cultural revo-lution, emptying the city like the Khmer Rouge with good manners.

There are Nepali journalists who predict just such a Maoist takeover, but that worst-case scenario is unlikely. The army will deploy, the old guard in Kathmandu will rally to defend itself, and India, China, and the United States will stir themselves from indifference. "The Maoists are a real problem," says University of California, Berkeley professor emeritus of political science Leo Rose, a leading Nepal expert. "But it's hard for me to see them overthrowing the present government. What are they offering? They don't have any achievements or accom-plishments. My own guess is they'll be an irritant, a problem, but not an alternative."

It is more likely that the Maoists will be undone by their own quest for ideological purity, by their faith in a violence that, as they them-selves admit, is not supported by the Nepali people. The U.S. Embassy in Kathmandu argues that there may be as few as 2,000 hard-core communists, and that, as an American diplomat there told me, the "masses" backing the Maoists "are really ordinary people more dis-gusted with circumstances than Maoist in ideology." Their support for the guerrillas is "wishful thinking in a desperate situation," as Nepali political scientist Vijaya Sigdel puts it. But the more the Maoists expand, the quicker the people will learn that opposing a corrupt gov-ernment is not the same as supporting a fanatical insurgency. Nepal can still evade the dark garden of Maoist dreams, but the exceptional kingdom is already losing its distance from the world, becoming instead a troubled, unexceptional place.

In the last days of the old Nepal, it is lovely to walk the strike-bound streets or roll about town in rickshas, pausing to watch aim-less bands of students and communists march listlessly through the city, lifting their fists, occasionally tossing a brick. There's something wonderfully feeble about the scene. Perhaps the Maoists' grim ferocity will yet founder in the traditional incompetence of Nepali politics. There is always the hope of farce, rather than tragedy.

I stop around the royal palace a few times, but nobody is allowed to visit. The Gurkha guards in puttees and plumed hats shoo me away, and I have to settle for looking through the fence at the lush grounds, the pine trees, and the ornamental gardens.

In a few days the king will be dead. Long live the king.

September 2001

Wild Things

My Son, the Manatee

W. HODDING CARTER

t was a hot and grimy Florida morning, and I was sitting on a derelict pier outside Melbourne, baby-sitting a dead manatee. The manatee, an immature male, had just been towed a mile through the water behind a marine patrol boat after washing up in some snowbird's back-yard, and skin was sliding off the poor thing like a blanched tomato. Two teenage boys, sucking on cigarettes, walked up and asked for per-mission to swim, having seen me get out of the patrol boat. "Sure, why not," I said, shrugging. The Intracoastal Waterway looked about as refreshing as a sewage ditch, but I wasn't in a helpful kind of mood. I glanced down at the partially submerged manatee, tied by its tail to the dock, rotting in the winter sun. The patrol officer had complained bitterly about having to waste his time on recovery missions, so upon my suggestion, he had left the manatee and me alone to wait for a state marine biologist. How could he stop people from speeding in no-wake manatee zones, he'd grumbled, if he spent three hours out of an eight-hour day on a dead manatee?

A sign declaring "Have Dead Manatee, Will Talk" must have been hanging over the dock. As the teenagers tentatively waded into the brown muck, a skinny, worn-out alcoholic teetered over from his broken-down pickup. "I've never seen one of these before," he declared, his Adam's apple bobbing like a freaked-out aquarium fish. His breath drowned me in sweet, fermented fumes. "I've always wanted to. I love wildlife." He peered down, nearly losing his balance. "Not doing so well, huh?"

"Yeah, this cold water, even though it's only in the midsixties, is pretty rough," I offered, passing on information I had only just learned myself. "It kills them, even."

"This one's not dead, though. Just hurting a bit, huh?" Oily fluid was oozing from the body and the odor of decay lingered in the air. After I broke the news, the man ambled away, shaking his head. "Oh, I wanted to see a live one. Never seen one of them."

That's what I went down to Florida to do, too—to see a very special live one named Brutus. You see, Brutus is my son. My youngest sister adopted him for me on my birthday last summer, coughing up $20 to the Save the Manatee Club, a Maitland, Florida–based conservation group dedicated to protecting this endangered species. The West Indian manatee, that less-than-streamlined marine mammal, was placed on the endangered-species list in 1973, threatened with wholesale habitat destruction. Up until the 1950s, the giant herbivores were plentiful enough to be hunted, but no one really has a clue how many there were at their peak—guesses range throughout the tens of thousands, and wandering manatees are almost impossible to count. But by 1973 there were likely fewer than a thousand left in this country, and scientists estimate the current Florida population at a mere 2,600, along with small pockets in the Caribbean and Central America. Their death rate rises each year.

The day Brutus's adoption packet arrived, I merely glanced through it desultorily. I read that manatees mate only every two to five years and their gestation period is 13 months. Plus they have a high infant-mortality rate. Didn't sound good. I read more. Manatees live in the shallows of both fresh and salt water, where pollution and development destroy their habitats. Boats hit them all the time. Well, that's awful, I muttered, and began wondering how best to remove chewing gum from my two-year-old's hair. But then something about Brutus's sad face and sunken eyes caught my attention.

As I read on, I noticed that Brutus, probably in his thirties, was very close to me in age, but we had even more in common. He likes water;

I like water. He eats nearly 200 pounds of hyacinths and various water plants a day; I've been known to eat 100 pounds of junk food. He weighs nearly 2,000 pounds; I weigh 170. He is quite the ladies' man, always chasing the girls. I . . . But what was this? The literature said that Brutus is "often found sleeping by himself." Was he sad? Bitter? Having a midlife crisis? (Manatees live up to 60 years.) We had to make sure he was OK. "Brutus, we're coming down to see you!" I cried, speaking also for my wife and three daughters. "We'll swim together. Take pictures. Make you feel like part of the family."

Before heading down to Florida, I figured I should talk to Jimmy Buffet. I'd noticed he cofounded the Save the Manatee Club in 1981 with then-Governor Bob Graham, and I hoped he'd have a word or two to pass on to Brutus. But his publicist's response struck me like a whirring propeller: "Jimmy is not available to participate," she said. "He is only making himself available for national television programs." Undeterred, I had her submit some questions for Jimmy anyway. "Do you have any message you might want to give Brutus or any of the other manatees you're helping to save?" I asked, and "Do you know anyone who might have been a manatee in a former life?" The publicist got back to me a few days later and said Jimmy wasn't answering the questions, not even the one about how he might begin a song about manatees. Hell, even I could do that:

> Nibblin' on eel grass,
> Watchin' some mare's ass,
> All of those big boats loaded with Bud.
> Swimmin' to warm springs, listenin' to props zing,
> See our backs—
> They're covered with blood.
> Wasted away again in Manateeville,
> Searchin' for our lost celebrity friend.
> Some people claim that he'll bring us to fame,
> But we know, this is surely our end.

Well, let's hope not, but prospects do look dire for the manatee, despite the efforts of the Save the Manatee Club and a cobweb of federal and state wildlife agencies. Between the club's adoption program, the state of Florida's Save the Manatee license plates, and other fund-raising efforts, millions of dollars are spent each year on rescue efforts, research projects, and educational programs (for humans, not manatees) from Florida to the Carolinas. But it's an uphill battle, waged against such well-connected foes as Wade Hopping, lobbyist for the National Marine Manufacturers Association, who last year called for the species's delisting because the manatees, he said, had made such a great comeback. Hopping speaks for boaters who don't like the no-wake—and even no-boat—zones posted in high-density manatee habitats. Meanwhile, the number of manatees killed by watercraft jumped 24 percent in 1999. Total deaths in Florida last year were 268, a quarter of those due to boat collisions. Most manatees die on impact or bleed to death from propeller cuts, but even broken bones can kill them. Their ribs are solid and heavy, not porous like ours, and when one breaks, it's like a hardwood board snapping in two. The resulting internal injuries can prove fatal.

But in a few of these no-boat zones, the manatees are doing quite well: the Crystal River National Wildlife Refuge and Brutus's wintering grounds in central Florida's Blue Spring State Park among them. Back in 1970, when motorboats were still allowed at Blue Spring, only 11 manatees retreated to its warm waters, which feed the equally languorous St. Johns River, on Florida's east side. Now more than a hundred gather there each winter, enough for scientists to classify them as one of three distinct Florida populations, the others being the east coast manatees, whose range stretches from Miami up to the Carolinas, and the west coast manatees, who travel from the Keys as far west as Alabama. For the St. Johns group, the main attraction is Blue Spring itself. Fed by groundwater seeping through limestone bedrock, the spring remains a constant 72 degrees: manatee heaven.

It sounded inviting, but I was told that swimming with the manatees was a no-no. "We consider it harassment," said Nancy Sadusky, spokeswoman for the Save the Manatee Club. Sensing my disappointment, she hastily added, "We do encourage Passive Observation—you can still hang out near the spring and take Brutus's picture."

* * *

Blue Spring State Park is 30 miles northeast of Orlando, and as we made our way south from our home in Maine, my wife, Lisa, and I tried to prep our kids about Brutus and his friends. Driving down McDonald's-Exxon-Comfort Inn-Jiffy Lube Lane in Orange City, toward the turnoff for the park, Lisa explained that Brutus, like most manatees, could be identified by his unique pattern of propeller scars.

"Why do the boats cut Brutus?" asked Eliza, who's four. Because the boats go too fast in shallow water, we answered.

Then Anabel, her twin, chimed in. "Is Brutus better?" Yes, yes, we said. Helen, our two-and-a-half-year-old, held her own counsel, staring mutely at her manatee book.

"But the boats might cut his back again, huh?" Eliza continued. Luckily we arrived at the spring before we had to answer.

"Bruuuuutus!" the girls yelled, running to the boardwalk that hugged the shore. "Where are you, Brutus?" A lush hammock of live oak and wax myrtle engulfed the bank, making it nearly impossible to see the 50-foot-wide spring. The girls pried their way past dozens of baffled tourists staring blankly down from the boardwalk at the vividly clear water, but all they could see were a few fat catfish and a small school of tilapia. Brutus, along with all the other manatees, was nowhere in sight. The park allows visitors to swim in the upper reaches of the spring run each day—just not near the manatees—and half a dozen people were already splashing around the narrow waterway. Human-manatee interaction wasn't a problem because, understandably, the manatees had left. Park rules state that were one to reappear, everyone would have to hop out of the water. But the manatees usually just leave sooner on their afternoon foraging runs into the 60-degree (or colder) river, traveling perhaps dozens of miles for food and, with any luck, a shallow pocket of warm water. Most get cold stress in water below 68 degrees; they develop internal infections and canker-like sores, similar to frostbite, on their extremities, which often lead to death. So the park tried to prohibit swimming but bowed to legislative pressure when swimmers and divers complained.

We waited around, hoping against hope that Brutus might show. But hours passed, and finally, dejected, we set up our tent in an RV site at the park. Thirty miles northeast of Orlando might be a great

place for manatees, but it's a little less so for humans. The area's sprawling development is inescapable and frightening, and during our entire
stay, beeping, churning construction equipment serenaded us wherever
we went. Florida has the country's fastest-growing population, and the
2,192-acre park made a poor beachhead in the fight to preserve some
semblance of tranquillity.

That afternoon, our friends Russell Kaye, Sandi Phipps, and their
five-year-old daughter, Lucy, joined us at our campsite. Russell and
Sandi had come to photograph the manatees. With all three suffering
from strep throat, they were no boost to our sagging morale. Our girls
were pouring topsoil over each other when my wife began grousing
that the tourists were ugly; Blue Spring gets up to 2,000 visitors a day
because of the manatees. "They're a blight on this beautiful natural
setting," Lisa announced.

"What makes us so beautiful?" I asked, still worried about Brutus.
A seemingly befuddled box turtle walked by.

"We're not," Lisa replied. "We're a blight too. We should all commit mass suicide."

"Not until I see Brutus," I said.

By the next morning, the manatees had returned. Putting down a muti-
nous clamor to abandon Blue Spring and head over to the Gulf Coast
to the mermaid-and-manatee show at Weeki Wachee Springs, Russell
and I accompanied park ranger Wayne Hartley on his daily head count.
Our sullen families watched the manatees from the boardwalk as we
made the rounds in a pair of canoes. Hartley said that Brutus returns
to Blue Spring every year, as my brochure had claimed, but he only
stays for a few days at a time and then disappears for weeks. "It's got
to be really cold to bring old Brutus in," he said. At 8:30 A.M. the air
temperature was a cool 50 degrees, so maybe Brutus had turned up.

A big man but no manatee contender, Hartley has been monitoring
the annual Blue Spring winter retreat for 19 years. One hundred and
thirty-one manatees had come up to Blue Spring this season, and he
knew nearly all of them by name. We paddled just a few yards past
the no-boat zone (PVC piping across the mouth of the spring) and hov-
ered over a bunch of manatees. It was extremely underwhelming. They

looked like sunken fat cactuses, as a result of sporadic bristly hairs dotting their bulbous backs. Eventually, one slowly rose to the surface, inches from our boat, revealing its stoppered snout, making me suddenly giddy. It was so close; it might be Brutus. The nose unplugged and a reverberating exhalation, like the spouting of a small whale, echoed across the still waters. Its breath smelled a bit like a deflating tire, only mustier.

"Brutus?" I asked.

"No, that's . . . Phyllis."

Another and another and another rose around us. Soon there were dozens of exhaling cactuses surrounding our canoes. I hadn't expected it to be like this, great clumps of them floating beneath us, conserving their energy, as we paddled overhead. One mother had not only her one-year-old calf close to her side, but also a pair of older adoptees vying for nourishment.

Hartley began a monologue of greetings that didn't stop until we were back on shore two hours later. "Glad to see you, Floyd. There you are, Jax. No, you're not Jax. Wait, yeah you are, tail buried in sand." Half of Jax's tail is missing, perhaps from a run-in with fishing line. Next to boating accidents, entanglement is the single biggest cause of injuries.

"There's Georgia," Hartley continued, taking pictures and recording distinguishing marks while he talked. I half expected him to give each manatee a friendly slap across the back, he reminded me so much of a local politician courting his constituents. "This is Georgia's third year back. Great success story. Picked up at 63 pounds. Six years at Sea World, released here." Georgia looked to be at least 1,500 pounds, if not more. "Problem is that Georgia likes people too much. She's even tried to climb steps out of the run to follow someone. She's taught her calf Peaches to like people, too." He swept his paddle over the water, indicating the whole lot. "The brats, I could beat them all," he said with affection.

Peaches, by the way, is a boy. You can tell by the proximity of the genitalia opening to the umbilical scar and anus. Males' are closer to the umbilical scar, females' to the anus. Of course, a manatee must roll on its back for you to see this.

One manatee took a shine to me and wouldn't leave my end of the canoe, nuzzling up to me and trying to touch my hand. "Oh, that's Unknown 11," Hartley said, glancing over his shoulder, noticing a tail scar. Unable to resist, I touched its head. According to the U.S. Fish and Wildlife Service, this was OK because the manatee approached me, but the state park did not condone such behavior. Unknown 11's skin was rougher than I thought it would be, almost like sandpaper. It came back for more—clearly very fond of me. Hartley said this behavior wasn't unusual. "The more they like hanging around people, the more they hang around boats, and thus the more they get hit," he cautioned. I asked if Brutus is like this. Hartley laughed. "Naw," he said. "Brutus is a real manatee. He moves away from the canoe, if he is awake. He's very calm, laid back, though."

We saw 72 manatees but no Brutus.

That night during dinner at Olive Garden (about the only place in town that serves salad), I got more grief, not only for keeping us in central Florida but seemingly also for the whole manatee situation.

"I wish they didn't give the manatees names," Sandi said. "What's with calling him Brutus? Or Louie? It anthropomorphizes them. It's kind of weird, don't you think? It makes you want to pet them."

Ashamed, I didn't mention touching Unknown 11.

Brutus didn't show up the next day, either. The weather had turned warm, with temperatures in the 70s and 80s during the day and only the low 50s at night. Weighing roughly a ton, Brutus, along with most of the other manatees, had little need for Blue Spring. So Russell and I headed over to Melbourne, on the Atlantic Coast, to watch a manatee recovery, which is how I ended up on a dock baby-sitting a dead manatee while Russell went off to meet the state marine biologist. Not surprisingly, our families opted to drive to Weeki Wachee.

About a half-hour after the patrol officer left me and my deceased charge, Russell and Ann Spellman, a redheaded biologist for the state-run Florida Marine Research Institute, pulled up towing her manatee rescue/recovery trailer. We dragged the corpse out of the water and loaded it in back of the trailer. All recovered manatees are given a necropsy to determine age and cause of death, and Spellman decided to do the postmortem right in the parking lot behind her office. The nearest pathology lab was three hours away, and she had to hurry to a meeting where she would be told that her already-meager budget was being cut.

"The first thing I like to do is cut the head off to get it out of the way," Spellman explained, as scores of flies swarmed around her and the manatee. She was squatting inside the trailer, which had a slick fiberglass coating so it could be easily hosed out. A pervasive stench clung to anything within range. Apparently breathing through her nose as well as her mouth, Spellman sliced through two layers of fat and muscle. Two more quick strokes of her poultry knife ("It has a good long handle," she said) and the young male's head was severed from its spine. The head slid a few inches on its own fluids and stared out in understandable disgust. "At least he's not a slimer," she said.

Pointing out puffy, white sores on the animal's flippers, tail, and head, Spellman theorized that it had died of cold stress. Barnacles clung to what was left of the manatee's skin, but there were no signs of recent boat scars.

She sliced through half a foot of flesh and found swollen lymph glands and other signs of infection that supported her initial evaluation. And seeing the manatee cut up, it no longer seemed so surprising that these animals cannot handle what seems like relatively warm water. Although there might be a foot of meat between skin and internal organs, there is shockingly little insulation. The amount of fat this creature had, less than an inch in thickness, would make a seal die of laughter. Russell, for example, has plenty more fat than a manatee.

As Spellman studied the carcass more closely, though, she began noticing odd things—a blood-red liver that should be brown, a collapsed left lung, two ribs out of place. She turned the animal on its side. An ugly white scar that we hadn't seen earlier stretched a foot across its back. "Boat," she said and then started digging around the ribs. Turned out there were six fractured ribs from the impact. Judging from its size, Spellman guessed the manatee to be a two-year-old that had perhaps still been nursing.

"I love animals, but it's like I'm a fireman," she said. "You don't see a fireman bawling his eyes out at the scene. You bawl your eyes out watching a stupid schmucky movie."

Spellman cleaned up the mess, stored the head to be sent off to a bio lab (where its exact age could be determined by growth rings in the ear bones), hauled the carcass to the local landfill, and headed off to her budget meeting. Since it was still extremely hot out and Brutus was nowhere to be found (I had called Hartley to check), Russell and I rushed across-state to catch the Weeki Wachee mermaid show. The girls had already seen the morning performance.

"They've got a summer mermaid camp," my wife gushed. "Their makeup stays on even when they're underwater. You should see how they hold their breath."

"Do they look anything like manatees?" I asked, refraining from pointing out that Brutus can hold his breath for up to 16 minutes. The manatees' order is called Sirenia and has long been associated with the mythical mermaids, as Lisa had reminded me earlier.

"No," she continued, her face flushed, "but to become a mermaid all I'd have to do is be able to hold my breath for two and a half minutes underwater while changing costumes . . . Did I tell you Elvis was here?"

The show, a musical rendition of *The Little Mermaid,* was mesmerizing. How did they get that makeup to stay on? One of the mermaids slid right past the underwater window cut into one side of the spring's deep cavern, but I definitely could not see how the mermaid/manatee myth ever started. Christopher Columbus, the first historical source for it, wrote that the mermaids he'd seen were not as handsome as artists had portrayed them. What an idiot! These mermaids looked nothing like manatees. To begin with, manatees' breasts are found under their front flippers and that certainly wasn't the case with the Weeki Wachee mermaids. And there weren't even any manatees around that day. "Those girls are so cute," the woman behind us said at the finale.

No one could say that about a manatee.

While you could barely even look at a live manatee at Blue Spring, the wild west coast was a different story. That night we stayed in a trailer at the Marine Park Inn on the Homosassa River a few miles up from Weeki Wachee. A huge billboard out on the road said, "Swim with the Manatees." This we had to see.

We rented a pontoon boat the next morning and slowly waddled up the river toward the mouth of Homosassa Springs—the main attraction for the hundred or so manatees that convene there on cold winter days. Not far from the mouth of the spring, in Homosassa Springs State Wildlife Park (which also features swamp tours and live hippos imported from Africa), nearly 20 tourist-choked pontoon boats and more than a hundred snorkelers were packed in an area half the size of a football field. Manateemania. Not only were these people swimming with about two dozen manatees, but they were also rubbing the manatees' bellies and backs. Some people looked like they were trying to have sex with the poor beasts. Others, like members of a hunting party, were chasing down retreating manatees, desperate not to let them get away.

An elderly couple paddled up next to us in their canoe. It turned out they were Manatee Watch volunteers. When they see unlawful behavior, the couple told us, they approach the swimmers and discourage them from breaking the law. A few minutes after we spoke, this duo broke up a gang of swimmers who had separated a mother from her calf. Mostly, though, they just paddled along, caring but ineffectual. According to the Crystal River National Wildlife Refuge, U.S. Fish and Wildlife officers in this area gave out only six tickets for harassing manatees in 1999, and in five minutes we witnessed about 70 infractions. Where were those guys?

We watched as snorkeler after snorkeler harassed the lugubrious manatees. "Hey!" one particularly goofy swimmer yelled out. "He's got my hand with his flipper and won't let go. He really won't!" Take him down, I silently pleaded. Take him down.

Lisa, Russell, and Sandi got in to take pictures and a couple of manatees approached them. The manatees performed headstands and even nudged them with their noses to get scratched and petted. Whether this was true affection or simply a result of years of being hand-fed lettuce by misguided tourists was hard to tell.

I jumped in, too. Like everyone else, I just had to get a look from underwater. Although I now knew that swimming with manatees is unhealthy for the species, the animal's giantness is powerfully compelling. "See, we're not all bad," you're thinking as one gets closer and closer. Then, you reach out and . . . another manatee is dead.

What the hell is going on here? I began to wonder. This is an endangered species. People shouldn't be touching endangered species. Boats shouldn't be able to motor up to endangered species and drop dozens of tourists in their lap. There shouldn't be signs on the highway exhorting people to swim with the goddamned endangered manatees. Go swim with a Weeki Wachee mermaid! What was the state of Florida doing to these poor, dumb animals? What was the U.S. government doing?

Hell, why not let people feed them, take them home as pets, shoot them even? I've read that the meat tastes pretty good; some people still poach them. Soak their tails in brine and have a party! It really wouldn't matter. They're not going to be around much longer anyway, except in aquariums and zoos.

The manatee I saw underwater seemed to know this. "I'm doomed," his sad face said, as I kicked to scare him away. I hopped out of the river, revved our engine as loudly as possible, and happily saw a few manatees splash down to deeper, safer water.

We returned to Blue Spring, still hoping to catch a glimpse of Brutus. It was our last day in Florida, and we had a few things we wanted to tell him.

We paddled out past the mouth of the stream and into the St. Johns. It is a wide river, stained brown with tannin, and it was unlikely we would see anything underwater. It was Sunday, and dozens of boats slowly motored up and down the river. Only a few disobeyed the no-wake rule.

Occasionally, one of us would call out, "Brutus!" and a flock of egrets would take to the sky. Once we startled a 12-foot alligator that was snoozing on the bank and the creature scurried directly toward our canoes. (Alligators, by the way, don't eat manatees; the lummoxes are just too big for their jaws.) Finally, when we'd been bitten by enough mosquitoes and the girls were scanning in all directions for attacking alligators, I stood in the canoe. I had been planning to make one last plea. Perhaps I'd started out as a deadbeat dad, but now I truly cared. I wanted to be there for him, the son I'd never known. But something profoundly different came out of my mouth. "Brutus!" I yelled. "Don't come back! We're not worth it!"

Brutus did come back, though. Two weeks later, Wayne Hartley e-mailed that he had returned. Like all manatees, he needs that warm water on occasion. Brutus has been coming to Blue Spring for at least 30 years and he probably will continue to do so until the day he dies. I hope I never see him.

May 2000

Does the
Mushroom Love
Its Plucker?

You may already know Larry. Remember the guy in the Cat-in-the-Hat hat selling Indonesian jewelry at Grateful Dead concerts from New England to California? The American guy doing judo moves in that Japanese punk-rock music video back in '86 on Japanese MTV? The guy in the plant store who had just closed a deal to import ten metric tons of Siberian ginseng from which he was going to make ginseng tea and ginseng beer? The guy passing out questionnaires to hitchhikers everywhere from Texas to Canada for the hitchhiker's guidebook he was working on in the early eighties? The guy who led forest walks during timber-sale protests in the northern Rockies, who knew everything about edible wild mushrooms and other nontimber forest products that he said are sometimes more valuable than the trees they're under? The guy on the top of the bus riding through Guatemala where the flat green roof of the jungle is often interrupted by Mayan pyramids overgrown with green? The guy selling hats his wife makes and whirligigs and braided wrist bands called *pulseras* at the Renaissance Fair in Moscow, Idaho, and at other crafts fairs last summer? That was Larry.

Larry Evans, the botanist, wild-mushroom expert, and entrepreneur, lives in the same city in northwest Montana as I do. Based on an informal survey I've taken, I would say that almost everybody in town knows Larry. He is 43 years old and has a salt-and-pepper beard and long hair that he wears in a braid. He dresses in loose, short-sleeve shirts with patterns designed by the late Jerry Garcia, and in striped red shorts, white socks, and black sneakers. On bright days he puts on two pairs of glasses—his usual prescription spectacles and over them a thin pair of wraparound shades. He is broad-shouldered and well built, and is six feet, one or two inches ("depending on the mood I'm in") tall. He sometimes adds to his altitude with the Cat-in-the-Hat hat, a red-and-white striped model perhaps two feet high. At the local farmers' market, where he sells wild mushrooms, plants, and garden produce on Saturdays from late spring to early fall, he is visible in the crowd from blocks away. People in town who don't know him by name usually recognize him when they hear him described. They say, "Oh, yeah—the mushroom guy."

If you ask Larry if he's serious about something he has just told you and he is, he'll reply, "I'm as serious as a heart attack!" If you tell him something he already knows, he'll say, "You're tellin' Noah about the flood!" In a cheery mood, he says, "Adios, amoeba!" instead of good-bye. Sometimes he'll pronounce the last few words of a sentence in a pursed-lip funny voice which is hard to describe. When he's talking about the latest evasive tactic of a timber company, for example, he'll repeat the timber company's explanation in this voice. It's irony, but old-fashioned, lighthearted, hippie-era irony rather than the hard-edged, ad-jingle irony of today.

If you ask Larry about mushrooms, he becomes excited and cagey at the same time. He's excited because, as he says, "I was born a mycophile." (*Myco*- comes from the Greek word for "fungus"; mushrooms are fungi.) "Some people are like that," he goes on. "Look at the people in any mushroom club, and you see that they can't help it. There's just this one percent of the population who if you show 'em a picture of a morel mushroom, they go ape." He's cagey, however, because people often assume that he is happy to part, free of charge, with mushroom information he has taken decades to acquire. I once made that mistake myself. Now I can't believe I ever did such a stupid thing. Not long after I moved to Montana, a mushroom-hunting friend of mine from back East noticed an article on mushrooms of the Russian Far East that Larry had written for a mycology journal. She told me the author lived in my town, so I found his name in the phone book and called him up and asked if he could recommend a good place for me to go looking for morels.

More amazing than the stupidity of this question, in retrospect, was how nice Larry was about it. He told me nothing, of course. But he didn't give me the short shrift my question deserved. I called him again from time to time, brought mushrooms to his stand at the farmers' market and asked him to identify them, and attended the mushroom lectures and slide presentations he offered at a garden-supply store south of town. Eventually, he told me all kinds of stuff—even, in a general way, where I might find morels. Sometimes I come across people who love a subject so much they will point the way into it even for strangers like me. Larry can make wild mushrooms seem as exciting and providential as windblown $20 bills scattered across your lawn.

English-speaking people traditionally fear and revile mushrooms. Our culture has generally considered them to be creepy, decay-loving, gloom-dwelling, and foul, in the province of witchcraft and necromancy. To us, they're akin to toads and centipedes and sightless fish, things we regard with an involuntary shudder. The English language reflects this distaste by providing hardly any common names for the many thousands of mushroom species that are indigenous to Great Britain and North America; mycophiles in the United States soon learn that to discuss mushrooms they must learn their Latin names. People who come from foreign places where wild mushrooms are prized are sometimes surprised to find how few Americans know or care about our abundant wild fungi.

My own interest in mushrooms came by way of Russia. It's my favorite foreign country, and Russians love wild mushrooms. Over there, everybody hunts for mushrooms—balding men in business suits, little girls in dresses, teenagers with backpacks, old babushka ladies. Russians took me on my first wild-mushroom hunt. My friends Alex Melamid and Katya Arnold, artists who emigrated to the United States in the late 1970s, look for mushrooms almost everywhere they go;

Katya has found them growing on indoor carpeting and on the floor of her car. She and Alex regularly search for mushrooms in several small public parks near their apartment in Jersey City, New Jersey. On one expedition they took along a young woman relative recently arrived from Moscow. When this young woman discovered a big patch of honey mushrooms growing at the base of a stump, her pale cheeks reddened, the pupils of her dark eyes enlarged, and she began to breathe hard. Her newly learned English abandoned her as she tried to tell me what wonderful mushrooms these were. I noticed her hands were trembling, a symptom I recognized from fly-fishing: Something similar happens to me when I spot a monster trout within casting range.

When Larry Evans talks about mushrooms, occasionally he veers in the next sentence into a story about the time he had to Taser a guy who was trying to beat him up in a village in Siberia. ("He attacked the mayor of this village while we were talking business, so I used some judo on him, so he came after me, so I gave him a few jolts of the Taser. It shocked him pretty good—he just stood there staggering like Frankenstein.") Or he will describe the beneficial possibilities of making paper products from nuisance plants like knapweed, or how the blossoms of the spiderwort plant change color when exposed to radiation (a property that has caused safety experts to plant spiderwort around food-irradiating plants to detect leaks), or where to buy scrimshaw carved on mastodon ivory, or how he just got a grant to use sheep to eat up a local infestation of leafy spurge.

And then in the next sentence he's talking about mushrooms again, and the digressions usually turn out to be not as far off the subject as they seemed. Perhaps this is because of the universality of mushrooms themselves. Fungi grow almost everywhere on the planet and have been around longer than almost any other life form. Larry balks at describing any living thing as "old"—all life forms, he says, continue to evolve and change no matter how successful they have been—but he concedes that fungi resemble the first multicellular beings more closely than do other present life forms. Fungi feed on organic matter, usually dead, and break it down into simpler structures that other organisms can use again. Some fungi make mushrooms; a mushroom is the fruit of a fungus, its means of distributing seeds (in this case, spores). A mushroom is not a plant, because it lacks chlorophyll and does not produce its own food. It needs no light to grow, which sometimes gives it an advantage over other life forms. For example, during the Cretaceous extinction, the catastrophic, possibly meteoric event 65 million years ago that darkened the atmosphere and killed off plants and the dinosaurs that depended on them, mushrooms survived. After thousands or millions of years, when the plant life re-evolved, the mushrooms were here waiting for them.

Most mushrooms launch their spores by hydraulic pressure—some from the face of their gills, some from tiny tubes or pores, some from the surface of wrinkles on the outside of the mushroom. A few mushrooms release their spores in a burst triggered by disturbances such as a gust of wind; if you pass your hand quickly above one of these mushrooms, the spores shoot out like a puff of smoke. Mushroom spores that land in the right circumstances germinate and eventually produce threadlike cells that combine into a network of filaments called a mycelium. The mycelium is the part of the fungus that eats, tunneling its way through organic matter and digesting as it goes. It is usually too minute to be seen, but when it's concentrated in one place it looks like a feathery white dusting. For some mushrooms, the individual mycelium can span hundreds of yards across. When the mycelium is well established, or when it has consumed the available nutrients, some of its threadlike cells come together in small masses of tissue that develop into fruiting bodies—what we call mushrooms—and the cycle begins again.

A few mushrooms feed on living matter such as insect larvae, other mushrooms, or trees. Some feed on dead or decaying things such as dung or fallen leaves or logs. Many mushrooms form a symbiotic relationship with the roots of living trees, in which the mycelium provides the tree roots with nutrients such as nitrogen or phosphorus and the roots provide the mycelium with moisture and sugars. The mycelium and the outside of the root combine so thoroughly as to create a tissue that is neither fungus nor plant. This tissue is called mycorrhiza, and it often encases roots until the roots themselves do not touch the soil. Trees such as Douglas firs and oaks are especially good hosts for mycorrhizal mushrooms. Many kinds of trees can be hosts, and the mushrooms have preferences. Mushroom hunters soon learn to look for certain kinds of mushrooms under certain kinds of trees. The mycorrhizal relationship is healthy for the trees as well, and trees with mushroom partners grow better than trees without. Many failures of reforestation have to do with an absence of mycorrhizal mushrooms, just as clear-cutting forests can be a disaster for the mushrooms that need the trees.

Larry grew up symbiotic with trees himself, on a Christmas tree farm in central Illinois. There were his father, a former grain broker; his mother, with a degree in biology; three younger brothers; and Larry. "All of us worked on the tree farm," he told me. "My second brother, Ron, is running it today. Most of the market's gone to plastic, though— 70 percent of all Christmas trees sold are plastic now. Us boys got paid subminimum wage to prune trees and fertilize and so on. I'm pretty proud of that phase of my life, actually. When I got to college I had an idea of how many hours of work it took for me to go to that school. But I can't say that the farm left me with a strong desire to go back to it."

Our conversation turned to the subject of reincarnation, which Larry believes in. We were sitting in his office, a room in the one-story ranch-style house he shares with his wife, Kris, on the west side of town. He likes to talk at his desk, surrounded by books and mushroom data in quantities that seem to block out the light. "I've always taken a great pleasure in plants, ever since I was a really young kid," he said. "I think that in a former time I might have been an herbalist in Asia, or maybe a Native American shaman. Growing up, I definitely knew I was having feelings that weren't tuned in to the place I was."

Larry's description of his youth is sort of vague. Those years seem to be important to him mainly for the escape velocity they helped him achieve. He went to college in Illinois for a year in the early seventies, quit, and headed west in his Subaru Ladybug looking for another college. He liked the environment of western Montana, the montane plant species unfamiliar to a boy from Illinois. The University of Montana had a good botany department. Plus, Missoula was a place you could live cheap, and Larry did, finding houses to fix up in exchange for rent, and dumpster-diving—looking for food in trash bins—with a few Missoula regulars he still sees around town today. He got his degree in biology, with a minor in microbiology, in 1979.

College turned out to be just a pause in his trajectory. "After I got my degree, starting in about '79, I hitchhiked all over the country," he said. "I've hitched in all 50 states except Hawaii." From a shelf he pulled down a copy of *Hey Now, Hitchhikers!*, a paperback guidebook written and typeset and published by Larry and his brother Don. "We passed out hitchhiking questionnaires to hitchers everywhere we went, and then we wrote up what we learned. But by the time the book came out in '82, the Reagan swing to the right had begun and almost no one was hitchhiking anymore. I felt like I was documenting a lost race."

He hopped freight trains, too, going back and forth across the country. A chart of his travels would look like a map someone scribbled on. By the late eighties he had crossed the Pacific and was traveling in Asia. In Japan he taught English and modeled; people liked to look at him because he's tall. He worked as an extra in Japanese soap operas and was featured in a rock video, but got tired of going for auditions and gave up that career. And so onward—to Indonesia, Thailand, China, India, Bangladesh. He lived next to a shiitake farm in Japan, cataloged mushrooms in Tibet, found his first truffles in Australia. Most years he wintered in Mexico. Between 1986 and 1990 he spent a total of just four weeks in the United States.

"I fell in love with mushrooms back in 1977," Larry said. "I took a course from the great mycologist Orson K. Miller, author of *Mushrooms of North America*. Pretty soon I had that book memorized. When I came back to Missoula in the early nineties after my travels, I began to hunt mushrooms around here on a regular basis and I opened my booth at the farmers' market. I've got a peddler's soul. I've sold stuff every place from jazz festivals to Dead shows (back when Jerry was alive) to just on the sidewalk somewhere. With mushrooms, what I sell isn't just the fungi, it's my reputation, because of course you have to be sure that what you're eating isn't going to kill you. My wife— we met when we were both traveling in Java in '89—has been eating mushrooms picked by me for seven years, and she's never gotten sick once. I've been sick from mushrooms only once myself, when I ate a piece of *Agaricus xanthodermus* by mistake. I threw up. It was no big deal."

In the corner of the windshield of Larry's pickup truck is a Grateful Dead decal with the band's logo encircling a large psychedelic-looking mushroom. Naturally, with Larry the subject of psychedelic mushrooms comes up from time to time. He usually doesn't mention it first himself; like most mycologists, he disdains the stoners' approach to the science, believing that psychedelic-seekers aren't interested in much beyond what gets them high. Also, the idea that mushrooms are merely a drug annoys him because it fits well with the general ignorance and phobias about mushrooms. His comments on psychedelics tend to be cryptic, and one understands that he knows more than he says.

On the subject of mushrooms that will kill you or just give you the miseries, however, he speaks with relish and at length. He describes the effect of Tippler's bane (*Coprinus atramentarius*), an edible mushroom that can cause the body to react strangely to alcohol: "Eat one of them and then have a beer, and your face will get flushed, you'll feel sick to your stomach, and you might end up paralyzed for two to three days." Some of the *Gyromitra* mushrooms, called false morels, contain monomethylhydrazine: "That's rocket fuel. It evaporates when you cook 'em, but you need a kitchen with good ventilation. People in Europe sometimes eat these for years until they build up a fatal dosage and suddenly die." The deadly *Amanitas*—the death cap and the destroying angel and others—he mentions with awe. "When you find those bad boys in the woods, you never see any animal bites on them. Most big mushrooms won't kill you, but an *Amanita* sure will. The toxins attack your kidneys and liver. You don't even want to know what happens after that. About 50 percent of the time, you die."

I asked Larry if there's an easy way to identify a hazardous mushroom, or a handy mnemonic, like the "leaves of three, let it be" rhyme of the plant world. "Well, don't eat any mushroom until you're sure what it is," he said. "Don't eat any the first time you pick it, don't eat any raw, keep different kinds of mushrooms separate when you're picking them, eat only a small portion of any mushroom the first time you try it, and try it twice, in case you're allergic—these are the basic rules.

The best way to identify a mushroom is to check it with an identification key in a good mushroom guide and make a spore print, or else bring it to an expert you trust, like me.

"Beyond that, there is no idiotproof method for determining which mushrooms are safe and which are not. Most boletes are safe and edible, and they all have pores rather than gills, which helps with identification. But then you've got boletes like *Boletus satanas*, Satan's bolete, which will definitely do a number on you. In the Northwest there are about 5,000 species of mushrooms, and we've studied maybe 800. Mushrooms are complicated; we're a pretty complicated life form ourselves, as far as that goes. But nowadays we think that everything should be idiotproof. An idiotproof world is a world only idiots would want to live in."

As a mushroom hunter, Larry is driven. One morning at the farmers' market I mentioned to him that I had seen a certain mushroom growing in some loose dirt and gravel by a concrete parking divider a mile or so away. When the market closed at noon, he packed up his wares and asked me to take him to it. We drove in his pickup to where I'd seen it. It was still there, and he picked it up and cried, "*Agaricus bitorquis!* I didn't think these guys were up yet!" We kept it to give the scent to his dog, Zora, a black German shepherd who can smell out mushrooms. Then we went to a place on the outskirts of town which he prefers I not be too specific about. It's a piece of vacant ground surrounded by a high chain-link fence. Larry asked me how I felt about trespassing as he cleared the fence in two leaps. I was willing but had a hard time getting over. His dog was running back and forth trying to get under. Larry bounded back across, gave me a boost, heaved Zora over, and crossed again.

The hard-packed dusty ground overgrown with last year's knapweed and wild lettuce looked unpromising. Larry said that *Agaricus bitorquis* often grows below the surface and is often called a duff humper for the way it pushes the earth above it. Immediately we found a few, then dozens, then *bitorquis* by the score. Crouching in the weeds, reaching into cracks in the ground, we came up with plump and ripe mushrooms with stout stalks and caps from about three inches to eight inches across. The cap of *bitorquis* is smooth and light gray to brown, and the gills are a chocolate brown like those of the domesticated, commercial *Agaricus,* its relative. As we filled our plastic shopping bags, Larry told me how delicious these are. Everywhere we turned, we found more. As we walked back to the road, Larry held his bag behind his back. "If anyone saw me coming out of here with a bulging bag, they'd know what I had and where I'd found it," he said.

We took the mushrooms to his house, and a few days later his wife took the *bitorquis* caps, sautéed them, stuffed them with cream cheese and crabmeat, baked them *en croute,* and served them as part of a wild-mushroom dinner that included chicken-and-shiitake-mushroom shish kebab and a salad of morels and fresh asparagus. It was the best meal I've eaten in the state of Montana. As I tasted the *bitorquis* caps, I kept thinking about the no-account shinnery ground from which they came.

"Larry is the most amazing person I ever met, and I'm married to him," Kris said when I joined her at the stove between courses. Kris is a milliner and a chef. Her last name is Love. She has blond hair, blue eyes, a turned-up nose, and a pleasantly raspy voice. "Before I knew Larry, when I walked in the woods I was like [eyes wide, expression spacey, staring up into the trees]. Now when I walk in the woods I'm like [eyes focused, head down, expression intent, looking at the ground]."

The same is true of me. I used to think of the woods as just a bunch of trees, and I stared into their upper story as if into a paradise of leaves, imagining tree forts and escape. Now, maybe because I'm too old to climb, maybe because Larry told me that more than half of a forest's living biomass is in its soil, I look more at the ground. I'm drawn to the tumbledown things—the curled-up shreds of bark, the dead logs that the mycelium is turning to powder, the crumpled cottonwood leaves, the dark and liquefying leaves from many summers ago, the broken branches, the soggy places, the yellow-green lichens, the creeping vines. I note the shrubs, the snowberry and serviceberry and dogwood and erigonum, and the dark-striped snakegrass, and the broadleaf grasses holding beads of dew in the places where they bend, and the glacier lilies and clematis and wild strawberry, and hundreds of plants I can't identify.

And sometimes among the jumble on the forest floor I find mushrooms—oyster mushrooms on a rotten log in terraces of oyster-scented white, or little brown no-name mushrooms rising on their long stalks through the ground debris like barrage balloons, or *Psathyrellas* with purplish caps tucked into the hollow of a rotten log, or every so often a morel. In the city in a fancy restaurant you might get one or two small morels as a garnish with your saddle of venison entrée, but they will be dried and rehydrated ones, their taste remote from what it once was. A morel is a roughly cone-shaped mushroom with a cap almost as wrinkled as a brain, intricately indented, and with a light-colored, sinewy-looking stalk. The yellow morel (*Morchella esculenta*) has a cap of an orange-yellow almost the exact color of fallen cottonwood leaves. The taste of sautéed morels on plain white toast with a glass of chardonnay embarrasses, spectacularly, the tastes of the foods you usually eat. And to come across one of these mushrooms, or a number of them, in the tumbledown forest understory is an experience of silent and towering outdoor emphasis. It's as if a huge chord has been struck. You want to sing, and the only reason you don't is that you might tip off any other morel hunters who happen to be in the area. The yellow morel in the grass under a young aspen tree, in some way, senses that it's cool and gourmet. It suggests that the whole cluttered forest floor, to the right palate, might be delicious too.

Earlier this summer, if you called Larry's number you got his machine. He was off doing a mushroom survey in the Kootenai National Forest for the Forest Service, he was seeing how the sheep were coming along with the leafy spurge, he was giving a mushroom lecture in Glacier National Park, he was attending a convention of the American Mycological Association. He was trying to think of what to do with all that ginseng he bought in Siberia a few years ago, now sitting in a warehouse in Salt Lake City. The ginseng and the idea of importing more nontimber forest products from Siberia were among his projects on hold. On the street in Missoula he ran into a friend who suggested a ten-day backpacking trip into the Bob Marshall Wilderness, and Larry began to calculate how he could work that into his schedule.

Also, he and his wife bought a restaurant. They were in it at all hours, redoing the decor and furnishings and planning menus and making the dozens of phone calls that opening a restaurant involves. The place they bought, the Black Dog, had been the only vegetarian restaurant in town. Some people worried that Larry and Kris might add meat to the menu. People would come up to them on the sidewalk, lower their voices, and ask, "Are you going to add . . . meat?"

Larry was not at the farmers' market every Saturday, but when he did show up, he had wild mushrooms by the score. He listed them on a small signboard, without prices, as if they were the important headlines in this week's news. His booth was so crowded that I could stand beside him unnoticed even by people who know me and listen to his spiel: "These big ones are the shimeiji mushrooms, *Lyophillum descastes,* the second most popular mushroom in Japan . . . Yes, ma'am, from right around here. Stevensville is the farthest I went for any mushroom on this table . . . That's a king bolete, I'm really proud of that, it's a two-pound mushroom, a beautiful thing. In Paris that'd be worth $30 . . . Do I think we'll still get morels this year? Hard to tell, but at elevation, anything's possible . . . These are the fairy ring mushrooms, that bunch there's about a buck's worth. They've got a delicious, nutty, almond thing going on with them, fry 'em up in oil or butter . . . Where did I find these morels? At the same old place—I mean, the old Same place! I'm the only Firesign-Theater-quoting vendor in the market . . . That bag is all dried oyster mushrooms and that other one is dried oyster mushrooms that I put through a brand-new coffee grinder. Add that powder to gravies or soups . . ."

Pulling out crumpled singles and fives, people bought shimeiji mushrooms with caps as big as hands, and a young giant puffball sliced vertically like a loaf of bread, and all the dried morels, and the oyster mushroom powder in a Zip-Loc bag, and fairy ring mushrooms in intricate little piles. By the end of the morning the imitation-wood top of Larry's folding table was almost bare. Only as the market closed did the group of customers and onlookers around him start to thin.

These signs of popularity cause me to worry: What if lots of people get interested in wild mushrooms, as happened recently to golf? I have learned that I am part of a vast generation and that we tend to overgraze. I asked Larry if he was concerned about the possibility that hunting mushrooms might become overpopular and suffer a decline. "I'm not too worried about crowding or other pickers," Larry said. "My real enemy is loss of habitat. Look at the landscape around here next time you're flying into Missoula. We're living in clear-cut heaven— that's still the main method of timber harvesting around here. Nobody wants to hear about selective cutting or logging mixed-age stands. The timber companies say it's too expensive, the usual complaint. Of course, when you take out a whole stand of trees, it destroys the mycorrhizal fungi. But it also destroys so much more. Certain lichens take 20 years to colonize a tree. We're ignoring links like this. And the timber harvest represents a single big payday that you won't be able to collect again for—what? Fifty years? A hundred years? Where, with mushrooms, it's a harvest that renews itself in just a year or a few years. Last year the Deschutes and Winema National Forests in Oregon made $330,000 from matsutake-picking permits alone. And the mushrooms that were harvested in Oregon and sent air-freight to Japan brought tens of millions of dollars to the state. Millions from mushrooms! And I'm not even counting the other nontimber forest products, the berries and ginseng and floral greens. When you get into mushrooms, you're hooked into the whole forest ecosystem, and you understand that a forest is rich far beyond its timber.

"Now, if I said all that sitting in an office at the biology department at the university, or in a forestry chair endowed by the Plum Creek Timber Company, do you think many people would pay attention to me? But out here on my own, dressing wacky and putting on a show and letting people see the great wild fungi from the forest—well, I think I've got the people's ear."

September 1998

I, Nature Boy

DAVID RAKOFF

I t is difficult in the extreme to construct either a Figure-Four or Paiute deadfall trap, to say nothing of having them work, in the dark, and in the rain, at 11 P.M., after 17 hours of lectures and demonstrations, during which one has already been taught (among other things) the Sacred Order of Survival—shelter, water, fire, food; how to make rope and cordage from plant and animal fibers; how to start a fire using a bowdrill; finding suitable materials for tinder (making sure to avoid the very fluffy and flammable mouse nest as it may contain hantavirus); how to recognize the signs of progressive dehydration; how to make a crude filter out of a matted clump of grass; how to distinguish between the common, water-rich grapevine and the very similar yet very poisonous Canadian moonseed; how to make a solar still out of a hole covered with a sheet of plastic (and how to continue the condensation process by urinating around the hole); and the Apache tradition of honoring those things one hunts, be they animal, vegetable, or mineral. All of this within the first day and a half of a Standard Class session at Tom Brown's Tracking, Nature, and Wilderness Survival School in the wilds of northwestern New Jersey.

The Standard is the first and most basic of 28 classes offered by the school, a Wilderness 101 of sorts—a weeklong, lecture-heavy, intensive introduction to primitive outdoor skills and nature awareness. The same skills and awareness found at the very heart of the bildungsroman that is the oft-told life story of Tom Brown Jr. Briefly, the story is as follows: Growing up in the Jersey Pine Barrens in the late 1950s, a young Tom spends almost every waking moment from the ages of seven to 18 in the woods under the tutelage of his best friend Rick's grandfather, Stalking Wolf, a Southern Lipan Apache from Texas. Brown's apprenticeship ends in 1967 upon his graduation from Toms River High School. He is designated 4-F by the draft board due to a chip of obsidian that had lodged in his right eye in his teens; years earlier, Stalking Wolf is said to have predicted that a "black rock" would keep the boy out of Vietnam. Over the next decade Brown takes odd jobs to make the money necessary to spend his summers testing his skills in unfamiliar environments across the country (the Tetons, the Dakota Badlands, Death Valley, and the Grand Canyon), living in debris huts and scout pits of his own devising, and subsisting on food he forages or kills himself. Eventually the young man re-emerges into society with a single-minded mission: to teach others and lead them back to the woods and a love of nature.

There have been digressions along the way. Brown has trained Navy SEALs in high-speed invisible survival and helped the FBI and state law enforcement agencies in tracking persons both missing and criminal. He solved his 600th case on his 27th birthday, a full year before the publication of his first book in 1978. *The Tracker* is a tale of an adventurous boyhood of limitless self-reliance in an unfathomably Arcadian wilderness. It makes for compelling, if not always easy to swallow, reading: part Richard Halliburton, part Carlos Castaneda, part *Kung Fu*. Grandfather, already an octogenarian in 1957 when Tom first meets him, appears as a man of almost Buddhalike wisdom with a penchant for posing oblique, seemingly insoluble riddles and laughing discreetly behind his hand as Rick and Tom, mired in narrow Western thought, fumble for answers.

It might not be Thoreau, but it is the key to the legend that Tom Brown may very well one day become, and certainly already is here at the Tracker School. Brown, 50, is a cult figure of international stature. The best-selling author of 16 books, whatever tracking Brown does now, be it for the crooked or the merely lost, is more of the armchair variety. Having trained tens of thousands of people at his school, he can call upon a global network of former and current acolytes when his tracking wisdom is requested.

Many of us here for the Standard—some 90 people from the United States and Canada, four from Austria, and a young woman all the way from Japan—are aspirants, yearning to join those ranks of expert trackers. Everyone is acquainted with Stalking Wolf. All have read at least part of Brown's oeuvre, be it one of the field guides to wilderness survival or to wild edible and medicinal plants, or perhaps the more spiritually oriented titles, such as *The Vision, The Quest, The Journey,* or *Grandfather.* According to the school's statistics, roughly 90 percent of us will return to take a more advanced course, starting with the Advanced Standard and branching off thereafter, perhaps to learn Search and Rescue, the Way of the Coyote, Intensive Tracking, or How to Be a Shadow Scout.

We are diverse in age and gender, and we run the gamut from the pragmatic to the ethereal; from the unbelievably sweet 18-year-old vegan boy from Portland, Oregon, to the gun enthusiast who brought his own supply of hermetically sealed decommissioned military MREs ("Bought 'em on eBay for ten cents on the dollar after the whole Y2K thing didn't pan out. Best au gratin potatoes I ever ate"); from the congenial soi-disant "hillbilly from West Virginia" in his fifties to the twenty-something physics major looking to drop out for a while. Most are friendly, intelligent, and environmentally and socially committed. More than a few are involved in education, in particular working with troubled teens in the wilderness. And, I am relieved to see, most are refreshingly immune to the pornography of gear. They radiate good health as they unpack bags of gorp, apples, whole-wheat pitas, and huge water bottles. I, too, have come prepared—with a deli-size Poland Spring mineral water, assorted candy bars, and four packs of Marlboro Lights.

I arrive on April 30, a beautiful, sunny, but very windy Sunday afternoon. We all spend the first few hours battling the strong breeze to pitch our tents, the placement of which is overseen by Indigo, one of the eight or so volunteers, alumni of previous Standard Classes, who help out for the week and in so doing refresh their skills and relive what was clearly for them a wonderful experience. Indigo, a rural New Jersey local, hovers somewhere between 50 and 70 years old. With her sun-burnished face, craggy features, and rather extreme take-charge demeanor, she is straight out of *My Antonia*. Still, she's not unfriendly, even as she tells one of the Austrians, his tent staked down and ready, "Uh-uh, mister. You gotta move it about four inches that way. We're making a lane right here." Indigo gesticulates like an urban planner dreaming of a freeway; she is the Robert Moses of Tent City.

It should be noted that we are not actually in the Pine Barrens, sacro-sanct locus of Brown's childhood in and around the town of Toms River. The Standard Class is held on the Tracker farm in Asbury, New Jersey, near the Pennsylvania border (not to be confused with Asbury Park, sacrosanct locus of the early career of that other South Jersey legend, Bruce Springsteen). Brown splits his time between here and the Barrens, but the farm at Asbury is better for teaching novices because of its rich biodiversity; the surrounding fields, meadows, and light forest, and the Musconetcong River, which flows a few hundred yards away, offer ample flora and fauna for this week of instruction. Aside from the barn, the central structure where the (hours upon hours of) lectures take place, the farm consists of Tom Brown's house, a dozen or so portable toilets, and a toolshed with an awning under which sits a row of chuck-wagon gas rings—our cafeteria. All activity is centered on the main yard, a scant acre of patchy lawn that lies between our nylon sleeping quarters and the barn. In the center of this is the all-important fire, which burns day and night, heating a large square iron tank with a tap, where we get hot water for our bucket showers.

Brown used to teach the Standard from beginning to end himself. These days, aside from evening and morning talks, he leaves the teach-ing responsibilities to his paid instructors, the most organically charm-ing group of people I've ever encountered. They're all affable, pedagogically gifted—there isn't a dud public speaker in the bunch—and chasteningly competent at the endless variety of primitive skills we're here to learn. They're a lovable crew of commandos straight out of central casting: Kevin Reeve, 44, director of the school, a John Goodman paterfamilias type who opted for early retirement from Apple Computer nine years ago after taking his Standard Class; Joe Lau, 31, resident flint-knapper—his stone tools are things of beauty—currently ranked second in ninjutsu in the state of New Jersey; Mark Tollefson, 32, plant expert, wild-edible savant, also in charge of food; Tom McElroy as the Kid—at 23, youth personified—a thatch-haired Tom Sawyer with an aw-shucks charm that belies his sniper's aim with the throwing stick; and Ruth Ann Colby Martin, 26, resident Earth Mother, who, it seems, can do literally everything, and is polymathically, beatifically dexterous, capable, strong, beautiful, and funny—Joni Mitchell as Valkyrie. Even though Ruth Ann has already run the Sandy Hook marathon on the day we meet her, she fairly glows. Let me be clear: As an avowed homosexual, I make it a practice to seek out the amorous embraces of men over those of women, and yet I fall heavily for Ruth Ann.

That first evening, the entire class gathers in the barn for an orientation session in which we are advised of the school's general guidelines and given our first taste of the ethos of the place, summed up by Kevin pointing to a sign above the stage. It reads, "No Sniveling."

"This is a survival school, not a pampering school," Kevin adds. As if on cue to reiterate the rustic authenticity of the place, a bat that lives in the barn swoops down over our heads. We are reminded to hydrate regularly and properly, and to beware the poison ivy that grows rampant on the farm. "And if you are taking any sort of medication to regulate your moods," Joe tells us, "we request that you stay on that medication while you're here."

All of the instructors chime in, in unison, their voices weary with hard-won experience: "*We wouldn't say it if it wasn't important.*"

Finally, we are warned about ticks and their dreaded Lyme disease. We are to check for the small black dots twice a day all over our bodies, particularly in those dark, warm, hairy places ticks apparently love. A proper self-scrutiny is demonstrated by one of the (clothed) volunteers, who takes to the stage holding a small hand mirror from the shower stalls. He moves it over and around his torso and limbs like a fan dancer, looking into the glass the whole time. As the coup de grâce, he shows us how to check our least accessible, most unwelcome potential Tick Hideout. Turning his back to us, he bends over, bringing the mirror up between his legs. "Ta-da!" he says, holding a triumphantly abject position. Everyone applauds.

We meet the man himself the following morning in a welcome lecture of sorts. Tom Brown is handsome and in great shape. With his silvering hair neatly parted on the side, trim mustache, and penetrating blue eyes, he resembles nothing so much as the scary, casually hostile, and emasculating gym teachers of my youth.

I'm only half right. Brown, while blessed with deadpan comic timing and a Chautauqua preacher's instinct for the performative flourish, also exhibits a disquieting and ever-present bass note of dwindling patience. This weird duality is an acknowledged fact. Kevin has warned us that Brown is "part mother hen, part drill sergeant." For the uninitiated, it can make for a fairly bizarre ride, sometimes in the same sentence. He begins with a little flattery, praising our very presence.

"The terms 'family' and 'brother- and sisterhood' do not fall flippantly from our lips."

That's nice, we think, prematurely warmed to our cores.

He continues. "Even my parents—when they call, the calls are screened. I talk to them when I want to. But you," he indicates us, snapping back to sweetness, "you speak my language. When I say to one of you, 'Hey, I heard a tree call your name,' you'll know what I mean. You're more than eight-to-five. I'm an alien out there," he says, meaning society. "But not with you. You're the warriors."

Happily, the Standard Class is not boot camp. We are not hiked miles and miles, made to gather firewood for hours on end, or required to test our physical mettle in any appreciable way. It's more intellectually rigorous. The days are long, from six in the morning to past 11 at night, largely spent in lecture, with hands-on experience making up only about 20 percent of our time. During breaks—primarily the time set aside for meals—we practice our skills. The yard outside the barn buzzes with pre-industrial activity: people making cordage, lobbing their throwing sticks at a shooting gallery of plush-toy prey, foxwalking and stalking slowly across the grass, and trying to start fires with bowdrills.

This last one is our primary milestone. The squeak of turning spindles and the sweet smell of smoldering cedar, occasionally followed by the applause of whatever small group might be standing nearby, is a constant. I make three attempts before success—but when it comes! The thrill of sawing the drill back and forth, watching the accumulation of heated sawdust, now brown turning to black, the thin plume that rises, the gentle coaxing of the tiny coal into fragile, orange life, the parental swaddling of that ember into a downy tinder bundle, the ardent, almost amorous gentle blowing of air into same, the curling smoke, and the final, brilliant burst into flames in one's fingers—its atavistic high simply cannot be overstated.

Recapturing and maintaining a sense of wonder is at the very heart of the Tracker School philosophy, which is in part "to see the world through Grandfather's eyes." In other words, in a state of complete awareness, living in perfect harmony with nature, attuned to what is known in the Apache tradition as The Spirit That Moves Through All Things. This awareness will provide the key to tracking animals, both human and otherwise. "Grandfather didn't have two separate words for 'awareness' and 'tracking,'" Brown tells us one morning.

No doubt. But Brown's subsequent description of a brief, hundred-yard morning walk from his house to the barn is so strange and omniscient, he calls to mind Luther and Johnny Htoo, the chain-smoking 12-year-old identical twin leaders of the Karen people's insurgency movement in Burma, with their claims of invisibility and imperviousness to bullets: "There had been a fox. The hunting had not gone well. She emerged at 2:22 A.M. Her left ear twitches. Another step, now fear, and suddenly the feral cat appears. She's gone!" We won't be able to reach this level by week's end, but apparently, we are told frequently by both Brown and the instructors, we will be able to "track a mouse across a gravel driveway."

"Full survival," in Tom Brown's world, has nothing to do with the amassing of alarming quantities of canned food, a belief that the government is controlled by Hollywood's Jewish power elite, home schooling, CBS reality-based programming, or Charlton Heston. Full survival means naked in the wilderness: no clothes, no tools, no matches. It is both worst-case scenario and ultimate fantasy. Worst case being that the End Days have come upon us, the skies bleed red, the Four Horsemen of the Apocalypse have torn up the flower beds, and we must fend for ourselves and our loved ones. The fantasy being that we've gotten so sick and tired of our consumer society that we just park our cars by the side of the highway, step into the woods, and disappear. An oft-repeated joke throughout the week is, "Next Monday, when you go in to work and quit your jobs . . ."

Being in the woods, we are told, will become an experience akin to being locked in the Safeway overnight. "The main danger in full survival is gaining weight," Kevin avers. Nature is a bounteous paradise for those who play by the rules. That would be nature's rules, not the government's. Since much of the nation's remaining wilderness falls under the protective jurisdiction of the National Park Service—whose rangers don't look kindly on the wanton building of debris huts, and killing and eating the animals—much of what we learn turns out to be illegal in what remains of wild nature.

Case in point: animal skinning. Even picking up roadkill requires a permit. On Tuesday evening, for the lecture on skinning and brain-tanning, Ruth Ann comes in wearing a fringed buckskin dress that she made herself. She tells us the story of coming upon a roadkill buck while taking a much-needed break from writing college papers. My immediate reaction the entire week to anything Ruth Ann tells me is eagerness and a wish to try whatever it is she is proposing. When she tells us how to slit the animal down the middle, and then to cut around the anus and genitals, and then to pull them through from inside the body cavity, I think, regretfully, "I wish I had a dead animal's anus and genitals to cut around and pull through its body cavity."

I almost get my wish. She dons a pair of rubber gloves, leaves the barn, and comes back bearing a very dead road-killed groundhog. It has already been gutted and the fur pulled down from the hind legs to just below the rib cage. She hangs it on a nail by its Achilles tendons. Grabbing hold of the pelt, instructor Tom McElroy—the Kid—pulls, using his entire body weight. Groundhogs, as it turns out, have a great deal of connective tissue. There is a ripping, Velcro-like sound as the fur comes down. McElroy briefly loses his grip and the wet animal jerks on its nail, spraying students in the front row with droplets of groundhoggy fluid. The bat flutters around the barn throughout.

Next comes the tanning. Almost nothing is better at turning rawhide into supple leather than the lipids in an animal's own brain, worked into the skin like finger paint. A further, utterly beautiful economy of nature is the fact that every single animal has just enough brains to tan its own hide. Ruth Ann made her own wedding dress from unsmoked buckskin, as well as her husband's wedding shirt. She has brought them to the lecture to show us. I expect her to look rough-hewn, disinhibited, and slightly tacky—like Cher—but when she takes the dress out of the box and holds it up against herself, it is lovely: soft, ivory, and impeccably constructed. My crush is total.

But there will be time for infatuation tomorrow. It is getting late, and as happens every night, my rage starts to set in around 10:45 when people refuse to stop asking questions. I'm desperate to get to bed, having concluded my approximately two and a half hours' worth of obsessively running to the can during breaks—prophylaxis against a groggy stumble through Tent City to the Porta-Johns in the middle of the freezing-cold night. A small cadre of exhausted fugitives has already disappeared, heading back to their tents slowly and silently, without flashlights. I join them.

Awareness starts small. Only when we understand the many mysteries that lie within the earth's tiniest, seemingly mundane details will we be able to track animals or people. "Awareness is the doorway to the spirit, but survival is the doorway to the earth. If you can't survive out there naked and alone, then you're an alien," Brown says one morn-ing, gaining volume as he goes. "You think the earth is going to talk to someone who is not one of her children?" he yells.

My guess is no. To that end, we are taken out to a meadow over-grown with heavy grasses, garlic mustard, and wild burdock, a place known as Vole City for its large population of small rodents. We each lie down and examine an area no larger than a square foot, digging down, exploring.

My classmates look very idyllic and French Impressionist, scattered about here and there, supine in the sunlight, lost in contemplative investigation. Myself, I sit up, terrified at the prospect of finding anything, especially a vole. The instructor shows me how to root around just underneath the grass to find their ruts. I use a stick to gingerly push aside the stalks and turn over the debris, picking out the dull sheen of a slug here, the progress of a tiny worm there. Thankfully, no voles. Warming to my task, I suddenly spy—dark, wet, and gray against the fresh green of a blade of grass—the unmistakable articulation of amphibian digits, a hand span no bigger than this semicolon; it is connected to a tiny amphibian arm, connected to a tapered amphibian head the size of a peppercorn. The gleaming, dead eye catches the sunlight. My heart in my mouth, I call the instructor back over and show him. He picks up the tiny sprig with the half-eaten salamander still perched on it and holds it four inches from his mouth, enumerating the various classifications of the creature: the coloring, the reticulations, the patterns, the species. The instructor tries, God bless him, to draw me into a Socratic dialogue, asking me questions about what I've observed. He points to the chewed-out underside of the demi-lizard. "What kind of teeth marks made those cuts? Are the edges scalloped? Look at the gnaw marks. That's a great find," he concludes, patting me on the back.

I show my salamander to those working near me in the field, and they show me what they've uncovered. I feign interest in one woman's small mound of unidentifiable animal scat. But we both know the truth: My corpse makes her find look like, well, a pile of shit. For a brief moment, I am Big Man in Vole City.

The instructor's matter-of-fact treatment of the dead salamander, the complete lack of any "poor little guy" moral component to its demise, speaks to what makes the Tracker philosophy unique. There is none of that falsely benign conception of nature as friendly, inherently good, tame, and prettified. Aldous Huxley, in his essay "Wordsworth in the Tropics," assails what he calls the Anglicanization of nature, the cozy revisionism of a force that is intrinsically alien and inhospitable: "It is fear of the labyrinthine flux and complexity of phenomena . . . fear of the complex reality driving [us] to invent a simpler, more manageable, and, therefore, consoling fiction."

At Tom Brown's Tracker School, there is a clear-eyed acknowledgment that things eat and get eaten. Ruth Ann, in telling us of the year she lived in the Pine Barrens in a house she made entirely by hand with cedar walls and a debris roof, gets straight to the point. "Whatever came into my house, I ate," she says. "Mice? We just threw 'em in the fire, burned the hair off, and ate them whole. They just taste like meat, and there's something to be said for that added crunch."

She's not being heartless; in fact, she's the very opposite. For every skill we are taught, whether it's harvesting plants, using our bowdrills, skinning an animal, or gathering forest debris, the first step in our instruction is always a moment of thanksgiving for the trees, the spirit of fire, the groundhog, the water. It's a strange adjustment to have to make, at first. I am not proud to admit that there was a moment at 5:30 A.M. on the fourth day of class when, serving on cook crew, I stood bleary-eyed with exhaustion—having only gotten to bed some five hours earlier because of a late-night lecture on wild edibles—and seriously considered killing the guy who led us in a 15-minute thanksgiving that included complimenting the rising sun for being "just the perfect distance away from us." There are worse things than acknowledging a continuum and connection between all things and staying mindful and grateful of our place therein, but it can be a hard concept to swallow before the coffee hits the system.

Even wide awake there are moments of fuzzy logic in this theory of interconnectivity. Kevin, our elder statesman, explains that the Apache tradition of being thankful to the prey will also result in a willing acquiescence on the part of the hunted. "Something that gives its life for your benefit does so with gladness, if you are humble," he intones. Isn't it pretty to think so. Ascribing complicit suicidal motives to the rabbit who licks the peanut butter from a deadfall bait stick—no matter how self-effacingly daubed on—seems a tad Wordsworthian to me.

But such doubts become ever fewer as the week progresses. From about Thursday on, the home stretch of the course, spirits are high. Most of us have gotten fire, and in a brilliant bit of Pavlovian pedagogy, the food improved markedly after the outdoor cooking demonstration. Despite the staff's urging us not to take what we are told at face value, to go home and prove them right or prove them wrong, we're all pretty jazzed and itching to head out into nature. That said, among the people I talk to there is also a growing skepticism about Brown himself. It has nothing to do with his credibility, the veracity of his life story, or even the purity of purpose of the Tracker School. Unfortunately, it's personal: Brown's drill sergeant persona thoroughly throttles his mother hen. As pleasant as he may be just after breakfast—and he frequently is sunny, sprightly, and very funny—if he addresses us after sunset, there is a darkness in him and a potential for ire that is frankly terrifying.

In one evening lecture, he talks about the necessity for us to "take bigger pictures," to see more of the world through our wide-angle vision, to sense things before actually seeing them. "Instead of going click, click, click," he minces, "go CLICK! CLICK! CLICK!" he suddenly roars. A few people actually flinch. Later on, in a moment meant to chide us for the persistence of our citified tunnel vision, he tells us that he has been observing us unseen from a perch on top of the tool shed. As we make our way to bed, we watch our backs, scanning our surroundings for heretofore unnoticed surveillance. One young man asks the group softly, "You guys ever see *Apocalypse Now?*"

It's too bad that Brown the Personage has this effect on some people, because when I interview Brown the Person on Friday afternoon, the next-to-last day of class, he turns out to be a nice, intelligent guy with an undeniably noble and admirable mission in life. "It would be my dream to go back into the bush and live and never have to face another aspect of society," he tells me as we sit at the kitchen table in front of a stone fireplace. "But that's not my vision, that's my dream. My vision is to reach as many people as I possibly can." Still, he remains adamant about not franchising the Tracker School despite huge enrollment. (Before Standard Classes swelled to close to 100 people, the waiting list was six years.)

By the time I meet him, though, my disenchantment has become fairly entrenched. It doesn't help that Kevin escorts me into the modest house that Brown shares with his second wife, Debbie, 33, and their two young children—and doesn't leave, joining Tom McElroy, who is sitting in a chair, weaving a jute bag on a small circular loom. They crack jokes, weigh in with opinions, engage in quiet conversations with one another; the phone rings; they pour themselves coffee. Pretty soon I realize I've come to the teachers' lounge.

Or is it a convocation of disciples? I ask Brown about the cult of personality that seems to be part of the Standard Class.

"Oh, I try to get rid of that real quick," he says. "I tell people right off, 'Don't thank me, thank Grandfather.' I'm a poor example. I am nobody's guru." Brown talks about how he, Kevin, Ruth Ann, and the crew have to make sure to keep "Tracker groupies"—those overenthusiastic few who try to volunteer just a little too often—at a healthy distance. "Boy, this would be very easy to turn into a cult, big-time," he admits, "and I just will not allow it to happen. That's the last thing I want to happen."

Noted. And yet, in almost every lecture, there is the requisite prefatory story from Brown's life: "When Tom was 12 years old, Grandfather told him, 'This is the year you will provide me with meat . . .'" The accrual of personal detail forms a gospel of sorts, and anecdotes are delivered in a hortatory, liturgical style. Granted, the stories are told to show the wisdom of Stalking Wolf, not Tom Brown, but the reflected glory of playing Boswell to Grandfather's Johnson (a term straight out of a traveling salesman joke) clearly has its attractions.

Attractions not callously exploited, it seems. There is no line of Tom Brown sportswear, no exhortation from Brown that I buy anything while I am there, that I "Think Different." At a very manageable 600 bucks for a week of food and instruction, the Tracker School is not the enterprise of the career opportunist. In person, Brown is not only not power-mad, but he comes across as almost as nice as one of his instructors.

I leave the house fairly won over. I return to Tent City and walk out into the field to gaze at the sun, now lowering in the late afternoon sky. I find one of my classmates standing in the grass in the honeyeyed light, enjoying a water bottle full of herbal tea. We stand there amiably and peacefully, mutually imbued with the soy milk of human kindness. He holds out the bottle of amber liquid, offering it to me, and says, "Rum?"

Our last supper is one of our own harvesting. I'm on burdock detail, digging the rough, brown, footlong roots out of the red clay of a nearby field with a fellow student. Back at the cooking shed in the main yard, all 90 of us spend an hour or so cleaning, scraping, and slicing. I have never had a meal so Edenic in its profusion and beauty: a salad of chickweed, violet flowers, pennycress, and wild onions; a stir-fry of burdock, dandelion, nettles, and wintercress buds; dandelion flower fritters; garlic mustard pesto over whole-wheat pasta (store-bought— cut us some slack); nettle soup; and spicebush tea. We are each given a trout to gut, wrap in burdock leaves, and place in the fire. After six days here, I approach this task with a strange relish. It is the best fish I have ever eaten.

The grand finale of the Standard is a nighttime sweat lodge. I generally try to avoid pitch-dark, infernally hot enclosures, but now that Brown is my new best friend I find his preamble so avuncular and sweet that I almost consider it. He tells us we are to enter in a clockwise direction, leaving the area behind him free for those among us who suffer claustrophobia. "The minute you want to get out, just say so and we'll open the doors," he proclaims. "I won't love you any less."

I resolve to do it until he cedes the floor to Joe Lau, the ninjutsu expert, who reads us the guidelines. When I hear "crawl in on your hands and knees," I realize that there is not Xanax enough in the world to make me enter the low, round, straw-covered structure. The other rules include taking off all metal jewelry that doesn't sit directly against your skin as it can heat up, swing back, and burn you pretty badly. And then there's the final admonition: "You are absolutely forbidden to pass wind in the sweat lodge," says Joe. "*We wouldn't say it if it wasn't important.*"

The students assemble in their bathing suits, and there is something strange and primal about this nearly naked crowd in the moonlight. Their progress into the lodge is slow, and it takes a while for everyone to crawl in. I can hear Brown beginning his incantatory singing.

I rise early on the last morning. I'm almost the only student awake. I ask if there's anything I can do, and one of the volunteers asks me to build up the fire. "Well, how the hell am I supposed to do that?" I think to myself. Almost as quickly, I realize I know precisely how to do that, and much more. I have never taken in more information in one week in my life. Can I track a mouse across a gravel driveway? I

couldn't track a mouse across a cookie sheet spread with peanut butter, but that's no matter. Despite Kevin's recantation in his final wrap-
up, when he begs us, *"Don't* quit your jobs, *don't* make any radical
decisions for the next three months, *don't* trash your relationships."
("How many of us did that?" Ruth Ann stage-whispers), I can't help
feeling like I could if I needed to, and survive. Lavishly.

Another student gives me a lift to the bus station. I count the road-
kills on the shoulder of the highway along the way. "I could do something with that," I think. "And that. And that." I resist the temptation
to ask my driver to pull over and let me out, so that I may part the
trees and step through, letting the branches close behind me as I keep
walking, until I can no longer be seen from the road.

October 2000

The Whale
Hunters

SEBASTIAN JUNGER

The last living harpooner wakes to the sound of wind. It has been blowing for two weeks now, whipping up a big ugly sea, ruining any chance of putting out in the boat. On this strong, steady wind, the northeast trades, European slave ships rode to the New World bringing 15 million Africans across the Atlantic. One of their descendants now creeps through his house in the predawn gloom, wishing the wind would stop.

The man's name is Athneal Ollivierre. He is six feet tall, 74 years old, as straight and strong as a dock piling. His hair rises in an ash-gray column, and a thin wedge of mustache suggests a French officer in the First World War. On his left leg, there's the scar of a rope burn that went right down to the bone. His eyes, bloodshot from age and the glare of the sun, focus on a point just above my shoulder and about 500 miles distant. In the corner of his living room rests a 20-pound throwing iron with a cinnamon-wood shaft.

Ollivierre makes his way outside to watch the coming of the day. The shutters are banging. It's the dry season; one rainfall and the hills will be so covered with poui flowers that it will look like it just snowed. Shirts hang out to dry on the bushes in front of his house, and a pair of hump-back jawbones forms a gateway beyond which sprawls the rest of his world: seven square miles of volcanic island that drop steeply into a turquoise sea. This is Bequia, one of 32 islands that make up the southern Caribbean nation of St. Vincent and the Grenadines. Friendship Bay curves off to the east, and a new airport, bulldozed across the reefs, juts off to the west. More and more tourists and cruise ships have been coming to Bequia, the planes buzzing low, the gleaming boats anchoring almost nightly in the bay, but at the moment that matters very little to Ollivierre: He's barefoot in the tropical grass, squinting across the water at a small disturbance in the channel. Through binoculars it turns out to be a wooden skiff running hard across the channel for the island of Mustique. It emerges, disappears, emerges again behind a huge green swell.

"Bequia men, they brave," he says, shaking his head. He speaks in a patois that sounds like French spoken with an Irish brogue. "They brave too much."

Ollivierre hunts humpback whales from a 27-foot wooden sailboat called the *Why Ask*. As far as he's concerned, his harpooning days are over, but he's keeping at it long enough to train a younger man, 43-year-old Arnold Hazell, to do it. Otherwise the tradition, and the last remnant of the old Yankee whaling industry, will die with him. When they go out in pursuit of a whale, Ollivierre and his five-man crew row through the surf of Friendship Bay and then erect a sail that lets them slip up on whales undetected. Ollivierre stands in the bow of his boat and hurls a harpoon into the flank of an animal that's 500 times as heavy as he is. He has been knocked unconscious, dragged under, maimed, stunned, and nearly drowned. When he succeeds in taking a whale, schools on Bequia are let out, businesses are closed, and a good portion of the 4,800 islanders descends on the whaling station to watch and help butcher, clean, and salt the whale.

"It's the only thing that bring joy to Bequia people," says Ollivierre, a widower whose only son has no interest in whaling. "Nobody don't be in their homes when I harpoon a whale. I retired a few years ago, but the island was lackin of the whale, and so I go back. Now I'm training Hazell. When I finish with whalin, I finish with the sea."

When a whale is caught, it's towed by motorboat to a deserted cay called Petit Nevis and winched onto the beach; the winch is a rusty old hand-powered thing bolted to the bedrock. Butchering a 40-ton animal is hard, bloody work—work that has been condemned by environmentalists around the world—and the whalers offer armloads of fresh meat to anyone who will help them. Some of the meat is cooked right there on the beach (it tastes like rare roast beef) and the rest is kept for later. The huge jawbones are sold to tourists for around a thousand dollars, and the meat and blubber are divided up equally among the crew. Each man sells or gives his share away as he sees fit—"Who sell, sell; who give, give," as Ollivierre says. The meat goes for $2 a pound in Port Elizabeth.

If there is a species that exemplifies the word *whale* in the popular mind, it's probably the humpbacks that Ollivierre hunts. These are the whales that breach for whale-watching boats and sing for marine biologists. Though nearly 90 percent of the humpback population has been destroyed in the last hundred years, at least half of the remaining 11,000 humpbacks spend the summer at their feeding grounds in the North Atlantic and then migrate south in December. They pass the winter mating, calving, and raising their young in the warm Caribbean waters, and when the newborns are strong enough—they grow a hundred pounds a day—the whales journey back north.

It is by permission of the International Whaling Commission, based in Cambridge, England, that Ollivierre may take two humpbacks a year. In 1986 a worldwide moratorium was imposed on all commercial whaling, but it allowed "aboriginal people to harvest whales in perpetuity, at levels appropriate to their cultural and nutritional requirements." A handful of others whale—in Greenland, Alaska, and Siberia—but Ollivierre is the only one who still uses a sailboat and a hand-thrown harpoon. These techniques were learned aboard Yankee whaling ships a hundred years ago and brought back to Bequia without changing so much as an oarlock or clevis pin.

"You came and put a piece of your history here, and it's still here today," says Herman Belmar, a local historian who lives around the corner from Ollivierre. Belmar is a quiet, articulate man whose passion is whaling history. He is trying to establish a whaling museum on the island. "Take the guys from Melville's *Moby Dick* and put them in Athneal's boat, and they'd know exactly what to do."

* * *

One day at dawn I drive over to meet Ollivierre. His house is a small, whitewashed, wood-and-concrete affair on the side of a hill, surrounded by a hedge. Except for the whalebone arch, it's indistinguishable from any other house on the island. I let myself through a little wooden gate and walk across his front yard, past an outboard motor and a vertebra the size of a bar stool. It's mid-February, whaling season, and Ollivierre is seated on a bench looking out across the channel. I stick out my hand; he takes it without meeting my eye.

By Bequia standards, Ollivierre is a famous man. Many people have stood before him asking for his story, but still I'm a little surprised by his reaction. Not a word, not a smile—just the trancelike gaze of someone trying to make out a tiny speck on the horizon. I stand there uncomfortably for a few minutes and finally ask what turns out to be the right question: "Could I see your collection?"

If you wander around Port Elizabeth for any length of time, a taxi driver will inevitably make you the offer: "Come meet the real harpooner! Shake his hand, see his museum!" A museum it's not, but Ollivierre has filled the largest room of his house with bomb guns, scrimshaw, and paintings. The paintings are by a local artist and commemorate some of Ollivierre's wilder exploits—ATHNEAL DONE STRIKE DE WHALE, reads one. As Ollivierre discusses his life, he slowly becomes more animated and finally suggests that I walk up to the hilltop behind his house to meet the rest of the crew.

A path cuts up the hill past another low wood-and-concrete house. Split PVC pipe drains the roof and empties into a big concrete cistern, which is almost dry. (Every drop of drinking water on Bequia must be caught during the rainy season.) At the top of the hill are some wind-bent bushes and a thatch-and-bamboo sun-break that tilts southward toward the sea. Four men sit beneath it, looking south across the channel. They gnaw on potatoes, pass around binoculars, suck on grass stems, watch the sky get lighter. In the distance is a chain of cays that used to be the rim of a huge volcano, and seven miles away is the island of Mustique. When the wind permits, the whalers sail over there to look out for humpbacks.

"Hello. Athneal sent me," I offer a little awkwardly.

The men glance around—there's been some bad press about whaling, even the threat of a tourist boycott, and everyone knows this is a delicate topic. An old man with binoculars motions me over. "We can tell whatever you want," he says, "but we can't do anything without Dan, de cop'm."

After Ollivierre, Dan Hazell, who bears some distant relation to Arnold Hazell, is the senior member of the crew. He's the captain, responsible for maneuvering the boat according to Ollivierre's orders. A young man named Eustace Kydd says he'll round up Dan and a couple of others and meet me at a bar in Paget Farm. Paget Farm is a settlement by the airport where the whalers live: ramshackle houses, dories pulled up on rocks, men drinking rum in the shade. Most of the men on the island make their living net-fishing. They go out before dawn and one crewman strings the nets along the ocean bottom—30 feet down with just two lungfuls of air, but it's a living. Later, the crew hauls in the catch, hoping to find snapper, kingfish, and bonita caught up in the twine.

I nod and walk back down the hill. Ollivierre is still in his yard, glassing the channel and talking to a young neighborhood man who has dropped by. They give me a glance and keep talking. The wind has dropped; the sun is thundering impossibly fast out of the equatorial sea.

Unfortunately for Ollivierre, the antiquity of his methods has not exempted him from controversy. First of all, he has been known to take mother-calf pairs, a practice banned by the IWC. In addition, Japan started giving St. Vincent and several neighboring islands tens of millions of dollars in economic aid after the imposition of an international moratorium on whaling in 1986. The aid was ostensibly to develop local fisheries, but American environmental groups charged that Japan was simply buying votes on the IWC. The suspicions were well founded: St. Vincent, Dominica, and Grenada have received substantial amounts of money from Japan, and all have voted in accordance with Japan's whaling interests over and over again.

Things came to a head last year when the IWC introduced a proposal to create an enormous whale sanctuary around Antarctica. The sanctuary would offer shelter to whales as the worldwide moratorium was phased out in keeping with growing whale populations. The

Massachusetts-based International Wildlife Coalition, headed by Dan Morast, threatened to organize a tourist boycott against any country that voiced opposition to the proposal, and in the end only Japan voted against it. St. Vincent, Dominica, and Grenada abstained from the vote, and the South Seas Sanctuary was passed.

But the controversy over Bequia is more emotional than a vote. Ollivierre has become the focal point for dozens of environmental lobbyists, for whom everything he does is drenched in symbolism. First there was Ollivierre's flip-flop: In 1990 he announced his retirement, but a year later he was back at it, sitting on his hilltop, looking out for whales. It was a move that angered environmentalists who thought they'd seen the last of whaling on Bequia. The reaction was compounded by Ollivierre's efforts to sell the island of Petit Nevis, the tiny whaling station that has belonged to his family for three generations; a Japanese businessman's offer of $5 million was an outrage. Of course, Ollivierre's personal impact on the humpback population is negligible. Morast's point seems to be more conceptual: that the land sale is just another form of bribery to encourage the St. Vincent representative on the IWC to vote for whaling.

And contrary to Morast's view, Ollivierre would love to retire. His joints ache, his vision is clouded, he's an old man. Harpooning is dangerous, and apprentices are hard to come by. Several years ago he trained his nephew, Anson Ollivierre, to harpoon, but Anson branched out on his own before even bloodying his hands. Now he's building his own whaleboat, and Ollivierre fears Anson will get his whole crew killed. So this year Ollivierre tried again, taking on Arnold Hazell. Hazell's great-grandfather crewed for Ollivierre's great-grandfather, and now, a hundred years later, the relationship continues. Since there are no whales to practice on, Hazell just hangs out at Ollivierre's house, listens to the old stories, soaks up the lore.

When Hazell has killed his first whale, Ollivierre will retire. And the antiwhaling community will have a new face upon which to hang its villain's mask.

A short time after meeting with Ollivierre and his crew, I drive down to Paget Farm. On the way I pass a new fish market, paid for by the

Japanese government as part of a $6 million aid package. According to the Japanese, it's a no-strings-attached token of affection for the Bequia fishermen. Past the market I turn onto a narrow cement road that grinds up a desperately steep hillside. At one end of the road is the sky; at the other end is the sea. The appointed bar is a one-story cement building halfway up the hill. I park, chock the wheels, and wander inside. It's as clean and simple inside as out: a rough wooden counter, a half-dozen chairs, no tables, a big fan. The walls are a turquoise color that fills the room with cool coral-reef light. A SAVE THE WHALES poster hangs in tatters on one wall, and a monumental woman opens soft drinks behind the counter. Five men are ranged at the far end of the room. They are dressed in T-shirts and baggy pants, and one has a knife in his hand. Captain Dan, too shy to speak, just looks out the window into the midday heat. Arnold Hazell greets me with a smile.

"In Bequia we don't have much opportunity like you in de States," he begins. "We grew up on de sea an live from de sea. Even if we don't cotch a whale for de next ten years, it will be good just to be whalin. Just to keep de heritage up. Japanese an Norwegians—they killin whales by the thousands, an those people could afford to do something else. They have oil, they have big industry, they have a better reason to stop." He pauses. "You know, we can put the boat out, we can talk to you, you can take snaps, but it a whole day's work for us. We need something back."

Luckily, I've been told about this ahead of time. It's a tourist economy—the sunshine, the water, the beaches, it's all for sale—and the whalers see no reason why they should be any different. A young man in dreadlocks steps in quietly and leans against the bar. He listens with vague amusement; he's heard this all before.

"A few years ago a French crew come here," says Eustace. "They come to make a film. They offer us thousands of dollars; they prepared to pay that. But we say no because we know they makin so much more on the film. Why should we work an they make all the money?"

After this statement, negotiations proceed slowly. Some careful wording, a few ambiguous phrases, and finally an agreement is reached: We'll meet at Friendship Bay tomorrow before dawn. "And," says Captain Dan, his eyes never wavering from the horizon, "you'll see the *Why Ask* fly."

In the distant past, most of the Caribbean islands were inhabited by the peace-loving Arawak people. Very little is known about them, because most were killed, and the rest were driven from the islands, by the Caribs, whose name comes from the Arawak word for "cannibal." Unfortunately for the Caribs, Columbus discovered their bloody little paradise within years of their ascendancy, and 200 years later most of them were gone as well. Bequia—dry, tiny, and poor—was one of their last hideouts, and when the French finally settled here, they found people of mixed Carib-African ancestry hiding in the hills. The Africans, as it turned out, had swum ashore from a wrecked slave ship, the *Palmira,* in 1675.

France ceded Bequia to Britain in 1763, and inevitably the Black Caribs, as they were called, were put to work on the local sugar and cotton plantations. Only free labor could coax a profit from such poor soil, and when the British abolished slavery in 1838, Bequia's economy fell apart. The local elite fled, and islanders reverted to farming and fishing—and eventually whaling—to survive.

The first Bequian to kill a whale was Bill Wallace, a white landowner's son who went to sea at age 15 and returned 20 years later with a New England bride and an armful of harpoons. As a child on Bequia he'd watched humpbacks spouting offshore during the winter months, and he didn't see why boats couldn't put out from the beach to kill them. Crews could keep lookout from the hilltops and then man their boats when they saw a spout. He recruited the strongest young men he could find and established the first whaling station on Friendship Bay in 1875.

There was nothing benevolent in Wallace; he was a tough old salt who was essentially out for his own gain. He'd lost his father shortly before leaving the island and had grown up in an industry that was considered brutal even by the brutal standard of the times. Whaling crews were at sea for three or four years at a stretch, under conditions that would have made prisoners of war balk. Captains had absolute authority over their men, and some were known to demonstrate it by occasionally whipping one to death. The crews themselves were no blessing, often largely composed of criminals, drunks, and fresh-faced kids just off the farm. It's easy to guess whose habits, after four years at sea, rubbed off on whom.

The only thing that kept such an enterprise together was the unspeakable danger that these men faced and the financial rewards of making it through alive. The largest whales in the world—blue whales—weigh 190 tons and measure up to 100 feet long. They have hearts as big as oil drums; the males have penises nine feet long. When scared, the first thing they do is thrash the water with their flukes. Enraged whales have been known to rush headlong at three-masted ships and sink them; the chase boats that put out after whales were light, fast, and no more than 30 feet long.

Harpooned whales often bolted at such speed that the rope would catch fire as it ran out through the chocks. A coil in the line could yank a man's arm off or pull him overboard. Sometimes the whale would sound and then come up through the bottom of the boat at full speed. A slack line was always a bad sign; the men could do little but peer anxiously into the depths and try to see from what angle their death would come. Inexperienced whalers were known to jump right out of the boat at the first sight of a whale. Others, intoxicated by terror, whaled until they grew old or were killed.

Four in the morning, the air soft as silk. I'm speeding along the dark roads in a rented jeep, slowing down just enough to survive the speed bumps. The northern part of Bequia is almost completely uninhabited, steep, scrub-choked valleys running up to cliffs of black volcanic rock. Shark Bay, Park Bay, Brute Point, Bullet. Between the headlands are white-sand beaches backed by cow pastures and coconut groves. Land crabs rustle through the dead vegetation, and enormous spiders spindle up tree trunks. The road passes a smoldering garbage dump, climbs the island's central ridge, and then curves into Port Elizabeth. The only signs of life at this hour are a few dockworkers loading a rusted inter-island cargo ship under floodlights. The road claws up a hill and then crests the ridge above Lowerbay—Lowby, as it's called—and starts down toward Friendship.

A dry wind is blowing through the darkness, and the surf against Semples Cay and St. Hilaire Point can be heard a mile away. I pull off the road near Ollivierre's house and feel my way down a steep set of cement stairs to the water's edge. The surf smashes white against the outer reefs; everything else is the blue-black of the tropics just before dawn. The whalers arrive ten minutes later, as promised, moving single file down the beach. They stow their gear without a word and put their shoulders to the gunwales of the *Why Ask;* she rolls heavily over four cinnamon-wood logs and slips into the sea. The wind has abated enough to sail to the preferred lookout on Mustique; otherwise we'd have to make do with the hill above Ollivierre's.

Within minutes they're under way: Captain Dan at the tiller, Ollivierre up front, and Biddy Adams, Eustace, Arnold Hazell, and Kingsley Stowe amidships. They pull at the 18-foot oars, plunging into the surf. Once clear of the reef they step the mast, cinch the shrouds, becket the sprit and boom. They scramble to work within the awkward confines of the boat as Ollivierre barks orders from the bow.

The *Why Ask* is heartbreakingly graceful under sail, as much a creature of the sea as the animals she's designed to kill. She was built on the beach with the horizon as a level and Ollivierre's memory as a plan. Boatwrights have used such phrases as "lightly borne" and "sweet-sheared and buoyant" to describe whaleboats of the last century, and they apply equally to the *Why Ask.*

The boat quickly makes the crossing to Mustique, where the crew spends half the day on a hilltop overlooking the channel. With an older whaler named Harold Corea stationed above Ollivierre's house with a walkie-talkie, they have doubled the sweep of ocean they can observe. In addition they often get tips from fishermen, pilots, or people who just happen to look out their window at the right moment. These people are always rewarded with whale meat if the chase is successful.

In the early days, between 1880 and 1920, there were nine shore-whaling stations throughout the Grenadines, including six on Bequia, and together they surveyed hundreds of square miles of ocean. They'd catch perhaps 15 whales in a good year, a tremendous boon to the local economy. In 1920, 20 percent of the adult male population of Bequia was employed in the whaling industry.

Five years later all that changed; a Norwegian factory ship set up operation off Grenada and annihilated the humpback population within a year and a half. Almost no whales were caught by islanders between 1925 and 1948, and none at all were caught for eight years after that. The whaling stations folded one by one, and by the 1950s only the Ollivierre family was left. Today the humpback population has recovered slightly—the IWC now considers the species "vulnerable" rather than "endangered"—but sightings off Bequia are still rare. Last year the crew put out after a whale only once; so far this season they have yet to see a spout.

The boat returns from Mustique in the afternoon with nothing to report. The crew shrugs it off: Waiting is as much a part of whaling as throwing the harpoon.

On those lucky occasions when Ollivierre spots a whale from Mustique, he fixes its position in his mind, sails to the spot, and waits. If there's no wind, the crew is at the oars, pulling hard against oarlocks that have been lined with fabric to keep them quiet. Humpbacks generally dive for ten or 15 minutes and then come up for air; each time they do, Ollivierre works the boat in closer. The harpoon, protected by a wooden sheath, rests in a scooped-out section of the foredeck called the clumsy cleat; when the harpoon is removed, it fits the curve of Ollivierre's thigh perfectly.

The harpoon is heavy and brutally simple. A thick cinnamon-wood shaft has been dressed with an ax and pounded into the socket of a throwing iron. The head itself is made of brass and has been ground down to the edge of a skinning knife; it is mounted on a pivot and secured by a thin wooden shear pin driven through a hole. Upon impaling the whale, the pin breaks, allowing the head to toggle open at 90 degrees, catching deep in the flesh of the whale. It's a design that hasn't changed in 150 years. The harpoon is attached to a nine-fathom nylon tether, which in turn is tied—"bent," as Ollivierre says—to the manila mainline, which is 150 fathoms long. The line passes through a notch in the bow, runs the length of the boat, takes two wraps around the loggerhead, and is coiled carefully into a wooden tub. The loggerhead is a hefty wooden block that provides enough friction to keep the whale from running out the entire tub of rope.

When a whale is pulling the line, Eustace scoops seawater over the side and fills the tub—otherwise the friction will set the loggerhead on fire. Meanwhile, Ollivierre takes his position in the bow, delivering orders to Captain Dan in a low, harsh voice. Above all they must stay clear of the tail: It's powerful enough to launch a humpback clear out of the water and could obliterate the boat in a second. Ollivierre's leg is braced against the clumsy cleat, and the other men are wide-eyed at the gunwales, the rank smell of whale-vapor in their faces. The harpoon has been rid of its sheath, and Ollivierre holds it aloft as if his body has been drawn like a bow, right hand cupping the butt end, left hand supporting it like some kind of offering. You don't throw a harpoon; you drive it, unloading it downward with all your weight and strength the moment before your boat beaches itself— "wood to blackskin"—atop the whale.

"De whale make no sound at all when you hit it. It just lash de tail and it gone," says Ollivierre. "Dan let go of everything an put his two hands on de rope. De whale have to take de rope from him; he have to hold it down."

A struck whale gives a few good thrashes with its tail and then tries to flee. It is a moment of consummate chaos: the line screaming out through the bow chock, the crew trying to lower the mast, the helmsman bending the line around the smoking loggerhead. Some men freeze, and others achieve ultimate clarity. "After we harpoon it, that frightness, that cowardness go from me," says Harold Corea, who at 63 is one of the oldest members of the crew. "It all go away; I become brave, I get brave."

Brave or not, things can go very wrong. Around 1970—Ollivierre doesn't remember exactly when—a whale smacked the boat with a fluke, staving in the side and knocking Ollivierre out cold. When he came to, he realized that the rope had grabbed him and turned his leg into a loggerhead. It sawed down to bone in an instant, cauterizing the arteries as it went, and nearly ripped his hand in half. Ollivierre refused to cut the rope because he didn't want the whale to get away, but finally the barnacle-encrusted fluke severed it for him. The boat returned to shore, and Ollivierre walked up the beach unassisted, his tibia showing and his foot as heavy as cement. Two men on the beach fainted at the sight.

There is no such thing as an uneventful whale hunt; by definition it's either a disaster or almost one. As soon as the harpoon is fast in the whale, the crew drops the mast and Dan tightens up on the loggerhead to force the whale to tow the boat through the water, foredeck awash, men crammed into the stern, a 20-knot wake spreading out behind. Too much speed and the boat will go under; too much slack and the whale will run out the line. (There is one account of a blue whale that towed a 90-foot twin-screw chaser boat, its engines going full-bore astern, for 50 miles before tiring.) Every time the whale lets up, the crewmen put their hands on the line and start hauling it back in. The idea is to get close enough for Ollivierre to use either a hand lance or a 45-pound bomb gun, whose design dates back to the 1870s. It fires a shotgun shell screwed to a six-inch brass tube filled with powder that's ignited by a ten-second fuse. Ollivierre packs his own explosives and uses them with tremendous discretion.

The alternative to the gun is a light lance with a rounded head that doesn't catch inside the whale; standing in the bow, Ollivierre thrusts again and again until he finds the heart. "De whole thing is dangerous, but de going in and de killing of it is de most dangerous," he says. He's been known to leap onto the back of the whale and sit with his legs wrapped around the harpoon, stabbing. Sometimes the whale sounds, and Ollivierre goes down with it; if it goes too deep, he lets go and the crew pulls him back to the boat. When his lance has found the heart, dark arterial blood spouts out the blowhole. The huge animal stops thrashing, and its long white flippers splay outward. Two men go over the side with a rope and harpoon the head to tie up the mouth; otherwise water will fill the innards and the whale will sink.

As dangerous as it is, only one Bequian has ever lost his life in a whaleboat: a harpooner named Dixon Durham, who was beheaded by a whale's flukes in 1885. So cleanly was he slapped from the boat that no one else on board was even touched. The closest Ollivierre has come to being Bequia's second statistic was in 1992, when the line caught on a midship thwart and pulled his boat under. He and his crew were miles from Bequia, and no one was following them; Ollivierre knew that, without the boat, they would all drown. He grabbed the bow and was carried down into the quiet green depths. Equipment was rising up all around him: oars, ropes, wooden tubs. He hung on to the bow and clawed desperately for the knife at his belt. By some miracle the rope broke, and the whole mess—boat, harpoons, and harpooner— floated back up into the world.

Ollivierre found his VHF radio floating among the wreckage and called for help. Several days later, some fishermen in Guyana heard a terrible slapping on the mudflats outside their village and went to investigate. They found Ollivierre's whale stranded on the beach, beating the world with her flippers as she died.

The next day, Ollivierre, Hazell, and Corea are back up at the lookout, keeping an eye on the sea. Corea, who was partially crippled by an ocean wave at age 19, is one of the last of the old whalers. Hazell is the future of Bequia whaling, if there is such a thing. They sit on the hilltop all morning without seeing a sign. No one knows where the whales are. A late migration? A different route? Are there just no more whales?

After a couple of hours Ollivierre is ready to call it quits for the day. If anyone sees a spout, they can just run over to his house and tell him. More than anything he just seems weary—he's whaled for 37 years and fished up until a few years ago. Enough is enough. He says good-bye and walks slowly down the hill. Corea watches him go and scours the channel one more time.

Hazell squats on a rock in the shade with half his life still ahead of him. He is neither old nor young, a man caught between worlds, between generations. Down the hill is a scarred old man who's trying to teach him everything he knows; across the ocean is a council of nations playing tug-of-war with a 27-foot sailboat. Hazell would try to reconcile the two, if it were possible, but it's not. And so he's left with one simple task: to visualize what it will be like to face his first whale.

A long winter swell will be running. The sunlight will catch the spray like diamonds. He'll be in the bow with his thigh against the foredeck and the harpoon held high. The past and the future will fall away, until there are no politics, no boycotts, no journalists. There will be just one man with an ancient weapon and his heart in his throat.

October 1995

And Old Views Shall Be Replaced by New

MARK LEVINE

Heaven is a vast and frozen place, and the westernmost waters of what the Chinese call the River to Heaven seep from a still pond at the base of a glacier in the northern foothills of the Himalayas, four miles above the distant sea in a province inhabited by nomadic yak-herders and half-remembered political exiles. For its first 2,000 miles, the stream drops unrelentingly—an average of about eight feet per mile—and scours through the limestone cliffs of Tiger Leaping Gorge in a nine-mile-long waterfall that has the habit of quickly transporting whitewater adventurers to some better, drier afterlife. The river absorbs huge tributaries and swells across the broad "red basin" of Sichuan Province, and then it dives into a final stretch of sheer canyons whose forested walls are home to shrieking monkeys and whose muddy banks are populated by more sedate creatures—rice farmers and fishers and coal diggers and souvenir vendors—who even now are hastening to pack their belongings into grain sacks and straw baskets and to begin a long march toward new homes. These people don't need to be reminded to take a last good look at everything around them: river, mountains, villages, temples, funeral mounds. Not far downstream, where the mustard-brown water emerges from the last of China's mythologized Three Gorges, a great wall is being raised from north to south, and the current of the Yangtze River, flowing at 90,000 cubic yards per second, bearing prodigious amounts of silt and sewage and the occasional waterlogged corpse, will soon be turned back toward its faraway source more surely than a horde of invading Mongols.

I've climbed through swirling dust to an inauspicious cement platform that marks the prospective crest of this new great wall, a 26-million-ton slab of concrete that will rise as high as a 60-story building above the riverbed and span a mile and a quarter from shore to shore. I'm overlooking Sandouping, Hubei Province, former site of a waterside farming village and current site of what may be the largest industrial undertaking in the history of the world. From this height, the great turbid flow of the Yangtze seems to veer below like an afterthought, nearly obscured in a haze of dump trucks and cranes and hydraulic excavators and pyramids of gravel and barges weighted down with American-built bulldozers.

This is what national obsession looks like: the future home of the Three Gorges Dam, named in honor of the most revered 120-mile stretch of river canyon in China—an imposing landscape that is slated, very shortly, to suffer unredeemable alterations. A river will become a lake, forested hillsides will become slopes of waterlogged stumps, farmland and ancient stone villages will dissolve into blurred reminiscence, a ribbon of countryside—stretching a distance equal to that between Los Angeles and San Francisco—will find itself abandoned to the blades of 26 massive turbines and converted to beautiful invisible electricity.

For now, the dam gestates beneath the tundra of the sprawling construction site. Everywhere I look the skin of the earth has been removed, and what remains is gristle and pale fractured land. My escort, Shen Wenfu, a slight and overeager man of about 30 with a thick scar on his right hand, is a propaganda officer for the China Yangtze Three Gorges Project Development Corporation, a government-established agency charged with overseeing the grandiose venture, and he affects deep emotion at the sight of the blasted landscape. "Five years ago," Shen says, "there was nothing here, only mountains and villages. Now you see the temporary ship lock and the coffer dam and the diversion channel. I feel very proud."

A few plots of terraced farmland remain on the green upper hill-
sides, perched directly above the shredded mountain walls of the dam
site, and a dozen peasants can be seen bending in the fields in their
blue suits and straw hats, seemingly oblivious to the excavated world
below. The scene lends itself aptly to musings on oblivion, because
despite the enormity of the dam site, and despite the legion of 40,000
workers who will live and toil on the project until 2013, from my vantage point at this makeshift sentry tower the overwhelming impression
is that of unreality, as if I were looking at a papier-mâché model of a
disaster, one that a good rain could wash away. The sky is white and
the sundered hills are white and the valley below is potted with white
craters and even the gigantic earthmovers that totter everywhere on
six-foot tires seem hushed and far away. "This dam is a dream for the
Chinese people," an official at the project's headquarters told me, and
like a dream the endeavor is propelled forward by its own logic. Unreality pervades the phenomenon that is the Three Gorges Dam, from
the mock political debate that ensured approval of the $25 billion proj-
ect, to the headlines in official papers saying things like "River Project to Improve Environment," to the numbed response of close to two
million people who are already being uprooted from their riverside
homes with promises of the good life to come in shining hilltop cities
that have yet to be built.

The mountains surrounding the dam site have been transformed into
billboards encouraging support for the dam, as if the hills were advertising their own destruction. Workers dragging explosives along the
gravel-strewn riverbanks are urged, "Struggle for Two Months and All
Will Be Better." Tourists packing the decks of cruise ships drift through
the eerie concrete maw of the site and are reminded, "Be Proud of the
Three Gorges Dam." Though the Tang Dynasty poet Tu Fu spent a
few ailing years in the Three Gorges region during the eighth century,
current sloganeers don't have much time for poetic obliqueness. ("The
state is shattered; mountains and rivers remain," Tu Fu once noted,
wrongly.) Time is running out in the Three Gorges, and happily so for
the dam builders, since the dam is a project being run, in part, on a
tight symbolic timetable. Shen, my personal propagandist, checks his
Motorola pager, adjusts his Playboy belt-buckle, and points to a sign

counting down the few remaining days until "the closure of the main river channel," when a temporary dam will divert the current, expose the floor of the river, and enable work to begin in earnest on the permanent structure.

According to officials, you have until November 16 of this year to see what a great river looks like when it flows unimpeded. "In China," says Wang Rushu, a senior engineer with the Three Gorges Project Corporation, "we have two exciting events in 1997. First is the return of Hong Kong to the Motherland. And second is the closure of the Yangtze River," which is often referred to as China's Mother River. It's a big year for Mother in China, and the country's genuine celebratory spirit has everything to do with a feeling of shaking off the final remnants of colonial garb and asserting dominion over Chinese territory and Chinese nature. China isn't suffering any guilty Western-style retrenchment from its idealistic nation-building mission, and I'm often regarded, pityingly, as a visitor from the past come to marvel at the future. "Mr. Mark," says Shen, "go home and tell your people the truth about this great Chinese dam."

To track the ripple of enthusiasm created by the damming of the world's third-longest river, it's advisable to start your journey, as I did, hundreds of miles upstream of the dam site, in the blighted, tremulous heart of central China, where Chongqing, a gloriously decrepit city of 15 million, sprouts organically from the hills at the juncture of the Yangtze and Jialing rivers. If you want to enjoy the spectacle of blind men competing to shine your shoes for a nickel, if you want to refresh yourself beneath a perpetual rain that stings the skin and smells like sour diesel, Chongqing will not disappoint. Fifteen hundred miles from the Yangtze's destination at the East China Sea, Chongqing is optimistically slated to become the hub of rampant development in the heretofore inaccessible and "backward" interior of China. The closure of the Yangtze will back up the river's eastbound flow for about 400 miles, creating a placid, 575-foot-deep reservoir with the disarming name of Three Gorges Lake. In a magical liquid jolt, the seedy river harbor of Chongqing will be reborn as a gleaming waterfront metropolis, and ocean liners will glide effortlessly across an artificial basin 25 miles longer than Lake Superior.

I could feel it collecting on my tongue, like the grit in Chongqing's breeze: the intimation that a cleansing flood is spreading inland and that this town, alive with desperate energy, is a chosen site awaiting the fulfillment of its destiny. Construction cranes dot the horizon and vacant skyscrapers hover over the chaos of the city below. A brand-new department store displays washing machines and big-screen TVs and a full stock of other dust-coated amenities that no ordinary Chinese could possibly afford. A man squats in an alley over a pail of blood, slicing eels, and a crowd of other men, clasping worn tools, waits for offers of odd day-jobs. Most foreigners stay in Chongqing only long enough to book passage on one of the tour boats whose three-day trips downstream through the Three Gorges originate here. A tiny old woman in a blue sailor's suit grabs my hand in the newly built ferry terminal and urges me, in a hoarse whisper, to reserve my berth while I still have a chance. "The river," she says, "is crowded with people who wish to see the Gorges before they disappear."

In the Chinese consciousness, the Three Gorges of the Yangtze evoke something like the physical awe of the Grand Canyon, crossed with the mysticism of a few thousand years of ornate history and legend. The Gorges are hallowed ground in China, the virtually impassable boundary between modern coastal regions and provincial outposts like Chongqing. In the Gorges, it's said, the broad, wallowing sweep of the river narrows to a perilous 35 feet at times, deepens, and pounds through a corridor of limestone cliffs 3,000 feet high that rise from the depths like massive stone bulwarks. The mute geography has survived wars and revolutions and famines and floods, but the Three Gorges Dam is designed to overpower the landscape.

I board the passenger ferry *Yao Hua*—"China Sunshine"—along with 700 Chinese, three German backpackers, and a psychologist from Buffalo, and since this is tourism Chinese style, dockside vendors are selling fried chickens' feet and roasted rabbits with teeth intact, and a barefoot woman scampers along hawking pickled eggs. Most of the Chinese passengers, who share rooms of eight wooden bunks, are already absorbed in card games and gambling before the boat leaves the dock. The harbor is cluttered with cruise ships jockeying for position among barges heaped with coal, and a fisherman works strenuously with a bamboo pole to unmoor his crudely patched rowboat from a sandbar. He's still quite stuck when the good ship *China Sunshine* pulls up anchor and discharges a clot of coal dust and sets off through the China smog.

The mood on the ship is jubilant. Only recently have a tiny percentage of Chinese achieved sufficient prosperity to head out on the tourist trail, and most of those I speak with on board—businessmen, minor government officials, retired factory workers—tell me this is their first vacation away from their hometowns. A travel agent from Henan Province who has named himself Wolf is accompanying a group of chipper tourists in orange baseball caps, and he provides me with an expert recitation of the benefits of the Three Gorges Dam: downstream flood control; the generation of enough electricity—16 nuclear reactors' worth—to provide a full tenth of China's current energy needs; improved navigation of the former river. On a more personal note, Wolf lets on that the common notion that the Three Gorges will begin to "disappear" behind the dam's floodwaters come November has created a lucrative tourism frenzy. (An internal memo from a state security agency refers to the enthusiasm as Three Gorges Fever.) In truth, Wolf admits, the upcoming channel closure, dramatic as it is, marks only an early step in an alleged 16-year process of gradual flooding. Where the Three Gorges Dam is concerned, though, the distinction between fact and symbolism has become extremely watery.

One after another the passengers strike stiff poses on deck as their relatives snap pictures against the backdrop of rolling pine-covered hills and rich burgundy soil. The broad banks of the river, covered with softball-size rocks, host an incongruous blend of barefoot fishermen and soot-streaked factories. Coal chutes drop down the hills alongside patches of farmland; a stream of effluents runs into the river from an open pipe 50 feet from where a woman collects water in wooden buckets. We're 36 hours upstream from the Gorges, and the glamorous scent of imminent destruction is in the air. My sailing companions and I mill restlessly in the humid dusk like early arrivals at a celebratory bonfire. We know that the valley we're passing through will be inundated by the waters behind the dam and that this obliterating tide will rinse through the streets of 13 cities, 140 towns, and well over a thousand peasant villages. As far as I can tell, no one finds this prospect less than exhilarating. "Those towns are poor and ugly," says one of my roommates, Feng, a harbor policeman who is missing the tips of three of his fingers and whose shirt is speckled with dried blood.

Follow the river 600 miles downstream from Chongqing, leaping like a magical ocean-bound fish over the ostensible Three Gorges Dam, and you will find the place in a city called Wuhan where the Yangtze River flows past the offices of the Yangtze Water Resources Commission. At one point in my travels I dutifully ventured to Wuhan to receive official instruction on the scheme to stop up the Three Gorges with a monumental concrete plug. My government-sanctioned escort, an adorable 21-year-old from Beijing's All-China Journalist Association named Liu, was met by her escort, who took us to a military guard station on Liberation Avenue, where we were joined by a third escort, who told me he would act as my translator and then escorted us up an elevator to a paneled boardroom where two more translators waited, their job, it seemed, to take notes and giggle and roll their eyes and otherwise to remain coy and silent during my meeting with their bosses, three high-ranking officials who sat on bulky leather sofas 20 feet away from me and drifted in and out of the room when they weren't speaking—one of them, in particular, returning to his seat with much more neatly groomed hair. Tea was served, stacks of business cards distributed, the principle of friendship between nations extolled, and much time devoted to mutual assurances that this chummy get-together bestowed great honor on all concerned, despite the fact that I was a member of the despised U.S. press who was sure to spread lies about their fetish.

The standard arguments for the dam present the project as an expression of the state's benevolence toward its people, a bountiful gift that will relieve the anxiety of those living in the Yangtze floodplain, make their air a little less sooty, and power the factories that drive the world's fastest-growing economy. Luo Zehua, a chief engineer at the Water Resources Commission, told me the dam should be seen as a humanitarian mission. "This project," he said, speaking in tones of exquisite boredom, "will improve the lives of people in the region. Each year, during flood season, 120,000 square kilometers of land, inhabited by

70 million people, are endangered by flooding. This is our first priority: Farmland and people have to be protected from the river." I stared
out the boardroom window, past an illuminated Mobil Oil sign, to the
fog-shrouded Yangtze. Two hundred miles below the dam, the river,
broad and contained by steep levees, looked tame enough to me—a
big, ugly, churning Mississippi cutting an inelegant path through a big,
ugly, industrial boomtown.

If it seems outlandish that the 12,000-member bureaucracy of the
Yangtze Water Resources Commission would focus its attentions on a
single river, it's worth considering that the Yangtze valley drains one-
fifth of China's area and is home to one of every 12 people on the
planet. Forty percent of China's grain, 70 percent of its rice, close to
half of its total industrial and agricultural output, are produced in the
Yangtze valley, mainly in the heavily populated lowlands downstream
of the dam site. And there's the rub. "As you know," Luo said, "we
have suffered extraordinary floods." One official told me that in the
past 2,000 years of documented history, the Yangtze has jumped its
banks in catastrophic fashion an average of once every decade. These
aren't water-in-your-cellar floods, either; about 300,000 people have
drowned in the swollen Yangtze this century. Wuhan, the city eight
floors below me, was under water for four months in 1931, in the
aftermath of flooding that killed 140,000 and left about 30 million
homeless.

Given the toll exacted by the Yangtze's caprices, it's hardly surprising that the issue of the Three Gorges Dam has long been bound up
with politics and emotion as much as with economics and technology.
In the early 1920s, two decades before the era of giant dams was born,
Sun Yat-sen, one of the heads of the Republic of China, dreamed up
the idea of mounting a wall of salvation across the Yangtze. His nationalist protégé, Chiang Kai-shek, liked the plan well enough, too, and
two generations later Mao Zedong himself was mooning rhapsodically
over the fantasy dam in his 1956 poem called "Swimming": "Great
plans are afoot. . . . / Walls of stone will stand upstream to the west /
To hold back Wushan's clouds and rain / Till a smooth lake rises in
the narrow gorges. / The mountain goddess, if she is still there, / Will
marvel at a world so changed."

Mao wrote the poem shortly after doing the backstroke across the three-mile-wide Yangtze at Wuhan, a feat he'd undertaken to inspire the young revolutionary nation with his vigorous example and to provide an old-fashioned demonstration of the supremacy of human will over nature. Thus emboldened, he initiated the Great Leap Forward, the attempt to radically accelerate the pace of China's industrialization, which is said to have resulted in starvation for 20 to 30 million Chinese and which featured an extravagant program of dam-building. China, which had virtually no dams in 1949 at the inception of the People's Republic, now boasts half of the large dams in the world and some 83,400 dams in all. These fail at a rate ten times higher than those of the rest of the world. One series of dam collapses, following a 1975 typhoon, reportedly killed 230,000 people, though no such death toll was ever confirmed by the Chinese government and is nowhere mentioned in the promotional materials of the Yangtze Water Resources Commission.

Nor, when you visit the Yangtze Water Resources Commission with your team of cheerful handlers, will you hear of any concern about cost overruns, though the dam's projected tally has more than doubled in the last few years and shows no sign of halting at its present estimate. "On schedule, on budget," you'll be told, and there's no use arguing. You won't hear about the prospect that the Yangtze's heavy flow of silt might clog and disable the dam's turbines, and you won't hear of the danger that reduced sediment flow downstream might deprive farmland of nutrients and cause massive riverbank erosion, and the very thought that holding back 50 billion cubic yards of water might cause an earthquake will be dismissed as science-fictional hyperbole, and you'll be offered nothing but patronizing assurances that endangered species whose habitats are to be flooded will be relocated with tender loving care. The dire warnings of the Chinese military to the effect that a large dam in a broad valley smack in the middle of the country might as well be painted with a bull's-eye, the better to allow the laser-guided missiles of China's enemies to take out 15 or 20 million folks with a single barrage—talk of these "unrealistic" and depressing concerns would ruin your tea party. Western-style environmentalism will be decried as a new form of imperialism designed to thwart the aspirations of developing nations, and you'll be reminded that until recently the barons of American industry and the princes of American politics were enthusiastic supporters of the dam. (Henry Kissinger will be spoken of in loving terms.) You'll also be relieved to hear, by way of openness, that "some people, it's true, have opposed the project out of a lack of understanding. After discussion, though, we gave them a better understanding, and now they share our opinions."

Since 1992, when the National People's Congress formally approved the dam during an unusually contentious session in which floor debate was forbidden, the project has basked in the glow of rousing official unanimity. This glow should not be underestimated, since it is produced by an 18,200,000-watt light bulb dangling above the Three Gorges, and when you stare into the glow for a long time—say, 84.7 billion kilowatt hours each year—you're bound to see spots before your eyes, which may impair your vision. If you sail through the narrows of the Three Gorges on the ferry *China Sunshine*, for instance, you may want to bring your sunglasses. For the dam, you understand, "is a touchstone," as He Gong, vice-president of the Three Gorges Project Corporation, told Chinese papers. "Nothing can stop it now."

"The riverboat captain," says riverboat Captain Zhang, "is involved in an ancient struggle with nature." I've stirred him from a nap on day two of my Yangtze cruise, and for want of a more private place to talk, he sits in my cabin on a cot, smoking and fingering the fine hairs on his chin and brooding over the challenges of his vocation. We're 120 miles downstream from Chongqing, 12 hours or so from the Three Gorges. "The river," continues the captain, "is very mysterious. It looks quiet and peaceful, but the surface is deceptive and the depths are very dangerous. There are many shoals and rapids, especially in the Three Gorges, and many hazards that are invisible to the eye." Captain Zhang, who is 41, has worked this stretch of the Yangtze for more than half of his life, and he says it took ten years of studying the river to master it. Not long ago, navigation through the Gorges was a more hazardous business, but the frequent use of dynamite to break up the rapids and clear obstacles has made the captain's burden somewhat lighter. There's not much sporting thrill involved in making it through the middle reaches of the Yangtze. No spray of river water will muss your hair, and you can comfortably shave during the ferry's least steady moments.

"The Chinese people have strong emotions about this river," says Captain Zhang. A map of the region is spread on his lap, and his long pinkie nail glides from one town to the next. "Zigui will be under water," he says. "Wushan will be flooded. Fengjie, too, will be inundated. Wanxian will be half-drowned. Zhongxian—inundated. Fengdu—inundated. Fuling—inundated." I ask him to point out the level that the dammed water will reach on the surrounding hills, and he gestures to a whitewashed house hovering a third of the way up the slope. "I think a little above that house," he says. We are 250 miles from the dam site.

"Why should I feel strange?" the captain says, reflectively, gazing out the window of my berth. A fisherman leans toward the water from a narrow ledge of rocks and gathers his nets. "Nothing will change very much. The mountains will still be here, the water will still be here. Old views will be replaced by new views."

A few hours ago, the ferry docked at the town of Fengdu, and I followed the other passengers off the boat through a gauntlet of souvenir vendors awaiting us in the predawn mist. For the past 1,200 years, Fengdu has been regarded in folk mythology as a gateway to the underworld; ghosts are said to congregate here before passing on to hell. About 50 Buddhist and Taoist temples, destroyed by Red Guards during the Cultural Revolution, once clustered in the mountains above town, housing sculptures with names like *Between the Living and the Dead* and *Bridge of Helplessness*.

I stopped on a street corner in Fengdu to eat a fried breadstick beneath a colorful banner urging the locals to "Remain Agricultural—Protect the Soil—Be Happy to Move," and it was there I met Li, a 60-year-old seamstress with thick white hair and a commanding voice. Li said that like her fellow townspeople she was indeed happy to move, and she waved to a spot far across the river where a barren construction site marked the future home of Fengdu. "Our new town will have the same name," she said, "and the government will build a bridge

across the river so that we can visit old Fengdu whenever we wish."
Except, of course, that old Fengdu will be accessible only to divers.
"The new city will be modern, and much richer," said Li. A crowd of
children in blue and white school uniforms had surrounded us, and
Li's voice grew shaky. "I will miss my home. It's hard for old people
like me to move, but until it happens it won't seem real. And who
knows, maybe I'll be dead by then."

I wandered through Fengdu, trying to avoid the dispiriting central
avenue, where a throng of vendors pushed trinkets. The town relies
on infusions of cash from the cruise-ship visitors, because there's no
industry to speak of and a population of around 100,000 to support.
The floodwaters of the Three Gorges Dam have been threatening the
Yangtze valley for so long that the entire region has slid from the map
of central economic planning, cut off from investment. This has had
the effect of ensuring long-lasting poverty, which makes it easier for
the dam-builders to argue that relocation can only benefit the people
being moved. "Look around," said one merchant, after I had slogged
through eight inches of muck to sit with him in his tiny cigarette shop
in the shadow of a huge limestone overhang. "Who would want to
live here?"

I drifted to the edge of town and came to a steep staircase cut into
the red sandstone of a cliff, and I began to climb, peering down at the
shallow steps, and after a while I looked to my side and saw a thin
fog riding low over the Yangtze, and saw the *China Sunshine* docked
along with five other cruise ships, and saw Fengdu spread out beneath
me like an improvised blueprint.

And I looked closely at this blueprint until it blurred at its edges,
and beyond the edges I saw a crease form in the pale eastern horizon
of Sichuan Province, widening as it approached, and lifting itself in a
great wave toward the city, and sprawling through the courtyards and
markets and groves of fruit trees, and wrapping Fengdu in a swift,
devouring embrace.

Xu was waiting for me at the top of the steps, sitting against a wall
on a slab of iron strung between two zinc buckets, dripping sweat onto
his cigarette. He was returning to his home in the hills, bearing steaming slops to feed his pigs. I had followed him to this point 250 feet

above the town, where surely, I thought, we had ascended beyond the last ring of destruction.

I was wrong. "Not high enough," said Xu, matter-of-factly. "Everything below us will be submerged, and then the water will continue to rise." Xu spoke so softly I had to lean forward to hear him, and when he finished his cigarette he flicked the butt into one of the slop-pails. "My ancestors have always lived here. We've never lived anywhere else. I'm sad to move, but it'll be OK. The government will build us a bridge and we can visit the old town whenever we like."

I said to Xu, jokingly, that at least in new Fengdu he wouldn't have to climb so many steps to bring food to his pigs. Well, he said, he was unsure if he'd be allowed to keep pigs there. "It will be modern, and much richer," he said, with a booming lack of conviction. I wondered if the dam-builders had been passing out inspirational tapes. The specter of the great distant unbuilt wall had thoroughly subdued Xu, who shared the broadly held Chinese belief that compliance is a virtue. "What difference does it make whether I want to go or not? When the government tells us to go, we'll have to go. The only choice is to remain and live underwater."

Chinese papers have lately run stories that hint at official awareness of a coming nationwide ecological crisis—stories about water shortages, soil erosion, respiratory ailments caused by foul air. The bureaucracies in charge of the Three Gorges Dam, on the other hand, who receive nothing but praise in the national press, have worked hard to cloak their monolith in a bright green mantle, insisting that the project's hydroelectricity can help alleviate the country's reliance on low-grade coal for three-quarters of its energy needs. Wang Rushu of the Three Gorges Project Corporation, author of the project's rosy environmental impact statement, says the dam's annual output of electricity is equivalent to that produced by burning 50 million tons of coal, without the accompanying discharge of greenhouse gases. That's the standard "clean energy" rationale for dams, and it has long served as a pious foundation for dams around the world. (Engineered reservoirs now hold five times as much freshwater as all the world's rivers.) There's a strong popular appeal to the notion that dams are environ-

mentally friendly, and one side of Wang's office is covered with a paint-
ing of the Three Gorges Dam that renders it as an enhancement of
nature, the centerpiece of a scene featuring a sparkling lake and sail-
boats and billowy clouds and lush forested hills and a waterfall whose
waters foam at the base of a benign concrete wall.

Nonetheless, a cottage industry devoted to criticizing the dam
sprang up in the West over the last five years. Groups like International Rivers Network, Canada's Probe International, and Human
Rights Watch bullied the World Bank—whose habit has been to lavish cash on large dams in developing countries—into retreating from
the project. (Sensing a messy international debate in the offing, the
Chinese decided against applying for World Bank funding.) The White
House, in a 1995 directive signed by Deputy National Security Adviser
Samuel Berger, shied away from "a project that raises environmental
and human-rights concerns on the scale of the Three Gorges," adding
that the United States "should refrain from publicly condemning the
Three Gorges project." The criticism from abroad has only bright-
ened the dam's nationalistic hue within China. "We don't need your
American money," Wang Rushu told me earlier. "We can build our
own dam."

While in Beijing to learn about the state of environmental advocacy
in China, I was eager to seek out some homegrown wisdom on the
controversial homegrown dam. I made lots of phone calls and heard
the phrase "sensitive issue" so many times it made my own ears sensitive. I took long cab rides to the gates of international aid agencies
and was passed scribbled messages through iron gates and had a thoroughly gleeful adventure in paranoia. "You'll have difficulty finding
anyone willing to talk to you about the dam," one potential Chinese
source told me. "That includes me." Finally, a furtive whisper directed
me to Pan Hongtao, a handsome, broad-shouldered man in his thirties who is a journalist and editor at a Beijing paper called *China Environment News*. Pan was busily assembling the Earth Day issue of his
paper—circulation 250,000—the old-fashioned way, with wooden
rulers, scissors, and tape. Such was the level of his preoccupation that
he refused to make eye contact with me once during our meeting. "I'm
sorry for wasting your time," he mumbled, by way of introduction.

He gestured for me to put away my notepad. "I'm not an expert, you see, and so I'm unable to provide you with any information."

I was charmed by Pan and by the way he trembled slightly when he spoke, and I told him I hadn't come to feed off his sources; I was just curious to know his own impressions of the Three Gorges and to hear about Chinese environmental issues from a Chinese perspective.

"I really don't have any impressions of the Three Gorges Dam," he said. "It's a sensitive issue. The paper receives reports issued by official agencies and runs articles based on these reports."

What happens, I asked, if a reporter learns of information that conflicts with an official report?

"That doesn't happen," Pan assured me. I was relieved. "Our only sources are official reports." I looked past Pan's glass-enclosed office to the crowded newsroom and wondered what the reporters there did all day.

Pan didn't offer me any tea. He wanted me out of his office. His colleagues were staring and his manner was positively morose. No, he said, he was unaware of any Western criticism of the dam. No, he wasn't in a position to comment on the level of environmental awareness in China or to hazard a guess on what the most pressing environmental issues of the day might be. He did confirm, modestly, that *China Environment News* was the leading such paper in China. I remembered a Chinese journalism student I'd met a few weeks earlier in Shanghai, where the Yangtze spills into the sea, who told me that the press has an obligation to be optimistic—even, at times, to resort to what she called "white lies." "We must avoid unnecessarily exciting the people," she said. Not surprisingly, Chinese papers are as bland and cheerful as cereal boxes, but Pan Hongtao did not seem cheerful when he ushered me from his office.

I had better luck with Liang Cunjie, a sprightly 65-year-old who runs Friends of Nature, China's first and only grassroots organization devoted to environmental issues, out of a nondescript one-room office on the edge of Beijing's Forbidden City. "There are a number of environmental groups that call themselves nongovernmental organizations," he told me, "but actually they are GONGOs, government-organized NGOs, controlled and run by the government." The all-volunteer group that Liang founded in 1994 counts about 300 members, is run on a shoestring, and focuses on consciousness-raising activities, like a recent tree-planting trip to an arid stretch of Inner Mongolia. He recognized the need to be "artful" in criticizing government policy if he wanted to pursue his modest goals, and this despite the fact that Friends of Nature is tolerated in the first place only because of Liang's admittedly "privileged" status—he's a former vice-president of the Chinese Academy of Culture and a member of an advisory body called the Chinese People's Political Consultative Conference, which he likens to an upper house of parliament and which others have called the "non-Communist Communist Party."

Liang said that since the Three Gorges Dam had received the official stamp of approval two years before his group came on the scene, it seemed impractical to mount a campaign of opposition. "The project is so politicized. It's not just a matter of engineering or hydro-science." The dam, Liang said, had grown into a central matter of national prestige for reasons that he claimed not to understand. "It's a mystery to me," he said. "It's just a dam. We have so many dams. Why is this particular one so important? There is no shortage of alternatives, either—we could build small dams on the tributaries and gain the same effects in flood control and energy production. Why build such a big project, when the results are unknown scientifically?"

For now, though, Liang's only means of combating grand symbolic schemes such as the Three Gorges Dam was to undertake small symbolic missions, like planting trees in the deforested wilderness. "After two days of painstaking work under the desert sun during the height of the summer, we planted about 2,700 trees. But when we were finished and looked back at what we'd done, we couldn't even find the so-called forest we'd just planted. Because this many trees in a desert is nothing."

Not far now to the Three Gorges: it's dusk on the Yangtze, day two of my river journey. I'm humming along with the tinny Chinese pop song that blares over the PA system of the *China Sunshine,* and I'm enjoying the stiff breeze on deck with a can of warm Tsingtao beer in hand, when I'm clipped on the side of the head with a Styrofoam carton of rice and soggy peppers. Passengers who've eaten in their rooms are tossing their takeout containers overboard, part of the ship's after-meal janitorial spectacle. The dining room staff clears leftovers onto the tablecloths, gathers the tablecloths into tidy bundles, and pitches them into the river. Trash cans are emptied into the current. Last night I followed two giggling crew members as they dragged a barrel of garbage to the back of the ship and heaved the entire thing toward the watery depths.

The surface of the river is adrift with Styrofoam. Chopsticks and plastic bottles jostle like comical toy boats. No amount of sentimental cooing over the Mother River can conceal the truth that she is dirty and smells very bad. The Yangtze valley has been inhabited for thousands of years, and the river has always served as the common washbasin and sewer and burial site for settlements along its shores. Traditional habits of dumping haven't much adapted to the rapid industrialization of the region over the past 20 years, and now it's not just night soil and chicken bones that ride the downstream current, but hefty amounts of mercury, arsenic, lead, and cyanide. When the river is closed off by the dam, Yangtze sturgeon, the world's largest freshwater fish, will have its upstream travel blocked, but at least the sturgeon will be spared some unseemly wading; on the other side of the wall the 265 billion gallons of raw sewage dumped in the river each year will have its passage to the ocean thwarted. And though the agencies in charge of the dam have promised solutions to this problem— they have solutions for everything—it doesn't seem that any funds have been allocated for water treatment plants. Bucolic Three Gorges Lake, many critics say, will assume the refreshing attributes of an enormous clogged toilet.

I'm awakened abruptly at four in the morning. Feng, the harbor cop, is sitting on his bunk staring at me through a cloud of cigarette smoke. He points out the window, and I see the sheer walls of Qutang Gorge, the uppermost of the Three Gorges, whitened against the night by a full moon. I rush to the deck and join a dozen other passengers, some wearing only sandals and underwear, and the wind is stinging, and the river slaps against the mountains, and although a thin pencil of black sky is visible through a crevice thousands of feet above, for a few ghostly moments it feels as if the world has been reduced to its elements and these elements are enclosed within the gorge.

The ship docks at Wushan, a town where the schedule for relocation has been painted on the sides of buildings, and I board a small motorboat for a tour of the Little Three Gorges—not to be confused with the other, more famous Three Gorges—on a tributary of the Yangtze. The tour guide is wearing black leather hot pants and halter and squawks through a megaphone and spends a great deal of time selling commemorative stamps to support the Three Gorges Dam. "No more Little Three Gorges in November," she announces, repeatedly. She leads us on a tour of the battlefield before the battle has commenced: a stone bridge 350 feet high, spanning the canyon, that will be dismantled; rich alluvial fields whose farmers will be shuttled to rocky highlands; a town, settled in the third century, lined with buildings from the Ming Dynasty, awaiting the flood; a tiny strip of shoreline where a hundred displaced peasants, selling skewered potatoes and packs of Three Gorges cigarettes, live in striped plastic tents. The canyon, free of the factories that hover over much of the Yangtze, is gorgeous and appalling. The water is pale green, reflecting layers of green hillside, and a handful of old women scrub their laundry with stones along the banks. Terraced farms dangle high above the river. The boat winds through narrow, claustrophobic passages. Monkeys scamper in treetops, and passengers crane their necks and whistle and wave. "I hope those monkeys can swim," I shout, and everyone laughs and the tour guide sends an approving wink my way.

At one stop I talk to an old peasant who stands in sandals made of rope in a pasture with his four goats. He doesn't know how old he is. He doesn't know where he'll be moved when the waters rise, except higher, where the soil is no good. He doesn't know how long his family has lived on this river, though the tour guide tells me, contemptuously, that the old man is a member of the Tujia minority, allegedly descended from the Ba people who settled the region as many as 8,000 years ago. And the tour guide points to a cave in a cliff wall, a thousand feet above the water, where one of about a hundred remarkable "hanging coffins" has been left by the Ba people. The Ba had the right idea, suspending their remains beyond the reach of enemies or starry-eyed dam-builders. The Ba coffins are among the few archaeological relics in the region that are sure to be saved from the Three Gorges Dam.

Back aboard the *China Sunshine,* the new views I've been told so much about begin to emerge. In Xiling Gorge, the third and longest of the Three Gorges, abandoned villages dot the hillside. An old woman in a tattered blue Mao jacket sits beneath an umbrella on the roof of a vacant mill, pointing accusingly at the passing ferry. "She's lost her mind," says one of my shipmates. "She should be reported to the authorities."

The river begins to widen. We're coming out of the Gorges, approaching the threshold between China's backwaters and its presumed destination in modernity, approaching the induced limit of the Yangtze, approaching a wall that has to rise in the imagination before it can rise on the riverbed. We're ten miles from the dam site. The hillsides have become quarries, deforested, dusty pink undersides exposed. Barges line the banks, piled high with rocks bound for the cement factory.

I spot a man clambering from a cave far up a cliff, and for a moment he seems like a flickering vision released from a hanging coffin, a feral creature left to fend for himself on a deserted ledge, picking a neurotic zigzagging path away from the cave. While I'm watching he disappears in smoke.

A blast echoes through the mouth of the canyon. "Explosion!" shouts a child on deck. The ship responds with a full-throated call from its horn. Shale slides down the mountain toward the river, trailing a great dusty wake. Rubble splashes into the river. Passengers cheer. We've made it through the Three Gorges before they disappeared; our journey along the banks of the condemned is almost over. It's time to get off the boat.

A few days later I'm granted a glimpse of the human future of the Three Gorges by following the curves of the Yangtze, this time by minibus, to the resettlement center of Maoping—"Mao Village"—a former farming community that looms above the Yangtze about a mile from the dam site. In the dam-builders' dreamscape, Maoping will become a lakeside town of about 35,000 devoted to dam-related tourism and light industry, and I've been brought here, with official permission, because Maoping is considered to offer exemplary proof of the bounties of forced resettlement. I'm walking through the mostly unpaved streets of the town-in-progress with Yang, a local resettlement officer in his early thirties who moves with the bearing of a capo. Teenagers leaning against idle backhoes bolt upright as we pass. "Construction began here in 1994," Yang tells me, "when there was only terraced farmland. Now the village is covered with buildings." It's true. There's a hotel with mirrored windows and a barren department store and the hollow shells of schools and offices and apartment blocks, all faced in white ceramic tile—enough architecture, vintage 1996, to make an American subdivision developer tremble with possibility.

Yang regards his job as a patriotic calling, and it's a hard job, too, because no industrial project has ever involved the relocation of such a large population—between one and two million, depending on whose figures you trust. New homes must be built, new jobs provided, roads and schools and hospitals designed, and order maintained. The state security apparatus has already drawn up plans for containing disturbances, though Yang assures me that "there are no people who refuse to move," to which my charming escort Liu adds, "The Chinese people are very meek." Resettlement bureaus have dispatched a corps of agents to go door to door throughout the "affected areas," persuading those in the dam's path to do the right thing and offering "education" to those reluctant to pack their bags. Yang says, "There are 1.2 billion people in China, so this is a very small number to affect." An official from the Yangtze Water Resources Commission says, "The Chinese believe in sacrificing for the good of the country." An official at the Three Gorges Project Corporation headquarters says, "We tell them, if you move one million, then we save 15 million from floods. Very easy. We move one, we save 15." And one after another of the passengers on *China Sunshine* says, "They're peasants. They'll be glad to move."

Yang takes me to a marketplace in Maoping and introduces me to an old man, a model of what the government hopes to achieve in its resettlement efforts. The man, retired from a machine factory, tells me that he lives in a modern building surrounded by neighbors from his former town and that he makes extra money by selling vegetables on a patch of land the government gave him. "Life is much better than before," he says. "There's more entertainment here for old people. Of course I miss my old home, but I'm proud to put the nation first."

I'm glad to meet the old man, and Yang is glad for me to meet him. Yang cares about the people he forces to move here, and positive feedback brightens his day. About the only thing the old man has to complain about are the cracked lenses of his eyeglasses.

Yang and the old man help to remind me that this dam—so easily condemned as environmental folly and callous nationalistic muscle-flexing—was born out of a visionary impulse that has as much to do with social engineering as with the engineering of a river. The project—I'm thinking, while Yang beams at me and the old man polishes his cucumbers—reflects a desire to improve on nature and on human nature both. It's not easy for an American of my generation, who has come of age in an era of downsized utopian ambitions and downsized dams, to credit the Chinese with pursuing the drive to transform themselves. The old man in the marketplace is surrounded by other old people, selling meat and noodles and milky blocks of tofu, and they're smiling at me and tugging at my shirt and they all seem grateful for the great dam to come.

And then I slip down a gully past a garbage heap to a shadowy lane where Yang warns me that I am unlikely to meet "representative" members of the relocated population. Undeterred, I call up to a random second-story window of a brand-new building and summon Ming Wa to come speak to me. Ming is a pretty young woman with long braided hair and crooked teeth who tells me she moved to Maoping from her ancestral home, a tiny village barely a mile away which has been folded up to make room for the dam. What kind of work did you do there? I ask.

"I was a peasant," she says. "I tended paddies and raised plants for cooking oil."

And what do you do now? I ask.

A lively conference ensues between Yang and my escort before Ming's response is translated for me. "Temporarily unemployed," I am told. Ming has been "temporarily unemployed" since arriving in Mao-ping three years ago. Her husband has gone off to a city half a day's bus ride away to look for work. She gets by on a state-provided allowance of about $8 a month.

"I didn't like farming," she says. "Few people do. It's very hard work. But at least I could raise plants and vegetables for food. Here, everything costs money. It's all money, money, money."

I remind myself: Nearby, in a marketplace, a happy old man is selling vegetables.

I ask Ming to describe the compensation package she has received from the government. Yesterday, Wang Rushu of the Three Gorges Project Corporation told me, emphatically, "We compensate the people who have to move. We give them $5,000 for every person—$5,000 for an old man, $5,000 for a child." He elaborated. "Before, these people are rather poor. They live in the mountains; they work in the fields. Now we give them money to build a new house, to get new furniture. For instance, a new freezer. New television. And we train them. Before, they were farmers; now they are workers, working in factories, iron mills, maybe, or maybe they work as drivers. So they think: I've got a new house. I've got new furniture and a new TV. And the government pays me $5,000. So yes, I'm very interested in resettling. That's what they think."

There is considerable deliberation between Yang and my escort before Ming reveals to me the deal her family cut with the dam-builders. Finally I'm told that Ming's family received about $1,500 to compensate for the loss of their house and their land. "A lot of money," my escort says to me.

"That is a lot of money," I say. A peasant family in this area is unlikely to earn much more than $40 a month. "What did you do with it, Ming?"

"We had to pay for our new apartment," Ming says. "But it wasn't enough money to pay for the apartment, so there was nothing left over."

Yang isn't looking very relaxed anymore, but luckily a sizable crowd has gathered to enjoy our conversation—since as far as I can tell, Mao-ping is full of the temporarily unemployed—and one of the onlookers opens a burlap sack full of live snakes, and my escort shrieks, and the crowd dissolves in hysterics.

So we retreat into Ming's building, climbing a flight of concrete steps with the aid of a plumbing pipe for a banister, and Ming shows off her immaculate and nearly bare concrete apartment. "I definitely prefer living in a modern house," she says. "My old house was made from wood and soil and had no water. But my old village was beautiful. A stream ran beside the village, and we were surrounded by forest. When the authorities came and told us we would be moved, I was loath to leave. I returned to the village once, shortly after we moved here, but there was nothing to see. It was all a construction site." Yang is glaring at Ming. Ming looks like she could talk all afternoon, if such things were permitted. "There's no way to kill the time," she says.

The next day, while in Wuhan, I relate Ming's story to a committee of dam-builders, and I am told, "This woman is not representative."

Ming Wa of Maoping, Damland, is still very much on my mind when I pay a visit on Dai Qing, the woman anointed in the Western press as the official martyr of the Three Gorges Dam. Like Ming Wa, Dai Qing too is "temporarily unemployed," as a result of the Three Gorges Dam. "I've lost almost everything," she tells me. "I'm still a citizen of China, and I still have the right to live in Beijing, but I have no job, no income, no medical insurance."

Dai is a witty and energetic woman in her early fifties who has traveled the elite circles of Chinese intellectual society. She is the adopted daughter of one of China's highest-ranking military officials; she was a onetime Red Guard; she was trained as a missile engineer; she wrote a column for one of China's most prestigious newspapers. In the late 1980s, buoyed by a liberalized political climate, she edited a collection of essays, called *Yangtze! Yangtze!*, that criticized the Three Gorges Dam from various technical perspectives. It reads like an innocuous enough book, of interest mainly to engineers, and her sources for the essays were high-ranking government officials whose objections to the project were practical, not ideological. Dai was not unaware, though, that water power and political power are sometimes vested in the same source. "I got involved in this issue not for scientific reasons," she says, "but to promote the freedom of speech." We sit in near darkness in her apartment. A computer and fax machine are covered in plastic. A small American flag is propped on a bookshelf. "But of course this dam is a political project, and a person who is against this project is thought to be against the Party and against the government."

The book was published in March 1989, and a few months later Dai, who says she "hates revolution," headed to Tiananmen Square to try to persuade leaders of the student movement that they had accomplished enough and that they ought to head back to their campuses. "What did I do during the June 4 incident? Practically nothing." Dai was arrested and sent to Qinchen prison, a notorious Soviet-built retreat for political detainees. She was never formally charged with wrongdoing, though in the post-Tiananmen haze she was held in solitary confinement for ten months and was frequently promised execution by her jailers. Dai insists that *Yangtze! Yangtze!*, which was banned while she was in jail, was the cause of her arrest. "The government wanted to show people who were against the Three Gorges project what might happen to them. And it worked. Right now, censorship in China is not too bad, but self-censorship is the rule."

Dai, who likes to say things like, "For the dictatorship, the dam is a symbol of central control," has become a media darling of the Western press, profiled in the *New York Times,* venturing abroad for fellowships at Harvard and colloquia in Copenhagen. The problem is that no one is listening at home. The dissident's celebrity she enjoys in the West is mirrored by the virtual anonymity she suffers in China. (Pan Hongtao, the silent journalist at *China Environment News,* was not alone in telling me he'd never heard of Dai Qing.) She inhabits the limbo reserved for the audacious, a much emptier place in China than the limbo reserved for the timid and dispossessed, where Ming Wa waits for compensation or consolation. "Even though my phone is tapped by the authorities," Dai tells me, "even though police are sometimes standing at my gate, I must remain in China. If I live abroad, I lose the power to criticize."

The pleasant voyage of the *China Sunshine* ends in Yichang, a city 30 miles downstream from the dam. Here is the headquarters of the Three

Gorges Project Corporation and a site to which foreign industrialists make regular pilgrimages in hopes of winning bids. My own pilgrimage is nearly complete. I pay an official at Dam Central a sum that represents a month's salary in China, and I'm led to a waiting van that speeds me at 80 miles per hour along impressive new infrastructure built to service the dam's construction: a new highway, closed to the public and guarded by armed police, attended by work crews also guarded by police; darkened tunnels that snake through the granite mountains; a gleaming bridge crossing the Yangtze and entering the site of the Three Gorges Dam. The bridge towers are emblazoned with the calligraphy of current premier Li Peng, a Soviet-trained engineer who is widely regarded as the henchman of Tiananmen Square and who is mocked by cynics for wearing his pants hitched high on his torso to evoke the image of Mao Zedong. I've reached my destination. Soldiers wave us in.

From ground level, the dam site looks like a shantytown, its rows of workers' barracks covered with tin and tar paper. Hard hats are a rare sight, and loafers seem to be the footwear of choice. In one direction work proceeds with sophisticated hydraulic drills, in another with picks and shovels. A few men nap in the shade beneath a bulldozer. Women sell dusty bottles of water. Transients drift through the site, pulling bamboo carts of rubble, but I'm not permitted to talk to these people—they're not "representative workers." I'm taken far and wide in the blazing heat on an absurd mission to find "representative workers," and when I find some I draw a blank. What do I ask them? What can they tell me? That the work is hard, but the wages—around $70 a month—are good? That they have come here far from home and miss their families, whom they visit once a year? That they are proud to work on a project that "means to modern China what the Great Wall meant to ancient China"? It's all true, and all I can do is wish them well. I hope they build a good dam.

I hope they build the world's best dam, in fact, and I hope that one small corner of the dam remains available for the inscription of some graffiti that commemorates the involvement of my own proud dam-building nation. If I'm ever to return here with a fat can of spray paint, I'll make a note that in 1944, the U.S. Bureau of Reclamation, whose dams have slackened the flow of all but 42 miles of the Columbia River, sent its chief designer to China to draw up plans for the Three Gorges Dam. I'll mention that in 1985, a consortium called the U.S. Three Gorges Working Group, comprising members from leading American industrial and financial concerns, proposed to the Chinese that the dam be built as a U.S.-China joint venture. I'll find a vibrant color with which to record Caterpillar's angry response to the Clinton administration's withdrawal of support for the project: "A politically correct export strategy," argued the peeved supplier, "can end up as a politically incorrect trade imbalance." And I'll give my paint can a final shake and append an asterisk with the name Bi as a reminder to those sometimes sanctimonious friends of the environment, including myself, who tend to get lulled into romanticizing the simple charms of the impoverished peasantry.

I met Bi on my last day in China, along a stretch of the real Great Wall, 70 miles outside Beijing at a place called Simitai. I'd gone there, to the rustic core of ancient China, where the land is plowed with oxen and cleared with handmade scythes, because I wanted to build a wall in my mind big enough to surround and overtake the wall rising above the Yangtze. I wanted to mute the chorus of voices I'd heard—those of officials, environmentalists, tourists, the displaced and the soon-to-be-displaced, the shrill and the complacent—and listen to the sound a wall makes when its only function is that of vague remembrance. Nixon famously told Zhou Enlai that American astronauts had seen the Great Wall from space, a claim as mythical as the notion that Hoover Dam remains visible from beyond. I suspect that the farther you sail from Earth, the more all walls must fade into the poignant insignificance of human dimensions. Some hold back rivers for a while, some hold back armies for a while. Some mark frontiers, some surround prisons. Some enclose the tombs of emperors and some enclose the vaults of bankers and some enclose the mud huts of peasants like Bi.

Bi joined me at the base of a mountain at the Great Wall at Simi-tai, and she trailed beside me for four hours beneath the midday sun. At Simitai, few efforts to preserve the wall have been made, and its granite sentry towers are crumbling, and the precipitous path that the wall follows across the spine of the mountains is littered with yellowed chips of stone. Bi took my picture with my camera, and she directed me around treacherous gaps in the trail, and at one point she gestured to a spot two valleys away which she said was her home and from which a thin plume of smoke rose. She sold me three bottles of water for 40 cents each. At the end of the day she sold me some postcards. Each of the 30 or 40 Westerners at Simitai that day was escorted by someone like Bi, a destitute local peasant for whom this form of entrepreneurship was the best chance of survival.

The wall stood there in a state of glorious incomplete collapse, holding nothing back, revealing nothing, and I stood on top of it and watched it define the landscape. It was a marvel. Its 3,000-mile expanse is said to be held together with mortar ground from the bones of the slaves who died building it. I looked down toward the valley, where a small dam had been built in a stream, and I followed Bi still higher, to the highest sentry tower, and I looked out across both sides of this wall that had divided the country, this wall that had been breached repeatedly, this wall that had stood for centuries as a symbol of oppression, this wall that endures now as an eroding token of archaeology.

October 1997

The Post-
Communist Wolf

DAVID QUAMMEN

t's two hours after sunset on this snow-clogged Romanian mountain, and in the headlight of a stalled snowmobile stand five worried people and two amused dogs. One of the dogs is a husky. Her
name, Yukai, translates from a distant Indian language to mean
"Northern Lights." Her pale gray eyes glow coldly, like tiny winter
moons. One of the worried people is me. My name translates from
Norwegian to mean "cow man" or, less literally, "a cattle jockey who
should have stayed in his paddock"—neither of which lends me any
aura of masterly attunement to present circumstances. The temperature is falling.

Unlike placid Yukai, we five humans are poorly prepared for a
night's bivouac in the snow, having long since abandoned most of our
gear in an ill-advised gambit to lighten our load and move faster. Three
of us—myself, the American photographer Gordon Wiltsie, and a German visitor, Uli Geertz, from the conservation group Vier Pfoten ("Four
Paws")—are on backcountry skis with skins, schlepping along steadily
behind a biologist named Christoph Promberger and his biologist wife,
Barbara Promberger-Fuerpass, who are driving the two snowmobiles.

Christoph is a lanky, 34-year-old German whose raucous black hair
and almond-thin, lidded eyes make him appear faintly Mongolian—

that is, like a young Mongolian basketball player with a wry smile. Though officially employed by the Munich Wildlife Society, he has worked here in the Carpathian Mountains since 1993, collaborating with a Romanian counterpart named Ovidiu Ionescu, of the Forestry Research and Management Institute, to create a new conservation program called the Carpathian Large Carnivore Project. Barbara, a fair-haired Austrian, joined the project more recently and is now beginning a study of lynx. Both of them are hardy souls with considerable field experience in remote parts of the Yukon (where Christoph did his master's work on the relationship between wolves and ravens, and where later they honeymooned), so they know a thing or three about winter survival, backcountry travel, problem avoidance, snowmobile repair. But tonight's conditions, reflecting an unusually severe series of January storms and an absence of other human traffic along this road, have caught them by surprise.

Gordon and I are surprised, too: that Murphy's Law, though clearly in force, seems unheard-of in Romania.

At the outset Christoph was towing a cargo sled, but that had to be cast loose and left behind. Even without it, the Skidoos have been foundering in soft six-foot drifts, and much of our energy for the past few hours has gone into pushing these infernal machines, pulling them, kicking them, cursing them, nudging them ever higher toward a peak called Fata lui Ilie, ever deeper into trouble. The sensible decision, after we'd bogged at the first steep pitch and then bogged again and again, would have been to turn back at nightfall and retreat to the valley.

Instead we went on, convincing ourselves recklessly that the going would get easier farther up. Ha. Somewhere ahead, maybe three miles, maybe five, is a cabin. We have one balky headlamp, a bit of food, matches, two pairs of snowshoes as well as the skis, but no tent and, since ditching even our packs back at the last steep switchback, no sleeping bags. The good news is that the forest is full of wolves.

"I believe the term is goat-fucked," Gordon says suddenly. "A situation that's so absurdly bad, it becomes sublime." Gordon's own situation is more sublime than the rest of ours, since he's suffering from a gut-curdling intestinal flu as well as the generally shared ailments—

cold hands, exhaustion, frustration, hunger, and embarrassment. "We could easily spend the night out here, without sleeping bags," he adds.

On that point I'm inclined to disagree: We could do it, yes, but it wouldn't be easy.

Christoph's mission with the Carpathian Large Carnivore Project is to investigate the biology and population status of Romania's three major species of predator—the wolf, the brown bear, the European lynx— and to explore measures that might help conserve those populations into the future. His immediate purpose, with this snow-trek toward Fata lui Ilie, is to use the cabin as a base for three or four days of wolf-trapping. The trapped wolves, if any, will be fitted with radio collars for subsequent tracking.

Since 1994, Christoph and his coworkers have collared 13 wolves, at least three of which have been illegally shot. Two have dispersed beyond the study zone, and four others have fallen cryptically silent, probably because their transmitters failed. One of the missing animals is a female named Timis, the first Carpathian wolf Christoph ever touched. Timis, the alpha bitch in her pack, was a savvy survivor, and she opened his eyes to the range of lupine resourcefulness in Romania. Originally trapped and collared in a remote valley near the city of Brasov, Timis and her pack soon relocated themselves closer and began making nocturnal forays into town. On Brasov's south fringe was a large meadow where they could hunt rabbits, and by skulking along a sewage channel, then crossing a street or two, they could find their way to a garbage dump, rich with such toothsome possibilities as slaughterhouse scraps, feral cats, and rats. In 1996, Timis denned near the area and produced ten pups. With the aid of a remote camera set 50 meters from the den, Christoph spent many hours watching her perform the intimate chores of motherhood. But times change and idylls fade. Timis disappeared, the fate of her pups is unknown, and in the enterprising ferment of post-Communist Romania, the rabbit-filled meadow is now occupied by a Shell station and a McDonald's.

At the time of our visit, only two wolves are still transmitting, one of which is a male known as Tsiganu, recently collared in another valley not far from Brasov. The wolf population of the Carpathians is sizable, but the animals are difficult to trap—far more difficult than wolves of the Yukon or Minnesota, Christoph figures—probably because their long history of close but troubled relations with humans has left them more wary than North American wolves. Romania is an old country, rich with natural blessings but much wrinkled by conflict and paradox, and history here is a first explanation for everything, including the ecology and behavior of *Canis lupus*. Go back 2,000 years, before the imperial Romans put their stamp on the place, and you find the Dacia, a fearsome indigenous people who referred to their warriors as Daois, meaning "the young wolves."

Just after World War II, wolves roamed the forests throughout Romania, even the lowland forests, with a total population of perhaps 5,000. They preyed on roe deer, red deer, and wild boar, but were also much loathed and dreaded for their depredations against livestock, especially sheep. In the 1950s the early Communist government, under a leader named Gheorghe Gheorghiu-Dej, sponsored a campaign of hunting, trapping, poisoning, and killing of pups at their dens to reduce the wolf population and make the countryside safe for Marxist-Leninist lambs. That anti-wolf pogrom worked well in the lowlands, which were more thoroughly devoted to agriculture and heavy indus-try. On the high slopes of the Carpathians, though, where lovely beech and oak forests were protected by a tradition of conscientious forestry and where dreams and memories of freedom survived among at least a few of the hardy rural people, wolves survived too.

The Carpathians also served as a refuge for brown bear and lynx. The bear population stands presently at about 5,400, a startling multitude of *Ursus arctos* considering that in all the western United States (excluding Alaska), where we call them grizzlies, there are only about a thousand. The wolf population, at somewhere between 2,000 and 3,000, represents a large fraction of all *Canis lupus* surviving between the Atlantic Ocean and Russia. Why has Romania, of all places, remained such a haven for large carnivores? The reasons involve accidents of geology, geography, ecology, politics, and the ironic circumstance that a certain Communist potentate, successor to Gheorghiu-Dej, came to fancy himself a great hunter. This of course was the pipsqueak dictator Nicolae Ceausescu, who for decades ruled Romania as though he owned it.

Born in the village of Scornicesti and apprenticed to a Bucharest shoemaker at age 11, Nicolae Ceausescu made his way upward as a gofer to early Communist activists during their years of persecution by a fascist regime. He served time in prison, a good place for making criminal and political contacts. He was cunning, he was ambitious and efficacious though never brilliant, he bided his time, sliding into this opening and then that one, eventually gaining ultimate control as general secretary of the Communist Party in 1965. He styled himself the Conducator, a lofty title that paired him with an earlier supreme leader, Marshal Ion Antonescu, the right-wing dictator who had ruled Romania during World War II. Ceausescu distanced himself from certain Soviet policies such as the invasion of Czechoslovakia in 1968, and thereby made himself America's favorite Communist autocrat, at least during the administrations of Nixon, Ford, and Carter. His manner of domestic governance remained merely Stalinism in a Romanian hat, but for a long time the United States didn't notice.

Ceausescu's dark little shadow cast itself across Romania for 25 years, with the help of his Securitate apparatus of secret police and informers, which included as many as three million people in a nation of just 23 million. Such institutional menace wasn't uncommon in the Communist bloc, of course, but it may have weighed more heavily here, due to a certain wary, fatalistic strain in the national spirit. Romania under Ceausescu had a few brave dissenters, but not the same sort of robust underground network of dissidents that existed in the Soviet Union or, say, Czechoslovakia. There's a nervous old Romanian proverb, counseling caution: *Vorbesti de lup si lupul e la usa.* Speak of the wolf and he's at your door.

Ceausescu's industrial, economic, and social policies were as wrong-headed as they were eccentric. Though he was Stalinist in style, he had that self-important yearning for independence from Moscow, and so he pushed Romania to develop its own capacities in oil refining, mineral smelting, and heavy manufacturing. During the 1970s his industrialization initiative sucked off a huge fraction of the country's GNP and generated a big burden in foreign loans; then in the 1980s he became obsessed with paying off those loans and made the Romanian populace endure ferocious austerity in order to do it. He exported petroleum products and food while his own people suffered in under-heated apartments without enough to eat. He instituted a systematization campaign, as he called it, which essentially meant bulldozing old neighborhoods and villages in order to force their inhabitants into high-rise urban housing projects, where he could better control the flow of vital resources. His systematization created a larger proletariat living amid ugly urban blight, and his industrialization resulted in some horrendous point-source pollution problems, such as the smelter at Zlatna and the gold-reprocessing plant at Baia Mare, which just recently let slip a vast wet fart of toxic sludge from one of its containment ponds into the Danube drainage, poisoning fish downstream for miles. But for some reason Ceausescu did not become obsessed with exporting timber, and so the Carpathian highlands remained wild and sylvan while other parts of the country grew grim.

The Conducator himself lived a life of splendorous self-indulgence and paranoia, like a neurasthenic king. He had food-tasters to protect him from poisoning. He had germ obsessions like Howard Hughes. He trusted only his wife, Elena, who was his full partner in megalomania and his chief adviser on how to govern badly. With her, he sealed himself away in palatial residences, letting the people see him mainly through stagey televised ceremonials. For bolstering his ego and political luster he depended also on occasional mass rallies, for which tens of thousands of citizens were mandatorily mustered to express—or anyway, feign—adulation. The last of those, on December 21, 1989, went badly askew and led to his fall. All the other Communist leaders who got dumped during that dizzy time, from Gorbachev down, were content to go peacefully, but Nicolae Ceausescu required execution.

Ceausescu's shadow still lingers in some places, including the snowed-over road that may or may not eventually carry us to Fata lui Ilie. The forest is thick. The spruce trees are large and heavily flocked with snow. While the Skidoos are mired still again, on another steep switchback below a ridgeline, I wonder aloud whether this route was originally cut for hauling timber.

"No, this was a hunting road for Ceausescu," Christoph tells me. "He'd fly in by helicopter. And his people would come in by four-wheel drive to organize the hunt." Among other fatuities, Ceausescu prided himself as a great killer of trophy-size bears. Although his name went into record books and his trophies can still be seen at a museum in the town of Posada, Ceausescu's actual accomplishments were contemptible: squeezing off kill-shots at animals that had been located, fattened, and baited for his convenience. The sad irony is that, so long as he arrogated the country's bear-hunting rights largely to himself, the bear population flourished. Records show that it peaked, at about 8,000 animals, in 1989. The end of that year was when the ground shifted for everyone— carnivores, citizens, and the Conducator himself. The people finally revolted, and Ceausescu, losing his nerve, tried to flee but was captured. On Christmas Day, before a firing squad, the great hunter got his.

Farther along, when we pass a spur road to Ceausescu's helicopter pad, I feel tempted to ski up and inspect it. But by now Christoph and Barbara are far ahead on the snowmobiles, Gordon is with them, and I'm skiing through darkness with only Uli's dim headlamp as a point of guidance. Ceausescu is dead, the bears are asleep, the new government is led by a center-right coalition of parliamentarians, the Carpathian forests are being privatized to their great peril, the currency is weak, the mafia is getting strong, and all idle contemplation of the pungent contingencies of recent Romanian history is best left, I realize, for a time when I'm not threatened by hypothermia.

The wolf known as Tsiganu was trapped on December 19, 1999, near a valley called Tsiganesti. The handling, collaring, and release were done by a Romanian wildlife technician named Marius Scurtu, a sturdy young man with an unassuming grin and a missing front tooth. Marius had blossomed into an important member of the Carnivore Project, absorbing well Christoph's field training in wolf capture and showing great appetite for the hard backcountry legwork. In recognition of his role, he was allowed to christen the new animal. Besides relating the wolf to that particular valley, the name he picked— Tsiganu—means "Gypsy."

At the time of trapping, Tsiganu weighed 95 pounds. He was notable for the lankiness of his legs and the length of his canine teeth. Since collaring, he has rejoined a small pack of four or five animals, though whether he himself is the alpha male remains uncertain. He now broadcasts his locator beeps on a frequency of 148.6 megahertz, and several times each week either Marius or another project technician goes out with a map, a radio receiver, and a directional antenna to check on him. Tsiganu seldom lets himself be seen, but from his prints and other evidence in the snow, a good tracker can learn what he has been doing. In the past month he has killed at least three roe deer, two dogs, and two sheep.

On a warmish day not long before our misadventure on the trail toward Fata lui Ilie, Gordon and I skied along with a tracker named Peter Surth. We followed him up a tight little canyon into the foothills above a village. It was slow travel, through wet heavy snow along the bank of a small stream, but within less than a mile we came to a kill. The rib cage and hide of a roe deer, partly covered by overnight snowfall, confirmed that Tsiganu and his pack hadn't gone hungry. Continuing upward, we passed an old log barn from which we could hear the companionable gurgles and neck bells of sheep, safely shut away behind a door. Moments later we met a man in country clothes, presumably the sheep-owner, trudging down a steep slope. Peter spoke a few words with him, then told us the gist of the exchange. Wolves, you want wolves? the man had said. Wolves we've got, around here. Lots of them.

We angled up a slope, rising away from the creek bottom. A half-hour of climbing brought us, sweating, onto a ridge. Peter took another listen with the receiver, catching a strong signal that seemed to place Tsiganu within 300 yards. Which direction? Well, probably there, to the northwest. But the tempo of beeps also indicated that the animal was active, not resting, and therefore his position could change fast. We hustled northwest along the ridgeline. When Peter listened again he got a much different bearing, this one suggesting that Tsiganu and his pack were below us, possibly far below, on the opposite slope of the creek valley we'd just left. Or maybe the earlier signal had been deceptive because of echo effects from the terrain. Or maybe this one was the echo.

Such are the ambiguities in tracking an animal that doesn't want to be found.

*   *   *

Not far from where we stood, pondering the whereabouts of Tsiganu, lay a snowbound hamlet of thatch-roofed cottages, conical haystacks, and a few shapely farmhouses with gabled and turreted tin roofs, all hung like a saddle blanket across the steep sides of the ridge. It was called Magura. It seemed a mirage of bucolic tranquillity from the late Middle Ages, but it was real.

Gordon and I had been there a few days earlier with another project worker, Andrei Blumer. In bright sunshine and stabbing cold, we had skied up from another valley on the far side, stopping to visit an elderly couple named Gheorghe and Aurica Surdu. The Surdus live in a trim little cottage they built 50 years ago to replace a 500-year-old cottage on the same spot, in which Aurica had been born. Aurica is a pretty woman of seventy-some years, with a deeply lined face and a wide, jokey smile. We were greeted effusively by her, Gheorghe, and their middle-aged son, another Gheorghe but nicknamed Mosorel, who himself had boot-kicked up through the snow for a Saturday visit. Passing from deep snowbanks and icy air into a small narrow room with a low ceiling, a bare bulb, and a woodstove upon which simmered a pot of rose-hip tea, we commenced to be steam-cooked with hospitality. Aurica, wearing a head scarf and thick-waled corduroy vest, spoke as little English as Gordon and I did Romanian, but she made herself understood, and her motherly eyes missed nothing. She stood by the stove and fussed cheerily while Andrei traded news with Mosorel, Gordon thawed his lenses, and I waited for my glasses to clear. *Have some rose tea, you boys, get warm. Here, have some bread, have some cheese, don't be so skinny.* The tea was deep-simmered and laced with honey. *Have some smoked pork. And the sausage too, it's good, here, I'll cut you a bigger piece, don't you like it? You do? Then don't be shy, eat.* We had set off without lunch, so we were pushovers. *Mosorel, give them some tsuica, what are you waiting for?* Mosorel, grinning broadly, poured us heated shots of his mother's homemade apple-pear brandy, lightly enhanced with sugar and pepper. *Tsuica* is more than just the national moonshine; it's a form of communion, and we communed.

Mosorel's right hand was swaddled in a large white bandage. It testified to a saw accident several months earlier, Andrei explained, in which Mosorel had sliced off his pinky and broken his fourth finger while cutting up an old chest for usable lumber. Mosorel is a carpenter, sometimes. Sometimes too he's a tailor; his nickname means, roughly, "Mr. Thread." Until the saw accident he had also been pulling shifts at a factory down in the nearby town. Like his parents, who still raise pigs, cows, sheep, onions, corn, beets, potatoes, and more than enough apples and pears for *tsuica*, Mosorel is a versatile man of diverse outputs. The hand injury didn't seem to dampen his spirit, possibly because some joyous aptitude for survival runs like a dominant gene through the family, homozygous on both sides of his parentage. As the sweet liquor spread its heat in our bellies, the talk turned in that direction—to survival, and how its terms of demand had changed.

During the Communist era, Gheorghe and Aurica Surdu had been required to supply 800 liters of milk each year to the state. Andrei translated this fact, Aurica nodding forcefully: Yes, 800. There were also quotas to be met in lambs, calves, and wool. Since the revolution, things had changed; no longer were Gheorghe and Aurica obliged to deliver up a large share of their farm produce, but market prices were so low that, rather than selling it, they fed their milk to the pigs. So, I asked simplemindedly, is life better or worse since the fall of Ceausescu? The talk rattled forward in Romanian for a few moments until Andrei paused, turned aside, and told me that Mosorel had just said something important.

"At least we're not scared now," he had said.

Just below the high village of Magura, at the mouth of the small river valley draining from Fata lui Ilie and other peaks, sits a peculiar little town called Zarnesti. Narrow streets, paved with packed snow at this time of year, run between old-style Transylvanian row houses tucked behind tall courtyard walls closed with big wooden gates. Horse-drawn sleighs jingle by, carrying passengers on the occasional Sunday outing. Heavy horse carts with rubber tires haul sacks of corn, piles of fodder, and other freight. Young mothers pull toddlers and grocery bags on metal-frame sleds. There are also a few automobiles—mostly beat-up Romanian Dacias—creeping between the snowbanks, and along the south edge of town rises, with sudden ugliness, a cluster of five-story concrete apartment blocks from the Communist era, like a histogram charting the grim triumph of central planning. Beside the train tracks sits a large pulp mill that eats trees from the surrounding forests, digests them, and extrudes the result as paper and industrial cellulose.

You can walk all afternoon along the winding lanes of Zarnesti, down to the main street, past the Orthodox church, past the pulp mill, looping back through the post-office square, and not see a single neon sign. There are no restaurants and no hotels, none that I've managed to spot, anyway. Yet the population is 27,000. People live and work here, but few visit. For years Zarnesti was off-limits to travelers because of another industrial plant in town, the one commonly known as "the bicycle factory." The bicycle factory was really a munitions factory, built in 1938, when Romania was menaced by bellicose neighbors during the buildup toward World War II. Later, in the Communist era, it thrived and diversified. It produced artillery, mortars, rockets, treads for heavy equipment, boxcars, and—yes, as window dressing—a few Victoria bicycles. For decades it was Zarnesti's leading industry. But the market for Romanian-made rockets and mortars has been wan since the disintegration of the Warsaw Pact, and the bicycle factory, which once employed 13,000 people, has laid off about 5,000 since 1989. At the pulp mill, likewise, the workforce has shrunk to a fraction of its former size. The town's economy now resembles a comatose patient on a gurney, ready to be wheeled who knows where. Still, Zarnesti is filled with stalwart people, and a few of those people are energized with new ideas and new hopes.

One new idea is large-carnivore ecotourism. It began in 1995, when Christoph Promberger was contacted by a British conservation group, working through a travel agency, that had heard about the Carpathian Large Carnivore Project and wanted to bring paying visitors to this remote corner of Europe for a chance to see wolves and bears. They came—not actually to Zarnesti, but to another small community nearby—and the money spent on lodging and food, though modest, was significant to the local economy. Two years later Christoph and his colleagues repeated the experiment as an independent venture. They welcomed eight different tour groups totaling some 70 people, who were accommodated in small *pensiunes,* vacation boardinghouses run by local families. By now the wolf fieldwork had come to focus on the wooded foothills and flats of the Barsa Valley, which stretches 30 miles into the mountains above Zarnesti. Although the likelihood of actually glimpsing a wolf or a brown bear in the wild is always low, even for experienced trackers like Marius and Peter, some nature-loving travelers were quite satisfied to hike or ride horses through Carpathian forests in which a sighting, or a set of tracks, was always possible. Large carnivores, it turned out, were attracting people who wouldn't come just for the edelweiss and primrose.

One of the *pensiunes* where the travelers stay is owned by Gigi Popa, a 46-year-old businessman whose trim mustache, balding crown, and gently solicitous manner conceal the soul of a risk-taker and a performer. Give him three shots of *tsuica,* a guitar, and an audience—he'll smile shyly, then hold the floor for an evening. Give him a window of economic opportunity—he'll climb through it. In the 1980s, Gigi worked as a cash-register repairman for a large, inefficient government enterprise charged with servicing machines all over Romania. The machines in question were mediocre at best and destined to be obsoletized by modern electronic versions. Gigi couldn't divine all the coming upheavals, but he could see clearly enough that mechanical Romanian cash registers were not a wave to ride into the future.

"After the revolution, I change quickly my job and my direction," Gigi says. He got out of cash-register repair and opened a small grocery and dry-goods store in the back of the house.

He was ready for the next step, not knowing what the next step might be, when Christoph told him about English, Swiss, and German travelers who would be coming to Zarnesti, drawn by the wolves in the mountains but needing lodging in town. Gigi promptly remodeled his home and his identity again. He became a *pensiune*-keeper, with four guest rooms ready the first summer and another four the following year. He now plays an important partnership role to the Carpathian Large Carnivore Project's program of tourism. Gigi's *pensiune* is where Gordon and I have been sleeping, for instance, when we're not sublimely geschtuck in the mountains.

One morning I ask Gigi the same question I asked Mosorel: Has the new order made life better or worse? "The good thing of the revolution is everybody can do what he have dreams," Gigi says. "Because everybody have dreams. And in Ceausescu time you can do no thing for your own. Must be on the same"—he makes a glass-ceiling gesture—"level. Everybody." Whereas now, he says, a person with initiative, wit, a few good ideas and a willingness to gamble on them can raise himself and his family above the dreary old limit. The bad thing, he says, is that free-market entrepreneurship involves far more personal stress than a government job in cash-register maintenance.

One day in the summer of 1999, Christoph and Barbara noticed a sizable construction job under way in the Barsa Valley, some miles upstream from Zarnesti. The foundation was being laid for a hundred-room hotel.

This was not long after Christoph had begun discussions with the town mayor about a vision of sustainable ecotourism for Zarnesti. The crucial premise of that vision was to let the Barsa Valley remain undeveloped while the infrastructure to support visitors would be built as small-scale operations down in the town. If the valley itself were consumed by suburban sprawl and recreational development, Christoph had explained, then the carnivore habitat would be badly fragmented if not destroyed, and the Large Carnivore Project would be forced to move, taking its ecotourism business with it. But if the Barsa habitat were protected, then the project could remain, channeling visitors to whatever small *pensiunes* might be available in Zarnesti. Everyone had seemed to agree that this was the sensible approach. Yet now the hotel construction revealed that someone else—an investor from the city of Brasov, 50 miles away—intended to exploit the area on an ambitious scale. And belatedly it was revealed that the town council had approved open-development zoning for the entire valley.

"So this was disaster," Christoph remembers thinking. "Absolute disaster."

Christoph himself had to leave the country just then for a short visit back in Germany. He and Andrei Blumer, who joined the project as a specialist in rural development, hastily shaped their best argument for valley protection, so that Andrei could present their case to the mayor. Zarnesti's mayor at the time was a man named Gheorghe Lupu, formerly an engineer in the bicycle factory before Romanian bicycles lost their tactical military appeal. Bright and unpretentious, his dark hair beginning to go gray, Mr. Lupu wore a black leather jacket at work, kept his office door open to drop-by callers, and described himself jokingly as a "cowboy mayor." About the problems of Zarnesti, though, he was serious. Tax revenues yielded only 10 percent of what they did before the revolution, he could tell you; the pulp mill had laid off 2,000 people, the bicycle factory even more; the sewage system and the gas-supply network needed work; the roads too cried out for repair. There was little basis to assume that this harried man would muster much sympathy for protecting wolf habitat—notwithstanding the fact that his own name, Lupu, translates as "wolf." But would he be able, at least, to grasp the connection between large carnivores, open landscape, and tourism? It was a tense juncture for Christoph, having to absent himself while the whole Barsa Valley stood in jeopardy.

Just before leaving for Germany, he received a terse electronic message on his mobile phone. It was from Andrei, saying: "Lupu stopped everything." The mayor had moved to reverse the council's decision. Let the tourists eat and sleep in Zarnesti, he agreed, and pay their visits to the wild landscape as day-trippers. He had embraced the idea of zoning protection for the valley.

But to announce a policy of protection is one thing; real safety against the forces of change is another. Barbara and I get a noisy reminder of that difference, in the upper valley, during an excursion to set traps for her lynx study.

We're twenty-some miles above Zarnesti, where the Barsa road narrows to a single snowmobile trail. Barbara has driven her Skidoo, loaded with custom-made leg-hold traps and other gear, me riding my skis at the end of a tow rope behind. In the fresh snow at trailside we've seen multiple sets of lynx prints, as well as varied signs of other animals—deep tracks from several red deer that came wallowing down off a slope, fox tracks, even one set from a restless bear that has interrupted its hibernation for a stroll. Late in the afternoon, just as Barbara finishes camouflaging her last trap, we hear the yowl of another snowmobile ascending the valley. At first I assume that it must be Christoph's. But as the machine throttles back, I see it's a large recreational Polaris, driven by a middle-aged stranger in a fur hat, with a woman on the seat behind him. Then I notice that Barbara has stiffened.

She exchanges a few sentences in Romanian with the stranger. He seems rather jovial; Barbara speaks curtly. The man swings his snowmobile around us and goes ripping on up the valley. When he's beyond earshot, which is instantly, Barbara explains what just transpired.

Claims he's from Brasov, she says. But he is not Romanian, to judge from his accent. Probably a wealthy Italian with a second home. When he heard what Barbara was doing—setting traps to catch lynx—he thought she meant trapping for pelts, and he acted snooty. When she added that it's for a radio-tracking study, he graced her with his patronizing and ignorant approval. Oh, you're doing wildlife research—OK. His ladyfriend, on the other hand, was worried. "She asked if it would be dangerous to continue, with all the lynx in here. Ya, it would," Barbara says caustically. "Keep out." The upper valley is closed to joyriding traffic, and those two have no business being here, Barbara explains. Unlimited motorized access, along with development sprawl and other symptoms of the new liberty and affluence, are now a damn sight more threatening to the lynx population—and the wolves, and the bears—than fur-trapping, judicious timbering, or even the crude, spoliatory hunting once practiced by Nicolae Ceausescu, with all his minions and helicopter pads.

Barbara has never before seen a recreational snowmobile in Zarnesti, let alone up here. "Aaagh," she says, as the roar of the Polaris fades above us. "It all starts with one. There are so many rich guys in Brasov now."

The following day, Christoph receives a disturbing piece of news by mobile phone from Marius: Tsiganu has been shot.

The details are still blurry, but it seems that a couple of boar hunters let fly at the wolf for no particular reason except his wolfhood. Probably they were poaching, since no gamekeeper was present, as mandated for a legitimate boar hunt. Tsiganu is wounded, hard to say how badly, but still on his feet at last report. Marius, having heard the shots, came upon the hunters a few moments later. Marius is still out there,

Christoph tells me, following a trail of radio beeps and blood spoor through the wet snow. Before long he will either find Tsiganu's fresh carcass or else run out of daylight without knowing quite what's what.

A day passes. Still there's no definite news of Tsiganu. On the morning of the second day, I set out tracking with Marius and two project assistants.

We park the Dacia truck on a roadside above a village and begin hoofing along a farm lane into the foothills. We follow a snow-covered trail on a climbing traverse between meadows, along wooded gullies, beyond the last of the farmhouses and the last of the barking dogs, past two men hauling logs with a pair of oxen. Marius moves briskly. He's a short, solid fellow with good wind and a long stride. He cares about this animal—both about *Canis lupus* as a denizen of the Romanian mountains, that is, and about Tsiganu as an individual. But Marius is a home-bred Romanian forestry worker, not a foreign-trained biologist, and his attitude is complexly grounded in local realities.

"Last year the wolf was killing for me two sheep," he says as we walk. "Because the shepherd was drunk. Was like an invitation to eat." Some farmers moan about such losses, Marius says, but what do they expect? That the wolf, which has lived as a predator in these mountains for thousands of years, should now transform itself into a vegetarian? As for hunters who would offhandedly kill a wolf for its fur, he can't comprehend them. "Also I am a hunter," he says. He shoots ducks, pheasants, wild boar, and in self-defense he wouldn't hesitate to kill a bear. But a wolf, no, never. It's much nicer simply to go out with his dogs, hike in the forest, and know that in this place the ancient animals are still present.

Two miles in, we pick up a signal from Tsiganu's collar. The bearing is south-southwest, toward a steep wooded valley that descends from a castle-shaped rock formation among the peaks above. Farther along, we get another signal on roughly the same line, and now the tempo of beeps indicates that Tsiganu is alive—at least barely alive, because he's moving. Here we split into two groups, for a better chance of crossing his trail. Marius and I continue the traverse until we find a single set of wolf tracks, then back-follow them up a slope. The tracks are deep, softened in outline by at least one afternoon's melting, and show no sign of blood. Yesterday? Or earlier, before the shooting? They might be Tsiganu's or not. If his, is the stride normal? Has his wound already clotted? Or is he lying near death with a slug lodged against his backbone, or in his lung, or in his jaw, while his packmates have gone on without him? Are these in fact his tracks, or some other wolf's? No way of knowing.

So we hike again toward the radio signal, post-holing our way through knee-deep crust. We round a bend that brings us into the valley below the castle-shaped peak. Here the radio signal gets stronger. We stare upward, scanning for movement. We see none.

Marius disconnects the directional antenna from the receiver. He listens again, using the antenna cable's nub like a stethoscope, trying to fine-focus the bearing. Again a strong signal. So we're close now. Maybe 100 meters, Marius says. He tips back his head and offers a loud wolfish howl, a rather good imitation of a pack's contact call. We listen for response. There's a distant, dim echo of his voice coming off the mountain, followed by silence. We wait. Nothing. We turn away. I begin to fumble with my binoculars.

Then from up in the beeches comes a new sound. It's Tsiganu, the gypsy carnivore, howling back.

December 2000

One Nation, Under Ted

JACK HITT

"The thing is, there's this red dot," says Beau Turner, standing quietly in a longleaf-pine forest on his Avalon Plantation, 25,000 red-clay acres half an hour south of Tallahassee. It's 6:30 on a late-spring morning, and the humidity is rolling in like a fog; already I regret the hot coffee in my hand. One of our chores today is to band some new woodpecker chicks with Avalon identification, but then the red dot came up and I was anxious to see it. Not much bigger than the head of a pin, the red dot is a nearly Zen idea of nature's beauty. It sits behind the ear of the male red-cockaded woodpecker, an endangered species that Turner has spent the last four years trying to reintroduce to this land.

"It's like a bird hickey," drawls Greg Hagan, a woodpecker specialist and former U.S. Forest Service biologist who bolted to Avalon four years ago to work with Beau. During mating season, the red dot gets shown off to the females, and it pretty much reduces them to shameless tramps. Hagan points to a towering pine, taking note of a shower of splinters catching the light. It's no red dot, but it's as close as we'll get. Following the wood chips up a column of sunshine, I finally see him. A red-cockaded woodpecker pecking away, foraging.

It is a lovely sight, and the work it's taken to put that bird in the upper story of this forest is critical to understanding why, at 33, Beau Turner is one of the most important conservationists working the land today.

Reintroducing the red-cockaded woodpecker has cost millions of dollars—probably tens of millions, if you consider that the bird is just part of a much larger attempt to restore Avalon's entire longleaf-pine ecosystem, which is in turn a mere fraction of the projects under Beau's management. The youngest son of cable magnate and billionaire Ted Turner, Beau is in charge of an unprecedented bid to return almost two million private acres to their original state of biodiversity—bringing bison back to tallgrass prairies, desert bighorn sheep back to New Mexico mountains, and wolves back to great swaths of the Rockies—in an effort to prove that responsible environmental stewardship can pay off, not only in beauty, but in bottom-line profits, a form of enlightened stewardship that Beau calls "holistic land management."

At Avalon, that translates into a massive program of weeding thousands of acres of invasive tree species and reintroducing the controversial tool of fire to revive the longleaf-pine forests that once thrived here. The hope is to establish selective harvesting of the pines in a land-management system that will do it all: make money, permit the Turners to preserve the plantation's historic use as a quail-hunting spread, and restore these woods to their ancient role as habitat for the red-cockaded woodpecker. So the red dot is an emblem of a larger-than-life ambition—the type of thing Americans have come to associate with the Turner name.

RCWs, as birders call red-cockaded woodpeckers, are "persnickety birds," says Hagan. They prefer to bore holes about 40 feet off the ground in tall, old, longleaf pines. The hole must be precisely 1-7/8 inches in diameter, not a fraction bigger or flying squirrels will climb in and depredate their eggs. And to keep out snakes and other ground predators, they like to peck little holes around the entrance so that the pine leaks its sap, a stubborn whitish glue.

When Hagan got started at Avalon in 1998, he built 40 RCW nesting chambers in his workshop and placed each box in a notch he chainsawed high up in a pine, complete with sap-mimicking white paint stripes. That year, he released ten young RCWs obtained from the Apalachicola National Forest; one pair flew off, but eight stayed, settling into Hagan's phony nests for a season before building their own. Each year Beau and Hagan have released another ten birds or so; the current population is near 45 birds, stable enough that the woodpeckers are beginning to breed.

"Check this out," Beau says. He and Hagan are looking at a small video monitor, part of a device Hagan dreamed up. On a long extendable pole, he's placed a tiny camera, like something David Letterman might fasten to the head of a monkey. He can dip its lens directly into an RCW nest. On screen, two chicks—bald and helpless—tumble over and over each other.

Hagan straps a narrow ladder to the trunk of the pine and climbs up in a safety harness, like a telephone man. At the hole, he uses a dental mirror to peer in, and another little device to scoop up the chicks in a tiny sling. He climbs down and carefully places a chick in Beau's hands. With the banding tool, Hagan marks the bird twice, once with a Fish & Wildlife number and again as an Avalon chick born this year.

"Take a look," says Beau, holding the little woodpecker in cupped hands. The bird is curious to behold, but so is the man. Beau's a boyish-looking adult, with a kid's flop of hair betrayed only by a few gray strands. His smile is wide and friendly. He's standing upright (and he's a good six-foot-three), reminding me not of his father but of Teddy Roosevelt in one of those vintage pictures of him beside a dead bull elephant, chest out, his smile wild with a primal Darwinian pleasure. Beau is holding a new kind of trophy animal, appropriate to this age: a blind, rubbery, neonatal chick with pin feathers, about two inches long, alive.

Multiply that chick thousands of times and you get an idea of the national scale involved here. From Ted Turner's original southwestern Montana spreads—the 22,000-acre Bar None and the 114,000-acre Flying D—the Turner empire has mushroomed to include 20 properties that dip into nearly every North American ecosystem. A quarter-million acres of Nebraska sandhills. Another 138,000 in South Dakota. Forty thousand in the Oklahoma tallgrass prairie. The Vermejo Park Ranch in northern New Mexico, at nearly 600,000 acres, is the largest ponderosa-pine ecosystem in private hands. It joins Turner's other New Mexico holdings—the 156,000-acre Ladder Ranch and 360,000-acre Armendaris Ranch, both near Truth or Consequences—to constitute 2 percent of the state's land. At 63, Turner is now the single largest individual land-owner in the country; his personal chunk of America is 1.8 million acres and growing. Compare that to The Nature Conservancy, the nation's largest land-conservation organization, which owns 1.6 million U.S. acres and manages 5.4 million more. The Turner empire is bigger than Delaware. It is enough mountain and valley and river and prairie that it could rank as the 48th-largest state.

This total does not include Ted's international property, two *estancias* in Patagonia and one in Tierra del Fuego totaling another 128,000 acres. Recently, the Patagonian estates have served as fly-fishing retreats for Ted, who's had sort of a bad year. In its January restructuring, AOL Time Warner put Turner out to pasture, and since then he's been about as easy to interview as the banished ruler of an autocratic kingdom. When his nervous chamberlains finally made the arrangements, Turner and I conversed via speakerphone, as his scribes took down Ted's pontifications to ensure accuracy on my part.

"I don't want all the land, I just want the ranch next door," Ted bellowed from his bunker at the CNN Center in Atlanta. "That's a joke, of course," he yelled, but of course he wasn't joking. Turner buys land almost compulsively because, he boomed, "we're heading for extinction at 90 miles per hour," because "humanity is an endangered species." As the brochures for Turner Enterprises proclaim, Ted's dream is to manage these vast lands "in an economically sustainable and eco-logically sensitive manner while conserving native species."

Like all moguls, Ted is a notorious man of action, and he gets prickly with questions that seek reflection. When I tossed him a bunny about his land philosophy, he barked, "You're the writer, I'm not getting paid to write this article!" When I tried flattering him about the wide range of carnivores now roaming the Flying D, he shouted: "We don't have any grizzly bears. We don't have any Indians!" That didn't sound quite right, so he tried again. "We have Indians *visit*! And we've had some grizzlies walk through, but we don't have any wolves, so we don't have all the animals there."

Ted Turner is one of our loudest citizens, which in this culture of cool television can be perceived as idiocy. He is also vulgar and reckless, qualities that obscure his more charming delphic gifts. Ted has pretty consistently put forward big, round concepts that later paid off: Whether it's shrinking the world into a global village through cable television or forgiving Jane Fonda or fretting about our debt to the United Nations, he has a way of seizing on an idea with dramatic action (inventing CNN, *marrying* Jane Fonda, donating a billion to the UN). Now, by his estimation, he's sunk at least $500 million into biodiversity and bison.

One could easily dismiss Turner's purchasing escapades and eco-rhetoric as money-wasting billionaire hoohah. (His net worth, estimated at $4.8 billion in late September, puts Turner 25th on *Forbes* magazine's list of the 400 richest Americans.) But when Turner, praised in the business media for hiring brilliant managers, handed the day-to-day implementation of his land ideas to Beau, the second-youngest of his five children, Ted's paired instincts—make money, save planet—found fertile ground.

Together with his dad, Beau has developed these ideas into what one might call the Turner ethic, a mingling of the southern tradition of hunting-based conservation, a businessman's eye for profit, and an environmentalist's appreciation of beauty and biodiversity. In any five-minute period, Beau can coo about the red dot, complain bitterly about the commodity prices for buffalo bellies and pine timber, point his finger at a darting white-tailed deer and go "bang," and improvise a symphonic paean to what the land looked like centuries ago.

When he talks about the past, the term "pre-Anglo" falls regularly from Beau's lips. It's a metaphor for discovery—for finding out what was lost in the East as we replaced millions of acres of forests with patchwork microenvironments, and in the West as we nearly eliminated bison, wolf, prairie dog, and other species from big-sky landscapes. If the work of colonial and industrial settling deflated once-thriving ecosystems in all these places, then the Turners seek nothing less than to reinstate the bustling climax landscapes that naturally thrived there. And in those redeemed ecosystems, to seize on what opportunities lurk for the entrepreneur. It's a view of nature guaranteed to thrill and piss off everyone from Greenpeace to the beef industry.

To dream up these ideas is one thing. But with Beau in charge, Ted is nailing them to the ground, trying to find out what happens in messy, mucky practice—a fact that impresses even critics who aren't always sure what the hubbub adds up to. "As I read what ecologists write, there's always a hypothetical 'what if' tone, because they can't do the experiment," says Frank Popper, a Rutgers professor known for his Buffalo Commons theory, the idea that the Great Plains' economic future lies in an ecological return to open prairie, and with it, bison. "Maybe what Turner is doing is a giant experiment—of how biodiversity would actually work, not in the lab or on a computer model, but on a scale that is appropriate for animals the size of buffalo and antelope."

If so, the Turners' vision "is of extraordinary importance," says Dave Foreman, Earth First! founder and leader of the Wildlands Project, an initiative that works with Turner and others to link large swaths of wildlife habitat. "Aldo Leopold said that 'one of the penalties of an ecological education is that one lives alone in a world of wounds.' The job of an ecologist is to be a land doctor. And some of the things they are doing on Turner's ranches are the cutting edge of healing the wounds."

Which is another way of saying that Ted Turner puts his money where his mouth is—and he rather famously has plenty of both.

Beau Turner's zeal for the outdoors is apparent the minute a housekeeper opens the front door at Avalon Plantation, with its columns and its stone dogs and a Civil War cannon out front. Piled in a great heap on the delicate furniture of the drawing room, anticipating Beau's later arrival, is a cargo hold of equipment: seven fishing poles, several rifles, boxes of ammo, a longbow, a crossbow, three tackle boxes, seven pairs of boots for every imaginable terrain, and a machete.

Beau's interest in the outdoors began on the family's plantations in South Carolina. Outside Charleston are two Old South spreads, Hope Plantation and St. Phillips Island, that Ted bought in the late 1970s. "I grew up hunting and fishing there," Beau says about Hope, "but it was Pop who encouraged us to really find out what was on the other side of the door." Given the inclinations of Turner *fils,* it was not much of a decision for Turner *père* to tap his youngest son to oversee the properties when it came time to divvy up the next generation's responsibilities. (All of Turner's other children—Laura Turner Seydel, 40; Teddy Jr., 38; Rhett, 35; and Jennie Turner Garlington, 32—are involved in the family's environmental work, but none to the same extent Beau is.)

"I remember the day I graduated from the Citadel," Beau says, recalling that spring of 1991. "Pop was talking to me afterwards about what to do next. I had been accepted to Wharton Business School. And he said I should think about the environment." Beau describes it as the turning point of his life, as if he can't quite believe he almost went to a fancy eastern business school. Instead he went to Montana State and started on a master's in wildlife biology.

By this time western ranches had become the bauble of choice for the billionaire crowd, but Ted wasn't buying livestock just to complete the cowboy postcard outside some 18-bedroom log mansion. Rather, he set out to redeem the buffalo—an interest that dated back to Ted the kid collecting buffalo nickels, and one that got a little eccentric as Ted maintained a proto-herd on his South Carolina land in the 1970s.

When Beau took over the species work in 1993, the operation snowballed. In 1992 Ted had added a New Mexico property, the Ladder Ranch, to the two Montana ranches, and in 1993 bought the 12,000-acre Snowcrest Ranch, southwest of Bozeman, Montana. The slow accretion of property continued, one or two ranches a year, with high marks like the 1996 purchase of the 580,000-acre Vermejo Park Ranch west of Raton, New Mexico. All the while the Turners were hiring scientists, adding bison, and developing restoration programs.

"Ted has said he would not have been so aggressive in the acquisition of land if not for the interest and abilities of Beau," says Mike Phillips, the star wildlife biologist hired away from Yellowstone National Park in 1997 to run the endangered-species programs. "Beau's biggest strength is his passion—unending passion and unending enthusiasm for proper land stewardship. This guy is caught hook, line, and sinker. He eats it, he breathes it, he sleeps it."

Today, if Ted is the visionary CEO of Planet Turner, Beau is the practical-minded CFO. From its headquarters in Bozeman, not far from the Flying D, the operation is broken down by mission: Turner Enterprises is a for-profit group trying to earn money from the properties by cutting timber, running big-game hunts ($13,000 per elk hunt at the high end), and ranching bison, whose lean meat is sold to upscale groceries and restaurants. The Atlanta-based Turner Foundation is the charitable arm, its trustees Ted and the kids, giving away $44 million in 574 grants last year to every environmental and population-control group imaginable, from $15,000 for Wild Alabama to $500,000 for the National Wildlife Federation. The Bozeman-based Turner Endangered Species Fund is the field operation for the properties, spending $1 million of Turner Foundation money last year on species-restoration programs for listed critters and greenery like the Mexican wolf and the blowout penstemon. As one employee told me, "Turner Enterprises makes the money, the Foundation gives away the money, and the Fund spends the money."

On the ground, each western ranch manager reports to a single chieftain, Russ Miller, who has managed the ranching business since 1992. His biodiversity counterpart is Mike Phillips, a renowned bigfoot in wolf restoration. Another sign of the scale the Turners operate on is the arrival of Mike Finley, the new president of the Turner Foundation, and former superintendent of Yellowstone, Yosemite, and Everglades National Parks. When the ranch managers get together twice a year, as they did this August in Bozeman, the agenda runs from bison herd projections to fire management to community outreach.

The main business is still bison. Ted now owns 8 percent of the country's population—27,000 head. With wholesale prices for live bison dropping, though, he recently decided to try to stimulate the demand side. He intends to open five restaurants next year called Ted's Montana Grill. Run by his eldest son, Teddy, Jr., and supplied by Beau, the Grills will sell bison burgers but also regular hamburgers and even chicken. "We've got a motto," Beau says slyly. "'Nobody beats our meat!'" It's not clear he's kidding.

When Beau and I sit down to dinner in the formal Avalon dining room that night, the cook serves osso buco—but of course the shanks are bison, not veal. Heavy with meat and bones, the fine porcelain plates are delivered by servants. "Do y'all eat the marrow with the meat like ya supposed to?" Beau asks, all chummy, as if he's not so sure about this fancy-ass osso buco stuff. He makes you feel like you either could eat the marrow and sip the exquisite cabernet at the table of a billionaire, or just put your elbows on the table and chew damn good meat with Beau. Whichever.

It's a southern thing, too. Any relationship, no matter how strained, weird, or antagonistic, has to be grounded in the habits of friendship—the back slap, a private detail, booze. After dinner, Beau asks me to put down the pad and just have a drink. We polish off another bottle of wine and talk about friends, wives—Beau married Texas interior designer Gannon Hunt in 1999—and family. I learn about his sister's heartbreak, a gravely ill child.

His ease can be disarming. At one point, I motion to a portrait of Vivien Leigh as Scarlett O'Hara in *Gone with the Wind*. The thing is nearly life-size, I say, just like the one in the movie.

"It *is* the one in the movie," Beau says, as if he'd just learned it himself. Then he jumps up to show me the purple stain where a drunken Rhett Butler shattered his wineglass just before he took Scarlett upstairs for what we might now call date rape. Beau says that his father "picked it up," as if Ted had found it at a yard sale.

When the weather comes up, I talk about the strange winter we had in Connecticut, and Beau cites the rainfall totals for northern Florida before dilating on the inaccuracies of the precipitation forecasts for the Dakotas. Rain was pretty good in the Northwest, he says, but he's concerned about the Southwest, particularly Arizona and New Mexico. There have been rain shortages in those states, which means the possibility of catastrophic fire.

There's a way to talk about the weather that marks you as a local—a knowledge of the immediate past, of the way it's supposed to be right now. Beau talks that way about half the country. He looks at tracts of land, entire states, the way I look at my backyard vegetable patch. As a garden.

Rattling around Avalon in his old Toyota truck, Beau's intimacy with the landscape shows. At one dried-up peat bog, he talks at length about what will replace it: a 360-acre lake he's restoring. At another lake he hops out into a biblical gathering of insects.

"Oh, hell, don't worry about those," he laughs as the swarms blacken us. "They're just hatchlings. They won't do anything." Unperturbed, he pulls out a fly rod. "How about a sportsman's shot?" he informs the photographer with me. "Let me catch a bass. Right here." He walks to the water's edge and starts examining the surface and the shadows. He casts, and two minutes later a fish is dangling on the line. Then he does it again, like a Saturday morning Bassmaster. The day wears on like this, Beau driving around the lumpy roads of his 25,000 acres, yakking endlessly. "Black bears like to cross through here," he says at one point, and sure enough, one appears, sees us, and rambles off.

We pull up to some thick woods. The stretch is dense with oak and magnolia; the underbrush is as tall as a basketball player—impenetrable without a machete.

"You'll never get a better view of past, present, and future than right here," he says. He asks me to look at this forest, and it just looks like "forest" to me, but then it becomes clear that these woods are supposed to be repellent. If I leave this land knowing anything, he wants me to know that this is wrong.

"Pre-Anglo, this land burned every year," he says. "Those hardwoods would never make it to this height. This should be longleaf pine." We continue on, bouncing up and down past different styles of forest, and then come to a clearing where bulldozers are shoveling ripped-up trees into piles to be burned.

"This is tung-nut tree," Beau says. "It's not a native species. It was planted in the forties to produce tung-nut oil. But it chokes out the longleaf pine." So, on about 3,000 acres, he's tearing out the tung trees and reseeding pine. We drive to a patch of newly reclaimed longleaf forest, where the tung trees have been removed, the hardwoods logged, and the floor cover burned to make it easier for the longleaf to come back.

"Look at that," Beau says. "It's amazing. What you're seeing is a work of art."

The man who taught Beau to see the land this way is just up the road at Beau's latest acquisition, an old 8,500-acre pine plantation. We hook up with Leon Neel, Beau's mentor, an originator of the Turner ethic, and a driving force in its implementation. Neel is an old-timer in this area, a 74-year-old environmentalist who's worked with loggers all his life. More important, he is a practitioner of fire ecology, the growing school of thought that fire was not just a part of the land "pre-Anglo," but—whether set by migrating American Indians, by lightning, or by Beau's employees today—a necessary part of wildlife management.

"You've got to understand how this works," Neel says in his smooth inland drawl. He grabs a small clump of longleaf in the grass stage. He explains how it closes up during a fire, protecting the tree's heart, and then shoots straight up above the usual fire line, beginning its ascent to the top of the forest canopy.

Longleaf pine produces beautiful, languid, 12-inch needles precisely to create the kind of fuel that will combust into fire every fall, destroying its competitors. The "hand of man," as Beau and Neel like to say, stopped the fires and deprived the longleaf of its main Darwinian advantage. It started to disappear as the unburned forests easily pushed it aside, and as mill companies clear-cut these woods to make room for fast-growing pulp trees like slash and loblolly pine.

On some level, there's a tree-hugging sensibility at work here: Neel and Beau look at these woods and can see the difference between overgrown hardwood and the cathedral spaces of a climax pine forest. But this is where Beau also earns the Turner in his name. "Longleaf is a really nice timbering wood for furniture," he says. "Slash and loblolly aren't." Beau believes he can profitably log these woods while maintaining the parklike cathedral conducive to quail and, at the tip of the pyramid, the red-cockaded woodpecker.

"Clear-cutting wrecks your soil, and that's just going to hurt you in the long run," says Beau, shouting now. "Economics and environmental sustainability go hand in hand, that's what we've learned." His mind now fixed on wrongheaded ideas, he recalls the story of a huge $50 million grant proposal that came to him. Some guy had created a hybridized Sahara-type grass that, in an arid environment, produces a wheat grain, a corn grain, and then another grain so that livestock could forage all year long. The perfect plant. He was surprised when

Beau asked where the nutrients for this miracle specimen would come from.

"He wasn't thinking it through," Beau says, actually pissed off. Then he lets loose with an almost comical "and um" that only Tom Wolfe could spell—"*aaaaannnd aaaahhhhhhmmmmm*"—before adding, "We can't go on like this. It's crazy." The accent, the tone, along with the disgust, frustration, and impatience, come together into quintessential Turneritude—and there's no mistaking who this boy's father is.

Raising woodpeckers in the East is one thing; restoring wolves and their chilling howl in the West is another. Out West, the sheer scale of land and humans' long, troubled history with large carnivores means that wildlife restoration is not a garden-club nicety, but a political act that jeopardizes a "way of life." The Turners have decided to champion the cow's shaggy rival as well as bears, wolves, prairie dogs, and other animals perceived as pests. When Ted Turner—an Easterner and a billionaire and a guy with woolly eco-theories—showed up next door, the Welcome Wagon didn't exactly wheel up to the ranch gates.

"In New Mexico, at least, he's thumbed his nose at local custom and culture," says Caren Cowan, the executive director of the Albuquerque-based New Mexico Cattle Growers' Association. "He's made statements that livestock or cattle should never have been raised in an arid climate like this. Given that we have three different ethnic cultures in New Mexico, some of which have raised livestock for up to 400 years, we feel that this is very insensitive to the local peoples."

Cowan, a frequent Turner critic, is not as worried about bison on Ted's property as she is about his reintroduction of undesirables to the neighborhood. "We have a lot more concerns with the endangered species he's propagating. This organization has taken strong opposition to the whole reintroduction of the Mexican wolf."

So far, Turner has never released a wolf on his property. He has only assisted—under provisions of the Endangered Species Act—the U.S. Fish & Wildlife Service, welcoming reintroduced wolves onto his land if they stray from public acreage, which they have done in New Mexico; maintaining captive holding or breeding programs for Fish & Wildlife on the Ladder Ranch and the Flying D; and monitoring Mexican wolves released into the Apache and Gila National Forests. But by hiring Yellowstone's Mike Phillips as the architect of his wolf program, Turner has invited the wrath of most, but not all, of his fellow ranchers.

One cattleman who finds Turner's notions worth studying is fourth-generation New Mexican Jim Winder, whose 125,000-acre Heritage Ranch sits ten miles south of Turner's Ladder Ranch. Winder heads the Quivira Coalition, a group of ranchers and environmentalists trying to create ecologically healthy rangeland. Like Turner, he welcomes reintroduced wolves onto his property; he spotted a large radio-collared male there just last summer. But he also understands ranchers' hostility. "The wolf presents itself as a cost to these ranchers," he says, "and the economics of ranching are basically slow starvation. Talking about wolf recovery is like taking a drowning man and pouring a cup of water on his head."

Winder isn't worried about bison replacing cattle. "That's still a specialty market," he says. "Most ranchers think it's a joke." But he has joined an increasing number of western ranchers who are trying the same sustainable practices—pasture rotation and natural grazing patterns—that the Turners use. "I don't believe their current business is economically wise," Winder says. "But what Turner does that's different is he puts a value on conservation. As I like to tell people, Ted Turner's got the money of a small government, but not the bureaucracy. He's able to accomplish a lot of things that an individual like me cannot."

Winder believes that, for landowners of modest means, ecology has to pay for itself. And groups like The Nature Conservancy are sympathetic. "There is sometimes a sense of all or nothing in the environmental community," says TNC president Steve McCormick from the organization's Arlington, Virginia, headquarters. "In some cases, 100-percent conservation is not possible. So if you can get 90 percent because the landowner is getting some economic return *and* is motivated to keep the environmental quality, then that's good. If the landowner thinks he has to either sell to conservationists or build condos, then the possibility of selling a few trees, for example, in a sustainable operation is much better." In other words, a third way.

"If ranchers weren't so damn pigheaded," Winder says, "they would be studying what Turner is doing and figuring out how to make money from it. Ted Turner is offering a life preserver for ranchers; if you want to ranch, you better be studying what he's doing. We are."

"The wolves are coming," says Mike Phillips, pointing to the mountains. On the outskirts of Bozeman, Phillips is cruising down the highway toward the Flying D in a pickup. "This is ground zero of the large-carnivore restoration movement."

Phillips, a sandy-haired 43-year-old, is pointing not at the mountains, but at the scattered homes, farms, and shops on the outskirts of town. "The wolves are right over that ridge," he says. "They're gonna be on the Flying D someday, with its bison, moose, and elk. But still, they'll leave and walk north into settled lands and into this valley and get stuck among human habitat. They're gonna eat people's boots and knock over trash cans and kill the cat. They will cause problems, but they won't cause as many problems as they're credited for."

Openly challenging the ranchers' perspective, Phillips wants to reintroduce the wolf—as in big bad—to the public. "Do you know how many sheep are killed every year by wolves?" he asks as we pass under the arch marking the property line of the Flying D. Before us unfurls a hilly range that eventually erupts into the 10,000-foot Spanish Peaks. "About six. And cows? About the same. Do you think that's low? OK, fine, double it. Now, do you know how many cows just die every year in the normal course of the livestock industry? About 30,000."

To listen to Phillips is to get the sense that all the difficulties of cattle ranching in the West, which are considerable, get blamed on the fanged mug of the wolf.

But the Turners' efforts to redefine the wolf haven't always won over environmentalists, either. Last year, their work with some Yellowstone wolves penned up on the Flying D drew fierce criticism from humane groups. Turner biologists, working with Fish & Wildlife, were testing Skinnerian ideas to create a generation of wolves with no appetite for livestock, trying the same methods used to rid Malcolm McDowell of sexual cravings in *A Clockwork Orange*. The wolves were fitted with electric collars, permitted to approach livestock, and then given a strong shock.

Andrea Lococo, Rocky Mountain coordinator of the national animal-protection group Fund for Animals, excoriated the practice. "We think it's absolutely ridiculous that we should try to alter the natural behavior of wild animals, particularly to benefit a private industry that uses public lands," she said. Reaction from the right was no better. "Wolves are killers by instinct," says Steve Pilcher, executive vice-president of the Helena-based Montana Stockgrowers Association, "and I doubt you can really take that out of them." Others were merely bemused: "I have to respect Ted's imagination," says The Nature Conservancy's McCormick, "but we haven't tried to do that. Our scientists would suggest it wouldn't work."

To the Turner camp, the experiment embodies a question that's at least worth asking: If adaptation in nature occurs all the time in the normal hustle of the ecosystem, then why can't we help adapt the wolf to provide *some* wildness but not too much? It sounds ridiculous, and typically Turnerian in its hubris, except that we've fully domesticated all kinds of animals and partially domesticated scores of others.

But a wolf? Phillips expected flack, and he got it. "No other private organization has ever gone shoulder to shoulder with the U.S. government and helped deal with the daily grind," he says. "Wolves are tough. They wear you down fiscally, they wear you down emotionally. Nobody likes you."

This morning, there are eight wolves being cared for on the Flying D—six pups, a mother, and a yearling—not free, but penned. They were killing sheep 60 miles away, so Fish & Wildlife removed them and accepted the Flying D's invitation to take them in. Phillips believes in a form of "soft release"—keeping them penned up for a while so they lose their homing urge. In the past, wolves that were "hard released" have wandered great distances to get home.

We pick up Beau at his ranch house and head over to a cluster of outbuildings. Phillips pops the door on a freezer truck parked to the side and, stiff as a board, a 300-pound buffalo calf falls out the back, stands miraculously like a ballerina *en pointe,* and then falls over and thuds into the dirt. Then out come a giant bison drumstick and a rib cage as preposterously large as the one that tipped over Fred Flintstone's car. The first chore of the morning, apparently, is to feed the wolves.

The truck jackhammers a few miles up and down hills until a fenced-off slope dramatically comes into view. The wolf pen has a perimeter fence to keep out the bison. Inside that is a 15-foot-high chain-link enclosure bent at the top to prevent climbing, and inside that is an electric fence. The gate is locked with a chain, latched with a bolt, and secured with a bungee cord. Phillips undoes them all. Quietly we drag carcasses and parts just inside the pen.

"Step over that," Phillips says, indicating the threshold at the gate. "It's hot." As he closes the gate behind us, the wolves react to our presence. They maintain their distance but take turns sprinting up and down the far length of the fence, really, really fast. We set out the gargantuan lunches and fill the water troughs. Then Phillips says, "Let's go have a look at them. Stay close."

As we walk toward the racing wolves, we have to be careful not to stumble on any of the dozens of gnawed hooves that litter the grass. Toward the other side, where the wolves apparently drag their food, the place is a crowded boneyard of ungulate feet. Above us, a half-dozen ravens watch from the trees, making a noise that sounds like a demented laugh track. I look across to see eight highly aroused wolves galloping back and forth, and I am thinking: That's an agitated mother wolf with six pups; they are hungry and penned in; we are moving toward them as an aggressive pack.

I don't have my Boy Scout manual on me, but if memory serves, none of this is particularly safe. Yet as we get closer to the pack against the fence, the wolves squeeze out to one side and race to the far fence by the gate, obviously terrified.

"They've gained a little weight," Beau says hopefully, as if he's talking about frail octuplets in the neonatal ward. Phillips examines the holes they've dug to sleep in. Some pups are in one of the wooden shelters. Phillips pops the top and we all stare in at a pup curled and sleeping. They are handsome animals. You want to pet them.

I definitely remember what the manual says about that.

*   *   *

On the Flying D, as at Avalon, Beau can look out the window at any view of the land and strike up a natural-history yarn. Throughout the morning, wildlife passes by as if we were on safari. An elk bugles, a coyote runs through, then a fox. The outsize shield of a bison's head slowly turns and regards us as we enter every slope or vale.

Given all this, I ask, what is the point of allowing wolves to thrive in a near-paradise of bison grazing lightly on the land?

"First off, deer and elk wouldn't be dying of chronic wasting disease," Beau says, mentioning the illness borne of overpopulation and lack of predation. "So there'd be less disease in the landscape." Then Beau and Phillips start riffing about the land out the window, citing some of the advantages they've seen and others that have been theorized around wolf introduction elsewhere.

With deer and elk populations in check, there'd be fewer coyotes and thus more mice and rodents and voles. Meaning more raptors and foxes. Hence a greater variety of carrion, so scavengers would benefit. Wolverine distribution, for example, is directly related to winter carrion supply.

"If ungulates behave differently because of the presence of wolves, then the plants experience a different fate," Phillips says. "There might be more aspen saplings that make it to adulthood. So then there'd be more beavers, and that might alter your water regime. We don't know how it will play out after that, but we want to discover, or rediscover, that effect."

How long will it all take? And who might it piss off along the way? We are all sitting on a little wooden bridge over Cherry Creek, far off from the wolf pen. Here the Turner ethic has already run afoul of many different interests. The Montana Fish, Wildlife & Parks agency, working with the Turners, would like to stock the river with westslope cutthroat trout. Sounds simple enough, but all hell has broken loose. The westslope cutthroat trout is an imperiled, though not listed as endangered, fish. It's native to Montana, but not to Cherry Creek. Actually, no fish is native to the creek, at least not the 70- to 80-mile portion in question, which stretches between a fountainhead lake and a waterfall. Because it's perfectly isolated and impossible to breach without the hand of man, it would be a great place for this delicate trout to dwell. The problem is that, years ago, rainbow and brook and Yellowstone trout were all stocked in this creek, and they now dominate the isolated section. To ensure that these tough trout won't drive off any reintroduction of westslope cutthroat, the state agency wants to chemically kill the invasive trout.

Naturally, there are plenty of environmentalists who see this as self-defeating madness. Since part of the creek flows through public lands, the public has standing to sue to halt the plan. A federal suit was withdrawn earlier this year due to overlap with other cases. But a state suit against Montana Fish, Wildlife & Parks and the Montana Department of Environmental Quality is still pending, charging violations of the state constitution and Water Quality Act. "The poison they want to use will also kill off the insect population and the amphibians," says Bill Fairhurst, spokesman for the Public Lands Access Association and the petitioner in both lawsuits. "They are not killing fish, they are killing an entire ecosystem."

"They have a point," says Beau. "They say, 'If you guys are all about historical conditions and the wisdom of nature, then the place was fishless in the first place.' True, but it's a dandy site for trout. And we're not willing to take a sense of environmental history to an absurd level if it means we'll lose a native fish."

On Cherry Creek, as on most of these lands, the difference between Turnerism and environmentalism could not be starker. Those suing don't trust the hand of man to fix our mistakes. The Turners believe that when the environment is busted, benign neglect is also a choice, and often a bad one. So they take action, cause trouble, get people talking. Maybe that's the point. "Our logic," says Phillips, "is if you can provide a stunning example of something, it sometimes prompts people to do things they would not have done otherwise. We're trying to excite and motivate others to be good stewards." According to The Nature Conservancy's McCormick, mini-Teds are already popping up. Telecommunications magnate John Malone is buying up his own empire and preserving it through conservation easements, legal riders in which, by relinquishing development rights, landowners can ensure their land's preservation in perpetuity. Several of Turner's properties, including the Flying D, the Bar None, and Avalon Plantation, carry easements through The Nature Conservancy; after Ted's death, the properties will go into a trust, which his children will manage until the last one passes away. Then the trust will revert to the Turner Foundation.

But the ambition stretches beyond the family's own growing acreage. The Turners are at the forefront of a movement to reinvent land management with an eye toward big-picture ecology—to blur the boundaries between public and private land and let vast migration corridors open up, allowing keystone species like wolves, grizzlies, elk, and mountain lions to take back the North American range. "The truth is that there is no way to build a large-carnivore conservation program without public lands," Phillips says, swinging his legs over the bridge. "No private landscape is big enough to support it. You must have both." In the end, he says, the Turners intend to continue linking up with efforts on public lands (which abut many of the family properties) to force a reconsideration of what we think when we think about wildness. On the Flying D, that might involve a pretty picture of bison grazing on a montane range, part of a robust system of flora and fauna that includes the natural stress of large carnivores and their natural predators, *Homo sapiens,* as well.

"I see a day when we'll add wolves to the hunt here," Beau says, "when the bison population supports it, maybe even needs it." Of course, on the Flying D, the wolf will never be the main force thinning the herd. Ted's Montana Grill will. And the hunting and fishing business will help maintain a balance in the aquaculture and among the game animals like elk, deer, and even wolf.

That's the business side. The aesthetic side, even the spiritual side, is to have a landscape teeming with as much biodiversity as the nutrient content in the soil and the dynamics of plant, bird, and mammal will permit. It is a neo-romantic view, one that sees a kind of beauty in the red dot of the RCW flitting among trees, made beautiful not by its mystery, but by our understanding of why it's there. After aeons of forcing the land to conform to our demands and economies, by backing off some of the ecosystems we do use, we might begin to see the dynamic of nature differently.

"The wolf is just another critter in the woods, if we understand what he's doing and why he's doing it," Beau says.

"No more right or wrong than a rabbit," Phillips adds. Just another animal on the land, trying to get along, like us.

December 2001

At Play

HAMPTON SIDES

O n Friday the 13th of February, the skies over Hakuba, Japan, are at last sun-streaked and cloudless. Up until this morning, these Nagano Olympics seem to have been cursed by the Shinto gods. Not enough snow. Too much snow. Too much fog. Sleet. Rain. There was even an earthquake, a 5.0 temblor—not powerful enough to do any real damage, except, perhaps, to a racer's concentration. The downhill event has been delayed by nearly a week. But this morning, at dawn, the officials tell the Olympians to wax their skis. It's show time.

Hermann Maier, wearing bib number four, is standing in the chute, immersed in the ritualistic tics of the countdown: digging in his skis, planting and replanting his poles. He wears a red-and-white spandex suit and a red crash helmet adorned with the eagle of the Austrian flag. The course, having been machine-spritzed with mist through the night, is now a long neck of blue ice, fast and slick, with the hard glint of chromium.

"I suppose," Maier says to me when I meet him at his gym in the Austrian Alps, "you're going to want to know all about the *sturtz*."

The what?

"The *sturtz*—the crash. The Americans only want to know about the crash. It's all they care about. Violence makes all the headlines in your country." The 25-year-old champion curls his lip in disgust. "There was an American photographer on the mountain. He didn't say, 'Hey, you all right?' He says, 'Hey, great picture!'"

But it *was* a great picture. The video of Maier's downhill crash was something like the Zapruder film of the Winter Olympics, microanalyzed for the exact moment of error and the exact moment when bones should have cracked, an alarming sports reel played and replayed in the craven knowledge that all of us, everywhere, especially Americans but probably even well-mannered Austrians, are beady-eyed rubberneckers who can't help ourselves. Here was a piece of footage lurid enough to replace the stale old "agony of defeat" clip at the start of *ABC's Wide World of Sports,* the one in which Yugoslavian ski jumper Vinko Bogotah endlessly pinwheels down the mountain during a 1970 contest in Obersdorf, West Germany. Maier's *sturtz* in Nagano was more than just a spectacular wipeout. It was an anarchic burst of kinesis that refreshed our understanding of why alpine skiing is so exciting to watch in the first place: the possibility of pure, white-knuckled calamity, the chaos lurking just behind the scrim of mastery and finesse.

Maier comes from a country where skiing is less a sport than a national science project, a country that produced two of the greatest theoreticians of motion, Ernst Mach and Christian Doppler. To crash, and to crash so crazily, so wantonly, is a most un-Austrian thing to do, and Maier remains deeply unhappy that he will be forever linked to such a messy encounter with the laws of physics. "If you ask me," Maier says, "I would prefer to be famous for winning two gold medals in Nagano rather than for my screwup."

Thus chary about going down in history as skiing's Olympic crash-test dummy, Maier has dedicated himself to putting in a steady, chaos-free season on the slopes of the world this winter. He not only aims to win the World Cup overall title for the second year in a row, but also plans to beat Swede Ingemar Stenmark's 1979 record of 13 World Cup victories in a single season and to prevail in a slew of events at the World Championships in Vail next February. And he intends to do it with deliberate and measured rationality. "You better believe it," he tells me. "I'm done with the crashing." He says this with a vehemence that protests too much, as if he suspects that certain bad habits can't be extinguished, as hard as one may try.

Besides, the *sturtz* has been good to Maier. It helped to carry him across a certain invisible line of demarcation into skiing superstardom. "In a way, the crash was the best thing that ever could have happened to him," says John Garnsey, president of the organizing committee for the 1999 World Championships in Vail and a jury member at Nagano. "If Maier had just won two Olympic golds, he'd be yet another great Austrian skier, known and respected by insiders everywhere, but not a household word—certainly not in this country. To succeed is boring. To fail spectacularly and then succeed—that's really something."

Maier is visualizing the line he set for himself during his inspection runs, but that was three days ago. In the aftermath of the storms, the course-setters had to pull the gates and then hastily reset them this morning, with no time to allow the skiers to reinspect. The Austrian coaches tell Maier that the course is just as it was before: Proceed as planned, no changes.

Yet in fact the course has changed—in a few places, dramatically so. At the first turn, there's a little bump that didn't exist at the inspection—"the mystery mogul," it will later be called—and after that a sharp drop-off followed by a gate that will require an abrupt left turn. To make it, Maier will have to pull back a little, stand up on his skis, slow down. But the way this new feature is situated, Maier, moving at nearly 80 miles an hour, won't be able to see it coming.

At some point or another, every skier crashes. Look at any expert's knees and you'll see the telltale scars, the butterfly stitches. Racers share a perverse and largely inexpressible addiction to the crapshoot of speed. Among themselves they don't need to talk about it, but when they try to communicate the sport's attraction to others not of the tribe, they have an annoying habit of talking about a thing called "the edge" as if it were a specific geographical place where they do most of their living, some impossibly remote principality tucked away behind distant mountains.

Maier is no exception. "It's true," he says in his characteristic mono-
tone, "I'm only happy when I'm skiing on the edge. It's the only place
where I can be. If you're not there, well, forget about it."

The difference is that by all accounts, Hermann Maier *does* push
the downhiller's brinkmanship just a little farther than it's ever been
pushed. He may train and prepare with cold, methodical thorough-
ness, but when he gets on a slope his lust for the attack seems to take
over. No one skis a tighter line, no one takes it so close to the precipice
of disaster. Before the Olympics, some skiers on the World Cup circuit
began to suggest that Maier, by always going at such a fearless, full-
throttle tilt, was merely flying on the fumes of good luck. To them,
what was even more astonishing than his Nagano crash was that it
didn't happen sooner.

If nerve were Hermann Maier's only attribute, however, he would
not have possessed the means to become the best all-around skier in
the world. During last year's World Cup circuit, he won 11 different
races in three separate alpine disciplines (giant slalom, Super G, and
downhill). Insiders have now begun to say that if Maier can avoid major
injuries over the next few years, he could become one of the greats—
a versatile champion on par with Jean-Claude Killy. Yes, he takes
immense risks, but he can back it all up with such raw power and with
such a commanding range of skills that the risks are worth taking.

His fellow World Cup skiers tend to speak of Maier with an awe
that's colored by a chilly note of incomprehension, as if they can't quite
decide whether Maier is entirely human.

"He is for sure not one of us," says Austrian teammate Hans Knauss.

"He is on another planet," says Andreas Schifferer, another Austrian teammate.

Says German downhill gold medalist Katja Seizinger, "He is beyond
this world."

Even Maier's longtime girlfriend, Petra Wechselberger, describes
him in similar terms: "He is a machine-man. He is some kind of
extraterrestrial."

This "otherworldly" verdict appears to be virtually unanimous. His
peers characterize Maier as a lone wolf, asocial to the core. "A lot of
people are intimidated by Maier," says U.S. gold medalist Tommy Moe.

"He's so intense and unfriendly, he's right on the edge of being rude. I've never once seen him say hello to the other skiers, not even a *wie gehts*. The guy's a robot, man."

Maier's various nicknames over the course of his short, spectacular career reflect this sense of his being a creature fundamentally apart—not just in terms of skill and manners, but perhaps even metabolically. "The Beast," they called him at first. Then "the Monster" and "the Alien." And, of course, the ultimate alias, the one that finally stuck during the Olympics and will probably never go away: "the Hermanator."

The name fits on so many levels that it's almost uncanny. Like Maier, the cyborg villain played by Arnold Schwarzenegger in the 1984 movie *The Terminator* possesses an action-figure physique, a calm and relentless efficiency, and an unnerving indestructibility. ("It doesn't feel pity or fear, and it absolutely will not stop—ever.") Schwarzenegger, of course, was born and raised in Austria. Like Maier, he is a power lifter, motorcycle enthusiast, and serious skier. It made perfect sense when, after the crash, Schwarzenegger publicly adopted Maier as a kind of poster robot of the slopes. "He is the Huh-mahn-nay-tuh," Schwarzenegger told the CBS television audience during an interview shortly after the crash. "And he'll . . . be . . . bahhk. He will tuh-mahn-nate all competition." Schwarzenegger proved to be right on this score, thus making the nickname seem prophetic.

After the Olympics, Schwarzenegger and Maier appeared together on *The Tonight Show*—the Hermanator and the Terminator together at last, sealing the connection forever, though that day was the first and only time the two have met.

"You guys look like Hans and Franz from *Saturday Night Live*," Jay Leno joked.

"Yes," Schwarzenegger agreed. "We've come to pump . . . you . . . up."

Maier, looking understandably confused by the reference, smiled a bewildered smile. Changing the subject, the Hermanator observed, to Schwarzenegger's chagrin, that he was only 12 years old when *The Terminator* was released.

These days, it's difficult to tell whether Maier is cultivating the Hermanator persona when he insists on remaining frustratingly unemotive, or if he's simply being himself. One day, for example, I asked Maier what he loves about skiing. What, for him, is its essential allure?

"Da speed," he replied. "I like to go fast."

OK, but . . . anything else?

"*Ja*, I like to win. If I lose, I'm not very happy."

In the final seconds of the countdown, Maier turns his head to the sky and hyperventilates, his face wreathed in the fog of his own exhalations. The electronic clock dweeps down to zero, and it's time. Maier snarls, and his cold blue eyes bulge fiendishly behind his Carrera goggles. He launches himself in one great heave, skates to pick up speed, and lowers into a full tuck. He's dropping like a stone now, gathering momentum, 30 miles per hour, 40, 50, 60, his skis chattering over the ice. Fifteen seconds into the run, he's still crouched low, his poles clutched tight under his arms, head thrust forward. This is the point where he should be tapping the brakes in anticipation of the first turn, but he doesn't—he's doing 65, 70, 75, and still picking up speed.

To understand Maier's singularity, you have to understand the dreadnought that is the Austrian Ski Federation.

In Nagano, the Austrian men won three of five gold medals and eight of 15 possible medals. Even more amazing, last year they did something that no other national team has done in the 30-year history of the World Cup: Austria took every alpine title there is to take, winning the downhill (Andreas Schifferer), Super G (Maier), giant slalom (Maier), slalom (Thomas Sykora), and the overall title (Maier). In the final World Cup standings, six of the top ten racers were Austrian.

Because his nation is expecting nothing less than an encore performance this year, Maier's time is considered a public asset, a precious commodity that must be husbanded and protected. When I told people in Salzburg that I was going up to the mountains to interview Hermann Maier, they were invariably puzzled. "How can this be?" they would ask. "He is in training."

Sure enough, when I meet Maier he is in training, spending 60 hours a week working out in the village of Obertauern, a ski resort lofted in a high alpine meadow an hour's drive from Salzburg. The gym where Maier trains, the Olympiastützpunkt, with its halogen-bright hallways, "therapy studios," and gurgling whirlpool lagoons, is like some technopolitan lair out of a Bond film. While being escorted to meet Maier, I catch glimpses of German heavyweight boxer Axel Schultz sparring and several members of the Japanese national ski team running on treadmills, their chests hooked up to winking banks of heart monitors.

The Hermanator is sitting in the café sipping an apple cider, surrounded by an entourage that includes his trainer, his agent, and the director of tourism for Salzburg. There's a fresh bead of blood on his left ear where the Olympiastützpunkt technicians have just extracted their sample for the daily lab analysis. Maier's dirty-blond hair is sweat-drenched (he's just finished a two-hour ride on a stationary bike), and a long trail of yellow fuzz connects his sideburns to the patchy goatee on his chin.

How are you? I ask.

"The training is going very, very well," he says in the clipped but sturdy English that he learned years ago while teaching Scandinavian skiers on the slopes above Flachau, his hometown. "I think I've got just the right formula. At the present time, I'm working mostly on the thighs." The members of his retinue nod their heads in approval.

The anxiety of success is thick in the air. Measured by the high standards of its past glories, Austrian skiing has only recently emerged from a long slump. As consistently good as the Austrian ski teams have been through the years, until Maier's breakthrough last season the country hadn't produced a true international superstar since Franz Klammer (who won his downhill gold in the 1976 Olympics), and it hadn't had an overall World Cup champion since Karl "The Great" Schranz in 1970.

Maier trains with the champion's fear, the constant awareness that everyone, including the other Austrian skiers, will be after him this year, that it's all his to lose. Six days a week, he speeds up the narrow serpentine roads from Flachau in his cherry-red BMW Z3 to Obertauern. Working like an automaton, he is intent on proving that he isn't just a single-season phenomenon.

Fame, to Maier, is an annoyance. Shortly after the Olympics, Austrian president Thomas Klestil presented Maier with the Gold Cross, the country's highest honor. Upon Maier's return from the World Cup circuit, the country held a welcoming ceremony in Flachau that was broadcast live to more than a million Austrians. At sunset, the heavens fluoresced with beams of laser light, and Maier wriggled down the slopes on his skis past a crowd of 10,000 villagers, a hero dropping out of the alpenglow like some Wagnerian god.

Maier hated all of it. If it were left up to him, there'd be no media and no fans, no endorsement obligations, no extraneous demands of any kind, only an empty room in which to train and an empty slope on which to prove he's the best skier in the world.

He resents the necessity of being surrounded by so many retainers and attendants—his "baby-sitters," he calls them. "Believe me," he confides to me when we have a moment to ourselves out in the Olympiastützpunkt lobby, "being famous hasn't made my life any easier. Every minute I'm dealing with the baby-sitters is one more minute I'm not training."

Sixteen seconds into the downhill, Maier hits the "mystery mogul" and is pitched a few feet into the air. He lands on his skis, but he's slightly out of kilter now and moving far too fast to make the steep left turn. He attempts a final, desperate correction, but it's too late. Maier sails over a little lip and plunges into a pockmark in the snow, his left ski snagging in the crust. And then, as if he has struck some invisible trip wire on a trebuchet buried in the mountain, Maier is catapulted into the blue skies of Japan.

Ski racing is a sport that knows few genuine surprises or upstarts, and this is especially true in Austria, where the best skiers are singled out at the age of 10 or 12 and given all the cosseting and technical support that the planet's most advanced skiing nation can lavish upon them.

Only two years ago, Hermann Maier was a relative nobody, an unpedigreed skier embarking on his first full season on the World Cup tour. He was an outcast throughout his teens and early twenties, a dark horse working in obscurity while his peers got the thoroughbred treatment. "He didn't do it the Austrian way, that's for sure," says Fritz Vallant, a coach for the Austrian national team. "He is the only one I know of who did it all on his own."

Flachau, a 750-year-old town of steep-roofed wood-and-stucco chalets and hexed barns and onion-domed churches, lacks the glamour of vaunted Tirolean resorts like St. Anton or Kitzbühel. Locals ski, or teach skiing, whenever they're not cleaning out stables or milking the Pinzgauer cows. The only industry of note is the headquarters of the Atomic ski company.

Hermann Maier, Sr., and his wife, Gertraud, still operate the ski school they've run for 35 years, the same one where Hermann, Jr., learned to schuss at the age of three. By the age of six he was already winning races. "He never liked to lose," says Frau Maier. "If he did, you had to leave him alone. You couldn't cheer him up."

But there was always one serious problem: He was way too small. At 16 he still weighed only 110 pounds. When he was 17, he shot up nine inches in a single year, but the spurt left him gawky, and the national coaches remained unimpressed.

Maier took a job as a bricklayer in Flachau and, after undergoing the rigorous certification process required before one can teach skiing in Austria, became an instructor at his parents' school during the winter. He'd rise at dawn, before the tourists took over the steeps, and bound up the mountain for a few quick runs on a giant slalom course he'd set himself. When he was 18, Maier did his compulsory military service, a six-month stint during which he lifted a lot of weights and endlessly ran through the Alps with a grenade launcher strapped to his back. Along the way, he'd been steadily bulking up, hitting 180 pounds by the age of 20. He never gave up his determination to compete at the top level, and in October 1995, vowing to make his mark as a professional ski racer, he laid his last brick.

In January 1996, a World Cup giant slalom race was held in Flachau. All the elite athletes from the international ski world had landed on Maier's doorstep, and Hermann was asked to be a "forerunner," which simply meant he would ski the giant slalom course before the race in order to help the officials work out the bugs. His first run out of the gate, Maier clocked a time of 2:20:19, which proved to be just one second behind Alberto Tomba, who was then the best skier on the World Cup circuit.

In a matter of weeks he won the EuropaCup title, and at last gained a spot on the Austrian team. A year later, in his first World Cup down-hill race, at Chamonix, he crashed and broke his left arm. He was still wearing a cast the following month when he won his first World Cup victory, in the Super G at Garmisch, Germany, and at the advanced age of 24 he was named skiing's Rookie of the Year.

"He's old," says Vallant, "but his head is fresh."

Vaulting heavenward, with a stout tailwind that seems to have picked up where his own kinetic force left off, Maier thinks, "You just lost the gold medal." For a brief moment he appears to be flying grace-fully, as though it's still possible that he could stick his landing and redeem his mistake, but then, as he reaches the apogee of his arc, it becomes clear that the trajectory is all wrong. Training, technique, and force of will mean nothing now. Maier furiously windmills his arms in a futile attempt to right himself; he's going head over heels, tumbling through space, on his way down toward the icy hardpack.

Maier tells me that his schedule may permit him to accept my invita-tion to take him and his girlfriend out to dinner later in the week.

To pass the time, I take to watching the "Wetterpanorama" broad-cast on Austria's TV 1, a show that's composed entirely of live feeds from one gorgeous alpine valley after another, a continuous spool of real-time vistas from Glocknerstrasse to Saalbach-Hinterglemm. On mountain summits all across Austria, TV cameras perpetually swivel back and forth, robotically capturing the scenery—dells, lakes, gla-ciers, snow-dusted peaks—in a droning metronomic gaze, 365 days a year. "Wetterpanorama" is both mind-numbingly dull and hypnotic, an ordered synthesis of nature and technology that seems essentially Austrian.

On the evening we've agreed to go out to dinner together, Petra Wechselberger swings by my hotel and rescues me from another "Wet-terpanorama" session. She picks me up in Hermann's new, cobalt-blue

BMW 325 convertible, and as soon as I hop in, she gives me the bad news.

"Hermann says he's sorry but he can't come," she announces. "He hates to go out to restaurants—too many people."

We drive over to an Italian place in the next dorp. Heads start to turn as we walk in, and gradually it dawns on me that people think we're on a date. It doesn't bother Petra. "They say Hermann and I aren't getting along anymore," she says. "There are rumors we're breaking up."

Petra is 24 and has long brown hair and a flawless olive complexion. She's a kindergarten teacher in town. "The kids tremble when they see Hermann," she says. "They look up at him in fear." She began dating Maier when she was 15.

Petra tells me she wants to get married and have children once Hermann's racing days are over. Clearly, however, she's growing impatient. "He trains and trains until he can no longer see straight, until he can no longer stand up," she says. "At the end of the day, he'll call me and say, 'Please, please, I'm so hungry!' He wants his food waiting when he arrives."

What's he like to eat?

"Macaroni and cheese most of all," she says. "He'll put away three plate-loads and then collapse in front of the TV."

What's he like to watch?

"Mr. Bean cracks him up. Mostly, he likes action movies. He says anything with Stallone is good."

What music does he like?

"He doesn't like music."

Books?

"No."

Does he go out with friends?

"He doesn't have friends, really, not close ones. Ever since he was a little boy, he's never been the type of person who needs other people."

Does he ever go skiing, you know, just for fun?

"That's the last thing he'd ever do. In the ten years I've known him, we've skied together four times."

Petra sighs and fixes a hollow gaze on the menu. "The years have just gone by," she says. "He's always exhausted. He never wants to go anywhere. He never wants to spend money or have fun. He just wants to train. Back and forth, back and forth, between Flachau and the gym. Sometimes I think the man is some kind of an alien."

His left shoulder and the back of his head make the initial contact. There is a concussive crunch and then a messy clatter of flying ski poles and snapped bindings. He bounces, somersaults, skids 50 feet before smashing into one snow fence, flips once more, and plows through another snow fence. It seems to go on forever. He pinwheels two more times and then lands facefirst in the deep snow along the margins.

After a few long, motionless moments, Maier pulls himself to his knees. Although he is in excruciating pain, he has the presence of mind to wag an index finger at a camera, so that his mother, back in Flachau, will know he's OK. He stands up, brushes off the snow, and flexes his shoulder to make sure nothing is broken. He waves away the worried officials, clicks back in, and skis the rest of the way down the mountain.

He has a bruised sternum, a dislocated left shoulder, a badly bruised disk in his lower back, and contusions everywhere. His right knee is soon hideously swollen, but early the next morning, Maier is back on a stationary bike, still training, still getting ready for the next race . . .

Three days after the crash, Maier astonished the world, first by showing up at the Olympic Super G course at all and then by winning it by a half-second margin. Three days after that, he won a second gold, this time in the giant slalom.

Maier watched the videotape of his Olympic crash for the first time over the summer, having forsworn a viewing all spring for fear it would affect his last few World Cup performances. His reaction was curious. Instead of being amused or horrified, he became cross with himself, irritated at his own negligence.

"I see the video and I say only one thing," he told me. "That man is out of order!"

November 1998

Life's Swell

The Maui Surfer Girls love each other's hair. It is awesome hair, long and bleached by the sun, and it falls over their shoulders straight, like water, or in squiggles, like seaweed, or in waves. They are forever playing with it—yanking it up into ponytails, or twisting handfuls and securing them with chopsticks or pencils, or dividing it as carefully as you would divide a pile of coins and then weaving it into tight yellow plaits. Not long ago I was on the beach in Maui watching the surfer girls surf, and when they came out of the water they sat in a row facing the ocean, and each girl took the hair of the girl in front of her and combed it with her fingers and crisscrossed it into braids. The Maui surfer girls even love the kind of hair that I dreaded when I was their age, 14 or so—they love that wild, knotty, bright hair, as big and stiff as carpet, the most un-straight, un-sleek, un-ordinary hair you could imagine, and they can love it, I suppose, because when you are young and on top of the world you can love anything you want, and just the fact that you love it makes it cool and fabulous. A Maui surfer girl named Gloria Madden has that kind of hair—thick red corkscrews striped orange and silver from the sun, hair that if you weren't beautiful and fearless you'd consider an affliction that you would try to iron flat or stuff under a hat. One afternoon I was driving two of the girls to Blockbuster Video in Kahului. It was the day before a surfing competition, and the girls were going to spend the night at their coach's house up the coast so they'd be ready for the contest at dawn. On contest nights, they fill their time by eating a lot of food and watching hours of surf videos, but on this particular occasion they decided they needed to rent a movie, too, in case they found themselves with ten or 20 seconds of unoccupied time. On our way to the video store, the girls told me they admired my rental car and said that they thought rental cars totally ripped and that they each wanted to get one. My car, which until then I had sort of hated, suddenly took on a glow. I asked what else they would have if they could have anything in the world. They thought for a moment, and then the girl in the backseat said, "A moped and thousands of new clothes. You know, stuff like thousands of bathing suits and thousands of new board shorts."

"I'd want a Baby-G watch and new flip-flops, and one of those cool sports bras like the one Iris just got," the other said. She was in the front passenger seat, barefoot, sand-caked, twirling her hair into a French knot. It was a half-cloudy day with weird light that made the green Hawaiian hills look black and the ocean look like zinc. It was also, in fact, a school day, but these were the luckiest of all the surfer girls because they are home-schooled so that they can surf any time at all. The girl making the French knot stopped knotting. "Oh, and also," she said, "I'd really *definitely* want crazy hair like Gloria's."

The girl in the backseat leaned forward and said, "Yeah, and hair like Gloria's, for sure."

A lot of the Maui surfer girls live in Hana, the little town at the end of the Hana Highway, a fraying thread of a road that winds from Kahului, Maui's primary city, over a dozen deep gulches and dead-drop waterfalls and around the backside of the Haleakala Crater to the village. Hana is far away and feels even farther. It is only 55 miles from Kahului, but the biggest maniac in the world couldn't make the drive in less than two hours. There is nothing much to do in Hana except wander through the screw pines and the candlenut trees or go surfing. There is no mall in Hana, no Starbucks, no shoe store, no

Hello Kitty store, no movie theater—just trees, bushes, flowers, and gnarly surf that breaks rough at the bottom of the rocky beach. Before women were encouraged to surf, the girls in Hana must have been unbelievably bored. Lucky for these Hana girls, surfing has changed. In the sixties, Joyce Hoffman became one of the first female surf aces, and she was followed by Rell Sunn and Jericho Poppler in the seventies and Frieda Zamba in the eighties and Lisa Andersen in this decade, and thousands of girls and women followed by example. In fact, the surfer girls of this generation have never known a time in their lives when some woman champion wasn't ripping surf.

The Hana girls dominate Maui surfing these days. Theory has it that they grow up riding such mangy waves that they're ready for anything. Also, they are exposed to few distractions and can practically live in the water. Crazy-haired Gloria is not one of the Hana girls. She grew up near the city, in Haiku, where there were high-school race riots—Samoans beating on Filipinos, Hawaiians beating on Anglos—and the mighty pull of the mall at Kaahumanu Center. By contrast, a Hana girl can have herself an almost pure surf adolescence.

One afternoon I went to Hana to meet Theresa McGregor, one of the best surfers in town. I missed our rendezvous and was despairing because Theresa lived with her mother, two brothers, and sister in a one-room shack with no phone and I couldn't think of how I'd find her. There is one store in Hana, amazingly enough called the General Store, where you can buy milk and barbecue sauce and snack bags of dried cuttlefish; once I realized I'd missed Theresa I went into the store because there was no other place to go. The cashier looked kindly, so I asked whether by any wild chance she knew a surfer girl named Theresa McGregor. I had not yet come to appreciate what a small town Hana really was. "She was just in here a minute ago," the cashier said. "Usually around this time of the day she's on her way to the beach to go surfing." She dialed the McGregors' neighbor—she knew the number by heart—to find out which beach Theresa had gone to. A customer overheard the cashier talking to me, and she came over and added that she'd just seen Theresa down at Ko'ki beach and that Theresa's mom, Angie, was there too, and that some of the other Hana surfer girls would probably be down any minute but they had a History Day project due at the end of the week so they might not be done yet at school.

I went down to Ko'ki. Angie McGregor was indeed there, and she pointed out Theresa bobbing in the swells. There were about a dozen other people in the water, kids mostly. A few other surfer parents were up on the grass with Angie—fathers with hairy chests and ponytails and saddle-leather sandals, and mothers wearing board shorts and bikini tops, passing around snacks of unpeeled carrots and whole-wheat cookies and sour cream Pringles—and even as they spoke to one another, they had their eyes fixed on the ocean, watching their kids, who seemed like they were a thousand miles away, taking quick rides on the tattered waves.

After a few minutes, Theresa appeared up on dry land. She was a big, broad-shouldered girl, 16 years old, fierce-faced, somewhat feline, and quite beautiful. Water was streaming off of her, out of her shorts, out of her long hair, which was plastered to her shoulders. The water made it look inky, but you could still tell that an inch from her scalp her hair had been stripped of all color by the sun. In Haiku, where the McGregors lived until four years ago, Theresa had been a superstar soccer player, but Hana was too small to support a soccer league, so after they moved Theresa first devoted herself to becoming something of a juvenile delinquent and then gave that up for surfing. Her first triumph came right away, in 1996, when she won the open women's division at the Maui Hana Mango competition. She was one of the few fortunate amateur surfer girls who had sponsors. She got free boards from Matt Kinoshita, her coach, who owns and designs Kazuma Surfboards; clothes from Honolua Surf Company; board leashes and bags from Da Kine Hawaii; skateboards from Flexdex. Boys who surfed got a lot more for free. Even a little bit of sponsorship made the difference between surfing and not surfing. As rich a life as it seemed, among the bougainvillea and the green hills and the passionflowers of Hana, there was hardly any money. In the past few years the Hawaiian economy had sagged terribly, and Hana had never had much of an economy to begin with. Last year, the surfer moms in town held a fund-raiser bake sale to send Theresa and two Hana boys to the national surfing competition in California.

Theresa said she was done surfing for the day. "The waves totally suck now," she said to Angie. "They're just real trash." They talked for a moment and agreed that Theresa should leave in the morning and spend the next day or two with her coach Matt at his house in Haiku, to prepare for the Hawaiian Amateur Surf Association contest that weekend at Ho'okipa Beach near Kahului. Logistics became the topic. One of the biggest riddles facing a surfer girl, especially a surfer girl in far-removed Hana, is how to get from point A to point B, particularly when carrying a large surfboard. The legal driving age in Hawaii is 15, but the probable car-ownership age, unless you're rich, is much beyond that; also, it seemed that nearly every surfer kid I met in Maui lived in a single-parent, single- or no-car household in which spare drivers and vehicles were rare. I was planning to go back around the volcano anyway to see the contest, so I said I'd take Theresa and another surfer, Lilia Boerner, with me, and someone else would make it from Hana to Haiku with their boards. That night I met Theresa, Angie, and Lilia and a few of their surfer friends at a take-out shop in town, and then I went to the room I'd rented at Joe's Rooming House. I stayed up late reading about how Christian missionaries had banned surfing when they got to Hawaii in the late 1800s, but how by 1908 general longing for the sport overrode spiritual censure and surfing resumed. I dozed off with the history book in my lap and the hotel television tuned to a Sprint ad showing a Hawaiian man and his granddaughter running hand-in-hand into the waves.

The next morning I met Lilia and Theresa at Ko'ki Beach at eight, after they'd had a short session on the waves. When I arrived they were standing under a monkeypod tree beside a stack of backpacks. Both of them were soaking wet, and I realized then that a surfer is always in one of two conditions: wet or about to be wet. Also, they are almost always dressed in something that can go directly into the water: halter tops, board shorts, bikini tops, jeans. Lilia was 12 and a squirt, with a sweet, powdery face and round hazel eyes and golden fuzz on her arms and legs. She was younger and much smaller than Theresa, less plainly athletic but very game. Like Theresa, she was home-schooled, so she could surf all the time. So far Lilia was sponsored by a surf shop and by Matt Kinoshita's Kazuma surfboards. She had a twin brother who was also a crafty surfer, but a year ago the two of them came upon their grandfather after he suffered a fatal tractor accident, and the boy hadn't competed since. Their family owned a large and prosperous organic fruit farm in Hana. I once asked Lilia if it was fun to live on a farm. "No," she said abruptly. "Too much fruit."

We took a back road from Hana to Haiku, as if the main road weren't bad enough. The road edged around the back of the volcano, through sere yellow hills. The girls talked about surfing and about one surfer girl's mom, whom they described as a full bitch, and a surfer's dad, who according to Theresa "was a freak and a half because he took too much acid and he tweaked." I wondered if they had any other hobbies besides surfing. Lilia said she used to study hula.

"Is it fun?"

"Not if you have a witch for a teacher, like I did," she said. "Just *screaming* and *yelling* at us all the time. I'll never do hula again. Surfing's cooler, anyway."

"You're the man, Lilia," Theresa said, tartly. "Hey, how close are we to Grandma's Coffee Shop? I'm starving." Surfers are always starving. They had eaten breakfast before they surfed; it was now only an hour or two later, and they were hungry again. They favor breakfast cereal, teriyaki chicken, french fries, rice, ice cream, candy, and a Hawaiian specialty called Spam Masubi, which is a rice ball topped with a hunk of Spam and seaweed. If they suffered from the typical teenage girl obsession with their weight, they didn't talk about it and they didn't act like it. They were so active that whatever they ate probably melted away.

"We love staying at Matt's," Lilia said, "because he always takes us to Taco Bell." We came around the side of a long hill and stopped at Grandma's. Lilia ordered a garden burger and Theresa had an "I'm Hungry" sandwich with turkey, ham, and avocado. It was 10:30 A.M. As she was eating, Lilia said, "You know, the Olympics are going to have surfing, either in the year 2000 or 2004, for sure."

"I'm so on that, dude," Theresa said. "If I can do well in the nationals this year, then . . ." She swallowed the last of her sandwich. She told me that eventually she wanted to become an ambulance driver, and I could picture her doing it, riding on dry land the same waves of adrenaline that she rides now. I spent a lot of time trying to picture where these girls might be in ten years. Hardly any are likely to make it as pro surfers—even though women have made a place for themselves in pro surfing, the number who really make it is still small, and even though the Hana girls rule Maui surfing, the island's soft-shell waves and easygoing competitions have produced very few world-class surfers in recent years. It doesn't seem to matter to them. At various cultural moments, surfing has appeared as the embodiment of everything cool and wild and free; this is one of those moments. To be a girl surfer is even cooler, wilder, and more modern than being a guy surfer: Surfing has always been such a male sport that for a man to do it doesn't defy any received ideas; to be a girl surfer is to be all that surfing represents, *plus* the extra charge of being a girl in a tough guy's domain. To be a surfer girl in a cool place like Hawaii is perhaps the apogee of all that is cool and wild and modern and sexy and defiant. The Hana girls, therefore, exist at that highest point—the point where being brave, tan, capable, and independent, and having a real reason to wear all those surf-inspired clothes that other girls wear for fashion, is what matters completely. It is, though, just a moment. It must be hard to imagine an ordinary future and something other than a lunar calendar to consider if you've grown up in a small town in Hawaii, surfing all day and night, spending half your time on sand, thinking in terms of point breaks and barrels and roundhouse cutbacks. Or maybe they don't think about it at all. Maybe these girls are still young enough and in love enough with their lives that they have no special foreboding about their futures, no uneasy presentiment that the kind of life they are leading now might eventually have to end.

Matt Kinoshita lives in a fresh, sunny ranch at the top of a hill in Haiku. The house has a big living room with a fold-out couch and plenty of floor space. Often, one or two or ten surfer girls camp in his living room because they are in a competition that starts at seven the next morning, or because they are practicing intensively and it is too far to go back and forth from Hana, or because they want to plow through Matt's stacks of surfing magazines and Matt's library of surfing videos and Matt's piles of water-sports clothing catalogs. Many of the surfer girls I met didn't live with their fathers, or in some cases didn't even have relationships with their fathers, so sometimes, maybe, they stayed at Matt's just because they were in the mood to be around a concerned older male. Matt was in his late twenties. As a surfer he was talented enough to compete on the world tour but had decided to skip it in favor of an actual life with his wife, Annie, and their baby son, Chaz. Now he was one of the best surfboard shapers on Maui, a coach, and head of a construction company with his dad. He sponsored a few grown-up surfers and still competed himself, but his preoccupation was with kids. *Surfing* magazine once asked him what he liked most about being a surfboard shaper, and he answered, "Always being around stoked groms!" He coached a stoked-grom boys' team as well as a stoked-grom girls' team. The girls' team was an innovation. There had been no girls' surfing team on Maui before Matt established his three years ago. There was no money in it for him—it actually cost him many thousands of dollars each year—but he loved to do it. He thought the girls were the greatest. The girls thought he was the greatest, too. In build, Matt looked a lot like the men in those old Hawaiian surfing prints—small, chesty, gravity-bound. He had perfect features and hair as shiny as an otter's. When he listened to the girls he kept his head tilted, eyebrows slightly raised, jaw set in a grin. Not like a brother, exactly—more like the cutest, nicest teacher at school, who could say stern, urgent things without them stinging. When I pulled into the driveway with the girls, Matt was in the yard loading surfboards into a pickup. "Hey, dudes," he called to Lilia and Theresa. "Where are your boards?"

"Someone's going to bring them tonight from Hana," Theresa said. She jiggled her foot. "Matt, come on, let's go surfing already."

"Hey, Lilia," Matt said. He squeezed her shoulders. "How're you doing, champ? Is your dad going to surf in the contest this weekend?"

Lilia shrugged and looked up at him solemnly. "Come on, Matt," she said. "Let's go surfing already."

They went down to surf at Ho'okipa, to a section that is called Pavilles because it is across from the concrete picnic pavilions on the beach. Ho'okipa is not a lot like Hana. People with drinking problems like to hang out in the pavilions. Windsurfers abound. Cars park up to the edge of the sand. The landing pattern for the Kahului Airport is immediately overhead. The next break over, the beach is prettier; the water there is called Girlie Bowls, because the waves get cut down by the reef and are more manageable, presumably, for girlies. A few years ago, some of the Hana surfer girls met their idol Lisa Andersen when she was on Maui. She was very shy and hardly said a word to them, they told me, except to suggest they go surf Girlie Bowls. I thought it sounded mildly insulting, but they weren't exactly sure what she was implying and they didn't brood about it. They hardly talked about her. She was like some unassailable force.

We walked past the pavilions. "The men at this beach are so sexist," Lilia said, glaring at a guy swinging a boombox. "It's really different from Hana. Here they're always, you know, staring, and saying, 'Oh, here come the *giiiirls*,' and 'Oh, hello, *ladies*,' and stuff. For us white girls, us haoles, I think they really like to be gross. So gross. I'm serious."

"Hey, the waves look pretty sick," Theresa said. She watched a man drop in on one and then whip around against it. She whistled and said, "Whoooa, look at that sick snap! That was so rad, dude! That was the sickest snap I've seen in *ages*! Did you see that?"

They were gone in an instant. A moment later, two blond heads popped up in the black swells, and then they were up on their boards and away.

Dinner at Matt's: tons of barbecued chicken, loaves of garlic bread, more loaves of garlic bread. Annie Kinoshita brought four quarts of ice cream out of the freezer, lined them up on the kitchen counter, and watched them disappear. Annie was fair, fine-boned, and imperturbable. She used to be a surfer "with hair down to her frickin' butt," according to Theresa. Now she was busy with her baby and with overseeing the open-door policy she and Matt maintained in their house. That night, another surfer girl, Elise Garrigue, and a 14-year-old boy, Cheyne Magnusson, had come over for dinner and were going to sleep over, too. Cheyne was one of the best young surfers on the island. His father, Tony, was a professional skateboarder. Cheyne was the only boy who regularly crashed at Matt and Annie's. He and the girls had the Platonic ideal of a Platonic relationship. "Hell, these wenches are *virgins,*" Annie said to me, cracking up. "These wenches don't want anything to do with that kind of nastiness."

"Shut up, haole," Theresa said.

"I was going to show these virgins a picture of Chaz's head coming out when I was in labor," Annie yelled, "and they're all, 'No, no, no, *don't!*'"

"Yeah, she's all, 'Look at this grossness!'" Theresa said. "And we're all, 'Shut up, fool.'"

"Duh," Lilia said. "Like we'd even want to see a picture like that."

The next day was the preliminary round of the Quicksilver HASA Competition, the fourth of eight HASA competitions on Maui leading to the state championships and then the nationals. It was a two-day competition—preliminaries on Saturday, finals on Sunday. In theory, the girls should have gone to bed early because they had to get up at five, but that was just a theory. They pillow-fought for an hour, watched *Sabrina, the Teenage Witch* and *Boy Meets World* and another episode of *Sabrina,* then watched a couple of Kelly Slater surfing videos, had another pillow fight, ate a few bowls of cereal, then watched *Fear of a Black Hat,* a movie spoofing the rap-music world that they had seen so many times that they could recite most of the dialogue by heart. Only Elise fell asleep at a decent hour. She happened to be French and perhaps had overdosed on American pop culture earlier than the rest. Elise sort of blew in to Hawaii with the trade winds: She and her mother had left France and were planning to move to Tahiti, stopped on Maui en route, and never left. It was a classic Hawaiian tale. No one comes here for ordinary reasons in ordinary ways. They run away to Maui from places like Maryland or Nevada or anyplace they picture themselves earthbound, landlocked, stuck. They live in salvaged boxcars or huts or sagging shacks just to be near the waves. Here, they can see watery boundlessness everywhere they turn, and all things are fluid and impermanent. I don't know what time it was when the kids finally went to sleep because I was on the living room floor with my jacket over my head for insulation. When I woke up a few hours later, the girls were dressed for the water, eating bowls of Cinnamon Toast

Crunch and Honey Bunches of Oats, and watching *Fear of a Black Hat* again. It was a lovely morning and they were definitely ready to show Hana surfing to the world. Theresa was the first to head out the door. "Hey, losers," she yelled over her shoulder, "let's go."

The first heats of the contest had right-handed waves, three or four feet high, silky but soft on the ends so that they collapsed into whitewash as they broke. You couldn't make much of an impression riding something like that, and one after another the Hana girls came out of the water scowling. "I couldn't get any kind of footing," Theresa said to Matt. "I was, like, so on it, but I looked like some kind of kook sliding around."

"My last wave was a full-out closeout," Lilia said. She looked exasperated. "Hey, someone bust me a towel." She blotted her face. "I really blew it," she groaned. "I'm lucky if I even got five waves."

The girls were on the beach below the judges' stand, under Matt's cabana, along with Matt's boys' team and a number of kids he didn't sponsor but who liked hanging out with him more than with their own sponsors. The kids spun like atoms. They ran up and down the beach and stuffed sand in each other's shorts and fought over pieces of last night's chicken that Annie had packed for them in a cooler. During a break between heats, Gloria with the crazy hair strolled over and suddenly the incessant motion paused. This was like an imperial visitation. After all, Gloria was a seasoned-seeming 19-year-old who had just spent the year surfing the monstrous waves on Oahu's North Shore, plus she did occasional work for Rodney Kilborn, the contest promoter, plus she had a sea turtle tattooed on her ankle, and most important, according to the Hana girls, she was an absolutely dauntless bodyboarder who would paddle out into wall-size waves, even farther out than a lot of guys would go.

"Hey, haoles!" Gloria called out. She hopped into the shade of the cabana. That day, her famous hair was woven into a long red braid that hung over her left shoulder. Even with her hair tamed, Gloria was an amazing-looking person. She had a hardy build, melon-colored skin, and a wide, round face speckled with light-brown freckles. Her voice was light and tinkly, and had that arched, rising-up, quizzical inflection that made everything she said sound like a jokey, good-natured question. "Hey, Theresa?" she said. "Hey, girl, you got it going *on*? You've got great wave strategy? Just keep it up, yeah? Oh, Elise? You should paddle out harder? OK? You're doing great, yeah? And Christie?" She looked around for a surfer girl named Christie Wickey, who got a ride in at four that morning from Hana. "Hey, Christie?" Gloria said when she spotted her. "You should go out further, yeah? That way you'll be in better position for your wave, OK? You guys are the greatest, *seriously*? You rule, yeah? You totally rule, yeah?"

At last the junior women's division preliminary results were posted. Theresa, Elise, and two other girls on Matt's team made the cut, as well as a girl whom Matt knew but didn't coach. Lilia had not made it. As soon as she heard, she tucked her blond head in the crook of her elbow and cried. Matt sat with her and talked quietly for a while, and then one by one the other girls drifted up to her and murmured consoling things, but she was inconsolable. She hardly spoke for the rest of the afternoon until the open men's division, which Matt had entered. When his heat was announced, she lifted her head and brushed her hand across her swollen eyes. "Hey, Matt!" she called as he headed for the water. "Rip it for the girls!"

That night, a whole pack of them slept at Matt's—Theresa, Lilia, Christie, Elise, Monica Cardoza from Lahaina, and sisters from Hana named Iris Moon and Lily Morningstar, who had arrived too late to surf in the junior women's preliminaries. There hadn't been enough entrants in the open women's division to require preliminaries, so the competition was going to be held entirely on Sunday and Iris would be able to enter. Lily wasn't planning to surf at all, but as long as she was able to get a ride out of Hana she took it. This added up to too many girls at Matt's for Cheyne's liking, so he had fled to another boy's house for the night. Lilia was still blue. She was quiet through dinner, and then as soon as she finished she slid into her sleeping bag and pulled it over her head. The other girls stayed up for hours, watching videos and slamming each other with pillows and talking about the contest. At some point someone asked where Lilia was. Theresa shot a glance at her sleeping bag and said quietly, "Did you guys see how upset she got today? I'm like, 'Take it easy, Lilia!' and she's all 'Leave me *alone*, bitch.' So I'm like, 'Whatever.' "

They whispered for a while about how sensitive Lilia was, about how hard she took it if she didn't win, about how she thought one of them had wrecked a bathing suit she'd loaned her, about how funny it was that she even *cared* since she had so many bathing suits and for that matter always had money for snacks, which most of them did not. When I said a Hana girl could have a pure surfing adolescence, I knew it was part daydream, because no matter how sweet the position of a beautiful, groovy Hawaiian teenager might be in the world of perceptions, the mean measures of the human world don't ever go away. There would always be something else to want and be denied. More snack money, even.

Lilia hadn't been sleeping. Suddenly she bolted out of her sleeping bag and screamed, "Fuck you, I *hate* you stupid bitches!" and stormed toward the bathroom, slugging Theresa on the way.

The waves on Sunday came from the left, and they were stiff and smallish, with crisp, curling lips. The men's and boys' heats were narrated over the PA system, but during the girls' and women's heats the announcer was silent, and the biggest racket was the cheering of Matt's team. Lilia had toughened up since last night. Now she seemed grudgeless but remote. Her composure made her look more grown-up than 12. When I first got down to the beach she was staring out at the waves, chewing a hunk of dried papaya and sucking on a candy pacifier. A few of the girls were far off to the right of the break where the beach disappeared and lustrous black rocks stretched into the water. Christie told me later that they hated being bored more than anything in the world and between heats they were afraid they might be getting a little weary, so they decided to perk themselves up by playing on the rocks. It had worked. They charged back from the rocks shrieking and panting. "We got all *dangerous*," she said. "We jumped off this huge rock into the water. We almost got killed, which was great." Sometimes watching them I couldn't believe that they could head out so offhandedly into the ocean—*this* ocean, which had rolls of white water coming in as fast as you could count them, and had a razor-blade reef hidden just below the surface, and was full of sharks. The girls, on the other hand, couldn't believe I'd never surfed—never ridden a wave standing up or lying down, never cut back across the whitewash and sent up a lacy veil of spray, never felt a longboard slip out from under me and then felt myself pitched forward and under for that immaculate, quiet, black instant when all the weight in the world presses you down toward the ocean bottom until the moment passes and you get spat up on the beach. I explained I'd grown up in Ohio, where there is no surf, but that didn't satisfy them; what I didn't say was that I'm not sure that at 15 I had the abandon or the indomitable sense of myself that you seem to need in order to look at this wild water and think, I will glide on top of those waves. Theresa made me promise I'd try to surf at least once someday. I promised, but this Sunday was not going to be that day. I wanted to sit on the sand and watch the end of the contest, to see the Hana girls take their divisions, including Lilia, who placed third in the open women's division, and Theresa, who won the open women's and the junior women's division that day. Even if it was just a moment, it was a perfect one, and who wouldn't choose it over never having the moment at all? When I left Maui that afternoon, my plane circled over Ho'okipa, and I wanted to believe I could still see them down there and always would see them down there, snapping back and forth across the waves.

Women Outside, Fall 1998

The Unbearable Lightness of Being the Boarder Queen

SARA CORBETT

She comes late, over an hour, hopping out of her SUV onto a downtown San Diego parking lot with her backpack and her skateboard like a kid out of a school bus—a small, spritelike woman sprung from an absurdly large car. This is Cara-Beth Burnside, the only person in vert ramp skateboarding to whom the words "female" and "menace" both apply. She is compact and darty, with longish, brownish hair, a wry, contained smile, and gold-flecked eyes that seem to rove constantly. When she is not on her skateboard—when she is, say, rummaging through the sale rack at Old Navy or eating veggie tacos at the beach in Cardiff—Burnside is often doing something she calls "mind-skating." She mind-skates all the time, perhaps because the world can only hold so much of her attention in a given moment. Behind those eyes, beneath the furrow in her brow and the droopy clothes that seem to pull her nearer to the ground, a part of Cara-Beth Burnside is always somewhere else, on a skateboard, somewhere high up and closer to perfection.

The SUV, on the other hand, is an earthly mother, one of those black, boxy GMC Yukons. It's the moving motel room that's carted Burnside up and down the West Coast for months now, lost in a bubble of Metallica when she's hyped, Neil Young when she's not, working the cell phone, blabbing away her 1,400 monthly minutes and then some talking to friends in SoCal vernacular—in which the vibes are good or bad or sometimes just "vibey" and a girl wakes up either stoked or not stoked for the day ahead. Tossed deep in the Yukon's posterior are the remnants of a life lived largely in motion—12 pairs of sneakers, a jumble of empty water bottles, some old newspapers, a scuffed-up helmet, two backpacks, a dirty T-shirt, a mound of knee pads, a tool box, a solitary crushed Bud can. From Mammoth to Orange County to Tahoe to Hood and back down again, homeless but essentially happy, she collects paychecks as both a pro skateboarder and snowboarder, a top performer in each endeavor.

So far the vibes have been positive. In the eight years she's been competing, Burnside has finished fourth at the Olympics on the snowboarding half-pipe, won the 1998 Winter X Games half-pipe title, and earned a bushel of snowboarding grand prix. She's also won every skateboarding contest available to women—or girls, as they will always be known, and always refer to themselves, in the board-sport universe, where to be a woman is to submit oneself to a distasteful austerity, while girlhood, with all its sunny freedoms, is something to hold on to forever. Burnside, whose sagging surf shorts and stringy ponytail can make her look 17, is often purposely evasive about her age, telling those who ask that she's "twentysomething." In fact, she's 31. But if being a veritable grandmother in her two teenager-dominated sports doesn't slow her down, she argues, why should she let others judge her by her age? While her male counterpart, X Games eminence Tony Hawk, recently announced his retirement from competition at 31, Burnside refuses to even acknowledge that she may have an athletic shelf-life. It would mean putting herself out to pasture before girl skateboarders get the chance to compete in contests like the X Games or the newly minted Gravity Games, where vert ramp studs like Hawk and Andy Macdonald have ollied their way to piles of cash—earning up to $18,000 in a single afternoon—not to mention serious national exposure. It's a frustrating situation. With few opportunities to compete, Burnside remains all but invisible, despite being, in Macdonald's words, "far and away the best woman skating on a ramp."

Today, however, is the All Girl Skate Jam, the only pro-level contest for women in the United States, held several times a year in different cities. In a roped-off corner of a San Diego street fair, with the odor of kielbasa and fried onions blooming in the warm mid-September air, about 80 girls sprawl like an occupying army. Mostly teenagers, they sit, butts parked on their boards, smoking cigarettes and sipping skinny cans of super-caffeinated Red Bull soda. There are girls in bikini tops and cutoffs, girls in wool skullcaps and flannel, in tattoos and tongue studs, in dreadlocks, in ponytails, and one—a pretty Asian girl wearing a daisy print T-shirt—in a green mohawk. Some warm up on a 12-foot-high vert ramp, others swoop and whir over the street course, a maze of benches, rails, ramps, and quasi-urban obstacles suitable for leaping, skimming, and otherwise appropriating in order to sling one's body and one's board into the air.

Burnside, who has been sitting on the pavement, strapping on her knee pads and stretching a sore back, suddenly points a finger. "Oh my God, what *is* that?"

A few feet away, a motorized figurine buzzes through the thicket of tanned legs and beat-up boards. This is Skateboard Shannen, a new remote-control toy from Mattel, enjoying its official launch at the Skate Jam. Skateboard Shannen is a plastic pixie doll with a neat fringe of flaxen hair, flawless skin, and expressionless blue eyes. She is 11 inches tall, wears baggy jeans and a pink tank top, and scoots around on a neon-green skateboard with hot-pink wheels. Mattel has sent a few marketing reps and set up an information table—"Turns in any direction! Awesome 360s!"—but Skateboard Shannen appears to be on her own today and having little impact on the life-size skateboard girls.

Instead, the girls are fixated on their cult heroes—women like Heidi Fitzgerald, 27, a big girl with a blunt dark bob, lots of tattoos, and an ugly gash on her left knee, and Ashley Mull, 19, a freckled blonde who attends a nearby public high school where skateboarding is offered as a for-credit class, and who has broken her wrist three times in the last six months. At the moment, she's soaring on the vert ramp, one arm encased in plaster. Leaning up against a chain-link fence is Elissa Steamer, a gruff-looking, 24-year-old string bean dressed in low-riding Levi's, considered to be the country's top female street skater. In 1998, at the first annual All Girl Skate Jam, Steamer confessed to a reporter that she'd never, not once in her life, skated with another girl.

At the top of this loose hierarchy is Cara-Beth Burnside. She doesn't smoke and she's got only one tattoo—a delicate yellow sunburst with her nickname, "CB," etched onto her left wrist. Sitting amid her younger compatriots' billowing cigarette haze and talk of raging beach parties, she appears relatively tame and vaguely all-American. Be assured, she knows how to rage—the five-year-old tattoo is the product, she says, of "lots and lots of tequila"—but with time she's grown more moderate, focused on keeping her body tuned. She swims and surfs and takes long hikes with her mom when she can. She lives on toasted soy patties and organic vegetables, visits a massage therapist twice weekly, and seems to be the only person at the Skate Jam who actually stretches before taking to the ramp. It'd be easy to mistake her for an athlete if that weren't "completely the wrong category," she says. Skateboarders, even obsessive ones like her, aren't athletes. Snow-boarders aren't really athletes, either, even though they've kind of been corralled in that direction. No, insists Burnside, what she does—what skateboarders and snowboarders do—is different from what people with coaches and training sessions and uniforms do. "We're not so heavy," she explains. "We're, I dunno how to say it . . . something else."

But what? As a woman, Burnside is caught in the margins of an already marginalized sport. With few exceptions, pro skateboarders are an impoverished lot—bunking together in ratty bungalows up and down the California coast, living off small stipends from sponsors, reveling in skateboarding's fuck-all image. But as the sport's popularity has grown, a handful of the best skaters have made their concessions to the mainstream, cashing in on marketing opportunities and educating themselves in public relations along the way. Cara-Beth Burnside may not be hawking Skateboard Shannens, exactly, but in a dual attempt to make an adult living and boost the visibility of girls in skateboarding, she's doing everything she can—from trade-show appearances to compulsive training—to ensure her longevity.

Silently, she straps on her silver helmet and carries her board to the vert ramp. The girls who have been warming up instantly clear away, leaving her alone in the massive masonite and plywood parabola. Shoving off, she pumps her legs powerfully a few times until she's rolling, until body and board have achieved a smooth pendulum-swing, climbing all the way to the upper deck and gradually to the air beyond. A crowd starts to gather, first 50, then 80, then 100 or more spectators, drawn from the street fair, all eyes on Burnside, who is looping high overhead—rocking, rotating, expertly skimming the air, then dropping back to her board with just enough time to anticipate her next trick.

Frontside 50-50. Handplant. Air-to-fakey. She's speaking an aerial language now, one that most of the spectators, mainstreamers with their cups of keg beer and kielbasas, can only compute in simple terms of speed, motion, and flight. This is what she's waited for, what all the mind-skating has been about. Dipping her knees, Burnside unleashes herself again, and the crowd holds its breath. This time it's a long, slow 360—an ecstatic *'scuse me while I kiss the sky* moment, gorgeous and arrested—before her feet find the board again, and she's sweeping with supreme confidence toward her next bite of air.

"I'm tiiiiiiiiiiired!" "My baaaaaack hurts!" These are Burnside's friends, and this is a sushi restaurant full of San Diego yuppies. The All Girl Skate Jam ended an hour ago, with Burnside pocketing a thousand bucks in a clear victory on the vert ramp, plus her very own Skateboard Shannen doll, which now resides in the shadowy depths of the Yukon.

The friends—three female surfer pals, fellow pro snowboarder Victoria Jealouse, and Burnside's 18-year-old niece and frequent sidekick, Sabrina—have shown up for the celebration, having missed most or all of the contest itself. This doesn't stop them from razzing the day's hero. Sprawled out around a back table with a collection of king-size bottles of Sapporo beer, they are busy inventing Skateboard Cara-Beth, real-life sister to Skateboard Shannen, a motorized doll in a dirty T-shirt who complains fiercely every time you pull her string.

Jealouse, Burnside's closest friend, lifts her head and howls at the ceiling in a whiny little doll voice: *"I need a massaaaaaaage!"* The surfer girls, Tiffany, Indigo, and Sheri—lean, sun-bleached blondes in their twenties—erupt in rowdy laughter, shredding the restaurant's subdued hush.

Burnside smiles sheepishly and thwacks Jealouse on the shoulder. So she complains a little sometimes, so what? The truth is she is tired, and her back *does* hurt. An afternoon on a vert ramp will do that to you, especially if you don't let up. In the last two years, Burnside's been to four All Girl Skate Jams and won the vert contest at every one, hands down. She's also jumped from one sport to the next without taking a break, moving from skateboard season to the snow just as most of her snowboarding rivals are returning from a good off-season rest. "It's hard to explain how amazing it is that she stays on top in two sports," says snowboarder Shannon Dunn, who narrowly edged Burnside out for a bronze in Nagano. "Nobody else out there, guy or girl, has Cara-Beth's energy."

Today, for example, she could've gone easy, could've pulled out a few old tricks and still taken the prize, but that's not what it's about for Burnside. If it were only about first place, she'd have gone soft a long time ago; the fact is that her closest skateboarding competitors are just mastering tricks she was nailing a year ago. What she's chasing is an image in her mind—the sweet spot, the perfect moment when time becomes elastic and the body performs flawlessly. While Burnside looks at what the men are doing for inspiration—the giant air and dazzling back flips that keep ESPN2 in business—the women are all looking at her. At the last Skate Jam, held in May in Rhode Island, Candy Kramer, a pretty, olive-skinned skater from Florida and a perennial runner-up to Burnside, videotaped Cara-Beth's impeccable gay twist—a fakey to forward 360-degree rotation with a one-handed grab—and spent hours on the couch at home, watching her perform in slow motion. "No matter how hard I work on it, I *still* can't go as high as she does," Kramer confesses, laughing. "I can't even come close."

This is the thing about Cara-Beth Burnside: She cannot be out-worked, even as the obvious motivations, like staying on top of the competition, slip away. Earlier today, Steve Van Doren, vice-president of promotions for the shoe company Vans, Burnside's primary sponsor, watched as she attempted a Caballaerial, a 360-degree fakey to forward rotation executed no-handed. Named for eighties skate-star Steve Caballero and known as the Cab for short, it requires rotational speed and deft footwork, and happens to be the kind of trick that separates male skaters from female. Burnside has had her sights set on the no-handed Cab for months—threshing it over and over in her mind, imagining it unfolding perfectly—even as she bided her time far away from the big ramps of southern California, doing some summer snowboarding in Oregon. Today she launched it once but lost her footing in midflight and crashed on the ramp. On the next go-around she tried again, and crashed again. Then another time, with the same result. By now her T-shirt was covered with skid marks from the ramp, her face hot and damp with exertion, her back starting to cramp. Even the crowd seemed anguished, watching her. But Burnside headed up the ramp again. Passing Van Doren on the way, she flashed a half-grin and a thumbs-up. He shook his head. "She's always like this," he said, bemused. "We'll have to drag her off that ramp."

"Cara-Beth's obsessed," says Jealouse. The two met six years ago in the parking lot at Mount Hood and became fast friends, traveling to World Cup snowboarding events and making appearances for Burton, their mutual sponsor. "She gets mad when she can't do something," Jealouse says. "She'll be walking up the half-pipe, kind of growling. People steer clear. They say, 'Gosh, is she even having fun?' But she is. She's just struggling to learn her tricks. If it was easy, it wouldn't be fun for her."

Her work ethic is the stuff of legend—the way she'll dodge the ski patrol at sunset, hiding in the trees to steal another 20 minutes to perfect her latest trick; the way she's literally had to crawl up the stairs after a particularly intense round of face-plants and dingers on the vert ramp. "She gets mad at the rest of the girls when we leave the skate park after two hours," says fellow skateboarder and All Girl Skate Jam founder Patty Segovia. "We stay out two hours and she stays four."

What motivates Burnside? Her friends have one answer: perfection. Burnside herself grows flustered trying to explain. She's not shooting to win one specific contest, beat a particular competitor, or achieve some definitive level of fame. Instead, it's that thing in her mind, the next trick, the next tantalizing, just-out-of-reach accomplishment that's eluding her. "You try and you try and you try for so long," she says, "and then one day you get it. You landed it. You're so high. *So high.*"

Her eyes soften at the thought, at the memory that comes attached to every trick she's ever nailed. "I kind of fiend for that."

Yet the pursuit of perfection has its costs: Two years ago Burnside fractured her collarbone, and six months after that she fractured her clavicle. There have been five concussions, too; if she were an NFL quarterback, she'd be retired by now. But she won't even think about quitting. After six years and more than 30 top-three finishes she's cut back on her snowboard competitions, abandoning the World Cup circuit altogether, though she still travels and competes in U.S. contests throughout the winter before switching her attention back to skateboarding. From the outside, it seems as if she's devised a life of perpetual youth, in which the language is a secret one shared only by devotees, whatever their sex. But where snowboarding is liberated— the opportunities for girls being virtually the same as for guys— skateboarding is not. This bugs Burnside. She's no suffragette, mind you, but she feels lonely having no one there to compete with, no squad of trash-talking upstarts looking to dethrone her, not to mention a lingering bitterness for the days when she was a true outsider, an interloper in a male world. There have been bad vibes, offhand comments, and one time, according to Patty Segovia, some guys kicked Burnside's skateboard right over the fence at the park. She's not a crier by nature, but away from the guys, at times she's sat down and cried.

Now, in the skate parks, they stop to watch CB, this small-framed girl-bullet who may or may not have a chip on her shoulder, who seems to live half the time in her mind. According to Andy Macdonald, who skates frequently with her in Encinitas, California, Burnside's bravado on the ramp has silenced any critics. "She goes for the harder tricks and she keeps at it," he says. "There's no other woman riding a ramp who even comes close to her. She's better than a lot of guys, and there's definite respect for her—maybe even some jealousy." By sheer force of will, Burnside has made people take notice of her. Not one for public speaking, she uses the ramp as her pulpit, a place where she can issue a call to girls who may be too intimidated to persist, to the sponsors who continuously insist that skateboarding's a dead market for girls; a place where she can be both eloquent and forceful. This is Burnside's thing. It's what keeps her flying and falling.

"A lot of people say she's hell-bent," says Segovia. "It's the perfect word for her, actually. She always tells me that you have to make change happen yourself, even when the resistance is huge. That's what she's doing. She's hell-bent."

Struggles aside, Burnside's life is a good one. She's on salary with Burton and Vans, gets clothing from Volcom, watches from Baby-G, and sunglasses from Arnette. Her signature shoe—the CB, by Vans—is selling more than 150,000 units a year. Plus she's seen the world: skateboarded Puerto Rico, surfed the Maldives, snowboarded everywhere from Chile to Japan, and turned her mostly vegetarian nose up at sauerbraten and liver all over Europe. How many 31-year-olds can say that?

There's a rootlessness that accompanies so much freedom, though. Tired of not having a home base, Burnside's been looking at real estate lately in Encinitas, a skateboard mecca not far from her hometown of Orange, though she and Jealouse are also toying with the idea of buying a house in Tahoe. But then, why sign the papers when you'd hardly ever be home anyway? Burnside, who often crashes at her parents' house in Orange County, is off to San Francisco next week to pose as a virtual model for a Sony PlayStation skateboarding game. Soon after that, she's taking off for a Skate Jam in Hawaii. Jealouse flew in from Japan just today and has only a few more days before she flies out for a Burton photo shoot in the Andes.

"We don't live anywhere!" Burnside laughs, expertly using her chopsticks to flip a piece of maguro into her mouth. "I mean, I have a storage unit I'm paying rent on, and there's not even good stuff in it!"

Buoyed now by sushi and beer and a few Advils, Burnside seems to have forgotten her aching back. The surfer girls have ordered more Sapporo. Jealouse has pulled out an instant camera she bought in Japan, one that produces little photos the size of postage stamps, and is pointing it at Sabrina, who leans over the table, making faces. Sherri gets out her cell phone and starts calling around to find tonight's party.

There is no talk of boyfriends, no discussion of the future beyond this one night. Instead, the girls bask in a healthy kind of ribaldry, a Peter Pan timelessness that springs from being suntanned, strongbodied, and mortgage-free. They're serious but not serious, athletes but not athletes, free—at least for the moment—to live from good time to good time. Victoria recalls the night they were all wrestling and Cara-Beth, a brown belt in karate, chipped one of Tiffany's teeth.

"But remember that time you threw a bar stool at me and Indigo?" Cara-Beth says to Victoria. "That was gnarly!"

Now a tug-of-war breaks out between Sabrina and Tiffany over one of Victoria's snapshots. Victoria takes a photo of Cara-Beth half-heartedly trying to intercede. The flashbulb pops. A beer bottle goes over. A water glass tips. Sherri continues to talk blithely on the phone. Two waiters come running, but the girls are deep into battle now, laughing raucously as the entire restaurant turns to look. They poke and slap at one another, while Victoria jumps on Sabrina for a piggy-back ride. Nobody kicks them out exactly, but it's clearly time to leave. They pay the bill and depart—a riotous female scrum, brawling past the silver-topped sushi bar and out into the dewy San Diego night.

When Burnside took her first glide on a skateboard, somewhere around 1978, it was cool for girls to skate. This was, by many accounts, skateboarding's heyday: The country's first skateboard parks opened in 1976 in Daytona Beach, Florida, and Carlsbad, California, and skating had become something of a national craze. Contests for young skaters—both boys and girls—flourished, particularly in the surf-happy towns along southern California's Highway 101. And Cara-Beth, a wiry ten-year-old from Orange County whose mother had started her on roller skates as a young girl, capitalized.

But no sooner had she gotten into it than the craze sputtered out. Plagued by clampdowns on zoning laws and staggering bills for liability insurance, the skateboard parks that had fueled the sport's meteoric rise were now, one by one, being forced to close. Its popularity on the wane, skateboarding went underground, becoming renegade, hard-core, and angry. It also became decidedly male.

"The girl thing just kind of died," says Cara-Beth. "So I did it for another year with the guys. I was around 13. I was good, but there was no direction. There was nothing for me to do." For years she did whatever sport could hold her attention—a season or two of flag football, several years of karate—and then became a star forward on her high school soccer team. Nothing, however, gave her the gravity-defying high that skateboarding had. After two years at Santa Rosa Junior College she transferred to UC Davis in 1989, where she played soccer for two seasons and graduated with a degree in human development in 1992. There were times she envisioned herself working with kids, maybe coaching sports, but somehow those things seemed like sacrifices.

By the time Burnside climbed back on a skateboard—encouraged by the extreme-sports craze, threatened by the prospect of becoming just another nine-to-fiver in a mundane world—the sport's hard edges had grown even harder. Even as she started doing skateboard demos and occasionally competing in pro-level vert ramp contests for guys, even as she got her first offers of sponsorship, she was aware of the inevitable dead ends that lay ahead. Her male counterparts were flying from one event to the next, getting drunk, stoned, and paid along the way. Yet the sponsors providing the guys' meal tickets told Burnside that they were sorry, but there was nowhere to send her, no place for her to compete. "It was like having a job," she says now. "You get to a certain level and it's . . . boring. You want to move up to the next level and you don't have the chance."

She'd heard stories, though, of a pack of free-flying girls who were getting paid to travel the world, compete for big prizes, and live the life Burnside was dreaming of, unwired and weightless. Only they were doing it on snowboards. Up till then, Burnside's experience on the slopes had been limited to some wobbly attempts at skiing. But here was an irresistible option. She began trekking to Tahoe on weekends, apprenticing herself to anyone who'd ride with her, and flailing her way through half-pipe contests. In 1993, a year after finishing college, she'd already picked up some snowboard sponsorship and a little bit of notoriety, having repackaged her vert ramp ferocity into highly technical and increasingly dazzling escapades in the half-pipe.

Burnside was a minor wonder, but like so many of her fellow aspirants she was also flat broke. She lived briefly with her older brother Scott in Orange, sleeping on a few blankets in one corner of his home office. She stood in parking lots all around Tahoe and begged early departers for their lift tickets. Sometimes she'd hike 45 minutes to get to a half-pipe without a ticket. In Oregon she worked at High Cascades Snowboard Camp, shuttling campers to and from the airport in a yellow bus, tending to their wrist sprains and bruised tailbones like a mother. And when camp finished for the day, she'd bound down the mountain to the cement skateboard park on the other side of the highway, to maintain her dual compulsion. "I was in my own world," she says now of her frenetic drive to master both sports. "I was on my mission."

She was so good it was uncanny. Within four years of first stepping onto a snowboard, Burnside was traveling around Europe and Japan for World Cup events, placing regularly in the top ten. In 1995 she was ranked second in the world. In 1996 she clinched the Big Air competition at the U.S. Open at Stratton in Vermont. In 1998 she grabbed the X Games half-pipe title and played a part in snowboarding's inauguration at the Nagano Olympics.

It's hard to pinpoint what forces shaped snowboarding into a more equitable pursuit than skateboarding. Veteran riders like Shannon Dunn and Victoria Jealouse have their own stories about living in obscurity, bombarded by indifference in a male-driven marketplace, but somewhere along the way their talent took root and was recognized, helping the sport to grow. Today 40 percent of snowboarders are female, compared to less than 10 percent of skateboarders.

Burnside's success in snowboarding raised her stature in skating, too. More and more, given the crossover marketing between snow- and skateboarding, sponsors were taking notice of what she could do. And she was gaining confidence in her own worth. When Vans went through a restructuring in 1996, Burnside worried that her already paltry monthly salary of $50 would get cut. But rather than grovel, she went in and asked for the moon. "She said, 'No, forget it. I'm gonna take in my videos and magazine shots and show them who I am,'" recalls Segovia, who accompanied Burnside to her meeting with Gary Schoenfeld, the new Vans CEO. What she wanted was a signature skate shoe, something Vans had done for only a few of its top male skaters. "She just packed all her pictures up one day and marched over to Vans to talk to the president," remembers Mary-Love Burnside, Cara-Beth's mother, laughing. "And she got her shoe."

A year later, Vans unveiled the original CB skate shoe, a thick-soled suede sneaker with a replica of Burnside's sunburst tattoo on the heel. This was followed by the CB2 and the CB3 models, now offered in a rainbow of colors and found in skate shops across the country. A fourth CB shoe is currently in the works; it will be more durable and designed for serious skateboarders, Burnside says, signaling what she thinks is a promising demand among female skateboarders for gear that's "more hard-core."

As happy, and well-paid, as this makes her, Cara-Beth is still waiting for a tough competitive challenge from another girl skater. Her sponsors have grown accustomed to what Steve Van Doren at Vans calls her "gentle lectures" about how important it is to develop the women's skateboard market. "CB is not outspoken," says Van Doren. "She's totally low-key about it. But she gets her point across. She'll say in this low tone, 'Gee, it'd be nice to have a pro contest here.'" They do seem to be trying—though not hard enough, by Burnside's reckoning. There could be more contests for girls, more sponsorship dollars made available, more marketing glitter sprinkled on the few top female skaters like herself.

Yet the brand-naming and the hunt for more exposure strikes at what's becoming a familiar paradox in alternative sports: A culture gets built around its very counterculturedness, and the sport loses its edge the second it hits even a tributary of the mainstream. Recalling her experience snowboarding at the Nagano Olympics, Burnside adopts a rebel whine: "We got there and we had to get *uniforms,*" she says, her voice dropping as she details each new assault on her freedom, the shackles borne by athletes but not by airborne elves. "We had to get all this *stuff,* and we were on a *time* thing—buses, planes, *interviews.*" Her only solace, she says, was that her mother and older sister were able to go and that in Japan you can buy beer out of hotel vending machines. Still, the Salt Lake Olympics now loom on the horizon. By December 1999, Burnside was off to a strong start on the snow, taking second at the Vans Triple Crown and third at the Mammoth Grand Prix. Asked whether she'll compete at the 2002 Games, her attitude deflates. "Well, probably."

Even if skateboarding remains safe from Olympic glory, its outlaw status is somewhat grounded in misogyny. It's rare to see more than a handful of girls at a skateboard park. Open any one of the popular skate magazines and you'll find that women, if they appear at all, show up in stories about strip bars or, for instance, in *Strength* magazine's Fantasy Forum, where porn-star columnists field letters that begin, "Dear Professional Leg-Spreader . . ." When *Thrasher* deigned to run a few photos of Segovia's All Girl Skate Jam in 1998, it was under the headline "More Buns Than Weenies."

Burnside waves that stuff off. "The guys who read those magazines aren't the guys who are going anywhere in skateboarding," she says. "It's all about getting drunk and picking up chicks. The guys who win contests work really hard at what they do. They're super-serious and mostly pretty nice." She does what she can to make skateboard parks friendlier and less "vibey," whooping encouragement to any girl who shows up to skate, offering advice when it's asked for.

Burnside's own encouragement came from her parents, Mary-Love and Fred, who drove her to early contests and never once suggested she take up something more feminine than skateboarding. These days, Mary-Love travels to many of her daughter's contests, along with Sabrina. Fred, sidelined by health problems that leave him unable to work, stays mostly at home. Even as she drops in and out of her family's life in Orange, seeking refuge from her itinerant existence, sleeping on the futon in her old tapestry-covered bedroom, Cara-Beth seems to have become the family caretaker—nagging Sabrina, who also lives in the house, to do her homework, fretting over her father's well-being, and worrying that her mother doesn't get out enough.

Sitting in a beach chair by the pool behind her parents' house, a low-slung bungalow in a middle-class neighborhood of Orange County, Burnside munches on a toasted soy patty. She's thinking about her future, what's out there beyond the snow and the skate parks. The truth is she can hardly imagine it, being so wrapped up in the day-to-day dance between her two sports and her slavish devotion to staying young and fit. (She sees a kinesiologist and an acupuncturist regularly, and keeps little bottles of goldenseal and other herbal tinctures stashed in her room.) Pressed on the subject, she makes some noises about maybe teaching kids to skateboard and snowboard someday when she retires, but that's all.

Once, not so long ago, the Burnside home looked out onto hilly farmland. When Cara-Beth was a kid, she had a pony named Sugar Babe that she'd ride out there for hours. But Sugar Babe's been gone awhile now, and the hillside has been claimed by subdivisions. Still, sitting in the sunlight after a swim, her wet hair spilled like seaweed across her shoulders and her skin glowing, it's difficult to imagine Burnside getting older, getting slower, retiring. She fidgets in her chair, her eyes roam. "I can't put myself on a time line," she says, staring for a moment at the hill above her parents' house. "Time lines put limits on you, and I guess I'm not the kind of person who deals very well with limits."

Another shimmery California afternoon, another chance to skate. Dressed in a blue Volcom T-shirt and shredded cargo shorts, Burnside has hit a late-day session at the Encinitas YMCA, which looks like any other YMCA except for the 35,000 square feet of fenced-in concrete sitting directly behind the preschool. It's a skateboarder's paradise, with an extensive street course, a ten-foot-deep pool for carving, and what's considered to be the best public vert ramp in the state, an 80-foot-long behemoth where the most hard-core of pro skaters regularly come to strut and fly. Burnside likes it here because from the top of the ramp she can glimpse a tantalizing blue sliver of the Pacific, about a mile away.

Today she's amped, ready to work. This is opposed to de-amped, which she was yesterday when she just wanted to sit by the pool in Orange and eat her soy patties. Spotting a few friends on the deck of the vert ramp, all guys and all pro skaters, Burnside climbs the stairs and says her hellos. She's greeted cheerfully, like an old friend. Her buddy Andy Macdonald, lean and dark-haired, slings an arm around her and excitedly relates tales of the recent all-guy Gravity Games in Providence, Rhode Island, where Tony Hawk crashed on a 540 and some other guy slammed so hard they had to give him an IV right on the ramp. "It was the gnarliest thing I've ever seen," Macdonald says as Cara-Beth nods, intrigued. "Blood was everywhere!"

Formalities dispensed with, she warms up on the street course, rock-eting over a bench and then sliding along a short railing, her skateboard clattering noisily as she goes. Other skaters, many of them boys under the age of 12, swoop and dive around her like busy gnats. Loosening up, she moves on to the pool, coasting like a ball bearing around its high rims, grabbing a little air when the fancy strikes her. A few younger girls show up to skate the pool, and Burnside pauses to say hey. As time passes, though, the sociability begins to ebb, the intensity grows. Everywhere it's a whirl of motion—skateboards whisking, bodies lifting and rabbit-kicking the air, waiting for gravity to pull them back to earth. Skateboard sessions tend to have a rhythm of their own, depending on who's skating that day. Today's is quickly evolving into a "snake session," a long sweaty grind where only the super-aggressive survive.

Burnside seems unaware of time altogether. She moves onto the vert ramp, joining about 20 guys on the upper deck, all of them with their boards hanging impatiently over the lip, waiting like vultures for their chance to drop in. The rule is you don't drop in till the last guy's fallen and gotten to his feet again. Then you've got to be quick, grabbing your opportunity before someone else grabs it away. Among the guys, Burnside is small but no less eager. She stands in her silver helmet, hands planted on knees, one foot on the board, and then leaps at her chance: Down, down the ramp she flies, then up, up into the air, drawing her knees to her chest and twirling wildly. "Yeah, girl," someone calls from the deck. "C'mon CB," says another, encouragingly.

She pops and fizzes in the air before them, a little ball of mercury doing her tricks—a 360, an alley-oop—and then she goes for the Caballaerial. One hip dips too low and she slams, skidding out on her knees and dodging the next skater, who's already dropped in. It goes like this for another hour. Each time Burnside slams, she bounces back to her feet and dashes up the stairs to the deck, quickly rejiggering her ponytail and waiting to take her next shot.

Before long their numbers have dwindled—to ten, then eight, then five, as one by one the guys pull their fatigued bodies off the ramp. The afternoon sun is waning; the ocean has turned an iridescent green. A YMCA employee emerges from a booth and calls up at those still skating: "Five minutes!"

Burnside waits as one guy drops in, then another, then another. It should be her turn next, but this, after all, is a snake session: The first guy takes another turn.

"Three minutes!" Seeing her window, she drops in and falls almost instantly. Damn! She bounds up the stairs again and leans in to wait.

"One minute!" The YMCA timekeeper has begun to slowly drag a chain across the vert ramp—the only sure way to drive the skaters off—and is marching with his watch held up in front of him as if to ward off demons.

One skater plunges and nearly barrels over the timekeeper. Burnside watches almost frantically. The chain covers over two-thirds of the vert ramp's length now. She's got about 15 feet and 15 seconds, but maybe that's all she needs. So she swings down and lets it all go— unspools her body without another thought, sashaying up the wall and into the darkening air.

She grasps it instantly, the moment's elasticity, the elusive Cab suddenly within reach. Her back arches; the board momentarily drops away. She won't quite land this one, catching the board again but eventually skidding out on her knees. And yet here in the air, in this singular instant, she feels the lure of perfection in her bones, like for just one second she's limitless and eternally young, frozen in exuberant flight.

March 2000

It's Gonna Suck
to Be You

STEVE FRIEDMAN

The first time he tried it, the vomiting started after 67 miles, and it didn't stop until six hours later. The last time, his quadriceps cramped at mile 75, so he hobbled the last quarter of the course. But Kirk Apt is a resilient, optimistic, obsessive—some might say weird—man who describes experiences like being trapped on an exposed peak during a lightning storm as "interesting," and that is why he's here, in Silverton, Colorado, cheerfully tucking in to a plate of pancakes, eggs, and bacon at 4 A.M., discoursing on the nature of fun while he prepares to take on, yet again, the most punishing 100-mile footrace in the world.

It's called the Hardrock Hundred Endurance Run, even though it's actually 101.7 miles long, and is known to the small and strange band of people who have attempted it as the Hardrock 100. Or, simply, the Hardrock. In 1992, the first year of the race, just 18 of 42 entrants finished. Today, nearly half of the 118 men and women who set off into the mountains will quit or be told to stop. Based on medical opinion, history, and statistical probabilities, death for one or two of them is not out of the question.

Apt could not look more pleased. "Enjoy yourself," he says to a fellow racer, a man staring fearfully at a strip of bacon. "Have fun," he blithely exhorts another, a pale woman clutching a cup of coffee, clenching and unclenching her jaw. Apt says "have fun" frequently enough to sound creepy. Even among other Hardrockers—many of them sinewy scientists from New Mexico's Los Alamos National Laboratory who tend to describe themselves with staggering inaccuracy as "mellow"—the 39-year-old massage therapist from Crested Butte, Colorado, is known as Mr. Mellow.

It's race day, the first Friday after the Fourth of July (the 2001 Hardrock will start on July 13), and Mr. Mellow is working over his pancakes at a worn wooden picnic table inside a café hunkered at the northern end of the only paved road in town. Silverton, population 440, is encircled by peaks, nestled at 9,305 feet in a lush mountain valley in the southern San Juans, at least an hour by way of the most avalanche-prone highway in North America from fresh vegetables, a movie theater, or a working cell phone. If you didn't know about the 15 feet of snow that falls here every winter, or the unemployment rate that's four times the state average, or the knots of bitter, beery exminers who gather at The Miner's Tavern toward the southern end of the paved road most every night to slurrily curse the environmentalists they blame for shutting down the mines and trying to ban snowmobiles downtown, you might think that Silverton was quaint.

Outside, the sky is a riot of stars, the air clean and cold and so thin it makes you gasp. Inside the café, it's warm and cozy, a perfect place for Mellow to break bread with Terrified.

"The most important thing about the race," Apt says, "is to remember to make sure to enjoy yourself." Yes, there can be crippling cramps and hair-raising lightning bolts—big smile—but there are also remote, deserted vistas, long and lonely treks up mountains and across ridgelines, precious hours spent alone among old-growth forest and fresh wildflowers.

It sounds cleansing. If you didn't know about the dozens of unusually fit people who every midsummer collapse into near-catatonic, weeping blobs of flesh, their faces and hands and feet swollen to grotesque balloons because entire clusters of the racers' capillaries are breaking down and leaking (more on that later), you might think the Hardrock was fun.

Apt unfolds his six-foot-one, 168-pound frame from the café's picnic bench. Broad-shouldered, long-legged, clear-eyed, and, above all, mellow, he strides out of the emptying restaurant. He won the Leadville 100 in 1995, and though he's completed six Hardrocks, he's never finished first. Maybe this will be the year. Maybe not.

Big, big smile.

"How lucky are we?" he says.

Five minutes before six, the sun still not up, the competitors are turning in small circles on the gravel road outside Silverton Public School, taking in the surrounding peaks, scanning the distance for answers to questions most people never even consider. "Will I be hospitalized before sunset?" for example. They will spend the next day and at least one sleepless night in the deepest backcountry, almost constantly above 10,000 feet, climbing, sliding, wading, hiking, staggering, limping, and occasionally running. (Unlike other 100-mile racers, the fastest and most fit of the Hardrockers will jog no more than 60 percent of the course.) They will face five mountain passes of at least 13,000 feet and one 14,000-foot peak. Those who complete the loop will climb and descend 66,000 feet (more than would be involved in climbing and descending Mount Everest from sea level, as the race organizers like to point out). A large number of racers will vomit at least once. One or two might turn white and pass out. The slower runners will almost certainly hallucinate.

One of the most horrifying Hardrock visions is often all too real. It occurs when a race official informs a racer that he or she is moving too slowly to finish within the prescribed 48 hours. Getting "timed out," whether at mile 75 or at the finish line itself, is a bitter experience. Just ask Todd Burgess, a 32-year-old newspaper-page designer from Colorado Springs. Five-foot-ten and 175 pounds, Burgess is cheerfully cognizant of his limitations and aspires only to finish and to enjoy himself along the way. So last year he snapped pictures, meandered in the wildflowers, gamboled through the old growth. But toward the end of the race, he saw that unless he hurried, he wasn't going to make it. He sprinted. He stumbled. He panicked. And when he crossed the line at 48 hours, three minutes, and 35 seconds—which means that, officially, he didn't finish at all—another racer told him, "It's gonna suck to be you for the next year."

It was a cruel thing to say, but, as it turns out, somewhat prophetic. For Burgess, the last year has been one filled with doubts, fears, and horrific training sessions—12-hour runs and 50-mile practice races and Sunday-morning sleep-deprivation workouts. While it *has* sucked to be him, it would suck more to be timed out again this year.

It's been said that recovering alcoholics and bulimics and drug addicts are disproportionately represented among Hardrockers, which is tough to confirm, but it makes sense if you consider that addictive tendencies and compulsive behavior would come in handy with the training regimen. It's also been said that full-time Silvertonians tend toward the same kind of ornery optimism and obsessive, clannish, and sometimes perversely mellow brand of masochism exhibited by many of the racers. That's equally difficult to nail down, but having spent the better part of two winters here, I can vouch for the general sound-ness of the theory. It's no surprise that Silvertonians and Hardrockers tend to get along.

A few dozen townspeople have awakened early this morning to see the racers off, partly because three Silvertonians are entered, including one of the Hardrock's most popular hard-luck cases, 52-year-old Carolyn Erdman, who has tried and failed three times to finish. Also at the starting line is the only Silvertonian ever to complete a Hardrock, Chris Nute. Nute, 33, will be pacing Erdman the second half of the race. He is not entered this year largely because of his wife, Jodi, 30, who is with him for the start and whom no one has ever accused of being mellow, especially when it comes to the Hardrock.

The year Chris Nute ran the Hardrock "was the only time I ever thought we might get a divorce," Jodi says. "I couldn't understand wanting to do that. The training time sucked. And it made me feel out of shape. It totally gave me a fat complex. I had a [terrifying] vision of the future: that I was going to be married to an ultrarunner."

Dawn. Race director Dale Garland yells, "Go!" and about 50 Hardrock volunteers and spouses and Silvertonians watch as Apt, Burgess, Erdman, and their fellow racers jog and walk down a gravel road, turn southeast, and then head into the mountains—and toward the cold and dark and pain.

*　*　*

Some 100-mile races are more famous. Many are more popular. Most have more corporate sponsors. None approach the Hardrock's brutality.

"This is a dangerous course!" warns the Hardrock manual, a fantastic compendium of arcane statistics, numbingly detailed course descriptions, grave warnings, and chilling understatement. When it comes to the temptation to scale peaks during storms, for instance, the manual advises, "You can hunker down in a valley for 2 to 4 hours and still finish; but if you get fried by lightning your running career may end on the spot."

Though a 44-year-old runner with a history of high blood pressure, Joel Zucker, died of a brain aneurysm on his way to the airport after completing the race in 1998, no one has perished during a Hardrock. But, according to the manual, "It is our general opinion that the first fatality . . . will be either from hypothermia or lightning!" (A Hardrock-manual exclamation point is rare as a Sasquatch sighting; one suspects typographical error, grim subject matter notwithstanding.)

"There's a reasonable chance somebody could die," says Tyler Curiel, 45, a Dallas-based doctor specializing in infectious disease and oncology who's run eleven 100-milers and "50 or 60" ultras (any race longer than 26.2 miles). "I've fallen into ice-cold water, almost been swept away by a waterfall, walked six hours alone at high elevations in boulder fields," he says of his Hardrock experiences. "Had I sprained an ankle then, I might have been dead. I almost walked off a 2,000-foot cliff in the middle of the night once. Two more steps, and I would have been dead for sure. And I'm fairly competent. So, yeah, there's a reasonable chance."

By late afternoon, after ten hours of climbing and sliding and "EXPOSURE" (the manual lists dehydration, fatigue, and vomiting as "minor problems," so racers tend to take capitalized nouns seriously), the fleetest and most fit of participants are a good five hours from being halfway finished. At this juncture—the fifth of 13 aid stations, Grouse Gulch, mile 42.4—one would expect the appropriate emotion to be grim determination. So it comes as something of a shock to onlookers when a slender young man named Jonathan Worswick skips through a light rain, down a narrow, switchbacking trail, and across a stream into Grouse Gulch at 4:27 P.M. He is smiling. The 38-year-old runner from England is on pace for a course record.

The Hardrock old hands are unimpressed. These are retired runners, longtime observers of ultrarunning, in demeanor and worldview much like the leathery old men who hang around ballparks in Florida and Arizona, sneering at the fuzzy-cheeked phenoms of spring and their March batting averages. The old hands have seen young studs like Worswick before. Seen them tear up the first half of the course, only to be seized later by fatigue, cramps, nausea, and a despair so profound they can't even name it. Besides, the promising dawn has turned into a chilly, wet afternoon. And this is Grouse Gulch. Dangerous things happen at Grouse Gulch.

It doesn't *look* dangerous: a wooden yurt 12 feet in diameter, a canvas elk-hunters' shelter with three cots and a propane heater, and a telephone-booth-size communications tent where a radio operator hunches over his sputtering equipment, all hugging the west bank of the fast-flowing Animas River.

But if you've just trekked more than 40 miles, climbed 14,000 feet and descended 10,000, confronted Up-Chuck Ridge ("ACROPHOBIA"), which is nearly three times as steep as the steepest part of the Pike's Peak marathon, tackled the 14,048-foot Handies Peak ("Snow fields, altitude sickness, fantastic views"), where through a freezing rain you looked out upon the world and pondered the sleepless night (or nights) and the long hours that lie ahead, and now you are staggering down rocky switchbacks through pellets of freezing rain . . . well, then Grouse Gulch is danger itself. And nothing is more menacing than its banana pudding.

If there is some Higher Power watching over Hardrockers, urging them on, then surely there is a corresponding demon, tempting them to stop. What the fiend wants is for them to taste the pudding. Not the oatmeal, or soup, or mashed potatoes, or individually prepared breakfast burritos (meat or vegetarian)—though all are tempting. No, the pudding, whose scent floats along the riverbanks and up the mountain slopes as easily as the Sirens' lethal song wafted over the wine-dark sea.

The pudding itself is creamy, smooth, not quite white, not quite brown. (The recipe is absurdly prosaic: one large package of Jell-O instant vanilla pudding mixed with four cups whole milk and three fresh bananas; makes eight servings.) But for the weeping runner who has been slogging up and down talus slopes and through marshes for 15 hours or so, the pudding . . . for that person, the pudding whispers to them.

"Stop," it whispers. "Rest." The rush of the river blends with the hushed static from the radio equipment, but the pudding won't shut up. "Don't go on," it whispers. "Have some more pudding."

Worswick wolfs a vegetarian burrito—he won't even look at the pudding—and leaves ten minutes after he arrives. Fourteen minutes later, Kirk Apt strides across the bridge, looks around the aid station, sits down, changes his socks, and frets. Things are taking too long; he's wasting precious minutes. By the time he is ready to go, Mr. Mellow is thoroughly agitated. When he leaves Grouse Gulch, he starts too fast, realizes he's too "amped up," and has to breathe deeply in order to regain the calm he regards as essential.

Apt spends less than ten minutes at Grouse Gulch.

Todd Burgess had planned to be here by 6 P.M., but at 10 he is still struggling down the mountain, thighs burning, tentative, taking baby steps, fearful of falling.

He enters Grouse Gulch at 10:12 and leaves at 10:28.

Carolyn staggers in at 10:30, loses sight in her left eye, then leaves at 10:36, two minutes ahead of her planned 43-hour pace.

Others—swifter, more accomplished, less tortured—are not so strong. Scott Jurek, 27, who two weeks ago won the Western States 100-miler, hits Grouse Gulch at 6:05 P.M. and takes a rest. He will not go on. Eric Clifton, who has won thirteen 100-milers since 1989, walks into the aid station two minutes later, and also stops for good.

Soaked and cold and exhausted, other racers hear the rushing river and the steady drizzle and the devilish gibberings of the Pudding Master, and they feel the propane heat, and then they cast their weary eyes on the cots, soft as dreams.

Twenty-three Hardrockers quit at Grouse Gulch.

Vomiting, cramping, collapsing, whimpering hopelessly before the devil's pudding, and/or surrendering to that despair so profound that it's difficult to name, are all variations, in Hardrock parlance, of bonking. Typically, when a runner bonks, he or she also quits the race, as Apt did when he couldn't stop puking in 1992. Sometimes a runner bonks and keeps going, and even finishes, as Apt did when his quadriceps cramped and he trudged the last 25 miles of the course in 11 hours in 1999. To continue after bonking earns a runner enormous respect among fellow racers, most of whom have bonked at some point in their running careers. These people appreciate speed, but they revere grit.

When male Hardrockers bonk, they tend to quit. This is accepted wisdom among the racers, as is the fact that women bonkers, in general, do their best to finish. A racer can bonk without timing out, and he can time out without bonking. All things being equal, it's better to have bonked before being timed out than the other way around. Non-bonking runners who are timed out—especially late in a Hardrock—suffer the fate of Todd Burgess (it sucks to be them).

The Ouray aid station, at mile 58 and an elevation of 7,680 feet, would provide an excellent place to quit. Though there is no pudding of any sort here, nor heated tents with cots, next to the aid station is a parking lot, and next to that, a highway. Silverton is less than an hour's drive away, in a heated car.

But there will be no quitting here for Jonathan Worswick, who arrives at 7:42 P.M., still leading, and leaves at 7:56. Not for Kirk Apt, who arrives at 8:20 and leaves at 8:27—"psyched," he says, "but in a relaxed, calm way."

Neither will there be any quitting for Todd Burgess, who trundles toward the aid station the next morning at 5:14. His pacer, Fred Creamer, urges Burgess to run the last mile or so to the aid station, but Burgess wants to conserve his energy until he eats something. He's sure that a meal will give him the boost he needs for the second half of the course. In Ouray he takes a bite of warm roast turkey, a long pull of Gatorade, and vomits.

Creamer asks Burgess if this has ever happened to him during a race, and when Burgess says no, Creamer considers ending their journey. But Burgess says he feels great. He *does* feel great. Creamer feels grave concern. They continue. Like Burgess, Erdman approaches Ouray in the predawn darkness, moving fast enough to finish in less than 48 hours, but just barely. No one—not the aid station volunteers and not pacer Chris Nute—entertains the slightest suspicion that she might quit in Ouray. Not that they wouldn't welcome such an event.

Erdman entered the race for the first time in 1997, when she was 48, eight years after she quit smoking and one year after she and her husband left their cattle farm in Wisconsin and moved to Silverton. Nute paced her that year, and she made it 85 miles before race organizers told her that she was moving too slowly and that she was done.

In 1998 she entered again. Four weeks before the event she ran a 50-mile warm-up race in Orem, Utah. Three miles into it she fell and scraped her left knee. There was blood, and a little pain, but she thought it was no big deal. By the time she finished, she could see her patella; she was shocked at how white it was. The doctor in the emergency room told her she was lucky he didn't have to amputate the limb. She spent a week in the hospital with intravenous antibiotics. Surgeons operated on her twice.

In '99 she was timed out at mile 92.

Erdman has long gray hair that she wears in a braid, the lean body of someone half her age, and brown eyes that sparkle with an intensity peculiar to religious leaders and Hardrockers. She runs ten miles a day, more in the midst of Hardrock training, through rain, snow, and blistering sun. Her dedication has unified Silvertonians—like many residents of small mountain towns, notoriously resistant to unification unless it involves railing against silent black helicopters and the craven jackbooted federal thugs who claim the choppers don't exist. But they're worried about her. Will she endure too much, just to finish? What if she doesn't finish?

Nute knows that Erdman would sooner end up on an operating table than quit, and that's one reason he's agreed to pace her. They're friends. He wants her to finish, but he also wants her to live.

After 13 minutes at the station, they walk along the Uncompaghre River out of Ouray and onto a dirt road, which they climb steadily through thick forest. The air is moist with dew and sweet with pine; birds are starting to sing. Though Erdman is falling further behind her 43-hour pace, and hasn't slept for a full 24 hours and won't for another 24, the approaching dawn invigorates her—for about two hours. Then she wants to take a nap.

Not a good idea, Nute tells her.

Leafy undergrowth and lush, grassy ground beckon. Just a few minutes lying in that pillowy green would be so nourishing, so healing. It would make her go so much faster.

Really not such a smart thing to do, Nute says.

She pleads. She whines. She begs.

Pacers are valuable precisely because they warn their charges not to surrender to their worst temptations—like gobbling fistfuls of ibuprofen and taking ill-advised naps. But Nute is also Erdman's friend, not to mention a fellow Silvertonian. OK, he says, one nap. They settle on seven minutes.

She nearly cries with happiness. She spreads her jacket, makes a pillow of her pack, and lies down in a perfect leafy spot. But it's not perfect enough. She picks everything up, moves to another leafy spot, and lies down again. Nute watches, looks at his watch; eight minutes have passed. She doesn't like the position of the pillow, so she adjusts it. Then she adjusts her jacket. Then her body. Three adjustments later, she sighs. It is a pitiable little sound.

"Go!" she chirps to Nute, who is sitting down, staring at her. "Start timing."

This is when Nute starts to worry.

Back in Silverton, Jodi Harper Nute is worried, too. She has watched over the past week as Chris has helped with various Hardrock tasks, handing out literature, signing in runners, helping pace Carolyn. Jodi watched him chat with other runners. She watched him study the course map. She watched him huddle with the old hands, doubtless revering grit.

And what she feared has come to pass. Just last night Chris told Jodi he wants to race again. (The couple has since moved to Durango, where less snow makes it easier to train.)

"Goddamit," Jodi says. "I can't believe this." Pause. "Yes, I can. I was wondering why I've been so pissy the past few days. Now I know why. God*dam*it."

While Jodi worries, Hardrockers trudge 10.4 miles and 5,420 feet up to Virginius Pass (elevation 13,100 feet), then 5.3 miles and 4,350 feet down into the aid station at Telluride. They have traveled 73.7 miles and have another 28 to go. Soon they'll have to tackle Oscar's Pass, 6.5 miles away and 4,400 feet higher. "Basically," says Jonathan Thompson, editor of *Silverton Mountain Journal,* the local biweekly, "straight up a friggin' mountain."

After Oscar's ("Acrophobia, exposure, cornice"), surviving runners will face Grant Swamp Pass, the most difficult climb of the course, a murderously steep scramble over boulders and loose scree ("rock and dirt that will slide back down the hill with each step you take"). It would be daunting on a day hike. Erdman has been awake, racing, for 31 hours. It's now one in the afternoon, and after she wolfs a slice of pepperoni pizza, she and Nute leave town, climbing, straight into the zone where Hardrockers too proud, too foolish, or too dense to quit often get themselves in danger. In 1998, as two-time Hardrock champion Dave Horton was ascending Grant Swamp Pass, a melon-size rock dislodged by a runner above fell and struck his right hand. "A little later," Horton, 51, wrote in his account of that race, "I noticed that my glove was soaked through with blood." After finishing (of course), he realized that it was a compound fracture.

Many runners ignore puffy faces, hands that have ballooned like boxing gloves, feet like clown shoes, telling themselves it's merely a lack of sodium or some low-level kidney failure. Probably not fatal. They'll try to ignore the moist rattling they hear with every breath. Chances are the swelling and rattling are the result of damage to the body's capillaries. High-altitude races tend to starve capillaries of oxygen, which makes them leak fluid, which pools in the racers' hands and feet. "The danger," says Curiel, the doctor from Dallas, "is that one of the largest capillary networks is in your lungs, and when those capillaries start leaking, you have difficulty breathing. Pulmonary edema. In a really bad case, your lungs can fill up with water and you'll drown."

Digestive problems barely merit consideration. Jonathan Worswick left Ouray still in the lead but vomiting every few miles and suffering stomach cramps and diarrhea. Mr. Mellow stalked him during the climb, enjoying the view, confident in his uphill power, even more confident that Worswick had expended too much energy too early. Just before passing Worswick and crossing Virginius Pass, Apt recalled later, "a mental shift occurred for me. I knew I was in this race, and really had a good shot at winning."

Worswick overtook him on the downhill to Telluride, but Apt was having fun. Just after beginning the brutal assault on Oscar's, Apt told his pacer he wanted to "get after it." Minutes later they blew by Worswick, who was too sick to fight anymore. He bonked. But he continued.

Burgess hasn't puked since Ouray, and though by midafternoon he's suffering fatigue, muscle soreness, chills, and a slight loss of motor coordination, he's still in the race.

Erdman? She regained her sight near Telluride. But three miles later, she begins to gasp.

She turns to Nute. "I'm not going to make it," she says.

Nute knows she might well be speaking the truth. He's been monitoring his watch, worrying as Erdman has slowed to a 40-minute-mile stagger. He's been despairing that she'll never make it out of the next aid station, Chapman, at 83.1 miles, before the cutoff time. But Erdman is the one who inspired Nute to run his first and, depending on Jodi, possibly only Hardrock. Plenty of people have told Erdman to stop. Nute's not going to be one of them.

"Let's sit down for a minute," Nute says. "Let's just process this. Let's do the math."

But what calculus of the spirit can take into account years of training, hours alone, broken bones, and the taunting of the devil's pudding? Has an equation yet been written so elegant that it can encompass impossible dreams?

They sit, and they sit some more. They peer upwards, above tree line, where the skies are black with monstrous storm clouds. Lighting crashes.

Erdman does the math. Instead of a number comes a word.

"All I can think," she says, "is why?"

She doesn't bonk, and she isn't timed out. But after 77 miles, Erdman drops out of her third and—she says—final Hardrock.

Ten miles from the finish, Todd Burgess forgets how to walk a straight line. Counting, he decides, will solve the problem. If he can put eight steps together, one ahead of another, without wavering, and name the number of each step, he won't swerve into the wilderness and be lost forever. He is sure of this. He counts aloud for an hour.

When he steps onto the abandoned rail bed that will take him the last two miles to Silverton, Burgess can see the gentle, aspen-covered hill ahead. Once he climbs that, he'll be able to look down into the town. He'll be able to see the finish line below. He knows he's going to make it. Only one thing can stop him.

He knows it's a silly fear, most likely the result of exhaustion and chills. If he knew about leaking capillaries, he might ascribe his anxiety to that. But Burgess's attempts at rationality won't banish a dreadful notion, born of sleep deprivation, or cellular rioting, or the desperate, fearsome need to finish in under 48 hours:

"This would be a terrible time for a nuclear bomb to fall."

Burgess isn't the only one losing his mind. Gigantic june bugs wriggle from the soil and onto the damp and wobbly legs of Hardrockers unlucky enough to find themselves on the course after dusk on the second day of the race. Ghostly condominiums waver on top of mountain passes. Severed elk heads bob in the arms of grinning aid-station volunteers.

It's probably not capillary leakage. The visions seem to visit the slower runners, the ones who have been awake the longest.

"We know that people who have been sleep deprived have been noted to have visual, auditory, as well as tactile hallucinations," says Dr. Clete Kushida, director of the Stanford Center for Human Sleep Research. "They can also suffer irritability, as well as changes in memory, focus, and concentration. And psychomotor deficits."

That's one way of putting it.

After 40 hours, phantom Texans in ten-gallon hats walk beside the sleepiest Hardrockers at 13,000 feet, drinking beer and laughing. Grass turns to snow, rocks morph into Chevy Suburbans, plants transmute into Gummy Bears and bows. Before he died, Joel Zucker saw Indians.

Burgess finishes at 47 hours, 41 minutes, and three seconds, the 58th of 60 finishers (none of them Silvertonians). Then he sits on the ground.

Race Director Dale Garland walks to Burgess and asks if he would mind turning off the digital clock when it hits 48 hours. "I think this is good therapy," Garland says.

Burgess sits next to the clock and stares at it. At 48 hours he pushes a button, but the clock keeps going. Burgess keeps sitting, staring at the running numbers.

Jonathan Worswick finishes sixth, at 30 hours, 46 minutes, 16 seconds.

Kirk Apt wins in 29 hours and 35 minutes—beating the course record by more than 35 minutes. His legs tremble, and he weeps. Some onlookers get teary, too, even a few of the old hands. They don't like to talk about it, but they know that some of the fastest finishers are the most patently competitive, the loudest, the least liked, and the most likely to quit when outright victory seems impossible. Then there's Apt, who bonked and walked the last 25 miles of the course last year, enjoying the scenic vistas and the lonely ridgelines. Cramped. Limping. Having fun.

Local newspaper reporters gather round the champion. It's almost noon, clear and sunny. Apt tells one note-taker that he consulted a nutritionist before this year's Hardrock and that his "homemade goos" (various combinations of blendered hard-boiled egg, potato, tofu, avocado, rice, yogurt, salt, honey, and chicken liver) helped him stay the course. He tells another, "I'm really not that competitive, but I saw I had the opportunity to win, so I thought, Why not?" He mentions that he ran about 60 of the 100 miles—"the flats and downhills, and I ran a few uphills, too."

The reporter from Durango has one last question.

"What interesting things happened in the race?" she asks.

Interesting things? Mr. Mellow grins.

"The flowers were just amazing."

July 2001

Mr. Sunset
Rides Again

ROB BUCHANAN

I n 1956, the novelist and Hollywood screenwriter Peter Viertel traveled to the Basque country of southwestern France to watch location shooting for director Henry King's *The Sun Also Rises*. Viertel, a friend of Hemingway's, had written the screenplay, but it wasn't long before his attention started to wander. Standing on the promenade in Biarritz, watching the perfect rollers churn past the Villa Belza, he decided to send home for his surfboard and, as legend has it, became the first man ever to surf France.

Viertel might not recognize La Côte Basque today. There are McDonald's now, and shopping malls as hideous as any in Orange County, and an autoroute, the A63, that rumbles with trucks headed north from Spain. And of course there are surfers, so many that in the summertime you can forget about finding an uncrowded break.

As ye sow, so shall ye reap, and all that.

And yet in the fall, if you drive just south of Biarritz on the old Route Nationale, it is sometimes still possible to stumble upon the swells of yesteryear. At least that's the way it feels when I pull into the parking lot at Lafitenia, a woodsy, secluded cove with a long, hollow, right-handed point break. Back in the midseventies, Lafitenia was a mandatory stop for American and Australian surfers on the Endless

Summer circuit, a hard-partying band who eventually morphed their vagabond act into today's World Championship Tour. A quarter-century later the place is, fittingly, the site of the Silver Edition Masters World Championships, a ten-day-long blowout that's part surf contest—it's the official world championships of seniors surfing—and part class reunion.

Sponsored by Quiksilver Europe, whose headquarters is nearby, the early-October event features 32 of the biggest names from surfing's storied past. The two favorites, for instance, in the 35-to-40-year-old "grommet" category ("grommet" being a mildly derisive term for an adolescent surfer) are Aussies Tom Carroll and Cheyne Horan, who not so long ago were starring on the regular circuit. (Carroll, 36, won the world title twice; Horan, 39, was a four-time runner-up.) But the real royalty here are the men competing in the over-40 division, the ones who launched pro surfing as a viable sport in the late 1960s and 1970s. They're a mostly Australian bunch that includes Wayne Lynch, the 47-year-old mystical guru whose preference for surfing on unortho-dox board designs back in 1968 helped kick off the shortboard revo-lution; Peter Townend, 46, whose methodical compilation of contest outcomes from around the globe resulted in the crowning of the sport's first world champion (himself, by sly coincidence) in 1976; and Wayne "Rabbit" Bartholomew, 45, the brash loudmouth who led the Aus-tralian Invasion of Oahu's North Shore in the midseventies, and got most of his teeth knocked out in the process.

But if you had to pick one über-kahuna out of this august lineup, it would probably be a diminutive 51-year-old American named Jeff Hakman, otherwise known as Mr. Sunset. As a teenage surf prodigy on Oahu's North Shore in the mid-1960s, Hakman mastered the fear-some break at Sunset Beach. He eventually became one of the premier big-wave riders and a tireless competitor who pushed the sport into a new, contest-oriented era. His real legacy, though, began after he retired from professional surfing in 1977 and founded Quiksilver USA, an off-shoot of the surfwear brand that originated in Australia, thereby blaz-ing the path for the marketing juggernaut that is today's surf industry. Hakman might have ridden that wave forever, all the way to tens of millions of dollars and a big house in Del Mar. But the need for an intense physical rush stayed with him after he'd left pro surfing behind, and when heroin and the high life replaced big waves as his ride of choice, the result was a 15-year off-and-on struggle with addiction, during which he nearly lost everything, including his life. It's a very different kind of legacy—with many semipublic wipeouts—and one that is still unfolding.

The past seems both near and far away as Jeff Hakman trots down to the beach at Lafitenia, a board under each arm. His hair is gray and close-cropped now, and there are some worry lines at the corners of his eyes, but he's the same height and weight as in his prime (five-foot-seven, 150 pounds), and he's still got the flat stomach and bouncy legs of a kid. And the smile, too: a big, boyish, gummy grin.

It's a sunny, blustery afternoon on the Bay of Biscay, and the swell, though sizable, is bumpy and confused. Hakman deliberates for a few minutes before choosing the longer of his two boards, a gun-shaped seven foot, two inches, and then launches himself through the nasty shore break. He sets up a bit outside the normal takeoff, hoping for something bigger and cleaner to roll through. After missing the first wave, and then the next, he settles for a choppy, flat one that backs off suddenly. It's a dicey takeoff, but he pops quickly to his feet, takes the step in stride, and pulls a deep, classically round bottom turn, his trademark.

"*Et voilà c'est parti!*" says the French emcee over the public-address system. "*C'est Monsieur Sunset même, Jeff Hakman.*"

A little cheer goes up in the hospitality tent, and the monster-lensed photographers down on the beach start to fire away. But Mr. Sunset doesn't do much with the wave. The judges are looking for snaps and big cutbacks, all the showy point-scoring maneuvers of professional surfing today. Hakman just swoops easily down the line, pulling more classical curves, his long arms winging wide and his hands dangling loosely.

No one in the crowd seems disappointed with this performance. Indeed, there's a smattering of applause as Hakman kicks out at the end of his ride. "He doesn't rip anymore," notes one French journalist admiringly. "He floats now. But underneath, you can still see the same style."

Masters surfing has only been around for a few years and isn't nearly as big a phenomenon as, say, the Senior PGA. In spirit, it's closer to seniors tennis—less an opportunity for a second career than a chance to do some character acting. Still, it is entertaining to watch yesterday's heroes disport themselves on the waves, and most of them can still rip. In the over-forties, Rabbit Bartholomew and Michael Ho, the quiet Hawaiian Pipeline specialist, handily win their first-round heats, as does Oahu-raised Bobby Owens, who now runs the Patagonia store in Santa Cruz (and who apparently spends a lot of time on the water, testing product). Six-foot-four Australian Simon Anderson, who was the first to market the three-finned surfboard, astonishes the crowd by throwing his legendary snaps on a board no longer than he is. Also drawing cheers is 49-year-old Reno Abellira, a former Hawaiian champion who has such a low center of gravity that he can still fit his slipper into extremely tight tubes and exit clean. Even the amiable Australian Ian Cairns, 47, a onetime big-wave star known as Kanga, who now sports an extra 30 or so pounds around his midriff, has no problem taking off in a mean beach break. Moreover, he seems to enjoy himself when he does. His wife videotapes him, and his old mates slap him on the back and offer him a "tinnie" of beer when the session's over. It's a feel-good experience all the way around.

From a spectator's point of view, however, the most interesting competition at the Masters probably takes place off the water. A lot of attendees refer to the event as a "gathering of the tribe," and the opening-night dinner, at a rustic Basque inn up in the foothills, has the feel of a giant potlatch, with old friends table-hopping, the Hawaiian contingent strumming away on their guitars, and heartfelt, boozy toasts to and by the hosts from Quiksilver Europe.

Still, as the days go by, it's hard to dismiss the idea that there are two overlapping clans within the tribe. Most conspicuous are the guys with haircuts and mortgages and good jobs, usually in the surf business. After a period of wondering what he was going to do with his life, Rabbit Bartholomew, for instance, wound up running the Association of Surfing Professionals, the sport's world body. Cairns is a surf-contest promoter who lives in southern California. Others are entrepreneurs, like Paul "Smelly" Neilsen, president of one of the biggest chains of surf shops in Australia. Then there are the apparel executives. Peter Townend is the global marketing director for Rusty, a California board and surfwear maker. Michael Tomson, a skinny 44-year-old guy who favors fatigues and T-shirts, is a former South African star who founded his own clothing company, Gotcha, 22 years ago in a rented house in Laguna Beach, California. Today, Irvine-based Gotcha is consistently ranked in the five top-selling surfwear brands internationally.

The other clan consists of the guys who are still mainly surfing, paddling, and "living the life." For the most part they're the seekers, slackers, and free spirits who tend to avoid the straight life, such as it is, for as long as they can. One day, talking to Reno Abellira, I ask him what he is planning to do after the contest. He's going to California, he says vaguely, "to clean out an apartment and maybe sell a car." Glen Winton, the notoriously reticent Australian star who became known as Mr. X, is disarmingly candid about his career ambitions. "Right now I'm working as a security guard at a shopping mall," he says, "but what I really want to do is to become a judge."

"So you're going to law school and all that?"

"No, no," Winton says, laughing. "I mean a surf judge."

Hakman is the one guy who doesn't quite fit into either category. Between heats, he moves through the competitors' enclosure, mingling easily with members of both clans. There's a lot of smiling and shoulder slapping, remembering swells and epic parties. But you also see an extra beat of watchfulness from his fellow surfers, an uncertainty as to who exactly Hakman is today. Sure, he's now got homes in two of the world's most beautiful places (Biarritz and Kauai), a lucrative but not-too-demanding job as the marketing guru—his actual title—for Quiksilver Europe, and, even more remarkably, a reborn career as an advertising icon for the company. But you still get the sense that, for some people, Hakman may have gotten a little too far out there to ever really come back.

In the contest program, Hakman is listed not as American, but Hawaiian. Although he was born in southern California and learned to surf in Palos Verdes, his father, an aeronautical engineer by profession but a passionate "waterman" at heart, relocated the family to Makaha, on the North Shore of Oahu, when Jeff was 12. Makaha was a rough town in those days, and *haoles* like Hakman could face a brand of hostility that made the "Valley go home" localism of Palos Verdes seem tame by comparison. "Even today," Hakman says, "the tourist board will tell you, 'Uh, don't go there.'" But Hakman had no problem mastering the vibe. "I'm not aggressive," he explains. "I always try to bend and flex around."

Within a year, Hakman was a regular in lineups up and down the North Shore. But he created his first real sensation in January 1963, when he and his father decided to paddle out at Waimea Bay on a 20-foot-plus day. Waimea is the North Shore's biggest regular break—double-high freight trains of moving water that, should you blow the takeoff or get caught inside, can hold you under for 30 seconds—and at that time only a few grown men had dared to surf it. It's impossible to overstate the raw courage of that moment: Hakman was barely 14 years old, and small for his age to boot, weighing in at under 100 pounds and not yet five feet tall. He shakily rode one wave, and wiped out on the second. Then, with the rest of the lineup looking on in disbelief, he paddled into another one, rocketed down the face, and made the bottom turn, and then kicked out into the channel. "It really wasn't that hard," Hakman recalls nonchalantly.

The wave that truly appealed to Hakman was at Sunset Beach, a notoriously hard-to-read break halfway up the North Shore. "It intrigued me and scared the shit out of me at the same time," he says. "Things move around a lot, depending on the size and direction of the swell. It's not like Pipeline, where there's one definite takeoff spot. It's faster and steeper, and there's so much more water. You can't halfway commit. You gotta put yourself right in the guts of it." By the time he was 15, Hakman knew the wave as well as anyone; it was, he says, "my backyard."

Two years later, in 1965, Hakman was invited to compete at Sunset in the inaugural Duke Kahanamoku Invitational. Dreamed up by a Honolulu nightclub promoter, the Duke was a new kind of surfing competition. It boasted an international field consisting of the 24 best surfers in the world. There was a television crew from CBS to film the event. And there was cash—not prize money, but appearance fees—for the contestants. It was, in other words, the precursor of modern professional contests.

The surf was an unruly eight to ten feet the day of the finals. Paddling out to the point, Hakman caught the first wave and then realized that the next set was coming from much farther left, on the outside. He got there first and came away with what one of the judges would later recall as the best ride ever seen at Sunset: a screaming tube that went on and on through several different sections of the wave as Hakman crouched in a cheater-five—the toes of one foot wrapped over the nose of the board. A few waves later, he pulled a similar stunt, and the judges had no choice but to give the world's first pro tournament title to a 17-year-old kid.

Hakman was characteristically modest about the moment. "I was overwhelmed," he says in *Mr. Sunset,* a recent biography written by Australian journalist Phil Jarrat that includes a portrait of surfing's formative era and selections from Hakman's extensive photo archives. When Hakman was pressed by his surfing pal Fred van Dyke to make a speech, Jarrat writes, he only managed to get out, "Ah, thanks, everybody. I'm ah, stoked! Is that OK, Fred?"

Thus began a ten-year period when Hakman was arguably the best competitive surfer in the world. "They called him Surf Chimp because of his short legs and long arms," says Gibus de Soultrait, editor of the French magazine *Surf Session* and, as the French often are, an avid student of obscure American subcultures. "He always took a high line on the wave that gave him a lot of speed, and being so small and having a low center of gravity, he never fell. That helps when you're surfing Sunset with no leash.

"Hakman was more competitive than his main rival in those days, Gerry Lopez," de Soultrait continues. "Gerry was a soul surfer, into the mystical side. Jeff was always a guy who wanted to win. The two of them were at the heart of the old debate about surfing—is it a sport or is it an art?"

If it was a sport, it wasn't a particularly organized one at the time. There was no official circuit, no overall points title, and very little prize money. Income, such as it was, came from endorsement deals with surfboard manufacturers, travel stipends from surf filmmakers, and all the other scams that enterprising world travelers dream up. In Hakman's case, that occasionally meant small-time drug-trafficking schemes—something that seemed like little more than heart-pounding capers at the time but, in retrospect, ultimately helped grease his slide. "It was acceptable to take a couple of ounces with you and sell them when you got somewhere, to pay for the plane ticket," Hakman says matter-of-factly. "The people who were doing it weren't bad people. Now it's much more organized, and the street scenes are so hard, but back then I thought those people and that life were glamorous."

Yet as Hakman worked the "international beach scene," both partying and purveying, he was mulling more conventional business ideas. One day in 1975, at a contest in Queensland, Australia, he had to borrow a pair of board shorts at the last minute. They were of a tight-woven poplin and cut with a much wider yoke than anything he'd worn before, and they closed with Velcro and a snap instead of ties. Plus they had a cool name—Quiksilver—and a catchy logo in the shape of a wave. "I remember thinking, 'Wow, these are pretty good,'" Hakman says. "Gerry [Lopez] and I took 'em back to Hawaii and told Jack Shipley, Lopez's business partner [in a surfboard and sandal business], to import some." Shipley did, and even though he had to sell the Quiksilvers at $17 a pair—$5 more than the going rate for board shorts—he sold out all 100 pairs in two weeks.

That winter, still pondering the board-short business, Hakman wound up at a place called Ulu Watu, in Bali, then the hot new surf spot. Drugs were a big part of the scene in Ulu Watu; the surfer who showed Hakman the place liked to quaff psilocybin mushroom milkshakes before every session in the waves. Hakman was taken aback when he found a bunch of his friends smoking heroin through foil, but by the time he left Bali, he admits in *Mr. Sunset,* he too "had a nice habit going."

Jeff Hakman's apartment in Biarritz is half a block from the Côtes des Basques, the clifftop promenade where Peter Viertel got his big idea back in 1956. It's an austere neighborhood of high walls and carefully trimmed topiary, a bit sedate, perhaps, for a surf legend and a legendary partyer. Then again, Hakman is a family man now. Six months a year he and his Australian wife of 12 years, Cherie, and their two children, Ryan, 17, and Lea, 7, live here; it's just a few minutes' drive to Hakman's office at the Quiksilver Europe headquarters. The other half of the year they're in Hanalei Bay, Kauai, where Hakman doesn't do much except surf.

The big sun-drenched apartment is empty today. Cherie and the kids have gone back to Hawaii so as not to miss the start of the school year. Hakman will rejoin them in a few days, when the contest is over, but in the meantime he's alone with a stack of surf videos, a big bowl of vitamins and food supplements in the kitchen, and on the dinner table, a copy of a book titled *Yesterday's Tomorrow: Recovery Meditations for Hard Cases.*

Hakman is a fundamentally shy man, but part of the recovery process, he knows, is being able to share one's story. And so, half-reluctantly, he begins talking. A year after that fateful stop in Bali, he explains, he made his bid for the Quiksilver name. It happened like this: Preparing for his annual Australian swing, he asked his board shaper to install an extra-thick fin, hollowed out to keep down the weight. Shortly before his departure, he filled it with three ounces of cocaine—not to use himself, but to trade for heroin, which was much cheaper than cocaine in Australia. By the time Hakman showed up for the 1976 Bells Beach Classic, the preeminent surf contest of the Australian season, he was already strung out. Yet two amazing things happened that week, although Hakman is a little shaky on the details. Not only did he win the tournament, the first time a non-Australian had done so, but he also somehow persuaded the owners of Quiksilver Australia to grant him licensing rights to their name, logo, and board-short design for the U.S. market, in exchange for 5 percent of the new U.S. company and 5 percent of its sales.

Hakman had been talking to a surfer friend he'd met in Ulu Watu, a USC business school graduate named Bob McKnight, about the Quiksilver idea. With the license secured, the two of them set about building a business. They began a series of mad drives up and down the coast between their makeshift factory in Orange County, the fabric suppliers in Los Angeles, and all the surf shops they could talk their way into. There was no time to surf, and Hakman forgot about heroin for a while, too. But then the old urge returned, and before he knew it a friend was showing him how to shoot it intravenously.

For the next couple of years, insists McKnight, now the CEO of Quiksilver USA, in Huntington Beach, California (the new location of its headquarters), he had no idea about Hakman's heroin habit. "Either I was naive," McKnight says, "or he hid it incredibly well." Whatever the case, the company grew, slowly at first and then with startling speed. By the early eighties, annual sales were approaching $5 million. Hakman began to have a lot of pocket money, and his taste for heroin grew apace; at one point, he says, it was costing him $500 a day.

Hakman is surprisingly unemotional as he tells the story. There's no self-recrimination or wistfulness. Instead, there's almost a sense of wonder, as if he were describing a particularly phenomenal day on the North Shore. He doesn't look to blame his addiction on anything, and he won't take the easy way out and say it was a need for adrenaline inherited from his big-wave surfing days.

"I wouldn't go so far as to say letting go of the belt is like dropping into 30-foot Waimea," he says. "That instant of dropping down a big gnarly face—it's very close, equally potent, but not the same. On the other hand, the same thing that got me addicted definitely made me a good surfer. You know, once you get a direction, you go and commit." He pauses again. "I thought I could handle it," he says. "But every addict thinks that—that they're different."

Early on, Hakman had begun selling small numbers of shares in Quiksilver USA to pay for drugs. After 1980, though, the trickle became a deluge. "At 30, I thought I was going to live happily ever after," he says, his eyes moistening for the first time. "I still had about a 33 percent share in the company." He stops and rubs his face with his hands, regaining control. "By '82, it was all gone. The third partner in the company finally said, 'Jeff, you gotta leave. This isn't working at all.' I went, 'That's understandable.' I had a six-month-old son and about $3,000, total."

Hakman stops again, thinking it over. "The last 10 percent I sold for $100,000," he says, the barest note of regret in his voice. "It's worth at least $15 million today."

* * *

Midway through the third day of the Silver Edition competition, the swell begins to drop, from eight feet to five feet at first, and then all the way down to three. Even so, the men compete that day, and the third round turns out to be a good outing for Hakman; he finishes second to Wayne Lynch. But day four dawns sunny, calm, and flat, and the contest is postponed until further notice.

What do old surfers do when there's no surf? Pretty much the same thing young surfers do. They play video games, smoke pot, and laugh their way around the hotel golf course, and they eat, drink, and tell stories—competitively, of course.

One day after breakfast, Joey Buran, a stubble-headed Californian who became a minister about 15 years ago, regales a small but appreciative crowd with tales of an epic day at Waimea Bay when he barely escaped death by scratching his way over set after set of monster waves. Once he found himself safely outside, however, he realized there was no practical way to get back in. The sun beat down. Buran started to have sharky thoughts. Eventually he began sobbing and praying for a miracle, whereupon a lone figure on a jet ski appeared. "And you know what the guy did?" Buran says. "He came speeding up, turned and threw me a shaka"—Buran rocks his outstretched thumb and pinkie in the Hawaiian salute—"and kept right on going."

A day later, at a raucous competition dinner, Hakman, sitting midway down the table sipping mineral water, ventures a story of his own. It's about a hitchhiker he once picked up in the midseventies, driving a lonely road in the Australian countryside. The guy was, without a doubt, one of the rudest people he'd ever met; every time Hakman tried a conversational gambit, the hitchhiker came back with the same response: "None of your fucking business." Suddenly there were flashing lights and a siren—the police. Hakman pulled over. Panicking, the hitchhiker dropped his bag, jumped out of the car, and sprinted into the woods with the cop in hot pursuit. Hakman looked at the suspicious package lying on the seat next to him, considered the delicacy of the situation, and took the only reasonable course of action: He peeled out and sped off into the night.

There's a brief silence. "OK, OK," says Dave Kalama, a Hawaiian tow-in star who's been flown in by Quiksilver to do water safety for the contest. "What was in the bag?"

"None of your fucking business," Hakman says, flashing that big gummy grin.

Everyone laughs, less out of amusement than relief that Hakman isn't dropping some real-life bombshell from his past. This is, after all, a guy who got hepatitis from dirty needles in the late seventies and who was high for the birth of his son in 1982. Two of his shooting buddies subsequently died of AIDS. One day around the same time, when he was at work at his Quiksilver office in Costa Mesa, California, a Mercedes pulled up out front and six gun-packing gangsters stormed upstairs into his office, not so gently inquiring as to the whereabouts of several ounces of missing drugs. All good stories, perhaps, but not particularly funny. For some, the tales bring back memories of those in the old circle who died from drug overdoses, a not insignificant number that included several of Hakman's own friends, his brother-in-law, and, in the early seventies, two of the best young surfers in Hawaii, Rusty Star and Tomi Winkler.

There are a couple of reasons why Hakman didn't join them. "He wasn't ultimately self-destructive," says Bob McKnight. "Every time he got to the bottom, he had that instinct to straighten out. Hakman's very street-smart, instinctual, with a total survivor mentality. His dad is like that too—the guy is a frickin' aquarium diver, out in deep water every day still. Jeff was trained to be like that."

The other reason Hakman survived is that his friends and family members watched out for him. And he found a savior—or a savior found him.

Half a mile up the road from Lafitenia, just across the A63 autoroute, is the Quiksilver Europe "campus." One look at the tasteful, neo-modernist lines of the new corporate offices and you know that surfing's mystical power to sell stuff has only increased by crossing the Atlantic. For the most part, what Quiksilver sells is clothing—casual sportswear with a youthful design flair. (Its "technical" pieces, like the trademark board shorts and wetsuits, actually constitute a small fraction of its business.) According to EuroSIMA, the industry's trade association, surfwear is now a $1.2 billion business in Europe. Quiksilver Europe's share is about $150 million, which makes it about half the size of Quiksilver USA. For now.

"Europe has more surfable coastline than Australia," says Harry Hodge, the 50-year-old man who brought Quiksilver to Europe and the company's president. "There's Scotland, Ireland, Wales, France, Spain, Portugal—even Sardinia and Italy now. And I can tell you they need board shorts in Italy. Badly."

If there's one person responsible for the resurrection of Mr. Sunset, it's Harry Hodge. Born and raised outside Melbourne, "Hollywood" Hodge (he bears a passing resemblance to the actor Don Johnson) was a surfer and a journalist whose lifelong dream was to make a surf film "as good as *Endless Summer.*" In the end, he did make his movie, *Band on the Run,* but it cost him everything he owned and was, he admits, "a complete commercial failure."

Hodge fell into a yearlong depression, but he eventually rallied and found a marketing job with Quiksilver Australia. In 1984, offered a chance to launch a new license in France, Hodge did the unthinkable—he looked up Hakman, with whom he'd partied during the glory days in Costa Mesa, and asked him if he wanted a chance to start over as a one-quarter partner in a new company called Quiksilver Europe. "I had no reservations at all," Hodge says. "Hakman knew the business. And I was young."

Hakman was nearby, at Burleigh Heads on the Gold Coast of Queensland, where he and Cherie had retreated after the debacle at Quiksilver USA. He had come a long way down in the world, clerking in a surf shop and teaching Australian kids and Japanese tourists to surf on his lunch hour, and when his old peers from the pro ranks came through, they could barely look him in the eye. But Hakman wasn't unhappy.

"I loved teaching the kids," he remembers. "I'd take an eight-year-old out, and after two hours he'd be laughing and smiling and riding waves, just stoked . . .

"So when Harry said, 'Do you want to do this Europe thing?' I didn't know. It wasn't like I was over the addiction. I was healthy and I'd cleaned up, but those little sensations were still prickling."

Armed with a war chest of $200,000 Australian that they'd raised themselves, Hodge, Hakman, Hodge's girlfriend, Brigitte Darrigrand, and a fourth partner, John Winship, set off to conquer Europe. "Brigitte's parents put their house up as collateral, and then a banker here was somehow convinced and gave us a loan," Hodge says. "Two years later we had a line of credit of 70 million francs, with no tangible assets." Meanwhile, Hakman was slowly slipping off the wagon. "I was good—well, so-so—for about a year," he recalls. "Then you just run into certain people, and sooner or later you're in trouble."

In late 1986 the company accountant came to Hodge scratching his head. "I'm looking at these gas receipts of Jeff's," Hodge says, "and he's bought enough fuel in the last three months to have driven around the world a couple of times." Hakman had been putting $20 of gas in his car but charging $100 on his card and pocketing the difference. Hodge and Darrigrand, furious at the betrayal, told Hakman that if it happened again, he was finished. "I got caught with the gas cards, then I got clean," Hakman says. "It's always the same cycle."

In 1988, unable to pay off their line of credit, the four partners started looking for help. They found a bittersweet solution in a buy-out offer from Quiksilver USA. "We basically sold the whole company, with an earn-out clause which we hit, for ten million," says Hakman. "We got stock options, but it's not the same as owning it. People say, 'God, you sold the company, how stupid!' But it was that close to being nothing. We had the fashion and we had the image, but none of us had a financial background."

With the sale complete, Hakman found himself with about $800,000 in the bank and not quite the same interest in running the business. Soon he was looking up old friends. "I was functioning, but it was a schedule from hell," he says. "I had to see my contact twice a day. I couldn't go to work without it, so I had to get him out of bed in the morning. Then I had to find him again at lunch. The problem wasn't when you were high. It was when you couldn't score. You're sweating, your nose is running, your voice is cracking. You're falling off your chair."

Hakman shakes his head, remembering the day the end came. "May 10, 1990," he says. "I got up, and I felt horrible. I turned to my wife and said, 'I don't think I'm in control.' I broke down and admitted it: I was scared." Cherie went to Hodge and told him Jeff was using again, and neither of them knew what to do. Rather than fire Hakman, as he'd promised, Hodge got on the phone. "I remember him yelling," Hakman says. "'Where's the place Elton John went? I want that place!'"

In his six weeks at Galsworthy Lodge, outside London, Hakman was subjected to an unsparing scrutiny and, perhaps more important, allowed to see the spectacle of other outwardly assured men and women paralyzed by their addictions. "Really elegant, refined people, guys in nice suits with good accents, who were helpless," he says. "Way worse than me."

"We both knew that we couldn't keep living like that," Cherie says. "I can't look back and say that it was easy, but we know what it is like to be human. We're lucky. A lot of people don't survive. We got through it, and the other end of all this has been great."

For close to a decade now, Hakman says, he's been clean.

The final weekend of the contest is at hand, and thanks to his decent showing in round three, Hakman now needs only a second-place finish in the last heat to make it through to the quarterfinals. The flowing, powerful Bobby Owens takes the early lead, as he has all week. Then Reno Abellira, who's been floundering at the back of the pack alongside Hakman, suddenly comes alive with a couple of nifty tube rides. But Hakman's first few waves look pretty good, too. In the spectator enclosure, the Quiksilver crew follows Hakman closely. "If he's not careful," says Hodge sarcastically, "he could wind up in the main event."

Abellira and Owens each get another wave, and Hakman slips into third place. Then, with two minutes left in the heat, a final set rolls in. Hakman almost takes off on the first wave, but it starts to break around him and then closes out entirely. He pulls back and spins to grab the second wave, but it's breaking too far to the left, and he can't quite paddle into it. The buzzer sounds, and that's it—he's out of the contest.

For Hakman, it's a victory nonetheless—one more step in the rehabbing of a legend. First, there was his job, which he describes as "sort of being Mr. Quiksilver, internationally," and which amounts to telling surfing stories at sales meetings, hanging out at trade shows, and offering an occasional design critique. Then there was the biography, which Hodge talked him into cooperating with as an act of therapy and as a way to recover his story.

Since its publication, the book has become something else—a strangely effective piece of marketing. (Though it has yet to find a U.S. distributor, *Mr. Sunset* has done surprisingly well, selling more than 20,000 copies overseas and over the Internet, and the Hollywood production company October Films has optioned it for the screen.) Just as Nike is quick to lap up anything that seems remotely cool about the NBA and The North Face leaps to outfit the next wave of mountain daredevils, Quiksilver can't help but stake out its territory. That means signing up obvious stars, like Kelly Slater, and hosting events like the Silver Edition Masters. But it also means reaching out to subversive heroes and prodigal sons like Jeff Hakman, because there's something authentic about them that no amount of white bread can match.

"We're not just some guy who looks like Jimmy Buffet with a parrot on his shoulder," says McKnight. "You get our guys together, Jeff and the other Hawaiians, and it's really real, man."

The next day, with Hakman looking on from the beach, the contest wraps up. Cheyne Horan edges out his old nemesis Tom Carroll in the under-40 finals, thereby claiming his first-ever world masters championship. (Later the same afternoon, he proposes to his girlfriend in a scene that he calls "way heavier than the final.") In the over-40 final, Rabbit Bartholomew manages to catch the wave of the tournament, a perfect, near-closeout tube ride. After what seems like ten seconds, he bursts out of the far end, pumping both fists, making the claim. The judges do what they must—they give him a perfect ten, and the victory.

The awards ceremony is held at Lafitenia, and afterward there's a pretty good party that doesn't end until past midnight. It's an idyllic scene: Hawaiian guitars, cold Buds (a delicacy in France), and the sun dipping low over the sea, just like in southern California. One might expect Hakman to skip out on the party, especially as it gets loud, but he winds up staying, hanging out with Hodge and the Hawaiians on the deck. He even has a beer. Though Hakman never had a real problem with alcohol, you can almost hear 12-step people everywhere gnashing their teeth. A beer! It's tantamount to starting up the heroin again! To the Aussies, though, it's just funny. "Hakman's having a beer!" Hodge yells. "Someone get a camera!"

Hakman has another beer, or two. He laughs at the jokes and tells a few of his own, but it's hard to figure out if he's truly having a good time. Maybe he is. But I have my doubts. Between jokes he gets a far-away look in his eyes, and soon he's backing out of the party. It's ironic, really. The guy who started the party is the first one to leave.

April 2000

Across the Disappearing Finish Line

BILL McKIBBEN

B arring the odd World War or Depression, being a man was once a fairly simple task. My grandfather, for instance, lived to be a well-adjusted 95—he visited Costa Rica on a banana boat at 90— by walking a few brisk miles every morning and avoiding between-meals snacks.

But it's not so easy anymore. Here are some things you need to know if you're going to be a healthy man, according to a recent issue of *Men's Health:* Chronic, day-to-day work stress can lower your sperm count by a third; a diet rich in garlic keeps your aorta flexible; vitamin B2 fights off migraines; shrinking your waist from 40 inches to 37 inches cuts diabetes risk in half; you can build your triceps by doing dips off the edge of a swimming pool; if you're determined to have sex in an elevator, a spokesman for the American Elevator and Machine Corporation recommends using a freight elevator ("Many lack security cameras, but check the ceiling to make sure"). Not only that—but negative sit-ups can build abdominal muscles faster than crunches.

None of this would surprise women. For a long time—say, three or four million years—being a woman was hard work. But sometime around 1985, when men in their underwear began reclining on Times Square billboards, manhood became nearly as time-consuming. A sampling of *Men's Fitness* covers over the past year promises "24 Ways to Customize Your Physique," "6 Dangerous Foods," "12 Instant Nutrition Fixes," "7 Best Biceps Builders," "Better Sex—10 Ways to Drive Them Insane," "7 Super Shakes for Peak Energy," "5 Awesome Back Wideners," "5 Ready-Made Seduction Dates," "20 Hospital Survival Tips," "6 Moves for Bigger Arms," and "50 Ways to Improve Your Life—Guaranteed."

I'd never paid much attention to this kind of thing before the winter of 1998, when at the age of 37 I embarked on, well, a quest. I decided to spend a year training pretty much full-time to be a cross-country ski racer—I knew I wouldn't win any races, but I wanted to understand my mind and body in new ways, before age closed certain doors. Maybe I was tired of living mainly through my head; maybe I was just freaked to be growing old. In any event, I found a coach, Rob Sleamaker, author of *Serious Training for Endurance Athletes,* who drew up a yearlong program that called for more than 600 hours of training—daily two-, three-, four-hour runs and skis, long bouts of uphill sprinting, my heart-rate monitor bleating softly all the while. Add to that endless sets of crunches and biceps curls and triceps extensions, and before much time had passed, muscles—not underwear ad–size muscles, but still—actually began to appear on my formerly smooth body.

And vanity began to infect my formerly oblivious consciousness. I found myself posing in front of the mirror as I shaved—flexing my pecs so they'd pop up and down, tensing my butt (my glutes, I mean) when I showered, feeling the indentations in my upper arm that marked the birth of my triceps. You couldn't really make out my washboard abs, but I could count the ridges of riblike muscle whenever I tightened my stomach. I read Arnold Schwarzenegger's 1977 autobiography, *Arnold: The Education of a Bodybuilder,* with new understanding.

Unlike Arnold's, however, the veins in my arms bulged like phone cords, not tug lines; my forearms bloomed from celery stalks to broccoli stalks. My wife, Sue, was the only one to notice I was sprouting muscle mass, and even she, in my opinion, paid far too little attention to the details of my emergent triceps. Of course, endurance athletes are not supposed to Popeye up—more muscle takes more blood to feed it, eventually reducing your efficiency. Still, self-image matters, I was finding out. As a boy, resolutely unphysical, I supposed I should exercise in order to get girls. I got girls anyway; eventually I got married and fathered a child and so fulfilled my genetic mandate, and the fact that I couldn't reliably open pickle jars did not prevent my DNA from passing down yea unto the generations.

And yet did I measure up to my forebears, those sturdy small-town Westerners, on the manliness scale? My father, growing up, had spent his summers at a log cabin on the edge of Mount Rainier—a place without lights or running water, in the shadow of the great Douglas firs. We'd visit the cabin every few years on some vacation driving trip, and usually we'd find my cousin Craig there. A mountaineer, Craig was forever heading off to Pakistan or Baffin Island or some other place with high icy cliffs to conquer. Sometimes he'd open his pack to show us his collection of carabiners, pitons, and ropes. Dad loved it—this was his fantasy life, long before Everest mania. But he'd reared us in the cushy suburbs of the East, where SATs counted more than sit-ups, and sometimes it seemed to me as if I was devolving, defying Darwin.

That summer, as I roller-skied and ran and lifted and interval-trained in preparation for the winter race season, Mom and Dad celebrated their 40th anniversary. Dad had recently retired after a lifetime as a journalist, and the whole family joined them at a slightly down-at-the-heels resort in the White Mountains that offered a shaggy nine-hole golf course out back. It was a great pleasure that summer to head out onto the green with my dad and my younger brother, Tom. I'd never played before, and I had no swing; they had to show me how to grip the club. But when I connected I had power—the ball would sail away into the middle distance. It didn't bother me that it went left or right or onto the neighboring fairway. I just liked the idea that it went long and strong.

The more I trained, and especially the more I began to race, the more I understood that my mind needed toughening at least as much as my body—that endurance was about going until it hurt, when the natural impulse was to slow down, and then deciding whether to listen to that impulse or not. Not long after my golf date with Dad, I went off to Australia, which has the planet's best August snow, eager to test out my hepped-up lungs. I'll never forget the morning of the Paddy Pallin Classic, a 25-kilometer race through the twisted snow gums and eucalyptus trees on the shoulder of 7,310-foot Mount Kosciusko, the continent's highest peak. I remember exactly how good it felt when the gun went off, how I bounded up the hills on my new legs, how I fantasized about catching the wave of skiers who had started five minutes before me—and how immediately I lost all that sweet focus at the first real sign of adversity. A racer came blowing by me, my chest tightened, and suddenly I was just plodding along, concentration gone. I still had some work to do.

But there'd been enough glimpses of transformation—races where for a few minutes I'd drop into the inescapable now of competition—to keep me going. When I came back from Australia, I began the longest, hardest month of my training schedule, an endless September that peaked one Saturday morning with a 238-minute run. My parents were visiting our Adirondack home, and they offered to watch my six-year-old daughter, Sophie, while I worked out. I ran and ran and ran some more, finally stumble-charging up the last rise, congratulating myself that from now on the whole year was downhill. I was peeling off my T-shirt and savoring the smug aura of finishing something hard when I noticed Dad. He was about a hundred yards away from Mom, walking back and forth, and he was lurching a bit. "He's testing himself," she said, with a frantic edge in her voice.

Slowly the story started to come out. In August he'd been hiking hard in the Cascades, feeling fine. But when he got home he'd begun stumbling a bit—and once fell right over. Some days, Mom added, he slurred his words. Dad had chalked it up to the late-summer humidity, or perhaps a sinus infection, and had rallied (and reassured) himself by walking faster, working up a sweat. But when I took him aside that afternoon he confessed that his right side felt weak. Could I have had a small stroke? he asked me. As soon as he said it, I felt myself starting to panic—it had never even entered my mind that at 68 he'd start to decline. But I knew it must be true; it would explain the balance, the speech, even a few recent mild displays of uncharacteristic temper.

I bade my parents good-bye with a sour taste in the back of my throat. The next day Dad phoned from home in Boston to say that his doctor was convinced that indeed he'd had a very mild stroke. He'd scheduled an MRI for later in the week just to make sure, but he told Mom and Dad to go ahead planning a trip to Mexico; I could tell from his voice that Dad was immensely relieved.

And I was too. I spent a little time thinking about the Meaning of It All—how your body would eventually betray you no matter how fit you got—and then I went back to work, because racing season was coming into distant view. The weather began to change; a front came through one of those early autumn nights, dropping temperatures down into the low thirties, threatening the tomatoes. The weatherman talked about "the possibility of sleet or snow on the high ridges." The S word hadn't been heard in these parts since early May, and it made me quiver inside.

I started stacking firewood in earnest that week, and while I was working Friday afternoon I looked up to see our dog, Barley, trotting toward me with something in her mouth. At first I thought it was a shoe, but when she dropped it for me I saw it was a hawk—dead, but utterly unmarked, a broad-wing, all strength and sinew. Sophie and I spread its strong, gray feathers, examined its powerful beak and talons, and then wrapped it in plastic and put it in the freezer so that she could take it to school. I went back to the woodpile.

When I looked up a few minutes later, Sue was standing there in the fading light with tears running down her cheeks. My mom had just called. Dad had a brain tumor, "an aggressive nonbenign tumor." They were operating on Tuesday. Just like that.

I hugged her for a long time, and then headed straight out into the woods, cursing and crying and carrying on. Mom said the doctor had told them that even with the operation "the long-term average survival" was 12 months, which put a new spin on the whole idea of long-term. For me, 12 months was a "training cycle." I was still sobbing when Dad came on the phone. "This is ridiculous, isn't it?" he said with a rueful chuckle. He'd been shaving when I called, and for some reason that made me even sadder. How do you manage to look in the mirror when someone has just told you that in a year you won't be there?

A couple of weeks before, I'd visited some actuarial Web site that let you calculate your likely life span. Didn't smoke, long-lived relatives, plenty of exercise, low cholesterol—when I tapped the final button it told me I was going to die at 93. I'm certain that Dad would have gotten the same result. He was strong and active; he'd just written his first book. But there was no little button on the actuarial table for something called glioblastoma, the most virulent form of brain cancer.

When we got to Boston the next day, the change was obvious. Six days earlier his speech had been a little slurred. Three days earlier he'd driven to church and chaired a meeting. Today, Saturday, his triumph had been walking the 20 yards to the Adirondack chairs in the backyard. His world was shrinking with incomprehensible speed. He told us about finding out the bad news: The surgeon had pronounced his death sentence, and then said he should choose. "I could get a big bottle of scotch and have a wonderful last night before going into a coma, or I could have this surgery and that would keep me going a little longer."

The night before Dad went to the hospital, as I was taking off his slippers to put him to bed, I could see the hard, veiny calves that only a month ago were powering him up high mountains in his native Northwest. They were useless now. Was he useless? What did it mean to lose your body in a week? And what would it mean, 24 hours hence, to lose some large chunk of your mind?

That next morning, at the hospital, Dad passed into another, yet-smaller world, where his abilities meant nothing. When the surgeon finally came for his pre-op visit, Dad asked only one question: "Will my personality change?"

"I hope not," the doctor said.

We watched as they wheeled him out of his room to the operating theater. It was after lunch before the doctor appeared to give us the news. Dad had come through surgery OK, but the pathology was exactly what he suspected: glioblastoma, grade four. The worst grade. He couldn't get it all; it had already spread to both lobes. Sorry. The next few months, the doctor said, would be "the good time," a phrase that would come to haunt us.

When they finally let us up to see him, Dad looked . . . beautiful. A turban of bandages wrapped his head, but beneath it his face was eerily young, as if he were in his twenties. The sparkle was back in his eyes. When we turned on the TV the Red Sox were leading the Indians in game one of their playoff series behind seven RBIs from Mo Vaughn. Dad was making jokes—he whose head had been sawed open and then the two halves pulled apart by traction. This much was clear: His personality had not changed, not one whit. Doubtless it would darken when the tumor recurred, when the swelling built up again. The hope, though, was that we'd bought ourselves a few months, a window of time to make peace with his passing. Nothing more.

And so we settled into the pattern of small victories and somewhat larger defeats that must mark most terminal illness. They shifted Dad to a "rehabilitation hospital" in the suburbs, where after daily morning trips by ambulance to the radiation ward he would return for afternoons of physical therapy. The therapy rooms reminded me of the world where I'd spent much of the last year—they were filled with weight machines, parallel bars, treadmills. But here, in place of the ersatz philosophy of the gym, real struggle prevailed. Dad's workouts, as tightly scheduled and as exhausting as mine, involved batting a balloon back and forth with the therapist, folding washcloths, unscrewing a jar top, kicking a ball. He could swing his right foot perhaps an inch, enough to nudge the ball along the floor, but no more. When he tried to steer his wheelchair, it inevitably drifted to the right till he hit a wall, reflecting the now-distorted architecture of his brain. His major triumph: learning to apply and disengage the wheelchair brake.

Through it all I kept running. I suppose I should have stopped, if only because it seemed in such poor taste, calibrating my body's improvement as Dad's withered away. But Dad had been the most interested in my project from the beginning. And there was nothing else to structure my life. No one expected me at an office. I was commuting between the Adirondacks and Boston, between my adult and boyhood homes (I was sleeping on the bed I'd slept on as a boy, the same bed Dad had slept on in his youth). There was no way I could write—when I tried to still my mind enough to string two thoughts together, I invariably began to weep. Only motion seemed to relax me.

I'd begun this compulsive exercising on the premise that I was at the tail end of my youth. Now it was all too easy to calculate that if I lived as long as my father was going to, I was already halfway used up. But I could feel the second half of my life starting in more complicated ways too. Identities long fixed shifted back and forth. Sometimes I was still his son. But then the next morning would dawn, and we'd need yet again to make some impossible decision: more radiation, say. Dad would doze off while the doctor was explaining the options, and we'd be left trying to figure out what he might want, what we might want. The goal of all the physical therapy diminished. Instead of teaching him to regain real function in his muscles, the single aim became training him to help in the process of transferring himself from bed to wheelchair, and vice versa. If he learned that, he could go home and Mom could take care of him by herself. The technique, as detailed and precise as a good cross-country skiing kick, involved lifting his butt an inch up off the bed and then sliding himself in two stages about a foot and a half into the wheelchair. He would push himself up on his knuckles, slide ten inches, rest 30 seconds till the panting subsided, then make the next assault. Each time he'd forget the sequence and need to be reminded; each time it left him red-faced and tired.

All this training, and for what? It wasn't like my training. I knew I was getting steadily stronger and fitter. Not Dad. He worked all afternoon stretching his rubber bands, lifting his tiny dumbbells, and yet his body decayed faster than he could build it up.

I went in to the rehab center one morning and found him in an uncharacteristic rage. Some doctor had wandered through that morning (one of the glories of managed care was that unknown doctors constantly drifted in and out of our lives) and remarked to him, on the basis of a handshake, that he was getting weaker. Dad was outraged, agitated. He didn't want to go to therapy that afternoon, but I talked him into it.

You followed your schedule no matter what; sometimes that seemed about all my year had taught me.

If I needed a metaphor for my autumn, it came in early November. Back in the Adirondacks for a week, I noticed some fresh new pavement on a back road on the far side of the Hudson River. Fresh pavement, to a roller-skier, exerts a nearly gravitational pull—smooth and fast, it's the next best thing to snow. What I hadn't noticed was just how steep the hills were. I was, as always, wearing a bike helmet, but I'd forgotten my knee pads, and the light was fading. Predictably, I went for it. For an hour I skied the hills, tucking for fast descents, powering up with short, choppy kicks, feeling pretty damn strong. And then, predictably, a dog ran out at the bottom of a hill just as a car passed on my left—and I was down in a second.

Predictably, I jumped up, in the way that guys do when they've fallen, as if to say, Oh, I meant to do that. I waved off the stricken driver—and as soon as he was out of sight I sat right back down to consider. True, my knees were bleeding dramatically, soaking my shredded tights, but on the other hand I had 90 minutes left in my workout. I'd snapped a pole, so I clearly wasn't going to keep skiing, but I had my sneakers in the car. And so—predictably?—I ran, knees bleeding and stiff. It was clearly stupid. Perhaps I just wanted to hurt, and to keep going through the hurt.

My road-scraped knees healed just in time for me to return to Lake Placid and the giant treadmill at the Olympic Training Center for the final readout on my year's training. I'd passed through this particular crucible in the spring, establishing my baseline numbers and learning just how much the test could hurt—you ran until you couldn't run anymore, or at least until you thought you couldn't. This time, rubber bit clenched in my mouth to catch my exhalations, I lasted two minutes longer than I had in April, but it didn't cheer me up. Because I knew I'd had another minute in me, if only I'd fought the pain a little harder. But when the treadmill tilted toward the gut-check stage, I couldn't keep going. It hurt, that's why.

My coach, Rob, professed delight. "You've had a 45 percent improvement in body fat, your lactate threshold is 25 percent better—your engine is burning hotter at a lower lactate production. It means you can ski at a faster pace longer." Part of me did feel exhilarated. It had worked the way it was supposed to, all those hours and miles. Mine was not the physique of a champion, but what I had done was maximize my genetic potential, grown about as powerful as my ancestry would allow.

But the day left me feeling unsettled. When things had gotten really tough, I had looked for a way out. My *heart* might have become more efficient, but my heart seemed no stronger.

Maybe it was because I was beginning to question whether endurance was such a grand goal anyhow.

From the moment I'd learned of Dad's first conversation with the surgeon—scotch or scalpel—part of me had been wondering whether we should be keeping him alive. We'd press the specialists with questions about whether his condition would improve, and all we'd get was the Ph.D. equivalent of shrugs. In the meantime, he was home, enduring, and Mom was, too. The HMO professed to believe that a couple of hours of nursing assistance a day was all Mom needed; never mind that Dad outweighed her by 80 or 90 pounds. She hired extra aides to come in the evening and help her get him out of bed; the next-door neighbor's son slept upstairs now just in case he rolled out of bed and she couldn't get him back in. New pills piled up almost daily; dosages changed with every visit to the doctor; Mom was awake by six to give him his first medicines, and still up at midnight to feed him the final batch. When I thought about the burden she was under, I doubted I could handle anything like it. And yet she kept going forward, forward, forward, like—well, like an elite athlete. In her case, though, it wasn't uphill intervals and mental imagery that had laid the base. It was year upon year of loving, so consistently that the giving had become instinctive.

As for me, if watching someone die could perform the same kind of magic, I wasn't sure I was ready for it. When the treadmill got steep enough, I started looking around for someone to turn it off.

Whenever we were with the doctors, no matter how much of a fog he seemed to be in, Dad would ask that they treat his cancer "aggressively." But one night, when I was talking to him very late, he said, "If it's going to be like this all the time, then there has to be a cutoff somewhere." Amen, I thought. Where's the guy with the switch?

We made it to Thanksgiving, and I spent the week in West Yellowstone—my longest absence from his bedside so far, a guilty vacation— at the annual cross-country training camp that fills the town with gaunt, wax-obsessed nordic racers trying to cope with the 6,600-foot altitude. I flew home on Friday, though, for a delayed turkey dinner, where we managed to convince ourselves that we had much to be thankful for and that, with Dad propped up at table's end, all was joy. After the pie settled, I went for a run and instantly understood why athletes are so eager to train at altitude. My body had compensated for the thin Montana air by adding extra red blood cells. I ran through suburban Boston on a high—no matter how hard I pushed, I couldn't make myself hurt. My heart-rate monitor showed I was working reasonably hard, but I could have been out for the lightest of jogs. I felt out ahead of my body, as if I was outrunning my feet.

Sadly, the corpuscles quickly disappeared, and with them the sense that I had become a minor deity. Worse than that, the East was still warm and bare as December began. The temperature hit the seventies on the first of the month. The pond by our house was filled with summery ripples. No need for the woodstove; we slept with the windows open.

It bothered me on many levels. For ten years I'd been a nearly full-time student of global warming—worrying, tracking the rising sea temperatures that were bleaching coral reefs, writing about the increase in the strength and frequency of hurricanes. But I felt it most personally come winter. Always my favorite of seasons, it had become deeply unreliable. As the man from Fischer Skis had told me in West Yellowstone, global warming had already damaged their business, interrupting every winter with long stretches of mud and thaw. Business would doubtless carry on; in fact, I'd just come across a series of economic forecasts proving, in the smug fashion of economists, that increases in the greens fees from golfers would outweigh the losses from declining ski sales. But I didn't want to play golf—I wanted to speed sublimely through the woods, riding on an outstretched ski, pushing with every muscle in my body. I wanted the annual remission from friction.

Rob had been pushing me to pick a final race to aim for, something grand enough to be worthy of this whole experiment—and he'd been urging me to think about the Norwegian Birkebeiner, the mother of all cross-country races, held each March on a course that runs over the mountains from Rena to Lillehammer. Open to all comers, it attracts thousands of Norwegians, and most of the world's best marathon skiers. As they race, they commemorate the pivotal event in Norway's 13th-century civil war. The Birkebeiners—Birchleggers— were the underdogs, "often in such dire need that they had nothing but the bark of birch trees as footwear." But they were determined that the rival faction, the Baglers, not capture Haakon Haakonsson, the toddler son of their dying king. So on Christmas Day 1205, two Birke- beiner skiers spirited him away on an epic journey across the moun- tains. The boy grew up to be King Haakon and to finally rout the Baglers, raising Norway to its medieval glory. And hence, each year in late March, racers pound those same grueling 58 kilometers, about 40 miles, mostly uphill, each carrying an eight-pound pack to match the weight of the young king.

I doubted I could go. With Dad dying, the prospect of a transatlantic trip seemed unlikely. And I wondered if I could even finish the race. But I still logged onto the race Web site and clicked the button for an application. Maybe Dad would get better for a while—maybe the "good time" would arrive. I knew I wanted to go; it sounded crazy, hard enough to justify this crazy year.

This crazy year in which winter seemed never to come. By mid- December we'd set up the Christmas tree at church and gone caroling in shirtsleeves. Finally, December 17 brought a little snow to the Adirondacks, and a few phone calls established that the Olympic trails at Lake Placid were partially open. They were barely covered, but it was skiing, and I kicked around and around the same short loops with the junior biathletes, guns strapped to their backs, and the local mas- ters skiers, all of us desperate for snow. The next day warm, foggy air melted big tawny patches in the snow, and it was back to the damn NordicTrack. December was shot.

We got through Christmas Day in Boston just fine—a lot of the ornaments hung at wheelchair height, testament to Dad's pleasure in the work—but then, tired from the strain of this last big celebration, Dad was all but comatose for a couple of days. "Were it my dad," said the surgeon, "I wouldn't do much more."

At which point Dad emerged from his fog for the first time all day to ask yet again that he be treated "aggressively." Which annoyed the hell out of me—some part of me wanted him to go away and stop bothering us. Stop making me feel guilty for not being more help to my mother; stop pulling me away from my family; stop stop stop being so damn needy, so unlike my father. Which, of course, left me feeling twice as guilty as before.

A snowstorm might have righted me. It usually does. A couple of hours alone in the woods, gliding along, pushing up hills and carving down them, breaking out into the open on Adirondack lakes and tucking back into stands of hemlock, reminding me of the proper order and scale of things.

By late January the ground was still bare, and Dad was setting off on a major journey. Each day he seemed to grow a bit more abstracted from his shrinking world. He was never short with any of us. If his grandchildren were on hand, he would watch them playing around his bed with deep delight, and he never ceased following Mom with his eyes.

Sometimes the world he was visiting seemed inscrutable. Once I asked him what he was thinking so deeply about, and he replied, in a loud voice, "Insects!" But he did tell Mom several times that he constantly saw a white line in front of his eyes. One morning, when he was more alert than usual and when we had the house to ourselves, I asked him if he could describe the line to me. He asked for a pencil and, gripping it tightly in his shaking hand, drew a wavering line about two-thirds of the way across the page and labeled it R. On the edge of the paper, he drew a wavering circle and with great effort wrote "W. Ocean" across it. (In a lifetime of writing, they were the last words he ever wrote.) The picture represented, he said, a "typical Western river" leading to a "Western ocean."

"And what does that ocean mean?" I asked.

"Infinity," he said. "Completeness."

He nodded off for a few moments and then woke back up. Why didn't the river connect to the ocean? I asked.

There were, he said, necessary tasks still to be done, but he couldn't find the words to say what they were.

"Is death more scary to think about or more peaceful?" I asked.

"More peaceful," he said emphatically, and then drifted back to sleep.

That night at dinner he seemed happy—we'd been discussing "ultimate truths," he told Mom, with just a little smile to let us know he knew how unlike him it was to discuss ultimate truths. But a new man was clearly taking shape before our eyes.

My own journey seemed all but irrelevant, dull even to me, but by now the training was so ingrained that I kept with it almost automatically. And Rob, the one person besides my wife whom I'd trusted with my resolve to mount a supreme effort in some race, kept trying to help me find the right venue.

The trip to Lillehammer seemed less likely than ever, but I came across a brochure for the annual Keskinada races in Ottawa, in late February. The theme for 1999 was Norway; they were trying to duplicate parts of the Birkebeiner in Canada, including sending off one wave of racers carrying eight-pound backpacks. Ottawa was only a quick trip from Boston; this one I figured I could make. And so the images that filled my mind on training runs were suddenly Canadian: the pine forests of the Gatineau Park, the 50-kilometer trail. There was finally a little snow on the ground, and Rob told me to prepare with a four-hour time trial two weeks before the race. Four hours is a long time, especially with none of the adrenaline of a race to distract you; I headed to the ski tracks and did the same five-kilometer loop 11 times, till I knew every soft spot in the snow. Every lap brought me by a pigpen filled with noisy hogs; I'd stop there and choke down some energy gel. When the clock finally stopped, I'd gone 55 kilometers, and proved to myself that at the very least I could manage the distances in the race ahead. And I'd done it with my pack on my back, like a true Birchlegger.

Almost in spite of myself, I could feel my body starting to peak. As the really long workouts of the fall dwindled in number and distance, and the brutal intervals built up my speed, power began to accumulate. I imagined that I knew what a racehorse felt like in the gate, pent-up energy ready to express itself. Long, hard uphill skiing left me feeling spent but not wasted; my body craved fuel and burned it evenly; I was eager for a test, impatient for the Ottawa race to arrive. I was, in fact, in the best physical shape of my life.

In the middle of all this, my friend John Race came to visit. We'd met when he guided me up Mount Rainier five years before. Intellectually curious the way I was physically curious, he'd nonetheless spent almost all his energy on things of the body and the spirit. He'd spent months on Mount McKinley, gotten within 500 feet of the top of Everest, climbed 26,000-foot peaks like Cho Oyu. Now he was hungry for intellectual growth, and he wanted to write about his experiences. He was playing on the path I'd been following since I could first remember, and I was playing on his. It made me think of the first notion Rob had taught me when we'd started working together a year before—each of us born to be balanced physically, intellectually, and spiritually.

It hadn't taken me long to figure out how linked all three could be. If exercise was about being physical, then racing—being willing to hurt, to go harder than you wanted to—had an obvious spiritual quality. But the neat progression of my idea ran into trouble when Dad got sick. He was clearly operating at some higher level now, but it wasn't because he was trying. Instead, it seemed to be because he was letting go. Not giving up, not dropping out, but slowly, methodically, patiently letting go of his life. Every so often, I kept trying to ask serious questions, to find out what was going on inside. Partly it was just my curiosity, but I sensed, too, that he enjoyed talking about it, liked the fact that someone acknowledged he was dying and that it was an interesting process. One day he muttered that he was trying to figure out if there was something beyond this "make-believe" world, if there was something beyond "next week." His metaphors, like the drawing of the river, tended always toward the outdoor, the concrete, toward the joys of the Western boyhood that had filled his imagination ever since. "I feel like I'm climbing," he told me slowly one day. "Like I'm climbing up a cliff."

"Are you near the top?" I asked.

"Getting there," he said, with a grin.

I thought of all the climbs we'd taken when I was young, in the mountains of Maine and New Hampshire; of the pleasure he'd taken in the Adirondacks when I moved there; of the long trip we'd taken with his brother and my brother around Mount Rainier. Every time I'd looked at him in those weeks on the Wonderland Trail, he'd been grinning. Climbing wasn't a struggle for him, didn't represent a battle or even a test. It was a great joy, because it carried you higher, to where the view was clearer. And more than that—though the grand view may have started you slogging in the first place, no one kept hiking for years unless he came to like the slog. Sometimes it's bittersweet to reach the top, because there's nothing to do but linger for a while and go back down. This time, however, he wouldn't need to descend.

I'd started this exercise of exercising in an effort to try on a new identity, the way a high school boy might try on meanness, or a college boy might grow a goatee. But now, watching Dad, I realized what a solid thing an identity is. He was unchanged even by this catastrophe— he remained as decent and egoless a man as I'd ever met. As for me, I'd examined my core from a different side, or placed it under light of a different wavelength, and found it to be much as I'd always known it: curious, eager, tempted by deep commitment but afraid of the effort and pain.

I could live with that—it had served me well so far—but now I wondered if I could die with that. Wondered if I could go as gracefully as my father was going, as bravely and yet as peacefully. What would it be like to reach the end of my life without regrets?

Dad took one last trip into the hospital, for one last MRI. The tumor had fired up again, the doctors said, started once more to grow. Don't even bother calling the ambulance if something happens, they advised— you don't want them sticking a tube down his throat. Mom listened, asked Dad if he had anything to say.

He looked up, and in a clear, conversational tone announced, "I have this fascinating vision of a white line along the edge of a riverbank."

So there was Dad, cheerful in the face of a brain tumor. And here I was, gloomy because I'd caught a cold two days before the big race in Ottawa, and was reduced to obsessively guzzling tea, sucking on zinc tablets, and fretting about compromised respiratory efficiency. But on race morning I was up at 5:45, and I was the first to arrive at Gatineau

Park. I splurged $30 at the ski-waxing booth and watched the ski techs patiently iron on purple and red and then a coat of klister because the tracks were icy. I took my skis outside, tried them for a few strides, and instantly felt my mood soaring—I had rock-solid kick and lustrous glide. They felt like perfect extensions of my legs, each twitch converted into forward momentum.

The starting pen for my wave filled with other backpack-carrying skiers, about 40 of us among the hundreds of more conventional racers. An official weighed the rucksacks, making sure they topped the infant-king-Haakon line on the scale. We shuffled back and forth in the tracks for a few minutes, trying to stay limber, until the Norwegian ambassador to Canada sounded the ceremonial horn and we took off.

Because of the packs, it was easy enough to keep my competition in sight. We hit the first long uphill, and my legs felt so strong I had to consciously rein myself in a little, remind myself I'd be out on the course for a good three hours. One by one I picked off the guys in my wave—a fellow carrying a blaze-orange knapsack, a fellow in camouflage Lycra, a fast-looking skier who somehow managed to fall on the first small downhill. Twenty minutes into the race, a fellow in a brown rucksack was in front of me, and I was pretty sure he was either second or third in my wave—in other words, if I passed him I'd be in the money. I stayed on his tail for a few minutes, pulling abreast occasionally, even chatting for a while to let him know the pace wasn't hurting me. And I passed him.

After that I was skiing by myself. The hills just kept on coming, and my form began gradually to erode; by the halfway point I was laboring. I stopped for a drink of water and a ClifShot, and the people manning the table seemed concerned. "You're shivering," said one. "Are you hypothermic?" Before they could ask again, I skied off.

At some point along the course, a photographer crouched, taking pictures of everyone coming by so that he could try to sell them at the banquet that night. Through his lens, I was just one more tired-looking guy stuck somewhere in the middle of an unimportant race. And yet for me it was an epic. I crouched down in my tuck and let my muscles recover for a few minutes as the trail tilted downhill. Then came a long flat. Finally, at about 40 kilometers, the trail turned back on itself, and for about 500 yards you could see the skiers right behind you. Oh, God—one had a brown backpack, the same fellow I'd passed nearly two hours before, now right on my tail, maybe 40 seconds behind. Worse, my limbs were slowing down—I couldn't muster more than a sluggish kick. I could feel myself about to give up, about to be passed, about to turn normal.

And then I didn't. I made it up one hill and coasted down the other side; after that, though I was shaky and absolutely drained, I managed to go hard. Not fast. But fast enough, because I was still passing people. Fast enough, because every time I looked over my shoulder, the tracks were clear. Eventually there was a sign by the trail and it said: "Finish 1,000 Meters." Did a thousand meters mean a kilometer? Ten kilometers? My hypoxic brain fuzzed the question around until suddenly the trail spit out onto an open field, and the finish was only a few hundred good old English yards away. I sprinted, I fell across the line, someone picked me up and wrapped a wool blanket around me. They said I'd come in second in my wave.

My father's race finished on March 3. Though his sickness had lasted barely six months, half the impossibly short "long-term average survival" the doctors had given us at the start, he had endured. He'd kept going.

I had spent a year thinking about endurance. Trying to understand it as a function of physiology, of lactic acid and capillary networks. Trying to understand it as the ability to fight through the drama of pain. But now I understood it, too, as a kind of elegance, a lightness that could come only from such deep comfort with yourself that you began to forget about yourself. Something no heart monitor would ever measure.

Dad died in time to let me go to Norway for the Birkebeiner. Once I'd thought that this would be the epic end of my saga, but now I knew that whatever epiphanies I'd been allotted had come at the edge of his sickbed. Now there was just the pleasure of enduring in a great crowd of others doing the same—old men, some of them 80 and 85, a little stiff in their Lycra, but still elegant. They'd been skiing these hills 50 years ago, tracking down Allied airdrops in the woods, and they did so still, for the sheer joy of it.

The course was brutal as advertised, and I was in no danger of letting loose another epic performance. But never mind. I went deep inside, kept track of my weakening calves and my tightening chest, measured my resources against the distance left to go. And it all came out just fine—a little over four hours of hard skiing, ending with a series of sharp downhills into the Olympic stadium filled with brass bands and cheering crowds. I finished just above the middle of my age group, which I declared a great victory, considering they were all Norwegians. But I took my conquest as quietly as everyone else—there was no whooping or hollering on the bus to the showers, just satisfied and tired smiles. The year was over, and it was time for a smoked salmon pizza and a bottle of Ringnes and some Tiger Balm to rub on my aching thighs.

The next morning dawned clear and cold, and Sue and Sophie and I went for another ski. And for the first time in a long time, it meant nothing at all.

November 2000

The Fall Line

JON KRAKAUER

James Gallien had driven five miles out of Fairbanks when he spotted the hitchhiker standing in the snow beside the road, thumb raised high, shivering in the gray Alaskan dawn. A rifle protruded from the young man's pack, but he looked friendly enough; a hitchhiker with a Remington semiautomatic isn't the sort of thing that gives motorists pause in the 49th state. Gallien steered his four-by-four onto the shoulder and told him to climb in.

The hitchhiker introduced himself as Alex. "Alex?" Gallien responded, fishing for a last name.

"Just Alex," the young man replied, pointedly rejecting the bait. He explained that he wanted a ride as far as the edge of Denali National Park, where he intended to walk deep into the bush and "live off the land for a few months." Alex's backpack appeared to weigh only 25 or 30 pounds, which struck Gallien, an accomplished outdoorsman, as an improbably light load for a three-month sojourn in the back-country, especially so early in the spring. Immediately Gallien began to wonder if he'd picked up one of those crackpots from the Lower 48 who come north to live out their ill-considered Jack London fantasies. Alaska has long been a magnet for unbalanced souls, often outfitted with little more than innocence and desire, who hope to find their footing in the unsullied enormity of the Last Frontier. The bush, however, is a harsh place and cares nothing for hope or longing. More than a few such dreamers have met predictably unpleasant ends.

As they got to talking during the three-hour drive, though, Alex didn't strike Gallien as your typical misfit. He was congenial, seemed well educated, and peppered Gallien with sensible questions about "what kind of small game lived in the country, what kind of berries he could eat, that kind of thing."

Still, Gallien was concerned: Alex's gear seemed excessively slight for the rugged conditions of the interior bush, which in April still lay buried under the winter snowpack. He admitted that the only food in his pack was a ten-pound bag of rice. He had no compass; the only navigational aid in his possession was a tattered road map he'd scrounged at a gas station, and when they arrived where Alex asked to be dropped off, he left the map in Gallien's truck, along with his watch, his comb, and all his money, which amounted to 85 cents. "I don't want to know what time it is," Alex declared cheerfully. "I don't want to know what day it is, or where I am. None of that matters."

During the drive south toward the mountains, Gallien had tried repeatedly to dissuade Alex from his plan, to no avail. He even offered to drive Alex all the way to Anchorage so he could at least buy the kid some decent gear. "No, thanks anyway," Alex replied. "I'll be fine with what I've got." When Gallien asked whether his parents or some friend knew what he was up to—anyone who could sound the alarm if he got into trouble and was overdue—Alex answered calmly that, no, nobody knew of his plans, that in fact he hadn't spoken to his family in nearly three years. "I'm absolutely positive," he assured Gallien, "I won't run into anything I can't deal with on my own."

"There was just no talking the guy out of it," Gallien recalls. "He was determined. He couldn't wait to head out there and get started." So Gallien drove Alex to the head of the Stampede Trail, an old mining track that begins ten miles west of the town of Healy, convinced him to accept a tuna melt and a pair of rubber boots to keep his feet dry, and wished him good luck. Alex pulled a camera from his backpack and asked Gallien to snap a picture of him. Then, smiling broadly, he disappeared down the snow-covered trail. The date was Tuesday, April 28, 1992.

More than four months passed before Gallien heard anything more of the hitchhiker. His real name turned out to be Christopher J. McCandless. He was the product of a happy family from an affluent suburb of Washington, D.C. And although he wasn't burdened with a surfeit of common sense and possessed a streak of stubborn idealism that did not readily mesh with the realities of modern life, he was no psychopath. McCandless was in fact an honors graduate of Emory University, an accomplished athlete, and a veteran of several solo excursions into wild, inhospitable terrain.

An extremely intense young man, McCandless had been captivated by the writing of Leo Tolstoy. He particularly admired the fact that the great novelist had forsaken a life of wealth and privilege to wander among the destitute. For several years he had been emulating the count's asceticism and moral rigor to a degree that astonished and occasionally alarmed those who knew him well. When he took leave of James Gallien, McCandless entertained no illusions that he was trekking into Club Med; peril, adversity, and Tolstoyan renunciation were what he was seeking. And that is precisely what he found on the Stampede Trail, in spades.

For most of 16 weeks McCandless more than held his own. Indeed, were it not for one or two innocent and seemingly insignificant blunders he would have walked out of the Alaskan woods in July or August as anonymously as he walked into them in April. Instead, the name of Chris McCandless has become the stuff of tabloid headlines, and his bewildered family is left clutching the shards of a fierce and painful love.

On the northern margin of the Alaska Range, just before the hulking escarpments of Denali and its satellites surrender to the low Kantishna plain, a series of lesser ridges known as the Outer Ranges sprawls across the flats like a rumpled blanket on an unmade bed. Between the flinty crests of the two outermost Outer Ranges runs an east-west trough, maybe five miles across, carpeted in a boggy amalgam of muskeg, alder thickets, and scrawny spruce. Meandering through this tangled, rolling bottomland is the Stampede Trail, the route Chris McCandless followed into the wilderness.

Twenty or so miles due west of Healy, not far from the boundary of Denali National Park, a derelict bus—a blue and white, 1940s-vintage International from the Fairbanks City Transit System—rusts incongruously in the fireweed beside the Stampede Trail. Many winters ago the bus was fitted with bedding and a crude barrel stove, then skidded into the bush by enterprising hunters to serve as a backcountry shelter. These days it isn't unusual for nine or ten months to pass without the bus seeing a human visitor, but on September 6, 1992, six people in three separate parties happened to visit it on the same afternoon, including Ken Thompson, Gordon Samel, and Ferdie Swanson, moose hunters who drove in on all-terrain vehicles.

When they arrived at the bus, says Thompson, they found "a guy and a girl from Anchorage standing 50 feet away, looking kinda spooked. A real bad smell was coming from inside the bus, and there was this weird note tacked by the door." The note, written in neat block letters on a page torn from a novel by Gogol, read: "S.O.S. I need your help. I am injured, near death, and too weak to hike out of here. I am all alone, this is no joke. In the name of God, please remain to save me. I am out collecting berries close by and shall return this evening. Thank you, Chris McCandless. August?"

The Anchorage couple had been too upset by the implications of the note to examine the bus's interior, so Thompson and Samel steeled themselves to take a look. A peek through a window revealed a .22-caliber rifle, a box of shells, some books and clothing, a backpack, and, on a makeshift bunk in the rear of the vehicle, a blue sleeping bag that appeared to have something or someone inside it.

"It was hard to be absolutely sure," says Samel. "I stood on a stump, reached through a back window, and gave the bag a shake. There was definitely something in it, but whatever it was didn't weigh much. It wasn't until I walked around to the other side and saw a head sticking out that I knew for certain what it was." Chris McCandless had been dead for some two and a half weeks.

The Alaska State Troopers were contacted, and the next morning a police helicopter evacuated the decomposed body, a camera with five rolls of exposed film, and a diary—written across the last two pages of a field guide to edible plants—that recorded the young man's final weeks in 113 terse, haunting entries. An autopsy revealed no internal injuries or broken bones. Starvation was suggested as the most probable cause of death. McCandless's signature had been penned at the bottom of the S.O.S. note, and the photos, when developed, included many self-portraits. But because he had been carrying no identification, the police knew almost nothing about who he was or where he was from.

Carthage, South Dakota, population 274, is a sleepy little cluster of clapboard houses, weathered brick storefronts, and shaded yards that rises humbly from the immensity of the northern plains, adrift in time. It has one grocery, one bank, a single gas station, a lone bar—the Cabaret, where Wayne Westerberg, a hyperkinetic man with thick shoulders and a rakish black goatee, is sipping a White Russian, chewing on a sweet cigar, and remembering the enigmatic young man he knew as Alex. "These are what Alex used to drink," says Westerberg with a smile, hoisting his glass. "He used to sit right there at the end of the bar and tell us these amazing stories of his travels. He could talk for hours."

Westerberg owns a grain elevator in town but spends every summer running a custom combine crew that follows the harvest from Texas north to Montana. In September 1990 he'd been in Montana cutting barley when, on the highway east of Cut Bank, he'd given a ride to a hungry-looking hitchhiker, a friendly young man who said his name was Alex McCandless. They hit it off immediately, and before they went their separate ways Westerberg told Alex to look him up in Carthage if he ever needed a job. "About two weeks later," says Westerberg, "he thumbed into town, moved into my house, and went to work at the elevator. He was the hardest worker I've ever seen. And totally honest—what you'd call extremely ethical. He set pretty high standards for himself.

"You could tell right away that Alex was intelligent," Westerberg continues. "In fact, I think maybe part of what got him into trouble was that he did too much thinking. Sometimes he tried too hard to make sense of the world, to figure out why people were bad to each other so often. A couple of times I tried to tell him it was a mistake to get too deep into that kind of stuff, but Alex got stuck on things. He always had to know the absolute right answer before he could go on to the next thing."

McCandless didn't stay in Carthage long—by the end of October he was on the road again—but he dropped Westerberg a postcard every month or two in the course of his travels. He also had all his mail forwarded to Westerberg's house and told everybody he met thereafter that he was from South Dakota.

In truth McCandless had been raised in the comfortable, upper-middle-class environs of Annandale, Virginia. His father, Walt, was an aerospace engineer who ran a small but very prosperous consulting firm with Chris's mother, Billie. There were eight children in the extended family: Chris; a younger sister, Carine, with whom Chris was extremely close; and six older half-siblings from Walt's first marriage.

McCandless had graduated in June 1990 from Emory University in Atlanta, where he distinguished himself as a history/anthropology major and was offered but declined membership in Phi Beta Kappa, insisting that titles and honors were of no importance. His education had been paid for by a college fund established by his parents; there was some $20,000 in this account at the time of his graduation, money his parents thought he intended to use for law school. Instead, he donated the entire sum to the Oxford Famine Relief Fund. Then, without notifying any friends or family members, he loaded all his belongings into a decrepit yellow Datsun and headed west without itinerary, relieved to shed a life of abstraction and security, a life he felt was removed from the heat and throb of the real world. Chris McCandless intended to invent a new life for himself, one in which he would be free to wallow in unfiltered experience.

In July 1990, on a 120-degree afternoon near Lake Mead, his car broke down and he abandoned it in the Arizona desert. McCandless was exhilarated, so much so that he decided to bury most of his worldly possessions in the parched earth of Detrital Wash and then—in a gesture that would have done Tolstoy proud—burned his last remaining cash, about $160 in small bills.

We know this because he documented the conflagration, and most of the events that followed, in a journal/snapshot album he would later give to Westerberg. Although the tone of the journal occasionally veers toward melodrama, the available evidence indicates that McCandless did not misrepresent the facts; telling the truth was a credo he took very seriously.

McCandless tramped around the West for the next two months, spellbound by the scale and power of the landscape, thrilled by minor brushes with the law, savoring the intermittent company of other vagabonds he met along the way. He hopped trains, hitched rides, and walked the trails of the Sierra Nevada before crossing paths with Westerberg in Montana.

In November he sent Westerberg a postcard from Phoenix, urging him to read *War and Peace* ("It has things in it that I think you will understand, things that escape most people") and complaining that thanks to the money Westerberg had paid him, tramping had become too easy. "My days were more exciting when I was penniless and had to forage around for my next meal," he wrote. "I've decided that I'm going to live this life for some time to come. The freedom and simple beauty of it is just too good to pass up. One day I'll get back to you, Wayne, and repay some of your kindness."

Immediately after writing that card, McCandless bought a second-hand aluminum canoe near the head of Lake Havasu and decided to paddle it down the Colorado River all the way to the Gulf of California. En route he sneaked into Mexico by shooting the spillway of a small dam and got lost repeatedly. But he made it to the gulf, where he struggled to control the canoe in a violent squall far from shore and, exhausted, decided to head north again.

On January 16, 1991, McCandless left the stubby metal boat on a hummock of dune grass southeast of Golfo de Santa Clara and started walking north up the deserted beach. He had not seen or talked to another soul in 36 days. For that entire period he had subsisted on nothing but five pounds of rice and what he could pull from the sea, an experience that would later convince him he could survive on similarly meager rations when he went to live in the Alaskan bush. Back at the border two days later, he was caught trying to slip into the United States without ID and spent a night in custody before concocting a story that got him across.

McCandless spent most of the next year in the Southwest, but the last entry in the journal he left with Westerberg is dated May 10, 1991, and so the record of his travels in this period is sketchy. He slummed his way through San Diego, El Paso, and Houston. To avoid being rolled and robbed by the unsavory characters who ruled the streets and freeway overpasses where he slept, he learned to bury what money he had before entering a city, then recover it on the way out of town. Snapshots in the album document visits to Bryce and Zion, the Grand Canyon, Joshua Tree, Palm Springs. For several weeks he lived with "bums, tramps, and winos" on the streets of Las Vegas.

When 1991 drew to a close McCandless was in Bullhead City, Arizona, where for three months he lived in a tent and flipped burgers at McDonald's. A letter from this period reveals that "a girl Tracy" had a crush on him. In a note to Westerberg he admitted that he liked Bullhead City and "might finally settle down and abandon my tramping life, for good. I'll see what happens when spring comes around, because that's when I tend to get really itchy feet."

Itchy feet prevailed. He soon called Westerberg and said that he wanted to work in the grain elevator for a while, just long enough to put together a little grubstake. He needed money to buy some new gear, he said, because he was going to Alaska.

When McCandless arrived back in Carthage on a bitter February morning in 1992, he'd already decided that he would depart for Alaska on April 15. He wanted to be in Fairbanks by the end of April in order to have as much time as possible in the North before heading back to South Dakota to help out with the autumn harvest. By mid-April Westerberg was shorthanded and very busy, so he asked McCandless to postpone his departure date and work a week or two longer. But, Westerberg says, "Once Alex made up his mind about something there was no changing it. I even offered to buy him a plane ticket to Fairbanks, which would have let him work an extra ten days and still get to Alaska by the end of April. But he said, 'No, I want to hitch north. Flying would be cheating. It would wreck the whole trip.'"

McCandless left Carthage on April 15. In early May Westerberg received a postcard of a polar bear, postmarked April 27. "Greetings from Fairbanks!" it read.

> *This is the last you shall hear from me Wayne. Arrived here 2 days ago. It was very difficult to catch rides in the Yukon Territory. But I finally got here. Please return all mail I receive to the sender.*
>
> *It might be a very long time before I return South. If this adventure proves fatal and you don't ever hear from me again, I want you to know your a great man. I now walk into the wild.*

McCandless's last postcard to Westerberg fueled widespread speculation, after his adventure did prove fatal, that he'd intended suicide from the start, that when he walked into the bush alone he had no intention of ever walking out again. But I for one am not so sure.

In 1977, when I was 23—a year younger than McCandless at the time of his death—I hitched a ride to Alaska on a fishing boat and set off alone into the backcountry to attempt an ascent of a malevolent stone digit called the Devils Thumb, a towering prong of vertical rock and avalanching ice, ignoring pleas from friends, family, and utter strangers to come to my senses. Simply reaching the foot of the mountain entailed traveling 30 miles up a badly crevassed, storm-wracked glacier that hadn't seen a human footprint in many years. By choice I had no radio, no way of summoning help, no safety net of any kind. I had several harrowing shaves, but eventually I reached the summit of the Thumb.

When I decided to go to Alaska that April, I was an angst-ridden youth who read too much Nietzsche, mistook passion for insight, and functioned according to an obscure gap-ridden logic. I thought climbing the Devils Thumb would fix all that was wrong with my life. In the end it changed almost nothing, of course. I came to appreciate, however, that mountains make poor receptacles for dreams. And I lived to tell my tale.

As a young man, I was unlike Chris McCandless in many important respects—most notably I lacked his intellect and his altruistic leanings—but I suspect we had a similar intensity, a similar heedlessness, a similar agitation of the soul.

The fact that I survived my Alaskan adventure and McCandless did not survive his was largely a matter of chance; had I died on the Stikine Icecap in 1977 people would have been quick to say of me, as they now say of him, that I had a death wish. Fifteen years after the event, I now recognize that I suffered from hubris, perhaps, and a monstrous innocence, certainly, but I wasn't suicidal.

At the time, death was a concept I understood only in the abstract. I didn't yet appreciate its terrible finality or the havoc it could wreak on those who'd entrusted the deceased with their hearts. I was stirred by the mystery of death; I couldn't resist stealing up to the edge of doom and peering over the brink. The view into that swirling black vortex terrified me, but I caught sight of something elemental in that shadowy glimpse, some forbidden, fascinating riddle.

That's a very different thing from wanting to die.

Westerberg heard nothing else from McCandless for the remainder of the spring and summer. Then, last September 13, he was rolling down an empty ribbon of South Dakota blacktop, leading his harvest crew home to Carthage after wrapping up a four-month cutting season in northern Montana, when the VHF barked to life. "Wayne!" an anxious voice crackled over the radio from one of the crew's other trucks. "Quick—turn on your AM and listen to Paul Harvey. He's talking about some kid who starved to death up in Alaska. The police don't know who he is. Sounds a whole lot like Alex."

As soon as he got to Carthage, a dispirited Westerberg called the Alaska State Troopers and said that he thought he knew the identity of the hiker. McCandless had never told Westerberg anything about his family, including where they lived, but Westerberg unearthed a W-4 form bearing McCandless's Social Security number, which led the police to an address in Virginia. A few days after the Paul Harvey broadcast, an Alaskan police sergeant made a phone call to the distant suburbs of the nation's capital, confirming the worst fears of Walt and Billie McCandless and raining a flood of confusion and grief down upon their world.

Walt McCandless, 56, dressed in gray sweatpants and a rayon jacket bearing the logo of the Jet Propulsion Laboratory, is a stocky, bearded man with longish salt-and-pepper hair combed straight back from a high forehead. Seven weeks after his youngest son's body turned up in Alaska wrapped in a blue sleeping bag that Billie had sewn for Chris from a kit, he studies a sailboat scudding beneath the window of his waterfront town house. "How is it," he wonders aloud as he gazes blankly across Chesapeake Bay, "that a kid with so much compassion could cause his parents so much pain?"

Four large pieces of posterboard covered with dozens of photos documenting the whole brief span of Chris's life stand on the dining room table. Moving deliberately around the display, Billie points out Chris as a toddler astride a hobbyhorse, Chris as a rapt eight-year-old in a yellow slicker on his first backpacking trip, Chris at his high school commencement. "The hardest part," says Walt, pausing over a shot of his son clowning around on a family vacation, "is simply not having him around anymore. I spent a lot of time with Chris, perhaps more than with any of my other kids. I really liked his company, even though he frustrated us so often."

It is impossible to know what murky convergence of chromosomal matter, parent-child dynamics, and alignment of the cosmos was responsible, but Chris McCandless came into the world with unusual gifts and a will not easily deflected from its trajectory. As early as third grade, a bemused teacher was moved to pull Chris's parents aside and inform them that their son "marched to a different drummer." At the age of ten, he entered his first running competition, a 10k road race, and finished 69th, beating more than 1,000 adults. By high school he was effortlessly bringing home A's (punctuated by a single F, the result of butting heads with a particularly rigid physics teacher) and had developed into one of the top distance runners in the region.

As captain of his high school cross-country team he concocted novel, grueling training regimens that his teammates still remember well. "Chris invented this workout he called Road Warriors," explains

Gordy Cucullu, a close friend from those days. "He would lead us on long, killer runs, as far and as fast as we could go, down strange roads, through the woods, whatever. The whole idea was to lose our bearings, to push ourselves into unknown territory. Then we'd run at a slightly slower pace until we found a road we recognized, and race home again at full speed. In a certain sense, that's how Chris lived his entire life."

McCandless viewed running as an intensely spiritual exercise akin to meditation. "Chris would use the spiritual aspect to try to motivate us," recalls Eric Hathaway, another friend on the team. "He'd tell us to think about all the evil in the world, all the hatred, and imagine ourselves running against the forces of darkness, the evil wall that was trying to keep us from running our best. He believed doing well was all mental, a simple matter of harnessing whatever energy was available. As impressionable high school kids, we were blown away by that kind of talk."

McCandless's musings on good and evil were more than a training technique; he took life's inequities to heart. "Chris didn't understand how people could possibly be allowed to go hungry, especially in this country," says Billie McCandless, a small woman with large, expressive eyes—the same eyes Chris is said to have had. "He would rave about that kind of thing for hours."

For months he spoke seriously of traveling to South Africa and joining the struggle to end apartheid. On weekends, when his high school pals were attending keggers and trying to sneak into Georgetown bars, McCandless would wander the seedier quarters of Washington, chatting with pimps and hookers and homeless people, buying them meals, earnestly suggesting ways they might improve their lives. Once, he actually picked up a homeless man from downtown D.C., brought him to the leafy streets of Annandale, and secretly set him up in the Airstream trailer that his parents kept parked in the driveway. Walt and Billie never even knew they were hosting a vagrant.

McCandless's personality was puzzling in its complexity. He was intensely private but could be convivial and gregarious in the extreme. And despite his overdeveloped social conscience, he was no tight-lipped, perpetually grim do-gooder who frowned on fun. To the contrary, he enjoyed tipping a glass now and then and was an incorrigible ham who would seize any excuse to regale friends and strangers with spirited renditions of Tony Bennett tunes. In college he directed and starred in a witty video parody of Geraldo Rivera opening Al Capone's vault. And he was a natural salesman: Throughout his youth McCandless launched a series of entrepreneurial schemes (a photocopying service, among others), some of which brought in impressive amounts of cash.

Upon graduating from high school, he took the earnings he'd socked away, bought a used Datsun B210, and promptly embarked on the first of his extemporaneous transcontinental odysseys. For half the summer he complied with his parents' insistence that he phone every three days, but he didn't check in at all the last couple of weeks and returned just two days before he was due at college, sporting torn clothes, a scruffy beard, and tangled hair and packing a machete and a .30-06 rifle, which he insisted on taking with him to school.

With each new adventure, Walt and Billie grew increasingly anxious about the risks Chris was taking. Before his senior year at Emory he returned from a summer on the road looking gaunt and weak, having shed 30 pounds from his already lean frame; he'd gotten lost in the Mojave Desert, it turned out, and had nearly succumbed to dehydration. Walt and Billie urged their son to exercise more caution in the future and pleaded with him to keep them better informed of his whereabouts; Chris responded by telling them even less about his escapades and checking in less frequently when he was on the road. "He thought we were idiots for worrying about him," Billie says. "He took pride in his ability to go without food for extended periods, and he had complete confidence that he could get himself out of any jam."

"He was good at almost everything he ever tried," says Walt, "which made him supremely overconfident. If you attempted to talk him out of something, he wouldn't argue. He'd just nod politely and then do exactly what he wanted."

McCandless could be generous and caring to a fault, but he had a darker side as well, characterized by monomania, impatience, and unwavering self-absorption, qualities that seemed to intensify throughout his college years. "I saw Chris at a party after his freshman year at Emory," remembers Eric Hathaway, "and it was obvious that he had changed. He seemed very introverted, almost cold. Social life at Emory revolved around fraternities and sororities, something Chris wanted no part of. And when everybody started going Greek, he kind of pulled back from his old friends and got more heavily into himself."

When Walt and Billie went to Atlanta in the spring of 1990 for Chris's college graduation, he told them that he was planning another summerlong trip and that he'd drive up to visit them in Annandale before hitting the road. But he never showed. Shortly thereafter he donated the $20,000 in his bank account to Oxfam, loaded up his car, and disappeared. From then on he scrupulously avoided contacting either his parents or Carine, the sister for whom he purportedly cared immensely.

"We were all worried when we didn't hear from him," says Carine, "and I think my parents' worry was mixed with hurt and anger. But I didn't really feel hurt. I knew that he was happy and doing what he wanted to do. I understood that it was important for him to see how independent he could be. And he knew that if he wrote or called me, Mom and Dad would find out where he was, fly out there, and try to bring him home."

In September—by which time Chris had long since abandoned the yellow Datsun in the desert and burned his money—Walt and Billie grew worried enough to hire a private investigator. "We worked pretty hard to trace him," says Walt. "We eventually picked up his trail on the northern California coast, where he'd gotten a ticket for hitchhiking, but we lost track of him for good right after that, probably about the time he met Wayne Westerberg." Walt and Billie would hear nothing more about Chris's whereabouts until their son's body turned up in Alaska two years later.

After Chris had been identified, Carine and their oldest half-brother, Sam, flew to Fairbanks to bring home his ashes and those few possessions—the rifle, a fishing rod, a Swiss Army knife, the book in which he'd kept his journal, and not much else—that had been recovered with the body, including the photographs he'd taken in Alaska. Sifting through this pictorial record of Chris's final days, it is all Billie can do to force herself to examine the fuzzy snapshots.

As she studies the pictures she breaks down from time to time, weeping as only a mother who has outlived a child can weep, betraying a sense of loss so huge and irreparable that the mind balks at taking its measure. Such bereavement, witnessed at close range, makes even the most eloquent apologia for high-risk activities ring fatuous and hollow.

"I just don't understand why he had to take those kinds of chances," Billie protests through her tears. "I just don't understand it at all."

When news of McCandless's fate came to light, most Alaskans were quick to dismiss him as a nut case. According to the conventional wisdom he was simply one more dreamy, half-cocked greenhorn who went into the bush expecting to find answers to all his problems and instead found nothing but mosquitoes and a lonely death.

Dozens of marginal characters have gone into the Alaskan backcountry over the years, never to reappear. A few have lodged firmly in the state's collective memory. There is, for example, the sad tale of John Mallon Waterman, a visionary climber much celebrated for making one of the most astonishing first ascents in the history of North American mountaineering—an extremely dangerous 145-day solo climb of Mount Hunter's Southeast Spur. Upon completing this epic deed in 1979, though, he found that instead of putting his demons to rest, success merely agitated them.

In the years that followed, Waterman's mind unraveled. He took to prancing around Fairbanks in a black cape and announced he was running for president under the banner of the Feed the Starving Party, the main priority of which was to ensure that nobody on the planet died of hunger. To publicize his campaign he laid plans to make a solo ascent of Denali, in winter, with a minimum of food.

After his first attempt on the mountain was aborted prematurely, Waterman committed himself to the Anchorage Psychiatric Institute but checked out after two weeks, convinced that there was a conspiracy afoot to put him away permanently. Then, in the winter of 1981, he launched another solo attempt on Denali. He was last placed on the upper Ruth Glacier, heading unroped through the middle of a deadly crevasse field en route to the mountain's difficult East Buttress, carrying neither sleeping bag nor tent. He was never seen after that, but a note was later found atop some of his gear in a nearby shelter. It read, "3-13-81 My last kiss 1:42 P.M."

Perhaps inevitably, parallels have been drawn between John Waterman and Chris McCandless. Comparisons have also been made between McCandless and Carl McCunn, a likable, absentminded Texan who in 1981 paid a bush pilot to drop him at a lake deep in the Brooks Range to photograph wildlife. He flew in with 500 rolls of film and 1,400 pounds of provisions but forgot to arrange for the pilot to pick him up again. Nobody realized he was missing until state troopers came across his body a year later, lying beside a 100-page diary that documented his demise. Rather than starve, McCunn had reclined in his tent and shot himself in the head.

There are similarities among Waterman, McCunn, and McCandless, most notably a certain dreaminess and a paucity of common sense. But unlike Waterman, McCandless was not mentally unbalanced. And unlike McCunn, he didn't go into the bush assuming that someone would magically appear to bring him out again before he came to grief.

McCandless doesn't really conform to the common bush-casualty stereotype: He wasn't a kook, he wasn't an outcast, and although he was rash and incautious to the point of foolhardiness, he was hardly incompetent or he would never have lasted 113 days. If one is searching for predecessors cut from the same exotic cloth, if one hopes to understand the personal tragedy of Chris McCandless by placing it in some larger context, one would do well to look at another northern land, in a different century altogether.

Off the southeastern coast of Iceland sits a low barrier island called Papos. Treeless and rocky, perpetually knocked by gales howling off the North Atlantic, the island takes its name from its first settlers, now long gone, the Irish monks known as papar. They arrived as early as the fifth and sixth centuries A.D., having sailed and rowed from the western coast of Ireland. Setting out in small open boats called curraghs, made from cowhide stretched over light wicker frames, they crossed one of the most treacherous stretches of ocean in the world without knowing what they'd find on the other side.

The papar risked their lives—and lost them in untold droves—but not in the pursuit of wealth or personal glory or to claim new lands in the name of a despot. As the great Arctic explorer Fridtjof Nansen points out, they undertook their remarkable voyages "chiefly from the wish to find lonely places, where these anchorites might dwell in peace, undisturbed by the turmoil and temptations of the world." When the first handful of Norwegians showed up on the shores of Iceland in the ninth century, the papar decided the country had become too crowded, even though it was still all but uninhabited. They climbed back into their curraghs and rowed off toward Greenland. They were drawn west across the storm-wracked ocean, past the edge of the known world, by nothing more than hunger of the spirit, a queer, pure yearning that burned in their souls.

Reading of the these monks, one is struck by their courage, their reckless innocence, and the intensity of their desire. And one can't help thinking of Chris McCandless.

On April 25, 1992, ten days after leaving South Dakota, McCandless rode his thumb into Fairbanks. After perusing the classified ads, he bought a used Remington Nylon 66—a semiautomatic .22-caliber rifle with a 4x20 scope and a plastic stock that was favored by Alaskan trappers for its light weight and reliability.

When James Gallien dropped McCandless off at the head of the Stampede Trail on April 28 the temperature was in the low thirties—it would drop into the low teens at night—and a foot of crusty spring snow covered the ground. As he trudged expectantly down the trail in a fake-fur parka, the heaviest item in McCandless's half-full backpack was his library: nine or ten paperbacks ranging from Michael Crichton's *The Terminal Man* to Thoreau's *Walden* and Tolstoy's *The Death of Ivan Illyich.* One of these volumes, *Tanaina Plantlore,* by Priscilla Russel Kari, was a scholarly, exhaustively researched field guide to edible plants in the region; it was in the back of this book that McCandless began keeping an abbreviated record of his journey.

From his journal we know that on April 29 McCandless fell through the ice—perhaps crossing the frozen surface of the Teklanika River, perhaps in the maze of broad, shallow beaver ponds that lie just beyond its western bank—although there is no indication that he suffered any injury. A day later he got his first glimpse of Denali's gleaming white ramparts, and a day after that, about 20 miles down the trail from where he started, he stumbled upon the bus and decided to make it his base camp.

He was elated to be there. Inside the bus, on a sheet of weathered plywood spanning a broken window, McCandless scrawled an exultant declaration of independence:

Two years he walks the earth. No phone, no pool, no pets, no cigarettes. Ultimate freedom. An extremist. An aesthetic voyager whose home is the road. Escaped from Atlanta. Thou shalt not return, 'cause "the West is the best." And now after two rambling years comes the final and greatest adventure. The climactic battle to kill the false being within and victoriously conclude the spiritual pilgrimage. Ten days and nights of freight trains and hitchhiking bring him to the Great White North. No longer to be poisoned by civilization he flees, and walks alone upon the land to become lost in the wild.

Alexander Supertramp
May 1992

But reality quickly intruded. McCandless had difficulty killing game, and the daily journal entries during his first week at the bus include "weakness," "snowed in," and "disaster." He saw but did not shoot a grizzly on May 2, shot at but missed some ducks on May 4, and finally killed and ate a spruce grouse on May 5. But he didn't kill any more game until May 9, when he bagged a single small squirrel, by which point he'd written "4th day famine" in the journal.

Soon thereafter McCandless's fortunes took a sharp turn for the better. By mid-May the snowpack was melting down to bare ground, exposing the previous season's rose hips and lingonberries, preserved beneath the frost, which he gathered and ate. He also became much more successful at hunting and for the next six weeks feasted regularly on squirrel, spruce grouse, duck, goose, and porcupine. On May 22 he lost a crown from a tooth, but it didn't seem to dampen his spirits much, because the following day he scrambled up the nameless 3,000-

foot butte that rose directly north of the bus, giving him a view of the whole icy sweep of the Alaska Range and mile after mile of stunning, completely uninhabited country. His journal entry for the day is characteristically terse but unmistakably joyous: "CLIMB MOUNTAIN!"

Although McCandless was enough of a realist to know that hunting was an unavoidable component of living off the land, he had always been ambivalent about killing animals. That ambivalence turned to regret on June 9, when he shot and killed a large caribou, which he mistakenly identified as a moose in his journal. For six days he toiled to preserve the meat, believing that it was morally indefensible to waste any part of an animal that has been killed for food. He butchered the carcass under a thick cloud of flies and mosquitoes, boiled the internal organs into a stew, and then laboriously dug a cave in the rocky earth in which he tried to preserve, by smoking, the huge amount of meat that he was unable to eat immediately. Despite his efforts, on June 14 his journal records, "Maggots already! Smoking appears ineffective. Don't know, looks like disaster. I now wish I had never shot the moose. One of the greatest tragedies of my life."

Although he recriminated himself severely for this waste of a life he had taken, a day later McCandless appeared to regain some perspective—his journal notes, "henceforth will learn to accept my errors, however great they be"—and the period of contentment that began in mid-May resumed and continued until early July. Then, in the midst of this idyll, came the first of two pivotal setbacks.

Satisfied, apparently, with what he had accomplished during his two months of solitary existence, McCandless decided to return to civilization. It was time to bring his "final and greatest adventure" to a close and get himself back to the world of men and women, where he could chug a beer, discuss philosophy, enthrall strangers with tales of what he'd done. He seemed to have turned the corner on his need to assert his autonomy from his parents. He seemed ready, perhaps, to go home. On a parchmentlike strip of birch bark he drew up a list of tasks to do before he departed: "patch jeans, shave!, organize pack." Then, on July 3—the day after a journal entry that reads, "Family happiness"—he shouldered his backpack, departed the bus, and began the 30-mile walk to the highway.

Two days later, halfway to the road, he arrived in heavy rain on the west bank of the Teklanika River, a major stream spawned by distant glaciers on the crest of the Alaska Range. Sixty-seven days earlier it had been frozen over, and he had simply strolled across it. Now, however, swollen with rain and melting snow, the Teklanika was running big, cold, and fast.

If he could reach the far shore, the rest of the hike to the highway would be trivial, but to get there he would have to negotiate a 75-foot channel of chest-deep water that churned with the power of a freight train. In his journal McCandless wrote, "Rained in. River look impossible. Lonely, scared." Concluding that he would drown if he attempted to cross, he turned around and walked back toward the bus, back into the fickle heart of the bush.

McCandless got back to the bus on July 8. It's impossible to know what was going through his mind at that point, believing that his escape had been cut off, for his journal betrays nothing. Actually, he wasn't cut off at all: A quarter-mile downstream from where he had tried to cross, the Teklanika rushes through a narrow gorge spanned by a hand-operated tram—a metal basket suspended from pulleys on a steel cable. If he had known about it, crossing the Teklanika to safety would have been little more than a casual task. Also, six miles due south of the bus, an easy day's walk up the main fork of the Sushana, the National Park Service maintains a cabin stocked with food, bedding, and first-aid supplies for the use of backcountry rangers on their winter patrols. This cabin is plainly marked on most topographic maps of the area, but McCandless, lacking such a map, had no way of knowing about it. His friends point out, of course, that had he carried a map and known the cabin was so close, his mule-headed obsession with self-reliance would have kept him from staying anywhere near the bus; rather, he would have headed even deeper into the bush.

So he went back to the bus, which was a sensible course of action: It was the height of summer, the country was fecund with plant and animal life, and his food supply was still adequate. He probably surmised that if he could just bide his time until August, the Teklanika would subside enough to be forded.

For the rest of July McCandless fell back into his routine of hunting and gathering. His snapshots and journal entries indicate that over those three weeks he killed 35 squirrels, four spruce grouse, five jays and woodpeckers, and two frogs, which he supplemented with wild potatoes, wild rhubarb, various berries, and mushrooms. Despite this apparent munificence, the meat he'd been killing was very lean, and he was consuming fewer calories than he was burning. After three months on a marginal diet, McCandless had run up a sizable caloric deficit. He was balanced on a precarious, razor-thin edge. And then, on July 30, he made the mistake that pulled him down.

His journal entry for that date reads, "Extremely weak. Fault of pot[ato] seed. Much trouble just to stand up. Starving. Great Jeopardy." McCandless had been digging and eating the root of the wild potato—*Hedysarum alpinum,* a common area wildflower also known as Eskimo potato, which Kari's book told him was widely eaten by native Alaskans—for more than a month without ill effect. On July 14 he apparently started eating the pealike seedpods of the plant as well, again without ill effect. There is, however, a closely related plant—wild sweet pea, *Hedysarum mackenzii*—that is very difficult to distinguish from wild potato, grows beside it, and is poisonous. In all likelihood McCandless mistakenly ate some seeds from the wild sweet pea and became gravely ill.

Laid low by the poisonous seeds, he was too weak to hunt effectively and thus slid toward starvation. Things began to spin out of control with terrible speed. "DAY 100! MADE IT!" he noted jubilantly on August 5, proud of achieving such a significant milestone, "but in weakest condition of life. Death looms as serious threat. Too weak to walk out."

Over the next week or so the only game he bagged was five squirrels and a spruce grouse. Many Alaskans have wondered why, at this point, he didn't start a forest fire as a distress signal; small planes fly over the area every few days, they say, and the Park Service would surely have dispatched a crew to control the conflagration. "Chris would never intentionally burn down a forest, not even to save his life," answers Carine McCandless. "Anybody who would suggest otherwise doesn't understand the first thing about my brother."

Starvation is not a pleasant way to die. In advanced stages, as the body begins to consume itself, the victim suffers muscle pain, heart disturbances, loss of hair, shortness of breath. Convulsions and hallucinations are not uncommon. Some who have been brought back from the far edge of starvation, though, report that near the end their suffering was replaced by a sublime euphoria, a sense of calm accompanied by transcendent mental clarity. Perhaps, it would be nice to think, McCandless enjoyed a similar rapture.

From August 13 through 18 his journal records nothing beyond a tally of the days. At some point during this week, he tore the final page from Louis L'Amour's memoir, *Education of a Wandering Man*. On one side were some lines that L'Amour had quoted from Robinson Jeffers's poem "Wise Men in Their Bad Hours":

Death's a fierce meadowlark: but to die having made
Something more equal to the centuries
Than muscle and bone, is mostly to shed weakness.

On the other side of the page, which was blank, McCandless penned a brief adios: "I have had a happy life and thank the Lord. Goodbye and may God bless all!"

Then he crawled into the sleeping bag his mother had made for him and slipped into unconsciousness. He probably died on August 18, 113 days after he'd walked into the wild, 19 days before six hunters and hikers would happen across the bus and discover his body inside.

One of his last acts was to take a photograph of himself, standing near the bus under the high Alaskan sky, one hand holding his final note toward the camera lens, the other raised in a brave, beatific farewell. He is smiling in the photo, and there is no mistaking the look in his eyes: Chris McCandless was at peace, serene as a monk gone to God.

January 1993

Fear of Falling

GREG CHILD

The first shot hits the cliff at 6:15 A.M. The sun is rising over Central Asia, sending shafts of daylight through the gaps in a ridge-line of craggy summits, brightening the steep, shadowy Kara Su valley of Kyrgyzstan's Pamir Alai range. Deep in sleep, their two portaledges dangling 1,000 feet off the ground, the four climbers barely react to the thump of lead hitting granite. But when the second report echoes through the gorge, Jason "Singer" Smith bolts upright.

"What the hell was that?" he shouts, donning his helmet instinctively, assuming the rifle crack is the clatter of rockfall.

"We're being shot at, Singer!" Beth Rodden calls out in alarm from the other portaledge.

"That's irrational," Smith replies. "It's probably local hunters."

Then the third bullet hits right between the two platforms. Rock chips fly out of the crater, spraying the climbers.

"That was definitely for us!" Rodden shouts.

The climbers are bunked high on Mount Zhioltaya Stena, a 12,000-foot peak in this rugged former Soviet republic. It is August 12, day two of a planned four-day ascent of the 2,500-foot Yellow Wall, and they are making their way up to a sheer headwall, looking forward to sinking their hands into a highway of cracks splitting the face. The quartet represents a remarkable pool of American climbing talent, friends from years on the rock-wall circuit out West. A self-assured 22-year-old Utah native, Smith lives in his van in California. He has made a slew of notable ascents, including a 14-day solo of the 4,000-foot big wall of Mount Thor, near the Arctic Circle on Canada's Baffin Island. His nickname, Singer, is derived from his penchant for stitching up kitschy clothing on an old sewing machine. Lying beside Singer is Texas-raised John Dickey, the team photographer. Bearded, lanky, and at 25 the old man of the group, he's a seasoned world traveler and, since he moved to California six years ago, a frequent back-country climber in the High Sierra. Rodden is a diminutive blond 20-year-old from Davis, California, with an angelic face that makes her look five years younger. Her appearance belies her toughness, how-ever; she is one of the very few women—and the youngest—to have climbed at the top 5.14 rating of difficulty. Her soft-spoken boyfriend and bunkmate, Tommy Caldwell, 22, is from Colorado. Built like a cross between a pit bull and a greyhound, he has laid claim to what is possibly America's hardest sport route, Kryptonite, a pitch near Rifle, Colorado, rated 5.14d. The group helicoptered into the Kara Su Valley from Bishkek, Kyrgyzstan's capital, two weeks ago, and they've got another good month of climbing to go. After they set up a base camp, Rodden and Caldwell began putting in this new route up the Yellow Wall while Smith and Dickey spent four days trekking down valley in an unsuccessful search for a telephone, to call about a lost duffel. Their journey had taken them past a Kyrgyz army camp and over a 14,00-foot pass, where they met yak herders who'd never seen foreigners.

The climbers peer over the edges of their portaledges and in the gath-ering light spot three men on the rubble-strewn slope below. The men wave their hands, gesturing that they should come down. The Ameri-cans yell to them to cease fire. Still sitting in their sleeping bags, they stare at each other with stunned expressions. Among them they can cope with any horror the mountains might dish out: avalanche, rock-fall, stormy weather; surely this situation can somehow be worked out, too. Hanging here they are sitting ducks, so they start to draw straws to see who'll go down first to meet the guys with the guns.

Dickey steps up to the plate. "I'll go," he volunteers.

They tie their ropes end to end and Dickey clips his rappel device onto the nylon strand. He eases over the edge of the portaledge and swings into the void, carrying down a Motorola two-way radio. As he departs he blithely suggests he'll offer the gunmen a cigarette, a gambit that the laconic Californian has found useful in the Third World for defusing tense situations.

The climbers can't figure out what the trouble is. The area they are in—a complex of high valleys dubbed the Ak Su region—has been visited every summer for 20 years by scores of Russian, European, and American climbers. Renowned for its huge sheets of tawny granite, the Ak Su has been called the Yosemite of Central Asia. All that is required to climb here is a frontier permit from the government of Kyrgyzstan, which the Americans have.

Dickey spins slowly as he rappels down. Twenty-five long minutes pass before he reaches the slope. Through a 200mm camera lens, Smith watches the handshakes between Dickey and the gunmen, sees them reject the proffered pack of cigarettes. Then Dickey radios up.

"These guys want you to come down. They just, er, well, you better come down. They want to go back to our base camp for, er, breakfast." Smith knows Dickey well enough to glean from his quavering tone that something is seriously wrong.

Smith clips his rappel device to the rope and slides down. On the ground he is confronted by two men—the third has left the scene. They are young; they wear fatigues and sport long black hair and beards. The men are packing Kalashnikov assault rifles, grenades, sidearms, and sheathed knives. Smith nervously shakes hands, and they trade names in a patois of gestures and the odd common word of English, Russian, and local dialect. The gunmen are Abdul, who seems to be the commander, and Obert. Smith sees that one is wearing a black Patagonia Gore-Tex jacket under his camo vest and a high-tech rucksack with a German label. Clearly these items were not mail-ordered; at the very least, the Americans figure, they are in the clutches of bandits. But Dickey also remembers seeing a short news story about Japanese geologists taken hostage here in 1999 by a group called the Islamic Movement of Uzbekistan, and the gunmen appear to fit the bill.

Rodden and Caldwell rappel down, and the gunmen indicate that everyone will head to the climbers' base camp, a mile down valley. Their tone is more matter-of-fact than menacing. They even smile occasionally. Yet there's no doubt who's in control. Half out of optimism, half out of a desire to suppress panic in the rest of the team, Dickey coolly reiterates that the gunmen just want some breakfast.

But when the climbers arrive in base camp they see that their tents, which they had sealed by tying the zippers together, are slit open at the walls. The third gunman—Isuf, or Su for short—is posted in the grassy meadow of camp, his weapon at his hip. He's wearing some of their clothing. A fourth man sits against a rock.

At first the Americans mistake this man for another bandit, until Caldwell and Rodden recognize him as Turat, a young Kyrgyz soldier who was friendly when he checked their permit a few days earlier. He's wearing civilian clothes now, and his face is stern. The Americans sit beside him, and when the gunmen aren't looking, Turat starts gesturing and scratching numbers in the sand. He manages to explain that he is a prisoner—taken off-duty, they judge from his dress. Next he holds up three fingers. Then he sweeps his hand across his throat.

"It wasn't hard to figure the math on this one," Smith tells me later. "There were three guys and one girl. I thought he meant that they'll take what they want from camp and then shoot the men."

"*Nyet, nyet,*" Turat insists when he sees the Americans' stricken faces. But the story he eventually gets across is hardly more encouraging: Yesterday he and three fellow soldiers were captured; the rebels executed his comrades, and they are keeping Turat alive as a guide. Turat points to his bloodstained pants—the blood of his friends.

Then Abdul summons Smith and Dickey to their big, yellow main tent. Inside, he and Obert are raiding the larder. They want to know the contents of each can and packet. A strange game of charades begins: When the rebels hold up a can of chicken meat, the climbers cluck, "bok bok bok." When they point to a strip of beef jerky they intone "moo."

What the rebels don't want is anything that smacks of "oink oink." And, as Dickey has learned, they are not into tobacco. Turat warns them in a mix of Russian and English not to offer them vodka, either—the Muslims don't drink.

The rebels order the climbers to stuff four packs with about 30 to 50 pounds each of cans, candles, sleeping bags, and clothing. Then they confiscate their four two-way radios. As he packs, Dickey turns to Singer. A crooked, nervous smile contorts his lips.

"We're hostages," he says flatly.

This valley, these mountains, this country: It is all remote, but it was widely believed to be safe. As Lonely Planet's guide to Central Asia encourages, "Most travellers vote Kyrgyzstan the most appealing, accessible, and welcoming of the former Soviet Central Asian republics," touting the incredible peaks of the central Tien Shan and Pamir Alai ranges. Tourism, the book continues, "is one of the few things Kyrgyzstan has to sell to the outside world." Certainly Rodden, Caldwell, Dickey, and Smith had been welcomed warmly here, and their expedition, backed in part by The North Face (which sponsors Smith and Rodden), had not ventured far off the beaten climbing path. In fact, I had climbed here myself in 1995, on an earlier expedition sponsored by The North Face, with Lynn Hill, Alex Lowe, and Conrad Anker. We found a pastoral scene of verdant meadows and a scattered population of seminomadic Kyrgyz—Islamic subsistence farmers who come here in summer, tending yaks and cows. We also found a slew of virgin routes on the stupendous walls of Peak 4810, Peak 3850 (so called for their heights in meters), and Russian Tower. Two Russian teams and another American group were also there, having helicoptered in from Tashkent, in Uzbekistan, and none of us encountered any hostility.

The next four years were equally calm, and Kyrgyzstan gained a reputation as Asia's hottest mountain playground. As recently as August 1999, the outfitter Mountain Travel–Sobek took trekkers to the same base camp where the climbers were kidnapped. But the frontiers of adventure, those last undiscovered and unspoiled places, are often the frontiers of political instability and civil conflict. They are often unspoiled not only because they are geographically remote, but also because they were historically frozen in place—for more than 50 years in Kyrgyzstan's case—by the geopolitical dictates of the Cold War. And now, as former outposts of the Soviet empire become hot zones of regional tension, they can also become dangerous to travelers. Fearing trouble, Mountain Travel–Sobek canceled its Ak Su trek this summer. And as Lonely Planet Online does warn adventure travelers heading for the boondocks of Kyrgyzstan, "There's a great temptation to hop off the bus in the middle of nowhere and hike into the hills, but this is not recommended if you value your life."

Indeed, Central Asia is a political powder keg—so much so that U.S. State Department officials refuse to even discuss the remote border regions of Kyrgyzstan, Tajikistan, and Uzbekistan on the record. But one official lists a Balkans-style litany of troubles: a five-year civil war that has killed 50,000 in Tajikistan; a weak Kyrgyzstan army; a repressive Soviet-style Uzbekistan government whose policies inflame the fundamentalist Islamic opposition. The most unstable element in this cauldron is war-torn, Taliban-controlled Afghanistan, now the world's greatest narco-state, churning out 4,600 tons of opium last year—even more than the Golden Triangle. Afghanistan is widely believed to be where militant groups like the Islamic Movement of Uzbekistan—the climbers' captors—get their training. Funding is handed out in the form of heroin. Rebels sell the drugs through pipelines to China, Russia, and Europe, and use the proceeds to buy arms from Russian, Chechen, and other sources. Much of this contraband is funneled across Central Asia's porous mountain borders, through high valleys like the Ak Su and Kara Su.

The IMU is a 1,200-man "cross-border, multinational fighting force," says Ahmed Rashid, author of the recent book *Taliban: Militant Islam, Oil, and Fundamentalism in Central Asia*. Mostly Uzbeks, the group's ranks include Afghans, Tajiks, Chechens, Pakistanis, emissaries from Saudi terrorist Osama bin Laden, and Filipino revolutionaries. The IMU, its Sunni Muslim membership having been repressed first by the Soviets and now by Uzbekistan's president-for-life, Islom Karimov, seeks to overthrow Karimov, who has detained up to 50,000 Muslim men from the country's Ferghana Valley. The ultimate goal is to create an independent Islamic state in the valley—one that, like Afghanistan, would adhere to the strictest eye-for-an-eye Sharia religious law. Led by Juma Namangani, an Uzbek warlord, the IMU operates out of the high mountains of Uzbekistan and Tajikistan, which embrace southwestern Kyrgyzstan from north and south. The Ak Su lies between their mountain stronghold and Ferghana, the object of their desire.

On August 23, 1999, IMU guerrillas poured over Tajik passes in the Pamirs into southwestern Kyrgyzstan, attacked Kyrgyz soldiers, and seized four Japanese geologists. The hostages languished in Tajik camps for 64 days until their release. The Japanese and Kyrgyzstan governments claim that no ransom was paid, but as sources in the U.S. State Department and the independent Central Asia Institute confirm, several million dollars may have changed hands.

If ransom was paid, then the climbers who flock to the Ak Su would represent an irresistible cash crop. And since the Japanese incident, the State Department insists, it has posted explicit warnings on its Web site about fighting and kidnapping risks in the area. When Smith, Dickey, Rodden, and Caldwell left the States on July 25, the site displayed a "Public Announcement" dated June 15, 2000, and, as it does for every country, a "Consular Information Sheet." Dated November 17, 1999, Kyrgyzstan's sheet cautioned U.S. citizens "to avoid all travel west and south of the southern provincial capital Osh." But these alerts stopped short of a full-fledged "Travel Warning," which advises Americans to avoid a country completely. The climbers read some, but not all, of this advice, and they interpreted much of it as outdated. They did not contact the U.S. embassy when they landed in Bishkek. Their Kyrgyz travel agent, Ak Sai Tours, made no mention of danger, nor did the helicopter crew that flew them to the Ak Su, nor did the Kyrgyz soldiers who checked their permits.

At around noon on August 12, Abdul orders his five captives to dismantle the base camp. When Turat tugs a long, sturdy aluminum tent stake out of the ground, he feels the pointed end with his finger and catches Smith's eye. It is clear that Turat wants to use the stakes as daggers. Earlier, he furtively signaled that he will try to kill the rebels if he can, and that there are 15 Kyrgyz soldiers in the valley and 17 rebels. Fighting is imminent.

Seeing the desperate look on Turat's face, Smith scans the ransacked base camp and decides that the odds are not very good. The three men carrying assault rifles are alert and wary. "No way, Turat," Smith whispers, shaking his head. "No way."

The climbers pack their leftover gear into duffel bags, and the rebels conceal these under pine boughs. Abdul indicates to them that they should carry their passports in their pockets. That's a good sign, Dickey thinks; it means they want us alive. Still, as they prepare to move out, they are terrified; their teeth are chattering. Rodden, as the only woman, is particularly apprehensive, her mind racing, thinking, "What'll these guys do to me?"

As they pack, Abdul comes across a photo of a smiling Beth and Tommy, arm in arm. He points to the young couple, and in sign language asks if they are together. "Yes—married," Dickey says instantly. If the rebels think Rodden is married, he reasons, maybe she'll be safer.

Then the radio squawks—a message from Su's nearby position on the small rise. Abdul orders everyone to scramble under trees, and seconds later the windy roar of a Russian-made Mi8 gunship fills the valley. The climbers watch as the dronelike helicopter flies toward the Yellow Wall and rises until it is level with the deserted portaledge camp. Abdul sees that Rodden is distraught; he shakes his finger at her and smiles, signing, "Don't cry." The chopper hovers long enough to see that the platforms are abandoned and then retreats down the Kara Su Valley, seemingly in the direction of the Kyrgyz army camp, 25 miles away, that Smith and Dickey had seen on their trek.

Abdul barks orders, and they quit base camp hastily. It is clear they are going on a long walk—probably, Turat is indicating, all the way to Uzbekistan, 50 miles north. About a mile from base camp they near the confluence of the Kara Su and the Ak Su, at which point the two rivers form the Karavshin. Scouting for soldiers, the rebels creep from one boulder to another along the riverside trail. Suddenly the helicopter makes another sweep and the climbers are ordered into the bushes. Leveling his rifle point-blank at Dickey, Abdul screams that anyone who attracts the attention of the helicopter crew is dead. Again the Mi8 departs.

As they walk, Smith tries to reassure Rodden. "Your concern is no longer Beth," he tells her. "I'm thinking about Beth from now on. All you are thinking about is whatever these men tell you to do. If you see a helicopter I want you to play James Bond and jump head-first into whatever tree these guys tell you to jump into. This is just a big giant video game and we are gonna turn it off in a couple of hours."

Quaking, Rodden nods.

The group traverses along the slope of a hill separating the Kara Su and the Ak Su Valleys. At this point Obert marches off down valley. At about 1 P.M. they stand 200 yards uphill from a mud-brick farmhouse. Beyond it a footbridge spans the Ak Su as it crashes downstream. Two Kyrgyz soldiers are outside the house, talking to the farmer. The rebels order their prisoners to sneak uphill through the trees; then Abdul urges them to run. When Rodden starts lagging under her pack, Smith grabs it. It is bright orange, a certain target. Twenty minutes later the group crests the hill. Gasping and sweating, they rest. Turat sits among the climbers, with the rebels watching from a few feet away.

"Over there," he signs to his fellow captives, pointing across the river. "Over there they kill me."

Sometime after 3 P.M. the shooting starts. The band of guerrillas and prisoners has stumbled downhill, across the bridge, and up the east side of the Ak Su Valley onto a steep, forested slope covered in boulders. The rebels have then split the hostages into two groups and hidden them under sprawling junipers. Another young rebel named Abdullah has joined them and the fighters have taken up positions among the rocks, laying, Dickey figures, an ambush. Everybody waits.

More soldiers are advancing up the hill, shouting to one another, when Abdul gives the order to fire. Within minutes two Kyrgyz soldiers are felled. Adbul's firearm is a cannon, a fast-action AK-74—more like an M-16 than the other rebels' AK-47s. Rodden, Caldwell, and Turat hunker behind a tree trunk, shielding their faces from the flying shell casings, ricochets, and rock chips. Ten minutes into the firefight Abdul scurries to the boulder and calls Turat's name. Turat is calm, Caldwell notices—"the toughest man I've ever seen," he'll say later—though it is clear the soldier is about to be executed. Caldwell has his arms around Rodden. She is weeping and shaking.

Turat turns to Rodden and, in the mix of words and hand signs with which they have learned to communicate, he tells her, "You, don't cry. I don't cry, and I am the one who will die."

Then he stands and walks toward Abdul, and the two disappear behind a car-size boulder 200 feet up the hill. The climbers hear two quick reports of a pistol, and then silence.

The battle continues, as Kyrgyz soldiers outflank the rebels. Abdul announces that everyone must move up to the boulder where Turat was taken. Dickey takes the lead, shouldering his pack and sprinting. The Kyrgyz soldiers draw a bead on him. Shots thump around his feet as close as nine inches. He sloughs off his pack and dives toward the boulder. The pack, lying on the ground, is riddled with bullets.

Smith runs to the boulder next; then Rodden. When she arrives, he twists her head away from Turat's corpse. Caldwell arrives last, chased by rifle fire, and wraps himself around Rodden like a shield. Behind the boulder now are the four Americans, Abdul, Su, and Abdullah.

"Abdullah was sitting against Turat's corpse," Smith will later recall. "He picked up Turat's arm and dropped it. Both he and Abdul laughed. Then Abdul kicked Turat's legs aside so he could make room to do his evening prayer. Bullets were raining over his head and he was kneeling, praying."

It is 4 P.M. when the first mortar round whistles in, exploding against the front of the boulder. The climbers huddle together in a ball of arms and legs. Heavy rifle fire zeroes in on them. When they look up they see Kyrgyz soldiers in positions 100 feet from the boulder. The whup-whup-whup of a helicopter, spotting overhead, adds to the noise. Smith is crouched over Turat's legs, wondering if he should pull the body over him and his friends. But the head wound is grotesque.

A third mortar round explodes 80 feet behind them at dusk, and Abdul makes them lighten their loads, ditching the packs and taking just a small sack with a few articles of clothing, credit cards, Turat's sleeping bag, a dozen PowerBars, and a handful of candy. This will be the total rations for six people for the next four days. At nightfall they run uphill, from tree to tree, through random fire. They march roughly four miles, heading north, downstream toward the Karavshin. They climb high on the rugged hillside to outrun the creeping light of the waxing moon, which backlights a skyline of shark-tooth peaks.

August 13, 3 A.M. The climbers have been moving for 18 hours. They shuffle forward like zombies. Abdullah has vanished into the night on another mission, and it is just Abdul and Su. At dawn the rebels stop beside a fast-flowing tributary of the Karavshin and order their hostages to crawl into two small caves.

Singer and Caldwell take one, with Su bedded down, gun in hand, at its mouth. Rodden and Dickey, with Abdul on guard, take the other. At first Dickey cannot believe that Abdul is serious when he motions them into "a small-ass little hole with a mud floor." The cave is 18 inches tall at its highest point. It is cramped for Rodden, who is five-foot-one, but Dickey, at six feet, can only lie with his knees to his chest. Spooning with Dickey, Rodden cries on and off all day. "Do you think anyone knows where we are?" she asks. "They're not gonna kill us, are they?" Dickey is as terrified as she. In the early afternoon, sun-warmed glacial melt swells the river, and the stream pours into the cave. Wallowing in four inches of ice water, in thermal undershirts, Dickey and Rodden shiver for 17 hours.

They emerge as the moon creeps over the opposite ridge. The food in their stomachs is long gone, replaced by lonely cramps; their captors are as hungry as they are. The rebels intend to cross the river, but fording it is out of the question—the rapids are Class IV. So Abdul and Su try to maneuver a log over the foaming torrent. They push the log halfway across; then it jams.

Suddenly Smith kicks off his shoes and wades into the waist-deep water. The current nearly overpowers him and the rebels call for him to return, shouting and gesturing, "danger, danger." Smith ignores them. He muscles the log toward the opposite bank, crouches atop a slick boulder, and steadies the log. Shouting above the roar, he motions for everyone to cross. Dickey goes first.

"What the hell was with that?" he asks.

"We gotta get out of here," Smith says.

Watching the rebels bungle the river crossing, Smith and the others realize that there are a lot of things they can do to help themselves. As

Smith will put it later, "One: They should think we were 100 percent behind their cause. Two: We should show them we were tough as nails because for all we knew they might eliminate the weak; somebody twists an ankle, they would kill them. Three: It would help if we were super-cool and helpful to them, because that would lead to . . . Four: They could trust us."

And indeed, as Abdul balances across the wobbling log he pauses at the final hop onto the boulder. Smith extends his hand and—to his astonishment—Abdul hands over his rifle. Smith passes the weapon to Dickey, then grips Abdul's hand. There is only one moment to react: Smith must kick the log out from under Abdul and send him into the rapids, and Dickey must flip the safety on the automatic and drop Su. If the idea works they are free; if not, Su will kill them. But the moment passes and Abdul reaches the bank.

The guerrilla smiles and praises Smith's courage. "You soljah?" he asks.

Half a PowerBar per day, brown, silty river water to drink, and cold, torturously confined bivouacs take their toll on the hostages as they spend the nights of August 14, 15, and 16 marching around cliffs and steep rubble on the east flank of the Karavshin Valley. On the third night they only get 400 yards before Smith collapses. Rodden sees that he's exhausted, so she takes out their last candy bar, a Three Muske-teers—how fitting, she thinks—breaks it into small chunks, and pushes it into his mouth.

They pass no huts, no farmers. None live this far up the steep hill-sides, and afraid of both the soldiers and the rebels, the locals give each faction a wide berth. Surreal moments abound. The whole val-ley, in fact, has turned nightmarish. On August 14 the hostages may have noticed the faint sound of a gun battle far down the Karavshin Valley. Rebel snipers had 30 Kyrgyz soldiers pinned in a crossfire in a narrow canyon. None survived. Later the Americans will pass that way and find blood-spattered rocks and a bullet-riddled field jacket. Dur-ing the next two weeks the conflict will escalate all along the Kyrgyzstan-Tajikistan border. Firefights will claim up to 48 Kyrgyz soldiers, 12 antirebel Uzbek soldiers, and 75 rebels. More foreigners

will be kidnapped. Elsewhere in the region, Russian border guards stationed near the Afghanistan-Tajikistan border will clash with rebels,
and a passenger on a train leaving Tashkent bound for Kyrgyzstan will
be arrested carrying 20 kilos of explosives.

But for all the climbers know, they are alone. Surely, they think, the
Kyrgyz army knows they've been taken: Helicopters are ever-present, and
one afternoon, as Rodden and Dickey lie hidden beside Abdul at the second bivouac, two soldiers walk to within a yard of them. Rodden's blond
hair is visible through the pine boughs. The men say something in
Kyrgyz and leave. But nobody moves: Abdul carries a grenade fixed to
his belt; if someone makes a move he pulls the pin and everyone dies.

Killing has become the main topic at Smith and Caldwell's bivouac.
Bashing in the rebels' heads with rocks, stealing their handguns, pushing them off cliffs, using choke holds and sharp sticks, punching them
in the larynx, and strangling them with bootlaces are all discussed.
Smith talks; Caldwell listens, quietly taking it in.

"How do you know all this stuff?" Caldwell asks.

"I hung out with thugs at school. I read *The Anarchist Cookbook*,"
comes the glib reply. Then Smith pauses and thinks about what is happening to his mind.

"Tommy, when I woke up today I realized I had lost all compassion for these men. I don't hate them. But I'm ready to do whatever it
takes to get out of here."

Caldwell nods.

That day Smith begins working on winning Su's trust. When helicopters appear he nudges him awake and helps to camouflage their
hiding places with more brush. On the move, he stops to lend his cap-
tor a hand on short cliffs, patting him on the back and telling him he's
a "good alpinista," much to Su's amusement.

Su clearly defers to Abdul, who looks ten years older than his
claimed age of 26. (The climbers doubt he's even called Abdul, in fact,
as the other rebels carefully avoid addressing him by name.) But, Smith
will say later, "At first Su scared me the most. He had a really blank
look on his face. But soon I was doing things like showing him my
passport, comparing ages and birth places with him. He told me he
was 19 and came from Tashkent."

By the night of August 16, day five, the group descends the hillside back to the Karavshin. To their amazement they start walking upstream, toward their Kara Su base camp. During the five-mile march the rebels shift into battle mode and fan out in front. The Americans consider running, but they know that in their weak condition—they are now out of food—they won't get far before they are mowed down. Yet the rebels are getting lax.

They cross the bridge near the battleground and enter the Kara Su Valley. Abdul gives the order to bivouac—in another set of coffinlike holes in the riverbank—and signals that he'll go ahead and kill some soldiers to get some food. Before he leaves he pulls Dickey's boots off his feet and tries them on. They are too large so he tosses them back.

"You fucker," Dickey sneers.

Then Abdul makes Smith hand over his insulated coat, leaving him in a T-shirt, angry and freezing. But what catches Smith off guard is Abdul's parting message—a mix of words and gestures that clearly means, "Su will protect you." As if he were now one of them.

Before a storm, climbers always sense tension. The changing weather charges the atmosphere with a last-chance sort of feeling. On August 17, the sixth day of captivity, clouds fill the sky. The temperature is near freezing, the air damp. Something's brewing. Before dawn Abdul returned with two stinking, greasy 40-pound sacks. One contains salty yak butter, the other balls of congealed yogurt—Abdul and Su, as desperate and starving as their charges, start in on the provisions, most likely taken from a farmer. The Americans each force down one or two of the rancid balls. In his bivvy cave Smith sits on the suitcase-size slab of butter, insulation against the cold rocks. For the first time in a long time, Caldwell prays.

At dusk they get under way again. Abdul explains that they must climb the rugged west side of the Kara Su Valley to a plateau 3,000 feet above. There they will rendezvous, waiting several days if necessary, with Abdullah and Obert—who the Americans think must be dead, judging from their radio silence these last two days and several distant bursts of fire. Eventually they will be taken north, to Uzbekistan, the hostages are told.

Then Abdul turns away, signing that he will catch up after he heads up to the Americans' base camp, where the stashed duffels hold fresh radio batteries. It is 10 P.M. From where they stand, at the foot of a perilously steep climb that they'll have to tackle without ropes, it is an hour to base camp, an hour back. Su is now their only guard; the hostages will have most of the night alone with him. As they begin to climb the succession of slabby cliffs and steep grassy slopes, Dickey turns to his companions and says, "We gotta whack this guy, tonight."

Stifled by rain clouds, the now full moon rounds the mountainside and bleeds onto the group as it reaches a point 2,000 feet above the river. The Americans and their guard climb a moderately difficult rib, a series of 5.2 pitches, flanked by glacier-carved cliffs. Smith and Dickey shadow Su the whole way, openly talking about finding a place to push him off. But they are each burdened with the heavy bags of butter and yogurt balls, and Smith has Turat's sleeping bag draped clumsily around his shoulders, like a shawl.

"We had all been talking about killing someone for days," Caldwell will remember, clearly uncomfortable with the memory, "but Beth had said to me she just didn't think I could emotionally handle it. So I was staying out of it."

"Alpinista!" Su orders Smith to the front. He waves his hand at the cliff as if to ask, "Which way?"

Smith heads up the 60-degree face, pointing out the handholds to Su, urging him on like a guided client. Su slings his AK-47 over his shoulder and scrambles up. A shove here would be fatal, and Smith steps into position to body-slam Su off the ledge. But the rebel skirts around him, oblivious, and starts up another step of rock.

"OK, this is it," Dickey says in a trembling voice. He hands Smith the sack of yogurt balls and climbs into position, just below Su.

"Come on, do it, John," comes a collective murmur out of the night. But Su moves beyond Dickey's reach. It is now midnight. They are near the top of the last cliff. Somebody has to do something.

Caldwell is thinking his friends might not do it. And he starts worrying about how they would survive a storm up here, worrying about Beth, wondering what will happen to them all in Uzbekistan. He turns to Beth and asks, "Do you want me to do it?" She doesn't say anything. Then he starts moving toward Su.

Fueled by a wave of adrenaline, Caldwell scrambles across the ledge and up the cliff. He reaches up, grabs the rifle slung over Su's back, and pulls. A faint breath of surprise, a sound like *whaaa*, escapes Su's lips. He is falling.

The rebel arcs through the circle of the moon, pedaling air. The climbers see him hit a ledge 30 feet down with a crack. Then Su rolls off into the darkness, over the 1,500-foot cliff to the river below.

Caldwell is screaming. Clambering up the cliff in seconds, he curls up in a ball and begins gasping, "Holy shit, I just killed a guy."

Rodden reaches him and embraces him. "How can you love me now?" Caldwell sobs. "After I did this?"

"You just saved my life, Tommy," she answers. "I couldn't love you more."

Then Dickey is shouting, "Let's go, let's go!" But Caldwell, the one least likely to have acted on their talk of killing Su, is beside himself.

"Tommy, listen to me," Smith shouts into his face. "We did nothing wrong. We just saved our lives. When we get home we'll say we all did it, OK? But right now we have to get the fuck out of here. Go!"

They take off at a frantic pace, moving diagonally downhill, occasionally pausing to console Caldwell and catch their breath. Then the sound of rocks sliding behind them stops their hearts and they run again, stumbling over scree until, at 1:15 in the morning, they reach the Karavshin.

Beside the river is a well-worn trail that Smith and Dickey recognize from their trek; from here it is 18 miles to the Kyrgyz army camp. They are nearly hallucinating from fatigue, yet they keep stumbling forward. A herd of cows, moonlit in their path, frightens them: They mistake them for rebels. The climbers hug the shadows, running from tree to tree.

Hours later, they cross a footbridge near a bend in the river; now they are just a mile and a half from the army camp and a few hundred yards from a forward outpost. They're on the home stretch. But suddenly three men—rebels—materialize out of the forest, one of them just 15 feet behind them. One shouts something, then the muzzle flash and crack of AK-47s fills the night. Yellow tracers fly past their heads.

Dickey dives behind a bush. Caldwell and Rodden hide behind a rock. Smith starts running, dodging bullets, but alone and in front he suddenly feels naked, and he turns and runs back to the others. The four collide and then run together toward the outpost. It occurs to Caldwell that rebels might be manning that, too, but there is no turning back. Then shots from the front streak over their heads. Shots in front, shots behind. They are in no-man's-land. A figure stands in the doorway of a nearby hut, aiming a rifle at them. Army or rebels? They can't tell. They dive into the dark hut anyway.

Smith is first over the threshold. "*Americanski! Americanski!*" he shouts, holding his hands high.

All they see are gun barrels. Heaving with fear the four sprawl facedown on the dirt floor. Hands frisk them. Then one of the dark figures detects that Rodden is a woman.

"Oh, madame!" the man says, surprised. He removes his hands from her and steps back apologetically.

"We almost made it," shouts Rodden, confused, thinking Abdul will step forward any moment.

"We did make it, Beth!" Smith cries.

Minutes later Kyrgyz soldiers are thrusting cans of sardines and canteens of water into their hands. The soldiers have turned back the rebels. It is 4 A.M. on August 18. The climbers have escaped.

If their ordeal took place in a mountainous black hole, the four Americans now step into a whirlwind. A hurried hike with soldiers through the blood-soaked canyon gets them to a helicopter that whisks them to the town of Batken. That morning, the U.S. embassy learns for the first time that Americans have been kidnapped. Dressed in ill-fitting Kyrgyz army fatigues—their clothes are in tatters and they have lost all their gear—the climbers appear on Kyrgyzstan's state-run TV. They are hailed as heroes. They board the private jet of President Askar Akayev. They fly to Bishkek, where they are met by U.S. embassy officials and they make their first calls home. While in Bishkek they learn they weren't the only climbers taken hostage: Six Germans, three Russians, two Uzbeks, and a Ukrainian either escaped or were rescued in military operations on August 16. By September 5, Minister Councillor Nurdek Jeenbaez of the Kyrgyz embassy in Washington, D.C., claims that the rebels have been pushed out of the area by his country's forces. Abdul, Obert, and Abdullah have most likely died fighting or faded back into the mountain passes of the Pamir. No one can say if Su's body has been found.

By August 25, all four climbers are home. When they hit the San Francisco tarmac, they slip back into their lives—or try. Caldwell and Rodden are reunited with their close-knit families, and Tommy is soon back up on the Colorado cliffs with his main ropemate, his father, Mike. Dickey and his girlfriend head to the Burning Man Festival in the Nevada desert. Smith returns to his Chevy van and to his job at The North Face, where he runs the A5 division, which makes high-end climbing accoutrements. And in press conferences, morning TV shows, and interviews, the four friends hedge around discussion of the death of Su. We all pushed him, they insist. That's the pact they had made; they would stick together.

Then one night Caldwell phones me from the Roddens' house in Davis. He has been reticent all along, reluctant to talk. This time, though, he sounds sure of himself. "This is the deal," he says. He takes a deep breath. "I was the one who pushed Su. It was something I wasn't prepared to do, so when I did it I was pretty shaken up. Jason and John said that we would say we all did it. That helped me a lot. I'm still coming to terms with it."

Smith is coming to terms with the experience in a different way. "When we reached the army camp," he tells me as we drive in his van to the Oakland airport in late August, "I said to everyone that if there was a week in my life I would want to relive, then this would be it. To experience every human emotion in such a short time, under those intense, life-threatening circumstances. I would gladly go back."

I have heard war veterans say such things. And I have said the same, in private, about peaks that took friends' lives and that I felt sure had been about to take mine. But veterans of combat and survivors of high-mountain accidents carry a burden that takes time to understand.

In the long run, Beth Rodden may be speaking for all four climbers when she admits to me, three weeks after their return to America, that she has begun having nightmares. "I see Abdul," she says. "I see weird concoctions of battles. My friends are in them, and I'm always running from something."

November 2000

Author's Postscript:

Shortly after the November 2000 issue of *Outside* went to press, it was discovered that the rebel named Su had survived his fall and had been captured by the Kyrgyz military. In March 2001 I traveled to Kyrgyzstan with former hostages Jason Smith and John Dickey, and interviewed Su—his real name turned out to be Ravshan Sharipov—in a prison cell in the headquarters of the former KGB, where he was awaiting trial on terrorism charges. He confirmed the events described in my article, as he also did in a subsequent interview with a reporter for NBC's *Dateline*. Sharipov was sentenced to death by a Kyrgyz court in the summer of 2001.

—*Greg Child*

The Boy Scout vs. the Mutant

BRUCE BARCOTT

On a stone buttress high above Montana's Gallatin River, Alex Lowe picks his way up a wall of layered gneiss warmed by the sun. Flakes of his climbing chalk drift down and speckle an old pine snag at my feet. A raven drifts by and crawks. Lowe's friend Jack Tackle, belaying at the foot of the wall, adjusts his sunglasses and suppresses a yawn. I catch the virus and yawn too.

Lowe rises along his single-pitch 5.11 route up the Skyline Buttress as smoothly as a man on an escalator. To say that Lowe climbs quickly, however, might imply that he projects a sense of urgency. In fact, photographer Gordon Wiltsie, who frequently climbs with Lowe, told me that the problem with shooting the man who is arguably the best climber on the planet is that his progress appears so effortless that it's nearly impossible to capture moments of graphic drama or tension. Sure enough, when Lowe reaches the wall's crux—the trickiest section—he overcomes it with a slight traverse and then a long stretch to a thin dime of a handhold. "What a day!" he yells after topping out. "God, I love this!" He rappels down the cliff and rejoins us. "I'm a little out of practice," Lowe announces as he clips out of the rope. Tackle snorts and rolls his eyes.

The two climbers trade places, but Tackle doesn't get six feet off the ground before the mendacity of Lowe's performance becomes apparent. Steps that seemed to be carved into the rock for Alex vanish as soon as Jack touches the wall. Cracks have closed, ledges have thinned, traverses have widened. Tackle is a superb climber, a local legend and one of Lowe's heroes, but he's simply not in the same league.

"Falling!" Tackle misses at the crux. Lowe crimps the rope and arrests the dangling climber.

"You hand-traverse left along the break, Jack," Lowe calls up. "Couple of thin edges for your feet, but good handholds."

After Tackle's climb, Lowe chooses a more difficult passage up the wall, and this time I see him with different eyes. For weeks I'd been asking his partners what sets Lowe above other elite climbers. Their answers often focused on his physiology—specifically, the arm strength that lets him hoist 200-pound haul bags up granite spires and hang from his ice tools for hours. But powerful guns are only part of it; he also possesses a cerebral delight in technical challenges. As a teenager growing up in Missoula, Lowe developed a passion for mathematics at the same time that he was falling in love with climbing, and neither enthusiasm has gone cold. On long expeditions, he'll pull out a copy of *Differential and Integral Calculus* and amuse himself by working the equations by headlamp. Watching him spider up the cliff, I can see now that the buttress isn't an objective he intends to conquer, but rather a problem he wants to enjoy. "Alex is constantly being entertained by the rock," explains Steve Swenson, who has accompanied Lowe on expeditions to Everest and Gasherbrum IV.

Late in the afternoon, a wintry breeze sneaks upcanyon and nips our fingers. Packing up for the drive back to Bozeman, Lowe and Tackle exchange climbing gossip and small talk, and soon another realm of knotty equations and exquisitely difficult balancing maneuvers enters the conversation: Lowe talks about how great it is to be home with his wife, Jenni, and the kids, and somewhat sheepishly admits that he just cleared a climbing trip with his wife before buying the ticket.

"I thought I'd do the chivalrous thing and offer not to go," he says.

Tackle tries not to smile. "It's called common sense, Alex."

Although the exchange is as casual and relaxed as Lowe's climbing seems to be, it reflects a persistent identity crisis, a 20-year tug-of-war between competing tendencies. It's as if two separate entities have battled for tenancy in his body. There is the Mutant, as Lowe's climbing partners have nicknamed him, in tribute to his otherworldly talent and his astonishing drive. And there is the Boy Scout, the diligent partner in a dual-career marriage and the stalwart father who holds tight to his humility and old-fashioned values in a climbing world populated with macho egotists and vagabond stoners.

This long-standing tension has produced an oddly patterned life. Lowe rode a prestigious scholarship to college but dropped out to climb in Yosemite and beyond. When his first son was born a decade ago, he buckled down and yoked himself to a family-man job as an oil-industry engineer. The nine-to-five life lasted until the day a chance to climb Everest suddenly materialized. The pattern, then, is that the Boy Scout holds a good job for a few months or years, and then the Mutant starts climbing the walls, erupts, and heads off for first-ascent nectar. Licking this contradiction may become his greatest maneuver yet. The two halves of Alex Lowe may never live in perfect harmony, but lately he has edged ever closer to the balance that has eluded him: composing outbursts of Mozartian climbing while tending a soul devoted to hearth and home. In short, he's figuring out how to set the Mutant free to bankroll the Boy Scout's cozy life.

Stewart Alexander Lowe is a terminally optimistic man of 40 years whose dark hair and geometric jaw give him a slight resemblance to Prince Valiant. Off the mountain, most of his friends have never seen him in anything more formal than a T-shirt, tennis shoes, and twill sports pants. He lives in Bozeman, Montana, with Jennifer Leigh Lowe, a painter, and their three sons (ten-year-old Max, six-year-old Sam, and two-year-old Isaac) in a 1920s craftsman-style house that Norman Rockwell would dismiss as a greeting-card cliché. He often employs the word "gosh" without irony, and his only vice is strong coffee—preferably lattes. With his lank, muscular physique and chronically sunny disposition, he walks and talks like a poster boy for climbing, which in fact he is. After rising from humble beginnings as an early-eighties big-wall rat, Lowe has become the unofficial captain of The North Face's so-called "dream team" of top climbers, which the outdoor company has put under full Nike-style contract. When climbing veterans like George Lowe (no relation) or fellow dream team member Conrad Anker hear of some young hotshot, their first reaction is, How does he stack up to Alex? "We're all at this one level of competition," says Anker, "and then there's Alex."

His résumé, though impressive, does not tell the complete story. He has climbed Everest twice. During K2's notoriously deadly season of 1986, he came within a thousand feet of the summit before being beaten back by the storm that claimed five lives. After posting the first winter ascent of the north face of the Grand Teton with Jack Tackle in 1984, he returned a few years later and did it again, solo, in a single day. He has put new routes up some of the toughest mountains in the world: the Himalayan 20,000-footers Kwangde Nup and Kusum Kanguru, the Peruvian peaks Taulliraju and Huandoy Este. He and Lynn Hill, also a member of The North Face's team, free-climbed (roped, but without mechanical aid) the Bastion, an immense 4,000-foot wall in a remote corner of Kyrgyzstan. Two years ago he teamed up with Anker to record the highly publicized first ascent of Rakekniven, a deadly-smooth granite knife that juts 2,000 feet straight out of the Antarctic ice cap. Last spring, with team member Greg Child, he paced Mark Synnott and Jared Ogden, a pair of young turks ten years his junior, up Great Sail Peak, a 3,750-foot virgin wall on the coast of Canada's remote Baffin Island.

Those are fine, but not world-beating, accomplishments. Among American climbers, Carlos Buhler has a more impressive Himalayan record, and Ed Viesturs boasts more experience at high altitude. But sheer loftiness and Seven Summits–style peak-bagging bore Lowe. "Alex could be much more famous if he'd spend more time climbing Everest or K2," says one of his partners, "but he'd rather spend his time climbing this unbelievable stuff out there."

It's the difficulty of that "unbelievable stuff" that drops his colleagues' jaws. At the tender age of 22 he cramponed his way up Hot Doggies, a radical new line of rock and ice in Rocky Mountain National Park—a feat that inspired climber Jeff Lowe (another example of the weird plenitude of mountaineering Lowes, also no relation to Alex) to introduce a new "M" (for mixed) difficulty rating. He laid the first spikes up Vail's fearsome Fang; recorded the first one-day ascent of

Andromeda Strain, a perverse mixed rock-and-ice route on Mount Andromeda, in Canada's Columbia Icefields; and posted solos of Root Canal (at the time, the toughest ice climb in the Tetons) and Mont Blanc du Tocul's Supercouloir. He has pioneered so many mixed-climbing ascents that he no longer keeps track. "The thing about Alex is, when he gets to these places, he doesn't look at the regular routes," says Synnott, who watched Lowe "do a bunch of sick stuff" in Synnott's Vermont stomping grounds before they shared the rope on Baffin Island in 1998. "He looks in between the routes and asks, 'Has anyone done that?' "

Inside the Lowes' downtown Bozeman home, Jenni's Western folk paintings hang on the walls of the living room, which is otherwise rife with signs of three boys underfoot. There are no tools of the climbing trade in sight; the only hints of Lowe's profession are the Tibetan prayer flags fading in a backyard tree and a dog named Anna (short for Annapurna). Essentially, upstairs is all Jenni and the boys; downstairs, in a basement apartment the Lowes used to rent out in leaner times, is an office-warehouse littered with haul bags, harnesses, ropes, and hardware—the Mutant's lair.

On the day I arrived, Lowe had just returned from a long road trip, and he was busy reacquainting himself with his family. It was Max's tenth birthday. When Lowe and I walked into the kitchen, Jenni was cooking seafood stew (Max's favorite), and Isaac, the toddler, began tugging at my arm, wanting to introduce me to his rocking horse, while six-year-old Sam beckoned me to a chair draped suspiciously with a towel. "Why don't you sit down right here?" he said.

After admiring Isaac's horse, I played the stooge, sat, and deflated the hidden whoopee cushion.

"BAH-ha-ha-ha-ha!" Sam exulted. "You had beans for dinner!"

"And what relative can we thank for bringing this treasure into our lives?" asked Alex, shaking his head and laughing.

"The boys talked me into buying it at Safeway the other day," Jenni said.

"How long was I gone?" Alex ventured quietly. "Twenty-one days?"

"I think it was more like a month," Jenni said.

"Wow. Long time."

"Too long," Jenni replied, gently, firmly.

Clearly, the reentry process has not yet been rendered seamless. In the previous weeks, Lowe had been fulfilling a commitment to visit The North Face shops around the country, show the new fall line, and give employees a chance to crag with the master. But the traveling poster boy had been restive. "I'm not spending enough time with Jenni and the kids," he kept telling his climbing mates.

The tug-of-war can become intense. If a climb isn't going to work, Lowe starts weighing days spent in a foul, damp tent against hours spent with his family. "Every cell down to the molecular level starts to twitch to get back to Bozeman," says Anker.

Less easy to know are the ways that the Mutant begins to make his demands after a long spell at home. In any case, Lowe was on his best behavior during Max's birthday dinner. Trying to instill some of his love of numbers in his eldest son, Alex coaxed Max into calculating how many children are born in the United States every day.

"So if a child is born every ten seconds, how many are born every minute?" Alex asked.

"Uh . . . six."

"And how many in an hour?"

"Three hundred sixty?"

"Gosh, that's great work, Max. How many in a day, do you think?"

This took some guessing, but eventually Alex guided him to 8,640.

After dinner Sam appeared with a violin and squelched out "Happy Birthday to You" for his older brother. Not to be outdone, Max put the fiddle to his chin and honored us with a tear-jerking rendition of "I'll Fly Away." Alex took it all in from the couch, sitting there smiling with his long legs splayed, his fingers knitted in back of his head.

"Maybe you should open your gifts now, Max," Jenni suggested.

Max ripped into the ribbons and wrapping and unveiled a graphite fly rod and reel, followed by scale models of the USS *Constitution* and Christopher Columbus's *Santa Maria,* and finally a copy of the *Macmillan Dictionary for Children.*

"Wow, that's pretty neat, Max!" Alex exclaimed when he saw the book.

"That one's from you, dear," Jenni said.

"Oh! Happy birthday, Max," he said sheepishly. "Boy. Guess I have been gone awhile."

Sitting amid wrinkled and torn paper on his living room floor, the Alex Lowe who wants to be home and wants to be away examined the rigging of the *Santa Maria*. "Look at this, Max," he said, holding up both models. "Look at the difference in size."

Lowe seemed to be calculating the 1492 odds: open ocean, unknown destination, only 128 feet of Spanish hardwood between the crew and oblivion. "Wow. They didn't even know what was out there." His tone was oddly intimate, as if he were admiring the new route a colleague had put up on Cerro Torre. "Pretty bold. Pretty audacious."

More than his new routes, first ascents, and pioneering mixed climbs, it's the way he climbs that has made Alex Lowe's legend.

"Alex's Grand Traverse is one of those stories that's taken on a life of its own in the Tetons," reports Doug Chabot, a guide with Exum Mountain Guides, where Lowe worked off and on for ten years. Most mountaineers hope to do the Grand Traverse once in their lives; many of the strongest climbers require at least 24 hours to complete it. Lowe squeezed it in between breakfast and dinner. "He came in one morning at Exum," Chabot recalls, "and when he found there wasn't any work that day, he took off in his tennis shoes and did the whole traverse by himself, climbing ten peaks. He was back by four that afternoon."

There are stories about ice climbs Lowe put up in Montana and Wyoming that nobody has ever repeated. There are tales of his showing up at walls all around the world and on-sighting routes the locals have been trying to solve for years. (A climber "on-sights" a route by climbing it with no prior knowledge.) There's the old yarn—confirmed—about the time he blew out the toe in his rock shoe halfway up Yosemite's El Capitan and completed the climb wearing it backward.

Part of his mystique derives from the perception that he has tapped into some inexhaustible life force. Climbers trade intelligence about his pull-up obsession—he gets itchy if he can't do 400 a day—as if they want to be assured it's nothing but hype. (It isn't.) On an expedition in Queen Maud Land, a stir-crazy Lowe dove into an Antarctic white-out equipped with only a shovel and a pair of skis. An hour later his companions stumbled out to find Lowe down in a freshly dug, eight-foot-deep pit, chinning himself on the skis. "Hey, guys!" he said. "How about a pull-up contest?"

When Lowe tells some of his own favorite stories, he tends to use the word "epic" a lot. To a climber, the word means something like "near total disaster." An epic is usually bad (as opposed to a "suffer-fest," which refers to an expedition during which inhuman conditions we're happily endured). Perhaps the granddaddy epic of them all was Lowe's June 1995 expedition to Mount McKinley, which gave the Mutant full license to express himself.

Lowe and Conrad Anker had planned an excursion up the Cassin Ridge, one of McKinley's most difficult routes. Lowe flew in to base camp on the Kahiltna Glacier a couple of days before Anker, and trekked up to the 14,000-foot camp to acclimatize. That night, for fun, he ran up to the summit with veteran American climbers Marc Twight and Scott Backes and McKinley's high-altitude doctor, Colin Grissom. Along the way, they passed three Spanish climbers bivouacked on the ice. "They'd sort of quit moving," Lowe recalls, "but they were still trying to climb up." The next day, with their tent shredded by the wind, the Spaniards radioed for help. "They were talking to somebody out in the Gulf of Alaska," says Lowe's friend Andrew McLean, who happened to be on McKinley at the same time. "All they could say was 'Rescue, rescue.'" Somebody got word to the Park Service, which called in an Army Chinook helicopter and asked Lowe, Twight, and Backes if they'd help out. Although a storm had struck the mountain, they agreed to try, and the helicopter pilot control-crashed the climbers onto McKinley's 19,500-foot-high "football field," the highest landing ever in a Chinook. "It was really scary," the not-easily-scared Lowe admits.

"They told us we had two hours to climb down the West Rib and get these guys back up," Lowe continues. The West Rib is a technical climb down a 50-degree slope of ice and rock. "By the time we got to them, one of the Spaniards had already fallen to his death. The other two weren't wearing gloves or hats. They were in the last stages of hypothermia—they were delirious—and their hands were frozen way up past the wrist." Twight and Backes went back up with the first climber, who could still walk, with the idea they'd return to help Lowe carry up the second man, who was in much worse shape. Lowe decided there wasn't time to wait.

"I stood him up, leaned him against me, and started up, but he just passed out, so I cut a chunk of rope, tied him directly into my harness—he was 20 feet below me—and just started climbing up this thing, dragging the guy. It was fully epic. When I reached the fixed ropes, I couldn't keep dragging him, but he wouldn't get up. So I finally picked him up, piggyback, and staggered uphill to 19,500 feet and carried him on to the football field. It was one of those things you do because you *have* to do it, one of those Herculean things where you get a lot of adrenaline going and you just do it." They all flew off to Talkeetna in the Chinook.

With the Spaniards safely thawing, Lowe returned to McKinley. Anker arrived at base camp the next day and was making purposefully slow progress to 14,000 feet, in order to acclimatize before their Cassin Ridge attempt. Lowe, who already had his high-altitude lungs, was antsy to get after something, anything. What to do, what to do? He decided to see if he could climb McKinley in a day.

"So I took off at midnight, got all the way up to the football field, about 500 feet below the summit, but the weather got really bad and I couldn't see anything, so I didn't quite make the summit." On his way down, Lowe passed a party of nine Taiwanese climbers at 17,000 feet. Soon afterward, despite whiteout conditions, the Taiwanese group tried to summit and became separated. Only six made it back to their camp. "The Park Service was like, 'Déjà vu,'" says Lowe. Once again, he was drafted, and he and Anker found one climber dead and towed two other half-frozen survivors down to safety. Apparently refreshed by their exertions, but without enough time left for their Cassin Ridge climb, Lowe and Anker attempted a single-day dash up nearby Mount Hunter, getting most of the way up its north buttress before running out of daylight. "That was kind of it," Lowe says, winding up the story with a shrug.

Sometimes the stories aren't so much epic as bizarrely comic. As Lowe climbed that summer on McKinley, his forehead bore the scar of a near-fatal fall the previous winter. The problem was an icicle in Hyalite Canyon, a few miles outside of Bozeman. Lowe, Tackle, and two others attacked it with ice tools, crampons, and screws. One pitch up (a pitch is half the length of a standard climbing rope, or about 100 feet), with Lowe swinging the lead and Tackle belaying, Lowe's entire section of ice broke free. With Tackle looking on, Lowe rode the ice 40 feet before crashing onto a ledge. Upon impact, Lowe's forehead whiplashed into the adze of his ice ax. He stood up, ecstatic at having survived, and shouted, "Fuck, man, I'm OK!" In fact, Lowe looked like a mangled victim in a Wes Craven movie; his companions could see that a broad section of his scalp was draped over one eye, exposing a section of skull. "Oh, man, you're not OK!" Tackle yelled back. "You're fucked up. Sit down!"

"We rappelled off and kinda taped the scalp back into place, and put a hat on, and taped around the hat, and started skiing out," Lowe recalls. "Kinda knew it was time to go to the ER. But we also knew it was going to be a long evening there, so we stopped down at the coffee shop and got lattes. It was great. My clothes were saturated with blood. We parked in the handicap spot in front of the coffee shop, marched right in, and then headed for the hospital."

"Alex was one of those little kids who never felt tame," says his mother, Dottie, a retired schoolteacher. She and her husband, Jim, raised Alex and his two brothers, Andy (older) and Ted (younger) in Missoula. "He always had trouble sitting still, was always the first one down the trail, always climbed the highest."

Jim, an associate professor of entomology at the University of Montana, often took the boys scrambling in Kootenai Canyon, and by the time Alex was in the fifth grade he started going off on his own. Several years later, Lowe hooked up with a U of M student named Marvin McDonald who, desperate for a partner to belay him on the walls of Blodgett Canyon, taught the 16-year-old the rudiments of climbing, using a sink-or-swim pedagogical technique. Soon Lowe was doing advanced multipitch routes with McDonald and starting to climb on his own with friends, using a ridiculously unsafe nylon rope he bought at a hardware store. He finished high school in 1976 with only one clear idea of the future: "All I knew was that I wanted to climb some more."

A chemical engineering scholarship took him to Montana State University in Bozeman, but Lowe's college career was geographically doomed from the start. Too many mountains beckoned through the classroom window. At the end of his sophomore year he dropped out, gathered his rack, and headed for the Sierra Nevada. Before he left, Dottie—who would spend the next 20 years praying for the safety of her son—anointed his VW bug with holy oil.

For Lowe, Yosemite in 1979 was "a place of dreams." The free-climbing revolution, in which young climbers eschewed the traditional hammered-in pitons for a purer, hands-and-feet-only esthetic, was taking place daily on El Capitan. Camp Four buzzed with climbing-mad kids like Lowe pitching their grubby tents alongside free-climbing masters like Ron Kauk, Jim Bridwell, and Dale Bard. He was the quintessential dirtbag. When his money ran out, Lowe engaged in the hallowed Camp Four tradition of scarfing: hanging out in the tourist cafeteria waiting for someone to leave a half-eaten stack of pancakes or sandwich behind.

He was "wandering aimlessly forward," as he recalls it, following a path that blossomed into a five-year climber's pilgrimage. When he had money he used it to get to Yosemite, the Canadian Rockies, New York's Shawangunks, Wales, the sea cliffs of Penzance, the Mediterranean Coast, and the French Alps. When he didn't have money— usually after a long spring, summer, and fall of climbing—he earned it roughnecking in the subfreezing Wyoming oil fields. In the winter of 1981–82, he and Jenni, whom he'd met a year earlier through a climbing buddy, hired on with a seismic exploration crew. "It was the perfect job for a climber," Lowe recalls. "Every day they'd fly us into high mountain areas in Colorado, Montana, Utah, and drop us off with cable, dynamite, and recording equipment. We were the flunkies there to roll the cable ahead of the geophysicist. We did that for about three months, saved another wad of cash, and bought plane tickets to London."

A Montana native and avid climber, Jenni was as hooked on vagabonding as Alex. Together they practiced the art of living cheap in mountain towns in England and France. "I really didn't think it would last," she says today, sounding bemused that she fell for this "kid"—Lowe is three years younger—who eventually won her heart with his "pretty boundless energy" and "unstoppable spirit."

For a while at least, the two climbers enjoyed an existence as carefree as anything Rimbaud or Kerouac tasted. "It's amazing how vivid those memories are," says Lowe. "Climbing was so vibrant and new, plus I was falling in love with Jennifer. I remember climbing all day on the granite sea cliffs near Penzance. The wild appeal: surf crashing at the base of the cliffs, seagulls crying around you. Jenni and I climbed a whole bunch of routes in the Alps. Most of these places have their climbers' haunts, and Chamonix had this foul place called Snell's Field. You could live in Chamonix and it didn't cost you anything. And most of the time you were out climbing—the North Face of Les Courtes, the Aiguille du Midi, classic alpine rock climbs."

When it was over, Alex and Jenni returned to the States so broke they had to hitchhike across North Dakota in a December blizzard to get home. The next spring they married, reality kicked in, and the new husband set about trying to find a steady career. He went back to Montana State University, finished his degree in applied mathematics, and in 1988 entered a graduate program in mechanical engineering. Meanwhile Jenni, who wanted to have kids and start a career as an artist, had given up climbing. Instead of finishing graduate school, Alex took a well-paying engineering job with Schlumberger Oilfield Services, the first solid career move of his life. "We thought our ship had come in," recalls Jenni, and none too soon. By this time their first son, Max, had arrived.

Lowe gave it his best shot, but he lasted barely a year. "It was just work all the time, which was cool," he says, "but then I realized I only got two weeks' vacation a year. That wasn't going to work." In the fall of 1990, when Hooman Aprin, a climbing buddy from Exum, offered him a slot on what turned out to be one of the first guided trips on Everest, Lowe bolted to Nepal and helped lead three of five clients to the summit. He celebrated Max's second birthday, jobless, on top of the world.

Lowe's subsequent stabs at a nonclimbing career followed a similar pattern: He'd stick with it for a year or two, then quit to climb or try something else. Quality-control engineer for Black Diamond, the climbing gear manufacturer. Snow avalanche forecaster. Exum mountain guide. In the early 1990s, after Sam arrived, Lowe was spending most of the year working as a private guide, and dashing overseas to tackle ambitious expeditions and climbs when the opportunity would arise. He was seeing less and less of his family, and spending more time guiding than climbing. Neither the Mutant nor the Boy Scout was getting what he needed.

Still, his reputation kept building, and Lowe capped off this period with a virtuoso display of sheer mountain steel. In 1993 he and Anker became the first westerners to compete in the Khan Tengri International Speed Climbing Competition, an annual race held on Kyrgyzstan's 22,950-foot Khan Tengri. The idea is simple, if suicidal. Thirty climbers start at the 13,000-foot base camp. Each is given a numbered padlock, which the racers lock onto a tripod at the summit to make sure nobody pulls a Rosie Ruiz. The fastest climber back to base wins. The only way to win is to go all out. "It's totally sketchy—I mean, people die doing this thing," Lowe says.

Lowe took the lead early and never looked back. Though unacclimatized and unfamiliar with the route, he smoked the field with a time of ten hours and eight minutes. In a competition in which climbers are usually separated by minutes, Lowe destroyed the previous Khan Tengri record by more than four hours.

The speed climb confirmed his stature among climbers but earned him little more than a plane ticket and all the vodka his Russian hosts could manage to pour down his throat. The big problem remained: Only a fool becomes a mountain climber to make money, at least in this country. Homebodies with mortgages, children, and fantasies of middle-class security are not often found among the rarefied upper echelons of the climbing profession.

Four years ago this picture changed for a lucky handful of marquee climbers. In 1995 William Simon, then president of The North Face, decided it was time for his company to back climbers the way other companies back baseball and basketball stars. Lowe, Anker, Greg Child, and Lynn Hill all became employees with travel budgets and full benefits. Lowe is expected to put in a certain number of days with sales reps and the R&D department, but the rest of the year he is free to climb.

After leeching off the Boy Scout for all those years, the Mutant finally got a job.

I meet him one morning in his basement office. It's 6 A.M. Jenni and the boys are still asleep upstairs, but he's been up working for three hours, which is standard operating procedure. When he's home in Bozeman he tries to devote the daylight hours to the boys, so he'll often rise at 3 A.M. for a "dawn patrol" run or ski up nearby Bridger Bowl, and be back at the house in time for breakfast. "It's hard to fit this many lives into one lifetime," he says.

I take the only chair in a spartan and tidy bachelor pad, furnished with a bookshelf, a Macintosh, a poster of Pakistan's Trango Towers, and a file cabinet stuffed with dossiers on mountains yet to be climbed. "Alex always has 15 things planned for the future," Jenni told me a few days earlier, so I thought I'd see if I could pry Lowe's to-do list out of him. After all, climbing's true icons—the names that resonate beyond the climbing shop—all have a single crowning achievement attached to their names. Heinrich Harrer had the Eiger. Hermann Buhl had Nanga Parbat. Tenzing Norgay and Sir Edmund Hillary had Everest. Reinhold Messner had his 14 8,000-meter peaks. Alex Lowe has a hundred mind-blowing ascents, but no One Big Thing that sticks in the public's mind.

If Lowe is plotting some paramount accomplishment to lift his reputation to that higher level, however, he's not saying. The Boy Scout keeps the file cabinet locked. He's just out to have a good time in the mountains, he insists. Anyone who climbs to make his name is climbing for the wrong reasons—and won't continue for long. "There are people who can't bear to fail," he says. "Those people are on the short track, as far as their careers go. You have to push hard, do hard things. But you also have to be able to say, 'OK, today's not the day.'"

Lowe is stimulated by danger, but he knows how to factor in fear as an element of the equation. "What I value is the soul-searching head game of getting a little out there," he says. The serious consequences integral to climbing only deepen his tie to the mountain and intensify the bond with his rope partner. "You go into a multipitch natural route, get a little scared, and the name sears itself into your mind." Given the high cost of a mistake, he says, a mountain apprenticeship should be long and slow, and it demands as much humility as strength and will. And acceptance, too: Together with the warmth and abundant affection in their marriage, Alex and Jenni share a kind of detachment—an understanding that his livelihood derives from calculated risk-taking—and a philosophical equanimity in the face of what could happen. She has spoken forthrightly of her ability to carry on alone if necessary. Meanwhile, Lowe sticks to the principle that has taken him this far: Let the Mutant race up the mountain, but make your crux decisions in light of the long view. Hard-core ambition is something you deal with down on the flats.

"I've definitely got lists of things I'd love to accomplish as a climber," he acknowledges, after I prod him further. "But let's face it: The world's full of climbers, and the realm of unexplored, unclimbed peaks is shrinking rapidly." In other words, he who blurts out his dream ascent is only inviting the world to spoil the party. It's no secret, however, that Lowe's attention for the past two years has been drawn to the Antarctic. The trip to Queen Maud Land in the winter of 1996–97 opened his eyes to the possibilities: an entire continent of mostly unclimbed—even unseen and unmapped—mountains. The main focus of his obsession is the Transantarctic Range, a spine of mountains as long as the Rockies that runs up the opposite side of the continent— a forbidding and insanely cold setting for the last big collection of first ascents on the planet. "The place is totally unexplored," he says excitedly, and he pulls out an article that includes the notes of a geologist-climber who was one of the first to set eyes on these mountains: "During the austral summer, the sun never sets, and mountaineering is limited only by your endurance and need for sleep."

And by a third factor: cash. Only one outfit, Adventure Network International, can get you there, and a round-trip ticket in their C-130

Hercules will set you back $30,000. The North Face and the National Geographic Society ponied up for the Queen Maud Land trip, but further expeditions may require Lowe to tolerate some odd collaborations. This winter he was planning to climb in the Transantarctics with Conrad Anker and the president of Adventure Network, Mike McDowell, a raffish Australian entrepreneur who made headlines last year by offering deep-sea tours of the Titanic. McDowell was waiving the price of the ticket so he could climb with Lowe. "He's kind of like your dad," Lowe told me. "He's got the keys to the car."

It's easy to see how irresistible Antarctica must be to Lowe. The challenge of the "great game" of climbing, he'll tell you, is pushing right up to the line where boldness and wisdom part ways, but "the ultimate attraction is the unknown. I want to climb routes that are remote and technically difficult. Climbing for me is all about solving the magnitude of the problem. The best projects are the ones with big question marks hanging over them."

He calls back in early December and leaves a message. "The rumors are true," Lowe says. He's just undergone reconstructive knee surgery. "I tore my ACL an hour before I left for the airport to head to South America. Had to bag the Transantarctic climb and come home." Irony ahoy: He tore it playing soccer with the boys.

He'd mentioned his knee problems before, but this time he confessed, "Actually, I first tore it six years ago jumping off some cliffs at Alta." His doctor had recommended immediate surgery, but Lowe had plans to climb Gasherbrum IV. He flew to Pakistan with his knee in a brace. Over the next six years his knee popped out a half-dozen times, and he'd coped. After the soccer incident, it didn't heal. He made it only partway to Antarctica before a Chilean doctor ordered him back home to the hospital.

Add a footnote to the library of Alex Lowe stories: He has done all this stuff—Rakekniven, Khan Tengri race, the dawn patrols—absent his left anterior cruciate ligament.

For now at least, the never-ending problem has been solved. The torn ACL has given him six months of quality rehab time with Jenni and the boys, with no nagging exploration itch. But when the knee heals, the Mutant plans to run wild. Lowe's 1999 datebook includes an expedition to the Great Trango Tower and a run up Tibet's Shisha-pangma, the 13th-highest mountain in the world. He and Andrew McLean plan to ski off the summit, making them the first Americans to schuss off an 8,000-meter peak. After that, it's back to Antarctica to enjoy his own personal sufferfest on some remote wall thousands of feet above the ice cap.

"It's really a blessing in disguise," he says. "Last time I did Trango, I had to walk up the Baltoro Glacier with a brace. I'll be able to dance up it this time."

March 1999

The Climber
Comes Down
to Earth

DANIEL DUANE

Drinking his third latte of the morning on our way to ski Alta, Conrad Anker looked, for a moment, content. I'd pulled him away from his glad-handing duties at the Outdoor Retailer trade show, and as we drove through Salt Lake City's suburban sprawl and into the frozen Wasatch Mountains, he seemed giddy at the prospect of some fresh air. Dark clouds hung low over the peaks, the snow-dusted road curved below shattered ribs of rock, and Anker, who lived nearby for a decade and a half, ripped apart a cinnamon bun and bubbled with nostalgia. Reaching across the dash, he pointed out an eagle's nest, then a mixed ice-and-rock route he'd once done in a single day, then a snow chute he used to ski in late spring—"Big GS-style turns," he recalled fondly, "not tips and tails."

A handsome, 38-year-old alpinist, with boyishly side-parted blond hair, close-set blue eyes, and a lantern jaw, Anker looks more like a high-strung surfer than a consummate mountaineer. With no hiker's thighs or gym-pumped muscles, there's a surprising lightness to his physique, and his head leans perpetually forward, as if straining into the future. A sometimes wry self-promoter who talks earnestly about saving the world, Anker also has the playful manner of the outdoors Peter Pan. Which makes sense, given that he has spent his entire adult life in a very particular America—an adventure-sports subculture in which status derives less from money than from talent at skiing, kayaking, and climbing, a subculture in which well-meaning environmentalist and anticonsumerist opinions make up an informal state ideology. Success begins with finding work flexible enough to let you play whenever the powder's deep, the ice is in, or the rock is dry. Greater success means making a living at some approximation of your game, like working ski patrol. True arrival means making a living doing the thing itself: travel, adventure, freedom.

Anker has been getting paid to play for most of a decade as a salaried, globe-trotting member of The North Face Climbing Team, and it's been a great ride. But lately he has been negotiating the transition from being the favorite partner of some of the world's great expedition leaders to becoming a leader himself. At the same time, he has had a painful reckoning with the costs of playing one of the world's most dangerous games—costs that include his own brushes with mortality, the untimely deaths of his three closest friends in the high mountains, and the strange fallout that those deaths have had in his life.

Turning down the car radio, Anker gestured at a band of granite called Hellgate Cliff. He told me that together with his first serious climbing mentor, the legendary Mugs Stump, he established a notoriously committed rock climb there, Fossils from Hell, in the 1980s. (Stump disappeared into a crevasse in 1992 while guiding clients on Alaska's Mount McKinley.) As we approached Alta, Anker remembered how he and another college climbing buddy, the underground hero Seth Shaw, had sometimes crammed an ice climb, a rock climb, and a few ski runs into a single day, even begged used lift tickets off skiers leaving Alta early. (Shaw was killed in May 2000 by falling ice, also in Alaska.)

"Wow!" he exclaimed as we rounded a snowbanked curve and a frozen waterfall swung into view. "Look at all the people on that ice climb! Wear your helmets today, boys!" Anker told me with evident pleasure that he and Shaw had held the round-trip speed record on that climb until Alex—Alex Lowe, Anker's best friend and a man once considered the best climber in the world—shattered it. In the fall of 1999, an avalanche struck Anker, Lowe, and a friend named Dave

Bridges on the flanks of Tibet's 26,291-foot Shishapangma. Anker ran one way and survived, but Bridges, 29, and Lowe, 40, headed another way and disappeared. Lowe left behind a widow, Jennifer, and three young sons.

Even Anker's most famous achievement is shadowed by ambiguities. In 1999 he joined the Mallory & Irvine Research Expedition to Mount Everest. That May, just above 27,000 feet, he found the 75-year-old remains of the British climber George Mallory. The discovery shed new light on one of the great unsolved mysteries of world exploration—what befell Mallory and his partner, Sandy Irvine, during the third summit attempt on Everest. But for Anker, who has put up important first ascents from Antarctica to Baffin Island, and who has no particular preoccupation with history, it was more a quirk of fate than the kind of cutting-edge climbing achievement of which he is most proud. Nevertheless, he was lionized in newspapers and magazines the world over; he coauthored (with David Roberts) a book on the Mallory expedition; and he has been on a near-constant speaking tour ever since.

By far the greatest change in Anker's life came shortly after the October 1999 memorial service for Alex Lowe, in Bozeman, Montana. In what must have been a bewildering and exhausting half-year, Anker had come straight back from Everest to spend five months cowriting the Mallory book, flown off to Shishapangma with Lowe, survived a battering in the lethal avalanche, and returned just in time to go on a book tour. Everywhere he went, according to Topher Gaylord, long-time director of The North Face Climbing Team, "people were giving Conrad so much support. But he had to go back alone to his hotel room every night, and it didn't bring Alex back, it didn't change anything. I think that's where Jenny and the kids became the best way of coping with losing Alex."

In a series of events that Anker understandably preferred not to discuss with a journalist, he eventually broke off his wedding engagement to an environmental lawyer named Becky Hall and became romantically involved with Jennifer Lowe. In December he proposed, and they plan to be married by the time this magazine arrives on the newsstands. Anker now lives with Jennifer and her sons in the Lowe home in

Bozeman—finding himself, in other words, husband-to-be to his best friend's widow and stepfather to three boys who lost their father while he was climbing beside Anker himself.

In Little Cottonwood Canyon that day, Anker did not dwell on his own and his new family's losses, and this was only partly because he knew that I already knew all the details. He also resolutely insists on a life-affirming view of his profession. In his Mallory slide show—the story of yet another young husband and father who died climbing— Anker doesn't mention the half-dozen mangled corpses that he came upon on Everest and that he describes in his book. He never shows the macabre photographs of himself looming over Mallory's grisly body. (He criticized this magazine for running one of these shots on its cover.) He sometimes even tells audiences, in all sincerity, things like, "If I can motivate just one of you to go home and plan just one climb tonight, I will have done my job."

Anker is, of course, a paid spokesman for The North Face and a man who has never known much beyond extreme alpinism. But one senses, too, that he feels a great compulsion, even obligation, to argue aloud that his chosen profession has been worthwhile and that Alex Lowe did not die foolishly—that his life's foremost pursuit is still as it has always seemed: good for body, soul, and mind, and inspired by grand purpose.

As I clunked across the Alta parking lot in telemark boots, Anker instructed me, teasingly, on how to carry skis—over one shoulder, tips down—so as not to look like a dork. Once on the mountain, he humored me on the mogul-free intermediate runs I'd said were my limit, but he dipped repeatedly off the trail, diving between steep trees and soaring, as airborne and playful as any teenager, back into sight. Anker has a reputation as a fantastic partner. Jochen Hemmleb and Jake Norton, for example, of the Mallory & Irvine Research Expedition, extol Anker as exceptionally hardworking and fun to be around, and all it took was a few runs that morning to see what they meant. When enthusiasm got the better of Anker, he steered me onto a series of experts-only bump runs through tight rock chutes, but I quickly forgot my irritation and terror in the sheer pleasure of watching someone ski the way you dream of skiing: as if your skis will never cross, your balance never falter, your reflexes never fail—as if the mountains, even at their steepest, are your best friends.

Indeed, Anker's two-page, single-spaced climbing résumé, with its emphasis on highly technical routes up good-looking mountains, must be the envy of all but a very small world elite. It includes a new route on the Russian Tower, in the Ak Su Himalaya, and desperate new big-wall lines both in Zion with Mugs Stump and on Patagonia's Torre Egger with Yosemite hardmen Steve Gerberding and Jay Smith. The list goes on: Cerro Torre; Ama Dablam and Lobuche, in the Khumbu Himalaya; a first ascent, with Lowe and the writer Jon Krakauer, of Queen Maud Land's Rakekniven.

Anker may not be quite world-class at rock, snow, or ice climbing, but his combined skills at all three put him in rarefied company. As photographer and mountaineer Galen Rowell told writer David Roberts in 1999, "Conrad can ski down virgin faces of big peaks in subzero Antarctica, climb El Cap routes in a day for fun, sport-climb 5.12, speed-climb up Khan-Tengri in the Tien Shan faster than the Russian Masters of Sport, climb the north face of Everest or Latok, ice-climb the wildest frozen waterfalls, and run mountain trails forever. Plus enjoy hanging out with his friends talking about other things besides mountains." For this reason, Anker is a much sought-after expedition member: On both Everest and his recent re-creation of Ernest Shackleton's traverse of South Georgia Island for an IMAX movie, with renowned alpinists Stephen Venables and Reinhold Messner, Anker was the designated technical climbing leader. (Their film, *The Endurance: Shackleton's Epic Journey,* premiered in February.)

Late in the day at Alta, when light snow flurries turned into a miserably cold wind, Anker plopped beside me on a lift and told me something I'd heard him say several times before: that Stump, Shaw, and Lowe had all been better climbers than he. It's a frank self-assessment: Anker has tended to play lieutenant to bigger names rather than headline expeditions himself. As a professional climber, he has also had to favor routes on which he has a reasonable chance of success and on which photographers and film crews can come along. Climbing's purist ideal—personified by Anker's very own mentor, Mugs Stump—is the two-man team moving fast with a minimum of gear, taking only enough pictures to prove what they've done, as Anker did for years with Seth Shaw. By contrast, caravan climbs like Anker's and Alex Lowe's National Geographic Society–funded first ascent of Rakekniven, with pressure for good photographs and a return on investment, require heavier anchors, more fixed ropes, and a slower schedule. Without criticizing Anker by name, last year's *American Alpine Journal* featured fierce denunciations of "Barbie mountaineering" and "business climbing."

Anker admits that professional climbers sometimes use power drills and fixed ropes with such abandon that it's akin to "hunting Bambi with a bazooka." He acknowledges that he and Lowe could have done Rakekniven in a single day, without drilling a bolt, instead of in four days with 28 bolts. But the role of alpha male is now wide open to Anker. He could easily pick one of climbing's "last great problems"— some hideous Himalayan north face—assemble a world-class team, and join the ranks of his sport's true immortals, climbers famous not just for stumbling across a dead guy on a trade route, but for hanging it all out in the most daring circumstances possible. Except, of course, that a lot of those immortal climbers have been turning up dead lately, and Anker now has the same incentive to stay alive that Alex Lowe did: Jennifer Lowe and her three sons.

As we rode Alta's Supreme lift for the last time that day, Anker's conversation reflected the painful complexity of this moment in his life. He remarked that he'd probably never have his own kids, then expressed his love for the kids he's now caring for—how he does homework with one, plays Lego with another, does Brio with the third. Moments later, he mused on a high-altitude big wall he hopes to do this summer in Pakistan, then wistfully described the last time he'd skied Alta with Shaw. Such a bittersweet predicament: fame shadowed by loss, dreams seeming obsolete just as they come true, sudden responsibility but also love, and opportunities to weigh against the well-being of a still-grieving family. As we disembarked, I wondered aloud if Anker couldn't use a run to himself.

"You don't mind?" he asked.

I didn't, and as I shuffled toward a groomed slope, I watched him slip under an out-of-bounds sign, take one look off what I was quite sure was a cliff, and vanish.

Anker was born in San Francisco in November 1962, but he grew up largely abroad. Anker's father, Wally, was an international banker who moved his wife, Helga, and four children first to Tokyo, then later to Hong Kong and Frankfurt, Germany. An avid mountaineer and skier, Wally also took the family on annual summer visits to Priest Ranch, the Ankers' California homestead, just outside Big Oak Flat, in the Sierra Nevada foothills. Later, in the mid-1970s, the teenage Anker boarded at the outdoors-oriented Colorado Rocky Mountain School.

Graduating in 1981, at age 18, he chose the University of Utah, at the foot of the Wasatch Mountains, and majored in commercial recreation. (Yes, the school's Department of Parks, Recreation, and Tourism really does offer such a degree.) Anker was more enthusiastic about fieldwork than homework and took seven years to finish his bachelor's degree. Along the way, he worked at the local North Face retail store and bicycled around Salt Lake City peddling homemade fleece hats to local shops for his fledgling outdoor-clothing company, Alf Wear. Anker took several semesters off to climb in Alaska with the soft-spoken, quietly driven Shaw, a classmate at the university. Starting in 1983, he also apprenticed himself to Terrence "Mugs" Stump, 31, a hard-living former college-football star (he played defensive back for Joe Paterno at Penn State before damaging his left knee) and one of the great American climbers of the period, renowned for his bold and visionary solos in the great ranges.

"I was like Grasshopper, listening to the master," Anker recalls. Up to that point, Stump was the most influential person in his life, "except for my parents," he says. For a time, Anker shared a house in Emigration Canyon, near Salt Lake City, with Shaw and Stump. Kevin Boyle, who started Alf Wear with Anker, recalls, "Their mentality was like, 'Hey, I can buy a bag of Bisquick, a thing of peanut butter, and I can live for a month and don't have to work, and now I can devote all my effort to climbing."

Out of college in 1988, Anker took Stump's advice and dedicated himself to life as a professional climber—a career that, in many respects, did not yet exist. He sold his interest in Alf to Boyle, switched from North Face retail clerk to product tester (meaning he got free stuff in exchange for telling them how well it worked), and made ends meet as a carpenter and high-access construction worker, scaling river dams and transmission towers. Like anyone who spends so much time in the mountains, Anker had his share of close calls. While attempting a new route on Alaska's Eyetooth in 1989, Anker and Stump, storm-bound on a portaledge, suffered for a week without food until the weather lifted. Then, in April 1991, Anker and Shaw flew to Alaska and grabbed the much-coveted first ascent of Middle Triple Peak. During their descent, however, Shaw fell 80 feet to the glacier below, surviving only because he landed in deep snow. A moment later, Anker also fell. Both men walked away, and the route made Anker's name in the American climbing community.

In 1992, the year Stump was killed, Anker claimed first ascents in Baffin Island's Sam Ford Fjord and Antarctica's Sentinel Mountains. In 1993, he joined Alex Lowe in the Khan-Tengri speed-climbing competition, in Kyrgyzstan. They'd met as coworkers at the Black Diamond store in Salt Lake City two years before, and they now became close friends. Shortly afterward, The North Face made Anker a founding member of The North Face Climbing Team. By 1995 he was living in Oakland, California, and managing the team full-time. Just two years later, he decided business was taking too much time away from his real work. Giving up his apartment, Anker had all his mail forwarded to his family's Priest Ranch and began a relentless series of climbing trips that culminated, at the end of the decade, in the search for Mallory and the fatal avalanche on Shishapangma.

Until early 1999, relative youth and luck allowed Anker to focus single-mindedly on the positive, upbeat aspects of his sport. That May, however, he began a protracted confrontation with climbing's hardest truths. The Mallory & Irvine Research Expedition, led by Mount Rainier guide Eric Simonson, represented the latest in media-friendly commercial climbing projects: a demonstration of emerging technology that can broadcast events from remote corners of the globe and a chance to feed the ravenous appetite for tales of disastrous adventures. Invited along as the technical climbing specialist, Anker had never been above 24,000 feet. He jumped at both the free ride to Everest and the enormous career opportunity.

At 5:15 on the morning of May 1, Anker and four others left Camp V for the "search zone," high on Everest's northeast ridge. Wandering around at 27,000 feet looking for two dead climbers was novel enough, and even slightly bizarre, given that the usual goal at that fatal altitude is a dash to the summit and down again. The prior Himalayan snowy season had been the lightest in a hundred years, and almost immediately Anker and his companions came across what one of them, Tap Richards, would later describe as "a virtual graveyard of . . . frozen bodies, a kind of collection zone for fallen climbers." Anker encountered a corpse in a purple nylon suit with its face eaten to the skull by goraks (ravenlike birds that haunt the high Himalayas). Finally, at about 11:45 A.M., he came across Mallory himself, wool-clad, frozen into the scree, and preserved well enough that bruises still showed through his skin. While the others emptied Mallory's pockets for clues, Anker lifted the body. He wrote later that it "made that same creaky sound as when you pull up a log that's been on the ground for years. It was disconcerting to look into the hole in the right buttock that the goraks had chewed. His body had been hollowed out, almost like a pumpkin."

A few days later, after a short rest, Anker and his teammates headed up again, this time to tackle the question of whether Mallory, without modern equipment, could have free-climbed the Second Step, a crucial obstacle near the summit. (En route they found the body of a woman from Telluride whose family had asked that they unclip her from the fixed ropes so that future climbers wouldn't have to step over her). Anker's difficulty on the Second Step led him to believe that Mallory could not have gotten past it; after summiting, he returned to Base Camp convinced that the two British climbers had perished before reaching the top.

Five months later, Anker had a much more devastating encounter with mountaineering's mortal consequences. In early October, Anker,

Lowe, and seven other climbers started up Shishapangma in an attempt to become the first Americans to ski down an 8,000-meter peak. According to Topher Gaylord, of The North Face (which also sponsored Lowe), Anker and Lowe had by this time become "the closest of friends—I mean true soul mates." For more than five years, the two had climbed together around the world and occasionally visited each other's families. Anker and Lowe were close enough in size to share climbing shoes, and they often zipped their sleeping bags together during bivouacs. Anker recalls that they also talked about becoming old men together. "You're going to come out to Big Oak Flat," Anker remembers telling Lowe, "and I'll come visit you, and we'll be in rocking chairs, reliving our youth." They shared the belief, Anker says, that "climbing's a wonderful thing, but if you don't come back again it's not worth it."

With every move documented in online postings and webcasts, the trip was precisely the kind of media spectacle that Anker and Lowe were tiring of, but they had so much fun together it hardly mattered. They would wake in the wee hours to brew coffee, e-mail home, and talk. "We're so in synch," Lowe wrote in a dispatch to Mountainzone.com, "words become superfluous—I'm awake—Rad's awake, my still, small voice speaks to me and echoes its words to Conrad. Partners are golden and Conrad's the motherload."

On October 5, 1999, the two partners, together with cameraman Dave Bridges, were crossing a flat section of glacier when they heard a crack high above. A huge avalanche began heading straight down toward the glacier. Lowe and Bridges ran downhill—Anker thinks they intended to jump into a crevasse—and Anker ran horizontally. Lying flat, he dug in his ice ax, only to be blown down the mountain. "It dragged me about 20 meters along the snow," Anker would later write. "It cut my head in four different spots, broke two ribs and stretched out my shoulder from the socket. During the course of this, I thought that I was going to die. Then light came and I realized I was alive." Holding his watch, Anker began searching for Lowe and Bridges, knowing that the last seconds of their lives were ticking away. Several hours later, Anker endured what he calls "the worst moment of my life." He used the expedition's satellite phone to call Jennifer Lowe.

*   *   *

Many career climbers, as they get older, yearn to come down off the mountaintop with something to say, some essential wisdom that will translate all those years of lonely, dangerous struggle into something of value to the rest of the world. Anker is no exception. Where most of the Shishapangma dispatches offer quick, sketchy impressions of the trip, Anker's tend to be thoughtful essays on moral matters— some serious, like his reflections on the Chinese occupation of Tibet, and some comedic, like his mock diatribe on the deplorable preponderance of fake plants (*"palm frondus plasticus, lilyus nylonus,* and *carnation imposteroti"*) in the LAX terminal. In *The Lost Explorer,* his Mallory book, Anker writes that he tries to use his slide shows and ski outings "to talk about being a good person, about how anger and hatred disrupt an expedition, about how sometimes it takes a little more effort to be positive than negative, but that it's ultimately life-enriching."

Last November, Anker traveled to a Marriott conference center in San Ramon, California, a few miles east of San Francisco Bay, to give what he called the "state of the union" speech at a sales conference for The North Face. A poster on the ballroom's back wall featured the perpetual ghost in Anker's life, Alex Lowe, dangling from a Baffin Island cliff. Anker stepped to the podium and began his presentation, "An Alpinist's View of the Fall 2001 Selling Season," by projecting a slide of himself high on the Grand Teton. Leaning toward his notes and furrowing his freckled brow, Anker declared, "A lot of the things we believe in climbing are very similar to what is there in business. There's a good metaphor that goes with doing business: doing an expedition, doing a climb." The targeted summit, apparently, was $240 million in annual sales. Successive slides interspersed more glory shots of Anker with the motivational steps common to climbing and high-end retail fashion: Identify the Goal, Select the Route, Create Your Team, Climb, Believe, Summit.

Anker was, admittedly, just doing his job—thus the hokey nature of his speech—but a messianic side to his character does seem to have blossomed since Lowe's death. He talks a great deal about using his fame to spread his "message," a loose amalgam of Buddhism, environmentalism, and adventure-sports boosterism. I once asked who his heroes were, and Anker replied, "Reinhold Messner, of course—but that's just a sports thing. My real heroes are the guys getting change done, like Mother Teresa, the Dalai Lama, Martin Luther King, Gandhi." As evidenced by his North Face speech, Anker has also been drawn to that most enduring of aging-climber axioms: *I have gotten to one extraordinary summit after another by adhering to principles that will see you through to your own summits, whatever they may be.*

It seems both ironic and natural that the one struggle in which those principles cannot help Anker is the job of reconciling himself to what climbing has cost him. He told me, for example, that the turnaround moment in his mourning of Mugs Stump came during the Khan-Tengri speed-climbing competition, when Anker saved a Russian climber's life. "I felt then," he said, "that there's something good to climbing, there was a meaning to it." Anker has saved quite a few lives in situations that he could easily have ignored. But the tortured logic of validating one climbing death by preventing another exposes the limits of climbing as a universal metaphor. What kind of game is redeemed by the opportunity it offers to save lives risked only in playing it?

Seth Shaw's death last May in Alaska, only seven months after the disaster on Shishapangma, brought Anker a new kind of regret. In a sense, he had long ago left Shaw behind. Shaw had stayed in Salt Lake City, working as an avalanche forecaster, and their near-fatal 1991 Alaska trip was the last time they climbed together. It was also, in the view of Durango climber Kennan Harvey, a good friend of Shaw's, "the last pure"—i.e., noncommercial—"expedition Conrad's done."

Anker was in Telluride, accepting an Adventurer of the Year award from Polartec, when he heard that Shaw had been killed. "Jenny and the little guys were there," Anker told me, "and at the time it was really hard to deal with it, because here I am—I've got the kids now, they want to go stay at a hotel with a swimming pool and watch the cartoons. And I realized how close Seth was to me, and we'd had a trip planned, and I'd backed out of it and decided to do a trip with Peter Croft and Galen Rowell instead . . ." Anker's attention wandered for a moment, perhaps distracted by what he'd implied—that he'd chosen a trip with a bigger-name partner and a bigger-name photographer.

Shaw, like Stump and Lowe, remains buried on the mountain where he died. Shaw's family and friends held a memorial service in Salt Lake City, planting a tree for him in Little Cottonwood Canyon, near a taller one planted for Stump in 1992. By most accounts Anker gave a beautiful eulogy, but Harvey, who attended the memorial, feels that there was something detached, almost impersonal, in Anker's delivery. "Conrad was out of touch there, because he'd had to move on," Harvey says.

Doug Heinrich, another old friend of Anker and Shaw, considers Anker's dilemma just "part of being a star. Your career, to a certain degree, takes the place of a lot of what sometimes seems mundane, like your day-to-day interaction with your friends. And once that's gone, it creates a huge void, especially when your friends pass away."

A few days after his North Face speech, just before he flew back to Montana, I met Anker for breakfast at a café in Berkeley. He was unshaven and looked exhausted. Twenty years of mountain sun and a year and a half of personal upheaval showed in the wrinkles around his mouth and eyes.

After coffee and eggs took the raw edge off his mood, I asked him to talk about what Alex Lowe had been going through toward the end of his life. Lowe, he said, had grown tired of back-to-back climbing expeditions, their canned commercial agendas, and of the time they took away from Jennifer and their three boys. Lowe's Shishapangma dispatches make frequent mention of his family, and he muses several times about the relatively frivolous nature of climbing. No one is in a better position than Anker to understand the bitter irony—that Lowe was preoccupied with climbing's calculus of selfishness just as the self-indulgence inherent in the sport was about to exact its greatest toll.

Later that morning, Anker drove us to the Berkeley Marina. Sitting on a bench under a chilly blue sky, he acknowledged how devastating the first six months after Lowe's death had been. At the suggestion of a friend at The North Face, he'd spoken to a therapist. "It was worthless," Anker said with palpable contempt. "Maybe I was defensive or angry, but she didn't get where I was coming from." In his anguish, Anker turned to Jon Krakauer and confessed he'd had thoughts of suicide. "I said, 'Jon, it's fucked up,' and Jon goes, 'Yeah, it's normal. You're just angry, and you feel like your friend's been cheated, or you've been cheated, and you're wondering why did it end up like this.'"

A hard wind blew across San Francisco Bay. His hands deep in his pockets, Anker told me that he'd found the most solace in the friendship of Gil Roberts, a San Francisco emergency-room doctor who was a member of the 1963 expedition on which Jim Whittaker became the first American to summit Everest. Roberts had been walking through the Khumbu Icefall beside a friend, Jake Breitenbach, when Roberts stopped to wipe his goggles. Breitenbach took a few steps forward, a block of ice fell on him, and he was never seen again. Hearing about Lowe's death, Roberts contacted Anker and talked to him about survivor's guilt—shortly before, as it turned out, Roberts discovered that he had metastasized melanoma and only a few months to live.

"Climbing is a good thing," Anker told me, switching abruptly from dazed emotion to his formal spokesman mode. "It's about the experience I had with Gil just before he died. We spent a day and talked about how death changes your view on life and makes you live life fuller."

It was an extraordinary thing to say: *Climbing is a good thing—it's about hearing a dying man's views on death.* And yet, why not? Climbing's relentless encounter with death appears to teach a twinned lesson. On the one hand, the sentiment captured in Psalm 103, which was read over the body of George Mallory high on Everest: "As for man, his days are like grass; as a flower of the field, so he flourisheth. For the wind passeth over it, and it is gone." On the other hand: Enjoy it while it lasts.

Bozeman, Montana, with snow thick on the surrounding Rockies and cottonwoods, and holiday lights on the eaves of all the Queen Annes just off main street, couldn't be a more picturesque mountain village. It also couldn't feel more like Alex Lowe's town. Barrel Mountaineering, down the street from the single-screen movie theater, has a kind of shrine to Lowe, with a signed poster hanging near a framed photograph of Lowe that someone has draped with white gauze. Barrel maintains a first-ascents binder in which local climbers, after establishing new routes, pen descriptions and attach photos. It might as well be Lowe's personal scrapbook. And when 1,400 people showed up late last year for Anker's Mallory slide show, it was a tribute to just how much Lowe mattered in the town in which Anker now lives with Lowe's family.

The boisterous audience quieted as Anker took the stage of the Bozeman High School auditorium. "As I'm sure some of you already know," he began, "Alex Lowe died in an avalanche last year." The auditorium fell silent, and Anker did a remarkable thing. "Alex died," he said, "and I survived, and I don't know why. By some miracle, I'm here, and in the memory of Alex, and of carrying on what Alex began with his family—Jenny and Sam and Max and Isaac—we're together." Anker paused then, as if to make sure everyone realized that he had just opened a slide show entitled "The Mystery of Mallory and Irvine" with a public declaration on the nature of his domestic and romantic arrangements. "And that's the best way that I can honor Alex . . . and I just thought that I'd say that and get that out there."

Shortly after Lowe's death, Anker talked about the loss of his friend with Tom Brokaw, on *Dateline NBC,* adding, "There's an unwritten thing that should one of the others make it through something, we would be there to help out." One can certainly imagine a warrior code by which duty demands that Anker look after Lowe's wife and kids. Anker has a strong desire to see—and to have others see—his actions as motivated by a clear moral purpose. I suspect that the appeal of climbing, for Anker, lies to some degree in its simulacrum of this clarity. When everything goes right, a climb can be very much the way he described it at the North Face sales conference—you always know exactly where you're coming from (the bottom), exactly where you're going (the top), and exactly what means you'll use to get there (gear, ability, and daring). But life has thoroughly undermined Anker's straightforward worldview, and no such surety is available in his current adventure, nor will it ever be again.

Anker later told me that Jennifer's once-skeptical friends were duly impressed by his words that night in Bozeman. (Jennifer Lowe declined to be interviewed for this article.) But who can really say if one best honors a fallen comrade by marrying his widow? Why even ask the question? Sir Edmund Hillary married the widow of a former expedition partner, and he ascribes the union to the very things that might well be drawing Anker and Jennifer together: mutual affection, common interests, a shared sense of loss.

The next day we spent the afternoon driving around town. Anker told me he'd been awake since 2:30 that morning—not the first time he'd alluded to missing sleep. He had a lot of organizational work to do for an upcoming Antarctica trip with Krakauer and a NOVA film crew, the subject of a PBS documentary on global warming scheduled to air in winter 2002. Around 8 A.M., Anker had walked the Lowe boys to school, and by noon, when he picked me up, he had already bought $800 worth of food for the expedition. The bed of his old Japanese truck—or, rather, Alex's truck, as Anker noted—sagged from piles and piles of plastic bags full of vegetable protein, nuts and dried fruit, brown rice, and black beans. We stopped first at a small sound studio where Anker recorded voice-overs for the IMAX film on Shackleton. We moved on to an office-supply store and then a mountaineering store. In each, people spotted Anker and asked about the Lowes. At the end of the day, we sat down in a bistro that hadn't opened yet. A waitress recognized Anker and gave us a booth.

Anker had been talking constantly about the Lowe boys. "One kid's one thing," he said, "but *three* kids, all boys and all hyperactive, bouncing off each other like neutrons—it makes a real challenge for Jenny. So Isaac and I do the alphabet, and Sam and I read, and Max and I do math, and it's a really good thing. I won't have children of my own, so that's . . ." His face tightened, and that "message" voice came back on again: "But overpopulation is the bane of our planet, and I'd always questioned the value of adding more souls to the world. So this is . . . These are good kids, and they deserve a chance to enjoy a normal childhood."

Someone cranked up "Jingle Bells" until it shook the empty room. When they'd turned it back down, Anker seemed slightly deflated. "I do feel bad leaving town now," he admitted, "especially over Christmas. You know what Max said? He's like, 'Dad was only here for two Christmases, and now *you're* going away for Christmas.' "

Daylight had faded from the snow-covered street outside. "We do talk about Alex every day," Anker said, "and things Alex did, and we do little special things for the boys, like work on the scrapbook and get out Alex's collection of old nickels." He added that he and Jennifer had been on a sort of tour of places she and Alex visited together—Telluride, Yosemite. "It's kind of taking the edges off," Anker said. "There's a lot of rough edges still . . ." His voice drifted, and he looked into his cup. "There's things that really set her off, and I could be wallowing in all this, but I've got to be a pillar of support to this family."

It occurred to me then that love, mourning, and Anker's ongoing life as a climber are all inextricably bound together right now. Anker has the difficult job of keeping his predecessor's flame burning for the family he calls his own—never will Anker be able to declare that he'd prefer not to hear about his wife's late husband again. After all, he too grieves for Lowe every single day. "For the first six months," he said, "it kind of felt like I'd lost my arm. There was this missing part of me. I would keep thinking, 'Well maybe the phone's going to ring and it's going to be him, saying, 'Yeah, yeah, what's up?'"

Anker had channeled his best memory of Lowe's voice, and it seemed to alarm him, as if he'd spoken Lowe back into being. "You know," Anker went on, "I still kept thinking, up until one year after the accident, that he was going to come back. I had these dreams that he would come back and he'd be like, 'What are you doing here?'" Anker's voice filled, for a moment, with genuine agony: "I'd go, 'Alex, man . . . here.'" With that, Anker leaned back and raised both hands in a resigned and desolate gesture of letting go, relinquishing any claim.

The waitress flipped over the "Open" sign, and I asked Anker if he'd ever thought about the disconnect between his turmoil and the picture of climbing he'd given to The North Face sales team.

"That's just the rosy side of climbing that people want to hear," he replied, shifting in his seat. "They don't want to hear that we all have demons somewhere driving us." Anker looked away briefly. "Putting yourself in that much harm's way, you've got to."

"To what degree did you feel like you were—"

"Lying through my teeth?" He laughed. "I don't think I was."

But could he ever communicate to such a group the things he's actually learned in climbing? About loss, loneliness, ambition?

"They wouldn't understand. I don't understand."

And how could he? Love is hard enough to find without questioning where we find it. Nobody knows an easy way to get over the deaths of people we care about. And while Anker does have a family counting on him for the first time in his adult life, he has also spent 20 years becoming a world-class climber. However he spins it in slide shows, his life has at its very core a deliberate dance with the reaper. "On Everest," he told me, "death is right there. It's sort of like you're underwater, and there's this sort of semipermeable membrane, this gel that surrounds you, because you have warm boots and gloves and an oxygen apparatus. But you can kind of push through this thing, and there's death right out there. All your energy becomes focused on living, on surviving. That's the allure."

Anker says he wants to do more film and TV work. He has talked The North Face into moving its climbing-hardware division to Bozeman, which could provide him with long-term security. And he talks about staying off avalanche-prone 8,000-meter peaks. This will not be easy. Anker is coming into his physical prime as a high-altitude climber; on the very biggest mountains, experience and endurance count for more than fast-twitch muscle speed. He finally summited Everest on the Mallory expedition, his first trip into the so-called Death Zone, that realm where the air is too thin for long-term human survival. In the process, he proved what every climber hopes to: that his body performs very, very well there. The moment for Anker to make a permanent mark is now.

And even if he chooses not to defy the critics of risk-averse, high-publicity commercial expeditions—what is sometimes called "guaranteed-outcome mountaineering"—Anker will still make a good living as a member of The North Face Climbing Team. He loves the mountains of Antarctica, and he dreams of accepting an invitation to join his hero, Reinhold Messner, on Cerro Torre, where Messner wants to repeat the famous Ferrari Route. Talking about it, Anker's eyes lit up—the pure climber thrilling to the next great vision.

But Cerro Torre and Antarctica are, of course, both in the Southern Hemisphere, where the climbing season coincides with Thanksgiving and Christmas, the very holidays that Anker doesn't want to miss again. He also knows that none of his friends died pushing their limits. Stump, Lowe, and Shaw all vanished in unforeseeable mishaps on relatively easy terrain. Their deaths argue that it is not the difficulty level that kills the best climbers, nor the presence of film crews, but the sheer amount of time they spend in the high mountains.

Night had fallen by the time Anker and I stepped back outside. Just before we parted, I pressed him with a final question. How would he feel about dying on this trip to Antarctica? Would it seem an honorable climber's death?

"No," he replied, "it would be really bad. I would just have let people down. For the person who dies, it's like a lightbulb going out, but the pain for people who are still there . . . It would be really quite foolish." His intelligent eyes widened, as if the possibility were terribly real. Then Anker wrapped both arms around himself, looked away, and said, mostly to himself, "I've got to keep my ass really safe."

May 2001

As Freezing Persons Recollect the Snow—First Chill—Then Stupor—Then the Letting Go

PETER STARK

When your Jeep spins lazily off the mountain road and slams backward into a snowbank, you don't worry immediately about the cold. Your first thought is that you've just dented your bumper. Your second is that you've failed to bring a shovel. Your third is that you'll be late for dinner. Friends are expecting you at their cabin around eight for a moonlight ski, a late dinner, a sauna. Nothing can keep you from that.

Driving out of town, defroster roaring, you barely noted the bank thermometer on the town square: minus 27 degrees at 6:36. The radio weather report warned of a deep mass of arctic air settling over the region. The man who took your money at the Conoco station shook his head at the register and said he wouldn't be going anywhere tonight if he were you. You smiled. A little chill never hurt anybody with enough fleece and a good four-wheel drive.

But now you're stuck. Jamming the gearshift into low, you try to muscle out of the drift. The tires whine on ice-slicked snow as headlights dance on the curtain of frosted firs across the road. Shoving the lever back into park, you shoulder open the door and step from your heated capsule. Cold slaps your naked face, squeezes tears from your eyes.

You check your watch: 7:18. You consult your map: A thin, switch-backing line snakes up the mountain to the penciled square that marks the cabin.

Breath rolls from you in short frosted puffs. The Jeep lies cocked sideways in the snowbank like an empty turtle shell. You think of firelight and saunas and warm food and wine. You look again at the map. It's maybe five or six miles more to that penciled square. You run that far every day before breakfast. You'll just put on your skis. No problem.

There is no precise core temperature at which the human body perishes from cold. At Dachau's cold-water immersion baths, Nazi doctors calculated death to arrive at around 77 degrees Fahrenheit. The lowest recorded core temperature in a surviving adult is 60.8 degrees. For a child it's lower: In 1994, a two-year-old girl in Saskatchewan wandered out of her house into a minus-40 night. She was found near her doorstep the next morning, limbs frozen solid, her core temperature 57 degrees. She lived.

Others are less fortunate, even in much milder conditions. One of Europe's worst weather disasters occurred during a 1964 competitive walk on a windy, rainy English moor; three of the racers died from hypothermia, though temperatures never fell below freezing and ranged as high as 45.

But for all scientists and statisticians now know of freezing and its physiology, no one can yet predict exactly how quickly and in whom hypothermia will strike—and whether it will kill when it does. The cold remains a mystery, more prone to fell men than women, more lethal to the thin and well muscled than to those with avoirdupois, and least forgiving to the arrogant and the unaware.

The process begins even before you leave the car, when you remove your gloves to squeeze a loose bail back into one of your ski bindings. The freezing metal bites your flesh. Your skin temperature drops.

Within a few seconds, the palms of your hands are a chilly, painful 60 degrees. Instinctively, the web of surface capillaries on your hands constrict, sending blood coursing away from your skin and deeper into your torso. Your body is allowing your fingers to chill in order to keep its vital organs warm.

You replace your gloves, noticing only that your fingers have numbed slightly. Then you kick boots into bindings and start up the road.

Were you a Norwegian fisherman or Inuit hunter, both of whom frequently work gloveless in the cold, your chilled hands would open their surface capillaries periodically to allow surges of warm blood to pass into them and maintain their flexibility. This phenomenon, known as the hunter's response, can elevate a 35-degree skin temperature to 50 degrees within seven or eight minutes.

Other human adaptations to the cold are more mysterious. Tibetan Buddhist monks can raise the skin temperature of their hands and feet by 15 degrees through meditation. Australian aborigines, who once slept on the ground, unclothed, on near-freezing nights, would slip into a light hypothermic state, suppressing shivering until the rising sun rewarmed them.

You have no such defenses, having spent your days at a keyboard in a climate-controlled office. Only after about ten minutes of hard climbing, as your body temperature rises, does blood start seeping back into your fingers. Sweat trickles down your sternum and spine.

By now you've left the road and decided to shortcut up the forested mountainside to the road's next switchback. Treading slowly through deep, soft snow as the full moon hefts over a spiny ridgetop, throwing silvery bands of moonlight and shadow, you think your friends were right: It's a beautiful night for skiing—though you admit, feeling the minus-30 air bite at your face, it's also cold.

After an hour, there's still no sign of the switchback, and you've begun to worry. You pause to check the map. At this moment, your core temperature reaches its high: 100.8. Climbing in deep snow, you've generated nearly ten times as much body heat as you do when you are resting.

As you step around to orient map to forest, you hear a metallic pop. You look down. The loose bail has disappeared from your binding. You lift your foot and your ski falls from your boot.

You twist on your flashlight, and its cold-weakened batteries throw a yellowish circle in the snow. It's right around here somewhere, you think, as you sift the snow through gloved fingers. Focused so intently on finding the bail, you hardly notice the frigid air pressing against your tired body and sweat-soaked clothes.

The exertion that warmed you on the way uphill now works against you: Your exercise-dilated capillaries carry the excess heat of your core to your skin, and your wet clothing dispels it rapidly into the night. The lack of insulating fat over your muscles allows the cold to creep that much closer to your warm blood.

Your temperature begins to plummet. Within 17 minutes it reaches the normal 98.6. Then it slips below.

At 97 degrees, hunched over in your slow search, the muscles along your neck and shoulders tighten in what's known as pre-shivering muscle tone. Sensors have signaled the temperature control center in your hypothalamus, which in turn has ordered the constriction of the entire web of surface capillaries. Your hands and feet begin to ache with cold. Ignoring the pain, you dig carefully through the snow; another ten minutes pass. Without the bail you know you're in deep trouble.

Finally, nearly 45 minutes later, you find the bail. You even manage to pop it back into its socket and clamp your boot into the binding. But the clammy chill that started around your skin has now wrapped deep into your body's core.

At 95, you've entered the zone of mild hypothermia. You're now trembling violently as your body attains its maximum shivering response, an involuntary condition in which your muscles contract rapidly to generate additional body heat.

It was a mistake, you realize, to come out on a night this cold. You should turn back. Fishing into the front pocket of your shell parka, you fumble out the map. You consulted it to get here; it should be able to guide you back to the warm car. It doesn't occur to you in your increasingly clouded and panicky mental state that you could simply follow your tracks down the way you came.

And after this long stop, the skiing itself has become more difficult. By the time you push off downhill, your muscles have cooled and tight-ened so dramatically that they no longer contract easily, and once con-tracted, they won't relax. You're locked into an ungainly, spread-armed, weak-kneed snowplow.

Still, you manage to maneuver between stands of fir, swishing down through silvery light and pools of shadow. You're too cold to think of the beautiful night or of the friends you had meant to see. You think only of the warm Jeep that waits for you somewhere at the bottom of the hill. Its gleaming shell is centered in your mind's eye as you come over the crest of a small knoll. You hear the sudden whistle of wind in your ears as you gain speed. Then, before your mind can quite process what the sight means, you notice a lump in the snow ahead.

Recognizing, slowly, the danger that you are in, you try to jam your skis to a stop. But in your panic, your balance and judgment are poor. Moments later, your ski tips plow into the buried log and you sail headfirst through the air and bellyflop into the snow.

You lie still. There's a dead silence in the forest, broken by the pumping of blood in your ears. Your ankle is throbbing with pain and you've hit your head. You've also lost your hat and a glove. Scratchy snow is packed down your shirt. Meltwater trickles down your neck and spine, joined soon by a thin line of blood from a small cut on your head.

This situation, you realize with an immediate sense of panic, is serious. Scrambling to rise, you collapse in pain, your ankle crumpling beneath you.

As you sink back into the snow, shaken, your heat begins to drain away at an alarming rate, your head alone accounting for 50 percent of the loss. The pain of the cold soon pierces your ears so sharply that you root about in the snow until you find your hat and mash it back onto your head.

But even that little activity has been exhausting. You know you should find your glove as well, and yet you're becoming too weary to feel any urgency. You decide to have a short rest before going on.

An hour passes. At one point, a stray thought says you should start being scared, but fear is a concept that floats somewhere beyond your immediate reach, like that numb hand lying naked in the snow. You've slid into the temperature range at which cold renders the enzymes in your brain less efficient. With every one-degree drop in body temperature below 95, your cerebral metabolic rate falls off by 3 to 5 percent. When your core temperature reaches 93, amnesia nibbles at your consciousness. You check your watch: 12:58. Maybe someone will come looking for you soon. Moments later, you check again. You can't keep the numbers in your head. You'll remember little of what happens next.

Your head drops back. The snow crunches softly in your ear. In the minus-35-degree air, your core temperature falls about one degree every 30 to 40 minutes, your body heat leaching out into the soft, enveloping snow. Apathy at 91 degrees. Stupor at 90.

You've now crossed the boundary into profound hypothermia. By the time your core temperature has fallen to 88 degrees, your body has abandoned the urge to warm itself by shivering. Your blood is thickening like crankcase oil in a cold engine. Your oxygen consumption, a measure of your metabolic rate, has fallen by more than a quarter. Your kidneys, however, work overtime to process the fluid overload that occurred when the blood vessels in your extremities constricted and squeezed fluids toward your center. You feel a powerful urge to urinate, the only thing you feel at all.

By 87 degrees you've lost the ability to recognize a familiar face, should one suddenly appear from the woods.

At 86 degrees, your heart, its electrical impulses hampered by chilled nerve tissues, becomes arrhythmic. It now pumps less than two-thirds the normal amount of blood. The lack of oxygen and the slowing metabolism of your brain, meanwhile, begin to trigger visual and auditory hallucinations.

You hear jingle bells. Lifting your face from your snow pillow, you realize with a surge of gladness that they're not sleigh bells; they're welcoming bells hanging from the door of your friends' cabin. You knew it had to be close by. The jingling is the sound of the cabin door opening, just through the fir trees.

Attempting to stand, you collapse in a tangle of skis and poles. That's OK. You can crawl. It's so close.

Hours later, or maybe it's minutes, you realize the cabin still sits beyond the grove of trees. You've crawled only a few feet. The light on your wristwatch pulses in the darkness: 5:20. Exhausted, you decide to rest your head for a moment.

When you lift it again, you're inside, lying on the floor before the wood stove. The fire throws off a red glow. First it's warm; then it's hot; then it's searing your flesh. Your clothing has caught fire.

At 85 degrees, those freezing to death, in a strange, anguished paroxysm, often rip off their clothes. This phenomenon, known as paradoxical undressing, is common enough that urban hypothermia victims are sometimes initially diagnosed as victims of sexual assault. Though researchers are uncertain of the cause, the most logical explanation is that shortly before loss of consciousness, the constricted blood vessels near the body's surface suddenly dilate and produce a sensation of extreme heat against the skin.

All you know is that you're burning. You claw off your shell and pile sweater and fling them away.

But then, in a final moment of clarity, you realize there's no stove, no cabin, no friends. You're lying alone in the bitter cold, naked from the waist up. You grasp your terrible misunderstanding, a whole series of misunderstandings, like a dream ratcheting into wrongness. You've shed your clothes, your car, your oil-heated house in town. Without this ingenious technology you're simply a delicate, tropical organism whose range is restricted to a narrow sunlit band that girds the earth at the equator.

And you've now ventured way beyond it.

There's an adage about hypothermia: "You aren't dead until you're warm and dead."

At about 6:00 the next morning, his friends, having discovered the stalled Jeep, find him, still huddled inches from the buried log, his gloveless hand shoved into his armpit. The flesh of his limbs is waxy and stiff as old putty, his pulse nonexistent, his pupils unresponsive to light. Dead.

But those who understand cold know that even as it deadens, it offers perverse salvation. Heat is a presence: the rapid vibrating of molecules. Cold is an absence: the damping of the vibrations. At absolute zero, minus 459.67 degrees Fahrenheit, molecular motion ceases altogether. It is this slowing that converts gases to liquids, liquids to solids, and renders solids harder. It slows bacterial growth and chemical reactions. In the human body, cold shuts down metabolism. The lungs take in less oxygen, the heart pumps less blood. Under normal temperatures, this would produce brain damage. But the chilled brain, having slowed its own metabolism, needs far less oxygen-rich blood and can, under the right circumstances, survive intact.

Setting her ear to his chest, one of his rescuers listens intently. Seconds pass. Then, faintly, she hears a tiny sound—a single thump, so slight that it might be the sound of her own blood. She presses her ear harder to the cold flesh. Another faint thump, then another.

The slowing that accompanies freezing is, in its way, so beneficial that it is even induced at times. Cardiologists today often use deep chilling to slow a patient's metabolism in preparation for heart or brain surgery. In this state of near suspension, the patient's blood flows slowly, his heart rarely beats—or in the case of those on heart-lung machines, doesn't beat at all; death seems near. But carefully monitored, a patient can remain in this cold stasis, undamaged, for hours.

The rescuers quickly wrap their friend's naked torso with a spare parka, his hands with mittens, his entire body with a bivy sack. They brush snow from his pasty, frozen face. Then one snakes down through the forest to the nearest cabin. The others, left in the pre-dawn darkness, huddle against him as silence closes around them. For a moment, the woman imagines she can hear the scurrying, breathing, snoring of a world of creatures that have taken cover this frigid night beneath the thick quilt of snow.

With a "one, two, three," the doctor and nurses slide the man's stiff, curled form onto a table fitted with a mattress filled with warm water which will be regularly reheated. They'd been warned that they had a profound hypothermia case coming in. Usually such victims can be straightened from their tortured fetal positions. This one can't.

Technicians scissor with stainless-steel shears at the man's urine-soaked long underwear and shell pants, frozen together like corrugated cardboard. They attach heart-monitor electrodes to his chest and insert a low-temperature electronic thermometer into his rectum. Digital readings flash: 24 beats per minute and a core temperature of 79.2 degrees.

The doctor shakes his head. He can't remember seeing numbers so low. He's not quite sure how to revive this man without killing him.

In fact, many hypothermia victims die each year in the process of being rescued. In "rewarming shock," the constricted capillaries reopen almost all at once, causing a sudden drop in blood pressure. The slightest movement can send a victim's heart muscle into wild spasms of ventricular fibrillation. In 1980, 16 shipwrecked Danish fishermen were hauled to safety after an hour and a half in the frigid North Sea. They then walked across the deck of the rescue ship, stepped below for a hot drink, and dropped dead, all 16 of them.

"78.9," a technician calls out. "That's three-tenths down."

The patient is now experiencing "afterdrop," in which residual cold close to the body's surface continues to cool the core even after the victim is removed from the outdoors.

The doctor rapidly issues orders to his staff: intravenous administration of warm saline, the bag first heated in the microwave to 110 degrees. Elevating the core temperature of an average-size male one degree requires adding about 60 kilocalories of heat. A kilocalorie is the amount of heat needed to raise the temperature of one liter of water one degree Celsius. Since a quart of hot soup at 140 degrees offers about 30 kilocalories, the patient curled on the table would need to consume 40 quarts of chicken broth to push his core temperature up to normal. Even the warm saline, infused directly into his blood, will add only 30 kilocalories.

Ideally, the doctor would have access to a cardiopulmonary bypass machine, with which he could pump out the victim's blood, rewarm and oxygenate it, and pump it back in again, safely raising the core temperature as much as one degree every three minutes. But such machines are rarely available outside major urban hospitals. Here, without such equipment, the doctor must rely on other options.

"Let's scrub for surgery," he calls out.

Moments later, he's sliding a large catheter into an incision in the man's abdominal cavity. Warm fluid begins to flow from a suspended bag, washing through his abdomen and draining out through another catheter placed in another incision. Prosaically, this lavage operates much like a car radiator in reverse: The solution warms the internal organs, and the warm blood in the organs is then pumped by the heart throughout the body.

The patient's stiff limbs begin to relax. His pulse edges up. But even so the jagged line of his heartbeat flashing across the EKG screen shows the curious dip known as a J wave, common to hypothermia patients.

"Be ready to defibrillate," the doctor warns the EMTs.

For another hour, nurses and EMTs hover around the edges of the table where the patient lies centered in a warm pool of light, as if offered up to the sun god. They check his heart. They check the heat of the mattress beneath him. They whisper to one another about the foolishness of having gone out alone tonight.

And slowly the patient responds. Another liter of saline is added to the IV. The man's blood pressure remains far too low, brought down by the blood flowing out to the fast-opening capillaries of his limbs. Fluid lost through perspiration and urination has reduced his blood volume. But every 15 or 20 minutes, his temperature rises another degree. The immediate danger of cardiac fibrillation lessens, as the heart and thinning blood warm. Frostbite could still cost him fingers or an earlobe. But he appears to have beaten back the worst of the frigidity.

For the next half hour, an EMT quietly calls the readouts of the thermometer, a mantra that marks the progress of this cold-blooded proto-organism toward a state of warmer, higher consciousness.

"90.4 . . ."

"92.2 . . ."

From somewhere far away in the immense, cold darkness, you hear a faint, insistent hum. Quickly it mushrooms into a ball of sound, like a planet rushing toward you, and then it becomes a stream of words.

A voice is calling your name.

You don't want to open your eyes. You sense heat and light playing against your eyelids, but beneath their warm dance a chill wells up inside you from the sunless ocean bottoms and the farthest depths of space. You are too tired even to shiver. You want only to sleep.

"Can you hear me?"

You force open your eyes. Lights glare overhead. Around the lights faces hover atop uniformed bodies. You try to think: You've been away a very long time, but where have you been?

"You're at the hospital. You got caught in the cold." '

You try to nod. Your neck muscles feel rusted shut, unused for years. They respond to your command with only a slight twitch.

"You'll probably have amnesia," the voice says.

You remember the moon rising over the spiky ridgetop and skiing up toward it, toward someplace warm beneath the frozen moon. After that, nothing—only that immense coldness lodged inside you.

"We're trying to get a little warmth back into you," the voice says.

You'd nod if you could. But you can't move. All you can feel is throbbing discomfort everywhere. Glancing down to where the pain is most biting, you notice blisters filled with clear fluid dotting your fingers, once gloveless in the snow. During the long, cold hours the tissue froze and ice crystals formed in the tiny spaces between your cells, sucking water from them, blocking the blood supply. You stare at them absently.

"I think they'll be fine," a voice from overhead says. "The damage looks superficial. We expect that the blisters will break in a week or so, and the tissue should revive after that."

If not, you know that your fingers will eventually turn black, the color of bloodless, dead tissue. And then they will be amputated.

But worry slips from you as another wave of exhaustion sweeps in. Slowly you drift off, dreaming of warmth, of tropical ocean wavelets breaking across your chest, of warm sand beneath you.

Hours later, still logy and numb, you surface, as if from deep under water. A warm tide seems to be flooding your midsection. Focusing your eyes down there with difficulty, you see tubes running into you, their heat mingling with your abdomen's depthless cold like a churned-up river. You follow the tubes to the bag that hangs suspended beneath the electric light.

And with a lurch that would be a sob if you could make a sound, you begin to understand: The bag contains all that you had so nearly lost. These people huddled around you have brought you sunlight and warmth, things you once so cavalierly dismissed as constant, available, yours, summoned by the simple twisting of a knob or tossing on of a layer.

But in the hours since you last believed that, you've traveled to a place where there is no sun. You've seen that in the infinite reaches of the universe, heat is as glorious and ephemeral as the light of the stars. Heat exists only where matter exists, where particles can vibrate and jump. In the infinite winter of space, heat is tiny; it is the cold that is huge.

Someone speaks. Your eyes move from bright lights to shadowy forms in the dim outer reaches of the room. You recognize the voice of one of the friends you set out to visit, so long ago now. She's smiling down at you crookedly.

"It's cold out there," she says. "Isn't it?"

January 1997

Dark Behind It Rose the Forest

RANDALL SULLIVAN

An image rushes back out of Santa Anita Canyon, more metaphor than omen, I hope, perhaps just a random bit of carnage to which I attach resonance.

I'm barely half a mile from the Foothill Freeway, looking over my left shoulder at the gorgeous lie that is Los Angeles after a rainfall. I steal a parting glance toward the most magnificent racetrack in America, laid out in geometric verdure, its lush grounds fringed with palm fronds that wear sunlight like a coat of lacquer. I can't see the hyacinths blooming, but I know they are, in a hundred festive colors.

The government-green Ford Bronco in which I am riding (the barrel of a 12-gauge shotgun hard against my thigh) continues its climb up Santa Anita Canyon Road along a center divider growing philodendrons with leaves the size of elephant ears. On each side of the road between cross streets with names like Hacienda and El Vista are low-slung, ranch-style homes. The lawns are so perfect they look as if they should be maintained not with mowers but with vacuum cleaners. In every other yard stands an orange or lemon tree, heavy with fruit. A white picket fence, freshly painted, surrounds the last house.

Just beyond, the road is straddled by a scabrous steel gate that closes each evening at 10 P.M. We pass through and enter a wide curve where I lean into a deadfall drop, looking down on red tile roofs and kidney-shaped swimming pools. The Bronco is still in second gear, but there's an abrupt sense of acceleration—almost of time travel—as the landscape is transformed in an instant.

The blue shimmer of swimming pools vanishes behind walls of red clay and granite, spiked with yucca, spilling clumps of chaparral. The pavement narrows, unwinding into a short straightaway, and there they are: the dead skunk, fresh roadkill stretched out across the center line, and the red-capped vulture that is eating its brains. The carrion bird reluctantly raises its bloody beak at our approach and flutters aloft, flapping its wings just above the Bronco until we pass, and then descends to finish its meal.

The stink will be there a week later; the memory will last a lot longer.

We are perhaps 200 yards into Angeles National Forest. It stretches the point to describe these 693,000 acres as wilderness. Wild they are, though, without question.

It was just a bit deeper into this canyon, two and a half miles off the pavement down a dusty fire lane, that Mike Alt met Mr. Potato Head. Alt, an LEO (law-enforcement officer) with the U.S. Forest Service, was surveilling the access route to a large marijuana garden one night when a car, running without headlights, drove up the gravel road and stopped right at the trailhead. Two men climbed out and threw a large plastic bag into the undergrowth. A supply drop, Alt figured, excited that after four nights in the woods he at last was getting some action. The bag, though, just sat.

Alt radioed to his supervisor, Rita Plair, that something wasn't right. Go ahead and check the bag, Plair told him. Alt is a man who likes to believe that he long ago passed the point where anything can surprise him, but even he was taken aback to open the bag and discover a human head, along with a pair of feet.

Unfortunately, Mr. Potato Head (the LEOs give names to all their cases) never would be fully reassembled. The two men who robbed and killed him were arrested a few days later, and one of them admitted cutting up the victim with a chainsaw but swore he couldn't remember what they had done with the rest of him.

Only the gruesome oddity of the Mr. Potato Head case was unusual, I am reminded by Chuck Shamblin, the LEO who is driving the Bronco up Santa Anita Canyon this morning. Discovering the bodies of murder victims is almost a routine thing for those who work in this forest, he says. (Two or three dozen such corpses turn up each year in the Angeles.) Of course, he adds, there's no way of knowing how many are never found. Careful killers bury their victims, and few are so helpful as that group of satanists who marked the spot with a large pentagram laid out in rocks, beneath which lay the remains of their human sacrifice.

They've been seeing more gang killings up here in recent years, Shamblin notes, and these too are ugly but obvious: a young man lying along the side of the road with a bullet hole behind his ear. Circling vultures and the stench of rotting flesh are usually what lead to the discovery of a dead person dumped close to the road. Shamblin wonders, though, about those who have been taken deeper into the forest, forgotten or overlooked.

"It would be interesting if all the bodies could stand up at once, so we could acknowledge them and do a head count," Shamblin observes. I nod; he's been described as a bit of a philosopher.

Fifty feet from the front door of Angeles National Forest headquarters in Arcadia, freeway traffic speeds east just above eye level, visible in fragmented blurs through a screen of eucalyptus and Canary Island pine. Not exactly my picture of a ranger station, I tell Shamblin when we return in the afternoon. He smiles. "Before, our offices were at the Hilton Hotel in Pasadena," he says. "This place is rustic by comparison."

At the very center of the building, in an office without windows, sits the desk where Rita Plair, one of two plainclothes special agents in the Angeles, has placed a large framed photograph of the LEOs under her supervision, all posing in camouflage (faces painted to match), brandishing shotguns and CAR-15 assault rifles with banana clips. Attached is a Post-it note that reads, "Prime Evil Forest."

The Forest Service officers who enforce the laws in this national forest are not exactly spokespersons for its recreational opportunities. I ask Plair about the best places to camp in the Angeles. She looks startled for a moment and then says, "You're asking the wrong person. I wouldn't take my family anywhere in there."

Lots of people do, though. Sixteen million people live in communities on the boundaries of the Angeles, and 30 million visitors a year make it the most heavily used—and abused—national forest. On some weekends, 90,000 vehicles crowd the roads into the Angeles, not all of them driven by people looking for traditional forms of recreation. Last year, 3,159 arrests were made in the forest, and crimes committed here reached double digits in such categories as murder, rape, carjacking, and arson.

"In almost every other national forest, the LEOs spend most of their time enforcing federal natural resource laws," Plair observes, "investigating things like illegal off-roading, tree cutting, theft of forest products, contamination of streams and rivers. We, on the other hand, spend most of our time enforcing state criminal laws. The way we put it is, 'Anything that happens in the city, happens here.'"

For instance, drive-by shootings. "We had one last summer where two groups came to the forest for an outdoor excursion," she recalls. "But then homies from one gang saw homies from another. Words were exchanged, shots were fired, and the next thing you know there's a high-speed car chase through the forest, people shooting at each other through windows." Two young men were wounded, but no one was killed. However, another gang shootout about a month later did rack up a fatality. "A couple of gangbangers got in a fistfight, and one of their friends pulls out a gun," Plair explains. "He fires off a shot but hits his own partner. So to make things right, he shoots and kills the other guy. The place was filled with picnickers, all screaming and running for their lives."

Even most natural resource crimes in the Angeles are subsidiary to some form of felonious activity. Mobile methamphetamine labs, operating mostly out of motor homes and travel trailers, have taken to using the back roads of the forest as places to cook, and their operators have poisoned several mountain streams with chemical waste. "We recently had one above the town of San Dimas where the guy had been dumping his chemicals for years into the reservoir that serves as the main water supply for the surrounding area," Plair recalls. "As it happened, we didn't have a strong federal case against the guy for drugs, but we got him big-time for natural resource contamination."

Hidden Springs and Big Rock Campground are favorite spots for gatherings of white-power groups with a membership base in the nearby communities of Palmdale and Lancaster, and there have been at least two cross burnings in that part of the forest during the last several years. Plair, who is black, has decorated most of one wall in her office with such items as a "White Power" poster that depicts a German soldier riding a Panzer tank like some hideously inflated skateboard, a White Patriot newsletter explaining that the Klan is not a hate group, and a photograph of graffiti that reads, "Niggers say 'OJ.' We say McVeigh."

Arson, which ranks second to marijuana cultivation cases in the number of man-hours consumed, seems to fascinate, confuse, and unsettle the LEOs more than any other crime they investigate. In part it's that they take this crime more personally; every one of the Angeles LEOs worked as a firefighter upon first joining the Forest Service. The deeper reason, though, is more mysterious, something the LEOs can barely indicate, let alone explain.

The majority of fires in the forest are deliberately set. Pyromaniacs, nearly always men, seem literally driven by demons, forces inside that flicker in their eyes and twitch under their skin. As Plair puts it, "Usually they have sexual problems they won't talk about." The second most common variety is what the Forest Service calls "grudge fires," blazes set by people angry at the government.

The 12 LEOs and two special agents who cope with these crimes, and whose jurisdiction encompasses a quarter of the most populous county in the United States, are but a tiny contingent even within the Angeles National Forest staff of 360, yet they face the same big-city problems as their 18,000 urban counterparts elsewhere in Los Angeles County. They are obliged also to investigate the $6 billion in pending civil claims against the Angeles, plus an array of criminal offenses that city cops never see—wildlife poaching, illegal mining, and marijuana farming on a vast scale.

Chuck Shamblin, a long-limbed man whose 54 years are belied by straw-colored hair and the appetite of a teenager, is not unfamiliar with adapting to difficult situations. In Vietnam he was one of the Army Special Forces soldiers known by the euphemistic job description Long Range Reconnaissance Patrol. A lot of people who were in Southeast Asia during those years will tell you the LRRP Green Berets, or "Lurps," were either the craziest or the bravest people on the scene, and certainly among the scariest.

When he left the military and joined the Forest Service back in 1970, however, Shamblin considered himself "a romantic." A national forest was one of the few places, he figured, where you could work outdoors, belong to a team, and serve what was truly a higher good. It seems incredible to him now, Shamblin admits, that until the early eighties, hardly any Forest Service employees carried guns. "In the whole state of California we had only a couple of armed officers," he recalls. "Our traditional mentality in the Forest Service was like the one I came in with, and this made us a little less realistic about dealing with what society had in store for us."

Recent experiences, for example, have taught the LEOs to make eye contact with virtually every woman they encounter in what Shamblin calls a mixed-gender situation. "To see if she has terror in her eyes," he explains. Carjackings, thefts, and sexual assaults often unfold sequentially, according to Shamblin. He has found "a number" of rape victims wandering on remote roads in this forest. "The most recent one started in Whittier," Shamblin says, "where the guy carjacked this woman, forced her to take money out of her ATM, then brought her up here to rape her." Before he could attack her, however, the woman escaped by jumping out of the car as it sped along Highway 39. "Bruised and cut, but not seriously injured," Shamblin recalls. "You want to tell someone like that how lucky she is, though she probably doesn't want to hear it."

These are circumstances that don't generally appeal to those who choose a career with the Forest Service. "When there's an opportunity to transfer to this forest," Shamblin concedes, "people are generally not receptive." After 27 years in the Angeles, however, he has learned to be a romantic and a realist at the same time. "We have to adapt to the world we live in," he explains. "All we can try to do at this point is protect the good things from the bad people."

If the LEOs tend to doubt that civilized values and scenic beauty can survive in this forest, the man in charge at headquarters, Michael J. Rogers, insists that the Angeles is the ultimate proving ground for the theory that nature can be saved from humanity's onslaught. Rogers, who has been forest supervisor since 1990, is an environmental evangelist for whom the glass is always half full—even when it's nearly empty. This forest is not merely a slow-motion apocalypse, he argues (often to members of his own staff), but a laboratory where those who hold the public trust can test themselves against the host of troubles that will eventually confront every park and wilderness area in the country.

In the Angeles, however, the future is now.

Angeles National Forest is spread mostly along the slopes of the San Gabriel Mountains, massive granite edifices that form the dramatic backdrop of Los Angeles in official photographs of the city (all taken on wind-scoured winter days when the smog is thin enough to permit a vista). The cluster of bare peaks that extend above alpine forests to form the San Gabriels' spine rises to more than 9,000 feet, an upsurge generated by the stupendous power of the San Andreas Fault, which continues to push this entire range north at the rate of two inches per year.

The amorphous sprawl of the most horizontal city on earth seems shockingly close when you look down on it from a southwest-facing vista point in the San Gabriels, yet impossibly far away for those who venture off-road to encounter its surviving herds of bighorn sheep or its large (and growing) populations of mountain lion and black bear. In this forest there are thousands of coyotes, bobcats, and gray foxes. There are western fence lizards and Pacific rattlesnakes, red-tailed hawks and band-tail pigeons. Those who make the drive to Pyramid Lake during nesting season can see dozens of majestic blue herons. The Angeles even harbors ringtail cats, creatures so elusive that few humans have seen one. Beginning in March and April, the meadows in these mountains become blooming fields of paintbrush and monkey flower, golden yarrow and bush lupine. At higher elevations, hikers can even find the rare red snow flower.

The traditional recreational opportunities offered by other national forests are abundant here. Camping, mountain biking, backpacking, and fly-fishing all draw devotees by the thousands. Every summer, scores of hikers ascend the highest peak in the San Gabriels, 10,064-foot-high Mount San Antonio, and in winter skiers can ride lifts all the way to the top of Mount Baldy.

Wholesome activities aside, Angeles National Forest is also the city's necropolis. The city being Los Angeles, of course, aspiring serial killers and soon-to-be-famous dead people receive far more media attention than the anonymous corpses that turn up in the woods with numbing regularity. Randy Kraft, the Claremont College graduate convicted of killing 16 people during the seventies and early eighties, dumped victims in the Angeles. So did the Hillside Strangler, Angelo Buono. Ron Levin, the fabulous Beverly Hills con man who became the first Billionaire Boys Club murder victim, was buried amid the chaparral and scree in Soledad Canyon, where coyotes found him before police could. Emmy Award–winning newsman Jeffrey Webreck was buried in the forest in 1991, killed by a soldier who claimed he was offended by Webreck's sexual advances. The legendary swindler Arthur Lee Evans, who once owned the largest brokerage firm in Orange County, was discovered in the Angeles—or at least his headless body was. The remains of the most recent celebrity victim recovered from the Angeles, model Linda Sobek, were found by Mike Alt and another LEO, Ken Harp, in a shallow grave near the Mount Pacifico Campground.

Disturbing as the discovery of a murder victim is, the LEOs clearly have been more shaken by those who come into this forest to kill themselves. The worst for Mike Alt was the man who made him his witness. It happened early one morning when Alt pulled into a turnout along the Angeles Crest Highway and saw a man standing on the edge of the precipice, holding a paper bag and taking in the view. "He waves at me," Alt says, "and I wave back: 'How's it goin'?' He looks at me for a second, then all of a sudden pulls this Smith & Wesson .357 out of the paper bag. 'Oh, shit!' I draw down on the guy, thinking maybe he's gonna kack me. I yell at him to put the weapon down. He looks right at me for a couple seconds, then puts the gun to his chest and pulls the trigger, right through the heart. He did it over his girlfriend."

Most of them do, says Alt, who finds especially infuriating "how fucking polite some of these bastards are." One in particular stands out, a man to whom Alt had given a traffic ticket one Saturday afternoon. Early the next morning, Alt recalls, he received a call to check out a complaint from some campers: A person parked in a van nearby had stayed up all night playing Barbra Streisand's "The Way We Were" over and over with the volume turned way up. Alt arrived at about 6 A.M. and found the man lying in the back of the van, dead from carbon monoxide poisoning. On the front seat the man had left four items: separate letters addressed to his ex-girlfriend, his mother, and his brother, plus the ticket Alt had given him the day before, a $20 bill attached to it with a paper clip.

The officers' involvement in a murder or suicide case is usually confined to the discovery of the body, since the investigations that follow are handled by Los Angeles County sheriff's deputies. Forest Service officers are left to deal with some grisly images, however. Like all cops, they use gallows humor to deflect the emotional consequences. Their connection to the land, though, seems to leave the LEOs haunted by the horror that accompanies the desecration of a serene landscape with mangled and bloody human remains.

Balzac's consummately cynical line about how behind every great fortune lies a great crime has been borne out better in Los Angeles than perhaps any other city on earth. And from the ridges above Soledad Canyon, in what is known as the Front Country of the Angeles, one is confronted by damning evidence of its truth.

This is the Los Angeles Aqueduct, flashing silver on the northern horizon as water siphoned from the streams of the eastern Sierra tumbles down through metal gates on its way to the lap pools of Bel Air. Beginning 84 years ago, this conveyance of water from rural Owens Valley to a desert city 233 miles to the south—one of the grandest thefts in U.S. history—not only made possible the development of the

San Fernando Valley, but also created the fortunes of the Chandler and Huntington families, whose wealth and influence would dominate Los Angeles during most of the twentieth century.

The light in Soledad Canyon is so harsh it hurts to look at the sky. Dry gulches and desiccated ridges cleave the earth in all directions. This barren ground seems ancient, like the humped back of some enormous prehistoric lizard lurking beneath the sod and asphalt that cover the valley floor, a sleeping beast that will awaken someday to remind the people below where it is they are living.

Turning south, I see the towers of Century City gleaming in the distance. I think of Joe Hunt, the Billionaire Boys Club leader and the most compelling criminal modern Los Angeles has produced. As a child, Joe hiked alone all through these canyons on the western end of the Angeles, creating a private domain along a streambed in Indian Canyon below Sugarloaf Peak. During the early eighties, Joe used to lead BBC members up here on "hunting trips" that were a kind of initiation ritual. From high ground, he invited his companions to look down upon Los Angeles and understand the city as a mirage of plentitude imposed upon a landscape of drought and erosion and seismic violence, a place where nothing is real except what people want. It was here, very near the spot where I am standing, that Joe and the Boys dumped the bodies after they began killing people to cover looming cash-flow problems.

My meditation on Joe Hunt is broken by gunshots, a short, static spit of bullets that seems to echo in broken reverberations through the arroyos and ravines all around me. My knees jelly for an instant, but when I hear the gunfire again, I feel certain it isn't close. All of the "designated shooting areas" in the Angeles Forest were closed by authorities in June 1996. So now people continue to shoot, anywhere they please. This at least has redistributed the devastation.

"Devastation" seems a paltry word, actually, when I consider Pigeon Ridge, for years the most popular of the free-for-all shooting areas in the Angeles. I first visited Pigeon Ridge more than 15 years ago, as a journalist in the company of the CEO Shooting Club, a group of corporate executives who prided themselves on owning the most lethal weapons available.

The noise, the chaos, and especially the trees are what I remember most about Pigeon Ridge. The black oaks and sycamores growing there had been literally shot to pieces; most of their lower limbs were missing, and the upper limbs were reduced to stubs. What was killing the trees, though, was lead poisoning, caused by the hundreds of bullets that had lodged in their trunks. In an entire afternoon at Pigeon Ridge, I saw exactly one pigeon, which was blasted out of the sky moments after its appearance.

When I return from Soledad Canyon to forest headquarters in Arcadia, Rita Plair tells me that more than a few people were killed at Pigeon Ridge before the designated range was closed. She recalls one shooting death she was summoned to investigate: "I arrive, and as usual it's chaos. Then I see these four gentlemen standing in a group, with a fifth man lying dead on the ground beside them in a pool of blood from a massive head wound. These four, though, are all still firing away, just like the 150 other people up there. I get one of the men to stop shooting and I ask him, 'What happened?' 'Well, he shot himself by accident.' They were his neighbors—one lived right next door—and they said he had pointed the gun at his head and fired, believing the trigger was on an empty chamber. So I call it in on my radio, and while I'm waiting for the coroner to get there, this man's friends, and everybody else up there, go back to shooting.

"After a while I can't take it anymore, so I approach this group again and ask, 'Doesn't it bother you?' And one of his friends says, 'Well, he can't hear us.' Another guy tells me, 'You think it's bad for you, we have to go back and tell his wife.'"

The LEOs are acutely aware of how well armed America has become. "In the entire time I've worked in this forest," Plair says, "I have never once stopped a car and not found a weapon in it. Not even once. Average people carry them because they think everybody else has one. And the awful part is, they may be right."

The Angeles LEOs have assigned one another nicknames drawn from the computer-animated movie *Toy Story*. Rita Plair is Bo Peep, and Chuck Shamblin is the Elite Green Soldier. The whole thing started, the others explain, when they realized Mike Alt was really Buzz

Lightyear, the *Toy Story* character who thinks he's a real person but in fact is only an action figure. His return to the job after severely injuring his neck and shoulder last autumn in a fall off a backcountry canyon rim to the base of a waterfall has only added to his legend. Not long ago, Alt worked seven-day weeks for four months straight; his wife of 18 years, who had long been threatening to divorce him, finally did.

At 47, Alt's square-cut build is starting to soften a little at the corners. Yet he still looks like a man born to wear the stiff cop's mustache that is his most prominent feature. He runs the drug investigations in the Angeles. What this means is "a lotta walks in the park," or "ground recon."

Alt refuses to carry "camping gear," as he disdainfully refers to it, on his overnight forays into the forest. His bedroll is a military poncho with a liner, carried on his belt. He insists on cold camping—no fires—and dines exclusively on MREs (military "meals ready to eat" rations). Such rigors seem to suit a man who has spent most of the past 30 years in the bush, beginning with his first tour of duty in Southeast Asia, where his work with Air Force Special Operations and "another government agency" during the Vietnam War is still, he says, classified.

Alt left the military in 1972, so disheartened that his only goal was to take the year's pay he'd saved up and "see if I could drink my way across the United States." One of his first stops, though, was a bar in Glendale, where he met another vet who had gone to work for the Forest Service as a firefighter. "He told me, 'It'd be perfect for you, man. Small teams, small unit, out in the bush.' I decided it was better than my first idea of becoming a professional alcoholic." After working his way up to fire captain and then turning to arson investigation, Alt joined law enforcement in order to keep doing what he does best: "Humpin' 16 hours a day in 90-plus degrees, with 50 pounds of gear on, over the steepest and most rugged terrain you can imagine, sleepin' in rocks or curlin' up in a sand bed," he explains with thinly disguised relish.

The heaviest concentration of marijuana gardens in California—and possibly the country—can be found in the Angeles. According to Alt,

Latin American crime families own and distribute most of the marijuana harvested here. They are the sort who don't expect but rather demand a return on their investment.

It isn't hard to find field hands. "A day laborer hired off the corner is gonna get $5 an hour to bust concrete," Alt observes. "When El Jefe pulls up in his shiny new truck and offers $100 a day, plus food, for work that isn't real difficult and will last weeks and months at a time, that sounds pretty damn good."

Almost all of the pot is planted at the midelevations of the Angeles, where oak, sycamore, and laurel can be trimmed and then rigged with ropes and pulleys to form a canopy that closes or opens with a couple of cranks on a hand winch. This makes spotting a marijuana garden in the Angeles from the air all but impossible. With chainsaws and machetes, growers can clear areas as large as the five-acre plot found last summer in Lost Canyon. Field hands carry in bags of potting soil and manure, working the ground by hand with shovels, and then install water lines, either flexible hoses or plastic pipes.

A total of 28,000 pounds of pot was seized by law enforcement in the Angeles last year. "We took 4,300 pounds of pot out of one garden," Plair recalls. Alt concedes, though, that they miss a lot more than they find. "You can walk a mile off the road, from almost any campground, and find a dope garden," he says.

People whose image of a Los Angeles canyon summons up one named Laurel or Coldwater have no concept of how rugged the landscape of the San Gabriels can be. From turnouts along even the paved roads in the Angeles you can stand on cliffs above near-vertical drops that disappear through thickets of undergrowth into ravines so deep they appear bottomless. "We've been in places here where you could literally throw a rock and hit the other side of a canyon, but it takes you four hours to get across yourself," Alt says. Yet field hands who tend the big pot gardens manage to transport 500-gallon water tanks and full sheets of plywood into even the most remote areas.

It was "resource damage" that first involved the Forest Service in marijuana investigations here. Those five acres in Lost Canyon once were covered with old-growth sycamores. And because rats and rabbits eat marijuana, the growers in the Angeles scatter the ground around their gardens with poison. Field mice and squirrels eat the poison also, and then pass it on to the red-tailed hawks and coyotes that hunt them. Larger animals are simply shot if they come too close. "At one garden last year we found a bear and seven deer, all shot dead," Plair says. "You go in and see something like that, it really affects you."

The Angeles LEOs are no less affected by some of the better-concealed hazards they discover. "The booby traps keep getting more sophisticated all the time," Alt notes. "Last year we went into a grove site and found ammo cans filled with C-4 explosives attached to detonation cords. We've found rat-trap shotguns and even pipe bombs."

Most of the weight Alt carries when he ventures off the forest's hiking trails consists of weaponry. On patrol in the bush, the LEOs arm themselves with CAR-15 assault rifles and sometimes shotguns, yet still often find themselves outgunned. Workers in the employ of El Jefe will use any weapon at hand to protect their crop.

Despite the risks of his job, Alt delights in matching wits with the endlessly ingenious pot farmers. Moreover, it is a curiosity of the Angeles that this stalker of men—a person who boasts he can "crawl up on you while you're eating lunch and put a gun to your head between bites"—knows the Angeles in ways most of the rangers assigned to the district stations never will. Motion and sound are what give you away in the forest, he explains, "so you're always moving real slow, and you're moving real quiet. And you walk into stuff. Like a couple of summers ago we're out on a three-man patrol and we step right into a herd of Nelson bighorn sheep. These big rams are standing all around us, 12 or 13 of 'em, less than ten feet away. They stayed right there until we tried to take pictures and the shutter on the camera set 'em off. Went straight up the vertical sidewall of the canyon."

It pleases some historians to report that barbarism existed in the San Gabriels long before Anglos came. After converting the native Tongva people who lived among these mountains in wickiups from hunter-gatherers into mission Indians, the Mexican Californios were mostly indifferent to the high country, except as a source of fresh water. The early hildagos, in fact, sent their caballeros into the mountains for only one purpose: to stalk grizzly bears. The horsemen lassoed the grizzlies and dragged them, slashing and lunging, into the grubby little empire of adobe huts and sandy wastes known in those days as El Pueblo de Nuestra Señora la Reina del los Angeles de Porciuncula. The purpose was to stage a public amusement, an extravaganza of gore that pitted bear against bull. The bear always lost.

White people did not show up in numbers in this high country until 1854, when a series of large gold strikes was made along the gravel shores of the San Gabriel River's East Fork. A boomtown was thrown up almost overnight, a ramshackle collection of sluice boxes and saloons, Long Toms and whorehouses, that stretched out for more than a mile along the river's edge. Eldoradoville, as the miners called the place, thrived for eight years and then was obliterated even more quickly than it had appeared, swept away by the unprecedented floods of 1862.

The mine entrances can still be seen along the river canyon walls, black holes that are especially vivid against a lurid background of graffiti tags. "4 Lokos Crew" and "Flaco Duarte" appear to have been especially active, I'm thinking, when Rita Plair, at the wheel of the Bronco this afternoon, remarks that she can't remember when the canyon walls have looked so clean. "I've seen it many times where you could drive up here and never even once see the faces of the rocks," she tells me, "just solid paint, layers and layers of it."

The Graffiti Clean Up Patrol completed its annual sweep of San Gabriel Canyon just two days ago, sandblasting the rocks and slapping fresh coats of paint on the public buildings. Already, though, dozens of new graffiti tags have appeared.

A tall, slender woman of 35, Plair seems almost fragile, until she shows a little of the tensile strength that made her an outstanding middle-distance runner who still competes in half-marathons. In this forest, Plair has been menaced by guns, knives, and anonymous death threats; she's faced down blacks who said she was a sellout and whites who called her a nigger. There isn't a flinch in her, though she winces occasionally.

The San Gabriel River, once filled year-round with trout, she points out, now yields a bounty of hypodermic needles and disposable diapers when its bottom is cleaned each year. Volunteers still talk about the year they pulled an entire dinette set from the river. "During summer, the stench in this canyon is overpowering," Plair says. "It's human waste, mostly."

On weekend afternoons during the hottest days of July, August, and September, "you'll see cars parked and double-parked all along Highway 39 for 25 miles," Plair tells me. "People just bail over the side down by the creek bottom to picnic, practically one on top of the other. It's truly a sight to behold—15 people in a pool of water the size of my desk. And what's in that water with them, you don't even want to think about."

Back when she was growing up in Georgia, Plair recalls a moment later, "My mother told my sisters and me, 'Tell me now if you plan to become a productive member of society. Because I would rather go to prison for homicide than turn another fool loose on the world.'" It isn't her own approach to parenting, Plair says, but 14 years in this forest have convinced her it works better than a lot of others.

Not so long ago, the part of her job Plair loved best was hiking into The Narrows, an area just off the East Fork of the San Gabriel River, to check on the "recreational" miners who congregate there. "But now, because of all the insanity we have to deal with right along the road, the days I could spend in the backcountry have disappeared," she says. "I used to forget I was right on the edge of a big city. These days, I have to remind myself I work in a forest."

As many as 30,000 people a day visit San Gabriel Canyon on weekends, and all of them, of course, come in automobiles. Plair's experiences with the teeming mass of day-trippers has made her, in the context of Forest Service orthodoxy, something of an environmental radical. The only way to keep an area beautiful, she now believes, is not to build roads there: "People who really love the land and nature are the same ones who don't mind hiking there."

Los Angeles at the end of the second millennium is perhaps the most multicultural city in history. Virtually every race, nationality, and ethnic group claims a constituency—and a competing interest. The metropolis that continues to spread beneath and beyond this forest is one where racial cohesion and ethnic cooperation are its best hopes for survival, and yet at the same time one where politically correct pieties serve only to obscure the real issues. It is a city where black males commit violent crimes at a per capita rate exceeding that of white males by more than ten to one, where the fastest growing ethnic groups are Asian and Middle Eastern. The coalition of Westside Jewish liberals and black councilmen from South Central that has controlled the political apparatus for nearly 20 years senses that the end of its time is near. The middle-class homeowners of the San Fernando Valley, feeling overtaxed and underserved, are in open revolt, threatening secession, while Latinos, who already constitute the largest ethnic bloc in Los Angeles (and soon will possess an absolute majority), are only now beginning to comprehend how little voice they have, given their numbers.

The forest, like the city, is overwhelmed. By early in the next century, the Angeles will contain more than 90 percent of all the undeveloped land left in Los Angeles County. As development saturates the surrounding landscape, the prospects for the kind of cultural amity and environmental awareness that could ease the overuse and crime in the Angeles seem increasingly remote. The Angeles LEOs see the forest deteriorating all around them, with no relief in sight, and the indifference they meet every day tempts them to a sense of futility. It seems remarkable to me that they have in their midst a true idealist, an impassioned preacher of hope. Stranger still, he happens to be the boss.

Forest Supervisor Michael J. Rogers is a native of Altadena, on the edge of the Angeles, and he hiked all through the San Gabriels when he was growing up in the forties and fifties. It was a magnificent place back then, he remembers, a sacred refuge from urbanization. As a college student, Rogers fought fires in the Angeles with the Chilao Hotshots, and he went on to work his way up the Forest Service ladder in a string of jobs in various forests in California and a stint in the national office in Washington, D.C. Rogers, now 58, lives in Altadena once again, and he still loves the forest he's in charge of. He has come to understand the Angeles, however, not as something separate from the city below, but as an intrinsic part of it. Which is why, he explains, he has devoted more and more of his energies to "the reforestation of Los Angeles."

"We've got generations of people now who have been totally removed from the natural environment," he tells me when we meet at forest headquarters in Arcadia. "The world they live in is concrete from one end to the other. So how can we expect them to appreciate and understand the forest?"

For several decades, Rogers acknowledges, the national forest has been doing less and less to provide environmental education to children in inner-city schools and to inspire kids with ranger-guided hikes and campfire talks. The current $15.7 million annual budget for the Angeles is $5 million less than it was receiving in the early 1980s, and burgeoning paperwork requirements have pulled employees off the trails and kept them deskbound. "We don't have a presence anymore on the ground, where we have a chance to interact with the public," Rogers says.

With less money to spend, Rogers has become an ardent advocate of community outreach. The April 1992 riots following the Rodney King verdict were a wake-up call for the Angeles, he argues: "We were not connecting well with the urban population, reminding them that the forest is where our water comes from, that trees clean the air." With the help of organizations such as the California Environmental Project, Rogers has poured his energies into an ambitious campaign to plant trees all over greater Los Angeles. He becomes emotional as he recalls the day the first trees were planted along Martin Luther King Boulevard in South Central. "Tom Bradley said he never thought he'd live to see this day, but when he saw the trees going in there were tears in his eyes."

And there may be some fiscal relief in sight. The Angeles, together with three other southern California forests, has begun to require that visitors who drive into the forest pay a $5-per-car daily user fee. Such user fees have been bitterly contested elsewhere, but virtually every public-interest group with a stake in the health of the Angeles has endorsed them here, where the money will go directly to the sites the public is visiting. "This will bring us back to a level of service we had a long time ago," Rogers enthuses. "I'm talking about back in the sixties."

Hearing Rogers talk in a rush about education and new programs and collective awareness, it is easy to be swept up in a wave of optimism. "Young people are starting to understand," Rogers declares. "I don't just believe, I *know* that if we reintroduce nature into these neighborhoods, we can restore this forest and transform this city."

But the LEOs smile with closed lips, shaking their heads, when they hear Rogers say that he already sees some small improvement in San Gabriel Canyon. They admire this man, recognizing implicitly that only someone like their own Mr. Rogers could ever change things for the better, yet at the same time they wonder if his vision of salvation would hold up under the psychological pounding they take every day. The cultural decay is so advanced, the criminal depredations so extreme, the environmental abusiveness so endemic, that pulling out of the downward spiral seems an implausible dream.

Rogers counters that healing by faith may be the only alternative to accepting defeat. "More and more national forests are going to become urban," Rogers tells me. "If we can't do it here, in Los Angeles, where the problems of the whole world have collected in one place, then we aren't going to do it anywhere."

What I know for certain is that visitors to the Angeles who love beauty and crave serenity should for the time being seek higher ground.

That means driving the Angeles Crest Highway. Despite all that exists at lower elevations, this road remains among the most spectacularly scenic in the country. It begins just above the affluent communities of Flintridge and La Canada, on a steep, winding climb that passes for miles through chaparral and an "elfin forest" of stiff shrubs and stunted trees. Above 4,000 feet, stands of digger pine and Douglas fir begin to appear among the live oak and California laurel. Higher up, these conifers are superseded by Coulter pine and incense cedar.

Alone in an open convertible, I drive for 20-minute stretches without seeing another vehicle, passing though granite narrows into vistas as breathtaking as Yosemite's. The air up here is thinner than down in the flatlands, of course, yet seems immensely richer, so thick with aromas that I begin to taste each breath.

The San Gabriel Timberland Reserve, later Angeles National Forest, was established in 1892. California's first federal forest preserve would be venerated during the years between 1895 and 1938, a period environmental historians call the Great Hiking Era. It was a time when people from the cities came to the mountains in unprecedented numbers, tramping in groups of two and three dozen over trails that previously had been little more than deer paths. Huge resort hotels were constructed in Rubio Canyon, atop Echo Mountain, at Crystal Springs. They've all long since closed.

I'm driving among stands of white fir and sugar pine by the time I reach the startlingly steep road that leads to the Mount Wilson Observatory, once considered the best place in the country for viewing the night sky. Above 6,000 feet, I begin to see Jeffery pines, magnificent trees that give off an odor like vanilla, hung with cones the size of watermelons.

I reach by far the finest campground in the Angeles, Chilao—"the one place in this forest where I'd consider spending the night," Plair admitted to me—set among thousand-year-old trees and expansive meadows, with superb views of the Big Mermaids and Strawberry Peak. Nearby is access to the Silver Moccasin Trail, the best hiking path in southern California.

After lunch at Newcomb's Ranch, where redwood logs six feet thick serve as bumpers between the gravel parking lot and the front door, I continue my climb, though it isn't far now to 7,018-foot Cloudburst Summit, where for the first time I can see lodgepole pines on the mountainsides.

Half an hour later, I begin my descent in rapture. For one who's flown into L.A. from a colder climate, the sheer sensual ecstasy of feeling the sun full on your face as you ride in an open car at elevations above 7,000 feet makes the trip worth the trouble. I reach the ridges of Upper Big Tujunga Canyon before it dawns on me that I haven't seen another human being in more than an hour.

It's another 30 minutes before I can comprehend that I'm still in Los Angeles County. This realization comes suddenly, though, when a yahoo in a Japanese sports car comes at me off a curve just below Red Box in a two-wheel drift, passing so close I can see the combination of belligerence and panic in his eyes.

A weird sight rises up about a mile above Switzers, where I pass a road crew filling potholes with fresh asphalt. One of the workers, I notice, is wearing a black leather sport coat and loafers with tassels. I know I'm not far from the city now.

By the time I reach Clear Creek, oak and laurel outnumber evergreens. Cars are coming the other way every few minutes or so, and more often than that as I descend below Dark Canyon. Everybody's driving so much faster down here than they were up in the mountains. I begin to feel the pressure, remembering that time is short.

"All rushing nowhere," I tell myself in an effort to keep the mood. It doesn't work, though; I feel dreadfully sober by the time I reach the chaparral, where for the first time I see trash thrown onto the side of the road.

For no reason I'm aware of, I start replaying my conversation with Mike Rogers, and after a few minutes I recover at least a little of the high I was on an hour earlier. Like him, I believe that the great drama of the nation runs along lines of tension formed by a blending of races and cultures, the balance of public interests with private ones, an ambition for transcendence in the finite context of our natures. If it's true, I can't imagine a better backdrop for the stage it should be played on than Angeles National Forest.

Five minutes later, I'm back on the freeway.

July 1997

Long Gone

**BRYAN DI SALVATORE
AND DEIRDRE McNAMER**

Gatorade was on sale at Safeway for 89 cents a 32-ounce bottle, and Mr. D's, just along Main, had knocked down country-style ribs to $1.39 a pound. The school district and the Gannett Grill needed cooks.

It was Thursday, July 24, 1997, in Lander, Wyoming, and the twice-weekly *State Journal* had thunked onto porches the afternoon before. Its lead story: Police Chief Dick Currah was pressing the city council to crack down on street parties.

Jesse Emerson of the Spirit Freedom Ministries would speak that evening about family alcoholism and drugs.

Here was a one-bedroom apartment for rent: $350 plus utilities. No pets.

Someone in northern California wanted a nanny.

By midafternoon, thermometers would crawl toward 90. It would be lip-cracking dry, under a ferociously blue sky. Clouds big as counties would bunch up to the northeast, where the Owl Creek Mountains meet the Bighorns, and just west, in the Wind River Range, Lander's backyard. They might shape themselves into massive anvils and shoot lightning down to the high plains. Or they might just light up gold as the sun fell away and be gone by morning.

To all appearances, it was going to be a spectacularly ordinary high-summer day.

What happened instead was something strange and nightmarish, the kind of nightmare that begins with innocuous moments that become harrowing only in hindsight. A casual good-bye kiss. Three quick glances at a wristwatch. A cheery wave.

It would be the day that a Lander resident named Amy Wroe Bechtel—24 years old, five-foot-six and 110 pounds, Olympic marathon hopeful, amateur photographer, friend, employee, daughter, sister, wife—fell off the face of the earth.

At the northwestern edge of Lander, past the Toyota dealership, on a rise above the tidy town, ten identical frame houses face the Wind River Range. Small and scraped-looking—former company houses from some gone-bust outfit in Rock Springs—they line one side of a street called Lucky Lane. The residents, many of them, are young, ardent, competitive rock climbers. An intense little bohemia of mountain-town athletes.

Todd Skinner, their de facto captain, lives in number ten with his wife, Amy Whisler, also a climber. Skinner, 39, has led four of the most notable first free ascents of recent years: Half Dome's northwest face, the Salathé Wall of El Capitan, Proboscis in the Yukon, and the Nameless Tower in Pakistan's Karakoram Range. Mike Lilygren, who accompanied Skinner on that 1995 Pakistan climb, lived last summer in number seven. (He recently moved in with his girlfriend down in town.) Skinner's sister Holly lives in number eight. And until July 24, Amy Wroe Bechtel lived with her husband, Steve, one of Skinner's Half Dome and Nameless Tower partners, in number nine.

When they woke on that morning, Steve and Amy faced a busy schedule. They had the day off from Wild Iris Mountain Sports, the local outdoor equipment store where both had part-time jobs. Steve's plan was to drive with his yellow lab, Jonz, to Dubois, 75 miles north, meet his friend Sam Lightner, and scout some possible new climbing routes at Cartridge Creek.

Amy drove her white Toyota Tercel station wagon to the Wind River Fitness Center, another of her part-time employers, and taught an hour-

and-a-half kids' class in weight training. She was upbeat, says owner Dudley Irvine, though "a little high-strung because she had a lot to do."

Indeed. Three days earlier, Amy and Steve had closed on a new house a mile toward the center of town from Lucky Lane, and she was busy organizing a 10k hill climb, scheduled for September 7. The runners would puff up a series of switchbacks not far out of town and then jump into Frye Lake and finish up with a picnic.

Her to-do list was long: run & lift, recycling, call phone co., electric, gas, insurance, get photo mounted or matted, flyers for race, get more boxes, mow lawn, call Ed, close road?, have Karn do drawing.

We know this: Amy taught the fitness class and picked up the center's recycling. She contacted the phone and electric companies. She stopped in at the Camera Connection on Main and asked owner John Strom about several photographs she planned to submit in a competition.

She was 11 days short of her 25th birthday, 13 months into her marriage—a radiant young athlete, small, lithe, determined, thoughtful, even-tempered, trusting. That's the capsule description and it varies not a whit, whether the describer is an acquaintance, like Strom, or a family member, or a close friend.

Strom, reserved and bespectacled, remembers that Amy was in running togs: yellow shirt, black shorts, running shoes. That she seemed cheerful and busy. That he sent her to the framing shop upstairs to see about matting. That it was midafternoon.

She talked with Greg Wagner at Gallery 331 about her photos. He says that in the course of 20 minutes or so, she looked at her watch two or three times. She left the store. Call it 2:30.

At this point, while quotidian life went one direction in Lander—while the shopper at Safeway reached for discount Gatorade and the fisherman eyed the gathering clouds and the golfer double-bogied the difficult fourth hole at the local municipal and Jesse Emerson rehearsed that evening's presentation—life for Amy went another.

At this point, everything about Amy Wroe Bechtel—her movements, her well-being, her very existence—becomes subject to speculation.

Lander is one of those pleasant, historically undistinguished western towns that borrows most of its reputation from what it is near and what it is not. It is 7,500 souls living a mile above sea level. Butch Cassidy was once arrested here. Its most famous resident was an old buckaroo, Stub Farlow, whose image atop a sunfishing bronc adorns Wyoming's license plates.

What it is near is the spectacular eastern front of the Wind River Range—fierce, sharp peaks that give onto gentler ones that give, in turn, onto the oceanic high plains. It is terrain of such starkly heroic proportions that it can make other American vistas—the silo-anchored fields of the Midwest, the nubby Appalachians, even the punched-up Pacific Coast Ranges—seem like the Land of Toys.

And what is Lander not? It's not rich-thick Jackson, 160 road-miles northwest—though like many small western towns with a view, it fears it may become that. Landerites cast wary glances at Jackson's log palaces, its sleek fleets of celebrities and wannabes and wealthy kids who fall from the sky in western costumes and $300 haircuts for some quality mountain time.

But truth be told, that's a transmutation Lander won't have to worry about any time soon. It has no downhill ski area and no prospect of one. Its snowfall, relative to much of the mountainous West, is sporadic and undependable, and its periodic winds are the kind of hellers that make it sad to go outside. ("Due to high winds please return carts to corral in parking lot," pleads a sign outside the Safeway.) Fishing is fine, but hardly world-class. Hunting is seasonal. Snowmobilers have been part of things for a long time, and the hipness quotient, measured in the New West by the ratio of cappuccino to Folgers, is negligible. The modest Magpie is still the only sit-down coffeehouse in town.

What else is Lander not, besides Jackson? It is not the gritty, extractive, assault-and-battery West of, say, Rock Springs. Or the university-town West that is Laramie. Or the strafed and struggling Indian West of the Wind River Reservation, just north of town.

Lander was the original home of *High Country News*, the feisty biweekly environmental newspaper (it moved to Colorado in the early eighties). In 1965, the National Outdoor Leadership School, which trains about 2,800 students each year in outdoor skills, was established in Lander. A few years before that, prosperity had descended on Lander in the form of a U.S. Steel iron-ore mine. In 1985, increasing foreign imports and other economic woes, so said U.S. Steel, prompted the company to pull out, putting 550 people out of work. The streets were suddenly dense with For Sale signs.

Lander, however, took stock. Regrouped. Hired some crackerjack community resource personnel and realized that its big selling points were its size, its civility, and its proximity to forest, wilderness, and mountains. NOLS stayed and prospered. The town promoted itself as a friend of small business. It aggressively advertised for "vigorous retirees." It expanded the golf course. It upgraded and modernized its sewer and water systems and remodeled Main Street with tasteful streetlamps, flower boxes, and litter baskets.

In the early nineties, the rock climbers began to arrive, drawn by some of the most accessible and difficult walls in America—notably the two-mile-wide dolomite, sandstone, and granite cliffs of Sinks Canyon, nine miles from town, and a higher area known as Wild Iris, with its 200 bleach-white climbing routes (featuring difficulty ratings from 5.9 to 5.14), 26 miles from town.

Business is good now, based mostly on recreation and light industry; growth is steady and calm. Lander keeps its boots shined and its troubles to itself.

The town's resident climbers—perhaps two-thirds of them male, most of them from west of the Mississippi—are a furiously healthy, adrenalinized, unironic group. They describe themselves as factionless middle-roaders of the sport—not the somber Brahmins, forever talking about how it used to be done, and not the young punks who scramble up the rock walls, headphones blasting, knocking a cliff all to hell in search of a few kicks.

The Lucky Lane bunch appears to waste little time on bad habits or generalized angst. Any outright oddnesses or furies seem to get channeled into climbing, and what's left over is small-town camaraderie (potlucks, fireworks on the Fourth), lots of rock-talk, and the edgeless high jinks of a platoon in the movies, of the spirited kids on the team bus. They tend to keep their doors unlocked and share equipment, climbing plans, social lives, workplaces. Skinner and Whisler are part owners of Wild Iris, the outdoor-gear store where Amy and Steve Bechtel and Mike Lilygren were on the payroll, and they own the house that Steve and Amy were renting. (Steve also works as a sales rep for DMM, a climbing hardware company, and for Stone Monkey action wear.)

At times, the in-without-knocking, post-collegiate communalism wore against Amy's need for privacy and order, according to Jo Anne Wroe, her mother. She wanted a home of her own and couldn't wait to move into the crisp ranch-style house they had just bought—an in-town place with flowers, a lawn, space for a darkroom. In fact, Amy's original plan for July 24 was to drive three hours north to her parents' home in Powell, Wyoming, to pick up furniture that her father, Duane, had been refinishing for the young couple.

Jo Anne remembers that Amy called the night before and said, "Would you feel really bad if I didn't come tomorrow? I've got about a million things to do, and it's my only day off." Jo Anne, her voice taut, adds, "Later I thought, Why didn't we just make her come that day? Those 'almost' moments. They're the things you think about."

Steve Bechtel says he returned from his rendezvous with Sam Lightner about 4:30 that afternoon to find the house empty. He and Amy were not in the habit of leaving notes about their whereabouts, and anyway, Steve had returned earlier than he'd planned. No reason for alarm. After a bit, he spoke with Todd Skinner and Amy Whisler next door, but they hadn't seen Amy since midday. He turned down an invitation to go for pizza with some of the Lucky Lane bunch, and waited. Had she gone climbing? No, her gear was still in the house. Had she gone to take some photographs? No, her camera was in the house. Her jeans and T-shirt were on the bedroom floor, and her running shoes were gone.

At about 10 P.M., he called her parents to see if perhaps Amy had driven there on the spur of the moment. When they asked him if anything was wrong, Steve, who later said that he was starting to worry at this point, replied with a casual white lie: "No."

Skinner and Whisler had gone to the 8:45 P.M. showing of *Con Air,* and they arrived home around 11 to find that Amy still wasn't back. By this time, Steve had called the Fremont County sheriff's office, which sent two deputies to the house, alerted the night shift, and began to organize a search-and-rescue team to head out at daybreak. Skinner and Whisler, meanwhile, went to look for Amy's car. They drove downtown, turned right at the Safeway, and followed what's known locally as the Loop Road, a 30-mile affair through the Shoshone National Forest.

At about one in the morning, Whisler used her cell phone to call Steve: They had found Amy's white Toyota Tercel station wagon at a place called Burnt Gulch, up in the mountains about 45 minutes from town. The car was unlocked. The keys were under Amy's to-do list on the passenger seat, next to her $120 sunglasses. Her wallet was not in the car. Nothing—except Amy's absence and the wallet's absence (she never carried it running)—seemed awry. It was as if she had simply parked the car and stepped away for a breath of night air.

Steve and his friend Kirk Billings grabbed lanterns, a sleeping bag, and matches and drove to Burnt Gulch. The little group arrowed flashlights past tree trunks, into blurry undergrowth. They called and called Amy's name, were answered with wind through the trees. They summoned more searchers.

Long before dawn and the arrival of the official search party, a dozen friends were looking for Amy-with-a-sprained-ankle, Amy-with-a-broken-leg, or Amy-attacked-by-a-bear. No attempt was made to preserve the integrity of what would later be presumed to be a crime scene. This was merely a lost runner. "I expected her to come stumbling out of the woods," said Billings. In retrospect, that assumption would seem disastrously naive.

Certain couples can look to outsiders like some platonic combination of health, beauty, and uncomplication. There is Amy in their wedding photo, smiling serenely, almost remotely—as if she's listening to a happy story she's heard before. Her pale blond hair is a shiny cap, her skin golden, her carriage slim and erect, her dress a simple, sleeveless column of white.

And there is Steve, strong-jawed and smoothly handsome in a tuxedo. And shorts. And Tevas. He's the cut-up, the counterpoint.

Steve and Amy met at the University of Wyoming in Laramie in December 1991, took exercise physiology classes together in the spring, and were dating by the fall of 1992.

Amy is the youngest of four closely spaced siblings, allies and friends during their growing-up years. Their father, Duane Wroe, 66, is a retired city administrator—intelligent, gaunt, testy, chain-smoking, a former big-time drinker (he gave it up 20 years ago). The family moved to Jackson in 1973, not long after Amy was born, and Duane was city manager there and later in Douglas and Powell. These days he keeps his hand in politics—he's been spearheading an initiative that would codify ethics requirements for Wyoming officeholders—and he tinkers with furniture and works on his and Jo Anne's modest house.

Jo Anne Wroe, 12 years younger than her husband, quiet-voiced, is a dark-haired version of her three tow-headed daughters. She can seem tentative, forthcoming, and insightful, almost in the same breath. She worked as a teacher of handicapped preschoolers for many years and now substitutes in the Powell school system.

A large photograph of Amy in kindergarten, part of the hallway display that Jo Anne calls her "rogues' gallery," shows a canny, appraising child of five, looking out from under a shock of white-blond hair. Even then, her parents say, she was thoughtful, orderly, highly focused—the kind of kid who sets goals and when she does, says Duane, "you better get flat out of her way."

Amy got the running bug in sixth grade. She wasn't, by all accounts, very good, but she kept at it through high school in Douglas and at the University of Wyoming. By her junior and senior years in college, Amy started winning everything in sight. She was captain of the UW cross-country and track teams, got named to the Western Athletic Conference's all-star team, and still holds the UW record in the 3,000 meters: 9:48.9. After college, she continued to compete in both regional and national competitions. In 1996, she ran the Boston Marathon in 3:08:33. Though Amy finished 41 minutes behind winner Uta Pippig, and though her time was 33 minutes behind the 1996 American Olympic marathon qualifying time, Steve Bechtel would matter-of-factly tell anyone who asked that his wife was hoping to qualify for the 2000 Olympics. He and her friends pointed to her heart, her drive. What, in the face of willpower like Amy's, is 33 minutes?

Steve, 27, grew up in Casper, the son of Thomas Bechtel, an architect, and Linda Bechtel, who is the director of a school for developmentally disabled children. Steve has a younger brother, Jeff, and an older sister, Leslie.

In his teens, Steve turned his back on team sports and skiing and pointed himself at rock-climbing, the sport that has obsessed him since. And like Amy, he progressed through sheer doggedness.

"Steve doesn't have the natural build of a climber," says Mike Lilygren, who was his college roommate. "You want to be lean, skinny, wiry, small, compact, like me. Steve is big, barrel-chested, and he's got those big legs to haul around."

Steve is talkative, quick, and according to his friends, engagingly zany. He knows by heart the lyrics to the complete works of They Might Be Giants. He programmed his computer so that when it came on, it screamed out one of Holly Hunter's lines from *Raising Arizona*: "Where's Junior?" By Lucky Lane standards, these are examples of full-frontal madcappery.

When it comes to his sport, however, Steve is known for a singularity of purpose unusually intense even for a big-wall climber. When Skinner began assembling a five-member team for the celebrated 1995 scaling of the Southeast Face of Pakistan's Nameless Tower—a 3,000-foot granite spear, also called Trango Tower—he picked Steve for his bulldog tenacity, his "mono-focus," his ability to Be Positive.

"An expedition team is an organic unit," Skinner says. "I guess I'm the mind; Lilygren, the good spirits, the sense of humor. Steve is the heart." Skinner speaks emphatically and with much eye contact. He is often out of town, giving motivational speeches to various organizations, corporate and noncorporate.

Steve was dropped from the expedition at base camp because of a severe sinus infection and eye hemorrhages. It was a bitter disappointment. The rest of the team spent two months on the Tower, waiting out storms in hanging tents or on narrow ledges, before completing an ascent in which they relied on no climbing aids—only their hands, their feet, and safety ropes.

If there is a moral to their adventures—and you hear it from the Lucky Lane climbers again and again—it is that tenacity buys victory, that you can hang for a long damn time four miles above sea level and still make the top, that hopelessness, failure of will, can be lethal.

Positive mental attitude. Focus. Your mind on the task, on the problem and nothing else. Quitting is not an option. Those were the mantras at Lucky Lane, even during the best of times. When Amy disappeared, climbing a cliff became finding a person.

"Amy is the summit," said Skinner, the motivational speaker, during the early days of the search. "We're trying to get to that point."

Getting lost or injured near Lander is like having your house catch fire next to the fire station. Scores of rescuers, fit and mountain-wise, live within a rifle shot of city hall. Amy's disappearance prompted an all-out response from the county's search-and-rescue volunteers, many of whom are NOLS staff and students; from Lander's extended climbing community; and from Amy and Steve's family members and a number of their college friends. By the weekend, the company of searchers grew to nearly 200.

"We know what we're doing," says Dave King, the Fremont County sheriff's deputy who became the case's lead investigator. "We have 50 activations a year. We have specialists in steep-angle searches, swift-water searches, cave rescues. We have trackers, air spotters, and what are called cadaver dogs, which supposedly can catch scents even under water. We can bring people out via Life Flight or horseback or on a stretcher. Me? I round up the volunteers. I provide the authority, and I take the blame for bad decisions, but I'm not the expert. I feel foolish sometimes—directing traffic that includes people who have written books about mountain search and rescue."

King is 41 years old, squarely and solidly built, with a spiky haircut that looks like something his 13-year-old daughter urged on him in the interest of with-it-ness. He's Lander born and bred, with such an engaging lack of bluster or antagonism that it's easy to overlook the fact that he keeps his cards very close to the vest. He summarizes, he confirms, he returns calls, he expresses his frustration at being literally clueless.

Investigators had discovered, on the bottom of the to-do list found in Amy's car, a milepost description of landmarks that she apparently jotted down, while referring to her odometer, along the first section of the proposed 10k race route—one more indication that Amy herself drove the Toyota up into the mountains before she disappeared. There-fore the search centered on the upper sections of the Loop Road, which begins as a paved highway flanked by ranchettes on the immediate out-skirts of Lander. It parallels the Popo Agie River through Sinks Canyon State Park, where visitors can watch the river vanish into a mountain cave and then walk a quarter-mile to watch it emerge at a quiet pond called the Rise of the Sinks. Water should make this underground trip in a few minutes—instead it takes two hours. More water emerges than has disappeared. Go figure.

Beyond Sinks Canyon, the pavement turns to gravel and switch-backs, rising 1,500 feet in six miles to Frye Lake—the hill climb Amy was scoping out for her 10k.

Still heading up through the Shoshone National Forest, the road passes campgrounds, firewood-gathering areas, Louis Lake, snowmo-bile and hiking trailheads. It crests above 9,000 feet and then descends to connect with Wyoming 28 near the skeletal mining hamlets of Atlantic City and South Pass City.

The Loop Road is essentially a horseshoe tipped on its ends. A vehi-cle has one way in, one way out. During the day, traffic is sporadic but not infrequent. At night, the Loop feels very empty, very close to the stars, suspended in a soft rush of treetop wind. About halfway along the road, in the westward shadow of Indian Ridge, the loop passes through a fire-thinned forest of lodgepole pines. A rutted side road used by fire-wood cutters heads off into the trees toward Freak Mountain. This is Burnt Gulch, the place where Skinner and Whisler found Amy's Tercel.

In the days that followed, searchers painstakingly staked out and scoured roughly 20 square miles around Amy's car. They almost liter-ally combed the five-square-mile area closest to the Toyota. They walked, four abreast, the length of the Loop. It was both a "wallet toss" search—covering the distance that someone could discard a wallet—and a "critical separation" search, in which volunteers, depending on the terrain, maintain only enough distance between them-selves so as not to miss anything: The "critical separation" might be ten yards on a sandy plain, ten inches in a rainforest.

Horses joined the hunt, and then the cadaver dogs and the national guard. ATVs scampered over the land. A search plane buzzed overhead. Helicopters, including one equipped with infrared sensors, thwacked over the mountains for hours, days. Radios crackled. Passing motorists were stopped and questioned. It went on from dawn to dusk for more than a week.

She should have been found.

If she had been attacked by a mountain lion or a bear, searchers should have found disheveled underbrush, scraps of clothing, blood, remains. If she had become injured or lost, the searchers—who went everywhere she could have managed to take herself—should have come upon her, and come upon her fast. It was a Rolls-Royce of an operation—nothing haphazard or skimpy about it—and it yielded not a flicker of Amy Wroe Bechtel.

The first day, the second day, the fifth day. Searchers returned to camp exhausted, pained, and baffled. There was not, according to King, a snip of cloth, a drop of blood, a single verifiable track, a sign of a scuffle—anything to indicate unambiguously that Amy was physically present, alive or dead, on the mountain. There were only a car, some keys, sunglasses, and a to-do list, with four of its 13 items checked off.

Landerites like to say that they live in a town that's free from big-city crime—the kind of random or serial mayhem that seems most possible when everyone's a stranger. But that's not strictly accurate. Beneath Lander's just-folks exterior is a town that, like most others, has not been able to fence itself off from trouble. A terrifying series of break-ins and rapes that began in the fall of 1993 prompted women's self-defense classes. In 1995, a self-described "hobo" was committed to the state hospital after being convicted of four of the attacks.

In February 1994, a local teenager was shot five times in the head and torso in the Sinks Canyon parking lot by a drug dealer who thought the victim was a police informer. The editorial headline: "Have Big-City Problems Invaded Our Secure Little Mountain Town?"

There have been unsolved murders. A woman and two children disappeared in 1980, and her blood-spattered car was found 30 miles outside of town; the bodies were never found. There was a brawl after the Lander-Riverton football game a few years ago. Shots were fired. Authorities confiscated bats, metal pipes, and a nine-millimeter pistol.

Still, Lander retains a sense of itself as a friendly, essentially innocent sort of place. Its motto could be "bad things happen, but they are not who we are." And always, the piney mountains just outside town have seemed some kind of antidote to human poisons and sorrows. That's where you could go to relax, to breathe in deep, to listen to your best self.

So, five days after Amy disappeared, when the search turned into a full-blown criminal investigation—when 25 FBI agents arrived from Denver and Virginia and from elsewhere in Wyoming, set up shop in the sheriff's office, and began to question anybody who knew anything about the young woman who seemed to have evaporated from their midst—Landerites reacted with fresh shock, followed by the scramble to impose some kind of logic on an inexplicable event. Very quickly, everyone seemed to have an opinion: the skinny, insistent drunk at the Gannett Grill who said the husband did it; the hacker on the 12th hole who was sure that someone with the wiles of a Ted Bundy had taken her away; the customer at a restaurant who said Amy was at the bottom of a nearby lake with a chain around her neck; the store owner who wondered if "maybe she just ran away." There was the half-remembered story of another young, athletic, blond woman named Ann Marie Potton, who vanished without a clue in British Columbia three years earlier after setting out for a hike on Whistler Mountain, and vague recollection of the "mountain men" who abducted a young blond athlete named Kari Swenson while she was jogging on a Montana mountain road in 1984. (In a curious coincidence, it turned out that one of Swenson's cousins is married to the owner of the Wind River Fitness Center, where Amy worked.)

Hikers and runners in the Lander area and beyond, especially women, began to look over their shoulders, to run in pairs or with dogs or with pepper spray.

And then the yellow ribbons appeared. Yellow ribbons on parking meters, on telephone poles, on trees, on tee-marker signs at the golf course: Come home, Amy. We're here. Come back, and the mountains will be safe again.

* * *

There are no yellow ribbons anywhere on the Wind River Reservation, which begins a few miles north of Lander. It is as if the Shoshone/Northern Arapahoe reservation occupies another country and another time, and the drama of Amy Bechtel plays faintly, far, far away.

Captain Larry Makeshine, at tribal police headquarters in Fort Washakie, heard about Amy's disappearance soon after it happened, but Fremont County authorities never contacted his office directly. Makeshine also heard that the FBI had sent in 25 agents, and he was mystified.

"I'm not questioning it," he said, several weeks after the FBI had come and gone, "but if I'm going to be quoted, I'd say I've never seen it done that way before."

Makeshine, a wry and circumspect man in his forties, said two agents from the FBI office in Riverton conducted interviews after several mysterious deaths on the reservation during the past year, including the hit-and-run homicide of Daniel Oldman, Jr., the teenage son of another tribal policeman. But Makeshine said that he doesn't know the status of those investigations, because "they didn't keep us posted."

Not far out of Fort Washakie, there is a little cemetery on a hillside where the Shoshone say Sacagawea, the heroic guide and interpreter for the Lewis and Clark expedition, is buried. A number of historians say otherwise—that the evidence points to an early death at Fort Manuel, far to the east in the Dakota Territory—but the Shoshone story is that she wandered for years after the expedition and came home finally to her people, who had long given her up for dead. They called her Wadzi-wipe: Lost Woman.

A month has gone by. Thousands of man-hours have been expended on generating publicity and following up on the hundreds of tips that have come in. By now, Steve and his friends have learned to discriminate between the promising and the ludicrous.

Two or three dozen psychics have offered their services. Some want money up front. Some just offer their insights. Some of the insights are theoretically helpful. "Let's say someone says, 'Check out a yellow mobile home off the highway ten miles from Lander,'" Steve says. "We can do that. If someone says, 'I see a white pickup in Utah,' well, tell me another."

Jim and Wendy Gibson, owners of Lander's Pronghorn Lodge, have told investigators they passed a slender blond woman wearing dark shorts running in the same direction they were traveling on the Loop Road—away from town—late on the afternoon of July 24. They had taken some visiting relatives, Nebraska flatlanders, up to the mountain for some predinner sightseeing.

"That's unusual," Wendy recalls saying as they drove by. "Someone running, way up here."

The runner was swift, swifter than any town jogger clomping the pounds away. Jim made a little joke: "She looks like she's running away from something."

On the way back to town, at Burnt Gulch, Wendy noticed a "dirty white vehicle" but had no reason to connect it with the young runner they'd seen earlier. Wendy remembers seeing "something red" in the car, something that reminded her of camping. A little farther toward town, they noticed a gray truck with half a load of logs and a man standing nearby, shirtless, holding a plastic container.

There was a report of gunfire on the night of July 24 at Louis Lake, eight miles from Burnt Gulch, and a voice yelling, "Come on, you sissy, do it, do it!"

A kid found a bottle in the river near Main Street in Lander. Inside the bottle was a note: "Help. I'm being held captive in Sinks Canyon. Amy." The handwriting, predictably, was not Amy's.

Wavery memories, contradictory as dreams. Dots to be connected. Frail clues. Cruel hoaxes. Shadows demanding to be tackled, to be pinned in place.

It is the end of August, then early September. Search headquarters has moved from the mountains and into town, and the taciturn, professionally noncommittal FBI agents, after an investigative blitz that lasted a week and a half, have returned to Denver and Cheyenne and Quantico.

A room in the sheriff's office has become the new command post. The walls are thick with time lines and topographic maps. In one corner sit three computers; in another, a small table with a pair of size-eight Adidas Trail Response running shoes and a mannequin torso wearing a yellow Stone Monkey T-shirt and black running shorts.

The concrete world of a physical search—gullies, cliffs, thick copses—has given way to the more abstract realm of an investigation: theories, networks, possible sightings, criminal profiles.

The vast majority of violent crimes against women are committed by a friend, an acquaintance, or a relative of the victim. The authorities quickly became interested in Steve and in a small number of men who had exhibited particular interest in Amy or her running career, but no one has emerged as anything approaching a clear suspect. Sam Lightner, the climber whom Steve drove to Dubois to meet on July 24, corroborated Steve's account of his whereabouts that day; still, no third party as yet has provided firm independent corroboration of the two climbers' account.

Meanwhile, Steve Bechtel and Amy's friends and relatives are doing what they compel themselves to do, acting as they have trained themselves to act.

They have converted Todd Skinner's garage on Lucky Lane into a search headquarters. The place is hot, cluttered, airless. Two women, including Steve's sister Leslie, stuff envelopes with canary-yellow flyers—a photo of Amy, her vital statistics, the date and place of her presumed abduction, a phone number to call, a heading: HAVE YOU SEEN AMY? $10,000 REWARD.

The group has mailed out or directed "satellite" volunteers to mail out more than 80,000 flyers. Addresses are gleaned from e-mail chain letters and Internet phone directories: bars, pawn shops, convenience stores, truck stops, motels, bus lines, Adopt-a-Highway sponsors, film processors. There is an Amy Web site; more than 200 other Web sites have links to it, and there is a goal of 1,000 links. The search is out of the woods, onto the computer screen.

Aphorisms are handwritten on the garage walls: "Miracles come after a lot of hard work." "You wouldn't want to quit and then find out later you only had inches to go . . ." Kipling's "If" is taped to a cupboard door.

A separate room at the back of the garage is the Lucky Lane climbing gym. One wall tips forward in a dizzying replica of an overhang. Mattresses cover the floor. On a side wall, scores of routes are listed by category: Easy, Tricky, Hard, Desperate, Savage, Hoss. Scattered randomly are yet more aphorisms: "Die Young! Die Strong!" "Life is Pain / I want to be insane." "No prisoners / No Mercy!" "You must Get Weak to get strong!"

In Steve and Amy's house, across the street, taped to the group's central computer, is another: "You've got a date with the ultimate burn."

There are few mysteries more potent than that of someone who vanishes without a clue, who seems to inhabit an ordinary day and then does not, who becomes the presumed victim of a crime only because the other alternatives seem less likely.

A missing person is not fully alive or fully dead. She does not age. She exists in a shadow land that we, the waiting, invest with both our fantasies and our nightmares. What if she simply slipped out of her life and started another from scratch? It's a theme that runs deep in America—the idea of leaving behind the complications and sorrows of one's day-by-day existence to make a fresh start as someone new, to lose one's past.

The FBI's National Crime Information Center listed approximately 35,000 adults missing at the end of 1997. But if history is any guide, the majority will return on their own or will otherwise be accounted for. Only 2 or 3 percent of the missing will turn into outright, long-term mysteries involving assumptions of foul play.

No one who has known Amy Bechtel seems to believe that she would simply cut all the traces and disappear, that she could impose that kind of open-ended pain on those she left behind. And so the imagination moves into a more dire realm, but one in which it is still possible to invest the missing person with the qualities of one's own, most survivable self. Maybe she is a prisoner, waiting for her chance. Or she is wandering in an amnesiac state but will someday recall her name and her history and reclaim them in triumph after a strange, long time in which she was lost to her searchers and to herself.

Beyond that, there is murder. That is the first terror-dream when a person is missing, and it is linked to a second: that of dying in such a way that one is never conclusively missed, never completely mourned.

Steve Bechtel enters the garage from across the street. He is wearing a T-shirt, shorts, sandals. In the weeks since Amy disappeared, his perennial tan has faded, though his face remains preternaturally smooth and unlined. His demeanor has taken on the alert exhaustion of an air traffic controller. With reporters, his manner is energetically neutral, like a young surgeon describing a harrowing operative procedure. A fancy new anesthetic gets the same buoyant description as the details of sawing through a limb. His cheerful tone of voice, his amiability, remains constant, whether he's talking about the details of rock climbing or the possibility that his wife has been raped and murdered.

"He's hurting," says his friend Marit Fischer, in Denver. "But he will never show them he is."

"Them" could be the reporters, or the volunteers in the garage. Or they could be those who are angry and confused by Steve's refusal to take a lie detector test.

Early on, the authorities—the FBI, chief investigator Dave King, sheriff Larry Matthews—and many townspeople and even Amy's parents took the position that if Steve was innocent, he had nothing to lose by sitting for a lie-detector test. Steve, most of his intimates, and his lawyer—Kent Spence, stepbrother of one of Steve's climbing acquaintances and son of *that* Spence, Gerry—felt quite differently. They said that Steve had already submitted to four formal interviews with the investigators, and they pointed to study after study about the unreliability of polygraph tests.

Further, Steve and Spence accused the cops of picking at straws in the wind, of relying on "profiles" of perpetrators, of wasting their energy badgering and frightening Steve when they could be tracking down potentially fruitful leads and suspects.

"The FBI in their usual sensitive manner attacked Steve Bechtel when they became frustrated with their failure to come up with any clues," Spence said shortly after taking on Steve as a client. "They pointed their cannons at him and accused him of being involved, when they had no evidence whatsoever."

Steve speaks of an FBI agent who he says told him, point-blank, just two weeks or so after the search for Amy began, "We have evidence you killed Amy." Steve uses the words "preposterous" and "unbelievable" to describe the situation. What he seems to be saying is that he has been put in a predicament in which he has to bear not only the loss of his wife, but the open-ended suspicion that he was her killer.

"This sounds strange, but we hope that she's been abducted," he says. "With that option, there are unlimited scenarios. One is that she was grabbed, raped, and killed . . ." He clears his throat. "We think that is unlikely. We think she's still alive, being kept alive, and has left the area. Maybe she has amnesia. That she is being kept by someone infatuated, obsessed with her. That is why we're making this a nationwide search.

"She's a very trusting person. She thinks that people are generally good. I think her thinking will change, has changed."

Nine miles from town, in the Sinks Canyon State Park Interpretive Center, among other exhibits, is a mounted photograph of a rock climber. The photo, shot by Amy Wroe Bechtel, placed third in the action category in a local contest. The climber, leaning against air, seems to be hanging onto the mountain by his very fingernails.

Two months after she disappeared, the Amy Bechtel Hill Climb took place. One hundred and forty-six runners stretched and shivered and high-stepped in a parking lot not far from Sinks Canyon State Park. Soon they would head off, climbing past killing switchbacks, toward Frye Lake, ten kilometers distant.

You know the drill: large dogs barking, tights, running shorts, sweat pants, ski caps, singlets, gloves, Marmot, Columbia, Patagonia, The North Face, pre-race babble.

There was Steve, greeting friends, being hugged. There were Jeff, Steve's brother, and Jo Anne and Duane Wroe, and Todd Skinner. There were Tom and Linda, Steve's parents, and Casey and Jenny, Amy's sisters.

Steve, in shorts, bareheaded, raised his hands and quieted the crowd. "Amy has wanted to do this race for a couple of years," he said. "She was always told the only people who would show would be eight of her former track teammates."

Laughter. Cheers.

"We're in this together. We know Amy's alive."

Cheers. Yes.

"OK . . ." His voice quavered. He paused. When he spoke again, it had returned to full strength.

"One last thing: Please wait for me after you get to the finish line."

Laughter.

Ray Candelaria, Lander Valley High School cross-country coach, said, "Runners, on your marks," and pointed his starter's gun to the sky.

We are not an especially admirable species. We are suspicious, violent, maladroit. We leave unholy messes wherever we go, despite our best intentions.

By the start of the hill climb, everyone was tired. They had been a long time on the mountain. Things had gone wrong. The original 800 number on the missing posters—all 120,000 of them—turned out to be invalid when dialed from out-of-state. Todd Skinner and Steve blamed the cops. The cops expressed surprise at this, claiming that Steve and Todd had told them the mistake wouldn't really matter, since a correct local number was also printed on the poster.

While the climbing community in Lander remained solidly loyal to Steve, things had unraveled badly among the family. Tempers had shortened. Alliances had frayed. A few weeks before the race, Amy's parents and siblings met with the FBI and the Fremont County sheriff's office and poured out their anxiety. Why were they so focused on Steve? Where was the investigation leading?

The authorities produced Steve's journals, or portions of them, selectively highlighted (or not—it depends on who's telling the story). As volatile and intriguing as the journals may be, they have not been made public, and the import of their contents varies wildly with the account of each possibly unreliable witness. Nels Wroe, Amy's brother, and his wife, Teresa, who is the director of a center for domestic-abuse victims, were shocked at what they felt were indications of violent tendencies in the writing, of obsessive thinking on Steve's part. Soon after, Nels restated—for a reporter from the Casper *Star-Tribune* and on a Wyoming public radio news program—his fervent wish that Steve would take a polygraph test. Duane Wroe agreed. Jo Anne said little. Amy's sisters, on the other hand, remained publicly loyal to Steve.

"It's not within me to be angry at someone for having feelings or thoughts and for dealing with them by placing them on a piece of paper," Casey Wroe-Lee told the *Star-Tribune.*

Nels said that Steve denied the journals' currency, that Steve said they were written in high school. Steve denied Nels's version of his denial and stated that while the entries do run up to a week or so before the disappearance, some of the disturbing entries were only gonzo song lyrics, written in high school.

Nels pointed out, as an example of Steve's obsessive jealousy, that Steve had refused to accompany Amy to Nels and Teresa's wedding because of the likely presence of a possible former boyfriend of Amy's.

Nels and Teresa didn't attend the hill climb. They said they didn't want to cause a stir, to have the families' choppy sorrows upstage an event that should focus exclusively on Amy.

So, as the runners headed toward Frye Lake, what had been envisioned as a day of sad but positive solidarity, of communal bolstering, had become—certainly for the families of Amy and Steve—grim, stiff, heavy, angry. The grand blue Wyoming skies had curdled.

Winter would arrive.

Steve would start working again at Wild Iris, and he would begin fixing up the house he and Amy have yet to occupy together. He described himself, wearily, as "functioning, able to work and continue living." When asked about his anger at the cops, at Nels, he said, "I don't really have the energy to get pissed-off at anyone these days."

The mouth of the Sinks was searched by divers. Old mine shafts in Atlantic City, Wyoming, were explored.

At a University of Wyoming football game, the scoreboard lit up with Amy's photo, the familiar phone number, the request for any information.

Todd Skinner and Amy Whisler headed south to their winter climbing headquarters in Texas. Skinner went on to Mali to climb Fatima, a 2,000-foot quartzite tower.

In mid-November, Skinner was asked about "Amy as the summit," about never giving up. He replied that in the absence of new clues, the primary task had become supporting Steve. "We never really started climbing anyway," he added. "We were stuck at the base of the mountain, walking in place."

Steve and Nels met at a race for Amy held in Laramie. They spoke briefly, cautiously, civilly.

Dean Chingman, a young Indian from Ethete, on the Wind River Reservation, went missing in early November. The search-and-rescue effort included search dogs and one airplane. Two FBI agents were assigned to the Chingman case.

Everyone waited for news from NASA on whether photographs that might have been taken by Russia's Mir space station on the day of Amy's disappearance would reveal new clues. Eventually word came that no such photos existed.

In mid-October, the FBI and the local investigators, having dropped their demand that Steve Bechtel submit to a polygraph test, asked him to come in for another general interview, but on the advice of Kent Spence, his attorney, he declined. "They're just trying to poke and poke, and hope that they get something," Spence said recently. "They've made it look like Steve has something to hide."

The Bechtel case was on the docket of a grand jury, convened in Casper in late November. Grand jury proceedings are unnervingly secret affairs. None of the officials involved would comment on the deliberations, though one of the subpoenaed witnesses said that the jury was mostly interested in a former acquaintance of Amy's whom authorities have been unable to locate.

The reward for information leading to the recovery of Amy Wroe Bechtel now stands at $100,000.

All these strands, these smears, shadows, whispers, shards—they have come to naught.

Early storms arrived, left. Deer hunters—objects of an intensive, dedicated, but fruitless flurry of Have You Seen Amy? publicity—came and went.

The Loop Road became impassable and was closed.

Winter lasts a long time in Lander. Forget the brochures, forget Jackson Hole. It is a punishing time. It is not the winter of whooping skiers and snowboarders, of fresh flocks of pink-cheeked tourists. It is unfathomably cold. It is knife-blade winds. It is the season of iron silence. Time to take shelter. To regroup. To gain faith—faith that the snow, the cold, will vanish. It has to.

It is also the season of memory's distortion. The golds of autumn become more golden; the greens of summer, greener; the warm, clear days, warmer, clearer.

But not this year, not in Lander. A woman is still lost. Friends and loved ones still grieve, wonder, rage: Where is Amy? And so her life, and the lives of those who care most about her, are suspended. In place of logic, movement, and resolution, there is stasis: a young face on a poster, a dusty Toyota station wagon, blinking cursors.

These won't do—not at all. They don't recall Amy, and they don't convey the knee-buckling anguish of this bottomless mystery. To glimpse even a measure of these things, you could return, perhaps, to a moment in September, nearly three hours after the first runner in the Amy Bechtel Hill Climb crossed the finish line at Frye Lake. The last four walkers are approaching the line as one, holding hands: Amy's mother, Jo Anne; Amy's sister, Casey; Casey's young daughter, Jillian; and Jillian's friend, Hanna.

Jo Anne Wroe's face is pulled long. She is limping. Strands of her rich black hair stick wet to her face. She looks bewildered, beyond exhaustion, like death itself.

March 1998

The Captain
Went Down with
the Ship

DANIEL COYLE

"L et's see if we can miss the reef this time," Joseph Hazelwood says
to me. Then he laughs.

That's the first thing you notice about Joe Hazelwood, the laugh.
It's not a laugh, actually; it's a joyless simulation of a laugh, a swift
propulsion of air through the nose that mimics laughter's cadence but
lacks its music, signifying neither joy nor scorn, but information.
Laughter is a vital element of the Hazelwood vocabulary. Dark eyes
bracketed by wrinkles, large bald head bobbing up and down, ever-
present Marlboro tilting dangerously from his lips, he wields mirth as
one might wield a friendly elbow: easing tension, forging a conspira-
torial mood, letting you know in no uncertain terms that he, along
with everybody else—better than everybody else—gets the joke. To be
Joe Hazelwood is to be preternaturally alert to double entendres, puns,
one-liners, coincidences, any flashing link between this moment and
that dark night in March 1989 when he was transfigured from an
anonymous but skilled professional into a lasting national symbol of
rank incompetence and drunken idiocy. When the opportunity for a
joke presents itself, he is coiled and ready, anticipating its arrival,
deflecting it with topspin, and then laughing his ersatz laugh—at the
joke, to be sure, but also at the irony of his telling the joke. To be Joe

Hazelwood is to be a connoisseur of irony, a seeker of veiled meanings. He may have lost his career, his ship, and his reputation, but he's still got perspective. He's still cool about it. Earlier today, Hazelwood was describing a different tanker run that he made through Prince William Sound. "We left Valdez fully loaded . . ." He pulls up short. "The ship, I mean—not me." The Marlboro tip glows and bobs.

We're in the Seamen's Church Institute, a tidy brick building in lower Manhattan that serves as a training center for merchant mariners. We've come here at my request from the midtown law office where Hazelwood works to take a spin in the bridge simulator. This full-scale, state-of-the-art device has been set up to replicate the conditions at midnight, March 23, 1989, a few moments before the *Exxon Valdez* bellied-up on Bligh Reef in Alaska's Prince William Sound and began disgorging 11 million gallons of crude oil, obliterating life on 1,244 miles of coastline, and forever altering the way in which we view the vulnerability of our wild places. Instantly overlaid by myth, the spill has become crystallized in the public imagination as the archetypal catastrophe, Captain Joseph Jeffrey Hazelwood its archetypal cause.

The captain is nothing if not punctual, so we arrived at five o'clock, exactly on schedule, and waited a few minutes while the simulator's operator booted up its Valdez program. Hazelwood was eager to get started: In order to catch his 6:24 train home to Huntington, Long Island, he calculated that he must depart here at 5:45, no later. Now, as our facsimile tanker approaches the facsimile reef, he steps comfortably around the bridge, eyeing the engine-order telegraph, tweaking the radar, confidently adjusting the dials and knobs. Satisfied, he steps back and checks his watch: 5:35.

Beyond the frames of five bridge windows, the mountains of Prince William Sound part to reveal a passage ten miles wide. Ahead, the monolithic main deck of the supertanker recedes toward the horizon. Winds are calm, skies dark, visibility eight miles. We've left the shipping lanes, just as the *Exxon Valdez* departed them in order to avoid ice. Off the starboard bow, a tiny red light pulses once every four seconds—Bligh Reef buoy. Radar shows that we're passing Busby Island, the spot where the tanker was to have begun its starboard turn back into the shipping lanes. An SCI captain named James Fitzpatrick, who has been informed of Hazelwood's time restriction, mans the helm.

"The moment of truth," Hazelwood says flatly. "Give me right 20."

"Right two-zero, Cap," says Fitzpatrick.

The ship begins to swing. Hazelwood does not look to the radar screen for proof; he waits to see it, as he later says, "to feel the turn." The red buoy light begins to slide across the windows, imperceptibly at first, then with silken rapidity. After two minutes, during which time we've advanced a bare seven-tenths of a mile, our 1,000-foot, 250,000-ton virtual supertanker—weighing 40,000 tons more than the *Exxon Valdez*—has turned on a dime. The buoy bobs innocuously off our port side. We've missed Bligh Reef by more than two miles.

Eyes on the horizon, Hazelwood speaks. "That's all you'd have to do. That's all anybody would have had to do."

"OK," says Fitzpatrick, picking up the note of finality. "Time to catch that train."

Hazelwood doesn't reply. The ship presses onward. Bligh Reef buoy disappears from view. Minutes pass.

"Uh, Captain . . ." The dutiful Fitzpatrick taps his watch, which shows ten minutes until six.

Hazelwood doesn't move. His head fixes on the horizon, eyes reflecting the radar screen's endless clocklike whirl.

"Give me left ten, midshipman steady," he says, ordering a course that will route the tanker back into the lanes, bound for Naked Island and the open ocean beyond.

"Left ten," echoes Fitzpatrick. Again, Hazelwood waits to feel the turn.

Somewhere beneath us, a subway rumbles toward Penn Station. Hazelwood lets it go. He stays on the bridge because eight years ago he didn't stay. He stays on the bridge because he is in purgatory and in purgatory you can laugh, or cry, or protest your innocence, but the only thing that matters is reliving your sin over and over until either you or God is worn out. And that's the other thing you learn about Joe Hazelwood: He's served notice to God that it's not going to be him.

*   *   *

"Welcome to my nightmare," he says.

It's my first meeting with Hazelwood, and he's standing in the cramped disarray of his 8-by-14-foot office, feet set wide apart, palms held out in parodic greeting. He's wearing a button-down oxford shirt, khakis, a Jerry Garcia–designed tie, and dress loafers, all of it enshrouded in the smoke and steam of his medicinal Marlboros and coffee. At 51, his body is that of a younger man: six feet, 180 pounds, broad shoulders tapering to a 34-inch waist, corded forearms below carefully rolled sleeves. Beneath the graying skein of beard, the face is small and childlike, with leathery skin crosshatched and furrowed by wrinkles, russet-colored eyes set in a wary squint, and obstinately protruding lower lip. He doesn't look at me as he talks, instead tipping his head toward the blue carpet. Eye contact comes in furtive volleys, to prevent the subtleties of his words from passing unnoticed or, worse, being misread for earnestness.

After a few minutes it becomes apparent that Hazelwood's not going to sit down. "I work standing up," he explains to his coffee cup. An old shipboard habit, and not his only one. "When I first came here, I walked around shutting every door in sight. Drove everybody nuts. Kept cleaning off my desk, too. As you can see," he indicates the avalanche of manila folders, sticky notes, and coffee-ringed napkins fanning out before him, "I've made the adjustment."

There have been other adjustments. The drop in salary from $100,000 to "enough to live on." The dearth of vacation. The daily 90-minute commute on the Long Island Railroad, or as he calls it, the Train of the Living Dead. "It's scary," he says. "I catch myself moving to the spot on the platform where the doors are going to be when the train stops." He places a long index finger to his temple and pulls the trigger. "I always swore I'd never be one of those guys."

Every morning begins the same way. "Let's see what disasters we've got today," he says, rattling open a copy of *Lloyd's List,* a maritime industry daily, and turning to the casualty report. Good news: capsized barge in San Francisco Bay, bulk carrier aground in Turkey, iron-ore carrier stranded in the Yellow Sea, cement-carrying barge near Guyana suffering "extensive damage" following a collision with an unknown submerged object. Hazelwood's job, among other things, is to negotiate settlements between cargo insurers, which his firm represents, and the parties liable for the losses, usually the shipping companies. Each morning brings a dozen or more new claims: delaminated plywood, sea-soaked paper, rancid plums, torn cellulose, rotting bananas. The files accumulate on his desk in great tilting stacks. Hazelwood makes a point of saying that he takes no joy in these incidents. He mentions this because he's aware, as he is aware of each Kafkaesque plotline in his post-spill life, that the more shipwrecks and groundings there are, the harder he has to work and (should you desire another level of irony) the larger his year-end bonus will be. When asked if he enjoys his present job, he hesitates and says yes. His desktop calendar, set on December 1995, is thickly brocaded with urgently penciled squares, triangles, circles, and other unidentifiable scratchings so deep that in places the paper is cut through.

"You'd be bored out of your skull watching me work," he warned me in an early phone conversation. "I know I am."

Hazelwood has been working at Chalos & Brown, the law firm that has defended him since the spill, for more than five years. Reserved and awkward in formal social situations, he excels in the manly woof and banter of proletarian office life, transmitting the universally comprehended vibe of the Good Guy, that can-do, sports-literate, shoot-the-breeze brand of heartiness that simultaneously draws people close and holds them at a distance. He isn't, he points out, an indentured servant. A reluctant Exxon picks up his legal bills, as it must under employment law in California, where Hazelwood signed on with the *Valdez*. (Democratically, Exxon also indirectly funds Hazelwood's criminal prosecution, since 85 percent of Alaska state revenues are derived from oil taxes.) Nor is he landlocked: His captain's license has been active since a nine-month Coast Guard suspension ended in 1991. After a brief string of temporary jobs—lobster fisherman, boat transporter—this job has the advantage of providing a staging area where Hazelwood can pursue the only vocation still open to him: defending himself in court. "Nobody in the maritime industry will touch him," says Michael Chalos, one of his lawyers and a college buddy. "Who could afford to take the PR risk? I mean, bang a dock and it's on the front page—'Hazelwood does it again!'"

In the hallway outside his office, 20 feet from his nameplate, a collage of newspaper clippings is pressed inside a black frame: DRUNK AT SEA . . . FATEFUL VOYAGE . . . OIL-SPILL CAPT FIRED . . . $1M BAIL LANDS OIL CAPT IN BRIG . . . More clips, hundreds more compiled by the firm, reside in two black scrapbooks inside his office. OFFICER SMELLED LIQUOR ON CAPT OF TANKER . . . SHIP MAY HAVE BEEN ON AUTOPILOT . . . OFF TO JAIL . . . SKIPPER'S RISE AND FALL . . .

"Good reading, isn't it," Hazelwood says over my shoulder.

It is, beginning with the trumpet-blare that the captain of the *Exxon Valdez* was, at the time of the accident, unqualified to drive his car in New York state because of drunken-driving violations. Then comes the *New York Times* page-one analysis that Hazelwood had probably set the ship on autopilot and gone below while third mate Gregory Cousins and helmsman Robert Kagan "desperately tried" to regain control. Then the stories that after the grounding, Hazelwood foolishly attempted to motor the ship off the reef, risking a possible capsizing and the spillage of millions more gallons of oil. And the dramatic courtroom depiction of the judge who compared the spill to the bombing of Hiroshima, set bail at $1 million, and sent Hazelwood to a night in prison before the bond was reduced.

Hazelwood flips through the binder as if it were a family album. His fingernail taps the page. "There's Kagan . . . there's Greg . . . there's a good shot of Mike Chalos . . . there's me in high school."

He chuckles. And why not? The world may know his secrets, but he can laugh, because he has found out the world's secret, one that allowed him to endure hatred, ostracism, ridicule, loss, and pain. The secret is this: Keep your mouth shut. Hazelwood believes in silence, believes in it with religious fervor, because it has served him in a way that no religion could or did; it has given him a power no one else had, power he has never relinquished. Aside from his lawyers and his testimony in the civil case, he has spoken to no one about what happened that night. Not reporters, not his best friend, not his brothers, not his wife, not his fighter-pilot father—especially not his father. What happened that night—more precisely, what Joe Hazelwood did, what he didn't do, and how he feels about it—belongs to him and no one else. He keeps his secrets, and for better or worse, they keep him.

On our final visit, he will tell me, "If there's one thing I've learned from this experience, it would be this: If you're ever in any kind of a touchy situation, do not say a word to anyone. Words can only hurt you."

The moment the *Exxon Valdez* touched Bligh Reef, Hazelwood's silence began. He gave no statements, permitted few interviews, declined to testify at the National Transportation Safety Board hearings and his 1990 criminal trial. "Hermetically sealed" was the term his lawyers used, and their obedient client disappeared onto the front page. His silence rescued Exxon, which needed a bogeyman; the press, which needed a reason; and the public, which needed a way to think about the unthinkable. He became a two-dimensional figure in a Puritan allegory, proof of the American theorem that history is character writ large. He evolved into a type, a handy referent for the loose cannon, the dangerous idiot. (Letterman's Top Ten Joe Hazelwood Excuse: "I was just trying to scrape some ice off the reef for my margarita.") The artistic pinnacle of the Hazelwood oeuvre was his nonspeaking role as divine idol of the Smokers, the scraggly, jet-skiing globe-wreckers of Kevin Costner's soggy 1995 future-pic *Waterworld*. "Be patient, Saint Joe, we're close," Dennis Hopper whispers reverentially to a gilt-framed portrait of the resolute-looking captain. "After centuries of shame, we're almost there."

That face—the shadowy beard, the child's stubborn lip, the brim of the driving cap darkening the already-sinister eyes—sets the tone of spill coverage. There's the usual spate of determinist profiles, in which Hazelwood's life is presented as dully predictable precursor: the 138 IQ, the cocky-ironic college yearbook motto "It Will Never Happen to Me," the college drinking escapades, the too-quiet manner—even his ship's Exxon Fleet Safety Awards for 1987 and 1988 are knowingly invoked.

Suitably enough, it was Hazelwood's words that sealed his fate, most notably through the spectacularly damning quote he gave the two Coast

Guard officers who boarded the ship the night of the spill. In four words, Hazelwood seemed to reveal that the reason for this spreading horror lay not in some mechanical or navigational problem, but rather in something that had broken loose inside him. The officer inquired what the problem was. Hazelwood replied, "You're looking at it."

"I mean, here they were, called out to a grounded tanker in the middle of the night, oil spewing all over the place, and they walk up and ask me what the problem is?" Hazelwood sweeps his arm grandly. "I said, 'You're looking at it'—as in, 'Hey, man, you're standing on it.' It wasn't an admission of guilt, but everybody interpreted it as such."

The few times that Hazelwood was quoted in the aftermath of the spill, he said nothing to vindicate himself or show remorse. When the judge in his criminal trial asked for an apology, Hazelwood declined. When Connie Chung asked if he could declare his innocence before a national television audience, he said he could say nothing either way about the case. He displayed a clinical detachment from what everybody else was fiercely concerned with: the otters, the salmon, the ecosystem of Prince William Sound, the spill's larger role as harkening call, along with the widening ozone hole and the disappearing rainforests, to the environmental movement's early-decade shift to center stage in the American consciousness.

Hazelwood seemed oblivious to the fact that his silence forever condemned him in the minds of many, oblivious to the proven truth of the political maxim that it's not the accusation, it's how you handle the accusation that matters. Among friends and acquaintances, the silence engendered much speculation. Was it guilt? Pride? Shame? Denial? Was he protecting someone? But to hear Hazelwood tell it, the matter is simpler: There's nothing to say.

"What am I going to do, write a book about a guy missing a turn?" His eyebrows arch cartoonily. "Books have a hero. I'm just a regular guy caught in a situation. There's a perception out there, and all the spin doctors in the world can't fix that perception. I'm not a bubbly person. I don't have an inner child I'm beating up. Go on *Oprah*? I just don't have it in me. The people who know me know what I'm about."

Occasionally, however, the shell of equanimity shows a few cracks. Though our time together has its agreed-upon boundaries (no questions about his actions leading up to the spill, no interviews with his wife or college-age daughter, no visits to his home), Hazelwood shows an increasing willingness to broach the accident and his feelings toward it. At those moments, which usually take place during his 20-minute walk from Penn Station to the office, his voice takes on the nasal, syncopated patois of middle-class Long Island. An unabashed bibliophile (another shipboard habit), he tosses off quotes from Oscar Wilde, Albert Einstein, Stonewall Jackson, Beryl Markham, and does a passable Bill Murray impression. The rhythm of the walk takes over, he's carried along in the hot swell of humanity, and for once his words flow unencumbered.

"You know, this thing happened the same spring as Tiananmen Square," he says, stopping to carefully stub out a cigarette. "That was big news for a day—then it was back to our regularly scheduled slamming of Captain Hazelwood. A year later you got Saddam dumping 40 million barrels of oil—150 times what was spilled in Prince William Sound—and he's setting the country on fire, and the guy's still getting better press than me?" On his fingers, he ticks off other accidents and tragedies that received less attention, including many larger oil spills that were virtually ignored by the press. "The way the media handles disasters is out of proportion. Like a friend of mine said after TWA Flight 800 went down: 'Good thing there weren't any fucking otters on board.'"

Then we're outside his building, in the shadow of its steel and smoked glass. "I've learned to keep my emotions out of it," he says, regaining his equilibrium. "This is a business, and emotions cloud your judgment. This is a technical problem, basically, and it's got to be dealt with in a technical way. Besides, it's like Eddie Murphy said in *Trading Places*: 'I'm a Karate Man—I bleed on the *inside*.'" He opens the door and smiles his good-guy smile, and it is utterly unconvincing.

The boxes are everywhere, stacked along walls, bowing bookshelves, and concealing the floor of Hazelwood's office, a tiny fortress of fact and belief. Together they form the bulwark of Hazelwood's legal argument that he was neither drunk nor negligent the night of the *Exxon Valdez* spill and that the real reason for the accident lies in an unfortunate combination of mundane events, happenstance, and human mistakes—the most significant of which were not made by Hazelwood. With few exceptions—and little fanfare from the media—the courts and Coast Guard have agreed, finding him innocent of criminal mischief, operating a watercraft while intoxicated, reckless endangerment, and misconduct. As he helps prepare the appeal to his civil charge of recklessness and waits for the Alaska Supreme Court to issue a decision on (brace yourself) the state's appeal of the appellate court's second overturning of Hazelwood's Class B misdemeanor conviction for negligent discharge of oil—a decision that will lead to either a new trial or, perhaps, the final dismissal of the criminal case—one would expect a level of anticipation, the heady possibility that one chapter might be coming to a close. But when I mention this, Hazelwood turns dour.

"What court do I go to to get my reputation back?" he says brusquely. "I'm not trying to impress anybody. I just don't want this hanging over my head. The damage is done. I've got to get on with my life."

Which mostly involves defending himself in court, a well-choreographed piece of tradecraft that Hazelwood and his attorneys know cold: Show how the accident happened, and then show that there is no evidence that Hazelwood's actions or behavior were anything less than normal; in short, let him blend innocuously into the larger context. Now, standing amid the boxes, Hazelwood moves through the key elements of his case with disarming ease. The evidence is all here, right here:

- Stripped to essentials, the *Exxon Valdez* hit Bligh Reef because it departed the shipping lanes to avoid ice—a maneuver executed by the *Brooklyn* and the *Arco Juneau* just hours before—and failed to turn back into the lanes before striking the reef.
- Third mate Gregory Cousins, testifying in the criminal and the civil trials, shouldered much of the blame for failing to execute the turn that Hazelwood had ordered. After outlining the maneuver and asking Cousins twice if he was comfortable making the turn, Hazelwood left the bridge at 11:50 P.M. Cousins phoned Hazelwood at 11:55 to say he was beginning the turn but then

failed to check that helmsman Robert Kagan followed his commands, spending precious minutes charting the ship's position.
Cousins was on the phone to Hazelwood, saying, "I think we're
in serious trouble," when they felt the first jolt a few minutes
after midnight.

"There was no reason to do what I did that evening," Cousins testified. "I shouldn't have allowed myself to become inattentive." Hoping to secure testimony against Hazelwood, the state gave Cousins
immunity against prosecution; plaintiffs in the civil suit did not press
charges against him lest he complicate their case against Exxon and
Hazelwood; the Coast Guard cited him for negligence and suspended
his license for nine months.

"To the public and the press, 'third mate' has the ring of 'cabin
boy,'" says Hazelwood. "Cousins was a trained, licensed navigational
officer, a good man. He's still a good man."

- Helmsman Kagan, when ordered to make the turn, did not execute it fully. Kagan earned the nickname Rain Man during the
  criminal trial for mixing up his right and left and for muttering
  to himself during cross-examination, "Why is he asking me that?
  I wish he wouldn't ask me that." Employment records showed
  that Kagan required "constant supervision."

"I put a lot of it on Kagan," says Paul Larson, who led the Coast
Guard investigation. "He does his job, and we're talking about something else today."

- The post-grounding radio transmissions in which Hazelwood said
  he was trying to "extract the ship from the reef" were mislead-
  ing. He only called for forward throttle—not reverse, as would
  have been necessary if he'd wanted to free the vessel. By keeping
  the ship pressed firmly against the reef, he minimized the spill
  and the danger to his crew.
- The blood tests that showed Hazelwood to be intoxicated were
  mishandled. Drawn ten and a half hours after the grounding

(because of variance in individual metabolic rates, most states, including Alaska, disallow any test performed more than three hours after an event), the blood was shipped to the lab in tubes without a chemical needed to keep the blood from fermenting, invalidating the results. In addition, the labels on the tubes were switched to make it appear as if they did contain preservative, a switch revealed by discrepancies in laboratory log entries.

Even in the criminal trial, before evidence of the blood mishandling had surfaced, state prosecutors were unable to persuade a jury that Hazelwood was intoxicated at the time of the grounding. By his own admission, Hazelwood drank "two or three vodkas" between 4:30 and 6:30 the night of the grounding. To account for his 0.061 blood-alcohol content ten hours after the accident, however, either (1) his blood-alcohol level upon boarding the ship had been .35, a level he could have achieved only by consuming 16 to 20 drinks in the course of the day, or (2) he had sneaked a few drinks sometime after boarding the ship at 8:25 P.M. With the testimony of 21 witnesses, including Cousins and the Coast Guard officers who first boarded the ship, that Hazelwood's behavior had not been impaired in any way, and with no hard evidence of shipboard drinking beyond two empty bottles of low-alcohol beer in Hazelwood's stateroom, the jury took little time in deliberating the intoxication charge.

As for his widely presumed alcoholism, Hazelwood can refer to records that show his physician had diagnosed him with "dysthymia, a subgrouping of depression, characterized by episodic abuse of alcohol," he says. "The perception is that I was a drooling idiot, carted off to the dry cleaners. I enrolled myself in a hospital-treatment program back in '85, went to the meetings, and stayed dry for several years. But as has been shown, alcohol had nothing to do with the grounding."

Other things did, though, and Hazelwood knows them by heart: the Vessel Traffic Service watchstanders, charged with monitoring the vessel's progress through the sound, who failed to spot the missed turn and who later tested positive for marijuana and alcohol; the abysmal state of the Alyeska Pipeline Company's spill-control equipment; the

ensuing circus of decision-making by Exxon, Alyeska, and state officials that let a possibly controllable spill get out of control. Accident
investigators call it an error chain, and Hazelwood can trace it back
as far as you like. What if Cousins had listened to lookout Maureen
Jones, who twice brought the Bligh Reef buoy to his attention during
the delay in executing the turn? What if Cousins hadn't, as a favor to
a friend, offered to work past midnight, when his shift was to have
ended? What if the ship hadn't gotten loaded more quickly than antic-
ipated and sailed two hours ahead of schedule? Hazelwood navigates
the possibilities as if playing a board game, effortlessly translating chaos
into a smooth, inevitable progression. He smiles ruefully, shrugs his
shoulders, rolls his eyes to the sky.

Then conversation turns, as it always must, to the central element
in the error chain, Hazelwood's absence from the bridge. Why did he
leave? To prepare departure messages to send to Exxon, he famously
explained. Why couldn't he have waited? Why didn't he know about
Kagan's shortcomings? How could he leave the bridge if there was even
the slightest chance of a mistake?

"I left," he says slowly, staring at the floor, "because there wasn't
a compelling reason to stay. I really can't comment further on that."

Hazelwood's lawyers argue that their client gave Cousins good
instructions, that other tanker captains had vacated the bridge at that
point in the voyage; that having been told the turn was beginning,
Hazelwood had no reason to suspect anything was amiss. It's an argument that might work in court, but not everywhere.

"It all boils down to the fact that Hazelwood wasn't on the bridge,"
says J. Samuel Teel, professor of nautical science at Maine Maritime
Academy. "I'm sure he's a great guy and a good captain, but he should
have been there and he wasn't. He's got to live with that."

"I say to this day it wasn't his fault. He just put too much trust in
certain people," says Captain John Wilson, an old Hazelwood friend
and shipmate. "Joe should have watched his mate a little bit closer."

"One of the finest tanker men I ever met," roars Captain Russ
Nyborg, a legendary San Francisco Bay skipper who served as a model
for young Hazelwood in his early Exxon days. "He left it to somebody else and somebody else screwed up. My wife and I were very

worried about him for a long time after it happened. He's so proud, you know, and he's had the shit kicked out of him." The old captain's voice goes rough with clumsily camouflaged concern. "So how's he doing, anyway?"

Months and years slid past, interest in the spill waned, and still Hazelwood kept to the shadows. He retreated to his wife and daughter and his cadre of Long Island friends, the ones who know him as Jeff, a childhood name that distinguishes him from his father. Never social (hosting one party in 14 years, according to a neighbor), he spent time reading, preparing for his defense, and occasionally sailing the 16-foot Hobie Cat he kept in the backyard. Friends worried about him, said he was quieter, more introspective. But at rare gatherings, they bull-shitted and talked sports and shipping just like always, and when they were sailing on Long Island Sound and passed a grounded boat and somebody said, "Little déjà vu, Jeffie?" Hazelwood waited through the silence and replied, "Haven't heard that one before," and everybody laughed loudly.

"Joe was a class act throughout this thing," says Jerzy Glowacki, chief engineer on the *Exxon Valdez* and one of Hazelwood's barmates in the hours before. "He's taken the full brunt of this, quietly, with dignity, under great stress, and I think he's able to do it because of his intelligence. He knows what is happening; he understands the reasons. I don't think he's able to shrug it off. I don't think he ever will. Whatever it is, he's carrying it inside, and I'm sure it's very heavy."

His parents wait and wonder, too. The summer after the grounding, his mother, a proper Georgia-bred Presbyterian, offered to arrange for a pastor to meet with him. When Hazelwood ran into the man at a funeral, the pastor said, "Whatever you did up there, God doesn't judge you." Hazelwood replied, "Sure as shit sounds like *you're* judging me," and walked off.

"I keep hoping Jeff will talk to me," Margaret Hazelwood tells me in her buttery accent. "I'll sometimes try to start such a conversation. I'll say things like, 'I wonder how I would have reacted in your situation.' But he won't talk." Hazelwood's 77-year-old mother sits with ankles crossed demurely in her impeccably furnished home in Huntington, where she and her husband raised two lawyers, a symphony conductor, and a tanker captain. Copies of *Canterbury Tales, Bartlett's Familiar Quotations,* and the *Oxford Companion to English Literature* perch near the piano. Three jade monkeys crouch on an end table: see no evil, hear no evil, speak no evil. Joe, the eldest, lives a few minutes away, and these days they see him often.

"To be honest," booms Joe Sr., a magisterial, blunt-spoken man with impressively muscled arms, "I don't think he really has handled it. He's caught up in the legal aspect of it—I mean, he won't go to the bathroom without consulting those fellows.

"Now here's a fact," he continues, leaning forward. "Somebody took a poll of all the tanker skippers who went in and out of Prince William Sound, and half of them said that they would have gone below at that point." He sits back and places an arm on the edge of the couch. "It was fate, luck, whatever you want to call it."

Joe Sr. knows about fate; specifically, how to kick it in the ass. He was a crackerjack pilot, first flying torpedo bombers for the Marine Corps in the western Pacific, then commercial jets for Pan Am's long-distance runs to South America, Cuba, Fairbanks, Tokyo, wherever. Every day was a mission: a 5:30 A.M. run followed by calisthenics followed by one or two hours studying flight manuals, approach patterns, and charts—not because it was mandatory, but because "that's what it took to be a good pilot." Joe Sr. was good enough to become the first commercial flight engineer to work past the age of 60. At 75, he looks raw and strong, still rising at 5:30 each morning to get his mileage in. His second son, Matthew, remembers his father saying that real accidents happen only to good pilots. What other people call accidents are actually mistakes.

"When Jeff was growing up, his father was flying," says his mother. "He would see the uniform, and it was something special. He saw his father strive to make every six-month check with everything perfect—and Jeff was the same way. He was so proud of his safety record. He felt he couldn't be less than perfect, ever."

She smiles in infinite understanding.

"All the children, they always tried to impress their father."

* * *

A brilliantly muggy June Sunday, and Hazelwood pilots his brown 1984 Chevy S-10 van along the jungly byways of Long Island's north shore. Festooned with rust, its starboard headlight housing patched with duct tape, the van cuts an incongruous profile as it chugs past the velvety lawns of towns like Cold Spring Harbor and Oyster Bay. Outfitted in a faded blue T-shirt, jeans, and decrepit flip-flops, he drives carefully, checking three times at a stop sign before proceeding. "Some people find it hard to believe," he says, "but I am a fairly cautious driver."

Generous in its concealments and discretions, Long Island is a good home for exiles. To the east stretches the old Gold Coast, Gatsby's East and West Egg. To the south, in Massapequa, resides Mr. Joey Buttafuoco. John Lennon had a house on the north shore, as did former tennis brat John McEnroe. Kerouac lived in Northport, just over the hill from Huntington. There's a palpable sense of refuge in the twisty roads and the Amazonian foliage, of secrets kept, of barriers not to be crossed. Different worlds can coexist, and that, as much as anything, is what Hazelwood enjoys. "You got the WASP thing with the super-rich, you've got the big-hairs with their Mr. T starter sets, and somewhere in the middle you've got schlubs like me."

After a few quick errands, he steers the van toward West Shore Marina in Huntington, where a childhood friend keeps a 33-foot sailboat. "If the wind's blowing, we'll take her out for a spin," he says, but when we reach the dock the air hangs thick and still.

He walks down anyway, past the buffed fiberglass haunches of $500,000 motor cruisers, past the blond woman in a jet-black bikini, to a sleek, teak-trimmed craft with a 45-foot mast. He checks the boat, running his hands over the standing rigging and cleated lines. The boat is named *Too Slick,* a fact that dictates a brief laugh.

Hazelwood comes to the marina often, sometimes to sail, other times just to hang around the boat and keep things shipshape. He's known around here for helping out when newbies need a hand.

"See that guy?" He points to a jowly man in a 42-foot Catalina. "He was having trouble docking that thing, pussyfooting it around, so I hopped aboard and we brought it in. Sometimes docking calls for a bold move."

Around the docks, Hazelwood finds the kind of moments he seeks, the kind of moments he lives for: to stand tall on some stranger's flying bridge and shoot the breeze about bold moves and Tiger Woods and the goddamn Yanks in complete and blessed anonymity. Anonymity, to Hazelwood, is the point of it all, the state of grace, the reward for his silence; he believes in its redemptive power more than he believes in himself, more than he believes in heaven, even more than he believes in the legal system. At moments like these, Joe Hazelwood does not exist; there are no jokes, no secrets, no history, no coincidences to anticipate. There's only a guy in flip-flops, a regular schlub, a man aware of nothing perhaps but the final crowning irony: In banishing the sins of the past, Joe Hazelwood is also banishing the very things that might set him free.

Gregory Cousins is back at sea, working as a mate for a private carrier. Robert Kagan, the only crew member on the bridge that night to receive no penalties, lives in Louisiana, having negotiated retirement from Exxon. ("He's been an emotional wreck since the spill," his wife says.) Exxon completed its most profitable year ever, with a net 1996 income of $7.5 billion. Prince William Sound now sports escort tugs, tanker-tracking systems, a variety of radar and radio beacons, and a 60-foot tower anchored to Bligh Reef that rises above the waves like a beckoning finger. The beaches look clean, but dig beneath the surface and you'll find oil.

Joe Hazelwood doesn't think much about the future. He'll get an Exxon pension in a decade or so. Maybe he'll travel. Maybe he'll move south, play golf. He's planning to sell his Hobie Cat. He doesn't use it anymore, and besides, he could use the money.

"It's still day by day for me," he says. "I can't imagine this ever being over. It's always there, like the albatross on the Ancient Mariner.

"Your watch is never over as captain," he continues. "Am I angst-ridden with guilt? No. Am I feeling responsible as a professional? Well, whether it's a mechanical failure or anything else that grounds you, it sucks."

As we walk back to the car, Hazelwood spots a 50-foot cabin cruiser revving clumsily into its slip. A fortyish woman in gold-encrusted sunglasses tweezes a deck line between flamingo-colored nails; her bald and sweating husband spins the wheel aimlessly. Hazelwood moves quickly, grabbing the decklines and snubbing them neatly around the dock cleats, positioning a fender, waving for the captain to back it in, tightening the lines. Then he's shaking hands with the husband, and the flamingo nails are applauding, and everybody's happy.

"How ya doin' today?" Hazelwood says, and then they do what Joe Hazelwood wants them to do, what he wanted all of us to do all along. They smile at him.

October 1997

Around the Bend

I See a Little Silhouetto of a Man

IAN FRAZIER

On one of the long motoring vacations my family used to take—five kids on a mattress in the back of the station wagon, our parents in front sharing the driving, heading down a highway in the Yukon Territories or on the Canadian prairies or some other far-flung place of the sort my father preferred—I saw my brother Dave writhing and wincing in pain. Of the siblings, I am the oldest, and Dave the second oldest. In those days, I found certain of his sufferings to be of scientific interest; on occasion, I even did what I could to increase them, just for the sake of experiment. In this case, I observed him screwing up his features, muttering to himself, and once in a while shaking his head like a horse in a cloud of flies. Finally I asked him what was wrong. "I can't stop thinking about the words 'inclined plane!'" he said. "No matter what I do they keep running through my head: inclined plane inclined plane inclined plane!" Our mother turned around and tried to comfort him, suggesting that he just think of something else, but Dave replied that trying to think of something else only caused him to think of inclined plane more. He sat there, beset and wretched, the golden inclined plains of Canada (or wherever) rolling past our station-wagon windows.

The day eventuated, as travel days do. We stopped at a point of interest, ate at a little restaurant in a little town, checked into a motel.

After the bouncing on the beds, the putting on of pajamas, the listening to of stories read by our father, Dave and I got into one twin bed and the three younger kids into the other. As the lights went out, and our eyes adjusted to the single beam falling through the opening in the door between our parents' room and ours, a wicked realization crossed my mind. "Dave," I whispered, "*inclined plane.*" I was rewarded with a moan like the moan of the damned.

The old saying about history occurring first as tragedy and the second time as farce seems to work in reverse order for me. Jokes I make, often at someone else's expense, have a way of turning up later as real and strangely less funny problems in my own life. My brother's affliction proved to be contagious: Getting a name or a phrase or a few bars of music stuck in my head has become one of the minor banes of existence for me. At certain moments, I have practically prayed for a distraction to dislodge whatever happens to be stuck, much as hiccup sufferers hope for an unexpected and curative fright. For years I lived in New York City and had distractions to spare; in New York, no idea survives in the mind for any length of time. But then I moved to a rural place where the distractions amounted to (1) the smell of pine needles and (2) time to put gas in the car. In such a distraction-free environment, idées fixes float through the air and catch in the folds of my brain like invisible wind-borne cockleburs.

One afternoon not long ago I was out fishing. The day was warm and sunny, the river clear and wadable, the fish rising. In short, nothing about the day or the fishing conditions needed improvement. As I worked my way up a brushy bank, I saw, in a patch of light among the bushes' underwater shadows, a large rainbow trout readjusting his position. He materialized in the patch of light so clearly that I could see his greenish-gold back, his regularly spaced black speckles, the flash of pink behind his gills. In the next second he was back in the shadows, invisible again. Almost simultaneously, I became aware that I was thinking obsessively of the name Barbaralee Diamonstein-Spielvogel.

Well, that did it. I knew how the rest of my fishing afternoon would go. "Barbaralee Diamonstein-Spielvogel . . . Barbaralee Diamonstein-Spielvogel," said my brain, matching the syllables to the mechanics of my cast. I looked about hopelessly for a change of subject. With a high-pitched cry, an osprey coasted overhead, plunged down, and Barbaralee Diamonstein-Spielvogeled a fish from the shallows. The Barbaralee Diamonstein-Spielvogel ripples widened and grew. Do you know who Barbaralee Diamonstein-Spielvogel is? I'm not sure I do. She's a society person in New York, I think. Her name is as infectious as pinkeye. Running now on inertia alone, I joylessly fished through the halcyon afternoon, inwardly, unstoppably praying,

Barbaralee Diamonstein-Spielvogel
Forgive us for what we have done.

Further, this is the kind of malady that qualifies the sufferer for no sympathy at all. That afternoon, I may have caught fish or I may not; I can't remember. I know that I arrived home when I had said I would, outwardly intact, with no obvious grounds for complaint. And yet inwardly, how flummoxed I was, how vexed! What could I answer my wife and children when they asked how I had enjoyed my afternoon? "It was OK, but I couldn't stop thinking of the name Barbaralee Diamonstein-Spielvogel." Or, more honestly and more pitifully, "Help me! The name Barbaralee Diamonstein-Spielvogel is about to drive me insane!"

Studies have shown (or would show, if they existed) that among outdoor enthusiasts between the ages of 40 and 52 who do repetitive-motion activities like rowing, long-distance cycling, jogging, or hiking, fully 37 percent have the words to the song "In-a-Gadda-Da-Vida" echoing in their brains. Those shrink-wrapped cross-country bicycle riders you see strung out for miles along state highways in the middle of the country are an internalized procession of the peskiest and most virus-like of Top 40 tunes from the past. Do you recall, by any chance, the robotic "I'm Telling You Now," by Freddie and the Dreamers? Almost certainly, cross-country bicyclists of a certain age do. The next time you see one stopped by the side of the road, pull over and roll down your window and sing a few bars of "I'm Telling You Now" for him. He may curse you and carry it with him all the way to Minneapolis-St. Paul. On the other hand, he may thank you for driving out what had been torturing him before, a song that went something like "Why do you build me up, Buttercup, baby, just to let me down, mmmm mmmm mess me around," and so on, to which he could recall only the tune and a smattering of lyrics but not the title or the name of the group. From the brain's point of view, imperfection of memory is no obstacle. The brain runs through the little it does recall quite cheerfully and endlessly just the same. It likes the dumbest things. Why doesn't it replay great symphonies, in full 100-piece orchestration? If we had only known, in the sixties, that these three-chord hit songs on the radio were going to accompany us into eternity—well, I'm sure back then we wouldn't have cared.

I carry guidebooks with me when I hike, to identify flora and fauna that catch my eye. Once identified, their names escape from me in an instant, like the names of strangers at a crowded party. Over the last year, I have learned the dogtoothed violet, the serviceberry bush, and the false morel mushroom—only a tiny percentage of all the specimens that I have looked up. Although I refer to a conifer guide when I'm cross-country skiing, I am still not trustworthy on the difference between a spruce and a fir. (Now I remember—a fir has short, flat needles, and a spruce has short, pointy needles that aren't as flat. I think.) But let the smallest piece of commercial-packaging trash appear along the trail, and I can give you the species, genus, and phylum every time. That fan of reflected light, for example, flickering stroboscopically in the rippling current of the creek, comes from a flattened part of a beer can on the creek bottom, a beer can that even at this distance I can identify as belonging to the genus Budweiser and the species Bud Dry.

That's the hard part: living with the realization that we have junk-filled brains. Much of the litter we bring with us into the wilderness is of the mental variety; past a certain point, our minds really cannot grasp places that are completely trash-free. The Fanta Grape soda can drawing bees in the middle of a supposedly pristine wilderness campsite provokes our outrage and disgust, of course. But underneath those feelings, and less comfortable to admit, is a small amount of recognition and even relief. The Fanta can is us, after all. In the nineteenth century, when the cult of the Scenic had just begun, advertisers (especially in New England) took to plastering giant advertising slogans on the scenery itself. Hikers who reached far-flung lookout points in the Adirondacks or the Berkshires would see the words VISIT OAK HALL on

a rock face in the prospect before them. (Oak Hall was a Boston clothing store.) Even more remarkable is how few of them seem to have
complained.

The other day, while enjoying one of my two distractions—putting gas
in the car—I noticed that a candy company had managed to set an
advertisement into the previously neglected space between the top of
the gas pump handle's grip and the base of the nozzle. It featured a
full-color photograph of a candy bar and the words, "Hungry? Try a
_____." I wondered: If I asked, do you suppose they would buy space
on the inside of my eyelids? Nowadays, advertisers no longer bother
to afflict the scenery. Today they think small and specific; they know
that the best medium is the individual consciousness itself. With so
much of our commerce trying to inveigle its tiny way into our waking and sleeping thoughts, some of it is bound to stick, adding to the
random detritus, songs and phrases and floating bits of near nonsense,
there already. We will never get rid of it all. We can only be thankful
that it follows its own slow cycle of decay; at least we no longer murmur, as we drift off to sleep by the campfire light, "See the U.S.A. in
your Chevrolet" or "Visit Oak Hall."

We can be thankful, too, that it stops with us. Most animals, for
example, do not like to watch TV. What a blessing that is! Bad enough
that the raccoons show up regularly to plunder the garbage cans out
back; how much worse if they showed up regularly in the branches by
the living room window to catch the Thursday night lineup on NBC.
With TVs in every cage and caged animals staring at them, zoos would
be even grimmer places than they already are. What we have in common with the rest of nature goes deeper than advertising, deeper than
words. One way to regard the annoying phrase stuck in the mind is
as a boundary marking where the not-human begins. The last time I
fished I caught big brown trout one after another, prehistoric-looking
battlers with banana-yellow bellies and inky spots the size of dimes on
their sides. Several of them jumped at me when they felt the hook,
appearing suddenly in the air and fixing me with their wild eyes. As I
revived them before releasing them, my two hands barely able to fit
around the cold, quick sides, I looked again and again at their eyes.

They held a concentrated intentionality, a consciousness I could only guess at. And yet I knew for absolute certain that (Everybody was Kung Fu fighting) unlike me the trout did not have the words (Those cats were fast as lightning) to a 1970s pop tune (In fact it was a little bit frightening) called "Kung Fu Fighting" (But they fought with expert timing) running through their brains.

February 1998

Is Just like Amerika!

BRAD WETZLER

I f it's true that you are what you eat, then I am a big, greasy kielbasa. I brought this on myself: For the past week I have been camping with a dedicated band of carnivores who favor canned meat and
an alarming variety of sausages. We're deep in the Brdy Hills, a rolling
patch of beech forest as charming as a dream, about 30 miles south
of Prague in the Czech Republic. The air is full of the smell of hon-
eysuckle, the buzzing of bees, the chirruping of bluebirds, and the siz-
zling of meat. The only human tracks within sight are our own.

But this is a curious bunch. There is Jerry, the frequently drunk
prankster who gets his kicks hiding pinecones in our sleeping bags. He
whispers that his real name is Vladimir, but tramps are only supposed
to go by their tramping names. Which is why "Jerry" is tattooed in
boldface on his right forearm. George, a starry-eyed guitar player, can
do a rendition of "This Land Is Your Land" in Czech that would make
anyone homesick for the hills of central Bohemia. Ace is a private in
the Czech army who always wears a Daniel Boone–style coonskin cap;
he sucked down too much rum last night and, while dancing to George's
intoxicating music, fell into the fire. Lucky for him Sheriff Tom was
still sober enough to pull him out. A one-armed bear of a man, Sheriff Tom is, at 45, the oldest hobo, and he happens to own the biggest

bowie knife, making him the logical choice to be the group's chief law-enforcement officer.

They are also a slovenly bunch. Empty sausage casings litter our campsite. Dirty clothes hang from branches. Camping gear—knapsacks, tarps, cooking kits—is strewn about like leftovers from a yard sale. The tramps themselves lounge in the dirt, sleeping, smoking, singing songs, telling stories . . . and eating meat. So far this week we've feasted on pork, beef, pork-beef sausage, ham steak, chicken, herring, sardines, smoked oysters, and plain old grilled meat, a gluey pink mush that comes in a can labeled "Grilled Meat." It's dinnertime on my fifth day with this group, and I've had enough—but that's only my opinion. Sheriff Tom insists that I keep up with my compatriots. He catches me sneaking away from the campfire and blocks my path, brandishing a bright-red, footlong salami in his one good hand. He's staring directly into my eyes. "Very . . . special . . . sausage," he says in deliberate, broken, heavily accented English. "You . . . will . . . enjoy . . . very much."

I ask what's in it. Sheriff Tom casts his gaze skyward, as if scanning the animal-cracker-shaped clouds to find the poor beast from which this sausage was rendered. "How you say . . . " Sheriff Tom says, sounding flustered. "I don't know. It is big, with hooves. Please. Eat!"

He hands me the sausage and motions for me to try it. Hesitant, I oblige, biting into the pasty gristle and rolling it around in my mouth. Then I make myself swallow.

"I know! I know!" Sheriff Tom suddenly blurts out as the sausage slides down my gullet. "It goes, 'Neighhhhhh!'"

The men I'm traveling with call themselves the Red Monkey Gang. They're a proud part of a nationwide movement called tramping, or *vandr* in Czech. As the name suggests, tramping is a takeoff on hoboing—the act of drifting from place to place by train or on foot. Real hoboing had its heyday during the Great Depression in the United States, when an estimated 1.5 million people lived on the loose. Most came to their vocation involuntarily, driven to the road by poverty and desperation. Nonetheless, hobos, like tramps, acquired a reputation for their carefree way of life, their predilection for booze, and a canon of whimsical folk songs and stories.

The Czech species of tramp, or *vandrak*, has the happy-go-lucky, alcohol-soaked aspects of the lifestyle down cold. But these are not bona fide, full-time tramps. The Czechs are dilettante vagrants: Recalling the lore of tramping, they embark on excursions in which they merely *pretend* to be down-and-out wastrels. Nor do they follow the hobo tradition with any commitment to verisimilitude; America's wide-open spaces have inspired many Czech "tramps" to dress up as cowboys or Indians or, just as bizarrely, World War II GIs. On weekends and during vacations, thousands of them hop trains (paying their fare rather than stowing away in boxcars), camp out under the stars, or rendezvous in the hills and at festivals, all the while singing Czech and American folk tunes. Most are middle-class working men with homes and families, though it's not uncommon to see women marching into the woods, too. Come Sunday night, everybody climbs back on the train and goes back to their day jobs.

Sounds like a pretty good life to me. So a few months back I flew to the Czech Republic and on a balmy Friday afternoon took a cab straight from Prague's Ruzyne Airport to Smichov Station, aka Tramp Central. There were tramps everywhere, relaxing on the ground, drinking in the train-station pub, strumming guitars. I bought a southbound ticket to the central Bohemian village of Revnice, which, I'd been told, was a jumping-off point for a lot of hobo outings. I boarded one of the shiny aluminum cars and, imitating the weekend tramps already on board, slumped on the floor with my backpack. "Ahoy," the other tramps said to me, using the traditional tramp greeting. (No one seems to know how ersatz hobos in the landlocked Czech Republic came to address each other as British sailors.) "Ahoy," I returned, and each one grasped my hand in the thumb-gripping, soul-style tramp handshake. We passed around a bottle of rum until Revnice, where I detrained.

Waiting at a bus stop just outside the station was a group of eight men wearing camouflage: tramps, I surmised. They introduced themselves as the Red Monkey Gang, welcomed me with handshakes and high-fives, and waved me on board the bus to Halouny. After five minutes, the bus let us off in a tiny hamlet consisting of a dozen or so stone houses with red tile roofs.

We shouldered our backpacks and set out up a steep hill in the direction of some thick green woods. The sun was beginning to set, and I was concerned that we'd be making camp in the dark. But having spent the better part of a day in the cramped middle seat of a 747, I relished the exercise and camaraderie of a group hike. In-country for only a few hours and here I was, trampin' with tramps!

After about 50 paces, though, Sheriff Tom motioned for me to remove my pack and pointed at a dilapidated stone building with a leaning front porch in front and a stinky outhouse in back. This was the Red Monkey Pub—U Cerveneho Paviana—the terminus, it turned out, of our hike. We entered and drank cold pilsner until 1 A.M., closing time, after which we set up camp in a small clearing behind the building. We spread our sleeping bags on the ground, crawled in, and woke up at noon, just in time for the pub to open.

For the next five days our routine was basic: sleep till 11 or so in the morning, skulk over to the pub for our noonday beer, pick wild mushrooms and blueberries, and hike. In the evenings we'd dine on sausage, drink rum, smoke cigars, and stare into the fire while George serenaded us with Czech versions of country-and-western songs.

Which brings us up to Saturday night and Sheriff Tom, who's holding me up with his sausage. I choke the entire thing down under duress while he watches, and then live with the consequences for the rest of the evening, sitting in a dyspeptic drowse beneath an incandescent full moon while George sings "King of the Road," "Hobo Bill's Last Ride," "Wabash Cannonball," and "Alaska, I Love You."

I'm still wide awake at 1:10 A.M., lying by the fire in my mummy bag, listening to Sheriff Tom's semidrunken snoring and trying to calm my aching stomach, when I hear a scream.

"*Kanec!*" somebody yells. It's Jerry the prankster, only now he seems in earnest. He trips over himself, lunging in my direction. "*Kanec!*" he shouts again.

I can hear grunting and heavy breathing, not all of it coming from my fellow tramps, who are frantically trying to free themselves from their sleeping bags. Suddenly a squadron of feral pigs crashes through the brush in single file. One, two, three, four, five. Noses to the ground, they begin to vacuum the campsite of its rubbish, eating sausage casings, residue in empty Spam cans, even dirty socks. Their beady eyes, glinting in flashlight beams, give them the look of crazed beasts from hell, and their razor-sharp tusks could rip flesh from bone. But then one pauses next to my backpack and I get a sense of proportion: These pigs are no bigger than Yorkshire terriers. Indignant, if more than a little relieved, I squirm out of my sleeping bag and prepare to defend our camp with honor.

Fortunately, I don't have to. The raid lasts less than a minute. Before anybody gets hurt, the pigs scurry off into the dark—presumably in the direction of another, even more slovenly, tramp site. The Red Monkeys saunter back to bed. When I crawl into my bag, a sharp object pricks my thigh and I grope after it: pinecone. I look over at Jerry, who is sitting up, grinning.

Tramp. Vagabond. Vag. Bum. Stew Bum. Profesh. Bindle Stiff. Alki Stiff. Roadie-Kid. Hobo. The wandering soul has countless names, many of them suggestive of sloth and indolence. The hobo (the term possibly a bastardization of a 19th-century vagrant's greeting, "Ho, beau!") is, one might say, prone to go long stretches without showering and unapologetic about his heavy smoking and drinking. He rides from city to city, from job to job—and sometimes he just rides for the peripatetic hell of it, gathering with fellow tramps in train yards and sleeping under bridges, outraging the local constabulary. Jack London, who as a youth spent eight months hoboing in 1894, wrote that the life of the road "entices romantic and unruly boys, who venture along its dangerous ways in search of fortune or in a rash attempt to escape parental discipline. It seizes with relentless grip the unfortunate who drifts with, or struggles against, the tide of human affairs."

Even in postwar America, nostalgia and wanderlust kept tramp wanna-bes hopping boxcars. Nostalgia eventually outweighed wanderlust, though, and tramping fully evolved into an idiosyncratic pastime, with aficionados in hobowear gathering like Civil War reenactors to sing the old songs of the road and swap pork-n-bean recipes. In keeping with the times, those who struggle against the tide of human affairs now have a support group: the 5,800-member National Hobo Association, which has a Web site (*www.hobo.org*), a magazine called *The Hobo Times* ($25 a year), and annual gatherings. The most recent conclave was in July in Elko, Nevada, where tramps spread out their bedrolls at a fairgrounds that, according to hobo.org, offered "electric power, showers and change rooms, and night lighting."

Unlike the Americans, however, the Czechs never really tramped out of necessity. From its start in the 1920s, it was a hobby—an amusing interpretation of American hobos and cowpokes. Marko Cermak, an outdoors writer and the unofficial historian of tramping in the Czech Republic, says the first tramps were lone-wolf types who headed for the hills after watching movie cowboys like Tom Mix and "Bronco Billy" Anderson battle Indians and herd cattle on the open range. These early Czech tramps would dress like cowboys, ride the trains to the edge of town, and sleep out under the stars "cowboy style," as Cermak calls it. It was a time when Europeans were developing an obsession with all things western through the novels of turn-of-the-century German writer Karl May, who never set foot in the American West but wrote of the high mesas and howling coyotes with a Prussian commitment to authenticity.

Taking a more laid-back approach to the western mania than their neighbors the Germans, who began organizing cowboy conventions and staging mock shoot-outs, the Czechs mixed up stories of hobos and cowboys-and-Indians into a happy stew and called it tramping. Teams of dozens, sometimes hundreds, of Czech hobos and cowboys established elaborate camps in the hills, where they elected sheriffs to keep order. (Some camps survive to this day, with cabins proudly named El Passo [*sic*], Jack London, Tacoma, and Cimarron.)

Over time, several factions formed. Some tramps, especially those with an ecological bent, began imitating the Indians they saw in American movies, dressing in elaborate costumes, carving totem poles, tanning hides with cow brains, and erecting tepees. Others specialized in canoe tramping, lugging their vessels onto trains and riding to their favorite rivers and lakes. After World War II, American movies inspired yet another vogue, one that is still prevalent today: the GI tramp. GIs dress in camouflage army fatigues (to blend in with nature, they say), black army boots, and dog tags.

To make any sense of all this—to form a rational connection between army-surplus getup, pub-oriented camping, and the Czech version of the "cowboy life"—you must put yourself in a bohemian frame of mind. The word "bohemian," with all its boozy, shiftless, rules-be-damned connotations, was born in this very region of Czechoslovakia— Bohemia, which comprises half the nation. Gypsies, otherwise known as Roma, or *Cikani* in Czech, have long been a significant minority here. (They make up 0.3 percent of the population today.) When Gypsies trekked beyond Bohemia into France during the 15th century, the French dubbed them Bohemians, and "gypsy" and "bohemian" became more or less synonymous. Bohemianism aside, the Czech Republic consumes more beer per capita than any other nation on earth—almost twice as much as the United States. This only helps make the country more fertile for tramping. In fact, the national anthem is fittingly titled "Where Is My Home?"

Even the Nazis and Communists couldn't keep the tramps down. Tramping groups were active in the underground resistance after Germany invaded Czechoslovakia in 1939; some who worked in munitions factories employed their prankster skills in the cause of freedom by mislabeling boxes so that German troops on the front lines got the wrong-size bullets. When the Reds took over in 1948, the apparatchiks felt sufficiently threatened by tramps to spy on the larger camps and break some of them up. Unsupervised assembly was outlawed—which, of course, only made tramping more attractive to the bohemian soul. In his 1990 book, *Disturbing the Peace,* Czech president Vaclav Havel recalled the role a group of tramps played when Russian tanks rolled into a small town north of Prague called Liberec in 1968, at the end of the Prague Spring. Led by a young man called The Pastor, the tramps took down all the street signs overnight to confuse the Russians. Another "poignant scene" involved the group standing guard at the town hall and singing the Bee Gees hit "Massachusetts." Havel writes: "I saw the whole thing in a special light, because I still had fresh memories of crowds of similar young people in the East Village in New York, singing the same song, but without the tanks in the background."

While disparate tramping groups went on to hold illegal rock concerts in the seventies and eighties, and in some cases went to jail for their provocative displays of affection for Western pop culture, tramping didn't face a real threat to its ethos until shortly after the Velvet Revolution in 1989. By the time the Czechs and Slovaks had parted ways, in 1992, the Czech Republic was already knee-deep in its attempts to graft a Western capitalistic head onto a moribund Eastern Bloc economic body. The transformation worked, for the most part, but it's had a sullying effect on tramping. Tramps who once scorned communism began to cast a yearning eye toward Western-style yuppiedom. Though hordes still tramp, the new economy has inspired careerism among many would-be hobos.

"Now everybody wants to make money," the bartender at the Red Monkey Pub told me. "They work long hours and don't have time to spend their weekends in the woods. They take vacations abroad. I think, too, that there is nothing to rebel against now." Up until the Velvet Revolution, she explained, tramps fancied themselves on the outside of society. "Of course," she said, brightening, "the young tramps, the 17-year-olds, rebel against capitalism now. So hopefully tramping won't disappear forever."

One hopes the bartender is right—that democracy, like Nazism and communism before it, will fail to take the bohemian out of the Bohemians.

I've grown tired of the Red Monkey Gang—bless their souls—and their slothful ways. On the morning of the sixth day, a pack of chipper, clean-cut tramps marches up to the pub, where we're seated on the front porch, and I quickly invite myself to join them. But saying goodbye to the boys is not easy. Sheriff Tom, I'm certain, has never had a more faithful sausage-eating mate.

"Why no more drink pivo with us?" he asks, gesticulating with his pilsner. "No like us?"

"Yes. Yes," I say. "I like you."

"No like our sausage?"

Well, now he's getting warmer. I mumble that my bum knee requires constant movement and move out. The new crew includes a couple of fresh-faced college students; a lanky young woman; a bony, English-speaking thirtysomething; and a hirsute middle-aged man. A hundred yards down the trail I look back—I shouldn't, but I do—and there is the Red Monkey Gang, waving a forlorn good-bye.

After a few minutes we stop, and the tramps introduce themselves. The two college kids are called Little Pid and Pad; it's never quite clear what "Pid" stands for, but "Pad" is Czech slang for "he who falls down a lot." Rita is Pad's girlfriend. The bilingual guy is the only one willing to give his real name: Pavel Bem, a talkative psychiatrist who's also the mayor of one of Prague's 15 boroughs. His nickname, Strevo, translates as "he who acts with extreme intentions." The leader, a six-foot-two bruiser with a thick beard, is simply Big Pid.

We grip thumbs, toast one another with the requisite shot of rum, and set off hiking down a potholed dirt road. Soon the road becomes a single rutted track in a green tunnel of clattering branches. It's late morning, but the farther we walk, the darker the woods get. The group plans to hike ten miles to Kytin, on the eastern slope of the Brdy Hills, and then head for Brdsky Kempy, "Valley of Brdy Camps," a narrow, heavily wooded canyon that isn't on any of my maps but, I'm reliably informed, was home to some of the earliest tramp camps, dating back to the 1920s.

Hiking with this new gang is like competing in a speed-walking contest. All five are former participants in the Czech scouting movement, and over the years they've spent a lot of time tramping in the Brdy Hills. Like most, they've perfected the art of traveling light. Each wears a small, threadbare green knapsack in which he or she carries a fluffy cotton sleeping bag, a cooking pot, a spoon, and ingredients for a few meals.

The path meanders between woods and fallow fields where quail and grouse flutter. According to a historical map of the Brdy Hills, during the thirties and forties, the most famous group in these parts was the Beer Volunteer Workers, a pack of about 150 tramps who wandered around dressed like American cowboys, carrying genuine Colt .45s. Their badge was a Boy Scout fleur-de-lis with a glass of beer in the center. The gang dwindled during the fifties, though, due to Communist harassment.

Strevo himself suffered under the regime; he was once jailed for two days without being told why. "You can't understand unless you've lived under a totalitarian government," he says. "You begin to question what the truth is. I think that's why Czechs are very outdoor-oriented. The TVs and radios constantly played propaganda. We had to get away from it. At least out here in the woods you could find some truth."

After three hours of hiking we come upon a fire ring nestled beneath a 40-foot rock face and a twisting rivulet. It's one of the early tramp sites. The wet air drenches my socks and shirt, and giant ferns bow down in the mist. "We are here," Big Pid says, taking the pack off his back.

We set our things down and begin gathering logs for a fire. I help the group string a tarp between two trees in case of rain and then unsheathe my nylon tent. I hardly have the first stake in the ground before Big Pid motions for me to stop. "There are no tents in tramping," he lectures, shaking his black beard. "You must see the stars." This didn't come up with the Red Monkeys, but then, I was never sober enough to try to put up a tent. I slide it back in its sleeve, but Big Pid isn't done yet. "And there are no gas stoves, fancy backpacks, and none of those PowerBars." He glares at my carbo stash. "We will show you real tramping food."

I thought I'd already seen real tramping food. Since we got to the campsite, we've been eating sausage and washing it down with rum. But sausage is just an appetizer for this crew. As Big Pid speaks, I watch him pull an entire roasted chicken out of his backpack, followed by an assortment of vegetables. He dismembers the bird and mixes up a stew over the open fire. The other tramps prepare meals in their own pots—everything from noodles to chicken casserole. Then, one at a time, each pot is set in the middle of the campsite. We stand in a circle and take turns bending down and spooning out a bite. For about an hour, the six of us share dinner and compliment the chefs. The evening's entertainment is a traditional tramping game: Standing nose to nose, we try to knock each other off balance. Big Pid, naturally, goes undefeated. Then we sprawl on the ground, light cigars, and pass a flask. As the fire dies down, a cuckoo fills the forest with its unmis-

takable call. *Cuckoo. Cuckoo. Cuckoo. Cuckoo. Cuckoo.* Five cuck-
oos. "Bad news," Strevo says. "According to the cuckoo bird you have
only five years left to live."

That's not very heartening, I say.

"If it's any consolation," he replies cheerfully, "we only have five
years, too."

"What? Do I look like I was in the Party?" exclaims a thin man dressed
in beads and buckskin, with blue streaks of war paint on his face. His
name is Jiri Kohout. I seem to have offended him by asking whether
he'd been a Communist.

My search for tramps has taken a side trip into *terra incognita*. I
have rented a minivan and, accompanied by my 19-year-old translator, Hana Kozakova, have driven to the small city of Plzen, about 60
miles west of Prague, in search of the more settled, rendezvous-
oriented, cowboy-and-Indian side of tramping. A rodeo is taking place
here, and I've been told I might find Indians. A good tip, as it turns
out: Within five minutes I bump into Jiri and his tribe next to the fun-
nel cake booth. His wife, Gabriela, son, Jarda, and daughter, Nikolka,
are dressed up like Lakota Sioux. I ask if he would be so kind as to
take me back to his tepee for a short powwow, and we walk down a
sidewalk to a small patch of grass outside the rodeo arena. There, next
to his car with bumper stickers that read "I Like American Indian Pow-
Wows" and "American Indian Hobbyist," are two tepees, outfitted
with colorful blankets and animal-skin rugs.

The Kohouts are here at the rodeo to perform a prayer dance at half-
time. It would be nice if they did a stop-the-rain dance. It's pouring,
putting a damper on the rodeo. A few moments ago a Czech cowboy
slipped in the muck and was gored by a bull. He's not badly injured,
but the ambulance siren is ruining any sense of authenticity. Meanwhile,
water is blowing in through the tepee's door, drenching the tom-toms
and blankets. Making the situation worse—at least from where I sit—
is Jiri's sidekick, a pale, burly, Indian-loving friend who is wearing chaps
sans underwear. He's inadvertently mooning the group while he tries to
close the tepee flap, eliciting groans from Jiri's son, a 16-year-old who
is chilling in Indian garb and a pair of Oakley sunglasses.

Oblivious to the commotion, Jiri launches into his story as if it were ancient cosmology. "Tramps and Indians were together at the beginning," he says wistfully, relating his thoughts through Hana. "But then something happened. Tramps became very dirty and smelly. And all that drinking was unsatisfactory to me. Indians aren't dirty. They are clean and smooth."

I notice that the Kohouts certainly are. Their blond hair is tightly braided, and their outfits are crisply pressed.

Jiri continues: He started dressing as an Indian 30 years ago, when, as a young man, he witnessed the horrible way in which Indians were treated in American westerns. "I knew then that Indians were my people," he explains. Already a veteran GI-style tramp, he began to wear Indian garb on outings. Soon he was erecting tepees in the woods, where he and his family spent weekends and holidays, living "the simple life" the way the Indians did. He beaded belts and purses for sale at Czech rodeos and other western-themed occasions. And he got himself a booking agent. Yes, he says, he's been to the States once, but he prefers being an Indian in the Czech Republic. "It's very good here," he says. "There are no snakes in Czech. It's much fewer dangers here."

I ask if being a Central European Indian opens him up for ridicule. "Yes, people joke about me being a blond Indian," he admits. He lights a cigarette and takes a deep, contemplative drag. "But I just stand proud. I give them no pleasure in teasing me."

As I prepare to leave, the Indians begin talking among themselves. Jiri looks concerned and takes me by the arm. "You understand, don't you," he asks, "that I am not a real Indian?"

What is this thing called the Wild West? John Wayne hunting Apaches? A faded denim jacket from the Don Imus catalog? Those who live there are forced to separate fact from myth. But in the Czech Republic, the myth remains untainted by reality. Czech tramps choose among happy clichés—footloose hobo, Marlboro Man, noble savage, GI Joe—celebrating wide-open America and throwing out the details. When I tell my new cowboy and Indian friends that I am from Santa Fe, New Mexico, the heart of Indian country, most of them seem to care not at all. They are more interested in showing me their new plastic pistol or horseshoe belt buckle.

Nonetheless, I don my armadillo bolo tie and head to the stark suburban neighborhood of Vestec u Prahy on the south side of Prague. There, in the middle of a cornfield, just beyond a row of housing projects, sits a weather-beaten ghost town called Westec City. Part theme park, part banquet center, Westec City represents the big-business side of Czech tramping; it pulls the ethos out of the woods and half-bakes it, hosting western-style barbecues and rodeos for corporate clients.

Tonight the partyers are from the Czech division of Microsoft. Cowgirls in cleavage-revealing western garb hand each guest a black cowboy hat and a mint julep at the door. Black-hatted executives and programmers line Main Street, a row of buildings labeled Saloon, Undertaker, and Post Office. As the sun sets behind the neighboring housing blocks, a tinny loudspeaker blasts the spaghetti-western theme song from *The Good, the Bad, and the Ugly*, and shutters creak in the wind.

A heat wave has descended on Central Europe, so I decide to wet my whistle with a drink in the Westec Saloon, hoping, as I've been promised, that I'll hear some good live music. Cowboys belly up to the bar, drinking the local brew. Faded wallpaper, round card tables, and a mounted deer's head make me feel like I've stepped into a scene from Kenny Rogers's *The Gambler*. A man in a cowboy hat is standing onstage, singing sad-sounding country-and-western songs in Czech, accompanied by a boom box. "What kind of music you got here?" I ask.

"Both kinds," says the barkeep. "Country and disco."

Through the window, I watch a man practice for the calf-roping event by tossing his lariat over anybody who passes by. I go outside and introduce myself. He tells me his name is Jaroslav Krchov, but his cowboy friends call him Dick. "That's spelled D-y-k," he says. Dyk, 33, has the callused hands of a cowboy. He sports a tattoo of his horse, Black-and-White, on his right arm. We arrange to meet the next day at the garage where he works as an auto mechanic and then drive out to his "ranch" on the outskirts of Prague.

When I pick him up in my minivan with Hana, Dyk seems a more subdued, blue-jumpsuited version of the gregarious cowboy I met at Westec City. We wind through narrow streets on the way to his house, past pubs and parks full of kids, and I ask him if anything is wrong. "I must tell you," he blurts. "My ranch is not like your ranches in the U.S. It is a very small ranch."

Five minutes later we are at the road's end, on a hill overlooking a busy expressway. "This is home," Dyk says, gesturing to a small, red-brick bungalow with a vegetable garden for a front yard. Behind it is a fence made of a few stakes and some twine. Four horses stand in stalls beside a pasture the size of a putting green.

Dyk walks over to his faithful Black-and-White, who is standing in the shade of a cherry tree. Wrapping his arms around the horse's neck, he recalls the first time he saw *The Treasure of the Sierra Madre*—the movie that made him, at age 19, a cowboy. Inspired, he found time apart from his mechanic's job to ride horses at a stable near his parents' home northwest of Prague and experiment with saddle repair. Over the next 14 years he built the stable behind his house, converted a delivery truck into a horse trailer, and began driving to rodeos in the Czech Republic and Germany. He spends a third of his $388 monthly salary on hay and oats, but his appearances at Westec City are for love, not money. Once a year he rides in the Czech Pony Express, in which horsemen race from town to town across the country, carrying real mail. He looks out across his quarter-acre spread and tells me that he plans to move his family to a bigger place farther from the city, with more space to practice his calf-roping and barrel racing. Capitalism has been good to Dyk and his clan. "It's much easier to be a cowboy these days," he says. "We no longer have to hide our cowboyness."

With my work finished and my pores oozing sausage grease, I find my way back to the train station at Revnice, where I first entered the Brdy Hills. It's a Sunday night, and homebound tramps are everywhere, in the train-station bar, sleeping on benches, strumming guitars, or nuzzling with sweethearts. Everyone looks half-dead: It's a scene from *Night of the Living Hobos*. Tomorrow the tramps will return to their jobs as clerks, mechanics, psychiatrists, and mayors.

For a brief but glorious time, I've laid myself down in the bohemian heart of camping. My extreme-sports-loving friends back in the States spend thousands on high-tech gear and strenuous expeditions that cannot possibly deliver the degree of comfort I got lying on the ground 20 yards from a pub. At every step my beer glass was full, my belly had meat, and my cigar was lit. Soap? Razor? I don't need no stinking razor. I've found the real, world-preserving wildness celebrated by that Yankee bohemian, Henry David Thoreau—the wildness not of place, but of what he called "foresters and outlaws." This is camping: eating junk, getting dirty, misbehaving. I've gone native: This boy is a tramp.

The train pulls into the station. I climb aboard and once again sprawl on the floor. As we pull out, the car begins to shake and clank in a satisfying rhythm. I'm just drifting off to sleep when a man dressed in ripped jeans and a torn army jacket, accompanied by a mangy dog with a metal muzzle, plops down next to me. He pulls an envelope full of tobacco out of his pocket and offers to roll me a cigarette. I decline, but look closer. Though I probably appear rather disgusting myself, this man looks much worse. He has clearly been on the road a long time, a lot longer than a couple of weeks. Wait a minute, I think— here's a *real* hobo.

He pulls out a stainless-steel hip flask and offers me a swig. I take a long pull and wipe my mouth with the back of my hand.

"*Dekuji,*" I say in thanks.

Realizing from my accent that I'm an American, he sits up, grabs his guitar, and begins to play: "This land is your land, this land is my land, from South Moravia to North Bohemia . . ."

It's time to go home.

November 2000

Dr. Pepper

RANDY WAYNE WHITE

Perfection is a goofball pursuit, one that's not only subjective but ultimately self-defeating: To find what you're looking for means the search has ended. Which is a shame, really, because roaming around looking for something is nearly always more fun than finding it. That's true of perfect waves and perfect countryside, and it's also true—God help me—of perfect hot sauce.

And yet I may have fouled my own premise here, because I think I've found a hot sauce that's uncomfortably close to perfection. I discovered it at its place of origin, a large, open-air building of tin and wood near the suburb of Mamonel, southeast of Cartagena, Colombia, on the road to San Jacinto, where out-of-work cartel guerrillas have lately turned their skills to the profitable business of kidnapping travelers or popping drivers in the head for quick cash.

But that comes later in the story. First you need to understand a few things about my interest in pepper plants and my search for the perfect hot sauce. In 1987, on my way to Australia, I spent a little time in Fiji. One day around noon, I put on running shoes and went for a jog through the steamy streets of Suva, the capital city.

Halfway through my run a tiny Indian man pulled his car off the road, hopped out, and called to me, "Sir—are you an American?" The insinuation was obvious: Only an American would be foolish enough to run at noon.

I nodded that I was and then listened dumbly as the man approached me and, without offering the slightest introduction or briefest preamble, said, "Oh, thank God I've met you. I've just been married, and an American will know. Please tell me, sir, what can a man do to cure premature satisfaction?"

This poor man was convinced that his discomfiture was a symptom of being oversexed and that he was oversexed because of a cultural dependence on spicy food. Hot peppers, he told me, were well-known aphrodisiacs. He'd been eating them in one form or another since infancy: "It was in my mother's milk, I tell you!"

His family grew its own peppers—a variety of *Capsicum annuum* peppers, similar to jalapeños, that he called by his own name, Bombay something-or-anothers—and he was addicted to the things.

"I eat them all day, and it has warped my thinking," the man told me. "It is difficult to concentrate at my work. I can think of nothing but sex! I am like a machine!" He paused for a moment and then made a small amendment: "A very, very fast machine. It is driving me mad. I love my wife very much, and we are both desperate. Isn't there some pill that you use in America?"

No, I said, but it seemed to me he was ignoring the obvious solution. "Why don't you stop eating all those hot peppers?" I asked.

It was at that instant, standing beneath a shade tree along the streets of Suva, that for the first time I received the peculiar dopester's stare of what in these faddish times is known as a chilihead. It was a frenzied look, as if I'd yanked a feeding heron up by the neck and held it eye-to-eye.

"Give up hot food?" he said. "For what, a woman?"

Yes, he may have been a crazed and offensive man, but I humored him—and for a very practical reason: I wanted some of those family peppers. I later persuaded him to give me a couple of them to take back to the States. After I got home I planted the seeds in the garden behind my house just to see if they would grow.

They did. They were pretty plants, too, producing a banana-shaped fruit that turned green, then yellow, then red. Looking at those plants made me think of running in Fiji and of the troubled man with his new wife, and it also caused me to project the long path those seeds had traveled: all the way from some little village near Bombay, probably across the Indian Ocean, past Australia to the South Pacific, and then around the rest of the world to my garden on the west coast of Florida.

That was the beginning of my search for the perfect hot sauce and the perfect pepper. It was not a difficult thing to collect seeds as I traveled to the far reaches of the world, and whenever I returned from a trip I would plant them.

A couple of summers ago, I walked a pepper fancier through my little garden. He was an Alcoa-lipped brand of chilihead, which is to say that the hotter the peppers, the better he pretended to like them. He came to the little red chili pequeños I'd pilfered from a bush in the Bahamas.

"These are nice," he said. "I've always liked these. Crush them up, they're good in beer." He was tossing the things down like M&M's.

Then we came to the two short rows that contain what I now know are the *C. chinense* varieties. I keep them separate from the peppers I actually use, because they don't have much taste and they're way too hot. Among them were several chunky black peppers from Southeast Asia that I myself had never had the courage to try.

The chilihead nonchalantly picked one of the black peppers and popped it into his mouth, and then his face began to change. It is said that the human eye does not convey emotion. Whoever said that hasn't watched a man recklessly eat a variety of *C. chinense*. The ocular lens cannot wrinkle, but it can bulge as if registering some hellish internal pressure, and that's exactly what I saw in the eyes of this chilihead.

"Mother of God!" he whispered when he could finally form words. "Man . . . that's good!"

I've never participated in these silly machismo ceremonies, which require the hot pepper eater to pretend he isn't in severe pain. Nor have I ever been interested in hot sauces that require users to dole out portions with an eye-dropper. But collecting pepper seeds and bottles of hot sauce has become an obsessive hobby of mine. I've grown to like the way certain chilies taste and smell, and I'm deeply fascinated by their long and oddly convoluted history. I've come to greatly enjoy the slow glow that originates at the mouth and spreads north and south (which may be why some believe they're an aphrodisiac).

Now, whenever I'm cooking, or whenever I'm standing out in my garden, I can relive all kinds of trips: Cuba, Australia, Jamaica, Indonesia, Thailand, and lots of other places where people grow and use the little darlings—and that includes just about every region on earth.

A lesson in travel is what hot peppers are. Ask a schoolchild what Christopher Columbus discovered in 1492, and he or she will say the Americas. Ask a chilihead, and the response will be "capsicums."

Capsicum is a genus of waxy fruits—all containing the potent alkaloid capsaicin—that are indigenous to a large tropical swath of the New World ranging from Amazonia all the way to Mesoamerica. These plants were called *chil* by the Aztecs, and they have been on the move ever since.

According to some archaeologists, the indigenous peoples of the New World have been cultivating and eating hot peppers for 6,500 years. When Columbus landed, capsicums were vital to the diet of many of the Native Americans he met. In a log from his second voyage, Columbus wrote of chilies that the "Caribs and Indians eat that fruit as we eat apples."

In 1492 there were fewer than a half-dozen species of *Capsicum* being cultivated in the Americas. In subsequent years, European explorers collected two principal species of peppers—*C. annuum* and *C. chinense*—from what is now the West Indies and Central and South America and steadily distributed them around the world.

Seeds from those original peppers probably followed the ancient trade routes, sailing from the Americas to Europe and Africa, on to India, China, and Thailand, where they were sold or traded by merchants who did not know they were revolutionizing the cuisines of the world for all time.

What was once a spice has nowadays become a way of life. There are hundreds of hot pepper societies around the world and hundreds of thousands of die-hard chiliheads who network on chili home pages on the World Wide Web. The present boom in the United States got started sometime back in the eighties, and it's proven to be one of those exceedingly durable trends, like fly-fishing and single-malt scotch, that won't let up. Not that I've paid much attention. My own interest in the subject continues to be random and solitary, though increasingly informed.

Recently, for instance, I learned that my Indian friend in Fiji wasn't the first person to believe that hot peppers are aphrodisiacs. According to Jean Andrews's excellent book *Peppers: The Domesticated Capsicums* (University of Texas Press) this myth got started sometime in the late 1500s, when Father Jos. de Acosta, a missionary, warned that their use "is prejudiciall to the health of young folkes, chiefly to the soule, for that it provokes to lust."

Chilies may be lust-provoking (we chili-eaters certainly hope so), but the missionary was sadly mistaken in calling them "prejudiciall to the health." We now know that one medium-size green chili pepper contains 130 percent of the recommended daily allowance of vitamin C—a higher concentration than citrus fruit. It's also known that capsicums can help prevent dangerous blood clots. There's increasing evidence that hot peppers can reduce inflammatory responses, including those in burns, some nerve disorders, and arthritis. Researchers at the National University of Singapore have even made claims that certain chilies can protect stomach cells against damage caused by alcohol and that they may also help prevent ulcers.

Not only that, but medical research has confirmed something dedicated chili-eaters have known all along: that we, in fact, enjoy an emotional "high." The burning sensation caused by peppers triggers the manufacture of endorphins, the body's own painkillers. The euphoria is similar to that enjoyed by long-distance runners and other endurance athletes who have yet to learn that they could feel just as good by curling up with a cold six-pack and a couple of habañeros.

There is no country on earth, I have discovered, that is too poor to cultivate chilies, and there is no citizenry so downtrodden that it will not cheerfully discuss and exaggerate the merits of its own local stock.

In the mountain city of Jalapa, Mexico—where it is widely believed that jalapeños originated—I obtained from a local man a small bag of what he said were seeds from the "original and authentic" jalapeño plant that only his family now possessed.

"My family has treasured and protected these pepper plants for at least 200 years," he told me. "Maybe more. You will not believe the heat in these peppers. It is a wild and ancient heat that touches the soul!"

Chilies may indeed touch the soul, but they contribute little to the intellect, as I once discovered during a trip to Vietnam. In the Central Highlands, I hired a car and driver to take me from Pleyku to Saigon. The Vietnamese are a great people, but their driving skills were handed down by a consortium of drunken French colonialists and former MiG fighter pilots, the net result being that the country's mountain roads are death traps.

My own driver was typical—a speed demon blithely unimpressed by the prospect of road carnage. Then I noticed a tiny bag of purplish black chilies on the seat beside me.

I suddenly imagined that I had a kinship with this lead-footed man: We shared the same obsession. If I could turn our journey into a collegial hunt for pepper seeds, I thought, perhaps my driver would back off the accelerator just a little.

I let him know what I wanted. His reaction was enthusiastic. Yes, he knew just where I could find some seeds from an incredibly hot black Vietnamese pepper—and then he mashed the gas pedal to the floor.

I knew only a couple of useful phrases in Vietnamese (for instance, *Toi khong phai nguoi nga*—"I am not a Russian"), but I knew enough about the country's drivers to ask a Vietnamese-American friend back in Hanoi what to say when I wanted to go slower.

Now I spoke the word: "Nhanh . . . Nhanh!"

My driver chuckled and we skidded through the next curve, going just as fast as we could go.

I tried again, yelling, "NHANH! NHANH!"

No response. We flew over hills and through villages, scattering curly-tailed dogs and cyclists and idiotic chickens.

Getting the man to slow down was hopeless, so I finally crawled over the seat and lay on the floor, resigned to the inevitable crash.

Yet we didn't crash. We found some pepper seeds, we made it to Saigon, and it wasn't until days later that I learned that my evil friend—thinking it was funny—had intentionally given me the wrong word for "slow."

"You dolt," my friend explained, "*nhanh* means 'faster.'"

"Great joke," I told him. "Hey—try one of these black peppers. They're mild as Nebraska squash."

I've planted and grown many chilies over the years, but in my travels I've taste-tested only several dozen of the hundreds of pepper sauces that are available around the world. Here are some hot sauces that I liked a lot, or at least that I found especially memorable: Red Extracto from Nicaragua, Majestica Hot Sauce from Singapore, Twin Elephants from Thailand, Tamarindo Pepper Sauce from Costa Rica, Congo Picante from Panama, Salsa Verde Picante from Cuba.

But recently, traveling through Colombia, I came across a local concoction that I believe was the best hot sauce I've ever tried. It was a pungent green, quite hot but not too hot. It had the fragrance of rich vinegar and crushed pepper blooms. It was simple. It was pure. Its name was Aji Amazona.

For me, successful travel requires serendipitous intersectings, and that's just what happened in Colombia. I was staying on the island of Manga, just off Cartagena, at a great little marina called Club Nautico. When I remarked upon the sauce, the marina's owner, an expatriate Aussie, replied, "Yeah—pretty good stuff, isn't it? I happen to know the guy who makes it."

Their little factory, Comexa, was a short taxi ride away from the marina, so I went to buy a case. I also met the proprietor, Jorge Araujo. "If you want to learn about peppers," Araujo told me, "I will show you."

Araujo took me out to the lush farming region where locals raised the chili peppers from which the hot sauce was made. As he drove, he remarked on the serious problems the area had been having with guerrilla kidnappers and bandits. Earlier that week, two German tourists had been robbed and murdered. I'd also heard that Colombian guerrillas were kidnapping as many as a thousand people a year, holding them for ransom.

Araujo said he knew nothing about this, though he did note that we weren't far from an area that "is not so safe." But all I saw were bright green fields and quiet villages and grinning children. Locals were selling buckets of wild honey, mangoes, and boxes of tamarind pods. Farmers were loading peppers, which would be packed with vinegar in tight wooden kegs and left to age for a year before processing.

Araujo told me that he had been in the wholesale pepper business, supplying produce to larger companies, when a "miracle" happened: an accidental cross-pollination.

"In the fields," he said, "our growers had cayenne peppers, but they also had a local variety called pipon, a big, red, stomachy variety that no manufacturer really wanted."

The pepper that resulted from this fortuitous cross-pollination was a rare specimen indeed. "It had a wonderful smell to it and a very bright color like no other I'd ever seen," said Araujo. "We called it the Accidental Pepper. But what could we do with it? We decided to try to make our own sauces."

Eventually Jorge christened this accidental hybrid "the Amazona." Named for the region where all chilies probably originated, it now follows its pre-Columbian ancestors on newer trade routes.

"Have you tried it?" Jorge asked.

I'd sampled the sauce back in Cartagena, I said, but I hadn't yet taken a bite of the actual pepper. And truth be told, I wasn't sure I wanted to. For all I knew, it could be perfect.

June 1997

MIKE STEERE

Demetri Coupounas hustles to get his things together after a morning hike and a quick shower. Peering out the curtains of a room at the Ramada in Salt Lake City, Coup, as he's known, can see that the August sky is getting dark and growly. If he and his wife, Kim, don't leave for the convention center right away, they're going to be schlepping boxes of order forms and catalogs through the rain.

Coup is here to set up and man the booth of his new company, GoLite, at the Outdoor Retailer Summer Market trade show. The country's largest gathering of manufacturers of adventure sports equipment, camping gear, and outdoor clothing, the OR show is where retail buyers come to decide what they're going to stock next spring. It's Wednesday, setup day for the show, which opens tomorrow morning at eight. But Coup, who fusses at Kim to get a move on, is already coming into entrepreneurial focus. "There's only one thing in my world right now," the 34-year-old businessman announces in his surround-sound baritone. "GoLite's launch." (Coup sang a cappella as a Princeton undergrad, and when he speaks, you'd think Mammoth Cave was doing a mike check.)

By the time Coup, at the wheel of his metallic tan 1994 Dodge Intrepid, nabs one of the few open parking spots near the Salt Palace Con-

vention Center, the clouds have turned Wagnerian. Coup and Kim shuffle to their back-corner space (200 square feet, $6,000) in a blocklong
white vinyl tent called Pavilion 2. As in years past, there's not enough
room inside the main hall for every exhibitor, so about 300 of the 860
manufacturers at the OR show display in two temporary, plywood-
floored shelters. The floor plan allots real estate by seniority, so all 194
of this year's first-timers are relegated to the hinterlands. Welcome to
Darwinian capitalism, outdoor style: Fledgling companies sit farthest
from the dense foot traffic and dealmaking they so desperately need
to join.

Coup and Kim weave through aisles packed with kaleidoscopic
kayaks, fleece wardrobes, putt-putting forklifts, and tabletop product
demonstrations that look like school science projects. When they first
lay eyes on their booth, which contractors have just assembled, they
beam like new homeowners. It's a $40,000 display unit—with light
maple trim and eight-foot-tall mirrors under a sign proclaiming the
company name—that announces a startup better-funded than most.
(So far, Coup has invested $600,000 of personal and family money in
GoLite.) This flashy upscale presentation will promote packs, tents,
and outerwear of severely minimalist design. GoLite, as the stripped-
down name implies, is a line of drastically lightweight trail products—
antigear gear, you might say—based on the specifications of a
graybeard Oregon hiking swami and author named Ray Jardine.
Indeed, Coup has come to sell a philosophy as much as a product.
"Ultralight," booms Coup, face jutting upward as it habitually does.
"I can't make money unless I've taken the loads off people. I like that."

If only Ma Nature would cooperate. Outside, the squall line coils
into ominous life, and people stand and gawp. But the bustling in the
tent continues, until suddenly the wind and racket intensify as a dirty
helix of debris swings directly toward the temporary structure, and a
woman near the door shrieks, "Tornado!" All hell breaks loose as
Coup and Kim dive under a section of flooring. The twister, roaring
at speeds of up to 157 miles per hour, flings kayaks skyward, pretzels
parking meters, skewers delivery trucks with metal beams, and shreds
the rectangular big-top like Kleenex. The tornado passes on, taking a
long swipe at a residential neighborhood and reducing several brick

houses to rubble before running out of juice in the foothills of the Wasatch Range.

The GoLite display is one of the few things relatively unscathed in a world gone Cuisinart. Coup's fine; Kim has a bit of ground-glass rash on her knees. There are scores of walking wounded, a few gravely injured, and one man who later died: Allen Crandy, a 38-year-old contractor from Las Vegas who just put together GoLite's booth. Coup and Kim help pull a beam off Crandy before the paramedics arrive. The tent pavilion has been wiped out.

A couple of hours later, the Coupounases stand fending off the omens in a Radisson Hotel room that belongs to Mark Thibeault, owner of the Bozeman, Montana–based agency that does GoLite's ads, graphics, and public relations. Coup, voice still booming, wonders aloud about replacing his Dodge, which caught a flying traffic signal, but he looks as if he's been pickled in his own adrenaline.

The show must go on. Two days after the tornado hit and minutes before the OR doors officially open (a day late), Coup is set up in a foster booth (#3524) in the glorious, fixed-roofed expanse of the Salt Palace's grand ballroom. He's doubling up with Erickson Outdoors, the contractor that actually makes GoLite's wares. Coup fiddles with a headless mannequin decked out in GoLite clothing and positioned under an open GoLite umbrella, the shock of the tornado now gone from his face. Head-on, he looks like a manic Tom Cruise. But then you notice a nose that slews to the right and, when observed in profile, becomes an avian shocker that shoots the Cruise thing to pieces. There's another likeness here too—Punchinello, from Punch and Judy. Picture Punch with black hair and a whisker shadow and you've got an official Demetri Coupounas hand puppet. One that is ready to spiel: Like most exhibitors, he has pushed catastrophe out of his mind. If he didn't, GoLite would be sunk.

"We lost a day to the tornado," he declares, warming up his sales fervor. "We're not going to lose a week."

GoLite got lucky. The twister handed Coup something no amount of money could buy: good OR real estate. But there's trouble lurking in the aisles. Despite all the media hype and big-bucks advertising centered on the presumption that outdoor gear is happenin', GoLite is entering a flat market. Industry-watcher Bob Woodward, who consults for outdoor companies and publishes a mercilessly frank insider newsletter called SNEWS, broods over this in a near-apocalyptic "State of the Business" editorial published just before the show. "We all have to accept that the market as we know it is going away," writes Woodward, who lives in Bend, Oregon.

The industry's annual sales, according to *Outdoor Retailer* magazine's State of the Market report, which is based on a survey of every shop attending its OR show, have dropped in recent years, to $4.8 billion in 1998 from $5.2 billion in 1995. The figure includes sales of tents, packs, outerwear, hiking boots, and climbing equipment—the bulk of the goods on display at the trade show—but not bass rods, firearms, and other hook-and-bullet accoutrements. It also does not include many of the hardgoods that most folks would consider to be outdoor gear—kayaks, bikes, in-line skates, skis, and snowboards, which together would make up a very healthy $7.2 billion market. But one that Coup isn't targeting. No, what GoLite's selling is high-end and wiggy backpacking gear, not the sort that Joe Sixpack can load up on at Wal-Mart, but stuff that will live or die in specialty shops, which sell about a third of what chains do. That means Coup is trying to bust into what is, at best, a $1.6 billion market.

Backpacking may have been the craze that got the masses into high-tech boondocking in the first place, but these days it's limited in popularity. Woodward says it's a more difficult sell now than it was in the 1970s, when he managed a shop in California. "We didn't have to compete with mountain biking," observes the 59-year-old pundit. "The whitewater kayak market was fledgling, and sea kayaks were a British phenomenon. Now all these things are vying for the consumer's attention." About 15 million Americans go backpacking once a year. But according to a study commissioned by the Outdoor Recreation Coalition of America, there were only 2.2 million backpacking enthusiasts in the country this year, slightly fewer than the number of avid canoeists, and a slide from 2.6 million in 1997. (ORCA defines a backpacking enthusiast as an adult who camps at least a quarter-mile from a trailhead, at least nine times a year.) Worse, opines Woodward, is that backpacking is largely a baby-boomer pastime, and the kids are buying toys to fuel their adrenaline. Woodward says he's heard stories of young staffers at REI referring to the backpacking department as "the geriatric ward."

The niche isn't the only thing old about GoLite's venture. OR vets have heard the ultralight drumbeat before and have watched companies march right into financial oblivion. Sierra West, a 1971 launch, is best remembered for its failed Lite Gear line. (The company survived by morphing into Big Dog Sportswear.) Mont-Bell faltered in the American market but lives on in its native Japan. The lone surviving ultralight purveyor, a New Hampshire mail-order business called Stephenson's Warmlite, has its own . . . issues. Founder John Stephenson hates clothing altogether, and so the catalog shows its models au naturel.

Some blame big-company dominance for the failure of ultralight; others point to an ingrained perception that light equals flimsy. Consumers expect gear to evolve by accretion, which explains why we have things like three-pound parti-colored rain jackets sewn of umpteen panels, and seven-pound webbing-festooned packs that look like intergalactic wedding dresses. More is an easier sell than less. And contrarian ideas, which consumers must buy to buy GoLite, are tougher.

On the other hand, what's wrong about GoLite could turn out to be right. "If any time is right, now is it," says Michael Hodgson, a respected industry gear maven and former technical editor for *Outdoor Retailer*. He thinks he's spotted a wave of resentment against overembellished clothing and gear, and thus a yen to buy light and plain. The fall 1999 Patagonia catalog, for instance, opens with a paean to simplicity and subtraction very much in the GoLite vein. Could it be a sign that Coup has a market wave to ride? Or is it that the big kahunas are going to get on their giant boards and plow him under?

Whatever the future holds, history says that Coup has assigned himself a hazardous mission. Mark Erickson, one-third partner and namesake of Erickson Outdoors, says that the industry offers "a high potential for self-delusion." Wildernessy business, like wilderness itself, tends to dazzle first-timers. The outdoor market can seem like a world entire, but rookies forget that its annual sales are less than half those of Toys "R" Us. People want in for all sorts of unbusinesslike reasons. But nobody in his right mind would get into industrial lubricants, say, for idealistic reasons, or because it was sexy. Or would he?

Coup and I are sitting at a walnut table by a window overlooking a pond and a small prairie-dog town at his rented town house in Superior, Colorado. I'm trying to get him to answer the question, "Why GoLite?" when he bolts from the table into another room and trots back with a copy of Ray Jardine's *The Pacific Crest Trail Hiker's Handbook*. The self-published paperback is less a trail guide than a sermon on a belief system that has come to be called the "Ray Way," complete with instructions for fabricating your own gear. GoLite is, essentially, the incorporation of Jardine's exhortation. Coup, already an avid backpacker, delved into the book and discovered his new calling in March 1998. He hands his talismanic copy to me, and I turn pages while Coup relives, via penciled margin notes, how he went from reader, to believer, to mad-dog entrepreneur.

Page 29: "Thou must lighten thy load if thou would reach thy destiny."

Page 45: "This book is excellent—I would be proud to have written it."

Page 89: The reader learns that a hiking sock's most important aspect is that it be thin, thus easy to wash and dry. Coup's got it covered: "My black dress socks would work well."

Page 167: Jardine tells of seven escaped prisoners who walked six and a half days across the Gobi Desert without water, and he uses the fact that only two died to illustrate his belief that humans can survive for quite some time without water. Coup's reaction? "Never give up."

Page 213: Where the book reports that the last grizzly bear spotted in California was in 1924, Coup has drawn a frowny face.

Page 276: Coup has made up his mind to backpack Jardine's hallowed route: "Kim and I should be able to enjoy the PCT in *under* three months."

Then he takes the book from me and flips back to a note up front made on his second reading. It was here that he shorthanded his destiny: "What about creating a company w/ Jardine to make his light-weight equipment!"

While his conversion sounds rash, Coup certainly had the chops to plunge into this with a straight face. After earning a degree in politics at Princeton and then working in Washington, D.C., on George Bush's inaugural committee, he went to Harvard and earned both an MBA and a master's in public policy from the John F. Kennedy School of Government. In 1992 he married Kim Riether, a native of New Jersey and a fellow Harvard brainiac Republican on the same career track. Coup's obsession back then was deficit-reduction policy, an outgrowth of his mathematical bent. At one point in our conversation he casually tells me that as we have been talking he has been simultaneously computing an infinite additive series called Fibonacci numbers. A Fibonacci is the sum of two previous Fibonaccis: $0+1$, $1+1$, $2+1$, $3+2$, $5+3$, and so on, equalling 1, 2, 3, 5, 8, and so on. The numbers are omnipresent elements in natural design—in nautilus shells, flowers, seed pods. It's safe to call Coup a numbers guy. Young Demetri, only child of a physician mom and a tax attorney dad in suburban Boston, ran a profitable sports book from the third grade on. He outscored all other ninth-graders in the Northeast in the American High School Mathematics Examination, after which his dad took him on as an investment analyst. His picks, among them Apple Computer, yielded returns in the seven figures, Coup says. Part of the pool is now his and at risk in GoLite.

After wrapping up his double-whammy diploma in 1994, Coup did a brief stint as a management consultant and then moved back to D.C. to be the policy director of the bipartisan Concord Coalition, an organization dedicated to eliminating the federal deficit. But then in 1997 he saw that the government actually would get out of the red (as it did in fiscal year 1998), and decided he needed to move on. Balanced-budget warlord Warren B. Rudman, the former Republican Senator from New Hampshire who cofounded the Concord Coalition, remembers Coup as a wonk on the rise. "I've always thought that someday Coup would get into politics," Rudman says over the telephone from Washington. "I'm not sure what the devil he's doing out there."

What he's doing at this moment is drowning organic toaster waffles in maple syrup (no butter—Coup and Kim are vegans) to tide him over until dinner. Out beyond the prairie-dog metropolis stretch miles of suburbifying rangeland. Look farther, though, and you see the first of the Rockies chewing up the last of the Plains and realize that this might not be a bad place to live. Kim, a cheery Nordic type whose energy level is on par with Coup's, listens in until she has to leave for work. Her temperament is right in sync with the image of her employer: She's chief operating officer of Up With People, an organization of travelling performers that she likes to call "the singing Peace Corps," and which has its world headquarters in nearby Broomfield.

The couple came here in July 1998, but they had known they'd wanted to move out west long before Coup conceived of GoLite. Back in the summer of 1995 they took a road trip and hiked the high points of 37 states. They'd already climbed New Hampshire's Mount Washington and were gunning for all 50. Their state-topping finale was a 1997 ascent of Mount McKinley, which they proclaimed the Zero Deficit Climb.

Still, you get the sense that it was the fresh challenge that drew Coup into GoLite. He says it took him 12 hours with Jardine's book to arrive at his epiphany. Within several weeks, he had drafted a proposal for the author, whom he'd never met. The nut: "I feel compelled to make contact to explore the possibility of producing packs, shelters, and sleeping systems along your specifications for the great mass of hikers and backpackers who would greatly benefit from reduced loads but who will not, for whatever reasons, make their own gear. . . . I am not just an MBA with a passing interest in turning my outdoor pursuits into profitable work. I am a passionate explorer." On April 14, 1998, he bleemed it to Jardine, in La Pine, Oregon, via e-mail.

Coup likes to say that Ray Jardine opened the GoLite R&D department years before there was a company. Born in 1944 and raised in Colorado, Jardine worked summers in Yellowstone and took up rock climbing in the Tetons. In college at Northrop University in Los Angeles he earned his degree in aeronautical engineering, and then worked at Martin Marietta near Denver for four years before quitting in 1970 to be a full-time rock rat. In 1974 Jardine designed and patented a camming device called the Friend, a staple of rock protection that remains the prototype for all the spring-loaded cams that climbers still use today. Partly through the use of his invention, he became a climbing demigod, with such credits as the first ascent of the world's first 5.13 route (The Phoenix, in Yosemite, in 1977). Then in 1981 he gave up climbing and dedicated himself to an omni-outdoor path that included, among other things, a three-year sailing voyage around the world with his wife, Jenny.

Starting in 1987, the Jardines embarked on a series of five summerlong through-hikes (the Pacific Crest Trail three times, and the Appalachian and Continental Divide Trails once apiece) that inspired Ray to make his own featherlight gear and to develop his anti-trail-tchotchke philosophy. Jardine's Pacific Crest guidebook has sold 20,500 copies, and by the mid-1990s it had created a cadre of ultra-light cultists who call themselves Jardinites. Even readers who had no intention of ever hiking the Pacific Crest Trail swore by the Ray Way.

When I visit him at his home in La Pine, Jardine worries that he looks sloppy from months of desk-work on his new book, *Beyond Backpacking,* and hours of fiddling with GoLite prototypes. But nothing shows except his strength. His cheeky face, coronaed by silver hair and beard, is elfin and mild. For a guy who is such a Calvinist on paper, he turns out to be an infectious, easy, multihour smiler.

Jardine claims he never wanted a cult following. "I don't like being a guru," he says in a soft lilt that contrasts the hard edge of his words. "I refuse." Nor does he need GoLite money. He says royalties from sales of the Friend plus his book sales keep him and Jenny where they want to be—far, far from the places where money rules. Especially places like the OR show, which they both abhor even though the industry it represents pays their way. "I wouldn't be caught dead in a place like that," says Jardine.

The last thing he ever expected—or wanted—was for some high-octane Republican pitchman to come thundering into his quiet. Coup's "bombshell" caught the Jardines two weeks before departure for a sea-kayak epic in the Canadian Arctic. Coup couldn't be ignored; he had more or less hologrammed himself into their house via e-mail, and then fax. "The first five pages were credentials," says Jardine, "which completely blew me away." (Kim's résumé was part of the package.) The Jardine household, immediately post-pitch, sounds like one of those Star Trek battle scenes where the shields are down and the reactor is going to blow. Says Ray, "We were going back and forth, 'No, no, no, we don't want this to happen.'"

But he didn't say no. And that was all the encouragement Coup needed. Jardine agreed to a deal for two reasons, the first of which was Coup's "business savvy." The second is related to the first, in that Coup positioned the idea as a way to help those poor souls who needed the stuff but wouldn't make it themselves. "This little thing in my mind said, 'Give the hikers a break,'" recalls Jardine.

From e-mail to binding agreement took only two weeks (the Jardines did make their trip) without Jardine and Coup ever meeting face-to-face. But during the negotiations, Jardine made known an odd wish: that Coup should sew his own Ray Way backpack, using the instructions in the Pacific Crest guidebook. Coup's reaction was equally unusual for a money guy: He did it. He drove all night from Boston to the Sicklerville, New Jersey, home of a sister-in-law who is a professional seamstress. In the course of 30 hours, Coup measured and cut fabric while she sewed; then he express-mailed Jardine the pack, which was really, Coup says, "an unwritten, unspoken contract contingency."

If GoLite was to have a prayer, its gear needed to say "buy me" to people who have never heard of Ray Jardine and who may not care to. Enter Erickson Outdoors. Among many other things, the company serves as GoLite's elocution school. Housed in an old pump factory near San Francisco Bay in Berkeley, Erickson Outdoors is a design and sourcing outfit with revenues of $9 million a year. The average consumer wouldn't be familiar with Erickson because its fabrications don't bear the name, but it's well known among the manufacturers at OR. That's primarily due to the combined expertise of its owners: Mark Erickson, Janice Fletcher, and Tom Mann, all of whom toiled at The North Face before leaving to form their company in the late eighties. At The North Face, Mark Erickson had codesigned the first geodesic dome tent, which led to the epochal VE-24. These days, Erickson Outdoors makes packs, sleeping bags, outerwear, and tents for clients such as CamelBak, Helly-Hansen, Land's End, L.L. Bean, and now GoLite.

Not that Coup's enterprise has all that much in common with Erickson's other clients. At least not yet. When he popped up at the Erickson booth during the 1998 trade show, Coup didn't exactly look like a contender. "Quite often, people have harebrained or ill-conceived ideas for products, and they're trying to get somebody interested in producing them," Erickson says. "Coup was, we thought, one of those guys. He came up to our booth, started picking our brains, asking us for our perspective on things." His suspicions were only confirmed when Coup, after a period of what Erickson describes as "haunting the booth," asked for impressions of the pack he'd produced at Jardine's behest. "He pulls out this stained, moth-eaten bag of nylon and proceeds to tell us about the virtues of ultralight camping," Erickson recalls. "We were polite. We engaged him, as we do by habit. He said thank you, and we thought that was the last we were going to see of that guy."

But Coup kept coming back, both over the remaining days of the show and afterward, and soon Erickson started to take him seriously. Two months after the August 1998 OR show, Erickson sat down with Coup and Jardine in Berkeley. (It was the first time the wonk and the swami had met in person.) The five-hour session resulted in a plan to start making stuff, thus kicking off a tristate game of Hacky-gear that's still going. Handmade Jardine originals issue forth from La Pine, Coup checks them out, and Erickson tries to render them commercial-mass producible, attractive, salable. But Jardine retains a prototype-killer clause: Should Erickson add weight, get flashy, or otherwise stray from the Ray Way, that version will be deep-sixed. Final approval, says Coup, requires two keys—both he and Jardine have to agree on each item. Getting to a launch has been, betimes, exasperating. Jardine says he spent "a thousand hours showing them how their improvements weren't improvements."

They do make changes, however. Mann, the company's materials expert and manager of overseas sourcing and production, has the greatest hands-on involvement. He also has an amazing facility for translating the nonverbal communications of equipment and clothing, to decipher the messages they're sending to the consumer. He's the Gear Whisperer.

Take the Breeze backpack, a cornerstone of the line. If you buy it, you've bought the Ray Way, because wearing a 15-ounce, frameless, hip-beltless pack with a conventional load—40 to 60 pounds—would be crippling. The $120 Breeze is intended, ideally—in Jardine's vision—to haul just 12 pounds. Since there wasn't much for Mann to work with in the way of amenities—he couldn't add daisy chains, wide shoulder pads, support stays—he concentrated on making the Breeze announce its strength, thereby refuting suspicions that light equals flimsy. The message comes across in the use of a super-strong black ripstop nylon, called Spectra, with a techie grid pattern of white lines. Mark Erickson had to fight for taxicab-yellow reinforcement stitching. He fought for the yellow, not the stitching, which was there all along but nonapparent. Now the rest of the GoLite line has contrasting reinforcement bar tacks, too. Even though Jardine balked at such visual enhancements, the Ray/Tom/Mark Way pack turned out to be tougher than the original and, most important, lighter—because it uses newer, more advanced materials.

Three months before GoLite's debut at the 1999 OR show, samples were being produced at factories in Korea, Taiwan, and China. They were followed by a first production run of, in most cases, 1,500 items for retail delivery. The GoLite starters: Breeze pack; Dome umbrella, $23; Newt rain jacket, $170; Coal insulated parka, $195; Bark shell jacket, $95; Trunk shell pants, $85; Nut fleece cap, $15; Pouch stuff sacks, up to $33; Cave two-person shelter (it's a tarp, not a tent), $185; and Nest bugproof inner shelter, $75. Total weight: seven pounds, 4.5 ounces. As of this writing, the Fur sleeping bag-oids (two pounds, $175) are still in the offing. We'll keep you posted.

Now comes the hard part, and Coup knows it. "There's an ultimate reasonable chance that we realize almost no sales," he says, savoring the risk like an Altoid. That, of course, means losing an enormous investment in time and money. Of the $600,000 that Coup committed by the eve of the OR show, $400,000 went toward the initial production run. If all of it is sold to retailers, GoLite will bring in more than $750,000—the standard factory-to-wholesale markup is 40 to 50 percent. (The markup from retailer to consumer is typically another 50 percent.) Not much left in the way of profit once you figure in marketing costs, Jardine's royalties, and other overhead.

Coup would love to break even on run number one. Before the bulk of his money returns, though, he'll have to shell out more on new factory orders and expenses. That's how he figures he'll have spent $1 million by the end of this year and why he has even more on tap to survive 2000. "In the plan, we come into the black next year. But then we go into the red again and come into the black again," he explains. "You go into the red in the second year for very good reasons: People have heard about you and they like it. So instead of making 1,500, you're making 3- or 4- or 5,000 products. Instead of making 12 models, you're making 20, 30, 50 . . ." A company could follow a more cautious, slow-growth plan, building on sales receipts rather than capital infusions. But slow, to Coup, looks like suicide, because it gives big competitors a chance to drive GoLite out of the game.

The goal for Coup's startup is $10 million in annual sales, but he has no idea if that's possible. The right-off-the-bat fall 1999 sales are gimmes: Merry Christmas, Jardinites. Then, things get thrilling. "If all the Jardinites there can be," says Coup, "are all the Jardinites there are now, I end up broken and bloody." Jardinites may, by God, be multiplying. We know for sure that marathon hikers are: A record estimated 3,000 people started the Appalachian Trail through-hike this summer, up from 1,800 last year.

Coup knows this tiny hard core won't keep GoLite breathing, but he has great hopes for "disappointed hikers," like himself and Kim, who once bailed out of an AT trip because they were miserable under the weight of their enormous packs. It makes perfect sense as you listen to the baritone logic, but upon further reflection, the strategy of selling something to people who hate it doesn't seem like a surefire recipe for success. "The thrust of marketing is you need more things to talk about," reasons Tom Mann. "They've turned that around and are giving a one-sentence message." The message, he says, is: "Get over it!" The "it" being attachment to all things not completely, literally, molecularly necessary.

But while the pack and the tent may speak too stridently, Mann says, "The apparel has broader appeal." This could be, in part, because clothes have to be, well, *wearable*. And if they're any good, as GoLite's seem to be, clothes this light—the Newt waterproof-breathable jacket, ten ounces; the Coal insulated coat, 18 ounces—are notable additions to the market. As for looks, the GoLite collection has a perverse sort of stylelessness that seems, for the moment, stylish. "We managed to sweeten it up, but still, the overall look is Plainsville," Mann says. "You might see a guy working at a filling station in it, but it's ultra-high-tech."

Coup hopes GoLite's wares will cross over into other weight-critical sports, such as climbing and cycling. But backpacking is central. The grand plan is to make hiking hew to the Ray Way, now also the Coup Way, thereby creating Coup's own market, which he'll dominate because he got there first with the most and the best. Of course, the outdoor world will be the judge of that.

Salt Lake City, the last quiet before the big doors open.

A fluorescent gloaming hangs high overhead in the Salt Palace. Coup, dressed Dan Quayle casual—dirt-free tennies, off-white chinos, belt embroidered with retrievers, polo shirt—is preparing to win over all comers to booth #3524. He tells me that he knows what failure would look like: "We're standing around and we're standing around, talking to each other." He's not exactly sure how to spot success, but he says he's more concerned about it over the long term than here and now.

Not that he wouldn't mind if GoLite caught some buzz this weekend. On a voodoo level, the OR show is nothing more than a vast, expensive rite to generate buzz. Buzz can bestow riches: In 1997, for example, the Canadian gear maker Arc'Teryx hit with a fiendishly clever new method of fabricating Gore-Tex outerwear in a $450-plus jacket. Thereafter, the company went from 55 employees to 270. "If that jacket had tanked at OR, I'm 90 percent sure it would have been the end of Arc'Teryx," says Jayson Faulkner, the company's sales and marketing vice-president.

To jump-start the process, Coup spent $150,000 with Thibeault, his promotion consultant, to make GoLite buzz. A chunk of it went to printing the slick catalogs, designed with punched-out holes toward the edges of the pages as a nod to ultralight. Some $9,000 went for a "belly band" ad wrapped around thousands of free issues of *Backpacker* magazine that its publisher handed out at the show. The front of the ad pictures bricks and a feather, separated by the fine-print question: "How much does enjoyment weigh?" The backside answer: "Next to nothing when it's 'Ray-Way'!" The GoLite logo is orange-on-black, computer-form type under a dome with a curving incision (representing a trail up a hill, I'm told). "It says, 'Big Player,'" Coup enthuses. "It says, 'For Real.' It says, 'The peacock has bright feathers!'"

And here come the first people to behold those feathers. Two guys slope down the still-quiet aisle, obviously with no commercial mission, and Coup advances to ask if they'd like to learn about GoLite. They would, either because they want to or because "no" is impossible. When a pitchee mentions someone else's ultralight gear, Coup roars back, "No, that was LIGHTweight. This is the first ULLL-tralight." Now and again he lets loose a cavernous laugh.

On the afternoon of the first day, Erickson says he's impressed at the steady stream of visitors: "Somehow Coup has been able to generate more than an average amount of interest from buyers. He's loving it." Meanwhile, as Coup rattles on, GoLite has a change of legend. Its story becomes his, not Jardine's. People want to know who the hell is this egghead gone feral. "How did you get into this?" one buyer asks Coup, and he looks enthralled by the answer. Michael Blenkarn, a designer at Arc'Teryx, swings by because he heard that Jardine would have some product at the show. He's impressed with the gear, but he's knocked out by Coup. "Had he spent the same amount of energy in the outdoor business that he did balancing the U.S. federal budget, he'd be deadly," Blenkarn tells me. "He's just changing mediums."

GoLite gets its first order, worth almost $10,000, from a two-store chain in Hermosa Beach. Still, the parade of tire kickers seems like the bigger story. The assistant manager of one mountain shop stops by and takes in the performance. "I'm really excited about the clothing," he declares. "That's really lightweight stuff." But he admits he's disinclined to recommend stocking GoLite because of the effort it would take to sell it. "You've got to make the customer believe you believe in it," he says.

But I see more hope in the Jardinites. I expected geezers in hiking sandals, but the truest believers I meet are two guys in their early twenties. I can't get a read on one because he develops a beagle-eyed fixation on Kim Coupounas. The other is a multi-pierced, Caucasian hiphop wonder who's wearing strange sneakers, black socks, mid-calf pants, and a dirt-colored T. "A friend turned me on to the PCT guide and, um, we just about worship the book as a Bible," he says. He starts giggling when he picks up a prototype sleeping system: "Is this the one that Ray used?" He says he's not sure whether the average consumer will bite, but he does see a possibility for the clothing that nobody had thought of: wilderness street wear.

The guy asks Coup if he sports the clothes around town. Coup looks confused: "I don't know the answer to that question." When the two stand close and talk, Erickson yells for somebody to get a camera. "I'm Gen X, but barely," Coup tells me later. "I don't get it completely."

No, you don't get it at all. Yet somehow GoLite has produced something this kid is dying to have. The Jardinite asks Coup to sell him a prototype Coal jacket because it's black, which GoLite doesn't plan to make; he can't stand the Fruit Loops end of the palette, like Chinese red. "It just stands out too brightly," he remarks. "If somebody were aiming a gun at me . . . " Good point. The GoLite universe changes entirely when he puts on the black coat. Everything plain and sturdy becomes resplendent—so bad it's good. For the first time, something GoLite makes sense and speaks in words that didn't emanate from Demetri Coupounas or Ray Jardine. The black Coal says "Street." Better yet, it says, "Screw you, Boomers, with your ridiculous techie coats of many colors and zippers galore and every other feature you've grafted on to junk up gear." What it says, is that this odd union of the number-gushing frontman and the ultralight-crusading guru has created a certain chemistry, one that might just make GoLite the coolest thing going at some OR show to come.

December 1999

The Low-Tech, High-Speed, Retro-Manic Simple Life

FLORENCE WILLIAMS

O h, to gallop strong and sure o'er the waving sedges of the plains! To drink in the sage-scented wind, to hold the reins in capable, callused palms! To streak gloriously—man and horse together— across the continent's flat heart, traveling in the very wheel-ruts of pioneer wagons, the very hoofprints of proud Sioux ponies. The freedom! The glory!

"Whoohee!" shouts Eustace Conway. "Canada! We've made it to Canada! Whoohee!" And by God, we have—up ahead, the border station between North Dakota and Manitoba looms above the wheat. Eustace Conway, brave redeemer of the tattered quilt of frontier values, wants the world to know that he has traveled farther and faster by horse-drawn buggy than any human ever, and is well on his way toward achieving nothing less than the first-ever circumnavigation of the Great Plains!

Luckily, Eustace, who is on leave from his day job as a North Carolina backwoods primitive and mountain man, doesn't mind the precious ticks of the sundial lost to border paperwork—a mere blip of bureaucratic pettifoggery in the unfolding drama of his retro-agrarian studliness. For their part, Curly and Hasty, Eustace's gelding steeds, seem grateful for the break. In only 17 days, this buggy has come 580 miles! Only 1,908 to go!

It is a windy day on a lonely stretch of highway, the laser-straight gravel roads we've been traveling giving way at the border to cracked blacktop. A few scattered trees, a clump in Canada, a clump in the States, lean slightly to the east. Muddy fields stretch in all directions, devoid of sentient life, save a few pintail ducks and two dough-cheeked Canadian border agents standing under their flag, grinning.

Their names are Dan and Bill, and they have never seen anything like this. "In my 12 years here, I have never seen anything like this," Dan says. "Have you, Bill?"

Bill shakes his head. Then he scratches it.

It's true. Here is one man's revivalist fantasy: a longhaired, wind-burned guy in a beaver-felt hat; at his side, his lissome, longhaired, windburned girlfriend, Patience Harrison, sans hat; and two tuckered horses hitched up to a refurbished 1830s wooden buggy, all followed by a rangy panting mutt named Spotticus.

Eustace lets loose his hillbilly guffaw. "I bet you haven't seen too many buggies cross this border!" he tells Dan and Bill.

Dan pulls out a Polaroid and takes our picture.

"Where'd ya start out from, then?" Bill asks with a faintly Northern European lilt.

"Well, we started 17 days ago in Hyannis, Nebraska, and came up through the Dakotas," Eustace drawls, launching into the same song and dance he has repeated daily for two weeks. Since I joined them a few days ago, Patience and I have been taking turns driving a tempo-rary support truck and riding with Eustace in the buggy, like a polyg-amist's wives heading West. Eustace always gets to ride in the buggy, because this is, after all, his inspired idea, and he's the one trying to set a land speed record. (Not that there's any existing record to break, not that the Guinness people have the slightest interest in a guy carv-ing big buggy doughnuts around the Plains.)

"And now we're heading west through Canada till we hit the Rock-ies," Eustace explains, "then south through Montana and Wyoming, then back to Nebraska."

Bill lets that sink in. "You're making good time then, eh? How far do you go in a day?"

This is the part where people either simply don't believe Eustace or think he's some sort of tormentor of horseflesh. "Between 30 and 60 miles a day," Eustace announces proudly.

Bill and Dan look at each other, incredulous. In case you don't know much about horses and pioneers, some perspective: Westward settlers were lucky to make eight to 12 miles a day, and they took Sundays off. And they were driving covered wagons. Horses harnessed to a light buggy, Eustace will tell you, can actually trot longer and go faster than under saddle. But 60 miles? Today, endurance horseback races might cover 50 or even 100 miles, but the races typically last only a day. This trip could take two months.

"Oof," says Dan.

"Uff-da," says Bill.

To strive to do that which has never been done, to gain enlightenment through physical suffering and prowess, to teach the misguided minions of industrialization a simpler life in unity with nature, to be loved and admired for all of these things, and someday—this is where the aptly named Patience might fit in—to impregnate a fair, worthy lass and raise robust progeny: These are the humble goals of Eustace Conway, 37.

When Eustace was 17, he walked out of the suburbs of Gastonia, North Carolina, and into a tepee in the woods, where he lived for the next 17 years as a hunter-gatherer. He gave up basic, inalienable American rights like TV and trash pickup. On Turtle Island Preserve—the 1,000-acre subsistence farm he muscled over the years out of the mountains near Boone—Eustace teaches workshops in primitive living and polishes his vision of a back-to-the-future agrarian utopia. His fervent hope is that his prairie odyssey will—never mind exactly how—spur folks to reconsider the wonders of an equine-powered economy and a simpler existence.

Eustace has been chasing heroic visions since the age of six, when he collected 140 pet turtles—more, he figured, than any other six-year-old on earth. In 1995, he and his brother Judson rode horseback across the country in a blistering 103 days. They ate roadkill. They set a world record. ("I asked around," says Eustace. "I found that nothing even came close.") He and his college buddy Preston Roberts—Eustace commuted from his tepee to Appalachian State University—followed up with a march around the Carolinas, setting another unofficial speed and distance record, this time for travel with a fully loaded pack mule. Eustace has told tales of these and other exploits to legions of schoolchildren and public radio listeners, because, like some flint-knapping performance artist, Eustace likes an audience. And audiences like him: He tells them about catching trout with his bare hands and sewing up a wound on his own face. A tentative book deal is in the works, and he is documenting this summer's buggy ride with a camcorder lent to him by Ron Howard's Imagine Films. At first Eustace stared at the camcorder the way Geronimo might have, but when he found the record button and the mini-screen gizmo that replays what he's shot, he whooped and hollered. "Dang!" he cried. "Look at that!" Now he's an eager point-and-shoot auteur.

"Most people would really hate this," says Eustace as he commands the horses to resume their trot after the border. Patience is idling along behind us in the truck. "Boys, trot!" he says, and they do. It's a marvel. Curly, a hardy blond American Bashkir, is pressing on despite a limp, bobbing his tired head like an oil rig. Hasty, a 15-year-old Morgan and former national endurance champion, is holding up fine after trotting for nearly 600 miles. There's no set itinerary or schedule: Each day at dawn, Eustace and Patience break camp, usually in a farmer's field, and then stop every ten miles or so for Indy 500-style water breaks. In the afternoons, when they rest for a couple of hours, the horses are so tired that they sometimes eat lying down and fall into a deep sleep. Then it's back in the harness till darkness falls, around 10 P.M.

When Eustace says, "Most people wouldn't understand why I keep driving this hard day after day after day," he's got that right. It's not that Eustace wants to achieve some deeper understanding of the pioneer experience. Though such matters interest him, Eustace would not even undertake this trip if it weren't for the stopwatch chance to do something better and faster than anyone else. "If this kind of thing had been done before," he says, "I wouldn't be interested. I have to do something *exceptional*."

We're back on the gravel now. A souvenir Canadian flag from our border buddies flaps in the breeze. The weather is nice today, and riding in the open air is fun, the perfect combination of smooth and springy. Perhaps the best part is the noise, the sound of shod hooves clacking along the gravel and the rhythmic wheeze of Spotticus as he trots along behind us.

"Grasslands are made for ungulates!" Eustace cries, warming up to his spiel. "The horse could solve so many of our modern problems—fossil fuel, traffic, social alienation." I'm straining to see it. I imagine myself wearing a prairie bonnet and clutching the Book of Mormon, and squint to summon up vistas of belly-high grass and herds of bison. But they're not here. A single-engine crop-duster plane shuttlecocks over a brown field, trailing chemical plumes. A coal-fired power plant on the horizon spews whorls of yellowish steam. There isn't even much grass left on this agro-savanna, just decayed stubble from last season's monocrop.

No matter. Eustace doesn't seem to notice the postapocalyptic feel of the place, the palpable weight of rust and disappointment and low crop prices. Farm after farm in the region has gone belly up, and families have abandoned their homesteads in droves. In Eustace's eyes, though, the failed prairie experiment has its bright side: The rural Plains are no more populated today than they were 100 years ago, when the frontier was declared closed. It is once again dead air, white space, the big blank. Eustace loves this.

"I had no idea it was so empty up here!" he crows.

The responsibilities of a celebrity primitive, even one in a hurry, include community outreach. News of our caravan has preceded us, and Eustace and Patience have been invited to speak to students in the tiny Manitoba farming town of Waskada: 98 kids, grades K-12, in a school due to close soon because of declining enrollment. Eustace hates to take time away from the road, but after one farmer feeds us a pork roast and another one puts us up in the bedrooms of his grown children, he feels obliged. Once in front of the kids, though, he's in his element. His twang becomes ever more slo-mo as he offers up a simplified version of his Thoreauvian mission: "The goal of my life is to set an example," he tells the children. "To say to people, 'Hey, you can live like this too, and there's something better to living without electricity than with it.' I want to get people's attention so they can follow their dreams." He describes his tools and accoutrements (including ax and knife, omitting sunglasses and Leatherman), the horses, the nice people everywhere they go. Most of the kids are rapt. Some are visibly perplexed.

"Why are you going around in circles?" a kindergarten girl asks.

"Doesn't your dog get tired?"

"Don't you ever get sick of each other?"

Picture this, kids: 12 hours a day, day after day after day, in some of the most god-awful wind and rain to hit the Plains in years. You wear one or two layers of long underwear, a layer of fleece, two wool sweaters, a hooded and lined Carhartt jacket and jeans, a lined raincoat, a poncho, rainpants, and three silk scarves. You pile on a wool blanket that a Sioux gave you in South Dakota, a heavy ripstop-nylon buggy skirt, and a blue tarp. You want to sit out the prairie-flattening storms, but you can't, because one of you is trying to set a world record for a category that does not exist. It's enough to send most of us into couples therapy. It's enough to make you want to rip each other's eyes out.

Patience and Eustace are no exception. They met three years ago, when Patience, then 23, was teaching second grade in Raleigh, North Carolina, and Eustace came to speak at the school. His lecture, about living in touch with nature, made her cry. When she visited Turtle Island, Eustace took her for a buggy ride through a homemade obstacle course and handed her the reins. "That's what I like about her," he says. "She's game for anything." Last year she quit teaching to travel in Africa before moving to Turtle Island to try out the Eustace lifestyle.

Now she can pluck turkeys and apply horse liniment and wash her clothes in a bucket. Patience, who grew up in Philadelphia and was once captain of Duke's field-hockey team, possesses two characteristics that Eustace values in women and horses: perseverance and a high threshold for pain. "We complement each other well," muses Eustace, lapsing into his animal-husbandry vocabulary when Patience is out of earshot. "That's why I thought I'd like to mate with her."

In the meantime, however, Patience is happy to play the role of Eustace's gregarious ambassador. It's Patience who waves to passing cars and makes cheerful conversation with farm families. Patience who does all the cooking and cleaning and horse-feeding and brushing.

But as Patience has been discovering, Eustace has some, well, out-dated ideas about men and women, along with some pretty outsized ideas about himself. "Eustace demands a lot of the people around him," she confides to me. "He likes to give orders, because that's just the way he is. I don't think he realizes how it sometimes sounds.

"He did once read *Men Are from Mars, Women Are from Venus* in an effort to understand his control thing," Patience continues. "It was really sweet. For a while he said things like, 'I can see I'm not vali-dating your opinion.' He sort of got over it, though."

To fully appreciate Eustace's transformation from suburban southern boy to mighty overlord of animals, nature, and women, you have to go back to 1924, when his grandfather, "Chief" C. Walton Johnson, founded Camp Sequoyah, a boys' camp outside Asheville, North Car-olina, "Where the Weak Become Strong and the Strong Become Great." Eustace spent his summers there, soaking up old Boy Scout manuals and Davy Crockett stories. His first words were "oak" and "maple."

If Camp Sequoyah succeeded in making Eustace Strong and Great, his relationship with his father, Eustace III—once a Sequoyah coun-selor, Eustace's Cub Scout leader, and now a retired chemical engineer who at 73 still runs up a local mountain twice a week—may have instilled some of the anxiety and insecurity requisite for any self-respecting record-breaking obsessive. "I cannot convey the extremity of my experience with my dad," says Eustace of his arcadian oedipal drama. "That's why I can push myself. Once, I was painfully cold on a camping trip and he said, 'Just run up and down.' That was all he said. Like he couldn't acknowledge that I was this little boy who needed his help. I entered manhood at four years old."

The natural world became both Eustace's solace and his Olympian arena. At 18, he helped lead a boys' group down the Mississippi River at flood stage from St. Louis to New Orleans in an Indian war canoe. At 19, he hiked the Appalachian Trail wearing a loincloth and living off snared grouse. He has never bought a roll of toilet paper in his life.

"Eustace always was different," sighs his mother, Karen, a former schoolteacher. "His father wishes he were more normal, and that's why he's always been so hard on him." The youngest of their three boys, Judson, makes his living as a guide in North Carolina and Alaska. Middle son Walton imports Russian art. Karen and her eldest have remained close, now that she has learned to accept wooden spoons as Christmas presents and the fact that Eustace will always be, as she puts it, "self-absorbed."

"He's such a good boy," she says, "but he was always headstrong and very demanding, wanting me to get him tomahawks and Indian outfits and wanting them right away. I certainly gave in a lot. Maybe it's my fault he turned out like this."

After a week of rain and wind and crop dusters, small breaks in the monotony of the Plains take on wondrous proportions. The blue-winged teal swimming in the flooded ditches, the occasional patch of grass, the clopping sounds of nineteenth-century travel.

Ever since we crossed into Canada, Curly has been limping, and Eustace figures he'll just stop and borrow a stand-in. While Patience tends to Curly and Hasty, Eustace and I drive over to see an enterprising man who's farming a trendy, if not appetizing, crop: pregnant mare urine, a key ingredient in estrogen pharmaceuticals. Walking right into the barn, Eustace introduces himself. "Mah name's Eustace, rhymes with 'useless,'" he announces in his fetchingest voice. Dan Meggison is a tall, lean redhead in his late forties, with gaunt cheeks and a wilted handlebar mustache. He studies Eustace, and then me with my pen in hand. "You're not them animal rights people, are you?"

Eustace laughs. "I've got to worry about them myself."

Dan relaxes and shows us around, and drama ensues. A new colt has somehow gotten on the wrong side of a barbed-wire fence from his mama, so while Dan parts the wire strands, Eustace coaxes him back through. It is in gestures like these that men like Dan and Eustace establish their common language, where Eustace proves himself not just a throwback Appalachian eccentric but a Man Who Knows Horses. Dan rewards him: "I've never had a colt named Eustace before." And this very minute, in the back pasture, a mare is lying on the ground, writhing and groaning. Dan slashes the amniotic sac with a pocketknife, grabs the foal's hooves—soft on the bottom, like lobster meat—and yanks. Out she splashes: Florence.

Hunkered over the wet filly, we are all rather proud of ourselves. Dan agrees to let Eustace borrow his draft mule, Clint, while Curly vacations at the farm for a few days. Mules are strong and tough, and Eustace is elated. He rubs his hands together like he's making fire and smiles. We celebrate over a lunch cooked by Heather, Dan's wife.

"Good sausage," I say, taking two more of Heather's offerings. Really, it's not that good, but I'm trying to be nice. "What is it?"

Dan pauses. "I was hoping you wouldn't ask," he says. I'm thinking, Please don't tell me, please don't tell me, but he does anyway.

"It's horse."

Eustace starts laughing.

Clint, it turns out, is a complete wanker. Not only won't he trot or pull the buggy, he acts as a drag on Hasty, who is battling some soreness of his own. Eustace is just about beside himself. It's already 3 P.M., and we're only six miles from the Meggisons' place. "Come up, boys," he pleads. "Step up." He prods Clint with the whip, but Clint is simply not interested. Finally another sympathetic farmer offers to lend us his family's mare and to trailer Clint back over to the Meggisons' farm. The substitute mare, Prairie, is terrified of the buggy, terrified of the few cars passing, and terrified of Eustace. Which means she runs. Fast. Even with Eustace holding her back, we are tearing down the road. So of course Eustace is now in a really good mood.

Amazingly, we make 39 miles before we pull over at a lonely wheat farm near the Manitoba-Saskatchewan border at dusk. The land is as flat as a Frisbee, the only lines breaking the horizon are the hulls of combines and aluminum silos and, way off, the tilted silhouettes of long-abandoned farmhouses.

Eustace pops a Stroh's. "Dang, girls, that's good!" He takes off his beaver hat and leans against the truck. "As my brother Judson would say, it's a perfect world."

Not for long. When we call Prairie's owners, they can't believe how far we've driven their mare. Thirty-nine miles! They are having a family coronary. She's not in shape! She hasn't trained for this! They want her back tonight, and they're going to pick up Curly and trailer him out for a horse exchange.

Sitting on the tailgate in the moonlight, Eustace's mood plummets. People just don't get Eustace, and this bugs him. "I am one of the most misunderstood men in the world," he says. Prairie looks just fine to him. "I love horses. I respect them, but I'm not lovey-dovey about it. They're work animals. I'll yell at them, I'll bite them, kick them in the nose with my knee. Horses want you to be dominant." He sighs. "Patience and I have both pushed ourselves extremely. Me, to tears and to near death. I wouldn't feel right asking these horses to do anything I hadn't done myself."

I try to picture Eustace biting a disobedient horse. I have to admit, I can see it. It's Eustace's dark side, the rage he reserves for keeping things in line. "Hasty wasn't a buggy horse at first," he told me earlier. "Even the Mennonites rejected him. But I turned him into one." I can imagine the relentless training, the sheer power of Eustace's will over that trembling champion, now a docile and efficient machine. Eustace lets you know, over and over, why his methods and worldview are the righteous ones, but the strange thing is that even when Eustace is being impossibly didactic, he's so damn likable. By and large, the good people of Saskatchewan are delighted with Eustace. They stop their Ford F250s by the side of the road and offer up bottles of wine and jars of homemade black-currant jam. And in turn Eustace seems delighted with everyone he talks to, every school group, every farmer, every woman.

But in the end, Eustace and these latter-day farmers couldn't be more different. One couple told us they took a vacation once, on their honeymoon, to Sioux City, Iowa. They bought a heifer. Eustace's primitivism, on the other hand, is uniquely contemporary, funded by the suburban school lecture circuit, college-enhanced, and enabled by the media. He's also not as one-dimensionally Cro-Magnon as people sometimes want him to be. Parts of the modern world fascinate him, like Redford movies, ripstop nylon, and duct tape. He positively gushes over the technological perfection of the five-gallon plastic bucket. When it comes right down to it, Eustace is an opportunist. And he's ambitious. "If I were really a Wall Street stockbroker instead of a mountain man, I'd be the leanest, meanest, richest one. That's just the way I am. I am a Type A mountain man."

Not surprisingly, it's hard to find a woman who will put up with a Type A mountain man for any length of time. After all, this is a man who didn't brush his teeth for ten years.

And one who is itching to fulfill his genetic destiny. Yep. Eustace is ready. He is dying to procreate. "I'd be happy to have at least seven kids," he tells me.

This alarms Patience. "I'd say it's just a little bit of pressure," she says one night while we're washing dishes, camped under the shadow of a cell-phone tower. She rolls her eyes. In fact, I catch Patience rolling her eyes quite a bit, like when Eustace tells her she can't bring along that jar of pickled peppers because it's too heavy, or when he dismisses her suggestion that maybe the horses should walk for a bit one evening. "I tend to be a controlling person also," she says, "but with Eustace, it's much easier to give up."

It seems clear that Eustace's central problem is that he has prehistoric needs but a modern libido. He needs to shack up with someone who can churn butter all day and follow orders. But he digs, really digs, the Spunky Modern Babe. Eustace got a big boost last year when *GQ* published an admiring article that emphasized his sheer redblooded manliness. Since then, he has received more than 100 letters from adoring women.

Eustace admits to me that some of these women sound pretty intriguing. "Patience is not ready for commitment," he adds. "She doesn't truly understand me." It's late at night. We're sitting in yet another bright farmhouse that has kindly taken us in. It's been raining, and we smell like wet wool. Patience is out in the barn. Eustace looks up from his beef stew and says, "The woman I really want to marry is Sacagawea."

"What about Pocahontas?" I ask. "She was from your neck of the woods."

He considers. "Pocahontas was romantic, which I like. But she had no backbone."

Leaving the buggy party as it trots west, I head back home to Montana for a while. I fly to Colorado and back. I see the new Star Wars movie. I paddle two clear mountain streams, eat sushi, and buy an outrageous pair of chunky black sandals at a mall.

When I next hook up with them, Eustace and Patience have been sitting in the buggy for 41 days straight. They've cut south through Montana, and we meet near a busted mining town called Musselshell, population 65. The horses look even bonier than before; their hair has rubbed off in spots under their harnesses, and Hasty's blood vessels wrap his body in long ropes thicker than my thumb.

"I've already blown any record out of the water!" Eustace proclaims, doing that fire-making thing with his hands again. "In the history of people with horses, not one's ever done what we've just done, ever. Period. Zero. We've done 1,500 miles now averaging 50 miles a day, and every day and every mile that we keep going just adds icing on the cake."

With only 988 miles and 18 days to go, Eustace has already begun plotting his next scheme, a buggy crisscrossing of New Zealand (because they really appreciate horses there) with Preston. Patience won't be joining them. She will probably not be joining Eustace on any more journeys, ever. Period. Zero. Patience has just about had it with Eustace. She puts this gently: "I think my parents don't quite believe Eustace is the right man for me, and my parents are usually right."

Alas, for now, one last ambition will have to go unfulfilled. "I don't see any babies happening anytime soon, unfortunately," Eustace mournfully tells me one morning as we trot past yellow fields of sweet clover. "If I could find the right woman to have babies, I'd be working on that."

So instead he's working on making it across two more states full of wheat and opportunities to spread the Eustace gospel. "I want to maintain a simple life," he insists, "even if I become famous, even if I make a movie or whatever. I still want to maintain a peaceful, quiet life in the forest."

As I step down from the buggy and say good-bye, I watch the simple life—complete with scrawny horses, future ex-girlfriend, box of camcorder cassettes, and yet another bad night's sleep—clop on into the sunset.

September 1999

King of the Dirtbags

MARK JENKINS

Yvon is leading. He's guiding his feet along a lip of rock, maneuvering himself out under an overhang. Positioned directly below the obstacle, he slides his hands up into a fissure and leans back. He holds himself horizontal, 700 feet of empty Wyoming air beneath him, studies the problem, and begins to climb.

He doesn't narrate the possibilities, nor does he appear to make any cerebral calculations; he just moves. His body—his hands and his feet coming in direct contact with the rock—will solve the problem.

He's focused; there's no wasted movement. His right hand shoots up and grabs an edge, quickly followed by his left hand, and then he steps up both feet. For a moment he is hanging upside down, crouched like a monkey about to leap for a branch. But he doesn't leap.

He pushes out with his legs and pulls in with his arms, and his body smoothly shifts to one side.

It would seem an awkward position for a man, pushing and pulling simultaneously, but somehow it creates a kind of dynamic tension, an internal, counterbalancing opposition. Yvon Chouinard is struggling precariously but also magnificently, paradoxically balanced. He's using a classic climbing technique called the lie-back: a difficult albeit direct solution to overcoming a crux. Another solid handhold, another foothold, and he rises gracefully onto the overhanging face. No hesitation, no desperation. Two more moves and he flows up and out of sight.

Then I hear him roar with delight.

"Don't bring those damn cams," Yvon had grumbled over the phone. "Don't need them. A few stoppers and hexes, that's enough. And don't bring those heavy ten-millimeter ropes. Ridiculous!"

He was just back from salmon fishing in Iceland. (Or was it trout fishing in Newfoundland? Or perhaps bonefishing in the South Pacific?) We were planning a climbing trip into Wyoming's Wind River Range. For 30 years Yvon had had his eye on a stunning, unclimbed line on the south face of 12,972-foot Mount Arrowhead. "And we don't need a tent," he bellowed. "I've spent a hundred nights in the Winds without a tent."

When I mentioned helmets, he scoffed at that, too, and said he'd only used one once or twice in his life. How about a headlamp? "I prefer to stumble around in the dark."

On the other hand, the fact that I wasn't intending to bring a fly rod represented a serious problem. "It's practically a crime to walk through the Winds and not fly-fish," Yvon said gravely. And when I suggested that a few cans of sardines and a tub of peanut butter would suffice for the week, he said tersely, "I'll do the cooking."

As a shakedown for an impending Andean expedition, I wanted to try using llamas. I volunteered to be the llama wrangler. Yvon had invited along two brothers from Hawaii, George and Kent Kam, so I figured the llamas could carry all our climbing gear and food, and said so. Yvon's response: "Don't need them."

We met at the Elkhart Park trailhead, on the west side of the Wind River Range, at noon on a forest-fire-dry day in August. I had the gear and the llamas, Josey Wales and Guy Sado; Yvon had the food and the Hawaiians, George and Kent.

It would be hard to find two more good-natured brothers than the Kams. They're Yvon's buddies from another of his life passions: surfing. George, 40, is as ebullient and outgoing as a maître d'. He had retired at the age of 32 after making a small fortune as a marketing manager for apparel companies in the surfing industry.

"It's just fashion, really," George said, smiling. "But everything's fashion. For every real-life surfer, or climber, or fly fisherman, there are a thousand wanna-bes."

Kent, 42, is quieter, but equally open. He had designed and built surfboards, then worked as a commercial pilot, and now is a firefighter in Honolulu, where he lives with his three-year-old daughter and his flight-attendant wife.

We weren't on the trail an hour, Guy Sado trotting along like a trouper and Josey Wales already showing ominous signs of being an outlaw, when out of the blue Yvon said, "Who needs a $450 raincoat?"

He was apparently reacting to the conspicuously outfitted backpackers we'd been passing on the trail, many of whom looked to be carrying the entire inventory of a small outdoor shop.

"What's wrong with getting wet!" Yvon cried.

When I reminded Yvon that Patagonia Inc.—the $223 million clothing company that he founded and owns, lock, stock, and barrel—sells precisely such items, he groused, "I know. I know. But they don't need them."

Hypothermia is what's wrong with getting wet, of course. And Yvon knows it—few men have spent more time in the mountains. Climbing together in Yosemite for a week last year, we'd talked for hours about shell design, and he'd gone on at length and in exquisite detail about the engineering of seams alone. Still, Yvon is prone to radical pronouncements. He's like an old philosophy professor of mine who started every class by posing a new existential problem: "Who can prove to me that the world wasn't created ten seconds ago, complete with memories, fossils, and computer files?"

"Yvon likes to say and do things for the shock value," says Doug Tompkins, a fellow climbing pioneer and businessman who has been Yvon's close friend for over 40 years. "It shakes people up. Gets them thinking."

While George, Kent, and I each carried a pack with shoulder straps and a hipbelt, Yvon carried his with a tumpline strapped across his

forehead. He learned this trick 20 years ago during a 45-day expedition across the Himalayas. He claimed the United Nations had done
a study on tumplines and found that, once your neck and back muscles were sufficiently developed, they were more efficient than shoulder straps and hipbelts. "I had chronic back pain until I started using
a tumpline," Yvon declared. He'd sent me one and I'd tried it, but
found I was walking miles staring at my feet instead of the landscape—
just like the women I'd seen humping conical baskets of rice all across
Asia.

On our first night in the Winds we camped in a brittle alpine meadow
beside seemingly fishless Seneca Lake. I put up our tent—Yvon had
relented on this issue—while he gave dryland fly-casting lessons until
dusk. Kent was a natural. George, in his enthusiasm, sometimes forgot the ten-and-two dictum. (Norman Maclean: "It is an art performed
on a four-count rhythm between ten and two o'clock.") I was no better with a rod than I had been as a kid.

After dark, sitting around the camp stove, Yvon said he knew a guy
in Bozeman, Montana, who lived for years in a stainless-steel, tubular
camper that you entered from underneath. He was a master welder
and was working on fuel-efficient stove designs at Yvon's bequest.

"You know, your average kitchen stove is a total piece of crap," he
said. "They're over 80 percent inefficient. Imagine if the pot set down
inside an insulated casing. The heat lost to the air would be minimal,
the fuel efficiency dramatically increased."

It was a good example of the way Yvon's mind works: constantly
questioning, rethinking, reformulating, innovating. As George told me,
"It's Yvon's instinctual quest for the best. He's always looking for ways
to improve everything. How to make it better, simpler, lighter, more
environmentally friendly. I don't know anyone like him. In everything
he does, he strives for perfection."

"You should hear him talk about board design," says John McMahon, a California stockbroker who's another one of Yvon's surfing buddies. "He wants to create the perfect surfboard."

It galls Yvon that most surfboards break so easily; he's offended by
anything that's disposable but doesn't have to be. Quality and simplicity have always been guiding principles for Yvon and his wife,

Malinda. Their son, Fletcher, 26, spends his days working on the problem, building and shaping surfboards in a shop less than a stone's throw from the shed in Ventura, California, where his dad once shaped pitons. Their daughter is a designer as well—says Yvon, "She has a very clear sense of what is practical and functional."

Where Yvon can sometimes be caught up in his own ideas, Malinda is the pragmatist. She interprets their vision, she sends the e-mails, she makes things happen. She is the nexus.

"Yvon has always been willing to push forward without a template," says novelist Tom McGuane, a passionate fly fisherman and a longtime friend. "He is not bound by psychological cintures like so many of us, but it is Malinda who has given him this freedom. Malinda allowed Yvon not to lose contact with his instinctive ability to take great leaps forward. She is always there. Malinda is a visionary just like Yvon, but she's the tactician, the one behind the scenes. Without Malinda, many of Yvon's ideas would never have seen the light of day. What Yvon and Malinda have, really, is a very productive, very creative partnership."

On our second day in the Winds, Yvon told us that "the most important thing I ever taught my kids was how to eat roadkill."

He explained: "We hit a sage grouse on the road one day when they were young, so we stopped and picked it up. I taught them how to skin it, then I taught them how to cook it, and we ate it. Then I taught them how to tie flies with the feathers. Then we went fishing with the flies and I taught them how to catch fish."

This was Yvon the survivalist talking now, another distinct character among the dozen or so of his multiple personalities. Designer, climber, writer, kayaker, environmental activist, lover of rivers and fish, philosopher, surfer, businessman, ascetic, aesthete—at the age of 62, he morphs from one role to the next effortlessly.

Here is Yvon the pessimist: "I knew Man was doomed when I realized that his strongest inclination was toward ever-increasing homogeneity—which goes completely against Nature. Nature moves toward ever-increasing diversity. Diversity is Nature's strength. Nature loves diversity."

And you don't get diversity without adversity, according to the Chouinard theory of the universe. We'd talked about this extensively in Yosemite.

"Adversity is what causes organisms to change and adapt," he'd said. "Adversity is the catalyst for evolution. Take away adversity and evolution stops. And what do you have then? Devolution: America."

Late that afternoon, we camped at the northern end of Upper Jean Lake, the south face of Mount Arrowhead looming above us. Yvon cooked the first of five straight dinners of his bowel-busting, carrots-and-onions tsampa. When Kent happened to mention the profusion of pine needles and dirt in the entrée, Yvon replied, "They're good for you!"

And then the lesson: "You know, I absolutely forbade my children from washing their hands before they ate. Weakens their immune system. You have to learn how to handle germs. I drink from every stream I fish for the same reason."

I asked him if he'd ever had giardia.

"Oh, God," he cackled. "So bad the farts would clear out a bus. But that's not the point. The point is, I'm trying to adapt myself to the environment. Not the other way around."

Later that evening I reconned our approach to the base of Arrowhead while Yvon gave George and Kent more fly-casting lessons. Studying the south face with my monocular, then swinging the lens down onto Yvon beside the lake, it occurred to me that he was far more focused on showing his Hawaiian pals how to cast than on climbing a new route.

"Yvon's a big-time sharer of knowledge," says John McMahon. "At this point in his life, I think he's more interested in teaching than doing."

The next morning, we rose at 5:30. I thought it a late start for climbing a new route, but Yvon seemed unconcerned. It took the four of us two hours to hike to the base of the south face. George and Kent intended to scramble to the summit via the west ridge, while Yvon and I had identified the gorgeous, curving line that creased the thousand-foot face. It went straight to the summit.

When Yvon discovered that, despite his admonitions, I'd brought a number of cams, he cut the biggest ones off the rack. He also cut a third of the slings and carabiners. He climbs with no helmet, no chalk, no tape, no headlamp, no sunglasses, no sunscreen. This is his way of adapting to the mountain.

"I've cut everything superfluous from my life," he declared.

Even though I knew it was yet another bit of Chouinard hyperbole, I still chewed on this sentence for the first several pitches of the climb. Yvon is a man who owns three homes: an oceanfront house in Ventura, an oceanfront home made from recycled materials on California's Central Coast, and a home in Wyoming with a jaw-dropping view of the Tetons. Yvon is a man who flew to South America five times last year just to fish. But he doesn't use chalk.

The climbing was pure fun, compelling but not difficult. We didn't say much. We simply climbed—smooth, in sync, swapping leads.

I was watching Yvon lie-back through the overhang on the sixth pitch, his movements poised and precise, when I remembered something else McMahon had told me: "You should see him surf. He just glides. He has no hesitation throwing himself out onto huge waves."

One time, I don't even remember what Yvon and I were talking about—writing, freediving, business—he suddenly said, "Forget about the end result. It means nothing. The end result is we die. What matters is the process. The process is everything."

It was hackneyed Buddhist rap, but here's the thing: Yvon, despite—or perhaps because of—his many contradictions, lives it. For Yvon it wasn't the fact that we were climbing a new route in the Winds; it was all about how we were doing it. To him the ascent became more elegant each time something unnecessary was eliminated. Gear, chalk, words, signals. He believes, with all his being, in the Saint-Exupéry line that regularly appears in Patagonia Inc. literature: "In anything at all, perfection is finally attained not when there is no longer anything left to add, but when there is no longer anything to take away."

We completed our directissima of Arrowhead's south face in three hours, and then spent the afternoon back at camp in a pleasing, post-exertion fog, erratically debating this and that. At one point I told Yvon that I thought Patagonia clothing was too expensive.

"Not compared to Calvin Klein," he responded.

He went on to defend his company by saying that, because of the renowned durability of Patagonia apparel, everybody from dirtbags to billionaires buys it.

"Dirtbags don't buy anything," I exclaimed. "They schwag it. I know—I used to be one."

"I still am one!" Yvon countered.

Now hold on . . . Yvon does wear the same old clothes for days on end. And he did sleep with his clothes on the whole week we were in the Winds. And no matter the protean conundrums of his mind, he's snoring in less than two minutes. And most of his climbing gear belongs in a museum. And he's completely satisfied eating sardines with a piton. And he doesn't need a shower. And he flies economy just like the rest of us. And he sleeps on friends' couches instead of paying for hotel rooms. And he drives vintage beater Toyotas. But . . .

"C'mon, Yvon, you're a multimulti-millionaire."

"I give it all away. I don't even have a savings account."

True, I already knew that Patagonia Inc. had given millions upon millions to environmental causes.

"But that's not even the point," he continued. "Being a dirtbag is a matter of philosophy, not personal wealth. I'm an existential dirtbag."

"You're not a dirtbag anymore, Yvon, you're a businessman. A very successful businessman. Dirtbags don't own companies. Somewhere along the way you must have wanted to be a businessman."

"Never!" There was real vehemence in his voice. "All I ever wanted to be was a craftsman."

"He's in denial," George told me later. "He's an entrepreneur. He's a capitalist. He just can't bear being lumped in with all those businessmen he doesn't respect.

"But he also *is* a dirtbag. It's a statement as much as anything else. You know those Patagonia ads—'Committed to the core'? Well, Yvon is the core."

*   *   *

The next day we continued trekking north. I was hoping we might make one more ascent, but I think Yvon had already gone back to trout-fishing dreams.

We stopped for lunch at Summit Lake. It was the geographic fulcrum, the halfway point between our start at Elkhart Park and our finish at Green River Lakes. George and Kent and I lolled in the tundralike hummocks while Yvon cast a line.

It was high noon, that unluckiest of fly-fishing hours, but a cutthroat took his fly and promptly snapped his 5x tippet. He replaced it with a 4x and immediately caught a one-pounder, then a pound-and-a-halfer. As he was popping the fish off the hook with a one-handed flick of the wrist, a big sloshing sound rolled across the water. Yvon looked back over his shoulder just in time to see the splash. In a seamless series of motions, he let go of the hook; began snapping the line in great big sky S's, streaking out more and more line; spun 180 degrees while the hook was floating in the air; cast, throwing all the line off the reel; dropped the fly bull's-eye inside the concentric circles; and caught a two-and-a-half-pounder before the one-and-a-half-pounder had time to swim away.

He issued his familiar, exuberant roar, and then allowed himself a brief commentary: "Now that's . . . that's fly-fishing."

Two hours later it was raining, and Josey Wales had sat down on the trail for the hundredth time. We'd climbed our climb and caught our fish and now the trip was about to fall apart, even though we were still a three-day walk from the trailhead. George volunteered to cajole and kick Josey along the trail while the three of us double-loaded Guy and hustled down to Three Forks Park.

The downpour kindly commenced only after we got our tents up. By the time we'd eaten Yvon's homemade tsampa, we were bone-cold and drenched. George and Kent hit the sack, but Yvon and I couldn't help ourselves. We hung around our miserable little campfire, choking on smoke, watching a heavy mist come off the high park grass and drift into the trees. We took swigs of Glenlivet and let ideas bounce and tumble around us.

Yvon told me about the time his son, Fletcher, speared a wild pig and cooked it using one of Yvon's recipes. He told me about his dream of inspiring the biggest companies in the world to give 1 percent of their gross sales to environmental causes, just like Patagonia Inc. does. He called it a revolution, and his eyes showed white in the dark.

"Imagine! Just imagine if Conoco and IBM and Microsoft and GM and United Fruit and Hughes all gave 1 percent. It would be billions of dollars. It could save the planet!"

("People criticize Yvon," says Tompkins, "but 99.9 percent of these people can't match what he's doing for the environment. Yes, he owns a big company and he could do more—I could do more, you could do more, we all need more courage to do more. But for everything Yvon takes out of this world, he gives back more than anybody I know. And that's the bottom line.")

Yvon, the maker of his own myth, was growing tired, but he had to tell me about this freediver he knows who has adapted himself so well to the underwater environment, has become so tuned-in, that fish will guide him to lobsters, that dolphins have saved him from shark attacks.

Yvon, a Henry David Thoreau and a Ralph Lauren and a Muhammad Ali all forged into one, was tired, but he wanted me to understand that sustainability is the only hope for the planet. "Sustainability, sustainability . . ." He repeated it like a mantra.

Yvon, the master of market semiotics, was so tired, but he said he has been trying to write a book for nearly a decade. "Writing is too hard," he complained. It's a book about business. What else. "You know what the business of most businesses in America is? To sell the business. The business is to sell the business. Cash out. Go golfing. Well, not me, goddamit."

We were standing hunch-shouldered in the dark, rain draining off the bills of our baseball caps, mist flowing into the black woods like a river, the campfire long since drowned. Yvon had to sleep now, but first he had to tell me something. "I am guilty." This in reference to his profligacy, for his burning fossil fuel to stand in icy water on some remote river and try to think like a fish instead of a human.

He was going to his sleeping bag now, but before he did he wanted to tell me his favorite joke. He'd told it to me before. "There once was this Zen master sitting on a small stone bench, studying his small Japanese rock garden . . ."

There are only five rocks in the master's garden. Each was chosen for its individual perfection, as well as its unique relationship to the other stones. One day a visitor comes to the garden. The visitor steps slowly around the tiny space, contemplating the rake-grooved gravel and the stones. Eventually the visitor turns to the Zen master and exclaims, "It is perfect." The Zen master shakes his head solemnly and says, "No, it will be perfect when there are only three stones."

Yvon chuckled and said good-night. I offered him my headlamp, but he waved it away and stumbled into the dark.

November 2001

Skating Home
Backward

BILL VAUGHN

While other men spend their power decades harvesting money for their golden years, I've devoted the prime of my life to a swamp. And not even a real swamp, not some righteous nightmare of cottonmouths and feral pigs, but a mere backwater, a slough, really, that meanders through our place in western Montana, rising and falling with the Clark Fork River nearby. In the summer the main channel of this marsh oozes sweet and fragrant between its walls of red dogwood and offers an array of refreshing temperatures as you plunge deeper to flee horseflies and the heat. Around Halloween it freezes. Then, with the vigilance of a patriarch whose family business is on the verge of going public, I stand guard over this ice till it melts in April, plowing off the snow, sealing the cracks, polishing its surface in the quest for a kind of perfection that's just not possible anywhere else, at least not for me. And when it is perfect and my skates sigh across its water-colored sheen, I can almost convince myself that everything's going to be all right.

When my wife, Kitty, and I moved into Dark Acres, our slough lay concealed under a midden of agricultural squalor. The ranch family that sold us a slice of its empire, huddled in the shadows of Black Mountain, had used this wetland for three generations as its own private dump. When you looked at its main channel you expected water; what you saw was junk and decay. But since we had the river to play in and didn't need no redneck swimmin' pool, we figured to bury this eyesore with fill. Maybe even install a nice tennis court on top.

But one morning during our first spring, I was drawn from the house by the hysterical barking of Radish, our red heeler. I supposed the racket was about an insubordinate magpie or a treed cat. But the thing making the dog insane turned out to be a western painted turtle. The size of *Atlas Shrugged,* she'd withdrawn into her shell to wait for all the gnashing to go away. Behind her in a sandy depression glistened four leathery white eggs. The turtle must have wandered away from the river, I guessed, or one of our mosquito havens, and lost her bearings. After a while four clawed feet emerged from the shell, then an ancient head in yellow and green and red. Radish growled and the hair on the ridge of his spine stood up like a mohawk. I put my arm around him. *There and so and well,* I said, reciting the mantra that always calms him down. The turtle waddled down the bank of the slough, out onto a rotten railroad tie through an obstacle course of brambles and beer cans, and, to my surprise, vanished with a wet slap, proving that this water was still alive. I pulled sand over her eggs with the toe of my boot.

It took me three years to clean the slough. I went after the lightest stuff first, standing on the banks to wrestle things from the tangle with a rake. Then, surrendering to the inevitable, I waded chest-deep across an uncertain bed to extract what I couldn't reach from shore. What refused to come to hand I fished out with a chain hooked to my old pickup. Each month more water opened to the sun. This progress, satisfying in ways I wouldn't understand until later, had no immediate reward beyond the fact that it was progress.

When this first stage was finished, I took inventory: 289 tires, a tractor, two riding plows, a ton of farm implement parts and horse tack and barbed wire and rotten hay, a heap of dolls, a medley of overstuffed furniture, the carcass of a Hereford, the skeleton of a beaver, and much festive plastic jetsam. Then there were endless chunks of timber washed from the forest floor into the slough when the river flooded once a decade. As it dried I reduced it with a chainsaw and stacked it into pyres. The night the Blue Jays beat the Phillies in the World Series I went around with a can of gasoline. The neighbors must have thought I was some kind of Canuck. The fires were still smoldering three days later.

Soon, some of the slough's former tenants began to return. A mated pair of mallards came first, winging around till they finally landed in the skinny stretch of water I'd opened. Then came a school of tiny black fish, a spotted frog, and a muskrat, only his nose breaking the surface to leave a hallucinogenic wake. Once I surprised a great blue heron standing on a log, one leg tucked as it eyeballed the place for snacks. It issued an indignant squawk so loud it made my heart flutter.

I was close to being finished with the restoration. Only a half-dozen cottonwood trunks were still floating around in the slough, and they were so massive the pickup couldn't pull them ashore. Standing in the water, working like a tug, I maneuvered these hundred-foot behemoths against the banks and anchored them to the brush with yellow rope while Radish took rides on their backs. The next day I rose from bed creaking as if I'd been gang-tackled by the Oakland Raiders and made my way down to the slough with coffee and a lawn chair. For the first time since I'd discovered it, I intended to sit by this water without feeling the neurotic obsession to make it better. And, in fact, it could no longer be made better. There wasn't even a stray leaf to mar its seamless length. The hideous reek of rotten hay that had greeted us when we moved in had been replaced with a perfume of pennyroyal and wild roses. I counted 29 turtles that had climbed onto my cottonwood trunks to take the morning sun.

Since the act of cleaning the swamp had also restored its health, I named it the Mabel, after my mother's mother. When she worked as a public health nurse in the fifties, one of Mabel's stops was a squatter's camp on Hill 57 above the outskirts of Great Falls, Montana, my hometown. Her patients were Blackfeet and Cree who weren't welcome on the reservations or wouldn't live there. Sometimes when I drift around in my rowboat or sit in the broadgrass to absorb the Mabel's serenity, I'm reminded of my grandmother. I remember the photographs she loved to take, hanging on the walls of the house my grandfather built. Most of these pictures, which won blue ribbons at the state fair, were portraits of the denizens of Hill 57. One was of a woman so old she could recount scenes from the Indian wars. I used to get mesmerized by that face, by the depth of the wrinkles and their number, an infinite crisscrossing of lines that mimicked the pattern of game paths after a rain. And next to this picture was one of a landscape that captured a creek in a cold snap radiating mist as it cut its way through fresh snow. It was the purity of this scene that appealed to me then—and that still appeals to me, a summation of my earliest Montana memories, a place sweetly indifferent to the camera, innocent and absent of malice.

On a frozen Sunday when I was ten, I stood in my PJ's decorated with rearing stallions and glared with contempt at the church clothes I'd flung on my bed. Here were wool slacks, a starched white shirt, a bow tie, a checkered sport coat, a pair of oxfords, and a ludicrous black fedora.

"Jesus fucking Christ!" my old man suddenly bellowed.

When I opened my bedroom door and looked around the house, I discovered it was empty. Dad had disappeared, and so had my six-year-old sister, Laura. The back door had been thrown open, admitting a wall of frigid air, so I went there to see what I could see. And what I saw left me utterly bewildered. There was the old man, butt-naked, his breath rising in angry clouds, charging down the snowy slope behind the house to Sand Coulee Creek, a ribbon of wind-polished ice winding through the shabby rural sprawl we called Rat Flats. I wrapped my arms around my bony self and stared.

When he got to the creek he fell to his knees and skittered across it like a fugitive in a prison flick. Had he caught on fire like those people you read about who suddenly burst into flames? Was he drunk?

Then I saw the hole, a devious blue crease. Suddenly uncoiling, he plunged his arm into it, his 225 pounds of muscle and sinew straining as he groped for something within. The air stunk of smoke from the coal furnaces everyone used. Danny, our Labrador, was out on the ice too, barking at the crease the same way he did when he trapped prairie rattlers against the chicken coop.

Dad lunged twice and brought forth a steaming thing in a fleecy blue snowsuit. Although I had begun to sense the importance of what was taking place, I had only one reference for what I was seeing: the breech birth of a neighbor's horse I witnessed that ended well when the man reached into the mare and yanked her astounded foal into the world. What Dad was now rushing back to the house wasn't a foal, of course. It was Laura. As he strode by, the sodden little doofus yowling in his arms, one of her skates trailing a lace, I saw that his face was lathered with shaving cream. Laura had disobeyed the rule about skating alone and was saved only because the old man happened to glance through the bathroom window as she crashed through the ice.

The next day I lay beside the crease and studied its architecture, fascinated by the fact that the ice had become as dangerous as it was fun. In the summer, the Sand Coulee was a simple, good-natured yokel whose water was clean enough to drink and harbored sunfish, crawdads, and even the occasional trout. We dropped into it every day from a tire swing roped to a box elder and poled around in it on our rafts and constructed elaborate mud cities on its shores.

In the winter, the creek became a different sort of sanctuary. It was a snap to skate the 300 yards from our place to the lagoon where the Missouri accepted the stream, but what I yearned to do was skate to the creek's headwaters, where I would live in tree houses and steal chickens from ranches. It wasn't just the easy pleasure of forward motion that seduced me when I took to the ice, but also the chance to escape all the unpredictable emotional weather back at the house. Yet I never got farther upstream than three miles. When I was old enough to mount a serious quest, it was too late. The creek began running the color of old blood, poisoned by acids and heavy metals leached from the coal mines. The frogs and the fish disappeared first, and finally the turtles. And then it dried up.

Instant snow removal is the key to perfect ice. This is a fact of winter in western Montana that I learned the hard way. I'd been spoiled as a boy by wind that whistled across the Sand Coulee so incessantly snow just didn't have the chance to pile up. But here on the Pacific side of the Continental Divide, wet, balmy fronts slug it out all winter with arctic air pushing south from Canada. Midnight rain can give way to two feet of morning powder the afternoon sun reduces to slush, which freezes by midnight. After hissy, pathetic gusts announce a front moving in, all this weather usually happens in a dead calm.

There is even the odd season when most ice doesn't thicken enough to skate on. That's never the case, however, with the Mabel. Its bed is insulated by the brush that surrounds it, like a beer cooler, so once it freezes it seems to absorb more cold and freeze even deeper. Snow left to melt on the surface of the slough will eventually freeze as well, causing leprous disfigurements—welts and pits and hedgerows, or the crumbly, porous stuff we call Crackers, or even the bulbous, lumpy outrage called Casserole. The object of snow management is Glaze, that flawless, diaphanous glass that can only be laid down when rain or thaw is followed by a hard freeze. Or when I can summon the energy to flood the ice from a hole I've chopped.

Of course, I knew none of this the day the restored Mabel was finally frozen and ready for business. I thought I was ready too. It had been three decades, but I was convinced that skating was as indelible a muscle memory as riding a horse. For a week the weather had been clear and sharp, with subfreezing lows and small melts in the afternoons. I put on knee pads and went down to the Mabel with a pair of old hockey skates bandaged with duct tape. I laid the skates on my lawn chair and walked onto the ice in my rubber pig-farmer boots with the sort of mincing steps you'd employ on a ledge. Radish cocked his head like a bird and pawed at the hard thing his swimming hole had become. As usual, he started barking. After I'd gone a few steps there was a groan as the Mabel adjusted to my weight and a rumbling crack that echoed back from the Bitterroot Range on the other side of the river. But after this scare I walked the length of my ice without incident, and then back, looking for devious blue creases. What I did find was Glaze nine inches thick. My pulse was racing. There was no longer any excuse to put it off.

I laced my skates and stepped forth with ankles wobbling and feet that felt bound. From the start there was forward motion, halting at first, no faster than a runaway Rascal in a nursing home hallway, but velocity that increased as I gained confidence. Then it all came back:

the angle of the stroke, the bent knees and stooped posture, the gliding rhythm. A neighbor doing breakfast dishes in her trailer looked
up, startled to see someone in the backyard. Or maybe what alarmed
her was the sight of a middle-aged man on skates. Her husband was
off sleepwalking through a 12-hour shift at the paper mill. I waved,
happy to be here instead of there.

I tried some backward skating, which I had begun to learn as a kid
because not knowing how put you at a disadvantage in hockey. But
when my feet nearly went out from under me, I decided I wasn't ready
yet for anything in reverse. Plowing ahead, I skated six laps, about
three miles, and then stumbled over to my chair, winded. My ankles
would no longer support me. Sweat rolled down my spine. I whispered
to my thudding heart, Whoa, there, big fella.

I woke up the next morning to discover that a foot of wet snow
had fallen overnight, with a ton more still coming down. In the Jungle, a four-acre briar patch between the Mabel and the river, the fire-
berry hawthorns were bent double under the weight.

I didn't worry about the effect of the blizzard on the Mabel because
I didn't know enough yet to worry. And besides, my feet were too sore
to skate anyway. But when I walked down that afternoon to admire
my fine green Glaze again, I was horrified to discover that not only
had the snow not been blown away as it always was on the Sand
Coulee, but the weight of it had fractured the ice and flooded the snow.
That night the temperature dropped to zero. Next morning my Mabel
was ridged and pocked and zitted, worthless to anyone except the
whitetails that crossed it to get from the forest to our haystack. But
by the end of the week a warm rain smoothed the Mabel's skin, and
when the temperatures dropped again my beautiful Glaze was back.

The next time it snowed I was all over the Mabel at once with a shovel.
I soon gave up the notion that I could clean off a quarter-mile of ice
by hand, but after a couple of hours I had opened enough to skate
laps. Then the shovel broke. Kitty came down once to watch me sweat
and steam in the sun.

"I'm training for the Elfstedentocht," I gasped.

"Say again?"

"The skating race in Holland. You know, from city to city."

At dinner I looked up from my corn bread to find her staring at me. "What."

"So you're going to waste all morning every time it snows?"

"Waste?" I said, patting my belly. "Yuppie scum pay good money for this kind of workout."

"Then why don't you shovel the driveway?"

Of course, fitness had nothing to do with it. But I couldn't explain the emancipation I felt when I skated on the Mabel, because I didn't understand it myself. I hoped its source was something profound, and not just a cliché: I was taking up juvenile sports in order to ward off the implications of my approaching 50th birthday and its promise of the desiccation to come; or I just wanted to feel again the breathless ardor a child feels as the game begins; or I was bored with the unfinished man I'd become and had fallen in love with the happy boy I now believed I had been. I figured it wouldn't take much of a shrink to identify the disenchantment with adult life underlying my affair with the Mabel and my reawakened love of skating, but where would that get me? I'd still have to clear off the ice. The solution, I realized, was way more cost-effective than therapy: Sears.

I found the snowblowers lined up like an armada of fighter planes. They ranged from a bantamweight with 3.8 horsepower to a ten horsepower gangster.

"What is it, sir, you are having to blow?"

I knew this voice instantly. When I turned around there he was, my favorite Bengali salesman. The birdsong of his accent wasn't any more Americanized than it had been when he'd sold me a clothes dryer a year earlier. ("You cannot go wrong, sir, with the Wrinkle Guard feature," he had promised.)

"Well, there's a patio," I said.

The salesman patted the baby bear model. "Very adequate for such a task."

"And a driveway. A long one."

He pointed to the mama bear version. "Five horsepower and many choices of blowing angles."

"And a quarter-mile of ice."

"Oh, my."

"For skating."

His eyebrows lifted and a smile of good fortune spread over his face as he slid the edge of one hand across the palm of the other.

In the end, of course, I went home with the papa bear model and two attachments. I knew Kitty would hit the roof, so I picked up a bribe. When she lifted the white figure skates from their box I saw that she'd been expecting something made of silk instead.

"What did you really buy?"

"A snow thing."

"You mean another shovel?"

"Not exactly."

I led her out to the pickup and my glowering new machine.

"If it keeps snowing like this we're going to need something to dig us out," I reasoned. I could see that this shot connected. In fact, we'd already been trapped once that winter and had had to hire a neighbor to plow the driveway.

When she asked the price, my answer was only 20 percent false. Her mouth fell open.

"Hey, I'll do the road right now," I offered. The snow was beginning to fall again.

The papa bear sucked up the six inches of dry powder on our driveway like a crackhead in a coke factory and then sprayed it contemptuously into a pasture. An hour later a raisin-colored overcast moved in, and the snow turned wet. I abandoned the driveway and hurried down to the Mabel to set loose the beast before my newest layer of Glaze was compromised. Things went like clockwork at first, but as the afternoon grew warmer the threads that stripped the snow from the ice and hurled it through the blower got clogged with slush. I cleaned them as best I could with a stick. Finally, blubbering and whining, the papa bear—triumph of American technology—just gave up. The ice I couldn't liberate began to sink under the weight of what would be a record snowfall.

By noon I was able to clear a path along the driveway for the pickup. Even in four-wheel drive I barely made it out. When I pushed the papa bear through the doors at Sears, my salesman saw me and hurried over, stricken. Snowblowers just don't seem to work very well against wet snow, I told him, though they are dynamite with powder. His eyes were liquid and sorrowful but totally uncomprehending. Then I felt a force at my back and turned around. Sears had fallen silent and dreamy and, except for one section of floor space, completely dark. And in that space, glowing with menace, was a column of riding mowers fitted with snow plows.

Look away, I told myself.

The following spring a black bear moved into the Jungle, attracted by its maze of hiding places and its wild raspberries. We saw him from time to time when he made his way from the vineries to drink from the Mabel. The horses would bolt in their pens, wide-eyed and snorting, but they soon grew used to bear-smell, and peace returned. I built a dock and spent the first hot afternoon of May throwing pebbles into the water for Radish to chase, an easy way to scour off the beggar's-lice he had gotten into. Then I jumped in myself for the helpless flailing I call swimming.

The Mabel froze early that fall. I fell twice trying to get down my strokes for skating backward, and my knee swelled up like a bag of microwave popcorn. After it healed I picked dead leaves off the ice every morning before they could absorb the sun and melt holes in the shape of themselves. Near Thanksgiving the heavens opened and a foot of perfect powder fell down. I thought: Snow, you bastard. I am no longer your slave.

Pheasants exploded into the air and dogs howled when I revved up my 15.5-horsepower Sears Craftsman riding mower with its automatic transmission and its Kohler Command engine and its four-foot snowplow. After I made quick work of the driveway, which pleased Kitty, I rumbled down the bank and onto the Mabel, the chains on the weighted back tires clattering ominously. In a half hour I was done. The Mabel sparkled.

The next day we had a hockey game. A dance professor accidentally smacked a crime reporter in the face with her stick and broke his nose. Radish rushed to lick the blood from the ice, rolling his eyes in pleasure.

During the holidays a horde of in-laws forgathered at Dark Acres to play cards and gossip about horses. On Christmas Eve, under a bone moon, we lit a bonfire and took to the ice for an hour of sport before our nightly games of pitch and boo-ray. Kitty looked dreamy as she sailed across the ice in her new skates. The kids sped around, hissing at the adults and pulling at Kitty's mother, whose knee pads and elbow pads and Carhartt coveralls made her look like the Michelin Man's wife.

When everyone else tired I decided to take one last spin alone. It was time. I glided to the far end of the Mabel, Radish at my side. Then, as the moon cast my shadow before me, I skated home backward.

January 2000

Contributors

BRUCE BARCOTT, an *Outside* contributing editor, is the author of *The Measure of a Mountain: Beauty and Terror on Mount Rainier* and the editor of *Northwest Passages: A Literary Anthology of the Pacific Northwest from Coyote Tales to Roadside Attractions*.

A longtime contributing editor to *Outside*, ROB BUCHANAN has written about adventure and travel for many publications, including *Sports Illustrated, Rolling Stone, Details,* and *The New York Times*.

Editor-at-large TIM CAHILL was a founding force behind *Outside* and wrote the "Out There" column for many years. Much of Cahill's writing for *Outside* has been collected in his books *A Wolverine Is Eating My Leg, Jaguars Ripped My Flesh, Pecked to Death by Ducks,* and *Pass the Butterworms: Remote Journeys Oddly Rendered*.

Outside correspondent W. HODDING CARTER is the author of *Westward Whoa*, an account of his journey down the Lewis & Clark Trail by boat, horse, and rental car, and *A Viking Voyage*, in which he attempted to re-create Leif Eriksson's discovery of Newfoundland in an open boat. He's at work on a book about the environmental restoration of the Everglades.

Australian mountaineer and *Outside* correspondent GREG CHILD has climbed some of the most challenging and dangerous Himalayan summits, including Mount Everest, K2, and Trango Tower. His 2002 book *Over the Edge* recounts the kidnapping of four American climbers in Kyrgyzstan in August 2000, a story he first reported in *Outside*.

SARA CORBETT has been a correspondent for *Outside* since 1994 and is a contributing writer for *The New York Times Magazine*. She is the author of *Venus to the Hoop*, a book about the United States' 1996 women's Olympic basketball team.

DANIEL COYLE is an *Outside* contributing editor. His book *Hardball: A Season in the Projects* was named *The Sporting News'* 1994 Book of the Year. His first novel, *Waking Samuel*, will be published next year by Bloomsbury USA.

BRYAN DI SALVATORE is the author of *A Clever Base-Ballist*, a biography of John Montgomery Ward, founder of the first union of professional athletes in 1878. DEIRDRE MCNAMER teaches creative writing at the University of Montana. Her most recent novel is *My Russian*, and she is currently at work on a new book set in northern Montana. The couple are married and live in Missoula.

DANIEL DUANE is a surfer, rock climber, and the author of *Caught Inside: A Surfer's Year on the California Coast* and the novel *El Capitan: Historic Feats and Radical Routes*.

HAL ESPEN is the editor of *Outside*.

Contributing editor IAN FRAZIER is the author of many books, including *Great Plains, Family,* and *On the Rez*. His latest is *The Fish's Eye*, a collection of essays about angling and the outdoors.

STEVE FRIEDMAN's work has appeared in many publications, including *Esquire, GQ*, and *The Washington Post*. He is co-author of the best-seller *Loose Balls: Easy Money, Hard Fouls, Cheap Laughs & True Love in the NBA*.

Correspondent JACK HITT contributes regularly to *Outside, The New York Times Magazine, Harper's,* and the public radio program *This American Life.*

EDWARD HOAGLAND, an essayist and novelist, is the author of numerous books, including the recently released *Compass Points,* a collection of auto-biographical essays, and *Notes from the Century Before,* an account of his 1966 excursion through the backcountry of British Columbia that was recently reissued by the Modern Library.

MARK JENKINS, *Outside*'s "Hard Way" columnist and reconnaissance agent, is the author of *Off the Map* and *To Timbuktu.* A collection of his *Outside* adventures, *The Hard Way,* was published recently by Simon & Schuster.

SEBASTIAN JUNGER is the author of the best-seller *The Perfect Storm,* a version of which first appeared in *Outside,* and *Fire,* a collection of his reporting from around the world.

Editor-at-large JON KRAKAUER is the author of *Into Thin Air,* a best-seller based on his eyewitness account of the 1996 Mount Everest tragedy. Krakauer won the 1997 National Magazine Award for Reporting for his *Outside* article detailing the event.

Contributing editor MARK LEVINE has traveled the globe for *Outside,* filing stories on mining waste in Montana, sorcery in Sumatra, and floods in Bangladesh. He is the author of two books of verse, *Debt* and *Enola Gay,* and he teaches poetry at the University of Iowa Writers' Workshop.

Frequent *Outside* contributor PETER MAASS is the author of *Love Thy Neighbor: A Story of War,* a memoir of his experiences covering the conflict in Bosnia. He has reported from a number of battle zones, most recently in Afghanistan.

BILL MCKIBBEN is the author of *Hope, Human and Wild* and *The End of Nature,* among many other books. The story selected for this anthology was an excerpt from his 2000 book *Long Distance: A Year of Living Strenuously.*

SUSAN ORLEAN is a staff writer at *The New Yorker*. She has written five books, including *Saturday Night* and *The Orchid Thief*. Her first story for *Outside*, "The Bullfighter Checks Her Makeup," is the title piece of her most recent book, a collection of profiles.

DAVID QUAMMEN wrote *Outside*'s "Natural Acts" column for 15 years and is now an editor-at-large. Quammen's columns have been collected in three books: *Natural Acts*, *The Flight of the Iguana*, and *Wild Thoughts from Wild Places*. He is also the author of *The Song of the Dodo*, a book about island biogeography; three novels; and a collection of short fiction. He is currently at work on *Monster of God*, a look at big predators and their relationships with humans.

Outside correspondent DAVID RAKOFF's collection of essays, *Fraud*, includes two stories that first appeared in the pages of *Outside*. A frequent contributor to *This American Life* and *The New York Times Magazine*, he has also written for *GQ*, *Harper's Bazaar*, and *The New York Observer*.

Contributing editor BOB SHACOCHIS's books include *The Immaculate Invasion*, a chronicle of the U.S. military intervention in Haiti, and the short-story collection *Easy in the Islands*, which won the 1985 National Book Award. He is at work on the second novel in the trilogy he began with *Swimming in the Volcano*.

Outside contributing editor HAMPTON SIDES is the author of *Ghost Soldiers*, a best-selling account of a World War II raid to rescue Allied survivors of the Bataan Death March. He edited *Why Moths Hate Thomas Edison*, an anthology of *Outside*'s "Wild File" columns, and is currently working on a book about the conquest of the Navajo people.

PETER STARK, a longtime *Outside* contributor, is the author of *Last Breath: Cautionary Tales from the Limits of Human Endurance*, an outgrowth of his essay in this anthology about the physiology of freezing to death. Stark also wrote *Driving to Greenland*, a collection of travel essays.

Outside correspondent MIKE STEERE has written for the magazine since 1986, on subjects ranging from piloting a motor yacht in Alaska to climbing Bolivia's 19,974-foot Huayna Potosi. He is a consultant for the Ford Motor Company–sponsored adventure magazine, *No Boundaries*.

RANDALL SULLIVAN is a contributing editor to *Rolling Stone*. He is the author of several books, including the recently published *LAbyrinth*, which investigates the deaths of Tupac Shakur and Biggie Smalls and the origins of the Los Angeles police scandal.

Contributing editor PATRICK SYMMES is the author of *Chasing Che: A Motorcycle Journey Through the Guevara Legend*. A frequent contributor to *Harper's*, he has also reported on guerrillas in Colombia and Cambodia.

PAUL THEROUX is the author of almost 40 books, including *The Great Railway Bazaar*, *The Happy Isles of Oceania*, and the recent novel *Hotel Honolulu*. His next book, a nonfiction account of traveling from Cairo to Capetown, will be published in the spring of 2003.

Contributing editor BILL VAUGHN's essay in this anthology, "Skating Home Backward," was nominated for a National Magazine Award in 2001. During his long career with *Outside*, Vaughn has written about feuds, *Survivor*, and his late-in-life quest to become an Eagle Scout.

Novelist WILLIAM T. VOLLMANN's twelfth book, *Argall*, published by Viking in 2001, is the fourth in his Seven Dreams series, a seven-volume history of North America.

BRAD WETZLER, a contributing editor to *Outside*, has written about the outdoors and current events for many publications, including *GQ*, *The New York Times Magazine*, and *Wired*.

RANDY WAYNE WHITE, a contributing editor, wrote the magazine's "Out There" column for eight years. His most recent collection of nonfiction is titled *Last Flight Out*. He also writes the popular Doc Ford mystery series; his latest Ford novel is *Twelve Mile Limit*.

FLORENCE WILLIAMS, a correspondent for *Outside*, writes about politics and the environment for various publications, including *The New Republic*, *The New York Times*, *Wired*, and *Mother Jones*.